An Evangelical Orthodox Guide to
CHRISTIAN THEOLOGY

SCRIPTURE ALONE

GRACE ALONE

FAITH ALONE

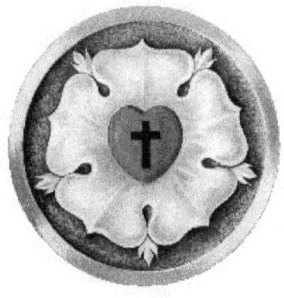

A Handbook for Pastors, Teachers, and Laymen

By Gary Ray Branscome

**In memory of William Tyndale
Who died a martyr's death for translating
The Bible into English.**

Christians are free to photocopy pages of this book for use in Bible Study, and even to reproduce [or translate] sections or chapters as long as 1- no changes, additions or deletions are made to the text, 2- proper credit is given for authorship, and 3- a business card size advertisement for the complete book is included. [Contact the publisher for advertisement text.]

© copyright Gary Ray Branscome 2021

Library of Congress
Lutheran News, Inc.
684 Luther Lane
New Haven, MO 63068
Published 2022
Printed in the United States of America
IngramSpark, TN
ISBN #978-1-7366844-5-0

Preface

By Gene Edward Veith

Christians need theology. Though we often hear "I just have a personal relationship with Jesus Christ" we need to know *who Jesus is*, *what He has done for us*, and *what He would have us do*. For that, along with all of the other issues that these questions raise—plus, the need to protect ourselves from the many false beliefs that could lead us astray—we need theology.

But theology is not philosophy, a set of ideas figured out by human ingenuity. Nor is theology just another academic discipline, a technical field for scholarly specialists. Nor is it something just pastors need to know. Yes, theology is an inexhaustible subject and rewards sophisticated study, but we laypeople need it too.

Christianity is a *revealed* religion. It has been said that the human mind can arrive at the correct conclusion that God *exists*, but, by itself, it can't know much *about* Him. That He loves us, for instance, or that He became a human being in Jesus, or that the Son of God died for our sins.

Because God is infinite and far beyond our comprehension, the only way we can learn about Him is if He somehow tells us what we need to know. And, according to Christianity, He *does*. He literally *tells* us, in human language that we can understand. That is to say, He gives us His Word.

His Word is written down in the Bible. Because of the immensity of that subject matter that God communicates, the Bible consists of various kinds of writing—history, laws, prophecies, poetry, letters—by various writers whom God has inspired. And in and through those words, accessible to anyone who can read or hear, God not only communicates truth about Himself and us, He speaks to us in such a way that He creates faith in our hearts.

Just as a "personal relationship" between friends involves talking with each other, we *can* have a personal relationship to Jesus: we speak to Him in prayer, and He speaks to us in His Word. But His Word is the foundation of that relationship.

And it is the foundation of theology. Strictly speaking, Christian theology is simply reflection on God's Word. We can think about God's Word, discover insights from it, see the configurations of what it reveals, and explore its depths. The result is theology.

To be sure, there are different theologies. Some Christians interpret God's Word in different ways and different groups of Christians have their theological commitments. Sometimes theologians try to "figure out" God's revelation to make it more understandable to the human mind. Some emphasize one statement from the Bible while explaining away other Biblical statements that testify to a more complicated truth. We should avoid such bad theologies, some of which squarely violate God's Word.

And when it comes to the church body we belong to, the one we trust to teach us and nourish us in our faith, we should find the one with the best theology. That is, the one that is best and most thoroughly grounded in God's Word.

In looking for that kind of church, I found the Lutherans. I remember, early in my instruction, when the pastor showed me the *Book of Concord*, the collection of creeds, catechisms, and confessions of faith that define Lutheran theology. I joked to the pastor, "Do you mean that I have to believe both *this* big book [the Bible] *and* this big book [the *Book of Concord*]?

He explained what I actually already knew, that the teachings of the *Book of Concord*, in the words of those who compiled it, are *"derived* from the Word of God" (Preface to the Christian Book of Concord, paragraph 10). Pastors from conservative, orthodox Lutheran churches take what is called a "quia" subscription to the *Book of Concord*, from the Latin word for "because." They believe in the theology expressed in the *Book of Concord* "because" it derives from the Word of God. Lutherans have their theology, but their authority is the Word.

Gary Branscome here has performed the valuable task of connecting theology back to the Word of God. Or, perhaps better said, of drawing out the theology taught by the Bible.

A key teaching of Christianity is the doctrine of the Trinity. This book shows how the Word of God teaches the Trinity—in the Old Testament as well as the new, in direct statements and in subtle details, in familiar passages and in passages you never realized.

Is a cultist or a progressive scholar denying the deity of Christ? This book shows the abundant Biblical evidence that Jesus Christ is both true God and true Man.

Today even many "evangelicals" are denying the Atonement, that Christ bore our sins on the Cross and paid the penalty for them with His sacrificial death. That is the "good news," the *evangel*, from which "evangelicals" derive their name. To draw back from that, in the name of "the new perspective on Paul," or defending God the Father from the charge of "cosmic child abuse," is to cut the heart out of the Gospel. But this book shows that Christ's Atonement permeates not just the writings of Paul but the entire Bible.

And so it goes with the way of salvation, the Christian life, the End

Times, and other issues, from the nature of angels to controversies over predestination.

What emerges is a theology shared by Luther, Tyndale, and other reformers, as summarized in the Reformation slogans "scripture alone," "grace alone," and "faith alone." But you don't have to be "Lutheran" to benefit from what Gary Branscome offers here. Not all readers—whether from different theological traditions or even all Lutherans—will agree with him on every point. But they will benefit from this immersion into Scripture.

Thus, the title of this book is *An Evangelical Orthodox Guide to Christian Theology*. The book is "evangelical," in the sense of the early Reformers who were called by that name, being focused on the "evangel," the gospel of salvation through faith in the work of Jesus Christ. It is "orthodox," in the sense of upholding the right doctrine of the historic church as set forth in the Bible. And it is a "guide," in the sense of leading the reader into the depths of God's revelation.

[FOOTNOTE: Dr. Gene Edward Veith is an author, scholar, and Professor of Literature emeritus at Patrick Henry College. He received his Ph.D. in English from the University of Kansas in 1979. Additionally, he holds honorary doctorates from Concordia Theological Seminary, Concordia University California, and Patrick Henry College. He served there as Dean of Academic Affairs and Provost, and was the Culture Editor of World magazine. He has written 20 books and over 100 scholarly works. Veith served previously on the faculty as Professor of English at Concordia University Wisconsin, as well as being the Dean of the School of Arts and Sciences and the director of the Cranach Institute.]

Endorsement

This book strikes a balance between biblical piety and academics. It presents us with Christian orthodoxy as an exciting and important challenge to live the biblical life honestly and vigorously. This book is a good contribution to the continuing charge to keep biblical faith alive in this present world. The author exhorts us all to godliness and humble submission to God. Gary Huffman, Baptist pastor.

Author's Foreword

Although I began writing this book a few months before my seventy-sixth birthday, as I began to write, a long forgotten prayer from my youth came to mind. I remembered clearly how that over fifty years earlier, at a time when I was earnestly struggling to learn and understand what the Bible taught, I prayed that I might one day be able to write a book that would help those struggling as I was. A book that would not just tell them what to believe, but show them what the Bible says. This book exists as an answer to that prayer.

The doctrine that God wants His church to believe and teach consists of those doctrinal truths clearly and explicitly stated in Scripture, and my comments are intended to point people to what the Bible says. Some may wonder why, time and again, I quote the Bible and then restate what it clearly says. My reason for doing that is to emphasize the fact that God wants us to learn and teach what He has said, not some man's explanation of what He has said.

While this book follows (with modification) the outline of John Theodore Mueller's "Christian Dogmatics," The content is new, and it is written in a way that lets the Bible speak for itself. Most of the Bible quotations are taken from the K.J.V.-2011 [Available from online-bible.net or branscome.org.] or an alternate reading of the same. Although the K.J.V.-2011 does not capitalize pronouns that refer to God, I have capitalized He, His, and Him when they refer to God.

Gary Ray Branscome

TABLE OF CONTENTS

A BIBLICAL APPROACH TO THEOLOGY
(Prolegomena)

The Nature and Concept of Theology
1. The Biblical Viewpoint of a Christian Theologian 1
2. Of Religion in General and the Rise of Secularism 3
3. The Christian Religion and Christian Theology 6
4. Theology Considered as Doctrine 9
5. The Theology of the Apostles 14
6. Law and Gospel 16
7. Vital Doctrines and Unanswered Questions 16
8. A Sound Approach to Theology 18

THE DOCTRINE OF HOLY SCRIPTURE

1. The Bible is the Only Source and Standard of Faith 22
2. Holy Scripture is the Word of God 28
3. The Inspiration of the Bible 30
4. The Holy Spirit's Relationship to the Writers 33
5. Attacks on the Doctrine of Inspiration 34
6. The Consequences of Denying Inspiration 36
7. The Properties of Holy Scripture 38
   A. The Divine Authority of Holy Scripture 40
   B. The Divine Power of Holy Scripture 43
   C. The Divine Purpose of Holy Scripture 46
   D. The Divine Sufficiency of Holy Scripture 47
   E. The Divine Clarity of Holy Scripture 49

THE DOCTRINE OF GOD

1. The Natural Knowledge of God 54
2. The Holy Trinity 57
3. The Doctrine of the Holy Trinity in Controversy 61
4. The Trinitarian Terminology of the Christian Church 64
5. The Holy Trinity Revealed in the Old Testament 66
6. God's Essence and Attributes 69
   1. The Doctrine in General 69
   2. The Passive Attributes 71
   3. The Active Attributes 75

THE DOCTRINE OF THE DIVINE DECREES

THE DOCTRINE OF CREATION
1. The Origin of All Things 82
2. The Order of Creation 83
3. The Six Days (Hexaemeron) 85
4. The Six Days of Creation Considered in Detail 86
5. The Unity of the Human Race 91
6. Special Questions Regarding the Creation Report 92
7. Creation an External Act of God 92
8. The Doctrine of the Age of the Earth 93
9. The Ultimate End of Creation 99

THE DOCTRINE OF DIVINE PROVIDENCE
1. The Guiding Hand of Divine Providence 100
2. The Objects of Divine Providence 101
3. Divine Providence and Secondary Causes 103
4. Divine Concurrence in Good and Evil Actions 104
5. Divine Providence and Free Will 106

THE DOCTRINE OF THE ANGELS
1. The Existence of Angels 111
2. The Name "Angel" 113
3. The Nature of the Angels 113
4. The Number and Ranks of Angels 118
5. Good and Evil Angels 120
6. The Holy Service of the Good Angels 121
7. The Evil Work and Eternal Punishment of Evil Angels 124

THE DOCTRINE OF MAN
A. Man Before The Fall
1. Man Created in the Image of God................................ 131
2. The Image of a Righteous God 132
3. The Divine Image and the Nature of Man 133
4. The Divine Image and Woman 135

B. The State Of Corruption
a. Of Sin in General 137
   1. Falling Short of the Glory of God 137
   2. The Divine Law and Sin 138
   3. The Causes of Sin 143
   4. The Consequences of Sin 144
b. Original (Inherent) Sin 147
   1. The Nature of Original Sin 147
   2. The Corrupt Mind and Will of Man 148
   3. The Cause and Universality of Original Sin 150
   4. The Effects of Original Sin 151

    c. Actual (Specific) Sins 152
       1. The Nature of Actual Sin 152
       2. The Causes of Actual Sin 154
       3. The Doctrine of Offense 156
       4. The Doctrine of Obduration 158
       5. The Scriptural Doctrine of Temptation 160
       6. The Classification of Actual Sins 162

THE FREEDOM OF THE WILL **172**

THE GRACE OF GOD TOWARD FALLEN MANKIND
  1. The Necessity of Divine Grace 176
  2. The Nature of Divine Grace 177
  3. Attributes of Justifying Grace 179
  4. Accurately Describing the Divine Will of Grace 183

THE DOCTRINE OF CHRIST

A. The Doctrine of the Person of Christ
  1. Introduction 185
  2. The True Deity of Christ 186
  3. The True Humanity of Christ 187
  4. The Personal Union 192
  5. The Communion of Natures 193
  6. The Communication of Attributes 194
    The First Genus 194
    The Second Genus 195
    The Third Genus 195

B. The Doctrine of the States of Christ
  1. Christ's State of Humiliation 196
  2. Erroneous Views Regarding Christ's Humiliation 197
  3. The Several Stages of the Humiliation 198
  4. The State of Exaltation 199
  5. The Several Stages of Christ's Exaltation 200

C. The Doctrine of Christ's Office
    a. The Prophetic Office of Christ 204
       1. Executing This Office in the State of Humiliation ... 204
       2. The Prophetic Office in the State of Exaltation ... 206
    b. The Priestly Office of Christ 208
       1. The Vicarious Atonement 213
       2. The Finished Work of Christ, and Faith 213
       3. Errors Pertaining to Christ's Vicarious Atonement ... 215
       4. The Priestly Intercession of Christ 219
    c. The Kingly Office of Christ 220
       Errors Regarding the Kingly Office of Christ 223

THE DOCTRINE OF SALVATION

THE DOCTRINE OF SOTERIOLOGY **225**

THE DOCTRINE OF SAVING FAITH
1. The Necessity of Faith 230
2. The Nature of Saving Faith 232
3. Knowledge, Assent, and Confidence 234
4. Why Saving Faith Justifies 235
5. Faith Viewed as a Passive Act or Instrument 236
6. Concerning True Faith and Living Faith 237
7. Faith and the Assurance of Salvation 238
8. Can the Believer Be Sure He Has Saving Faith? 240
9. The Faith of Infants 242

CONVERSION, OR THE BESTOWAL OF FAITH
1. The Scriptural Basis of the Doctrine 243
2. Conversion According to Scripture 245
3. The Beginning and End of Conversion 247
4. The Efficient Cause of Conversion 248
5. The Means of Conversion 250
6. The Internal Motions in Conversion 253
7. Conversion Is Instantaneous 255
8. The Grace of Conversion Is Resistible 256
9. Conversion According to Law and Grace 257
10. Continued Conversion 258
11. Sustained Conversion 260
12. Divine Monergism in Conversion 263
13. Synonyms of Conversion 266

JUSTIFICATION BY FAITH
1. Justification According to Scripture 268
2. Justification by Faith Alone 270
3. Why Justification by Faith is Central 272
4. Terminology That Guards Against Error 275
5. Justification and Works 277
6. The Effects of Justification 279

THE DOCTRINE OF SANCTIFICATION AND GOOD WORKS

1. The Nature of Sanctification 282
2. The Efficient Cause of Sanctification 285
3. The Inner Motions of Sanctification 286

4. The Means by which We are Sanctified 289
5. The Necessity of Sanctification and Good Works 290
6. The Imperfection of Sanctification in This Life 293

The Doctrine of Good Works
1. The Nature of Good Works 295
2. The Works of the Heathen 298
3. The Christian's Growth in Good Works 299
4. The Reward of Good Works 304
5. The Great Value of Good Works 309
6. Perversion of the Doctrine of Good Works 311

Sanctification and the Christian Life
1. The Christian Life and the Cross 313
2. The Christian Life and Prayer 316
3. The Christian Life and the Hope of Eternal Life 320

THE DOCTRINE OF THE MEANS OF GRACE
1. Identifying the Means of Grace 322
2. The Means of Grace in General 323
3. Errors Regarding the Means of Grace 325
4. The Importance of the Means of Grace 327
5. The Means of Grace and Forgiving Sin 329
6. The Means of Grace in the Old Testament 331
7. The Means of Grace and Prayer 333

THE LAW AND THE GOSPEL
1. The Difference Between Law and Gospel 335
2. The Law and Gospel Considered as Opposites 336
3. The Close Connection between Law and Gospel 337
4. The Art of Distinguishing Between Law and Gospel ... 339

THE DOCTRINE OF PRESERVATION 341

THE DOCTRINE OF HOLY BAPTISM
1. The Divine Institution of Baptism 343
2. Baptism in the Light of the Gospel 345
3. What Makes a Baptism Valid 347
4. Baptism a True Means of Grace 349
5. The Use of Baptism 351
6. Whom the Church should Baptize 352
7. The Administrants of Baptism 355
8. The Necessity of Baptism 356

9. Regarding Baptismal Customs 356
10. The Baptism of John the Baptist 358

THE DOCTRINE OF THE LORD'S SUPPER
1. The Divine Institution of the Lord's Supper 359
2. A Ceremonial Proclamation of the Gospel 360
3. The Words of Institution 362
4. The Material Elements in the Lord's Supper 363
5. The Lord's Supper as a Means of Grace 365
6. Who may be Admitted to the Lord's Supper? 366
7. The Necessity of the Lord's Supper 367

THE DOCTRINE OF THE CHURCH AND MINISTRY

THE DOCTRINE OF THE CHRISTIAN CHURCH

A. The Church Universal
1. God's Heavenly Kingdom 369
2. Erroneous Doctrines Concerning the Church 371
3. The Properties of the Christian Church 372
4. The Glory of the Christian Church 374
5. How the Church is Founded and Preserved 375

B. Concerning Local Churches
1. God's Earthly Kingdom 377
2. The Divine Institution of Local Churches 378
3. Church and State 379
4. Orthodox and Heterodox Churches 383
5. Heterodox Churches and True Discipleship 385
6. The Limits of Spiritual Fellowship 386
7. Separatists, or Schismatics 388
8. The Representative Church 389

THE DOCTRINE OF THE PUBLIC MINISTRY
1. The Christian Pastor 389
2. Pastors and the Priesthood of All Believers 391
3. The Public Ministry is a Divine Appointment 392
4. Is the Public Ministry Necessary? 393
5. The Call into the Ministry, and Ordination 394
6. The Christian Ministry is Not a Spiritual Estate 396
7. The Authority of the Public Ministry 397
8. Antichrists and The Antichrist 399

THE DOCTRINE OF ETERNAL ELECTION
1. Chosen by God 401
2. How Believers are to Consider Their Election 402
3. The Objects of Eternal Election 405
4. The Relation of Faith to Eternal Election 406
5. The Purpose of the Doctrine of Eternal Election 407
6. Holy Scripture Teaches No Election to Damnation 408

THE DOCTRINE OF THE LAST THINGS
1. Temporal Death 410
2. The Soul between Death and the Resurrection 413
3. The Second Advent of Christ 415
4. The Resurrection of the Dead 419
5. The Final Judgment 422
6. The End of the World 423
7. Eternal Damnation 424
8. Eternal Salvation 427

A BIBLICAL APPROACH TO THEOLOGY
Prolegomena

The Nature and Concept of Theology

1. The Biblical Viewpoint Of A Christian Theologian

"**God so loved the world, that He gave His only begotten Son, that whosoever believes on Him should not perish, but have everlasting life,**" and God so loved the world that He gave us the Bible to testify to that fact (John 3:16 and 5:39). As it is written, "**All the prophets testify of Him, that through His name whoever believes in Him will receive forgiveness of sins**" (Acts 10:43). Moreover, because God wants us to have confidence in what the Bible says, the Bible in all of its parts is the Word of God. And, the only valid purpose of theology is to faithfully organize and present what God has said, without adding to or taking from the plain meaning of the words.

However, because, "**There is no other name under heaven given among men, [other than that of Jesus Christ] by which we must be saved,**" Satan has "**blinded**" those who do not believe to the truth of the gospel, and confuses them, to keep them from coming to faith in Christ (Acts 4:12, 2Corinthians 4:4). Because of that blindness, many do not read the Bible because they think that what it says is all a matter of opinion. Others read their own ideas into the text while explaining away any passages that contradict their opinions. In contrast, **a truly Biblical theology will accept the words of Scripture as they read, allowing the plain grammatical meaning of the words [the same meaning that you are putting on my words as you read this] to stand. And, will make the doctrine that God has clearly and explicitly stated in the text the doctrine it sets forth.**

Christ's words, "**If you continue in my word, you are truly my disciples; and you will know the truth, and the truth will make you free,**" tell us that we are not really Christ's disciples if we do not continue in His Word, but instead look outside of Scripture for doctrine, or read unscriptural ideas into the text (John 8:31-32). The

words, "**No truth of scripture comes from any private explanation,**" tell us that no God-given truth comes from man-made explanations of the text (2Peter 1:20). I am not talking about the plain meaning of the words, but made up explanations such as the "gap theory". That kind of explanation is the word of man not the Word of God! And, the words, "**If they do not speak according to this word, it is because there is no light in them,**" tell us that any opinion that contradicts what the Bible plainly says is false [not light] (Isaiah 8:20). **The three verses just quoted tell us:**
    1-that the doctrine God wants us to get from His Word consists of what the words say,
    2-excluding all man-made explanations, and
    3-understood in a way that agrees with everything else that the Bible says.

Furthermore, because God has caused every truth necessary for our salvation to be plainly stated Scripture, those truths that are clearly and explicitly stated in Scripture are to be the standard by which all of the more obscure passages of Scripture are interpreted. **No obscure passage of Scripture should ever be interpreted to teach any doctrine not taught in the clear passages of Scripture.** Those who interpret unclear passages to contradict what is taught in the clear passages obscure what is taught in the clear passages thus hindering the work of salvation.

Jesus condemned the Pharisees for, "**Teaching for doctrines the commandments of men**" (Mark 7:7). Those man-made commandments [traditions] were an addition to God's Word, and thus contrary to the words, "**Do not add to His words, lest He reprove you, and you are found to be a liar**" (Proverbs 30:6). At the same time, the words, "**You completely invalidate the commandment of God, in order to keep your tradition... Making the word of God of no effect,**" tell us that when traditions are aimed at getting around what the Bible says, they take away from Scripture (Mark 7:9-13). And, that is condemned by the words, "**If any man shall take away from the words of the book of this prophecy, God shall take away his part out of the book of life**" (Revelation 22:19).

In contrast to the legalism of the Pharisees, **the Sadducees were rationalists. However, by claiming, "That there is no resurrection, and that there are no angels, or spirits," they were also taking away from Scripture** (Acts 23:8). **And, Jesus rebuked them by saying, "Are you not deceiving yourselves, because you do not know the scriptures, or the power of God?... In regard to the dead, and the fact that they rise: haven't you read in the book of Moses, how God spoke to him from the bush, saying, I am the God of Abraham, and the God of Isaac, and the God of Jacob? He is not the God of the dead, but the God of the living: therefore you are badly mistaken" (Mark 12:24-27).

Today, things have not changed. We still have legalists [like the Pharisees] who place great importance on obedience to men and man-made rules, while explaining away some passages of Scripture. And, we still have rationalists [like the Sadducees] who reject what the Bible says whenever it does not agree with their ideas. **Both legalists and rationalists have been deceived by a heart that is "deceitful above all things"** (Jeremiah 17:9). And, Christ's words, **"O fools, and slow of heart to believe everything the prophets have said,"** warn us not to follow their example (Luke 24:25).

2. Of Religion In General And The Rise Of Secularism

The philosophers of this world have never fully agreed on what "religion" actually is. Some of them think of it as rules and obligations. Others think of it as how God is worshipped, or as an ideology. The Apostle Paul, speaks of the **"Jewish religion,"** and calls the Pharisees the **"strictest sect"** of that religion (Galatians 1:13, Acts 26:5). James speaks of religion in terms of bridling the "tongue" and not deceiving the "heart", and calls visiting "the fatherless and widows in their affliction," and keeping "oneself unpolluted by the world" **pure religion** (James 1:26-27). Some years ago, I talked to a young man who used the cliché "Christianity is not a religion, but a relationship," as an excuse for not attending church. I understand the point that the people who use that cliché are trying to make [we are saved by faith in Christ, not a set of works], but that cliché is just a word game because religion is more than just works, and flippant definitions like that can easily become an excuse for not doing the will of God. The truth is that no one has ever come up with one comprehensive definition of religion that fits every religion.

In the past, evangelical theologians have taught that there are only two religions in the world. That definition lumps all non-Christian religions together as religions of the law (or works), while contrasting them with Christianity, with its emphasis on grace. And, there is truth to that distinction because man-made religions see things in terms of what men need to do, rather than what God has done for us. However, the rise of secular religions in the last century has changed all of that. And, many of the problems that Christians face today stem from a failure to understand and come to grips with that change.

The secular religions center around worship of the goddess "mother nature" disguised as science. This becomes obvious whenever those who embrace secular religion give "nature" credit for our senses, for our intelligence, or for life itself. By claiming that nature is our creator they are making nature their god, thus honoring **"the creation more than the Creator,"** which is idolatry even if a statue is not used (Romans 1:25). To give one example: A recent issue of "The Readers Digest" contained the statement, "That wonderous invention of nature: the canine nose" (March 2021, page 56). Other publications contain many similar statements, and that deification of nature has become the official state religion of our government. The proof of what I say can be seen in the fact that our government promotes and finances that religion in the name of education and science.

One of the doctrines of secular religion is the claim that the universe is billions of years old. Another is the claim that life came from non-life. And, a third is the claim that all the life forms on earth can be explained by simple life forms gradually morphing into more complex life forms. Furthermore, all of those doctrines are assumed to be true without the rigorous testing that sets science apart from philosophy. The purpose of such rigorous testing is to prove untested assumptions wrong – because that is the way real science advances. However, nature worshippers just interpret circumstantial evidence to support their ideas while explaining away anything that does not fit. In short, they interpret the scientific evidence the way cults interpret Scripture.

Let's start with the claim that life came from non-life. The scientific evidence against that claim is so strong that evolutionists try to avoid discussing it, at least with creationists. Nevertheless Darwin believed that life originated in a warm little pond. That is why they get excited whenever they think they see evidence of water on Mars. So let's take a look at the scientific evidence.

At one time it was widely believed that maggots would spontaneously generate in meat. In order to test that "hypothesis," Francesco Redi (in 1660) devised an experiment, consisting of jars that contained meat. One jar was open another jar had a piece of cheesecloth stretched across the top, and a third was closed. Maggots not only did not appear in the meat that was in the closed jar, but flies were actually observed laying maggots on the cheesecloth. Two centuries later, many still believed that bacteria would spontaneously generate in broth. In order to test that hypothesis, Louis Pasteur (in 1859) devised an experiment that utilized several long-necked flasks containing beef broth. The necks on some of the flasks were straight, while others were bent in an s-curve. As predicted, bacteria only infested the broth that was in flasks with straight necks. When the flasks had curved necks, the bacteria stuck to the side of the neck, and could not get to the broth. Those experiments, coupled with the invention of a dust-free box at the end of the nineteenth-century, convinced the scientific community that life does not come from non-life. Atheists know that. And, that is why, when the atheist Richard Dawkins was interviewed for the movie "Expelled," he suggested that life may have been seeded on earth by life forms that evolved elsewhere in the universe. That is atheist mythology not science.

When we look at the fossil record, we find that about forty percent of the fossilized life forms are **not extinct**. We find fossilized frogs, dragonflies, turtles, figs, cats, and thousands of other species that are virtually identical to their modern day living counterparts. In other words, the fossil record tells us that they have not evolved. That is scientific fact! However, when we encounter a fossilized life form that **is extinct** atheists often claim that it evolved into something else. There is not any scientific evidence to support that claim. They just make it because it fits their religion, and because we do not have a living specimen that we can hold up to disprove it. Take for example their claim that dinosaurs evolved into birds. There is not one scrap of evidence that dinosaurs ever evolved into anything. In fact, modern birds have been found in the same rock layers as dinosaurs. So the claim that dinosaurs morphed into birds is atheist religion, not science.

As to the age of the earth, many of the claims made about radiometric dating are false. In fact there is much evidence that the world cannot be as old as the evolutionists claim. While most of it is too technical to go into here, it is available through such research organizations as "The Creation Research Society" or "Answers in Genesis". I could add much more, but this is a book of theology, not science or apologetics. Nevertheless, it is important to understand that Christians do not reject the "facts of science," we just interpret those facts to agree with the truths that are clearly and explicitly stated in Scripture. In contrast atheists interpret the same facts to agree with their secular religion. And, the following verses describe what happens when a nation turns away from the True God.

"Professing themselves to be wise... They changed the truth of God into a lie, and worshipped and served the creation more than the Creator... For this cause God gave them up to vile affections: for even their women exchanged the natural use for that which is contrary to nature: And likewise also the men, leaving the natural use of the woman, burned in their lust one toward another; men with men doing what is shameful, and receiving in themselves that recompense of their error that was fitting. And even as they did not like to retain God in their knowledge, God gave them over to a reprobate mind, to do those things that are not right; Being filled with unrighteousness of every kind" (Romans 1:22-29).

REMEMBER
Opinions may contradict the Word of God,
but the facts never do.

3. The Christian Religion And Christian Theology

The particular set of beliefs basic to the religion of any society will shape the worldview of the people who embrace those beliefs. That in turn will determine the way people interact with each other, and that interaction produces a culture. That culture in turn will shape the institutions that are created, both governmental and religious. The so-called "culture wars" that people have been talking about stem from the fact that the adherents of naturalistic religion are trying to push Christians and Christian influence out of the public sector. They yell that they want religious freedom, when they really mean freedom from Christian influence. If we really had religious freedom in this country, a Christian congressman could stand up in congress and say, "I am introducing this bill to outlaw abortion because I believe that it is contrary to the Word of God," and everyone would say, "Put it to a vote, he has just as much right to his opinion as anyone else". The idea that any society can be religiously neutral is a delusion. The government-financed schools and universities that indoctrinate students in the atheist worldview constitute an atheist state religion, and atheist/agnostic professors are its priests.

Because Christians have the unchanging Word of God, we should all be able to agree. However, believers not only have to deal with a heart that is **"deceitful above all things, and desperately wicked,"** but Satan is continually trying to create division and confusion in order to lead people away from God's Word (Jeremiah 17:9). In our society he has used that division to turn many from the Bible to science, on the mistaken assumption that science can answer questions that the Bible cannot.

In reality, many disagreements among Christians are about what the Bible does not say, rather than what it does say. Churches divide over music, dress, ecclesiastical government, vestments and so forth. And, when it comes to disagreements about what the Bible does say, the disagreement is usually caused by someone reading ideas into the text, not the text itself. Such differences will only be resolved when all involved allow those truths clearly and explicitly stated in Scripture to be the standard, while rejecting any ideas or interpretations that contradict that standard. And, that is the standard this theology follows.

If you think that you go by the Bible, ask yourself if you are willing to accept the following passages of Scripture unconditionally or want to explain one or more of them away. **"In six days the LORD made heaven and earth, the sea, and everything that is in them, and rested on the seventh day"** (Exodus 20:11). **"No man can come to me, unless the Father who has sent me draws him: and I will raise him up on the last day"** (John 6:44). **"We have an advocate with the Father, Jesus Christ the righteous. He is the propiti-**

ation for our sins: and not for ours only, but also for the sins of the whole world" (1John 2:1-2). "My kingdom is not of this world" (John 18:36). "We are in the one who is true, in His Son Jesus Christ. He is the true God, and eternal life" (1John 5:20). "The Lord is... not willing that any should perish, but that all should come to repentance" (2Peter 3:9). "Without faith it is impossible to please God" (Hebrews 11:6). "We are sanctified through the offering of the body of Jesus Christ once for all" (Hebrews 10:10). "A man is justified by faith without the deeds of the law" (Romans 3:28).

Those who explain away any statement of Scripture have rejected God as their authority. To all of them the Bible says, "**He who is of God hears God's words... you do not hear them, because you are not of God**" (John 8:47).

"Christianity alone provides the solid empirical base for a sound approach to the universe and a valid relationship with its Creator and Redeemer... The case for Christianity is overwhelmingly powerful. Creationism receives greater and greater support in the philosophical community and differs radically from the obscurantist efforts of atheists to argue that time and 'mutation' somehow have the power to change empirical reality. Historical evidences of the miraculous life and resurrection of Jesus Christ put Christianity in the category of analytical meaningfulness without significant parallel when compared with the other major world's religions, to say nothing of the cults and speculative philosophical isms." [Dr. John Warwick Montgomery, Quoted from Christian News, 12/6/2021, pages 1-2.]

Only One Way of Salvation

One thing that could, and should, unite Christians is the way of salvation. The words, "**To give His people the knowledge of salvation by the remission of their sins, through the tender mercy of our God,**" plainly tell us that we are saved by forgiveness [not works] and that forgiveness is a gift of God's "mercy" [grace] (Luke 1:77-78). Furthermore, the words, "**All the prophets testify of Him, that through His name whoever believes in Him will receive forgiveness of sins,**" testify to the fact that salvation has always been through faith in the Messiah [Christ] (Acts 10:43). The words, "**I know that my redeemer lives, and that He will stand at a future time upon the earth,**" tell us that Job was trusting in Christ (Job 19:25). And, the words, "**The covenant *concerning faith in Christ*, that was confirmed by God at the time of Abraham, cannot be nullified by the law, which came four hundred and thirty years later,**" tell us that the law did not change the fact that salvation has always come to believers through faith in God's promise of forgiveness in Christ (Galatians 3:17). Yet, in spite of what the Bible plainly says, a number of sects prefer to teach wild conjecture about salvation being different in different periods of history.

One problem people have is in understanding the role of animal sacrifice. However, in the third chapter of Galatians, the Apostle Paul explains that, **"The law was instituted as a schoolmaster to bring God's people to faith in Christ"** (Galatians 3:24, a paraphrase). That means that God's grace never came through keeping the Law or sacrificing animals. On the contrary, in ancient Israel the "law," both civil and religious, worked as a schoolmaster. The civil law condemned sin, and the sacrifices required the people to confess their sins and look to God for mercy. By those sacrifices God taught the people that forgiveness is not cheap. And, because God instituted those sacrifices as a type of Christ's ultimate sacrifice, He counted faith in the promise of forgiveness that He had connected with the sacrifice as faith in Christ (Luke 11:50-51, Gal. 3:17, 24). David trusted in that promise, saying, **"I have placed my faith in your grace [mercy]; my heart will rejoice in your salvation"** (Psalm 13:5). And, that promise of grace (mercy) is why **God said, "I desired mercy, and not sacrifice"** (Hosea 6:6).

> "Whatever is not taken from, or whatever goes beyond, Holy Scripture is neither religion nor theology, but human speculation." (John Theodore Mueller, "Christian Dogmatics," page 30.) And, the only way we can eliminate error from our theology is by eliminating the human element.

Biblical Theology

The only way a theology can be truly Biblical, is for it to organize and set forth those truths clearly and explicitly stated in Scripture, "Line upon line; here a little, and there a little," **without adding to or taking from the words of Scripture** (Isaiah 28:10). While the word "theology" is not defined by Scripture, I use it as described above, in reference to what the Bible says, and knowledge of what the Bible says.

The words, **"The anointing that you have received from Him remains in you, and you do not need anyone to teach you: but the same anointing teaches you about all things,"** speak of a spiritual guidance that everyone who understands the way of salvation has received, at least in part, for it is the Holy Spirit who enables us to understand the way of salvation (1John 2:27). However, the Holy Spirit not only opens our eyes to understand the way of salvation, but gives some the ability to think theologically. I am not talking about philosophy, but the ability to think Biblically. As it is written, **"We are not adequate in ourselves to think that we can accomplish anything in our own strength; but our ability is from God; who** has also made us able ministers of the new testament" (2Corinthians 3:5-6).

The Apostle Paul said, "**I was made a minister, according to the gift of the grace of God given unto me by the effectual working of His power**" (Ephesians 3:7). Speaking of that God-given ability, Dr. John Theodore Mueller said, "Theology must first be found in the soul of a person before that person can teach and present it either by word or in writing." ("Christian Dogmatics," page 32.) For that reason, it is impossible for an unbeliever to be a theologian in the Biblical sense, even if he has learned the doctrines. And, because the soul of a Christian theologian is inhabited by and receives aptitude from the Holy Ghost, some describe the God-given ability of a theologian as a "habitude". Of that, Dr. John Theodore Mueller said, "Theology is a practical habitude of the mind, comprising the knowledge and acceptance of divine truth, together with an aptitude to instruct others toward such knowledge and acceptance and to defend such truth against its adversaries." // "The theological habitude further includes the ability to refrain from all human opinions and thoughts on God and divine things, to draw all doctrines from Holy Scripture, and thus to teach nothing but God's Word." ("Christian Dogmatics," page 33-34.)

Do not misunderstand me. I am not saying that we do not need human teachers. Although the Holy Spirit did teach the Apostle Paul directly, Paul already knew the Old Testament, and knew it well. However, Paul was an exception to the rule. All of the other Apostles learned at the feet of Jesus. Timothy learned at the feet of Paul. (Gal. 1:17, Acts 1:16-26, Acts 20:4, 1Cor. 4:15.) And, one important reason that the Holy Spirit uses others in His training is to bind believers together so that we "all speak the same thing, and that there are no divisions" (1Corinthians 1:10). That is why the Apostle Paul met with the other Apostles, to make certain that he was teaching the same doctrine that they were teaching – thus setting an example for us (Gal. 2:2). And, that is why those who are being taught by the Holy Spirit will be willing to listen to what other believers are saying, and will check it against Scripture (Acts 17:11, Isaiah 8:20).

4. Theology Considered As Doctrine

While teaching false doctrine is a sin, we must stress the fact that having the correct doctrine is not what makes us righteous in the sight of God, and having it does not make us better than anyone else. Since none of us has a perfect understanding of what the Bible says, we need to be humble. As teachers of God's Word we want to handle His Word in a responsible way, without being indifferent to what is taught or confusing our own opinions with the Word of God. That requires a precise knowledge of what Bible does or does not say. And, the only people who have that knowledge are those who realize that God wants us to teach what He has said, not what we (or others) think about it.

That being said, the entire body of doctrine, everything necessary for our salvation, is plainly stated in Scripture in passages so clear that they need no interpretation. God has not given us His truth in the language of the philosophers and scholars of this world, but in the language of shepherds, farmers, fishermen, and tentmakers. And, the doctrine set forth in its passages is the standard against which every interpretation and every human opinion must be judged. As it is written, "**If they do not speak according to this word, it is because there is no light in them**" (Isaiah 8:20). Furthermore, Bible history is central to everything the Bible says. In fact, rightly understood, the Bible is a book of history, not a religious text. It not only gives us a reliable record of all historical events pertinent to our salvation, but includes an historical archive of psalms sung, proverbs spoken, prophesies made, visions seen, and letters written.

Once I learned the doctrinal truths that are plainly stated in Scripture, I was able to see that all of those truths center around, and relate to, seven historical events. **Those events are, creation, the fall, the virgin birth of Christ, Christ's death, Christ's resurrection, Christ's ascension, and Christ's return.** What sets these events apart is the fact that they all have a deep spiritual significance for every man woman and child on earth. All of them have something to do with our relationship to God. And, that spiritual significance is clearly and explicitly stated in Scripture.

The Biblical record of creation is the foundation for everything else that the Bible says. It tells us where the universe came from, where life came from, God's original intent for man, the origin of marriage and so forth. The spiritual significance of creation lies in the fact that we were not created with a sinful nature, and the fact that because God created us we are accountable to Him. Here are a few of the Bible passages that clearly tell us what the spiritual significance of creation is.

The words, "**God saw every thing that He had made, and, behold, it was very good**," tell us that God did not create us with a sinful nature (Genesis 1:31). The words, "**Behold, as the clay is in the potter's hand, so are you in my hand, O house of Israel**," tell us that we belong to God (Jeremiah 18:6). And the words, "**Men will account for every idle word that they speak, on the day of judgment**," tell us that we must all account to God (Matthew 12:36).

While **the Biblical record of the fall** tells us how sin entered into the world, its spiritual significance lies in the fact that Adam's sin brought condemnation on us all. The entire law of God relates to the fall, because it reveals that condemnation. The flood of Noah also relates to the fall because it reveals God's wrath against sin – although it is also a type of the final judgment. Here are a few of the Bible passages that clearly tell us what the spiritual significance of the fall is.

Since God created us without sin, the words, **"The heart is deceitful above all things, and desperately wicked,"** reveal how our nature has changed as a result of the fall (Jeremiah 17:9). The words, **"All have sinned, and come short of the glory of God,"** tell us that the effect of the fall extends to all men (Romans 3:23). And, the words, **"Just as sin entered the world by one man, and death by sin; so death passed upon all men, because all have sinned,"** plainly tell us that sin entered the world as a result of the fall, and the fact that people die is proof that they are sinners (Romans 5:12).

While **the Biblical record of Christ's virgin birth** tells us that Christ is different, the spiritual significance of His birth lies in the fact that He was born the sinless Son of God. Here are a few of the Bible passages that clearly tell us the spiritual significance of His birth.

The words, **"Behold, a virgin shall be with child, and shall bring forth a son, and they shall call His name Emmanuel, which being interpreted is, God with us,"** tell us that because of Christ's unique birth He is God (Matthew 1:23). The words, **"Unto us a child is born, unto us a son is given: and the government will be on His shoulders: and His name will be called Wonderful, Counselor, The mighty God, The everlasting Father,"** again tell us that Christ is God (Isaiah 9:6). The words, **"He committed no sin, nor was deceit ever found in His mouth,"** // **"For God made Him who knew no sin, to be sin for us; so that we might be made the righteousness of God in Him,"** tell us that Christ was without sin (1Peter 2:22, 2Corinthians 5:21). And, the words, **"He appeared in order to take away our sins; and there is no sin in Him,"** again tell us that Christ was without sin (1John 3:5).

While **the Biblical record of Christ's death on the cross** tells us how He died, the spiritual significance of His death lies in the fact that He died for our sins. Here are a few of the Bible passages that clearly tell us what His death means for us.

The words, **"I want to remind you of the gospel… How that Christ died for our sins according to the scriptures,"** tell us that Christ died for our sins, and that fact is central to the gospel (1Corinthians 15:1-3). The words, **"God commends His love toward us, in that, while we were yet sinners, Christ died for us,"** tell us that Christ died for us while we were yet sinners (Romans 5:8). The words, **"By His own blood… He entered once for all into the holy place, obtaining eternal redemption for us,"** tell us that His blood was the price of our redemption (Hebrews 9:12). The words, **"We are sanctified through the offering of the body of Jesus Christ once for all,"** tell us that we are "sanctified" through the sacrifice [offering] of His body (Hebrews 10:10). And, the words, **"The blood of**

Jesus Christ His Son cleanses us of all sin," tell us that His sacrifice [blood] cleanses us of all sin (1John 1:7).

While **the Biblical record of Christ's resurrection** from the dead tells us that He rose again the third day, the spiritual significance of His resurrection lies in the fact that it was the seal of His victory over death, and in the fact that because He lives we will live also. Here are a few of the Bible passages that clearly tell us the spiritual significance of His resurrection

The words, "**If we preach that Christ rose from the dead, how can some of you say that there is no resurrection of the dead? For if the dead do not rise then Christ did not rise. And if Christ did not rise, our preaching is a waste of time, and your faith is worthless,**" tell us that Christ's resurrection is central to the gospel (1Corinthians 15:12-14). The words, "**Jesus... was delivered for our offences, and was raised again for our justification,**" tell us that Christ "was raised again" so that we might believe, and believing be justified through faith in Him (Romans 4:24-25). The words, "**Jesus said to her, I am the resurrection, and the life: he who believes in me will yet live, even though he is dead,**" tell us that because He lives He will raise all who trust in Him from dead (John 11:25). The words, "**The hour is coming, in which all who are in the graves will hear His voice, and will come out;**" tell us that because He lives He will raise "all who are in the graves" (John 5:28-29). And, the words, "**The Lord himself will descend from heaven with a shout, with the voice of the archangel, and with the trump of God: and the dead in Christ will rise first: Then we which are alive and remain will be caught up together with them in the clouds, to meet the Lord in the air: and so shall we ever be with the Lord,**" give us a description of our resurrection – Which can only take place because Christ has risen (1Thessalonians 4:15-17).

While **the Biblical record of Christ's ascension** into heaven describes what took place, the spiritual significance of His ascension lies in the fact that He 1- sent the Holy Spirit, 2- is our advocate before the Father, and 3- will return again. Here are a few of the Bible passages that clearly tell us the spiritual significance of His ascension.

The words, "**It is to your advantage for me to go away: for if I do not go away, the Comforter will not come to you; but if I depart, I will send Him to you,**" tell us that the outpouring of the Spirit on the day of Pentecost took place because Christ ascended into heaven (John 16:7). The words, "**Christ who died, yea rather, who was raised from the dead, is at the right hand of God, and also intercedes for us,**" tell us that having ascended into heaven Christ makes intercession for us as our mediator and advocate before God (Romans 8:34). And, the words, "**The same Jesus, that has been taken up from you into heaven, will come back in the same** way that you saw Him go into heaven," tell us that because Christ ascended into heaven, we can be assured that He will return (Acts 1:11).

While **the physical return of Christ is yet in the future**, its spiritual significance lies in the fact that when He returns all men will rise from the dead, and all will be judged. For those who trust in Christ there will be no condemnation, their tears will be wiped away, and they will live forever with Christ. However, all unbelievers will be condemned. Here are a few of the Bible passages that clearly tell us the spiritual significance of His return.

The words, **"He commanded us to preach to the people, and to testify that He is the one whom God has appointed to be the Judge of the living and dead,"** tell us that Christ is the one who shall judge both the living and the dead (Acts 10:42). The words, **"I charge you therefore before God, and the Lord Jesus Christ, who will judge the living and the dead at His appearing,"** tell us that Christ will judge the living and the dead when He returns (2Timothy 4:1). The words, **"There is therefore now no condemnation for those who are in Christ Jesus,"** for **"The blood of Jesus Christ His Son cleanses us of all sin,"** tell us that we who trust in Christ will not be condemned when we are judged (Romans 8:1, 1John 1:7). The words, **"God will wipe every tear from their eyes; and there will be no more death, or sorrow, or crying, neither will there be any more pain: for the former things have passed away,"** tell us that after the resurrection those who trust in Christ will never again experience pain or sorrow (Revelation 21:4). And the words, **"Come, you who are blessed by my Father, inherit the kingdom prepared for you from the foundation of the world,"** tell us what Christ's return means for believers (Matthew 25:34). In contrast, the words, **"Depart from me, you cursed, into everlasting fire, prepared for the devil and his angels,"** tell us what Christ's return means for unbelievers (Matthew 25:41).

While I could quote many more passages, my point is that these seven historical events are central to the message of salvation in Christ and thus central to work of world evangelism. For that reason, anyone who denies, calls into question, or contradicts Bible history is hindering the work of salvation, and should be avoided by every believer. As the Apostle said, **"Those who know God accept what we say, those who are not of God will not accept what we say. That is how we can distinguish the spirit of truth from the spirit of error"** (1John 4:6). That being understood, it is significant that the oldest creed of the Christian church, the *"Apostle's Creed,"* summarizes these historical events.

The Apostles' Creed
I believe in God the Father Almighty, Maker of heaven and

earth.

And in Jesus Christ, His only Son, our Lord; who was conceived by the Holy Ghost, Born of the Virgin Mary; suffered under Pontius Pilate, was crucified, dead and buried; He descended into hell; the third day He rose again from the dead; He ascended into heaven and sits on the right hand of God, the Father Almighty; From thence He shall come to judge the quick and the dead.

I believe in the Holy Ghost; the Holy Christian Church, the communion of saints; the forgiveness of sins; the resurrection of the body; and the life everlasting. Amen.

5. The Theology Of The Apostles

Because the Bible is the Word of God, it only contains one theology, one unified body of doctrine. In the past that was rarely questioned. However, some who have been influenced by secular religion, with its denial of the supernatural, interpret the statements of some Apostles to contradict others. In contrast, the words, "**All the prophets testify of Him, that through His name whoever believes in Him will receive forgiveness of sins,**" tell us that all of the prophets agree in their testimony of Christ (Acts 10:43). And, the words, "**The Spirit specifically says, that in the future some will depart from the faith, giving heed to seducing spirits, and doctrines of devils,**" warn us against listening to those who teach otherwise (1Timothy 4:1).

That being said, God prepared the way for Christ by moving "**All the prophets**" to "**testify of Him**" (Acts 10:43). And, the Old Testament (which was all the Apostles had) clearly sets forth all of the doctrines that I summarized in the previous section. The words, "**God saw that the wickedness of man was great in the earth, and that every imagination of the thoughts of his heart was only evil continually,**" told the Apostles that after the fall man was no longer good (Genesis 6:5, see Gen. 1:31). The words, "**Unto us a child is born, unto us a son is given... and His name will be called Wonderful, Counselor, The mighty God,**" told them that Christ was God (Isaiah 9:6). The words, "**He was wounded for our transgressions, He was bruised for our iniquities: the punishment that brought us peace was upon Him; and by His stripes we are healed,**" told them that His death was the atonement for our sins (Isaiah 53:5). The words, "**My own familiar friend, in whom I trusted, who did eat of my bread, has lifted up his heel against me. But you, O LORD, be merciful to me, and raise me up,**" speak of Judas and Christ's resurrection (Psalm 41:9-10).

And, the words, "**Who has ascended up into heaven, and come down?... what is His son's name, if you can tell?" speak of Christ's ascension (Proverbs 30:4-5). These and a multitude of other prophesies make it clear that the Apostles had the same Bible-history centered theology that we have. And, that theology is reflected in the words of the New Testament.

In his epistle to the Romans, the Apostle Paul begins his presentation of the salvation message with the words, "**All men, both Jews and Gentiles, are all under sin**" (Romans 3:9). He then follows that statement with a number of quotes from the Old Testament, beginning with the words, "**There is none righteous, no, not one**" (Romans 3:10 and Eccl.7:20). (See, Psalm 14:1-3, Psalm 5:9, Psalm 140:3, Psalm 10:7, Isaiah 59:7-8, Psalm 36:1.) Those quotes form the basis for his doctrine of Universal Condemnation, and he summarizes them with the words, "**Therefore no flesh will ever be justified in God's sight by the deeds of the law**" (Romans 3:20).

Beginning with the words, "**But now the righteousness of God apart from the law is revealed, being witnessed by the law and the prophets,**" he then transitions into the doctrine of Justification by Faith (Romans 3:21). That doctrine points to "**The righteousness of God which comes through faith in Jesus Christ,**" and ends with the words, "**Therefore we conclude that a man is justified by faith without the deeds of the law**" (Romans 3:22, 28).

In the fourth chapter of Romans, Paul presents the doctrine of Imputed Righteousness, which clarifies and expands upon the doctrine of Justification by Faith. In chapter five, he summarizes the Doctrine of the Atonement (verses 6-11), and that leads to his Doctrine of the Fall and redemption, which contrasts the effects of Adam's fall with the effects of Christ's atonement (Romans 5:12-21). I could go on and on, but the point I want to make is that the doctrine that God wants us to believe and teach is not a matter of opinion, but is plainly stated in Scripture.

For that reason, a truly Biblical theology does not consist of principles and concepts abstracted from the words of Scripture, but the actual words of Scripture, arranged by topic and presented in a way that agrees with all of the other doctrines that are plainly stated in Scripture, "**Line upon line; here a little, and there a little**" (Isaiah 28:10). That being the case, the root of much theological controversy is not disagreement about what the Bible says, but disagreement about what conclusions should be drawn from what the Bible says. And, Satan will always try to cause division and undermine faith. So expect it (1Corinthians 11:19). The important thing is what God says, not what men think, or the conclusions they draw.

6. Law And Gospel

In his epistles, the Apostle Paul devotes two chapters to the proper relationship of law to gospel. Those two chapters are the third chapter of Romans, and the third chapter of Galatians. In both of those chapters he tells us that trying to keep the law will not make anyone righteous in the sight of God. To the Romans he says, "**No one will ever be justified in God's sight by doing what the law requires: because the law is what makes us aware of our sins**" (Romans 3:20). And, to the Galatians he says, "**It is clear that no one is justified in the sight of God because of the law, for, the just shall live by faith**" (Galatians 3:11).

Now, to be justified is to be absolved of guilt, pronounced innocent, found blameless, or declared to be righteous. **Therefore, one key part of Paul's doctrine of the proper relationship of law to gospel, is that the law cannot make anyone righteous**. And, if it cannot make us righteous it cannot save us. Does that mean that the law is worthless? Not at all! The Apostle Paul goes on to answer that question by saying, "**Do we then cancel the law through faith? Absolutely not: On the contrary, we establish the law**" (Romans 3:31). That is why Evangelical Christians use the law to expose and condemn sin while pointing people to what the Apostle Paul called, "**The righteousness of God apart from the law... the righteousness of God which comes through faith in Jesus Christ to all and upon all who believe**" (Romans 10:3, and 3:21-22).

Paul goes on to explain the righteousness "**which comes through faith in Jesus Christ,**" by saying, "**All have sinned, and come short of the glory of God; Being justified freely by His <u>grace</u> through the <u>redemption</u> that is in Christ Jesus**" (Romans 3:23-24). And, how does God's "grace" and Christ's "redemption" make us righteous? That question is answered by the words, "**We have <u>redemption</u> through His blood, the <u>forgiveness of sins</u>, according to the riches of His <u>grace</u>**" (Ephesians 1:7). In short, it is the forgiveness of sins that makes us righteous in the sight of God. That is why it is written, "**Christ is the end of the law for righteousness to every one who believes**" for "**The blood of Jesus Christ His Son cleanses us of all sin**" (Romans 10:4, 1John 1:7).

7. Vital Doctrines And Unanswered Questions

In theology a distinction is made between those doctrines that form the very foundation of the Christian faith, vital doctrines that cannot be denied without undermining faith and subverting the work of the gospel: and those doctrines which are not the foundation of saving faith. For example: our salvation does not depend upon knowing that

David was king, or that Paul was beaten with rods. However, that does not mean that those doctrines are unimportant, or that we should tolerate those who attack or deny them.

First of all, everything recorded in the Bible was placed there by God for a reason. Therefore, every attempt to attack, deny, or explain away something the Bible says is an attack on God, and no church worth its salt will tolerate such attacks. Secondly, in the past some churches have allowed people to attack and deny vital doctrines of the Christian faith while justifying that denial with the claim, "it does not affect salvation". One doctrine that I am thinking of specifically is the doctrine of creation. In fact, I might say creation and the flood because denying either one of them undermines faith in Christ.

The Bible not only records the events of creation in straightforward historical narrative, but whenever it is referred elsewhere in Scripture, it is referred to as historical fact. For example: In answering a question about divorce, Jesus referred to creation, saying, "**Have you not read that He who made them at the beginning made them male and female**" (Matthew 19:4).

Those who counter what the Bible says about creation and try to get around it only do so because they have been influenced by a bogus history of the world that is disguised as science. They obviously place more stock in the opinions of men than the Word of God. You may have encountered people who claim to be Christian even though they reject what the Bible says about creation. However, if they are Christian, it is only because they are harboring a contradiction in their mind, and have not taken their rejection of creation to its logical conclusion. Otherwise it would destroy their faith. A person who rejects what the Bible says about creation while still regarding the Bible as the Word of God is not thinking clearly. It is totally inconsistent for someone to reject what the Bible says about creation and yet regard Jesus [who referred to it as fact] as God. It is totally inconsistent for someone to reject what the Bible says about creation while accepting the doctrine of the fall and redemption, and that doctrine is basic to the gospel (Romans 5:12-21). And, Christ condemns all such inconsistency with the words, "**O fools, and slow of heart to believe everything the prophets have said**" (Luke 24:25).

Even if rejecting what the Bible says about creation does not instantly bring God's condemnation and wrath, it tends to undermine faith and often results in children who walk away from the faith. My point is that everything that the Bible says is important. No part of it can be denied without consequences. And, everyone who contradicts and explains away any statement of Scripture, is "**Making the word of God of no effect**" (Mark 7:13).

Unanswered Questions

Another issue theologians have to deal with has to do with questions about matters on which the Bible has not spoken. In many cases those questions have to do with indifferent matters; that is matters that do not involve a moral issue, and are neither commanded nor forbidden by God's Word. In such cases the rule is that we do not add to or go beyond what the Bible says. If the Bible does not address a particular issue, then that is what we should say. However, modern technology often creates moral dilemmas that have to be addressed. Two of those are cloning and in-vitro fertilization. Matters such as that are not morally neutral because they destroy lives. In regard to in-vitro fertilization that is obvious because the process is to fertilize several human eggs, select the one wanted and kill the rest. That is murder! Cloning is prone to cause miscarriage and deformity, and for that reason it is not being promoted like it was a few years ago. However, I want to stress the fact that no one has the right to just teach anything he pleases about matters that Scripture does not address. When it comes to moral issues, Christians need to take the moral high ground, and stand for what is high, good, pure and right. **Believers should never use the silence of Scripture as an excuse to rationalize matters that are contrary to "the law written in their hearts,"** (Romans 2:15). Our desire should always be to exalt Christ, and to that end our views and conduct should always conform to, **"Whatever is true, whatever is honest, whatever is just, whatever is pure, whatever is lovely,"** and **"whatever is of good report"** (Philippians 4:8).

"Every one who sets aside the clear testimony of God's Word in a single point rejects the entire Word of God as the only source and standard of faith." (John Theodore Mueller, *Christian Dogmatics*, page 54)

8. A Sound Approach To Theology

As I have previously mentioned, and feel that I cannot stress enough, **the doctrine that God wants us to teach is what He has said**, not what men think. And, the meaning He wants us to place on His words is the same meaning that you are placing on my words as you read this, the plain conversational meaning of the words. That is what Paul was trying to get across when he said, **"Do not go beyond what is written"** // **"We have not written anything to you, other than what you read"** (1Corinthians 4:6, 2Corinthians 1:13).

The plain conversational meaning of the words includes all of the normal figures of speech that are in everyday use [or were when the Bible was written]. However, people who attempt to get around what the Bible says by inventing figures of speech and exotic "poetic" languages unknown to history are condemned by the words, **"The time will come when they will not endure sound doctrine"** (2Timothy

4:3). That being said, I offer the following quotations which reflect **a sound approach to theology**.

"|All exegesis, whether it be in general the unfolding of the sense of Scripture or in particular the explanation of (or rather the attempt to explain) the more difficult passages of Scripture, is based on the fact that the entire Christian doctrine is revealed and set forth in Scripture passages so clear that the learned and the unlearned alike can understand them; they do not stand in need of "exegesis" for explanation. If Scripture did not have this quality, it would not be for all Christians, "a lamp unto their feet and a light unto their path," nor would all Christians be able to establish the truth of their faith by Scripture, and in the light of Scripture mark and avoid false teachers.|" (Dr. Francis Pieper, *Christian Dogmatics*, Vol. 1, pages 359-360)

"The Christian doctrine is not produced by the theologian; all that the Christian theologian does is that he compiles the doctrinal statements contained in Scripture (in the text and context), groups them under their proper heads, and arranges these doctrines in the order of their relationship." (Dr. Francis Pieper, *Christian Dogmatics*, Vol. 1, pages 51-52)

"Hence a true Christian exegete must possess the following qualifications: a) He must regard the whole Bible as the inerrant Word of God; b) he must treat Holy Scripture as a book which is clear in itself; c) he must conscientiously point out the real sense of the text; and d) he must be able to refute the erroneous human opinions which false teachers or misguided orthodox theologians have foisted on the text." (John Theodore Mueller, "*Christian Dogmatics*," page 139)

"The whole Christian doctrine is revealed in Scripture passages that need no exegesis, but are an open book alike to the learned and the unlearned and can be so readily translated that the translator cannot go wrong unless he has made up his mind to depart from the original." (Dr. Francis Pieper, *Christian Dogmatics*, Vol. 1, page 347)

"Whoever attempts to shed more light on dark passages of Scripture than Scripture itself offers in its clear passages is adding to God's Word. And whoever obscures clear passages by bringing in obscure passages is taking away from God's Word." (Dr. Francis Pieper, *Christian Dogmatics*, Vol. 1, pages 364-365)

"We go astray in our exegesis of Scripture as soon as we think that the historical background given in Scripture needs to be supplemented by material from secular history and permit this supplementation to have a decisive influence on our exegesis." (Dr. Francis Pieper, *Christian Dogmatics*, Vol. 1, pages 366)

"| Correctly defined, open questions are such questions as inevitably arise in our study of Scripture doctrines but are not answered by Scripture at all or at least not clearly. And Scripture enjoins us to let them remain open questions. If we presume to answer them and ask men to accept our opinion as divine truth, we would be rejecting those Scripture passages which forbid us to add anything to God's Word. Every true theologian must learn not only to speak, but also to keep silence. He should speak where and as far as God's Word speaks; he should hold his tongue where God's Word is silent. He who has not learned this art of silence and dares to speak where God's Word is silent is condemned by Jeremiah 23:16: "**Thus says the Lord of Hosts, Hearken not unto the words of the prophets that prophesy unto you; they make you vain; they speak a vision out of their own heart and not out of the mouth of the Lord."|**" (Dr. Francis Pieper, *Christian Dogmatics*, Vol. 1, pages 93-94)

"The requirements of the divine will should not be altered by man, nor should His Word be changed to please the carnal heart." (John Theodore Mueller, "*Christian Dogmatics*," page 395)

A truly Biblical hermeneutic looks at what the words of Scripture say, not opinions about what those words might mean or what conclusions should be drawn from them. In short, the doctrine that God wants us to get from His Word consists of what His words actually say, not what men think. And, the truth of what they say is an objective fact that can be verified simply by reading the verse.

When the Reformation began, Martin Luther's confidence was not in himself, or in shaky interpretations of Scripture, but in the objective truths so plainly stated in Scripture that they needed no interpretation. Those plainly stated truths of Scripture are known in Reformation Theology as the **seats of doctrine**, and they are the foundation of orthodox Theology. Furthermore, because Bible doctrine consists of what the Bible says, not what men think, we can list the seats of doctrine for a particular topic. For example, the Biblical doctrine of divorce is given in Deut. 24:1, Mal. 2:15-16, Matt. 5:31-32 & 19:7-9, and 1Cor. 7:12-15. And, the doctrine consists of what those words actually say, not opinions as to how they should be applied..

The sum total of all the Bible passages that clearly state a doctrinal truth is known in theology as the "**analogy of faith**" (the standard of faith). That standard is the authority by which all interpretations, conclusions, and opinions of men must be judged (Isaiah 8:20). The Bible is perfectly clear. It is the sin darkened heart of man that confuses the issues, and creates controversy. And, it is sinful pride that causes men to pass off their own word as God's Word, or exalt it over the Word of God.

Many see nothing wrong with brushing aside and explaining away what the Bible says. Nevertheless, in the eyes of God that is rebellion, and the words, **"They rebelled against the words of God, and despised the counsel of the most High,"** // **"Rebellion is as the sin of witchcraft, and defiance is as iniquity and idolatry,"** condemn it (Psalm 107:11, 1Samuel 15:23).

SCRIPTURE ALONE

THE DOCTRINE OF HOLY SCRIPTURE
(De Scriptura Sacra)

1. The Bible Is The Only Source And Standard Of Faith

Throughout history there has been one and only one way of salvation, and that is through faith in God's promise of forgiveness in Christ, **"For there is no other name under heaven given among men, by which we must be saved"** (Acts 4:12). And, the words, **"Search the scriptures; for in them you think that you have eternal life: and they are they that testify of me,"** tell us that Scripture was written to testify of Christ (John 5:39). Furthermore, because salvation has been through faith in Christ from the beginning, the true church of Jesus Christ, the sum total of all who are saved through faith in Him, existed long before the day of Pentecost, long before Scripture was written. That is why we are told that **it was by faith that, "Abel offered to God a better sacrifice than Cain," and by faith that, "he was declared to be righteous"** (Hebrews 11:4). And, that is why the Bible says, **"If there had been a law given that could have given life, righteousness truly would have been by the law. But Scripture has concluded all under sin, that the promise might be given to those who believe, through faith in Jesus Christ"** (Galatians 3:21-22).

Long before the Bible was written the words, **"And a son was also born to Seth; and he called his name Enos, then men began to call upon the name of the LORD,"** tell us that men knew about God and were calling upon Him at that time (Genesis 4:26). However, after God had His prophets put His Word in writing, His people were warned **"You shall not add to the word which I command you, nor shall you take anything from it"** (Deuteronomy 4:2). [See Deut. 12:32, Josh. 1:7 and 23:6.] Only God can add to His Word. And, the words, **"You are... built upon the foundation of the apostles and prophets, Jesus Christ himself being the chief corner stone,"** tell us that the completed Scriptures, the writings of **"the apostles and prophets,"** are the **foundation** for our faith (Ephesians 2:19-20), for it is, **"Through their word,"** that we "believe" (John 17:20). As it is written, **"Faith comes by hearing, and hearing by the word of God"** (Romans 10:17).

Because the Bible was written so that, **"You may know that you have eternal life, and that you may believe in the name of the Son of God,"** Satan is continually at work trying to lead people away from what the Bible says (1John 5:13). And, he generally does that by substituting some other authority disguised as reason, tradition, or new revelation.

Human Reason

The absurdity of man attempting to make his own mind the arbiter of all truth can be illustrated by comparing our puny sin-corrupted mind to that of an ant. Suppose that you could communicate with an ant. Suppose further that you gave that ant a revelation, telling it things about the world and yourself that it could never possibly know apart from that revelation. What would you think of that ant if it then said, "I don't know if I believe everything you have said. I will decide for myself which parts to believe or reject"? Would you think that ant was stupid and egotistic? Well that is exactly what God thinks of people who react to His Word that way. That is why Jesus said, "**O fools, and slow of heart to believe everything the prophets have said**" (Luke 24:25). And, that is why the Bible says, "**Professing themselves to be wise, they became fools**" (Romans 1:22). We have a God whose knowledge is so great that the, "**hairs of your head are all numbered**" (Luke 12:7). So great that compared to Him we are far lower than an ant is when compared to us. Or as Job put it, "**How much less man, who is a maggot? and the son of man, who is a worm?**" (Job 25:6).

At this point someone is likely to say, "God has given us our mind and the ability to reason, and He expects us to use it," and that is perfectly true. However, we need to know the limitations of our knowledge, and be aware of how easily our own sinful heart can deceive us. As it is written, "**The heart is deceitful above all things, and desperately wicked: who can know it?**" (Jeremiah 17:9). That is why theologians make a distinction between the **ministerial and the magisterial** use of reason. The ministerial use of reason is the humble attempt of a believer to learn and accept what God has said in His Word. In contrast, the magisterial use of reason involves every attempt of man to claim knowledge beyond his ken, to profess himself to be wise, to set his own opinions over the Word of God, to make his own worldview the arbiter of truth, or to invent his own religion. Of all such attempts the Bible says, "**The wisdom of this world is foolishness with God**" (1Corinthians 3:19).

From the point of view of man's ignorance and sinful pride the Gospel itself is foolish. As it is written, "**The world through its wisdom did not know God... But we preach Christ crucified, a stumbling block to the Jews, and foolishness to the Greeks; But to those who are called, both Jews and Greeks, Christ the power of God, and the wisdom of God. Because the foolishness of God is wiser than men; and the weakness of God is stronger than men**" (1Corinthians 1:21-25). Therefore, we need to counter every attempt of sinful man to exalt man's word over God's Word, to cast doubt on the words of Scripture, to contradict what the Bible says, to interpret the Bible to make it fit human opinion, or to read unscriptural ideas into the words of Scripture. The words, "**If you continue in my word, you are truly my disciples, and you will know the truth, and the truth will make you free**," tell us that those who are truly Christ's disciples will never look outside of His Word for spiritual truth, or attempt to supplement what the Bible says (John 8:31-32).

Now as I mentioned before, God expects us to apply our reason to learn and accept what He has said in His Word. However, the words, "**We have not written anything to you, other than what you read**," tell us that the message God wants us to get from His Word is nothing other than what the words plainly say (2Corinthians 1:13). In other words, He wants you to place the same meaning on His words that you are placing on my words as you read this, for I am not writing to you anything "other than what you read". Furthermore, the words, "**No truth of scripture comes from any private explanation**," tell us our made-up explanations are worthless (2Peter 1:20). The only valid explanations of any passage of Scripture are those God has given us in Scripture. For example: If someone reads the words, "**Christ died for our sins**," and does not understand what they mean, it would be foolish for him to just make up an explanation. Instead, he should just accept what those words say as true, and ponder them as he continues to study God's Word. If he does that God Himself will give Him understanding as he reads other passages, such as, "**He was wounded for our transgressions, He was bruised for our iniquities**," or "**Blotting out the handwriting of ordinances that was against us, which was contrary to us, and took it out of the way, nailing it to His cross**," or "**The blood of Jesus Christ His Son cleanses us of all sin**" (Isaiah 53:5, Colossians 2:14, 1John 1:7). In short, the safest explanation of any passage is to say that it means the same thing as another passage. If we do that, even if we are wrong our explanation will still be the Word of God.

The context of any word or statement of Scripture has to do with the flow of thought from word to word and sentence to sentence. For example: in the passage, "**God called the light Day, and called the darkness Night. And the evening and the morning were the first day**," the word "day" appears twice (Genesis 1:5). And, each time the meaning of the word "day" is different. However, the context tells us exactly what is meant each time. Nevertheless, some who want to get around various statements of Scripture have started calling human opinion as to what the words of Scripture meant to people living back then "the context". As a result, they wind up exalting man's word over God's Word, thus making Scripture conform to their own opinion. Whatever men think they know about the culture and customs of Bible times is the word of man, not the Word of God. And, the words, "**If you <u>continue in my word</u>, you are truly my disciples**," tell us that we are not to look outside of Scripture for doctrine, and that those who read ideas found outside if scripture [the word of man] into Scripture are not truly disciples of Christ (John 8:31).

The words, "**Bringing into captivity every thought to the obedience of Christ,**" tell us that man's word should never be placed above the Word of God (2Corinthians 10:5). As far as God is concerned, any scientist who contradicts what God's Word says is just as ignorant as that ant I previously mentioned. Those who, in the name of reason, claim that miracles are impossible because they contradict "the laws of nature" only show their ignorance because **intelligent beings override "the laws of nature" all the time**. For example: It is contrary to the laws of nature for wood, clay, plaster and other materials to form themselves into a house. Because it is contrary to "the laws of nature" it will never happen by itself. However, **intelligent beings cause what would never happen naturally to happen**. Likewise, in the case of miracles, God uses His intelligence and ability to cause something to happen that would never happen on its own.

Those who, in the name of reason, claim that the Bible cannot be the Word of God because it contradicts itself, again only show their ignorance. While it is true that an actual contradiction would be an error, very often things that appear contradictory to us only appear contradictory because of our ignorance. For example: Suppose that you heard me say, "The Mississippi river flows south from Minnesota to the Gulf of Mexico," and later say, "I stood on the bank of the Mississippi river and watched it flowing north on its way to the sea". If you jumped up and said, "Ah ha, you contradicted yourself," you would only be showing your ignorance, because the Mississippi river does flow north in some places, one of them being in the northwest corner of Tennessee. The point I am making is that just because something seems like a contradiction to our puny finite minds does not mean it actually is a contradiction. And, when it comes to God's Word there are no real contradictions, only passages that men interpret to contradict when they could just as well be interpreted to agree.

Those who, in the name of reason, claim that what the Bible says cannot be true because it contradicts science again only show their ignorance. If they would actually look at the evidence, they would find that even though the opinions of men often contradict Scripture, the facts never do. Facts may be interpreted to contradict Scripture, but in every case they could just as well be interpreted to agree with it. Moreover, much of what is currently called science is nothing more than atheist religion being passed off as science. For example: Charles Darwin believed that life originated in a warm little pond. At the time he thought that idea was scientific, but it now contradicts science. A number of experiments by Francisco Redi (1626-1697), Louis Pasteur (1822-1895), and others convinced the scientific community that life does not come from non-living chemicals. Nevertheless, atheist religion – falsely called science – continues to hold to Darwin's dream of a warm little pond (1Timothy 6:20). Likewise, Darwin (who knew nothing of genetics) saw small changes in animals (such as finches with different size beaks) and assumed that such changes had no limit. However, modern genetics tells us that there is a limit. Because of that limit one kind of animal cannot change into an entirely different kind. Nevertheless, atheist religion – falsely called science – continues to claim that all life evolved from non-living chemicals (1Timothy 6:20). The atheists have no evidence! In fact, the evidence is against them. They simply reject the evidence, and **"Holdback the truth in unrighteousness,"** as the Bible says (Romans 1:18).

The Traditions of Men

When it comes to the authority of the "Church" or tradition, we need to distinguish between indifferent matters – matters neither commanded or forbidden by God's Word – (such as the color of the carpet), and matters on which God's Word is clear. The words, **"To the law and to the testimony: if they do not speak according to this word, it is because there is no light in them,"** tell us that no "Church" has the authority to contradict what the Bible says (Isaiah 8:20). As it is written, **"If anyone teaches otherwise, and will not agree with sound teaching, even the words of our Lord Jesus Christ, and the doctrine that is in accord with godliness, he is proud, knowing nothing"** (1Timothy 6: 3). As far as tradition is concerned, many traditions are benign, and a respect for tradition often gives people a sense of stability and permanence. However, the words, **"If they do not speak according to this word, it is because there is no light in them,"** tell us that traditions which contradict the Word of God are of the devil (Isaiah 8:20). The tradition of the Pharisees often amounted to nothing more than rationalizing sin. Of such tradition Jesus said, **"Why are you transgressing the commandment of God by your tradition?"** (Matthew 15:3). And, the words, **"If you continue in my word, you are truly my disciples,"** tell us Christ does not want us looking for truth outside of His Word (John 8:20).

The words, **"Do not be called masters: for you have one Master, even Christ,"** tell us that Christ's Word (the Bible) should be the highest authority in any "Church" (Matthew 23:10). Those who are unwilling to accept that rule often appeal to the words, **"Stand fast, and hold the traditions which you have been taught, whether by word, or our epistle"** (2Thessalonians 2:15). However, because the truth will never contradict itself, **no tradition actually taught by the Apostles will ever contradict what the Bible says**. And, the words, **"You shall not add to the word which I command you, nor shall you take anything from it,"** tell us that any tradition that adds to God's Word or explains away what it says is not of God (Deuteronomy 4:2). "The Christian Church has no authority whatever to teach any doctrine besides and beyond the Word of its divine Master Jesus Christ, laid down in the writings of His prophets and apostles." (John Theodore Mueller, *"Christian Dogmatics"*, page 94.)

New Revelations

The words, **"Even if we, or an angel from heaven, preach any gospel to you other than what we have preached to you, let him be accursed,"** warn us of the danger inherent in "new revelations" (Galatians 1:8). Since everything necessary for our salvation is set forth in Scripture passages so clear that they need no interpretation, nothing further is needed for our salvation. If an alleged revelation affirms what the Bible already says then it is superfluous. If it contradicts what the Bible says it will only hinder the work of the Gospel. In the past, false prophets, popes and others have claimed to be guided by God when they were contradicting His Word. However, the words, **"Let God be true, but every man a liar;"** tell us to regard anyone who contradicts what the Bible says as a liar (Romans 3:4). And the words, **"Do not add to His words, lest He reprove you, and you are found to be a liar,"** for, **"All liars, will have their part in the lake that burns with fire,"** should make every false prophet tremble, for, **"It is a fearful thing to fall into the hands of the living God"** (Proverbs 30:6, Revelation 21:8, Hebrews 10:31). Am I saying that a false prophet can never be saved? Not at all! God may, **"Give them repentance bringing them to a realization of the truth"** (2Timothy 2:25). However, they need to realize how serious their sin is. And, the words, **"It would be better for him to be thrown into the sea, with a millstone tied around his neck, than for him to cause one of these little ones to fall away,"** should be a warning to them all (Luke 17:2).

That brings us to another kind of new revelation that is widespread in American churches, the claim that God is speaking in, "A still small voice". The voice that these people hear is not an audible voice, but a "voice" in their head. However, the Bible says nothing about voices in the head! It is called, "A still small voice" because that is the way God's word to Elijah was described in 1Kings 19:12, at least in the King James translation. However, there is nothing in that passage, or anywhere else in Scripture, that speaks of an inaudible voice in the head. The English Standard Version translates those words as, **"A low whisper"**. That being said, I have experienced what seemed like an inaudible voice, as many others have. Sometimes, when praying about a matter I would be reminded of a Bible passage, or assured that things will be alright. Nevertheless, when people start seeking God's direction apart from His Word they open themselves up to satanic deception. That really came across to me some years ago when

I encountered people who claimed to believe in salvation by grace, but lived in constant fear that God would punish them if they did not "obey" every command that He gave them through "A still small voice" in their head. That is nothing more than a warmed-over version of works righteousness. I have also encountered people (and been told of others) who claim that God told them do things that were clearly contrary to His Word (like divorcing their spouse etc.). I have encountered others who claimed that God had given them an interpretation of Scripture, when their interpretation did not fit the context or the grammar, and contradicted what the Bible said elsewhere. All such interpretations are condemned by the words, "**He who has my word, let him speak my word faithfully**" (Jeremiah 23:28). "**Jesus said... If you continue in my word, you are truly my disciples**," and those words tell us that a true disciple of Christ will never look outside of God's Word for guidance (John 8:31). Furthermore, the words, "**No truth of scripture comes from any private explanation**," tell us that the Holy Spirit will never give us our own private explanation of something He said in Scripture (2Peter 1:20). And, the words, "**We have not written anything to you, other than what you read**," tell us that God wants us to pay attention to what His words say, instead of looking for explanations (2Corinthians 1:13). Rather than giving us explanations the Holy Spirit opens our eyes to see what the words plainly say – the meaning that is there for everyone.

2. Holy Scripture Is The Word Of God

Unlike all other books in the world, the Holy Bible (the Scriptures of the Old and New Testaments) is the Word of God. It is the Word of God in the same way that the writings of George Washington are his word, and the writings of Abraham Lincoln are his word. Through the words, "**Search the scriptures; for in them you think that you have eternal life: and they are they that testify of me**," Jesus tells us that the Bible was written to testify of him (John 5:39). And, the words, "**Man shall not live by bread alone, but by every word of God**," tell us that God gives us everlasting life through His Word (Luke 4:4). As it is written, "**Faith comes by hearing, and hearing by the word of God**" (Romans 10:17).

The words, "**Unto them [the Jews] was committed the word of God**," tell us that the Hebrew Scriptures are Word of God (Romans 3:2). Jesus' words, "**Everything must be fulfilled, that was written in the law of Moses, in the prophets, and in the psalms, concerning me**," tell us that because the Old Testament is the Word of God, "everything" it says about Christ had to be "fulfilled" (Luke 24:44). [Note: the phrase, "In the law of Moses, in the prophets, and in the psalms," refers to the three divisions of the Hebrew Bible, and was a way of saying, "In all of the Scriptures".]

Regarding the fulfillment of God's word, the words, "**Until heaven and earth pass away, not one letter or stroke will pass from the law, until everything has been fulfilled,**" tell us that even the letters and strokes are the Word of God, and that all that is written will be fulfilled (Matthew 5:18). The words, "**All this took place, to fulfill what the Lord had spoken by the prophet, saying, Behold, a virgin will be with child, and will bring forth a son, and they will call His name Emmanuel,**" tell us that Christ was born in fulfillment of Scripture (Matthew 1:22-23 - See Isaiah 7:14). The words, "**Fulfilling what was spoken of the Lord by the prophet, who said, Out of Egypt have I called my son,**" tell us that the words of the prophet were the words of God, and the flight of Mary, Joseph and Jesus to Egypt took place in fulfillment of Scripture (Matthew 2:15 - See Hosea 11:1). The words, "**None of them is lost, except the son of perdition; that the scripture might be fulfilled,**" tell us that Judas betrayed Christ in fulfillment of Scripture (John 17:12). And, the words, "**Do you think that I cannot call on my Father, and He would at once give me more than twelve legions of angels? But how then would the scriptures be fulfilled, that say it must be so?**" tell us that Christ's own suffering and death took place in fulfillment of Scripture (Matthew 26:53-54).

The words, "**Lord... You said through the mouth of your servant David, Why do the heathen rage, and the people plot in vain?**" tell us that the words of David (quoted from Psalm 2:1) were spoken by God (Acts 4:24-25). The words, "**The Holy Spirit rightly said to our fathers through Isaiah the prophet,**" tell us that words spoken by Isaiah the prophet were spoken by the Holy Ghost (Acts 28:25). [See Isaiah 6:9.] The words, "**As the Holy Ghost says, Today if you hear Him speak do not harden your hearts, as in the rebellion,**" tell us that the words of Psalm 95:7-8 are the words of the Holy Spirit (Hebrews 3:7-8). The words, "**What advantage then has the Jew? or what profit is there in circumcision? Much every way: chiefly, because the words of God were entrusted to them,**" call the scriptures entrusted to God's people in the Old Testament, "the words of God" (Romans 3:1-2). And, the words, "**To the law and to the testimony: if they do not speak according to this word, it is because there is no light in them,**" tell us that those who contradict Scripture have "no light in them" (Isaiah 8:20).

Consider carefully the words, "**Of which salvation the prophets have enquired and searched diligently, who prophesied of the grace that should come unto you: Searching what, or what manner of time the Spirit of Christ which was in them did signify, when it testified beforehand the sufferings of Christ, and the glory that should follow. Unto whom it was revealed, that not unto themselves, but unto us they did minister the things, which are now reported unto you by them that have preached the gospel unto you with the Holy Ghost sent down from heaven; which things the angels desire to look into," (1Peter 1;10-12). Those words tell us that the same "Spirit of Christ" who spoke through the prophets, was speaking through the apostles.

The words, **"Therefore, brethren, stand firm, and hold fast to the instructions that you were taught, either by what we said, or our letter,"** tell us that the writings of the apostles carry the same God-given authority as if they were speaking in person (2Thessalonians 2:15). The words, **"You want proof that Christ is speaking through me,"** tell us that Christ was speaking through the apostles (2Corinthians 13:3). The words, **"If any man thinks that he is a prophet, or spiritual, let him acknowledge that the things I write to you are the commandments of the Lord. But if any man will not hear what I have said, refuse to hear him,"** tell us that the words of the apostles are the words of God, and we should not listen to those who refuse to heed what they say (1Corinthians 14:37-38). The words, **"Those who know God accept what we say; those who are not of God will not accept what we say. That is how we can distinguish the spirit of truth from the spirit of error,"** tell us that those who will not accept what the Bible says have a spirit of error (1John 4:6). And, the words, **"You are no longer strangers and foreigners, but fellow citizens with the saints, and the household of God, and are built upon the foundation of the apostles and prophets, Jesus Christ himself being the chief corner stone,"** accord the Old testament writings of the prophets equal authority with the New Testament writings of the apostles (Ephesians 2:19-20).

3. The Inspiration Of The Bible

What the Bible says about its divine inspiration is not just an opinion, but an essential part of the Gospel message. God uses the passages of Scripture that testify to its inspiration to assure troubled hearts of His love, His mercy, and His promise of forgiveness in Christ. As it is written, **"The Spirit Himself bears witness with our spirit, that we are the children of God"** (Romans 8:16).

If you have a Bible program on your computer, and **do a search** for such phrases as "thus saith the Lord", "the word of the Lord", "the Lord said", or "the word of God" you will find dozens of Bible passages that testify to the divine origin of what the Bible says. Furthermore, we are told that, **"The words of the LORD are pure words** [i.e. not mixed with man's word], as silver tried in a furnace of earth, purified seven times," and given the promise, **"You shall keep them, O**

LORD, you will preserve them from this generation forever" (Psalm 12:6-7). And, the words, "**All scripture is inspired by God,**" tell us that every word of scripture comes from God (2Timothy 3:16). For, "**Prophecy did not originate of old by the will of man: but holy men of God spoke as they were moved by the Holy Ghost**" (2Peter 1:21).

The words, "**We have not received the spirit of the world, but the Spirit that is of God; that we might know the things that are freely given to us by God. That is what we speak, not in words taught by man's wisdom, but those taught by the Holy Spirit,**" testify to the fact that the Apostles were speaking words given to them by "the Holy Spirit" (1Corinthians 2:12-13). The words, "**You want proof that Christ is speaking through me,**" testify to the fact that Christ was speaking through the Apostle Paul (2Corinthians 13:3). And, the words, "**If any man thinks that he is a prophet, or spiritual, let him acknowledge that the things I write to you are the commandments of the Lord,**" testify to the fact that what Paul wrote was the Word of God (1Corinthians 14:37).

When the Bible tells us that, "**All scripture is inspired by God,**" the phrase translated "inspired by God" means "God breathed" in the original Greek. And, that means that it owes its origin to God even though it was recorded by men (2Timothy 3:16). When the Bible says, "**Holy men of God spoke as they were moved by the Holy Ghost,**" it is telling us that it was the actual words (not just ideas) that were inspired (2Peter 1:21). Moreover, the phrase, "spoke as they were moved," is not limited to oral communication. The deaf often speak through sign language, and I am speaking to you through the words you are reading. Furthermore, because the Doctrine of inspiration is an essential part of the Gospel message, those who attack it, deny it, or water it down endanger souls. As it is written, "**I do not pray for them alone, but also for those who will believe on me through their word;**" (John 17:20).

The words, "**If they do not listen to Moses and the prophets, they will not be convinced, even if someone rises from the dead,**" tell us that our salvation depends upon believing what the Bible says (Luke 16:31). As it is written, "**Faith comes by hearing, and hearing by the word of God**" (Romans 10:17). Moreover, the words, "**You are... built upon the foundation of the apostles and prophets, Jesus Christ himself being the chief corner stone;**" tell us that our faith is founded on the word of "the apostles and prophets" [i.e. the Bible] (Ephesians 2:19-20). And, the words, "**If you continue in my word, you are truly my disciples, and you will know the truth, and the truth will make you free,**" tell us that the truth that makes us free, the truth of the Gospel, is not to be found outside of God's Word (John 8:31-32).

King David said, "**The Spirit of the LORD spoke by me, and**

His word was in my tongue" (2Samuel 23:2). And, the words, "**They were all filled with the Holy Ghost, and began to speak in other languages, as the Spirit enabled them,**" tell us that the Holy Ghost did not just give those present at Pentecost ideas, but the actual words needed to express them (Acts 2:4). While it is true that God will, in answer to prayer, sometimes help pastors and other believers find the words needed to communicate the truths of Scripture, those who would reduce divine inspiration to mere assistance undermine the work of the Gospel by casting doubt on God's word, thereby endangering souls. To all of them God's warning is, "**Whoever offends one of these little ones who believe in me, it would be better for him if a millstone were hung around his neck, and he were drowned in the depth of the sea**" (Matthew 18:6).

Because the Bible is the inspired Word of God we can **know** that what it says is true. And, that is just what the words, "**I have written these things to you who believe in the name of the Son of God; that you may know that you have eternal life,**" tell us (1John 5:13). Furthermore, even though man's word is often broken, because Scripture is the Word of God, Jesus said, "**Scripture cannot be broken**" (John 10:35). Because every word of Scripture is inspired by God, "**It is easier for heaven and earth to pass away, than for one letter of the law to fail**" (Luke 16:17). "**For I tell you truly, Until heaven and earth pass away, not one letter or stroke will pass from the law, until everything has been fulfilled**" (Matthew 5:18). That is why the Apostle Paul could say, "**I worship the God of my fathers... believing everything that is written in the law and in the prophets**" (Acts 24:14).

The words, "**The promises were made to Abraham and his seed. God did not say, and to your seeds, as referring to many; but, And to your seed, referring to one which is Christ,**" tell us that not only the words but the form is determined by God (Galatians 3:16). [See Genesis 22:18 and 26:4.] Furthermore, because we know that the promised "seed" of Abraham was Christ, we also know that God's promise to multiply that one "seed" is fulfilled in all who are the children of Abraham through faith in Christ. As it is written, "**If you belong to Christ, then you are Abraham's seed, and heirs according to the promise**" (Galatians 3:29). That Includes all in ancient Israel who trusted in Christ (the Messiah).

Lastly, the words, "**Holy men of God spoke as they were moved by the Holy Ghost,**" tell us that divine inspiration included not only the command to write, but also the divine impulse to write (2Peter 1:21). Because of that divine impulse, "**prophecy did not originate of old by the will of man,**" but by the will of God (2Peter 1:21). Therefore, "**Let God be true, but every man a liar**" (Romans 3:4). "**To the law and to the testimony: if they do not speak according to this word, it is because there is no light in them**" (Isaiah 8:20).

4. The Holy Spirit's Relationship To The Writers

All of the passages that tell us that the Lord (or the Holy Spirit) spoke by the prophets reveal the relationship of Holy Spirit to the Holy writers. The words, **"All this took place, to fulfill what the Lord had spoken by the prophet,"** and the words, **"Fulfilling what was spoken of the Lord by the prophet,"** tell us that the Lord was doing the talking even though the words came through the prophet (Matthew 1:22 and 2:15). The words, **"Lord... You said through the mouth of your servant David,"** and the words, **"The Holy Ghost long ago spoke by the mouth of David,"** tell us that what was spoken was the Word of God even though it came through David (Acts 4:24-25). And, the words, **"As the Holy Ghost says, Today if you hear Him speak, do not harden your hearts, as in the rebellion, during the time of testing in the desert,"** tell us that the words of the Psalm being quoted are the words of the Holy Spirit (Hebrews 3:7-8 and Psalm 95:8).

History may very well remember our age as an age of skepticism, an age when many were so infatuated with their own thoughts that without ever speaking one word through divine inspiration they denied its supernatural aspects, limited (in their minds) God's ability to control what was said, and described inspiration in terms of their own experience. To all who are guilty of that charge God says, **"O fools, and slow of heart to believe all that the prophets have spoken"** (Luke 24:25). "Hasn't God made the wisdom of this world foolish?" (1Corinthians 1:20) **Hasn't God "Scattered the proud in the imagination of their hearts"?** (Luke 1:51) If you encounter such skeptics, do not be deceived, on the contrary, **"Let God be true, but every man a liar"** (Romans 3:4). For it is written, **"If they do not speak according to this word, it is because there is no light in them"** (Isaiah 8:20).

"It is fundamentally vital that we realize that this Bible is Christ's Word, God's Word, a divine Book; that, unlike the many volumes published in the United States last year, here is a book that came into existence not 'by the will of man,' but, as the apostle tells us, by the immeasurable and unending love of God to give His weak and inconsistent children a positive and unfailing guide through the perplexities of the here into the hereafter. — Externally, of course, the Bible has much the same appearance as any other volume of its size and proportions. But because it is God-breathed; because, as we are expressly assured, 'all Scripture is given by inspiration'; because the men who wrote the various books of the Bible; spoke as they were moved by the Holy Ghost,' we believe that the Bible, as 2,600 different passages of the Old Testament and 526 different references in the New individually claim, presents to us the Word of God, written by men who were chosen and supernaturally endowed by God for that purpose and who, through the divine process of inspiration, were given the exact, literal messages they have recorded for us." (Dr. Walter A. Maier, from the sermon, "*Christ's Estimate Of The Scriptures*," 1930.)

5. Attacks On The Doctrine Of Inspiration

For centuries the Bible was only available to scribes and scholars. During that time the common people had little or no access to it. However, almost as soon as it was translated into the language of the people, and made available by the printing press, Satan raised up men to attack it.

The words, "Faith comes by hearing, and hearing by the word of God," tell us that faith in the words of Scripture and faith in Christ go hand in hand. And, because they go hand in hand Satan is intent on destroying people's confidence in Scripture. Very often the men Satan uses are highly respected, have positions of influence, and are regarded as scholars. Nevertheless, the words, **"Those who are not of God will not accept what we [the Apostles and Prophets] say,"** tell us that such "scholars" are not of God (1John 4:6). The words, **"There must also be heresies among you, to reveal those who are approved by God**," tell us that they are not approved by God (1Corinthians 11:19). And, the words, **"If anyone teaches otherwise, and will not agree with sound teaching, even the words of our Lord Jesus Christ, and the doctrine that is in accord with godliness, he is proud, knowing nothing... from such withdraw yourself**," tell us that we should not listen to them or have any fellowship with them (1Timothy 6:3-5).

Writing over a century ago, before the Second World War, Dr. John Theodore Mueller said: "In Germany there is at the present time hardly a single outstanding university professor who still upholds the doctrine of verbal and plenary inspiration. This all but universal denial of inspiration is one of the saddest chapters in the history of the Christian Church; for every one who repudiates the inspiration of the Bible subverts the foundation upon which the Christian faith rests and falls under the condemnation of God. In the last analysis all objections to the inspiration of the Bible flow from the carnal, unbelieving heart." ("Christian Dogmatics," page 108). In my opinion, that apostasy in Germany was one of the reasons that the people were so willing to follow Hitler.

Those who deny that Scripture is inspired because the individual writers differ somewhat in style and diction "**err, not knowing the Scriptures, or the power of God**" (Matthew 22:29). What they fail to understand is that every person has their own personal language. My vocabulary is bound to differ somewhat from yours. And, God prepared the men that He chose to write down His words, by molding their vocabulary, and giving them the style and diction He wanted to use. What skeptics miss is that, "God's unique style is indeed noticeable throughout Holy Scripture, which bears the ineffaceable imprint of its divine Author on every page. The simplicity, majesty, and sublimity of the Biblical style are found in no book written by men; in fact, the style of the Bible is so unique that there is only one Holy Bible in the world. We may apply to Scripture the words that were spoken with regard to our Savior: '**Never man spoke like this man,**' John 7:46." (J. T. Mueller, "*Christian Dogmatics*", page 109.) The words, "**It is easier for heaven and earth to pass away, than for one letter of the law to fail**," tell us that every letter is there because God put it there (Luke 16:17). There are no uninspired parts.

All of the attacks on Scripture are condemned by the words, "**O fools, and slow of heart to believe everything the prophets have said**" (Luke 24:25).

Some have argued that research on the part of Luke precludes inspiration. But, what research Luke may have done does not change the fact that it was God who moved Him to write it down. As it is written, "**Holy men of God spoke as they were moved by the Holy Ghost**" (2Peter 1:21).

Some have argued that variant readings in copies of scripture disprove inspiration. But, those variant readings are in copies (not the original), and they affect only a tiny percentage of the readings. Furthermore, we have God's own promise that He will "Preserve" what He has written (Psalm 12:6-7).

Some have argued that alleged contradictions disprove inspiration. However, I have already explained that just because two statements seem contradictory to our puny sin-corrupted minds does not mean that they actually contradict. Many times we simply lack the information needed to understand how they fit together. In fact, the words, "**Do not answer a fool according to his folly, or you will be like him. Answer a fool according to his folly, or he will be wise in his own conceit,**" are God's way of telling us that just because two statements appear to contradict does not mean they actually contradict (Proverbs 26:4-5).

Some have argued that seeming historical discrepancies in Scripture disprove inspiration. However, in the last century so many specific claims of historical inaccuracy have been proven false that I am surprised that anyone would still use that argument. A little over a century ago historians were claiming that the Hittite kingdom never existed. Then archeologists discovered it. Not many decades ago some claimed that Pontius Pilate did not exist. Then a stone was found with his name on it. The truth is that as long as secular scholars do not have non-biblical evidence for something the Bible says, they think they can accuse that Bible of being wrong without any danger of their lie being exposed. To all of them **Jesus says, "O fools, and slow of heart to believe everything the prophets have said**," (Luke 24:25). As Christians we know that the opinions of men are often wrong, but the Bible never is.

Some have argued that inaccurate quotations of the Old Testament by writers of the New disprove inspiration. However, that is silly because they are trying to impose their rules on God. Sometimes the Apostles translate from the Hebrew. Sometimes they quote from the Greek Septuagint translation. Sometimes they quote the Septuagint corrected by the Hebrew. And, sometimes they restate the text in their own words. However, in every case they are saying exactly what the Holy Spirit moved them to say (2Peter 1:21).

And finally, some have argued that Paul's statement, "**To the rest speak I, not the Lord**," disproves inspiration (1Corinthians 7:12). However, all Paul is saying is, "This is my counsel on a matter that God has not specifically spoken on". Furthermore, his words, "**If any man thinks that he is a prophet, or spiritual, let him acknowledge that the things I write to you are the commandments of the Lord**," tell us that God caused Paul to include that counsel in Scripture (1Corinthians 14:37).

6. The Consequences Of Denying Inspiration

The satanic attack on Scripture has taken its toll on many churches, especially those with a history of affirming some passages of Scripture while explaining away others. As a result, practicing Christians make up a far smaller portion of our population than they previously did, and many who pass themselves off as Christian scholars do not feel bound to regard anything the Bible says as sacred.

One very visible aspect of that departure from Scripture is the world's denial of the first chapters of Genesis – God's record of creation, and the age of the earth. And, because that denial is forcefully advanced many are taken in by it. Nevertheless, the words, "**He who is of God hears God's words... you do not hear them, because you are not of God**," tell us that those who reject what the Bible says about creation are not of God (John 8:47).

What Christians who have bought into the lie of evolution and millions of years fail to realize, is that by rejecting what the Bible says about God creating all things in six days, they are rejecting the God who made everything "**In six days**," and replacing Him with a god of their own fabrication – a god who used evolution (Exodus 20:11). In short, **they change "the truth of God into a lie**," (Romans 1:25). As a result, those churches that reject the Genesis record, eventually slide down the slippery slope of rejecting the truth of Christ's virgin birth, His atoning sacrifice, and His resurrection while going on to condone all sorts of satanic behavior (immorality, abortion, homosexuality and even the farce of homosexual "marriage"). To all of the so called Christians who have gone that route, God says, "**They commit adultery, and walk in lies: they strengthen the hands of evildoers, so that no one repents of his wickedness: all of them are like Sodom in my sight, and the people of the city like Gomorrah**" (Jeremiah 23:14).

The words, "**This is a trustworthy statement, worthy of complete acceptance, that Christ Jesus came into the world to save sinners**," tell us that the very reason Christ came into the world was to save sinners (1Timothy 1:15). However, those who reject the Bible's record of creation and the fall have no reason to believe the Bible when it says, "**By one man sin entered into the world, and death by sin; and so death passed upon all men, for that all have sinned**," and, therefore, have no reason to believe the Bible when it says, "**As through the sin of one judgment came upon all men to condemnation; even so through the righteousness of one the free gift abounds to all men bringing justification and life**" (Romans 5:12 and 18). In short, rejecting what the Bible says about creation and the fall undermines the Gospel.

The words, "**Faith comes by hearing, and hearing by the <u>Word of God</u>**," the words, "**Being born again, not of corruptible seed, but of incorruptible, by the <u>Word of God</u>**," and the words, "**He chose to <u>give us life</u> through the <u>Word of Truth</u>**," all tell us that those who reject God's Word cut themselves off from God's "gift" of faith and eternal life (Romans 10:17, 1Peter 1:23, James 1:18).

The words, "**If you remain in me, and my words remain in you, ask whatever you wish, and it will be done for you**," tell us that those who reject God's Word forfeit Christ's promise of answered prayer (John 15:7). And, the words, "**Truly, truly, I tell you, if a man keeps My word, he will never see death**," tell us that those who reject God's Word forfeit the promise of never seeing death (John 8:51).

The words, "**You have the words of eternal life**," tell us that God's words are the source of eternal life (John 6:68). The words, "**Sanctify them through your truth: your Word is truth**," tell us that we are sanctified through the Word of God (John 17:17). The words, "**Blessed rather are those who hear the word of God, and keep it**," tell us that God's Word is a source of blessing (Luke 11:28). And, the words, "Truly, truly, I tell you, **He who hears my word, and believes on Him who sent me, has everlasting life, and will not come into condemnation; but has passed from death to life**," give all who trust in God's Word His own promise that we "will not come into condemnation" (John 5:24).

Lastly, those who reject God's word, reject, "**The wisdom that is from above," the wisdom, "**God ordained before the world to our glory,**" the wisdom, "**Which none of the rulers of this world knew, for had they known it, they would not have crucified the Lord of glory,**" the wisdom of which it is said, "**Eye has not seen, nor ear heard, nor has it entered into the heart of man, the things that God has prepared for those who love Him**" (James 3:17, 1Corinthians 2:7-9). And, the future of all who reject those blessings of God's Word is described in the words, "**It is a fearful thing to fall into the hands of the living God**" (Hebrews 10:31).

7. The Properties Of Holy Scripture

Up to this point our focus has been on the divine origin of the Bible, its inspiration, and the fact that every part of it is God-breathed. I pointed out that the words, "**It is easier for heaven and earth to pass away, than for one letter of the law to fail,**" tell us that even the letters were inspired by God (Luke 16:17). However, because the Bible is the Word of God it also possesses certain properties or attributes which we will now look at.

The first two properties that I call to your attention are the divine **truthfulness and unity** of Scripture. While the sections following this one will focus on some of the other attributes of Scripture, because these two properties are closely related to, and dovetail perfectly with, the doctrine of the inspiration of Scripture, much that can be said about them has already been said.

Regarding **the truthfulness of Scripture**, because the Bible is the Word of God, and "**God... cannot lie,**" all that the Bible says is true (Titus 1:2). And, all of the Bible passages that testify to the divine inspiration of Scripture also testify to its truthfulness. As to its truthfulness, Jesus Himself, in prayer to the Father, said, "**Your word is truth**" (John 17:17). In the Psalms we read, "**Your law is the truth,**" // "**Your word is true from the beginning: and every one of your righteous judgments endures forever,**" // "**the word of the LORD is right, and you can trust everything He does**" (Psalm 119:142,160 and Psalm 33:4).

Regarding **the unity of Scripture**, even though God moved men to write down the words, because the words were inspired by God the Bible is the Word of God. And, because God is its real author, the Bible only contains one theology, His theology. And, His Word testifies to that fact when it says, "**All the prophets testify of Him [Christ] that through His name whoever believes in Him will receive forgiveness of sins**" (Acts 10:43). Jesus Himself said, "**Search the scriptures; for in them you think that you have eternal life: and they are they that testify of me**" (John 5:39). David said, "**I have trusted in your mercy [grace], my heart will rejoice in** your salvation" (Psalm 13:5). Paul taught, "**Nothing other than those things that Moses and the prophets said would happen**" (Acts 26:22). Isaiah said, "**Whoever believes in Him [Christ] will not be ashamed**" (Isaiah 28:16, Romans 10:11). And, the Apostle Paul tells us that "**The covenant *concerning faith in Christ*, that was confirmed by God at the time of Abraham, cannot be nullified by the law, which came four hundred and thirty years later, so as to make the promise of no effect, for if the inheritance comes by the law, it is not given by promise, but God gave it to Abraham by promise**" (Galatians 3:17-19).

One attack on the inspiration of Scripture that I have not yet dealt with is **the attack on the divine unity of Scripture**. This attack assumes that the Bible is not inspired by God, and, therefore, that there must be a natural explanation for its existence, and that the men who wrote it must have had differences in their thinking. Some who accept that assumption then let their imagination run wild, twisting some statements to contradict others when they could just as well be interpreted to agree. And, by doing so they only show their ignorance, because they violate one of the fundamental rules of Bible interpretation, the rule that no passage of Scripture should ever be interpreted to contradict what the Bible says elsewhere. As it is written, "**If they do not speak according to this word, it is because there is no light in them**" (Isaiah 8:20).

The people I have in mind pick out statements made by different Apostles, and then claim to see different theologies, theologies that only exist in their minds. Others imagine that the first two chapters of Genesis give different accounts of creation, even though Christ's words, "**He who made them at the beginning made them male and female**, and said, **For this reason a man will leave father and mother, and will be united to his wife**," quote from both chapters as from one account (Matthew 19:4-5). Others ignore the historical evidence pointing to Moses as the writer of the first five books of Scripture, and then, out of pure fantasy, fabricate different writers for different parts of the Pentateuch. Of course their entire construct is nothing more than the product of an overactive imagination (a fairy story), yet they prefer their lie to the truth. For that reason, their attack on the unity of Scripture is a perfect illustration of the words, "**God... has scattered the proud in the imagination of their hearts**" (Luke 1:47, 51). And, the words, "**Those who know God accept what we [the apostles and prophets] say, those who are not of God will not accept what we say**," tell us that those people are not of God (1John 4:6).

A Guide to Interpreting God's Word

The properties of Holy Scripture guide us in our interpretation of Scripture. For example: Because one of its properties is its **unity**, we should never interpret one passage of scripture to contradict another. Because it has the **authority** of God behind it, we should conform our thinking to it while rejecting any interpretation that contradicts what it says. Because its **purpose** is to testify of Christ, we should interpret all that it says in the light of its testimony of Christ. Because it is **sufficient**, containing everything needed for our salvation, we should never try to supplement what it says, or read unscriptural ideas into it. And, because it is **clear**, the meaning God intends for us to get from it is exactly what the words say, nothing more, the plain grammatical meaning of the words, the same meaning that you are placing on my words as you read this.

A. The Divine Authority of Holy Scripture

Because the Bible is the Word of God, it is the highest authority in the Christian church, an authority that can and should be the only source, standard and judge of all that is taught in our churches. That authority, the authority of God's own Word, has a twofold function. **1-** In the life of a believer that Word convicts the heart of sin, while assuring the contrite (those who are sorry for their sin) of God's mercy and forgiveness in Christ. **2-** In the life of the church, that Word exposes doctrines that are not taught in Scripture, while condemning doctrines that contradict Scripture. [See Micah 3:8, Psalm 34:18, Romans 15:4, Acts 17:11, Isaiah 8:20.]

God's Word in the Life of a Believer

Because Scripture is the Word of God, it is empowered by God to accomplish His will. Of course, part of that will is to bring people to faith. However, after He has brought them to faith, His Word will be at work in their hearts, enabling them to see sins that they were formerly blind to, teaching them to shun those sins instead of making excuses for them, and assuring them of forgiveness in Christ, while bringing them to a greater knowledge of God and a better understanding of the Gospel. And, the authority of His Word plays a part in that. As it is written, "**We continually give thanks to God, because, when you received the Word of God that you heard from us, you did not receive it as the word of men, but as it is in truth, the Word of God, which <u>effectively works in you who believe</u>**." (1Thessalonians 2:13).

The words, "**Do not be conformed to this world: but be transformed by the renewing of your mind**," and the words, "**Bringing into captivity every thought to the obedience of Christ**," tell us that our minds and our thinking – our entire worldview – should be **conformed** to the Word of God (Romans 12:2, 2Corinthians 10:5). At the same time, the words, "**Making the Word of God of no effect** through your tradition," warn us of the danger of making excuses for sin instead of repenting and turning away from sin (Mark 7:14). And, the words, "**Christ did not send me to baptize, but to preach the gospel: not with words of worldly wisdom, lest the cross of Christ be made of no effect**," warn us that unbiblical thinking can undermine the work of the gospel (1Corinthians 1:17).

God's Word in the Life of the Church

Just as God's Word should be the highest authority in the life of the believer, it should be the highest authority in the church. All teaching should be in agreement with it, and anything that contradicts what it says should be rejected. As it is written, "**To the law and to the testimony: if they do not speak according to this word, it is because there is no light in them**" (Isaiah 8:20).

However, in order for God's Word to have its rightful place in the life of the church, and the preeminence that it deserves, **we must distinguish clearly between what God says and what men say**. When the prophet Jeremiah said, "**The prophet who has a dream, let him tell a dream; and he who has my word, let him speak my word faithfully**," he was speaking out against all who pass their own word, their own opinions, off as the Word of God (Jeremiah 23:28). When Jesus said, "**You completely invalidate the commandment of God, in order to keep your tradition**," He was speaking out against all who rationalize sin, and make up excuses aimed at getting around what the Bible says (Mark 7:9). Yet, the practice of teaching opinion as doctrine while explaining away any passages of Scripture that contradict that opinion is widespread in American Churches. You ask where. Where does the Bible say that Christ will raise up believers before the "**last day**"? I tell you that it is not in the Bible! In fact Christ said the opposite. Christ said, "**Every one who looks to the Son, and believes on Him, may have everlasting life: and I will raise him up on <u>the last day</u>**" (John 6:40). Yet, if you point out that verse to those teach the opposite they will explain it away, just as the Pharisees that Christ was speaking to in Mark 7:9 explained away God's Word. Many also teach a false gospel, telling people that they can live in sin and still be saved. However, the Bible says, "**Walk in the Spirit, and you will not fulfill the lust of the flesh, for the flesh lusts against the Spirit, and the Spirit against the flesh: and they are opposed to each other: so that you cannot do the things that you would**" (Galatians 5:16-17). Or, as John put it, "**Whoever has been born of God does not continue in sin; for His seed remains in him: and he cannot sin, because he is born of God**" (1John 3:9).

The point I am making is that we can know for certain exactly what the Bible says, or does not say. However, you will never be able to know what the Bible says unless you can tell the difference between what the words actually say, and the ideas you read into them. And, you will never be able to know what the Bible says until you are willing to reject any interpretations that contradict what the words say. There is no place for self-deception! As it is written, "**Blessed is the man to whom the LORD does not impute iniquity, and in whose spirit there is no self-deception**" (Psalm 32:2).

God's Word is Our Standard

The words, "**If they do not speak according to this word, it is because there is no light in them**," tell us that Scripture is the standard that everything taught in the church should agree with (Isaiah 8:20). Nothing taught in our churches should ever contradict what the Bible says. And, when the Apostle Paul says, "**Having gifts that differ according to the grace that is given to us, let us use them: if prophecy, prophesy according to the standard of faith**," he is emphasizing the fact that what is taught as God's Word (prophesy) should agree with what the Bible says about faith in Christ (Romans 12:6). As it is written, "**The testimony of Jesus is the spirit of prophecy**" (Revelation 19:10). [See John 5:39, Acts 10:43.]

When we reject and condemn a doctrine that contradicts what the Bible says, we are using Scripture as a judge. The words, "**Those who know God accept what we [the apostles and prophets] say, those who are not of God will not accept what we say**," condemn those who refuse to submit to God's judgment (1John 4:6). As do the words, "**If anyone teaches otherwise, and will not agree with sound teaching, even the words of our Lord Jesus Christ, and the doctrine that is in accord with godliness; He is proud, knowing nothing**," (1Timothy 6:3-4).

Beware of False Prophets

With the words, "**Beware of false prophets, who come to you in sheep's clothing, but inwardly are ravening wolves**," Christ authorizes every believer to judge what is being taught, and to reject those who contradict what the Bible says (Matthew 7:15). The Apostle Paul was not offended when the Jews at Berea, "**Searched the scriptures daily, to see whether**" the things that he was teaching were so. On the contrary, he commended them (Acts 17:11). And, he urged the believers at Corinth to judge what he was teaching, saying, "**I speak as to wise men, judge for yourselves what I say**" (1Corinthians 10:15). At the same time, it is important to know, that believers are to judge what is taught, by what the Bible plainly says not by their own opinions or private interpretations. Those who presume to pit their own opinions against the Word of God are guilty of being, "**Prophets of the deceit of their own heart**" (Jeremiah 23:26). As it is written, "**If any man speaks, let him speak according to God's Word**" (1Peter 4:11).

Translations

Because translations are not inspired by God, the original Hebrew and Greek text of the Bible is the authority by which all translations must be judged. However, a good translation of the original text is just as much the word of God as the original text. Therefore, while a pastor should know what the Hebrew or Greek text says, he should never use that knowledge in a way that undermines the confidence the people have in their translation, or gives them the impression that the Bible is a dark book that can only be understood by those who understand Hebrew and Greek. In the words of John Theodore Mueller, "The gap between the original text and its translations must not be widened unduly, so as to create doubts regarding their authority; for the language of Scripture is in most instances so direct and simple that any translator who performs his work conscientiously is compelled by the clear and direct language of Scripture to reproduce the sense of the original." (*"Christian Dogmatics"*, page 132)

The Cannon of Scripture

There are at present a number of publications and false documentaries spreading the lie that certain books have been removed from the New Testament. The truth is, those books were never accepted by the Christian church, and were never a part of the New Testament. Contrary to what these people claim, the four Gospels, and the Epistles of Paul have been universally accepted by the Christian church from the very beginning. The Gospels of Matthew and John were written by Apostles. The Gospel of Mark was written under the supervision of Peter. And, the Gospel of Luke and book of Acts were fully approved by Paul. There were a few people in the early centuries who questioned Hebrews (because the author is not named), the second and third epistles of John (because they seem like private letters), James and Jude (because even though they were brothers of Christ they were not prophets), and the book of Revelation (because of its strangeness). Nevertheless, those books were all widely accepted from the beginning. Let me also add that the books included in the New Testament did not become Scripture because of a decision made by the Church of Rome, but God compelled Rome to accept the books He had inspired.

B. The Divine Power Of Holy Scripture

Because the Bible is the inspired Word of God it has power, the power of God, behind it. And, God works through it to accomplish His will. As it is written, "**I am not ashamed of the gospel of Christ: for it is the power of God to salvation to every one who believes; to the Jew first, and also to the Greek.**" (Romans 1:16).

And, again, "**So will the word that goes out of my mouth be: it will not return to me empty, but it will accomplish what I want, and it will achieve what I sent it to do**" (Isaiah 55:11).

The words, "**He has given you life, who were dead in trespasses and sins,**" tell us that it is God who gives us life. (Ephesians 2:1). Because we are by nature "**dead in trespasses and sins,**" we can do nothing to make ourselves alive. That is why the Bible says, "**No one can say that Jesus is the Lord, but by the Holy Ghost,**" (1Corinthians 12:3). That is why the Bible says, "**Man does not live by bread alone, but man lives by every word that proceeds out of the mouth of the LORD**" (Deuteronomy 8:3). And, that is why the Bible says, "**Faith comes by hearing, and hearing by the word of God**" (Romans 10:17).

From man's point of view it sometimes does look like we are making a decision to believe. However, the words, "**No man can come to me, unless the Father who has sent me draws him,**" tell us that apart from the work of God no one ever could or would make the right decision (John 6:44). In fact, without God's help Satan would quickly fill us with doubt, and destroy our faith. Therefore, just as God works through His Word to bring us to faith, He works through His Word to strengthen and preserve our faith. That is what Paul was talking about when He said, "**I have planted, Apollos watered, but God gave the increase**" (1Corinthians 3:6). The words, "**The Spirit Himself bears witness with our spirit, that we are the children of God,**" tell us that our assurance comes from the witness of the Holy Spirit in our heart (Romans 8:16). The words, "**Toward us who believe, according to the working of His mighty power,**" tell us that it is the power of God that brings us to faith, and the power of God that keeps us in faith (Ephesians 1:19). And, the words, "**Faith comes by hearing, and hearing by the Word of God,**" tell us that God works through His Word to bring us to faith, and to keep us in faith (Romans 10:17).

Sometimes those whom God brings to faith in Christ feel an inner joy or excitement that they refer to as "a salvation experience". However, because not all Christians have such an experience we should never equate an experience with salvation. **We are saved by faith in Christ, not experience**. The emphasis has to be on faith in Christ, not what we feel. Whenever churches loose sight of that fact, they not only cause Christians who have not had an experience to doubt their salvation, they also lead the unsaved to seek an experience instead of pointing them to Christ. And, when that happens there is a danger that people who do not trust in Christ will convince themselves they have had a salvation experience, when they have not.

Any valid experience of joy or excitement resulting from the Holy Spirit's assurance of forgiveness in Christ should be regarded as a fruit of faith, rather than faith itself. Many Christians, especially those who have grown up in the faith, go through life without having such an experience. However, they know they are saved because they are trusting in what Christ did, not what they do, to get them into heaven. In contrast, it is often those who had a hard time understanding the way of salvation, those who have been burdened with guilt, or those who have been trying to please God with works that experience joy when they finally understand that salvation depends on what Christ did, not what we do. What's more, a genuine "salvation experience" is far different from the carnal excitement sought after by the whoop and holler crowd. The excitement sometimes associated with faith in Christ might be described as the happiness of a joyful reunion, the relief of having a great burden lifted from the mind, and the fascination of something that you are eager to learn more about all rolled into one. Martin Luther described that experience in these words. "Then I grasped that the justice of God is that righteousness by which through grace and sheer mercy God justifies us through faith. Thereupon I felt myself to be reborn and to have gone through open doors into paradise. The whole of Scripture took on a new meaning. (From the book, "*HERE I STAND,*" by Roland H. Bainton, page 49.)

The words, "**Being born again, not of corruptible seed, but of incorruptible, by the Word of God, that lives and abides for ever**," tell us that we receive the new birth through the "Word of God" (1Peter 1:23). And, the words, "**Nor do I pray for them alone, but also for those who will believe on me through their word**," tell us that we are brought to faith through the Word (John 17:20). However, the words, "**Christ did not send me to baptize, but to preach the gospel: not with words of worldly wisdom, lest the cross of Christ be made of no effect**," tell us that the words of Scripture do not effect a change in the heart in a natural way, through elegance or appealing to reason, but in a supernatural way, "**That your faith should not rest in the wisdom of men, but in the power of God**" (1Corinthians 1:17 and 2:5).

The words, "**What is the exceeding greatness of His power toward us who believe, according to the working of His mighty power**," tell us that the Word of God does not just tell us how to be saved, but actually converts us as the power of God works through it to bring us to faith in Christ (Ephesians 1:19). That is why the Bible calls the gospel, "**The power of God to salvation to every one who believes**" (Romans 1:16). Moreover, just as we are saved by the power of God, we are kept by the power of God. As it is written, "**Blessed be the God and Father of our Lord Jesus Christ, who in His great mercy has caused us to be born anew to a living hope through the resurrection of Jesus Christ from the dead, to an inheritance that is incorruptible, and undefiled, and will not fade away, reserved in heaven for you, Who are kept <u>by the power of God</u> through faith unto salvation which is waiting to be revealed at the end of time" (1Peter 1:3-5).

Nevertheless, the words, "**O Jerusalem, Jerusalem, you who kill the prophets, and stone those who are sent to you, how often I longed to gather your children together, as a hen gathers her chicks under her wings, and you would not,**" tell us that the Word of God can be resisted (Matthew 23:37). As it is written, "**You stiff-necked and uncircumcised in heart and ears, you always resist the Holy Ghost: as your fathers did, so do you**" (Acts 7:51). And, again, "**We preach Christ crucified, a stumbling block to the Jews, and foolishness to the Greeks, But to those who are called, both Jews and Greeks, Christ the power of God, and the wisdom of God**" (1Corinthians 1:23-24).

C. The Divine Purpose Of Holy Scripture

God tells us in Scripture why He caused the Bible to be written, the purpose He intends for it to serve, and what our response to it should be. In short, it was written to testify of Christ (Jn.5:39), the purpose it serves is not only to testify of Christ but bring us to faith through that testimony (Jn.20:31), and our response to the law should be to humble ourselves before God and repent (1Jn.1:9), while our response to the gospel should be to believe God's promise of forgiveness in Christ (Mk.1:15), and to believe that forgiveness cleanses us of all sin making us righteous in the sight of God (Rom.3:28). In the paragraphs that follow we will look at the Bible passages just cited, plus several others.

The words, "**This is a trustworthy statement, worthy of complete acceptance, that Christ Jesus came into the world to save sinners,**" tell us that Christ came into the world to save us (1Timothy 1:15). At the same time, the words, "**The Son of man did not come to be served, but to serve, and to give His life a ransom for many,**" tell us that Christ died to provide that salvation (Matthew 20:28). And, the words, "**I want to remind you of the gospel... upon which your <u>faith rests</u>... how that Christ died for our sins according to the scriptures, and that He was buried, and that He rose again the third day according to the scriptures,**" tell us that our faith rests upon the testimony of God's Word ["the gospel"], and that Christ died and rose again in fulfillment of that Word (1Corinthians 15:1-4). [See Mark 10:45 and 1Tim. 2:6.]

The words, "**Search the scriptures; for in them you think that you have eternal life, and they are they that testify of me,**" and the words, "**These are written, that you might believe that Jesus is the Messiah, the Son of God; and that believing you might have life through His name,**" tell us that the Bible was written to testify of Christ, so that we might have eternal life through faith in

Him (John 5:39 and 20:31).

The words, "**All the prophets testify of Him, that through His name whoever believes in Him will receive forgiveness of sins,**" tell us that "all of the prophets" testify of Christ (Acts 10:43). The words, "**Beginning at Moses and all the prophets, He expounded unto them in all the scriptures the things concerning Himself,**" tell us that Jesus taught His disciples to look for that testimony in Scripture (Luke 24:27). And, the words, "**I have written these things to you who believe in the name of the Son of God; that you may know that you have eternal life, and that you may believe in the name of the Son of God,**" tell us that Scripture was written so that we could "know" that we have eternal life in Him (1John 5:13).

How the Purpose of Scripture Applies to Its Interpretation

When Christ said, "**These are the words that I spoke to you, when I was still with you, that everything must be fulfilled, that was written in the law of Moses, in the prophets, and in the psalms, concerning me,**" the words, "in the law of Moses, in the prophets, and in the psalms" were a reference to the three parts of the Hebrew Scriptures (Luke 24:44). Therefore, those words of Christ testify to the fact that He regarded the entire Hebrew Old Testament as the Word of God. And, He was the one who would know! Moreover, because Scripture was written to testify of Christ, we should interpret everything that the Bible says in the light of what it says about Him. In theology that is known as a Christological (Christ centered) approach to Bible interpretation. In his epistles, the Apostle Paul gives us several examples of Christological interpretation as he interprets the Old Testament in the light of the Gospel. And, that approach to interpretation fits together perfectly with what I have already said about the theological unity of Scripture.

D. The Divine Sufficiency Of Holy Scripture

Because the Bible was, "**Written, that you might believe that Jesus is the Messiah, the Son of God, and that believing you might have life through His name,**" and because "**All the prophets testify of Him, that through His name whoever believes in Him will receive forgiveness of sins,**" We know that God designed the Bible to include every thought, every idea, every doctrine that we need to know in order to be saved (John 20:31, Acts 10:43).

The words, "**From infancy you have known the holy scriptures, that are able to make you wise unto salvation through faith in Christ Jesus,**" and the words, "**Nor do I pray for them alone, but also for those who will believe on me through their** word," tell us that what the Bible says is **sufficient** to bring us to salvation through faith in Christ (2Timothy 3:15, John 17:20). Therefore, there is no need to add to it, or supplement what it says. In fact, because it is sufficient, all attempts to change it, improve upon it, or supplement what it says will only hinder the work of salvation. That is why the Bible says, "**I testify to every man who hears the words of the prophecy of this book, If anyone adds to them, God will add to him the plagues that are written in this book. And if anyone takes away from the words of this book of prophecy, God will take away his share in the tree of life**" (Revelation 22:18-19).

The words, "**Go into all the world, and preach the gospel to every creature. He who believes and is baptized will be saved; but he who does not believe will be damned**," tell us that the gospel is sufficient to bring men to faith in Christ (Mark 16:15-16). While, the words, "**All scripture is inspired by God... That the man of God may be perfect, thoroughly equipped for every good work**," tell us that the Bible contains everything necessary for our spiritual growth (2Timothy 3:16-17).

The words, "**We are telling you what we have seen and heard, so that you may have fellowship with us, and the fellowship we have is with the Father, and with His Son Jesus Christ. And what we write to you is written, that your joy might be complete**," tell us that the testimony of Scripture is sufficient to bring us into fellowship with God (1John 1:3-4). While the words, "**Teaching them to observe everything I have commanded you**," with the words, "**Do not add to His words, lest He reprove you**," tell us that the Bible contains everything necessary to teach new believers "to observe everything" Christ has commanded (Matthew 28:20, Proverbs 30:6).

However, even though the Bible contains everything necessary for our salvation, the words, "**For what we now see is like a dim reflection on a glass; but then we will see face to face: now I know in part; but then I will know even as I am known**," // "**O the depth of the riches both of the wisdom and knowledge of God! How unsearchable are His judgments, and His ways past finding out**," tell us that there is much that we do not know, and cannot know this side of heaven (1Corinthians 13:12, Romans 11:33). Furthermore, just as the Bible does not, and cannot, reveal all spiritual knowledge; it does not, and cannot, contain all earthly knowledge. And, the words, "**No truth of scripture comes from any private explanation**," warn us not to explain Scripture in a way intended to make it support ideas that are not already taught in the clear statements of Scripture (2Peter 1:20).

E. The Divine Clarity Of Holy Scripture

God's Word is to be believed not debated, faithfully taught not twisted to make it agree with the opinions of men. Because the Bible was written so, "**That you may know that you have eternal life, and that you may believe in the name of the Son of God,**" the meaning God intends for you to get from His words is nothing other than what those words plainly say (1John 5:13). Or, as the Apostle Paul put it, "**We have not written anything to you, other than what you read**" (2Corinthians 1:13). It is true that God's Law needs to be applied, and men may disagree on how it is to be applied. It is also true that there are many things that we do not understand. However, every doctrine necessary to our salvation is so clearly and explicitly stated in Scripture that it needs no interpretation. For that reason, the only interpretation you need when reading Scripture is the same interpretation you are putting on my words as you read this, the plain grammatical meaning of the words. In other words, **I am not writing "anything to you, other than what you read"**.

Having said that let me make it clear that I am not denying that there are passages that are hard for us to understand. **The clarity of Scripture does not lie in our ability to fully understand what is said, but in the fact that the meaning God intends for you to get from His words is not hidden or mysterious, but is nothing "other than what you read"** (2Cor. 1:13). In other words, the words of Scripture mean just what they say. For example: If an article you were reading contained this statement, "A keratolytic drug used in the treatment of skin disorders," you might not understand that statement. But that would not mean that the author had some hidden meaning. On the contrary, the words mean exactly what they say, and they are explained by what the article says elsewhere. And, it is the same way with Scripture. If we encounter a passage that is hard to understand, instead of professing ourselves to be wise by making up an explanation, we should humbly admit our ignorance and allow the passages that are so clear that they need no explanation to cast light on the unclear passage. And, we do that by interpreting the unclear passages to teach the same doctrine that is taught in the clear passages of Scripture.

The words of the psalmist, "**Your word is a lamp to my feet, and a light to my path**," // "**The entrance of your words gives light; it gives understanding to the simple**," reveal the clarity of Scripture, for a dark book can never be a source of light or understanding (Psalm 119:105, 130). The words, "**The law of the LORD is perfect, converting the soul: the testimony of the LORD is sure, making wise the simple**," tell us that the Bible is clear enough to make "wise the simple" (Psalm 19:7). While the words, "**And we have a more sure word of prophecy; to which you do well to pay attention,** as to a light that shines in a dark place," speak of Scripture as a light (2Peter 1:19). And, the words, "**Therefore seeing that we have such hope, we speak very clearly,**" tell us that the words of Scripture have no hidden meanings (2Corinthians 3:12).

Regarding 2Corinthians 3:12 let me add that the KJV translates the phrase containing the Greek word "parrhesia" as, "Great plainness of speech," and translates that word as "plainly" in, John 10:24, John 11:14, John 16:25, and John 16:29. While Lenski translates 2Cor. 3:12 as "Having, therefore, such hope, we continue using full openness of speech". Lenski explains that translation by telling us that the phrase, "full openness of speech," "Means speaking with full openness, withholding nothing, without reservation of any kind" [i.e. nothing hidden] (Lenski's commentary on First and Second Corinthians, page 935.)

The words, "**These were of better character than those in Thessalonica, in that they received the word with all readiness of mind, and searched the scriptures daily, to see whether these things were so,**" tell us that the Bible's testimony of Christ is so clear that the Jews at Berea had no difficulty finding it in Scripture (Acts 17:11). And, the words, "**From infancy you have known the holy scriptures, that are able to make you wise unto salvation through faith in Christ Jesus,**" not only tell us that the words of Scripture are plain enough for a child to understand, but that they are also sufficiently clear to make one, "**wise unto salvation through faith in Christ Jesus**" (2Timothy 3:15).

The words, "**Search the scriptures; for in them you think that you have eternal life: and they are they that testify of me,**" would not make any sense if what the Bible says was just a matter of opinion (John 5:39). The same holds true for the words, "**Abraham said to him, They have Moses and the prophets; let them hear them**" (Luke 16:29). And, for the words, "**Therefore, brethren, stand firm, and hold fast to the instructions that you were taught, either by what we said, or our letter**" (2Thessalonians 2:15).

Christ's words, "**If you continue in my word, you are truly my disciples, and you will <u>know the truth</u>, and the truth will make you free**," presuppose the clarity of scripture, for it is only because the words of Scripture are clear that those who continue in them can "know the truth" (John 8:31-32). As do the words, "**If they do not speak according to this word, it is because there is no light in them,**" for it is only because the words of Scripture are clear that we can tell if someone is speaking "according to" them or not (Isaiah 8:20).

Those Who Reject the Clarity of Scripture

Throughout history there have been many who have been blind to the clarity of Scripture, many who rejected it outright, and many who have attacked it. The words, "**The minds of those who do not believe have been blinded by the god of this world,**" tell us that those who do not believe have been blinded (2Corinthians 4:4). The words, **"Israel, which followed after the law of righteousness, has not attained to the law of righteousness. Why? Because they did not seek it through faith, but through the works of the law,"** tell us why the Jews were blinded (Romans 9:31-32). They were blinded because they were so intent on making themselves righteous, that they were not willing to admit their sin and look to Christ for forgiveness. And, many today are blinded by their fixation on works righteousness.

However, a fixation on works is only part of the reason for their blindness. The words, **"Those who know God accept what we say; those who are not of God will not accept what we say. That is how we can distinguish the spirit of truth from the spirit of error,"** tell us that they are also blinded by the fact that the Holy Spirit is not in their hearts, and because they are unwilling to accept anything in the Bible that condemns them or disagrees with their opinions (1John 4:6).

In the world today, much opposition to the clarity of Scripture comes from those who are unwilling to accept what the Bible says about Creation and the age of the earth. The Bible is perfectly clear, but they deny its clarity because they no longer believe what it says, but are unwilling to admit it.

For example: The words, **"In six days the LORD made heaven and earth, the sea, and everything that is in them, and rested on the seventh day: for that reason the LORD blessed the Sabbath day, and made it holy,"** are perfectly clear (Exodus 20:11). Anyone, having average intelligence, can see that the days being spoken of are days of the week. That is made abundantly clear by the context. And, the only people who say, "Well we don't know how long a day was," are those who do not want to accept what the Bible says.

Because God knew that these people would create doubts about the length of the creation days, He plainly tells us that **"The evening and the morning were the first day,"** while saying the same for each of the following creation days (Genesis 1:5,8,13,19,23,31). And, if that is not enough, by the words, **"God separated the light from the darkness. And God called the light Day, and called the darkness Night. And the evening and the morning were the first day,"** God defines evening and morning as a period of darkness and light (Genesis 1:4-5). My point is that the Bible is perfectly clear. The darkness is in the heart of man, which is, **"Deceitful above all things, and desperately wicked,"** not in Scripture (Jeremiah 17:9).

"Holy Scripture never states mere 'general principles' from which the Christian theologian or the Christian Church must 'develop' the doctrines; for it is not a book of 'general principles' but of doctrines. In order that the theologian may be kept from teaching false doctrine, he must constantly bear in mind that he is to teach nothing but what Scripture itself teaches in clear words... The Christian exegete must scrupulously refrain from foisting upon its sacred text his own subjective views" (John Theodore Mueller, "*Christian Dogmatics*", pages 138-139.)

How the Clarity of Scripture Applies to Its Interpretation

The Word of God is clear because God loves us and is, "**Not willing that any should perish, but that all should come to repentance**" (2Peter 3:9). However, Satan wants just the opposite. Because Satan hates us he wants people to ignore what the words of Scripture actually say while reading their own ideas into the text. And, one of the ways he does that is by convincing them that the doctrine of the Trinity is not found in Scripture. So I will use the doctrine of the Trinity to illustrate how the clarity of Scripture applies to Bible interpretation.

While it is true that the word, "Trinity" is not found in Scripture, that word is simply the name we ascribe to a body of doctrinal truths that are each clearly and explicitly stated in Scripture. For example:

1. The words, "**Don't we all have one father? Hasn't one God created us**," give us the doctrine that **the Father is God** (Malachi 2:10)
2. The words, "**We are in the one who is true, in His Son Jesus Christ. He is the true God, and eternal life**," give us the doctrine that **the Son is God** (1John 5:20).
3. The words, "**Why has Satan filled your heart to lie to the Holy Ghost... you have not lied to men, but to God**," give us the doctrine that **the Holy Ghost is God** (Acts 5:3-4).
4. The words, "**There is one God; and there is none other but He**," give us the doctrine that **there is only one God** (Mark 12:32).

In stating those four doctrines I in no way want to imply that the passages I quoted are the only passages of Scripture that teach those doctrines. Nor do I wish to imply that those four doctrines are all there is to the doctrine of the Trinity. There is far more. However, **those four doctrines constitute the heart and core of the doctrine of the Trinity**. And, the point I want to make is that **each of them is clearly and explicitly stated in Scripture**.

I also want to call attention to the fact that those doctrinal truths are not all found in one place, but are scattered through Scripture "**here a little and there a little**". For it is written, "**To whom can he teach knowledge? and who will he enable to understand doctrine?... for truth must be upon truth, truth upon truth; line upon line, line upon line; here a little, and there a little**," (Isaiah 28:9-10).

One cult that denies the doctrine of the Trinity claims that the Holy Spirit is just God's "active force". Of course, that is just something they made up. However, we reject it because the words, **"He who searches our hearts knows the mind of the Spirit,"** tell us that the Spirit has a mind (Romans 8:27). The words, **"The Spirit himself makes intercession for us,"** tells us that the Spirit intercedes for us (Romans 8:26). The words, **"The Spirit specifically says, that in the future some will depart from the faith,"** tell us that the Spirit speaks (1Timothy 4:1). The words, **"The Comforter, who is the Holy Spirit, whom the Father will send in my name, will teach you all things,"** tell us that the Spirit teaches (John 14:26). The words, **"Do not grieve the Holy Spirit of God,"** tell us that the Holy Spirit can be grieved (Ephesians 4:30). And, the words, **"Why has Satan filled your heart to lie to the Holy Ghost,"** tell us that the Holy Spirit can be lied to (Acts 5:4). Because having a mind, making intercession, speaking, teaching, and being grieved etc. are the characteristics of a personal being (not a force) we refer to the Holy Spirit as a person. And, since the same can be said about the Father and the Son, we refer to the Father, Son, and Holy Spirit as three "Persons" rather than three Gods. That terminology is used in order to avoid contradicting the fact that there is only One God. So again, what God wants us to teach is plainly stated "line upon line" as the Bible teaches (Isaiah 28:9-10).

Because the doctrine that God wants us to believe and teach is clearly and explicitly stated in Scripture, everything else that the Bible says is there to support that doctrine, and nothing that is taught in the hard to understand passages of Scripture will contradict what is taught in the clear. For that reason, all of the hard to understand passages need to be interpreted to teach the same doctrine that is taught in the clear passages. And, those who interpret the hard to understand passages in a way that contradicts what is taught in the clear passages should not be listened to. As it is written, **"If they do not speak according to this word, it is because there is no light in them."** (Isaiah 8:20).

SCRIPTURE ALONE

THE DOCTRINE OF GOD
(De Deo)

1. The Natural Knowledge Of God

The Bible tells us that **God "Alone is immortal, dwelling in the light that no man can approach; whom no one has ever seen, or can see"** (1Timothy 6:16). And, because "no one has ever seen, or can see" God, apart from divine revelation, no human being can know that He exists, or know anything about Him. However, the words, **"The invisible things of Him from the creation of the world are clearly seen, being understood by the things that are made, even His eternal power and Godhead; so that they are without excuse,"** tell us that God has revealed Himself to men through the things that He created (Romans 1:20). And, that raises the question: Why do men fail to see the evidence?

The words, **"The heart is deceitful above all things, and desperately wicked: who can know it?"** tell us that men are more likely to deceive themselves than face the truth (Jeremiah 17:9). And, the words, **"When they knew God, they did not glorify Him as God, nor were they thankful; but became vain in their imaginations, and their foolish heart was darkened. Professing themselves to be wise, they became fools, and changed the glory of the incorruptible God into an image made to resemble corruptible man, and birds, and four footed beasts, and creeping things,"** tell us that when it comes to God self-deception seems to be the rule (Romans 1:21-23).

Has anything changed since those words were written? No! Not at all. **Utah is full of people who have "Changed the glory of the incorruptible God into an image made to resemble corruptible man,"** and idolatry is still widespread (Rom. 1:23). But, what about the atheists? The atheist professor Richard Dawkins answers that question with the words, **"Biology is the study of complicated things that give the appearance of having been designed for a purpose"**. ("The Blind Watchmaker" page 1, paragraph 2.) Those words tell us that he sees the evidence even if he chooses to deny it.

However, consider carefully his words, **"Things that give the appearance of having been designed for a purpose"**. Ask yourself: Do those things appear to a dog or a horse like they have been designed for a purpose? Of course not! It is our reason that tells us that they have been designed, and reason also tells us that for every design there is a designer. Dawkins has simply rejected reason preferring to deceive himself. And, the words, "**The heart is deceitful above all things**," tell us why he prefers darkness to light, and why the knowledge of God revealed in nature is not enough to save souls (Jeremiah 17:9).

The words, The "**Lord of heaven and earth... has made of one blood all nations of men to live on all the face of the earth, and has determined their appointed times, and the boundaries they live in, so that they should seek the Lord, in the hope that they might grope for Him, and find Him, although He is not far from any one of us. For in Him we live, and move, and have our being; and some of your own poets have said, We are His offspring**," also testify to the witness of God in nature (Acts 17:26-28). However, the words, "**He [God] did not leave Himself without witness, in that He has shown kindness, and given us rain from heaven, and fruitful seasons, satisfying our hearts with food and gladness**," tell us that men **not only** should see the evidence of God in nature, but should see His goodness in the fact that He provides them with rain, good crops and food (Acts 14:17). Sadly, however, the words, "**But the natural man does not accept the things of the Spirit of God: for they are foolishness to him: and he cannot understand them, because they are spiritually discerned**." explain why sinful man is blind to the evidence (1Corinthians 2:14).

The words, "**When the Gentiles, who do not have the law, do by nature the things contained in the law, they, not having the law, are a law to themselves: Who show the work of the law written in their hearts, their conscience also bearing witness, and their thoughts the mean while accusing or else excusing one another**," tell us that the Law of God written on the heart [although blurred by sin] is a third way that God reaches out to the lost (Romans 2:14-15). And, the words, "**Who knowing the judgment of God, that those who commit such things are worthy of death, not only do the same, but have pleasure in those who do them**," tell us that men are more likely to ignore or excuse sin than cry out to God for forgiveness (Romans 1:32). Moreover, if they have rejected the True God for an idol, even if they do cry out their cries will be to a god who cannot hear (Jeremiah 2:28).

The Natural Knowledge of God is not Enough

The words, "**Nor is there salvation in any other, for there is no other name under heaven given among men, by which we must be saved [than Jesus Christ]**," tell us that the natural knowledge of God is not enough to save the lost (Acts 4:12). The words, "**The natural man does not accept the things of the Spirit of God: for they are foolishness to him: and he cannot understand them, because they are spiritually discerned**," tell us why the natural knowledge of God is not enough (1Corinthians 2:14). The words, **"The fleshly mind is hostile to God: for it is not subject to the law of God, nor indeed can be,"** tell us that our sinful mind is by nature in opposition to the things of God (Romans 8:6). And, the words, **"Since... the world through its wisdom did not know God, it pleased God to save those who believe through the foolishness of preaching,"** tell us that because the natural knowledge of God is not enough, the only way to save people is through preaching the gospel (1Corinthians 1:21). As it is written, **"Faith comes by hearing, and hearing by the word of God"** (Romans 10:17).

The reason that the natural knowledge of God is not enough is this. Even if a lost person came to believe in the God who created all things, and earnestly desired His forgiveness, that person could not be saved unless God revealed to him **the promise of forgiveness in Christ**. The words, **"Scripture has concluded all under sin, that the promise might be given to those who believe, through faith in Jesus Christ,"** tell us that all who trust in Christ are trusting in that promise (Galatians 3:22). The words, **"If the inheritance comes by the law, it is not given by promise: but God gave it to Abraham by promise,"** tell us that Abraham was saved through faith in that promise (Galatians 3:18). The words, **"I will put hostility between you and the woman, and between your seed and her seed; it will bruise your head, and you will bruise His heel,"** gave Adam and Eve that promise of a deliverer (Genesis 3:15). And, the words, **"That the blood of all the prophets, which was shed... from the blood of Abel unto the blood of Zacharias,"** tell us that Able was a prophet, and, therefore, (like Abraham) one who had God's promise of forgiveness in Christ (Luke 1:50-51).

But The Natural Knowledge of God is Still Useful

Even though the natural knowledge is not enough to save the lost, it still has a purpose in God's plan. First of all, the Law of God written on the heart is often the basis of civil law. Secondly, that law (in our conscience) is often what convicts the lost of sin, preparing them to receive the gospel. The following dialogue by the Apostle Paul gives us an example of how he used the natural knowledge of God as a tool for evangelism.

"As I passed through, and saw your objects of worship, I found an altar with this inscription, TO THE UNKNOWN GOD. Therefore I proclaim to you, the one whom you worship in ignorance. The God who made the world and everything in it, since He is Lord of heaven and earth, does not dwell in temples made with hands; Nor is He served by men's hands, as though He needed any thing, since He Himself gives to everyone life, and breath, and everything else; And has made of one blood all nations of men to live on all the face of the earth, and has determined their appointed times, and the boundaries they live in; So that they should seek the Lord, in the hope that they might grope for Him, and find Him, although He is not far from any one of us**" (Acts 17:23-27).

However, as useful as this may be in evangelism, whenever we do not define who God is, Satan is quick to introduce a false definition, and thus a false god. For that reason, in describing God it is always important to describe Him as the God who has revealed Himself in Scripture, the one God who is Father, Son, and Holy Ghost.

2. The Holy Trinity

Although the truth of God's triune nature is revealed throughout Scripture, the fact that only one God exists is the foundation and cornerstone of the doctrine of the Trinity. We find that fact emphasized in the first words of the Shema, "**Hear, O Israel: The LORD our God is one LORD,**" in the words, "**There is but one God,**" and in many other places (Deuteronomy 6:4, 1Corinthians 8:6).

The words, "**Has a nation ever changed its gods, which are not really gods? but my people have exchanged their glory for what is worthless,**" tell us that all other gods are not real and are worthless (Jeremiah 2:11). The words, "**We know that an idol has no real existence in the world, and that there is no God but one,**" tell us that all gods other than the one true God do not actually exist (1Corinthians 8:4). The words, "**The LORD the King of Israel, and His redeemer the LORD of hosts, says; I am the first, and I am the last; and there is no God but me,**" tell us that the Father ("The LORD") and Christ ("His Redeemer") are one God (Isaiah 44:6). [I will deal with that further in the section on the Trinity revealed in the Old Testament.] And, the words, "**You should turn from these fantasies to the living God, who made heaven, and earth, and the sea, and everything in them,**" make it clear that the heathen can only be saved if they turn away from their false gods (Acts 14:15). In short, from beginning to end the Bible stresses the fact that there is only ONE GOD.

At the same time, the Bible plainly teaches the threefold nature of God. In the first epistle of John we read, "**There are three who bear record in heaven, the Father, the Word, and the Holy Ghost: and these three are one**" (1John 5:7). Now, I specifically chose that verse because it is attacked by many. I could defend it by pointing out that those words are found in Old Latin Bible manuscripts dating back to the fifth century, in Vulgate manuscripts dating back to the eighth century, and it was quoted by Cyprian in the third century (200-258AD). However, let us examine it in the light of what the Bible says.

The words, "**Loved by <u>God the Father</u>, and kept by Jesus**

Christ," tell us that the Father is God (Jude 11). Therefore, the Father bears record in heaven. The words, "**In the beginning was the Word, and the Word was with God, and <u>the Word was God</u>**," tell us that the Word is God (John 1:1). Therefore, the Word bears record in heaven. The words, "**The Spirit of the living God**," tell us that the Holy Spirit is God (2Corinthians 3:3). Therefore, the Holy Ghost bears record in heaven. At the same time the words, "**There is but one God**," tell us that there is only one God (1Corinthians 8:6). So every part of the verse, "**There are three who bear record in heaven, the Father, the Word, and the Holy Ghost: and these three are one**," is clearly taught in Scripture, and, therefore, is the Word of God (1John 5:7). Furthermore, the words "**these three are one**," in Latin would be saying "**these tri are une**," and that is where we get the term **tri-une [i.e. three-one]**. The word Trinity is just another way of expressing the word triune.

The word "Trinity" is the name we give to a body of doctrinal truths that are each clearly and explicitly stated in Scripture. For example:
1. The words, "**Don't we all have one father? Hasn't one God created us**," give us the doctrine that **the Father is God** (Malachi 2:10).
2. The words, "**We are in the one who is true, in His Son Jesus Christ. He is the true God, and eternal life**," give us the doctrine that **the Son is God** (1John 5:20).
3. The words, "**Why has Satan filled your heart to lie to the Holy Ghost... you have not lied to men, but to God**," give us the doctrine that **the Holy Ghost is God** (Acts 5:3-4).
4. The words, "**There is one God; and there is none other but He**," give us the doctrine that **there is only one God** (Mark 12:32).

In stating those four doctrines I in no way want to imply that the passages I quoted are the only passages of Scripture that teach those doctrines. Nor do I wish to imply that those four doctrines are all there is to the doctrine of the Trinity. There is far more. However, those four doctrines constitute the heart and core of the doctrine of the Trinity. And, the point I want to make is that each of them is clearly and explicitly stated in Scripture.

As you can see, **the Bible plainly tells us that the Father is God, the Son is God, the Holy Spirit is God, and that there is only One God. <u>Therefore, that is what God wants us to believe and teach.</u>** However, the idea of three being one is totally alien to our way of thinking. In fact, in our universe it is impossible for three to be one. However, God transcends our universe. Although present everywhere, He exists in a different dimension, a spiritual dimension where Three can be One. Nevertheless, one false teacher after another has attempted to come up with some explanation aimed at reconciling what the Bible says about God with man's ignorance. One such attempt claims that the Holy Spirit is nothing more than, "God's active force". We reject that claim because the Bible tells us that the Holy Spirit has a "**mind**" (Romans 8:27), "**speaks**" (1Timothy 4:1), **teaches** (John 14:26), can "**grieve**" (Ephesians 4:30), and can be "**lied to**" (Acts 5:3-4). Because **having a mind, speaking, teaching and so forth are the qualities of a personal being** (not a force), we speak of the Holy Spirit as a "Person". Since the same can be said about the Father and the Son, we refer to the Father, Son, and Holy Spirit as three "Persons" rather than three Gods. That terminology is used in order to avoid contradicting the fact that there is only One God.

Because Satan is continually at work trying to lead Christians away from what the Bible plainly says, and because the heart of man is "**deceitful above all things**," we need to stick to what the Bible says (Jeremiah 17:9). (See John 8:31-32.) That means that when the Bible says that **the Father is God, the Son is God, and the Holy Spirit is God** we need to teach **that each of them is the one true God**, without trying to compromise what the Bible says in a vain attempt to make God's Word fit our own puny little finite way of thinking. Compared to God, the most brilliant man is as ignorant as a worm. Therefore, we reject every attempt by man to deny that Christ is God, or to portray Him as only part of God rather than fully and completely God. The same holds true for the Father and the Holy Spirit. God wants us to teach what His Word says, without trying to make it fit our way of thinking. As it is written, "**He who has my word, let him speak my word faithfully.**" (Jeremiah 23:28).

The words, "**Who, being by nature God, did not see equality with God as taking something that was not His**," tell us that Christ is equal to the Father (Philippians 2:6). The words, "**That all may honor the Son, even as they honor the Father. He who does not honor the Son does not honor the Father who sent Him**," tell us that both the Father and the Son are to be honored as God (John 5:23). And, the words, "**Whoever denies the Son, does not have the Father: but he who acknowledges the Son has the Father also**," tell us that those who deny that Christ is God do not have the Father as their God (1John 2:23).

The words, "**Philip said, Lord, show us the Father, and that will be sufficient. Jesus replied, Have I been with you all this time, without your knowing me, Philip? he who has seen me has seen the Father; how then can you say, Show us the Father? Do you not believe that I am in the Father, and the Father in me? the words that I speak to you do not come from me: but the Father who lives in me, is carrying out His work. Believe me when I say I am in the Father, and the Father in me: or else believe me on account of my works**," tell us that to see Jesus is to see the Father, and to hear Jesus is to hear the Father

(John 14:8-11). And the words, "**That you might have the full assurance of understanding, and know the mystery of God, and of the Father, and of Christ**," tell us that the relationship of Christ to the Father is a mystery, and, therefore, something beyond our ability to understand (Colossians 2:3). For that reason, men need to simply teach what the Bible says, without "Professing themselves to be wise" by making up explanations (Romans 1:22).

Because Father Son and Holy Spirit are all one God, we need to realize that all true worship is directed at all three, even if we name only one, such as when we begin the Lord's prayer with the words, "**Our Father who art in heaven**" (Luke 11:2). The words, "**He who does not honor the Son does not honor the Father**," warn us against ever trying to worship one to the exclusion of the other two (John 5:23). And, because the Father, the Son and the Holy Spirit are all one God, they all share the attributes of God. For example, the words, "**I will always be with you, even to the end of the world**," tell us that Christ is **omnipresent** (Matthew 28:20). The words, "**Jesus came to them, and said, All power is given to me in heaven and in earth**," tell us that Jesus is **omnipotent** (Matthew 28:18). And, the words, "**Of Christ In whom are hidden all the treasures of wisdom and knowledge**," tell us that Christ is **omniscient** (Colossians 2:2-3)

At the same time, the Bible makes it clear that the Father, Son, and Holy Spirit each have distinct roles, and a distinct place that is not shared by the other two. For example: the words, "**Jesus immediately went up out of the water: and, the heavens were opened to Him, and He saw the Spirit of God descending like a dove, and lighting upon Him, and a voice from heaven, said, This is my beloved Son, in whom I am well pleased**," speak of each person of the Trinity doing something different (Matthew 3:16-17). The words, "**God so loved the world, that He gave His only begotten Son**," tell us that it was the Son who died on the cross, not the Father (John 3:16). And, the words, "**They were all filled with the Holy Ghost, and began to speak with other tongues, as the Spirit gave them utterance**," tells us that it was the Holy Spirit that was poured out on the day of Pentecost, not the Father or the Son (Acts 2:4). At the same time, because there is only one God, whatever is done by one person of the Trinity is not done to the exclusion of the other two.

> We worship one God in Trinity, and Trinity in Unity; neither confounding the Persons nor dividing the Substance. For there is one Person of the Father; another of the Son, and another of the Holy Ghost. But the Godhead of the Father, of the Son, and of the Holy Ghost is all one: the glory equal, the majesty coeternal. (From the Athanasian Creed.)

3. The Doctrine Of The Holy Trinity In Controversy

Although the doctrine of the Holy Trinity embodies truths that are plainly stated in Scripture, throughout history Satan has attacked it with a fury. He has attacked it through those who deny that only one God exists, and through those who deny or explain away what the Bible says about God the Son or God the Holy Spirit. He has attacked it through false religions, such as the Muslims who spread their religion by the sword, killing, enslaving and persecuting Christians along the way. And, he has attacked it through false prophets and through **fools "professing themselves to be wise"** (Romans 1:22). Against all such attacks the Bible warns, **"There were also false prophets among the people, just as there will be false teachers among you, who will privately introduce damnable heresies, even denying the Lord who bought them, bringing swift destruction upon themselves"** (2Peter 2:1).

Those who deny that there is only one God have to explain away passage after passage of Scripture. However, the words, **"Those who know God accept what we [the inspired writers of Scripture] say; those who are not of God will not accept what we say. That is how we can distinguish the Spirit of truth from the spirit of error,"** tell us that all who explain away statements of Scripture have a spirit of error, and should not be listened to (1John 4:6). As it is written, **"To the law and to the testimony: if they do not speak according to this word, it is because there is no light in them."** (Isaiah 8:6).

Regarding the fact that there is only one God, the words, **"Master, you have spoken the truth: for there is one God; and there is none other but He,"** plainly state that truth (Matthew 12:23). The words, **"There is one God, and one mediator between God and men, the man Christ Jesus,"** again tell us that there is one God (1Timothy 2:5). And, the words, **"You believe that there is one God; you do well: even the demons believe, and tremble,"** tell us that even the demons believe that there is one God (James 2:19).

Those who deny that there is only one God have been known to quote the words, "There are gods many, and lords many," but they are pulling that statement out of context (1Corinthians 8:5). In context that verse says, **"When it comes to eating meat that has been offered in sacrifice to idols, we know that an idol has no real existence in the world, and that there is no God but one. For even if there are so-called gods, whether in heaven or in earth, (as There are gods many, and lords many,) Yet for us there is but one God,"** so those words are saying the opposite of what they claim (1Corinthians 8:4-6). And, to all who think that they can just make the Bible say what they want it to say, God says, **"Woe unto those who are wise in their own eyes, and think they are** shrewd... Their root shall be as rottenness, and their blossom shall go up as dust: because they have cast away the law of the LORD of hosts, and despised the word of the Holy One of Israel" (Isaiah 5:21,24).

Those who go in the other direction by denying that there are three distinct persons, usually deny the deity of Christ. However, the words, **"Unto us a child is born, unto us a son is given: and the government will be on His shoulders: and His name will be called Wonderful, Counselor, The Mighty God, The everlasting Father, The Prince of Peace,"** plainly tell us that Christ is God while emphasizing His unity with the Father (Isaiah 9:6).

The words, **"Surely you are our father, even though Abraham does not know us, and Israel does not recognize us: you, O LORD [Jahweh], are our father, our redeemer; your name is from everlasting,"** tell us that our redeemer is Jehovah (Isaiah 63:16). And, the words, **"Behold, the days come, says the LORD, when I will raise to David a righteous Branch... and this is the name by which He will be called, The LORD [Jahweh] Our Righteousness,"** ascribe the name Jehovah or Jahweh to the descendant of David, namely Christ (Jeremiah 23:5-6).

The words, **"Before you brought the mountains into existence, or formed the earth and the world, even from everlasting to everlasting, you are God,"** tell us that God is from eternity (Psalm 90:2). While the words, **"But you, Bethlehem Ephrathah, though you are little among the thousands of Judah, yet out of you will He come forth unto me who is to be ruler of Israel; whose origin is from long ago, from everlasting,"** tell us that Christ has existed from eternity (Micah 5:2). So we see that the Bible equates God with Christ by ascribing eternal existence to both.

The words, **"I saw the dead, small and great, stand before God; and the books were opened: and another book was opened, which is the book of life: and the dead were judged according to what they had done, as it was written in the books,"** tell us that God will judge all men (Revelations 21:5). At the same time, the words, **"The Father does not judge anyone, but has committed all judgment to the Son,"** tell us that when we are judged by God, it will be God the Son (not God the Father) who will judge (John 5:22).

The words, **"Don't we all have one father? Hasn't one God created us?"** tell us that God the Father is our creator (Malachi 2:10). The words, **"The Spirit of God has made me, and the breath of the Almighty has given me life,"** tell us that God the Holy Spirit is our creator (Job 33:4). The words, **"All things in heaven and earth, both visible and invisible, were created by Him, whether they be thrones, or jurisdictions, or provinces, or authorities: all things were created by Him, and for Him, and He is before all** things, and by Him all things have their existence," tell us that God the Son is our creator (Colossians 1:16-17). And, the words, "**Who, being by nature God, thought it not robbery to be equal with God: but made himself of no reputation, and took upon Him the nature of a servant, and was born as a man,**" tell us that God the Son is equal to God the Father (Philippians 2:6-7). In fact, if God the Son was not equal to God the Father He would not be fully and completely God. That is why all attempts to portray the Son as subordinate to the Father wind up with more than one God. And, that is how we know that when Christ says of Himself, "**My Father is greater than I,**" He is speaking of Himself according to His human nature in His state of humiliation (John 14:28).

Those who portray Father, Son, and Holy Spirit as three modes or faces that God puts on, wind up explaining away all of the Bible passages that speak of Father, Son, and Holy Spirit as distinct from each other. For example: The words, "**Jesus lifted up His eyes to heaven, and said, Father, the time has come; glorify your Son, so that your Son may also glorify you,**" tell us that the Son is not the Father (John 17:1). The words, "**I will ask the Father, and He will give you another Comforter, that He may remain with you forever,**" tell us that the Son and the Spirit are distinct from the Father (John 14:16). And, the words, "**When the Comforter comes, whom I will send to you from the Father, even the Spirit of truth, who proceeds from the Father, He will testify of me,**" again tell us that the Father, Son and Holy Spirit are distinct persons within the One true God (John 15:26).

We know that the Holy Spirit is a person, not just a force, because the words, "**The Spirit specifically says, that in the future some will depart from the faith,**" tell us that the Holy Spirit speaks (1Timothy 4:1); the words, "**He who searches our hearts knows the mind of the Spirit,**" tell us that the Holy Spirit has a mind (Romans 8:27); the words, "**The Holy Spirit, whom the Father will send in my name, will teach you all things,**" tell us that the Holy Spirit teaches (John 14:26); the words, "**Do not grieve the Holy Spirit of God,**" tell us that the Holy Spirit can grieve (Ephesians 4:30); and the words, "**Why has Satan filled your heart to lie to the Holy Ghost,**" tell us that the Holy Ghost can be lied to (Acts 5:3). Those are all the qualities of a personal being, not a force.

We know that Christ's divine nature is distinct from that of the Father because the words, "**In the beginning was the Word, and the Word was with God, and the Word was God,**" tell us that Christ [the Word] not only was God but was with God (John 1:1). We know that Christ is "the Word" because the Bible says, "**The Word was made flesh, and dwelt among us**" (John 1:14). And, we know that Christ existed from eternity because Christ said, "**Truly, truly, I tell you, Before Abraham was, I am,**" and because the words,

"You, O LORD, are our Father, our Redeemer; your name is from everlasting," tell us that Christ [our Redeemer] "is from everlasting," (John 8:58, Isaiah 63:16).

The Bible tells us that, "**The minds of those who do not believe have been blinded**" (2Corinthians 4:4). And, Satan has several ways of blinding those he wants to keep in darkness. He blinds some by making them think that they are smarter than everyone else. That keeps them from listening to those who try to point out their errors. He blinds some by making them think that the Bible is full of deep mysterious statements. That gets them so busy looking for something profound that they fail to see the plain meaning of the words. He gets some into cults that lead them to twist and explain away many truths of Scripture. He leads some to filter everything the Bible says through the Godless philosophy of naturalism. And, he leads all of them to think that they are good people, or that the rules they keep make them good. It is those who have been blinded by Satan who are not satisfied with the Doctrine of the Trinity as it is plainly stated in Scripture, and as it has been taught by the Christian church for two-thousand years.

4. The Trinitarian Terminology Of The Christian Church

Although the doctrine of the Trinity is clearly taught in Scripture, those who refuse to accept what the Bible says often try to hide their disagreement by redefining the words of Scripture. We see that today in the way cults redefine Biblical terms in order to appear Christian. We also see it in the way theistic-evolutionists redefine the words of Genesis. Historically Christians have regarded that sort of doublespeak as dishonest. Nevertheless we have to deal with it, and the ancient church countered that sort of double talk by adopting terms that false teachers would not accept.

In 325AD church leaders from all over the Roman empire met in the city of Nicea to deal with the followers of Arius, who denied the deity of Christ. Like many "liberals" today, the followers of Arius hid their rejection of Scripture behind Christian terminology. For example: They would say that Jesus is the son of God, but denied that Jesus had a divine nature and existed from eternity. Of course the Bible says the opposite. The words, "**Out of you will He come forth unto me who is to be ruler of Israel; whose origin is from long ago, from everlasting,**" tell us that Christ is from everlasting (Micah 5:2). I could quote other passages, but what I want to stress is that the ancient church countered that problem by adopting a creed (recited during every worship service) that included words the Arians would not accept. That creed is known today as the Nicene Creed, and that creed (with minor variation) is recited by traditional Christians around the world.

The Nicene Creed

I believe in one God, the Father Almighty, Maker of heaven and earth and of all things visible and invisible.

And in one Lord Jesus Christ, the only-begotten Son of God, begotten of His Father before all worlds, God of God, Light of Light, True God of True God, Begotten, not made, Being of one substance with the Father, By whom all things were made; Who for us men and for our salvation came down from heaven And was incarnate by the Holy Ghost of the Virgin Mary And was made man; And was crucified also for us under Pontius Pilate. He suffered and was buried; And the third day He rose again according to the Scriptures; And ascended into heaven, And sits on the right hand of the Father; And He shall come again with glory to judge both the living and the dead; Whose kingdom shall have no end.

And I believe in the Holy Ghost, The Lord and Giver of Life, Who proceeds from the Father and the Son, Who with the Father and the Son together is worshiped and glorified, Who spoke by the Prophets. And I believe one holy Christian and Apostolic Church. I acknowledge one Baptism for the remission of sins, And I look for the resurrection of the dead, And the life of the world to come. Amen.

The wording of this creed is carefully thought out, so let me explain some of its statements. The words, "**I believe in one God, the Father Almighty, Maker of heaven and earth,**" simply restate the words, "Don't we all have one father? Hasn't one God created us?" (Malachi 2:10). Those words were never intended to deny what the Bible says about Christ and creation (Col. 1:16). Everything cannot be included in a brief creed. Those words were intended to affirm what the Bible says about Creation, while the words, "**Maker of heaven and earth and of all things visible and invisible,**" were intended to make it clear that, unlike Christ, angels are created beings.

The purpose of the phrase, "**Begotten of His Father before all worlds,**" is to affirm the fact that Christ did not come into existence when His human nature was begotten in the womb of the virgin Mary, but that He existed as God the Son from eternity. It is not saying that Christ's divine nature was begotten, but that He existed before anything was created.

The purpose of the words, "**God of God, Light of Light, True God of True God,**" are to emphasize the fact that Christ is true God. The words, "Light of Light," relate to the words, "**God is light, and in Him there is no darkness at all**" (1John 1:5).

The purpose of the words, "**Begotten, not made, Being of one substance with the Father,**" is to emphasize the fact that Christ is not a created being. The idea is that a created being would be made of a different substance than its creator. For example: If you create something in your own image such as a statue, it would not be made of the same substance that you are made of. But, your natural son would be made of the same substance you are made of. Therefore, to say that Christ is of one substance with the father, is to say that He is by nature God. However, unlike a human father and son, there is only one divine being, not two or three. The three are one!

If some of this wording seems strange, realize that it was necessary in order to expose those who were undermining the gospel by denying Christ's deity. And, it worked! If you travel to Egypt, you will find that the Coptic [Egyptian] Orthodox Church — which has endured Moslem persecution for well over a thousand years, and only recently has been allowed to have its own church buildings — still uses this creed, as do traditional churches around the world.

The word trinity is simply a name we give to all that the Bible tells us about God — with emphasis on the fact that the Father is God, the Son is God and the Holy Ghost is God, yet there is only one God. Moreover, **because "The heart is deceitful above all things, and desperately wicked," we should never attempt to supplement what God has revealed about Himself with ideas dreamed up by men** (Jeremiah 17:9). God wants us to teach His Word as He revealed it, **"Line upon line, line upon line; here a little, and there a little,"** not our ideas (Isaiah 28:10). Because Trinitarian terminology has played such an important role in preserving this doctrine, Christians need to understand the terminology, use it and defend it. Those who think that they can improve on it only cause suspicion, conflict, and division. Moreover, because **"The heart is deceitful above all things"** we need to continually remind people that God transcends our universe (Jeremiah 17:9). Although He is present everywhere, He exists in a different dimension, a spiritual dimension where Three can be One. And, it is just as foolish for someone to think that he can explain the truth about God by making up explanations, as it would be for him to think that he can discover the name of my next door neighbor by making up a name.

5. The Holy Trinity Revealed In The Old Testament

Although the doctrine of the Holy Trinity is clearly taught in the New Testament it is not alien to the Old Testament. On the contrary, the Old Testament lays a strong foundation for it. And, even though it is not explained in the Old Testament, there were some Jews of that era who realized that its pages reveal a plurality within the One True God, and even evidence of a threefold nature.

The Hebrew language has more than one word for God. In addition to the name Jahweh or Jehovah, there is the more generic term "Elohim" which is found throughout the Old Testament. And, unlike the name Jahweh (which is closely related to the Divine name "I Am," and can be translated as "He Who Is") Elohim is the plural form of the word "Eolah" which means "God". That being understood, let us look at the first words of the Shema (the Jewish Creed).

"Hear, O Israel: The LORD our God, is one LORD!" Deuteronomy 6:4

As we examine that statement, we find that the word translated, "LORD" in both occurrences is the name Jehovah, which is emphatically singular, while the word "God" is a translation of the plural word Elohim. If we look at the meaning of the names, that verse could be translated as **"Hear, O Israel: He Who Is our Gods, is one God"**. Furthermore, the word translated, "one" is the Hebrew word, **"echad"** which signifies a compound "one". That word is used in the sentence, "For this reason a man will leave his father and his mother, and shall cleave unto his wife: and they shall be **one** flesh" (Genesis 2:24). It is also used in the sentence, "Join both of them together as a single stick; and they will become **one** in your hand" (Ezekiel 37:17). Now, the Jews do have another word which signifies a solitary "one", and that word is **"yachid"** — which is usually translated into English as "only". That word is used in the sentence, "Take now your son, your **only** son Isaac" (Genesis 22:2). It is significant that Moses used the word "echad," not "yachid," in Deuteronomy 6:4.

Father Son and Holy Spirit

The Old Testament uses the terms Father Son and Holy Spirit in reference to God.

The words, **"Turn, O backsliding children, says the LORD... I thought you would call me, Father; and would not turn away from me,"** identify God with the word father (Jeremiah 3:14, 19). The words, **"If I am a father, where is my honor?... The LORD of hosts says this,"** identify God with the word father (Malachi 1:6). The words, **"The LORD says... for I am a father to Israel,"** identify God with the word father (Jeremiah 31:7, 9). The words, **"Don't we all have one father? Hasn't one God created us?"** identify God with the word father (Malachi 2:10). And, the words, **"You, O LORD, are our father, our redeemer; your name is from everlasting,"** again identify God with the word father (Isaiah 63:16).

The words, **"Unto us a child is born, unto us a son is given: and the government will be on His shoulders: and His name will be called Wonderful, Counselor, The mighty God, The everlasting Father, The Prince of Peace,"** identify God with the word son (Isaiah 9:6). The words, **"The LORD said unto him... I will have mercy on the house of Judah, and will save them by the LORD their God,"** speak of the God who has mercy, and the God who saves, as if they are distinct from each other (Hosea 1:7). The words, "**You, Bethlehem Ephrathah, though you are little among the thousands of Judah, yet out of you will come one who will rule in Israel for me; whose origin is from long ago, from everlasting**" identify God with one who will be born in Bethlehem [a Son] (Micah 5:2). And, the words, "**Behold, a virgin will conceive, and bear a son, and will call His name God with us,**" again identify God with the word son (Isaiah 7:14).

The words, "**Create in me a clean heart, O God... Do not cast me away from your presence; or take your Holy Spirit from me,**" speak of God's Holy Spirit (Psalm 51:10-11). The words, "**He [God] said, Surely they are my people... But they rebelled, and grieved His Holy Spirit,**" speak of God's Holy Spirit (Isaiah 63:8, 11). And, the words, "**The Spirit of the LORD spoke by me, and His word was in my tongue,**" tell us that the Spirit of the Lord is not a mere emanation from God, but one who speaks (2Samuel 23:2).

Isaiah 48:12-16

"Listen to me, O Jacob and Israel, whom I called; **I am He; I am the first, I am also the last. My hand has laid the foundation of the earth, and my right hand has spread out the heavens: when I call them, they stand forth together... Come near to me, listen to this; From the beginning I have not said anything in secret; from the time that it was, there I am: and now the Lord GOD, and His Spirit, has sent me.**" [Comment: notice that the one who is speaking is the one who "**Laid the foundation of the earth**", and "**spread out the heavens**". Yet His words, "**The Lord GOD, and His Spirit, has sent me,**" speak of two more who are God.]

Some Other Passages

The words, "**God said, Let us make man in our image, after our likeness... So God created man in His own image, in the image of God He created him,**" speak of God in the plural "**our** image," and then in the singular "**His own** image" (Genesis 1:26-27).

The words, "I heard the voice of the Lord, saying, **Whom shall I send, and who will go for us?**" speak of God in the singular "Whom shall I send," and then switch to the plural "who will go for **us**" (Isaiah 6:8).

The words, "**The LORD God said, Since man has become like one of us, to know good and evil,**" have Jehovah speaking as more than one, saying "like one of **us**" (Genesis 3:22).

The words, "**Your throne, O God, is for ever and ever: the scepter of your kingdom is a righteous scepter. You love righteousness, and hate wickedness: that is why God, your God, has anointed you with the oil of gladness above your companions,**" address God in the first line, and then speak of God His God (Psalm

45:6-7).

The words, "**The messenger of Jehovah said to her [Hagar], Return to your mistress... And she called the name of Jehovah who spoke to her, The God who sees me**," identify "The messenger [angel] of Jehovah," as Jehovah (Genesis 16:9 and 13).

The words, "**The LORD said to my Lord, Sit at my right hand, until I make your enemies your footstool**," speak of more than one Lord (Psalm 110:1).

The words, "**Holy, holy, holy, is the LORD of hosts: the whole earth is full of His glory**," tell us that Jehovah is thrice holy indicating a threeness in the one Lord (Isaiah 6:3).

In addition, many see the Aaronic blessing (Numbers 6:24-26), with its threefold reference to Jehovah as an indication of God's threefold nature.

> "The LORD bless you, and keep you:
> The LORD make His face shine upon you,
> and be gracious to you:
> The LORD lift up His countenance upon you,
> and give you peace."

Genesis 18:1-3

"<u>The LORD</u> appeared to Abraham in the plains of Mamre: as he sat in the tent door during the heat of the day, and he lifted up his eyes and looked, and, lo, <u>three men</u> stood by him: and when he saw them, he ran from the tent door to meet them, and bowed himself toward the ground, and said, <u>My Lord</u>, if now I have found favor in your sight, I pray you, do not pass by your servant." [Notice that when the LORD (**singular**) appeared to Abraham, **Abraham saw "three men**," ran to them, bowed, and said **"My Lord" (singular).**]

Although this verse has been used to illustrate the Trinity, because the Bible says "No man has seen God at any time," this appearance of God is better viewed as a pre-advent appearance of Christ along with two angels, the same two angels that later visited Lot in Sodom (John 1:18).

6. God's Essence And Attributes

The Doctrine In General

God has revealed Himself in Scripture as **the only God**, the Living God, the one who unlike all others exists from eternity supreme and perfect, "**The God of gods, and Lord of lords, a great God, mighty and terrifying, who does not regard persons, or take bribes.**" // "Who is the blessed and only Potentate, the King of kings... <u>Who alone is immortal</u>, dwelling in the light that no man can approach; whom no one has ever seen, or can see" //

"He is before all things, and by Him all things have their existence." (Deuteronomy 10:17, 1Timothy 6:15-16, Colossians 1:17). Therefore, even though the Bible sometimes uses the name god or gods in reference to false gods and authorities, it makes a distinction between the One True God and so-called gods. Making it clear that, **"An idol has no real existence in the world, and that there is no God but one"** (1Corinthians 8:4-6).

Furthermore, the names that God applies to Himself in Scripture are not mere titles, but a description of God Himself in terms of His fundamental nature, attributes and works. That is especially true of the name Jahweh or Jehovah, which has its origin in Scripture, and sets the God of the Bible apart from all others. That name shares its origin with the divine name "I Am" and can be translated as "He Who Is". Through the words, **"God said to Moses, I AM WHO I AM: therefore you will say to the children of Israel, I AM has sent me unto you,"** God reveals Himself as an eternal being (Exodus 3:14). Through the words, **"God also said to Moses, Tell the children of Israel, The LORD God of your fathers, the God of Abraham, the God of Isaac, and the God of Jacob, has sent me unto you,"** God reveals Himself as the God of Abraham, Isaac, and Jacob (Exodus 3:15). And, the words, **"I am Jahweh: that is my name: and I will not give my glory to anyone else, or my praise to graven images,"** explain why the divine name Jahweh or Jehovah is never applied to any created thing (Isaiah 42:8).

When we describe a man, we might describe him according to his being (origin, looks), his accomplishments, or his attributes (kind, honest etc.). However, none of these things describe his essential core being. Accomplishments may be faked, looks and personality can change, and even one's origin may be wrong since some people are never told that they were adopted. In contrast, Biblical descriptions of God's origin ("I Am"), accomplishments, or attributes reveal His essential core being, things that will never change. As it is written, **"I am the LORD, I do not change"** (Malachi 3:6).

The words, **"There is no other God besides me; <u>a just God</u> and a Savior,"** tell us that God is **just** (Isaiah 45:21). The words, **"The LORD is longsuffering, and <u>of great mercy</u>,"** tell us that God is **merciful** (Numbers 14:18). And, the words, **"God is not a man, that He should lie,"** tell us that God is **truthful** (Numbers 23:19). Those are three of God's attributes. However, when those attributes are ascribed to any man (when we say that someone is just, merciful or truthful etc.) the best we can find in man falls far short of perfection. It is not so imperfect that it is entirely unrelated to what God has revealed about Himself. In fact, the shortcomings we see in men help us to appreciate God all the more. Nevertheless, the attributes we ascribe to men are gifts of God not part of their essence, and may be lost. A person may cease to be just, a person may cease to be merciful, a person may cease to be truthful, a person may even cease to live, but God never changes.

In learning what God has revealed about Himself in Scripture it is important to adhere strictly to what the words say without letting the imagination run wild. The words, **"What we now see is like a dim reflection on a glass; but then we will see face to face: now I know in part; but then I will know even as I am known,"** remind us of our own ignorance, and the danger of assuming that we know more than what the Bible actually says (1Corinthians 13:12). For example: much harm has been done by those who twist what the Bible says about the goodness of God into an excuse to sin, or twist what the Bible says about God's hatred of sin into a denial of the gospel. In short, we need to let Scripture define God's attributes.

The Passive Attributes

It would be difficult, if not impossible, to compile and exhaustive list of God's attributes. Not only because we know so little, but also because human language uses synonyms to describe things. For example: The words, **"He, [God] being full of compassion,"** reveal God as **compassionate**, while the words, **"Blessed is the LORD: for He has shown me His marvelous kindness,"** tell us that God is **kind** (Psalm 78:38, Psalm 31:21). The question is: Do we treat kindness and compassion as two separate attributes, or as synonyms? Or do we treat God's kindness as one aspect of His compassion? Since the purpose of this Theology is to look at what God says in His Word, not what men think, I will not attempt to answer those questions, or make an exhaustive list of attributes. Instead I will focus on attributes that are fundamental to our knowledge of God.

The attributes that I have listed as passive are those that have to do with who God is, rather than what He does. They are His **eternity, unity, omnipresence, infinity, glory, inscrutability, perfection, immutability, and indivisibility.**

Eternity – The words, **"From everlasting to everlasting, you are God,"** tell us that God has always existed, and will always exist (Psalm 90:2). The words, **"Thus says the LORD the King of Israel, and His redeemer the LORD of hosts; I am the first, and I am the last; and beside me there is no God,"** tell us that no God existed before God (Isaiah 44:6). And, the words, **"Now to the eternal King, the immortal, invisible, and only wise God, be glory and honor for ever and ever. Amen,"** tell us that God is **eternal, immortal, invisible and wise** which are all attributes of God (1Timothy 1:17). [See Psalm 102:27, Deut. 33:27, Isaiah 9:6, Gen. 21:33, Isaiah 40:28, 2Cor. 5:1.]

Unity – The words, **"There is no God but Me,"** tell us that there is only one God (Isaiah 44:6). The words, **"God is a Spirit,"** tell us that the One God is "a Spirit" — singular (John 4:24). And the words, **"I am He: no God was formed before me, and there will be none after me,"** tell us that no God came into existence before God, and none ever will (Isaiah 43:10).

Omnipresence – The words, **"Can anyone hide himself in a secret place where I will not see him? asks the LORD. Don't I fill heaven and earth? asks the LORD,"** tell us that God is present everywhere (Jeremiah 23:24). The words, **"Where can I go to escape your spirit? or where can I flee to escape your presence? If I go up into heaven, you are there: if I make the grave my bed, behold, you are there. If I take the wings of the morning, and stay at the most distant parts of the sea; Even there your hand will lead me, and your right hand will hold me,"** tell us that there is no place where God is not present, and nothing that He does is done without Him being present (Psalm 139:7-10). And, the words, **"In Him [God] we live, and move, and have our being; and some of your own poets have said, We are His offspring,"** tell us that He is with us at all times (Acts 17:28). And, because God is present everywhere, He cannot be measured or confined. However, even though God is present in all of His creation (including in us) the creation is not joined to Him, or a part of Him as pantheists imagine. Instead God is distinct and separate from His creation as the Bible plainly says.

Infinity – The attribute of infinity tells us that God is not only eternal and present everywhere in space, but that He transcends both space and time. The words, **"In the beginning [of time] God created the heaven [space] and the earth,"** tell us that God created space and time (Genesis 1:1). The word "heaven" is not referring to the sun, moon and stars, because they were not created until day four. The words, **"You, even you, are LORD alone; you have made heaven, the heaven of heavens, with all their host, the earth, and all things that are in it, the seas, and all that is in it, and you preserve them all; and the host of heaven worships you,"** tell us that God made heaven [space] so His dwelling place transcends space (Nehemiah 9:6). The words, **"With the Lord one day is as a thousand years, and a thousand years as one day,"** tell us that God is not bound by time (2Peter 3:8). The words, **"The angel... swore by Him who lives for ever and ever, who created heaven, and everything in it, and the earth, and everything in it, and the sea, and everything in it, that time should be no longer,"** seem to be saying that time will end (Revelation 10:6). And, the words, **"So shall we ever be with the Lord,"** tell us that our life with God will never end (1Thessalonians 4:17).

Glory – The words, "**Who is like you, O LORD, among the gods? who is like you, glorious in holiness, awesome in splendor, doing wonders?**" speak of God's glory and holiness, both of which are attributes (Exodus 15:11). The words, "**I will speak of the glorious splendor of your majesty, and of the wonderful things you have done,**" tell us of God's glory and splendor (Psalm 145:5). The words, "**May His glorious name be blessed for ever: and let the whole earth be filled with His glory,**" tell us that God's name is Glorious (Psalm 72:19). And, the words, "**Be watchful to do all the words of this law that are written in this book, that you may fear this glorious and fearful name, THE LORD YOUR GOD,**" again tell us that God's name is a glorious name (Deuteronomy 28:58).

Inscrutability – The word "unsearchable" is sometimes used for this attribute of God. The idea is that God is unfathomable, that our minds are too little to fully understand Him, His thoughts, or why He does what He does. The words, "**O the depth of the riches both of the wisdom and knowledge of God! How unsearchable are His judgments, and His ways past finding out!**" Tell us that God's judgments are unsearchable (Romans 11:33). The words, "**Great is the LORD, and greatly to be praised; and His greatness is beyond our comprehension,**" tell us that God's greatness is beyond our ability to comprehend (Psalm 145:3). And, the words, "**I realized that a man cannot find out the meaning of all the work God requires under the sun: because even though a man works hard to discover it, he will not find it; yea even though a wise man claims to know it, he is not able to discover its meaning,**" tell us that we cannot understand why God does what He does (Ecclesiastes 8:17).

Perfection – The words, "**Be perfect, even as your Father who is in heaven is perfect,**" tell us that God is perfect (Matthew 5:48). God's perfection includes His attributes of righteousness and holiness. However, it also includes what are sometimes called God's negative attributes — the fact that He does not have any of the faults we see in men. For example: The words, "**God is not a man, that He should lie,**" tell us that God will not lie (Numbers 23:19). And, the words, "**The LORD redeems the soul of His servants: and none of those who trust in Him will be condemned,**" tell us that God will not betray our trust (Psalm 34:22).

Immutability – The words, "**O my God... Long ago you laid the foundation of the earth: and the heavens are the work of your hands. They will perish, but you will endure: yea, all of them will grow old like a garment; you will change them like**

clothes, and they will pass away: But you are the same, and your years will never end,"** tell us that God does not age, or change with time as the things He has created do (Psalm 102:24-27). The words, **"Every good and perfect gift is from above, and comes down from the Father of lights, who does not change, or shift as the shadows,"** tell us that God does not constantly change like we do (James 1:17). The words, **"A man has many plans in his mind; nevertheless the LORD'S plan will stand,"** tell us that nothing can stop what God has determined to bring to pass (Proverbs 19:21). And, the words, **"I am the LORD, I do not change; that is why you sons of Jacob have not been destroyed,"** tell us that Jahweh [He Who Is] does not change, either according to His existence or the plan being carried out by His divine will (Malachi 3:6). Therefore, whenever the Bible speaks of God changing His mind, such as when it says, **"I am sorry that I made Saul king,"** those statements need to be understood in a way that is consistent with God's divine foreknowledge and eternal purpose (1Samuel 15:11).

Indivisibility – The attribute of divine indivisibility (sometimes called divine simplicity) affirms the fact that God does not consist of matter and form, as created things do. While a man is the sum total of his parts, eyes, ears hands etc., **"God is a Spirit"** (John 4:24). And, because God is a Spirit, He is invisible. As it is written, **"Now unto the King eternal, immortal, <u>invisible</u>, the only wise God, be honor and glory for ever"** (1Timothy 1:17). Therefore, it would be wrong for us to portray God as some sort of exalted man consisting of parts (hands, eyes etc.) In fact, the words, **"Professing themselves to be wise, they became fools, and changed the glory of the incorruptible God into an image made like to corruptible man,"** condemn those who portray God as an exalted man (Romans 1:22-23). That being the case, whenever the Bible speaks of God's hands or eyes etc., we need to realize that His hands and eyes are not just parts of God, but are everywhere He is. So, when the Bible says, **"The eyes of the LORD run to and fro throughout the whole earth,"** it is not saying that God has two eyes, but that He sees everything (2Chronicles 16:9). Moreover, because the eyes of God are everywhere He is, He sees every person on earth at the same time. And, He sees each person in such detail that "the very hairs" of their head "are all numbered" (Matthew 10:30). Likewise, when the Bible says, **"This comes from the hand of God,"** it is not saying that God has two hands (Ecclesiastes 2:24). On the contrary, because God's hands are wherever He is, when He created the stars there were not just two hands at work. In fact, if we speak of hands at all we would have to say that when He created the stars trillions upon trillions of microscopic hands were at work fashioning subatomic particles from nothing, atoms from subatomic parts, and stars from atoms.

The Active Attributes

The attributes that I have listed as active are those that have to do with how God deals with us or what He does. They are life, knowledge, wisdom, will, holiness, justice, honesty, power, and goodness.

Divine Life – The words, "**The LORD is the true God, <u>He is the living God</u>**," tell us that unlike all idols, our God is alive (Jeremiah 10:10). The words, "**Who alone is immortal, dwelling in the light that no man can approach**" tell us that God is immortal (1Timothy 6:16). The words, "**In Him we live, and move, and have our being; and some of your own poets have said, We are His offspring,**" tell us that God is the source of our life (Acts 17:28). The words "**The hour is coming, and now is, when the dead will hear the voice of the Son of God: and those who hear will live. For as the Father has life in Himself; so He has granted the Son to have life in Himself,**" are not just telling us that God is alive, but that He alone has the power to give life (John 5:25-26). And, the words, "**They became fools, and changed the glory of the incorruptible God into an image made to resemble corruptible man,**" tell us that God is incorruptible (Romans 1:22-23). [See also: Deut. 32:39, 1Tim. 1:17, Acts 14:15 and 17:25, Heb. 10:31, 1Tim. 3:15 and 4:10.]

Divine Knowledge – The words, "**The eyes of the LORD are everywhere, watching the wicked and the good,**" tell us that God sees all things (Proverbs 15:3). The words, "**Your eyes saw me, before I was formed; and in your book all the days of my life were written, before they ever took shape, before any of them began,**" tell us that God knows all that will happen (Psalm 139:16), The words, "**If for any reason our heart condemns us, God is greater than our heart, and knows all things,**" tell us that there is no limit to God's knowledge (1John 3:20). And, the words, "**O LORD, you have searched me, and known me. You know when I sit down and when I get up, you understand my thoughts from far away. You watch over my travels and my rest, and know all my ways. Before there is a word on my tongue, O LORD, you know all about it,**" tell us that God knows everything about us (Psalm 139:1-4).

The words, "**There is a God in heaven who reveals secrets, and is making known to king Nebuchadnezzar what will be in the future,**" tell us that God knows the future (Daniel 2:28). The words, "**And you, Capernaum... if the mighty works, that have been done in you, had been done in Sodom, it would have remained to this day,**" tell us that God even knows what might have happened, but did not (Matthew 11:23). And, the words, "**Do not let anyone say when he is tempted, I am tempted by God: for God cannot be tempted with evil, nor does He tempt anyone,**" tell us that God does not cause men to do evil things, even though He knows what they will do (James 1:13). [See 1Sam. 2:3, 1Kings 8:39, Psalm 7:9, Ps. 34:15, Ps. 139"1-2, John 21:17, John 2:25, Isaiah 66:2, Matt. 6:32.]

Divine Wisdom – The words, "**Now to the eternal King, the immortal, invisible, and only wise God, be glory and honor for ever and ever. Amen**," tell us that God is wise (1Timothy 1:17). The words, "**O LORD, how many are the things you have made! in wisdom you have made them all: the earth is full of your creatures**," tell us that the design we see in all created things is evidence of God's wisdom (Psalm 104:24). The words, "**O the depth of the riches both of the wisdom and knowledge of God! how unsearchable are His judgments, and His ways past finding out!**" tell us that God's wisdom is beyond our ability to understand (Romans 11:33). While the words, "**Every good and perfect gift is from above, and comes down from the Father of lights, who does not change, or shift as the shadows**," and the words, "**If anyone of you lacks wisdom, let him ask God, who gives to all men generously**," tell us that all true wisdom comes from God (James 1:5 and 17).

Divine Will – The words, "**Who has known the mind of the Lord**? or who has been His counselor?" tell us that God has a mind (Romans 11:34). The words, "**For this is the will of God, even your sanctification, that you abstain from sexual immorality**," tell us that God has a will (1Thessalonians 4:3). The words, "**The LORD tries the righteous: but He hates the wicked and anyone who loves violence**," tells us that God hates wickedness (Psalm 11:5). The words, "**We must all appear before the judgment seat of Christ; so that each may receive the things done in the body, according to everything he has done, whether good or evil**," tell us that it is God's will to condemn sin (2Corinthians 5:10). And, the words, "**He who believes on Him is not condemned: but he who does not believe is condemned already, because he has not believed on the name of the only begotten Son of God**," tell us that God will condemn all who do not trust in Christ (John 3:18). In understanding God's will it is important to stick strictly to what God has revealed in His Word (Pr. 30:6, Rom. 1:22).

Divine Holiness – The words, "**I am the LORD your God: you shall therefore sanctify yourselves, and you shall be holy; for I am holy**," tell us that God is Holy, the words, "**This is the will of God, even your sanctification, that you abstain from sexual immorality**," tell us that God wants His people to be holy [set apart from the world, sanctified] (Leviticus 11:44, 1Thessalonians 4:3). The words, "**The LORD is righteous in all His ways, and holy in all His works,**" use holiness as a synonym for righteousness (Psalm 145:17). The words, "**Abraham answered and said, Behold now, I, who am but dust and ashes, have taken upon myself to speak to the Lord,**" tell us that because God is holy we should approach Him with reverence (Genesis 18:27). And the words, "**We were reconciled to God by the death of His Son,**" // "**In whom we have free and confident access to God through faith in Him,**" tell us that is only through the forgiveness that is ours in Christ that we have access to our holy God (Romans 5:10, Ephesians 3:12). [See Deut 32:4, Lev. 11:44, 1Pet. 1:15-16, Isaiah 6:3, John 12:41, Ex. 3:5, Romans 5:1.]

Divine Justice – The words, "**Be careful what you do: for you do not judge for man, but for the LORD, who is with you in the judgment. Therefore now let the fear of the LORD be upon you; take heed what you do: for there is no injustice with the LORD our God, or respect of persons, or accepting gifts,**" tell us that God is fair and just in all of His decisions, and will condemn all judges who are not just (2Chronicles 19:6-7). The words, "**You shall not make unrighteousness judgments: you shall not respect the person of the poor, nor honor the person of the mighty: but in righteousness shall you judge your neighbor,**" tell us that just judgments are righteous judgments (Leviticus 19:5). The words, "**The ungodly will not stand in the judgment, nor sinners in the congregation of the righteous,**" warn the ungodly that because God is just they will be punished (Psalm 1:5-6). The words, "**Because of your hard and impenitent heart you are stockpiling wrath for yourself in the day when the wrath and righteous judgment of God is revealed; For He will render to every man according to his deeds,**" warn the unrighteous of their need to repent (Romans 2:5-6). And, the words, "**The Lord Jesus shall be revealed from heaven with His mighty angels, In flaming fire taking vengeance on those who do not know God, and who <u>refuse to accept the gospel</u> of our Lord Jesus Christ: Who will be punished with unending destruction away from the presence of the Lord, and from the glory of His might,**" remind us that because God is just He has provided a way of receiving forgiveness through "**the gospel of our Lord Jesus Christ**" (2Thessalonians 1:7-9). [See Psalm 92:15, Hosea 14:9, Ps. 19:7, Isaiah 45:23, Ps. 119:137, Romans 1:32, Acts 17:31.]

Divine Honesty – The words, "**God is not a man, that He should lie; nor the son of man, that He should repent: has He said, and shall He not do it? or has He spoken, and shall He not make it good?**" tell us that God is unfailing in speaking the truth and in keeping His promises (Numbers 23:19). The words, "**Heaven and earth will pass away, but my words will not pass away,**" tell us that what God has promised will never fail (Matthew 24:35). The words, **"Let God be true, but every man a liar... That you might be justified in your sayings, and might overcome when you are judged,"** // **"Looking to the hope of eternal life, that God, who cannot lie, promised long ages ago,"** tell us that we need to believe God's Word not man's word [i.e. science, tradition etc.] if we want to escape God's judgment (Romans 3:4, Titus 1:2). And, this is God's promise, **"Whoever believes in Him [Christ] will not be ashamed,"** on the day of judgment (Romans 10:11). [See Psalm 146:6, 2Sam. 7:28, Isaiah 65:16.]

Divine Power – The words, **"Jesus looked at them, and said to them, With men this is impossible; but with God all things are possible"** tell us that nothing is impossible for God to do (Matthew 19:26). [See Gen. 18:14, Mark 10:27, Luke 18:27.] The words, **"The LORD made the heavens by His word; and all the stars by the breath of His mouth... Let all the earth fear the LORD: let all the inhabitants of the world stand in awe of Him. For He spoke, and it was done; He commanded, and it stood fast,"** tell us that God's power is revealed in His creation (Psalm 33:6-9). However, the words, **"An evil and adulterous generation seeks after a sign; but no sign will be given to it, but the sign of the prophet Jonah,"** tell us that even though God can do all things, He does not use His power arbitrarily (Matthew 12:39).

In the past, enemies of God [See James 4:4] have tried to confuse believers by saying, "If God cannot lie, steal, die, or make a stone that is too big for Him to lift, then there are some things that He cannot do". That sort of reasoning only shows their ignorance, for by the miracle of the virgin birth God took upon Himself the nature of man in the person of Christ Jesus. In the person of Christ it was possible for Him to lie or steal but He did not. As man there were many stones that He could not lift. And, as the God-man He did die. He died in our place so the we could have forgiveness. As believers, there are many things that we do not understand, however, in regard to those who use such arguments God warns us, **"Beware lest any man take you captive through hollow and deceptive philosophy"** (Colossians 2:8). "If they do not speak according to" God's "Word, it is because there is no light in them" (Isaiah 8:20).

Divine Goodness – The Bible passages that reveal God's goodness include those that speak of His compassion, love, mercy, grace, longsuffering and so forth. That being understood, the words, **"God so loved the world, that He gave His only begotten Son, that whosoever believes on Him should not perish, but have everlasting life,"** clearly reveal God's goodness (John 3:16). The words, **"You, O Lord, are a God full of compassion, and gracious, longsuffer-**

ing, and plenteous in mercy and truth," are aimed at assuring those with a repentant heart of God's mercy (Psalm 86:15). The words, **"You, Lord, are kind, ready to forgive; and full of mercy for all those who call on you,"** urge the lost to seek God's mercy (Psalm 85:5). The words, **"Do you despise the riches of His goodness, forbearance and patience; not knowing that the goodness of God leads you to repentance?"** tell us that God's longsuffering gives us time to repent (Romans 2:4). And, through repentance God reveals, **"The exceeding riches of His grace in His kindness toward us through Christ Jesus"** (Ephesians 2:7) **"In whom we have redemption through His blood, the forgiveness of sins, according to the riches of His grace"** (Ephesians 1:7). [See Psalm 145:9, Ps. 36:6-7, Ps. 86:15, Ps. 103:8, Eph. 2:4, Rom, 8:28]

More on God's Attributes

God is Compassionate. 1Kings 13:23, Lamentations 3:22-23, Psalm 78:38.

God is Faithful and True. Joshua 21:45, 2Samuel 7:28, Psalm 19:9, Isaiah 25:1.

God is Gracious. Nehemiah 9:31, Isaiah 30:18-19, Exodus 34:6.

God is Incomprehensible. Job 36:26, Job 37:5, Psalm 40:5, Psalm 139:6.

God is Incorruptible. Leviticus 11:44, Malachi 3:6.

God is Invisible. Job 23:8-9, 1Timothy 1:17.

God is Jealous. Exodus 20:5, Deuteronomy 32:16.

God is Longsuffering. Numbers 14:18, Psalm 86:15.

God is Merciful. Exodus 34:6-7, Numbers 14:18, Psalm 36:5, Psalm 136, Psalm 106:1, Psalm 13:5.

God is Righteous. Ezra 9:15, Psalm 145:7 & 17.

God is Upright. Psalm 25:8, Psalm 92:15.

THE DOCTRINE OF THE DIVINE DECREES

The purpose of this section is to focus on certain lasting commitments or decrees that God has made. These ongoing decrees are to be distinguished from external acts of God, (such as Christ changing water into wine) that only occupy a brief period of time. The Bible speaks of three such decrees the decree of creation, the decree of redemption, and the decree of predestination.

The Decree of Creation

The decree of creation is that commitment God made from the beginning, not only to bring all things into existence, but to sustain them according to His divine plan.

The words, "**Praise the LORD from the heavens: praise Him from the heights. Praise Him, all you His angels: praise Him, all His hosts. Praise Him, sun and moon: praise Him, all you stars of light. Praise Him, you highest heavens, and you waters above the heavens. Let them praise the name of the LORD: for He commanded, and they were created. He has also set them in their places forever: He has made a decree which shall not pass**," use the word "decree" in regard to what God has created (Psalm 148:1-6). The words, "**He gave to the sea His decree, and would not let the water flow further than He ordained: when He laid out the foundations of the earth**," tell us that the limits of the sea are determined by God's decree (Proverbs 8:29). The words, "**God has known all that He will do from the beginning of the world**," tell us that before God created He was committed to carrying out a plan (Acts 15:18). And, the words, "**God, who in the past spoke to the fathers at various times and in different ways by the prophets, has spoken to us in these last days in the person of His Son, whom He has appointed heir of all things, and through whom He made the universe. Who being the brightness of His glory, and the true image of His nature, and sustaining all things by the word of His power, when He had by Himself made purification for our sins, sat down on the right hand of the Majesty on high**," not only affirm the deity of Christ, but also tell us that God not only created the universe, but also sustains it "by the word of His power" (Hebrews 1:1-3).

The Decree of Redemption

The decree of Redemption is that commitment God made from the beginning to send Christ to redeem lost mankind, whose fall He has foreseen, but not caused.

The words, **"This Jesus, being delivered up by the predetermined plan and foreknowledge of God, you have taken, and by the hands of wicked men have crucified and slain,"** tell us that God allowed the Pharisees to arrest Jesus, because that was His plan from the beginning (Acts 2:23). God did not cause the Pharisees to crucify Christ, but He knew they would, for they had placed themselves under Satan's control by rationalizing their sins instead of repenting (Compare Mark 7:9-13 with John 8:44). The words, **"When the time had fully come, God sent forth His Son, born of a woman, born under the law, to redeem those who were under the law, that we might receive the adoption of sons,"** tell us that God sent Christ into the world at the time He did because of His plan to redeem those who are condemned by the law (Galatians 4:4-5). And, the words, **"In whom we have redemption through His blood, the forgiveness of sins, according to the riches of His grace. Which He has lavished upon us with all wisdom and understanding, having made known unto us the mystery of His will, according to His kind intention which He has purposed in Himself. That in the distribution at the fullness of times He might bring all things together, both which are in heaven, and which are on earth; under one head in Christ,"** tell us that Christ accomplished the plan God had from the beginning (Ephesians 1:7-10).

The Decree of Predestination

The decree of predestination is that commitment God made from the beginning to work through His Word to bring multitudes to salvation through faith in the forgiveness Christ won for us. Predestination and election will be treated at greater length when I deal with that doctrine. They are dealt with here only as eternal decrees of God

The words, **"The Lamb slain from the foundation of the world,"** tell us that it was God's plan from the very beginning for Christ to die for the sins of the world (Revelation 13:8). The words, **"He [the Father] has chosen us in Him [Christ] before the foundation of the world,"** tell us that God did not choose us before He decided to send Christ to die for our sins, but chose to save us **"in Him"** that is "in Christ" (Ephesians 1:4). The words, **"No man can come to me, unless the Father who has sent me draws him,"** tell us that we do not choose God, He chooses us (John 6:44). And, the words, **"We are bound to give thanks always to God for you, brethren beloved of the Lord, because God has from the beginning chosen you to salvation through sanctification of the Spirit and faith in the truth. To this end He called you by our** gospel, to obtain the glory of our Lord Jesus Christ," tell us that God calls those He has chosen "through the gospel," and saves them through "faith in" the gospel's promise of forgiveness in Christ (2Thessalonians 2:13).

At the same time, the words, "**As I live, says the Lord GOD, I have no pleasure in the death of the wicked, but want the wicked man to turn from his way and live,**" tell us that God does not want anyone to be lost (Ezekiel 33:11). The words, "**God... has made of one blood all nations of men to live on all the face of the earth, and has determined their appointed times, and the boundaries they live in, so that they should seek the Lord, in the hope that they might grope for Him, and find Him, although He is not far from any one of us,**" tell us that God wants all men to seek Him and find Him (Acts 17:24-27). The words, "**Everyone whom the Father gives me will come to me; and I will never turn away anyone who comes to me,**" tell us that God will never reject those who want to be saved (John 6:37). The words, "**O Jerusalem, Jerusalem, you who kill the prophets, and stone those who are sent to you, how often I longed to gather your children together, as a hen gathers her chicks under her wings, and you would not,**" tell us that God actively reaches out to those who reject Him (Matthew 23:37). And, the words, "**God speaks time and again, yet man does not notice,**" tell us that the lost turn a deaf ear to the word of God (Job 33:14). Therefore, those who are lost are lost by their own fault, and not because God did not want them.

The Doctrine Of Creation

1. The Origin Of All Things

The words, "**In the beginning God created the heaven and the earth,**" tell us that time, space, and matter originated with God (Genesis 1:1). The words, "In the beginning," denote the beginning of time, and the words "heaven and earth" are the Hebrew way of saying "all that exists," or "the entire universe". And, that is a reference to space, because the stars were not created until the fourth day. In other words, the Bible is telling us that space and time did not exist until God created it.

The reason time and space are intertwined is because, for time to exist there must be a place (space) where time is passing. Likewise, for space to exist movement must be possible, and movement takes time. This relationship of space and time is generally known as the "space-time continuum". Furthermore, if time did not have a beginning we would never have arrived at this point in time. Those who question this may imagine that time has always existed, but they fail to understand the meaning of "infinite". If time was infinite, then no matter how far back in time you went there would always be an infinite amount of time before that. There would be no beginning. However, the Bible tells us that there was a beginning.

The words, **"The invisible things of Him [God] from the creation of the world are clearly seen, being understood by the things that are made, even His eternal power and Godhead,"** tell us that God created time to be eternal and space to be infinite in order to illustrate the fact that He is both eternal and infinite (Romans 1:20). Moreover, because time and space were created by God, they both illustrate His triune nature. Like God, space consists of three parts (three dimensions) often spoken of as length, width and height. Likewise, time consists of three parts past, present and future. In both cases the three are one! In fact, it is impossible for space to exist without all three dimensions. Those who dispute this may try to imagine a two-dimensional existence where everything is as thin as a piece of paper. However, they forget that paper has thickness. If you take all of that thickness away nothing will remain. Space must exist as both three and one or it will not exist at all.

The words, **"The heavens declare the glory of God; and the sky displays His handiwork,"** tell us that all we see in the sky is the handiwork of God (Psalm 19:1). The words, **"The universe was created by the word of God, so that what is seen was made of what is not seen,"** tell us that God did not create the universe from pre-existing matter (Hebrews 11:3). The words, **"God... gives life to the dead, and calls into existence things that do not exist,"** tell us that when God created He called into existence that which previously did not exist (Romans 4:17). And, the words, **"All things in heaven and earth, both visible and invisible, were created by Him, whether they be thrones, or jurisdictions, or provinces, or authorities: all things were created by Him, and for Him, and He is before all things, and by Him all things have their existence,"** tell us that God created everything that exists outside of Himself (Colossians 1:16-17). Therefore, in opposition to pagan naturalism, which ascribes creative power to matter (evolution), the Bible tells us that God created everything that exists outside of Himself.

2. The Order Of Creation

The words, **"In the beginning God created the heaven and the earth,"** tell us that God first created time, space, and matter (Genesis 1:1). The words, **"God said, Let there be light: and there was** light," tell us that God created light before He created the sun (Genesis 1:3). The words, "**And God said, Let the earth bring forth grass, plants yielding seed, and the fruit tree yielding fruit after its kind, whose seed is in itself, upon the earth: and it was so,**" tell us that God filled the earth with plants before He created the sun, moon and stars (Genesis 1:11). The words, "**And God said, Let there be lights in the expanse of the heaven to separate the day from the night; and let them be for signs, and for seasons, and for days, and years,**" tell us that God created the light between the heavenly bodies and earth at the same time He created the heavenly bodies, otherwise we would not even know that most of them were there (Genesis 1:14). The words, "**And God said, Let the waters team with living creatures that have life, and let birds fly above the earth in the open expanse of heaven,**" tell us that God created sea creatures and birds before He created land creatures (Genesis 1:20). The words, "**And God said, Let the earth bring forth living creatures after their kind, cattle, and creeping things, and beasts of the earth after their kind: and it was so,**" tell us that God made land animals (Genesis 1:24). And, God created man on the sixth day, the same day that He created the land animals (Genesis 1:26-31).

It should be obvious that the order of creation taught in Scripture is totally incompatible with the evolutionary scenario. According to the Bible the land was created under water, not in a molten state. The earth and plants were created before the sun. Birds and whales were created before land animals, and man was created on the same day that land animals were created. Furthermore, because it is God, not man, who decides what is true and what is not true, the words, "**To the law and to the testimony: if they do not speak according to this word, it is because there is no light in them,**" tell us that all truth will agree with the written Word of God (Isaiah 8:20). In other words, **the opinions of men may contradict what the Bible says, but the facts never do.**

The Bible tells us that, "**The heart is deceitful above all things, and desperately wicked,**" and one way Satan uses the deceitfulness of the human heart to blind people to the truth of God's Word is by causing them to confuse their own fallible opinions with fact (Jeremiah 17:9). And, glaring confusion is obvious when it comes to the evolutionary delusion. When Darwin observed that different finches had different beak sizes, that was observable fact. When he assumed that given enough time small differences (such as beak size) could change one kind of animal into an entirely different kind of animal, that assumption was science fiction, not observable science. When Darwin observed warm ponds full of bacteria, that was observable fact. When he assumed that life originated from non-life in a warm little pond, that was science fiction, not observable science. In fact, **the entire**

evolutionary scenario consists of science fiction, not fact. Evolutionists simply interpret the facts to make them fit their science fiction scenario in the same way that cult people interpret the words of Scripture to make them fit their cultic beliefs. So forget the interpretations and stick to the facts.

The assumption that life could originate form non-life has been tested experimentally and rejected. Experiments by Francesco Redi (1660), and Louis Pasture (1859) coupled with the invention of a dust-free box at the end of the nineteenth-century, convinced the scientific community that life does not come from non-life. Likewise, research into genetics has shown that the amount of change possible in any living organism (such as change in beak size) is limited by the genes. Nevertheless, those who have made evolutionary science fiction their religion could care less about the facts. When Atheist professor Richard Dawkins (who knows that life does not come from non-life) was interviewed by Ben Stein for the movie "Expelled," he attempted to get around the scientific evidence by suggesting that space aliens brought life to earth (more science fiction), and that interview is in the film. Therefore, do not be intimated by the assertiveness of those who reject the Bible. Their entire worldview is a house of cards, consisting of one assumption stacked on another, and their seeming confidence is the result of satanic delusion.

3. The Six Days (Hexaemeron)

The words, "**In six days the LORD made heaven and earth, the sea, and everything that is in them, and rested on the seventh day, for that reason the LORD blessed the sabbath day, and made it holy,**" tell us that in six days God made "heaven and earth, the sea, and everything that is in them" (Exodus 20:11). The words of Genesis chapter one, "**The evening and the morning were the <u>first</u> day,**" (verse 5) "**The evening and the morning were the <u>second</u> day,**" (verse 8) "**The evening and the morning were the <u>third</u> day,**" (verse 13) "**The evening and the morning were the <u>fourth</u> day,**" (verse 19) "**The evening and the morning were the <u>fifth</u> day,**" (verse 23) and, "**The evening and the morning were the <u>sixth</u> day,**" define the word "day" by telling us that each of those six days had an evening and a morning (verse 31). And, the words, "**God said, Let there be light: and there was light. And God saw that the light was good: and God separated the light from the darkness. And God called the light Day, and called the darkness Night. And <u>the evening and the morning were the first day</u>,**" tell us that "the evening and the morning" consisted of a period of darkness and light (Genesis 1:3-5).

I have just summarized what God's Word plainly says about creation, and therefore, what God wants His church to believe and teach. However, Satan wants just the opposite, and one way Satan blinds people to the truth of God's Word, is by causing them to regard the plain meaning of the words as nothing more than an interpretation. Furthermore, those who treat the Biblical account of creation as an interpretation are not being honest, because they are not trying to teach what the Bible says, but trying to make it agree with atheist ideas.

Evolution proper is atheistic and immoral, while theistic evolution is neither in accord with Scripture nor with the basic principles of evolution proper. To deny the inspired character of the Book of Genesis means to contradict the testimony of the divine, omniscient Christ, who accepted also this book as canonical. (Dr. John Theodore Mueller, "Christian Dogmatics," page 181)

4. The Six Days Of Creation Considered In Detail

The First Day

Holy Scripture describes the first day in these words, "**In the beginning God created the heaven and the earth. And the earth was without form, and empty; and darkness was upon the face of the deep. And the Spirit of God moved upon the face of the waters. And God said, Let there be light: and there was light. And God saw that the light was good: and God separated the light from the darkness. And God called the light Day, and called the darkness Night. And the evening and the morning were the first day**" (Genesis 1:1-5).

The expression "in the beginning" refers back to the moment this world began to exist. There was no "beginning" before that moment, because God does not have a beginning. And, there was no pre-existing matter before that moment, because nothing outside of God existed. The words, "**God separated the light from the darkness**," tell us that when God created light He caused it to shine on one side of the earth, so that there was an, "evening" and "morning". And, God specifically tells us that "the evening [dark] and the morning [light] were the first day," because He wants us to know that the first day was the same kind of day as any other day with an evening and morning.

Note: The words, "**He that descended is the same also that ascended up far above all heavens**," describe the dwelling place of God as being "far above" what was created on the first day (Ephesians 4:10). As it is written, "**Lord... Before you brought the mountains into existence, or formed the earth and the world, even from everlasting to everlasting, you are God**" (Psalm 90:1-2).

The Second Day

Holy Scripture describes the second day in these words, "**And God said, Let there be an open expanse in the midst of the waters, and let it divide the waters from the waters. And God made the expanse, and separated the waters that were under the expanse from the waters above the expanse: and it was so. And God called the expanse Heaven. And the evening and the morning were the second day**" (Genesis 1:6-8).

Moses describes the expanse above the earth in two ways. When he writes, "**Let birds fly above the earth in the open expanse of heaven,**" he is describing the lower expanse as it appears during the day (Genesis 1:20). When he writes, "**Let there be lights in the expanse of the heaven to separate the day from the night,**" he is describing the higher expanse that contains the moon and stars as well as the sun, and is best seen at night (Genesis 1:14). For that reason, I understand the words, "God... separated the waters that were under the expanse [atmosphere] from the waters above the expanse [atmosphere]" in terms of the expanse as it appears during the day. That tells me that the earth was originally covered with fog, and that God separated the water below the atmosphere [water in the sea] from the water that is above the atmosphere [water in the clouds]. The idea that there may have been a vapor canopy above the atmosphere at that time is possible, but highly speculative.

The Third Day

Holy Scripture describes the third day in these words, "**And God said, Let the waters under heaven be gathered together unto one place, and let dry land appear: and it was so. And God called the dry land Earth; and the gathering together of the waters He called Seas: and God saw that it was good. And God said, Let the earth bring forth grass, plants yielding seed, and the fruit tree yielding fruit after its kind, whose seed is in itself, upon the earth: and it was so. And the earth brought forth grass, and plants yielding seed after their own kind, and trees bearing fruit, in which is their seed, after their kind: and God saw that it was good. And the evening and the morning were the third day**" (Genesis 1:9-13).

The words, "**let dry land appear**," tell us that the entire earth was originally under water. All of that water rushing off of the earth in just one day would have stirred up a lot of sediment, and that sediment may account for those layers of the earth's crust that do not contain any fossils — there could not be any fossils at that time because living things had not yet been created. The words, "**Let the earth bring forth,**" are not saying that plants just appeared, but that they "sprouted forth," growing very rapidly. In fact, on the very day they were created they were "**yielding seed,**" and "**bearing fruit**".

The Fourth Day

Holy Scripture describes the fourth day in these words, "**And God said, Let there be lights in the expanse of the heaven to separate the day from the night; and let them be for signs, and for seasons, and for days, and years: And let them be lights in the expanse of the heaven to give light upon the earth: and it was so. And God made two great lights; the greater light to rule the day, and the lesser light to rule the night: He made the stars also. And God set them in the expanse of the heaven to give light upon the earth, And to rule over the day and over the night, and to divide the light from the darkness: and God saw that it was good. And the evening and the morning were the fourth day**" (Genesis 1:14-19).

The words, "**He made the stars... to give light upon the earth**," tell us that when God created the stars He created the **light from the stars**. And, because God wanted that light to accurately reveal the stars He had created, Adam and Eve would have seen the stars exactly as they were at that time.

The Bible plainly tells us that God created both the earth and light before He created the sun, and all of the actual data agrees with what the Bible says. Foolish men may claim that the earth was originally a molten blob, but the earth's continents rest on granite, and granite only forms in the presence of water. In fact, if granite is melted it reforms as rhyolite. Furthermore, the earth's granite contains trillions of microscopic radiohalos caused by the breakdown of polonium 218. Since polonium 218 atoms break down in less than three minutes there is no way that granite could have formed slowly. It had to be hard within three minutes of the time it formed or the radiohalos would not be there. To quote Dr. John Theodore Mueller, "We know so little concerning astronomical data that it is both foolish and unscientific to supplement, correct, or criticize Scripture on the basis of human speculative systems." ("Christian Dogmatics," page 183) **The opinions of men may contradict what the Bible says, but the facts never do**.

The Fifth Day

Holy Scripture describes the fifth day in these words, "**And God said, Let the waters team with living creatures that have life, and let birds fly above the earth in the open expanse of heaven. And God created great whales, and every living creature that moves, which the waters brought forth abundantly, after their kind, and every winged fowl after its kind: and God saw that it was good. And God blessed them, saying, Be fruitful, and multiply, and fill the waters in the seas, and let fowl multiply in the earth. And the evening and the morning were the fifth day**" (Genesis 1:20-23).

Not only did God create the whales and birds before He created the land dwelling animals, He created them all in one day, a day that had an evening and a morning. Furthermore, the words, "**God saw that it was good**," tell us that His creative process did not involve suffering and death — because suffering and death are evils, and what is evil can never be called good. (See Deut. 31:17) The words, "**Sin entered the world by one man, and death by sin**," tell us that suffering and death is in the world because of man's sin, not because God made it that way (Romans 5:12). And, because Satan was behind Adam's sin, he is the one who is to blame for suffering and death. Therefore, those who worship a god who used evolution to create are worshipping the one who caused suffering and death, not the God of the Bible.

The Sixth Day

Holy Scripture describes the sixth day in these words, "**And God said, Let the earth bring forth living creatures after their kind, cattle, and creeping things, and beasts of the earth after their kind: and it was so. And God made the beasts of the earth after their kind, and cattle after their kind, and every thing that creeps upon the earth after its kind: and God saw that it was good. And God said, Let us make man in our image, after our likeness: and let them have dominion over the fish of the sea, over the birds of the air, over the cattle, over all the earth, and over every creeping thing that creeps upon the earth. So God created man in His own image, in the image of God He created him; male and female He created them. And God blessed them, and God said to them, Be fruitful, and multiply, and replenish the earth, and subdue it: and have dominion over the fish of the sea, and over the fowl of the air, and over every living thing that moves upon the earth. And God said, Behold, I have given you every seed bearing plant, that is upon the face of all the earth, and every tree, with seed in its fruit; to be your food. And to all the animals of the earth, and to all the birds of the air, and to every living creature that creeps upon the earth, I have given every green plant for food: and it was so. And God saw every thing that He had made, and, behold, it was very good. And the evening and the morning were the sixth day**" (Genesis 1:24-31).

Scripture then focuses on the creation of man with the words, "**And the LORD God formed man from the dust of the earth, and breathed into his nostrils the breath of life; and man became a living soul... And the LORD God caused a deep sleep to fall upon Adam, and he slept: and He took one of his ribs, and filled up its place with flesh; And out of the rib, which the LORD God had taken from the man, He made a woman, and brought her** to the man" (Genesis 2:7,21,22).

When the Bible describes man as being made of clay, such as when it says, "**O LORD, you are our father; we are the clay, and you are our potter,**" it is using a metaphor (Isaiah 64:8). However, whenever the Bible describes what we are made of without using a figure of speech, it uses the word "dust". The word "dust," in the Hebrew language, denotes the smoke-like wisps of dust stirred up by the feet when walking on a dry dirt road. Since many individual particles of that smoke-like dust are too small to be seen without magnification, if we had to translate the word, "molecules" into ancient Hebrew, we would translate it as "dust". Understood that way, the words of Genesis 2:7 are telling us that, "**The LORD God formed man from the molecules of the earth,**" and the words, "**Let the earth bring forth living creatures,**" could be understood as telling us that God created land animals from the molecules of the earth (Gen. 1:24). That has led some to wonder if all matter was created on the first day, and everything else, including the sun, moon and stars, then created from that matter. But, that is speculation, not something the Bible says.

The words, "**The LORD God... breathed into his nostrils the breath of life; and man became a living soul,**" tell us that man consists of two parts, body and soul (Gen. 2:7). Some regard spirit as a third part (Compare 1Thess. 5:23 with Gal. 3:2). And, the Bible does speak of both "soul" and "spirit," but it also uses those terms as synonyms (See Job 7:11, Isaiah 26:9, Matthew 10:28, Luke 1:46-47, compare 1Peter 3:19 with Rev. 6:9).

God's words to Adam, after he sinned, "**Cursed is the ground for your sake... Thorns also and thistles will it bring forth to you,**" tell us that animals and plants which are harmful to man only became so after the fall (Genesis 3:17). The Bible does not tell us if the corruption of sin caused certain plants and animals to develop poison, or if man (and animals) lost their immunity to that poison. However. The words, "**God saw everything that He had made, and, behold, it was very good,**" tell us that harmful characteristics were not present before the fall (Genesis 1:31).

The fall of man is closely related to the creation account. And, the fall of man, along with the results of that fall, is the reason Christ came into the world. For that reason the Biblical record of creation and the fall lies at the very heart of the Gospel. For, "**Just as sin entered the world by one man, and death by sin... even so through the righteousness of one the free gift abounds to all men bringing justification and life**" (Romans 5:12,18). I am not saying that a person cannot be saved unless he believes that God created the world in six days, but I am saying that **rejection of what the Bible says about creation is inconsistent with faith in Christ, and destructive to faith**. And, if it does not destroy a person's faith, it is only because his thinking is inconsistent. That is why

Jesus said, "**Had you believed Moses, you would have believed me: for he wrote of me. But if you do not believe what he wrote, how will you believe my words?**" (John 5:46-47).

The words, "**If you continue in my word, you are truly my disciples,**" tell us that those who are truly Christ's disciples will not reject what His Word says, look outside of that Word for the truth about Creation, or interpret His Word in the light of ideas that come from outside of His Word (John 8:30). The words, "**My sheep hear my voice, and I know them, and they follow me,**" and the words, "**Those who know God accept what we say,**" tell us that Christ's sheep will accept what the Bible says (John 10:27, 1John 4:6). (See Luke 24:25.)

5. The Unity Of The Human Race

The words, "**The LORD God had not caused it to rain upon the earth, and there was no man to till the ground,**" describe the earth as it was just prior to God's creation of Adam (Genesis 2:5). And, those words tell us that there were **no people** on the earth before Adam and Eve. The words, "**Adam called his wife's name Eve; because she was the mother of all living,**" tell us that there were no people prior to God's creation of Eve, and that she is the mother of every human who has ever lived, or will live (Genesis 3:20). And, the words, "**God who made the world and everything in it... has made of one blood all nations of men to live on all the face of the earth,**" tell us that all the "nations of men" are descendents of Adam and Eve (Acts 17:24,26). In other words, there were no people before Adam and Eve, and there never were people that were not fully human (half animal, or half angel). [Regarding angels, compare Heb. 1:13-14, Luke 24:39, Matt. 22:30.]

The words, "**It is not good that the man should be alone,**" tell us that Adam was alone before God's created Eve (Genesis 2:18). The words, "**Adam was first formed, then Eve,**" tell us that Adam was the first human formed (1Timothy 2:13). And, the words, "**The LORD God caused a deep sleep to fall upon Adam, and he slept: and He took one of his ribs, and closed up its place with flesh; And of the rib, which the LORD God had taken from man, He made a woman, and brought her unto the man,**" tell us that God took living tissue from Adam, and that the life of Eve was derived from Adam, just as the life of a child is derived from its parents (Genesis 2:21-22).

6. Special Questions Regarding The Creation

While the Bible does not explicitly tell us when the angels were created, the words, "**In six days the LORD made heaven and earth, the sea, and <u>everything</u> that is in them**," the words, "**All things in heaven and earth, both visible and invisible, were created by Him**," and the words, "**Thus the heavens and the earth, and everything in them, were finished**," tell us that "everything" was made during the six days of creation, and that would include angels (Exodus 20:11, Colossians 1:16, Genesis 2:1).

Just as the life of a child is derived from its parents, so <u>the soul of a child is derived from its parents</u> through propagation. The words, "**On the seventh day God ended His work**," tell us that God is not creating more souls, just as He is not creating more animals (Genesis 2:2). Instead all that is born comes from what was originally created. Likewise, the words, "**Behold, I was shaped in iniquity; and in sin did my mother conceive me**," tell us that David's mother conceived **him**, not just a body that he later occupied (Psalm 51:5). Those who claim that God creates a new soul for each body, have God corrupting souls by placing them into sinful bodies, and into homes where they are taught idolatry. And, the false claim that an unborn child does not yet have a soul has been used to justify murder (abortion).

The words, "**Our God is in the heavens: He has done whatever He has pleased**," tell us that God did not have to create the universe, and it is not some sort of emanation from Him as pantheists imagine, but He created all things for His glory just as His Word says (Psalm 115:3).

The words, "**God saw every thing that He had made, and, behold, it was very good**," tell us that none of the evil we now see in the earth, death, suffering, calamity, hardship is in the world because God created it that way (Genesis 1:31). In short, God created a perfect world. However, that does not mean that this world is the best of all possible worlds. The new heavens and new earth that God has promised will be far better. As it is written, "**Eye has not seen, nor ear heard, nor has it entered into the heart of man, the things that God has prepared for those who love Him**" (1Corinthians 2:9).

7. Creation An External Act of God

In theology a distinction is made between the **internal** and **external** acts of God. For example, when God forgives our sins, that forgiveness takes place in God's heart, so it is an internal act. In contrast, when God made water come out of a rock (after Moses hit it, Exodus 17:6) that was something God did that was external. In the same way, God's decision to make and sustain the universe was an internal commitment, while His actual work of creation was external.

Because the Father Son and Holy Ghost are one God, all three were equally involved in the work of creation. The words, "**Don't we all have one father? Hasn't one God created us?**" tell us that the Father is our Creator (Malachi 2:10). The words, "**All things in heaven and earth, both visible and invisible, were created by Him [Christ]**," tell us that the Son is our Creator (Colossians 1:16). And, the words, "**The Spirit of God has made me, and the breath of the Almighty has given me life**," tell us that the Holy Spirit is our Creator (Job 33:4). However, because the Bible plainly says, "**There is one God**" // "**No God was formed before me, and none will be after me**," we do not have three Creators, but only one, "**These three are one**" (Matthew 12:32, Isaiah 43:10, 1John 5:7).

"O the depth of the riches both of the wisdom and knowledge of God! How unsearchable are His judgments, and His ways past finding out! For who has known the mind of the Lord? Or who has been His counselor? Or who has first given to Him, that it might be paid back to Him again? For of Him, and through Him, and to Him, are all things: to whom be glory for ever. Amen" (Romans 11:33-36).

8. The Doctrine of the Age of the Earth

The delusion that grips our present age is so virulent that instead of answering the skeptics with a resounding "Thus saith the Lord," many turn on Scripture in a vain attempt to make its words agree with the ignorance of man. They act as if God did not know what He was doing when He caused the words of Genesis to be written, and try to make the Bible say what it clearly does not say, and never was intended to say. Nevertheless, God knew from the beginning what the skeptics would be saying. He knew they would claim that the earth is millions of years old. And because of His love for us, because He did not want us to be deceived, He designed the book of Genesis to exclude any possibility of "millions of years". Furthermore, He wants us to believe and teach exactly what His Word says, not what men think. As it is written, "**If they do not speak according to this word, it is because there is no light in them**" (Isaiah 8:20).

The words, "**In six days the LORD made heaven and earth, the sea, and everything that is in them, and rested on the seventh day: for that reason the LORD blessed the sabbath day, and made it holy**," tell us that **the seven days of Genesis were one week in length** (Exodus 20:11). However, God did not stop with just telling how long it took to make the heavens and earth. He included a detailed linage of each generation from Adam to Abraham. And, that linage gives us a record of the age of the earth that brings us right up to the era of recorded history.

Genesis Chapter 5:1-32

1 This is the book of the generations of Adam. In the day that God created man, he made him in the likeness of God;

2 Male and female He created them; and blessed them, and called their name Adam, on the day when they were created.

3 And **Adam lived an hundred and thirty years, and fathered *a son* in his own likeness, after his image; and called his name Seth**:

4 And the days of Adam after he had begotten Seth were eight hundred years: and he begat sons and daughters:

5 And all the days that Adam lived were nine hundred and thirty years: and he died.

6 And **Seth lived one hundred and five years, and begat Enos**:

7 And Seth lived after he fathered Enos eight hundred and seven years, and fathered sons and daughters:

8 And all the days of Seth were nine hundred and twelve years: and he died.

9 And **Enos lived ninety years, and begat Cainan**:

10 And Enos lived after he begat Cainan eight hundred and fifteen years, and begat sons and daughters:

11 And all the days of Enos were nine hundred and five years: and he died.

12 And **Cainan lived seventy years, and begat Mahalaleel**:

13 And Cainan lived after he begat Mahalaleel eight hundred and forty years, and begat sons and daughters:

14 And all the days of Cainan were nine hundred and ten years: and he died.

15 And **Mahalaleel lived and sixty-five years, and begat Jared**:

16 And Mahalaleel lived after he begat Jared eight hundred and thirty years, and begat sons and daughters:

17 And all the days of Mahalaleel were eight hundred and ninety-five years: and he died.

18 And **Jared lived an hundred and sixty-two years, and he begat Enoch**:

19 And Jared lived after he fathered Enoch eight hundred years, and begat sons and daughters:

20 And all the days of Jared were nine hundred and sixty-two years: and he died.

21 And **Enoch lived sixty and five years, and begat Methuselah**:

22 And Enoch walked with God after he begat Methuselah three hundred years, and begat sons and daughters:

23 And all the days of Enoch were three hundred sixty and five

years:

24 And Enoch walked with God: and he *was* not; for God took him.

25 And **Methuselah lived one hundred and eighty-seven years, and begat Lamech**:

26 And Methuselah lived after he begat Lamech seven hundred and eighty-two years, and begat sons and daughters:

27 And all the days of Methuselah were nine hundred and sixty-nine years: and he died.

28 And **Lamech lived one hundred eighty and two years, and begat a son**:

29 **And he called his name Noah**, saying, This *one* will bring us relief from our work and *from the* toil of our hands, because of the ground which the LORD has cursed.

30 And after he begat Noah Lamech lived five hundred and ninety-five years, and begat sons and daughters:

31 And all the days of Lamech were seven hundred and seventy-seven years: and he died.

32 And **Noah was five hundred years old: and Noah fathered Shem, Ham, and Japheth**.

[Comment: You will notice that this linage is carefully worded to preclude any claim that some generations may have been omitted. The key factor in determining the amount of time which transpired is the number of years that passed between the birth of each patriarch and the birth of his son. Therefore, we have an exact record of the time, and when we add up the years, these verses tell us that **Noah was born one thousand and fifty six years after the creation of Adam, and his sons were born five hundred years after that**.]

Genesis Chapter 11:10-26

10 These *are* the generations of Shem: **Shem *was* one hundred years old, and begat Arphaxad** two years after the flood:

11 And Shem lived after he begat Arphaxad five hundred years, and begat sons and daughters.

12 And **Arphaxad lived thirty-five years, and begat Salah**:

13 And Arphaxad lived after he begat Salah four hundred and three years, and begat sons and daughters.

14 And **Salah lived thirty years, and begat Eber**:

15 And Salah lived after he begat Eber four hundred and three years, and begat sons and daughters.

16 And **Eber lived four and thirty years, and begat Peleg**:

17 And Eber lived after he begat Peleg four hundred and thirty years, and begat sons and daughters.

18 And **Peleg lived thirty years, and begat Reu**:

19 And Peleg lived after he begat Reu two hundred and nine years, and begat sons and daughters.

20 And **Reu lived thirty-two years, and begat Serug**:
21 And Reu lived after he begat Serug two hundred and seven years, and begat sons and daughters.
22 And **Serug lived thirty years, and begat Nahor**:
23 And Serug lived after he begat Nahor two hundred years, and begat sons and daughters.
24 And **Nahor lived twenty-nine years, and begat Terah**:
25 And Nahor lived after he begat Terah an hundred and nineteen years, and begat sons and daughters.
26 And **Terah lived seventy years, and begat Abram**, Nahor, and Haran.

[Comment: A comparison of Genesis 5:32, 7:6 and 11:10 tell us that Noah was five-hundred and two years old when Shem was born. This chapter tells us that there were three hundred and twenty years between the birth of Shem and the birth of Terah, the father of Abram (Abraham, Gen. 17:5). So **Terah was born one thousand, eight-hundred, and seventy-eight years after the world was created**.]

Genesis Chapter 11:32 and 12:1-4
32 And **the days of Terah were two hundred and five years: and Terah died** in Haran.
1 Now the LORD had said unto Abram, Depart from your country, and from your kindred, and from your father's house, to a land that I will show you:
2 And I will make of you a great nation, and I will bless you, and make your name great; and you will be a blessing:
3 And I will bless those who bless you, and curse him who curses you: and in you all the families of the earth will be blessed.
4 So Abram departed, as the LORD had told him; and Lot went with him: and **Abram was seventy-five years old when he departed from Haran**.

[Comment: Since Terah was two hundred and five years old when he died, and Abram (Abraham) was seventy five years old at that time, we know that Terah was about one hundred and thirty years old when Abram was born. Therefore, **Abraham was born approximately two thousand and eight years after the world was created**.]

Genesis 21:5 And **Abraham was one hundred years old, when his son Isaac was born** unto him.
Genesis 25:26 And after that his brother came out, and his hand took hold on Esau's heel; and his name was called Jacob: and **Isaac was sixty years old when she bore them**.

[Comment: These verses tell us that Isaac was born when Abraham was one hundred years old, and Jacob (Israel) was born when Isaac was sixty years old. **Thus Jacob was born approximately two thousand one hundred and sixty-eight years after the world was created**.]

> Genesis 47:28 And **Jacob lived in the land of Egypt seventeen years: so the whole age of Jacob was one hundred and forty-seven years**.

[Comment: **Thus Jacob died in Egypt approximately two thousand three hundred and fifteen years after the world was created. And, if he entered Egypt seventeen years earlier, he entered Egypt about two thousand two hundred and ninety-eight years after the world was created**.]

The words, "**Now the time the children of Israel dwelt in Egypt, was four hundred and thirty years. And it came to pass at the end of the four hundred and thirty years, on that very day, all the LORD'S people marched out of the land of Egypt**," tell us that the Children of Israel left Egypt about **two thousand seven hundred and twenty-eight years after the world was created** (Exodus 12:40-41).

The words, "**In the four hundred and eightieth year after the children of Israel came out of the land of Egypt**, in the fourth year of Solomon's reign over Israel, in the month Zif, which is the second month, **Solomon began to build the house of the LORD**," tell us that Solomon began to build the temple 480 years after the children of Israel left Egypt (1Kings 6:1). Now some other dates given in Scripture may indicate that this 480 years does not include the forty years wandering in the wilderness, or the years under Joshua. However, if we just add the 480 years to what we have, that would mean that **Solomon began to build the temple three thousand two hundred and eight years after the world was created**.

The words, "And the temple was finished throughout in all its parts according to all its specifications in the eleventh year [of Solomon's reign], in the month Bul, which is the eighth month. So he **[Solomon] was seven years in building it**," (1Kings 6:38). **That brings us up to 3215 years after the world was created**.

Now as to recorded history, **the dedication of Solomon's Temple is generally dated at or around 970 BC**. Jewish sources tell us that Temple stood for 410 years. The date given for the siege and fall of Jerusalem is 588-586 BC. The captivity of most of Judah began twenty years prior to that. And, **the date given for the return of the Jews to Israel is 536 BC**. Those dates leave some questions. However, **Adding the 3215 years to the date when Solomon's temple was dedicated would mean that the world**

was created in the year four thousand one hundred and eighty-five BC.

Some Other Dates

As I mentioned, because of some other dates given in Scripture, and those contained in some ancient translations, we cannot be absolutely certain of the exact age of the earth. However, **there is no room in Scripture for millions of years**. The Septuagint translation adds one hundred years to the ages of some of the Patriarchs, but that would not make the world much older. Here are a few other dates.

Genesis 15:13 And the Lord said to Abram, Know with certainty that for **four hundred years** your descendants will be strangers in a land that is not theirs, and will serve them; and they will afflict them.

Acts 7:6 And God told him this, That his descendants would be strangers in a foreign land; and that they would enslave them, and mistreat them for **four hundred years**.

Acts 13:19-21 After He had destroyed seven nations in the land of Canaan, He divided their land to them by lot. And after that He gave them judges for about **four hundred and fifty years**, until Samuel the prophet. And afterward they asked for a king: and God gave them Saul the son of Kish, a man of the tribe of Benjamin, for **forty years**.

2Samuel 5:4 David was thirty years old when he began to reign, and he reigned **forty years**.

Galatians 3:17 The covenant *concerning faith in Christ*, that was confirmed by God at the time of Abraham, cannot be nullified by the law, which came **four hundred and thirty years** later, so as to make the promise of no effect.

In his massive work, "THE ANNALS OF THE WORLD" James Ussher correlates the Biblical timeline with recorded history, and in so doing has calculated the year of Jacob's death at 1689 BC and the date of creation as 4004 BC. That differs a little from the date given above, which calculates the year of Jacob's death at 1863 BC, which is at least 174 years earlier. And, if the 480 years mentioned in the words, "In the four hundred and eightieth year after the children of Israel came out of the land of Egypt," began at the time Israel finished coming out of Egypt, instead of the date they left, the date of Jacob's death could have been forty to eighty years earlier than that. See Joshua 24:29.

"The question is not: Is this or that doctrine clearly stated in the Confessions? But: Is this or that doctrine set forth in God's Word? If it is set forth in Holy Writ, it is for this reason a church dogma, even though not a word is said about it in the Confessions of the church. The reason for this is not difficult to perceive. The Christian Church is not the lord of God's doctrine, but only its servant. Its paramount purpose is not to create new doctrines but to preach the doctrines which its Lord has revealed. The dogmatician who draws his teachings from any other source than Holy Scriptures perpetrates an inexcusable fraud upon the Church... Christian ministers, teachers, and missionaries must proclaim to their hearers God's Word, not their own, so that... not one doctrine is taught that is not in agreement with Holy Scripture." (Christian Dogmatics, by John Theodore Mueller, pages 62, 63.)

Christians should not be troubled by claims that the earth is millions of years old. Careful measurements of earth's magnetic field reveal that it is growing weaker. Since there is a limit to how strong a magnetic field can be, if the earth was millions of years old its magnetic field would have disappeared ages ago. The earth's rotation speed is also slowing down, and the moon is moving away from the earth. This cannot have been going on for more that a few thousand years. And, the presence of vertical tree trunks in the sedimentary layers of the earth's crust show that those layers were formed rapidly. More could be said, but **no matter how ardently the opinions of men disagree with what the Bible says, the facts never do**.

9. The Ultimate End Of Creation

The words, "**The heavens declare the glory of God; and the sky displays his handiwork,**" and the words, "**Who has known the mind of the Lord?... For of Him, and through Him, and to Him, are all things: to whom be glory for ever,**" tell us that the ultimate end of all creation is the glory of God (Psalm 19:1). However, the glory that belongs to God is not the egotistic glory sought by sinful men, but the glory deserved by the one who created all things "very good," and has provided salvation for those who were by nature "hostile to God" (Gen. 1:31, Rom. 8:7)

The words, "**The LORD has made all things for Himself**" // "**Our God is in the heavens: He has done whatever He has pleased,**" tell us that God created all things for Himself (Psalm 16:4 and 115:3). The words, "**The heaven of heavens, belongs to the LORD: but He has given the earth to the children of men,**" tell us that even though God created man for Himself, the world is for man's benefit (Psalm 115:6). And, the words, "**Not to us, O LORD, not to us, but to your name give glory, because of your mercy and truth,**" tell us that God is to be glorified not only because He made us, but also because of His mercy in Christ Jesus (Psalm 115:1).

"**Praise the LORD. Sing to the LORD a new song, and His praise in the congregation of saints. Let Israel rejoice in Him who made him: let the children of Zion be joyful in their King. Let them praise His name with dancing: let them sing praises to Him with the tambourine and harp. For the LORD takes pleasure in His people: He glorifies the humble with salvation. Let the saints rejoice in this glory: let them sing aloud on their beds. Let the high praises of God be in their mouth**" (Psalm 149:1-6)

The Doctrine Of Divine Providence

1. The Guiding Hand Of Divine Providence

God not only created the world, He is actively involved in it, like a hand in a glove guiding, sustaining and directing the course of events. If sin had never entered the world, all things would work together perfectly. However, because of sin God withdrew some of His sustaining power. And, even that was an act of His love, aimed at making us aware of our sin, and need of His mercy.

The words, "**Cursed is the ground for your sake,**" tell us that the struggle for survival that we now endure is for our "sake" or benefit (Genesis 3:17). And, the words, "**In the sweat of your face you will eat bread, till you return unto the ground; for out of it you were taken: for you are dust, and to dust you will return,**" tell us that the struggle for survival should be a constant reminder of our mortality, and need for God's mercy (Genesis 3:19).

The words, "**You [God] sustained them [Israel] for forty years in the wilderness, so that they lacked nothing; their clothes did not grow old, and their feet did not swell,**" give us an idea of how much better the world would be if man had never sinned (Nehemiah 9:21). While the words, "**Your Father who is in heaven... causes His sun to rise on the evil and on the good, and sends rain on the righteous and on the unrighteous,**" tell us that God has not withdrawn entirely, but is still at work in the world, providing food and water for all, even those who hate Him (Matthew 5:45). And, the words, "**He did not leave himself without witness, in that He has shown kindness, and given us rain from heaven, and fruitful seasons, satisfying our hearts with food and gladness,**" should remind us that no matter how hard we work to provide food, if God did not create the plants and give rain there would be no food (Acts 14:17).

The words, **God "Has made of one blood all nations of men to** live on all the face of the earth, and has determined their appointed times, and the boundaries they live in; So that they should seek the Lord, in the hope that they might grope for Him, and find Him, although He is not far from any one of us: For in Him we live, and move, and have our being," tell us that God, by His providence, has determined the boundaries of the nations, in the hope that they might seek Him and find Him (Acts 17:26-28). The words, "**You make springs send water into the valleys that run among the hills. They provide drink for every beast of the field: the wild donkeys quench their thirst. Beside the waters nest the birds the air, who sing among the branches. You water the hills from your palace: the earth is satisfied with the fruit of what you do. You cause the grass to grow for the cattle, and plants for man to cultivate: so that he may get food from the ground; And wine to make the heart of man cheerful, and oil to make his face shine, and bread which strengthens him**," tell us that many of the things that we take for granted, and assume just happen, only continue because God is at work (Psalm 104:10-15). And the words, "**The king's heart is in the hand of the LORD, like the rivers of water: He turns it whichever way He wants**," should remind us that God is in control (Proverbs 21:1).

2. The Objects Of Divine Providence

The words, "**All things in heaven and earth, both visible and invisible, were created by Him** [Christ]... **and by Him all things have their [continuous] existence**," tell us that God's providence is not limited to His care for mankind, but includes all that God has created, down to the smallest detail. (Colossians 1:16-17).

In reference to the verse just quoted, R. C. H. Lenski — whose commentary on the New Testament is widely regarded as the best in dealing with the Greek — has this to say:

> Two additional statements complete the immense thought so far expressed: "and he [Christ] is before all things whatever (no article), and all the things that exist (again the article) have their permanence in connection with him," in connection with whom they were created in the first place. Creation and preservation naturally go together. The latter is highly pertinent here. No created being in the universe is independent of Christ. All are "through him and for him so that he is before them," and **all of them have their continuous existence only "in connection with him**. ("The Interpretation of St. Paul's Epistles to the Colossians, to the Thessalonians, to Timothy, to Titus and to Philemon" page 58.)

The words, "**Consider the lilies of the field, how they grow; they do not labor, or spin: Yet I am telling you, That even Solomon in all his splendor was not dressed like one of these... if that is how God clothes the grass of the field, that is here today, and is thrown into the fire tomorrow, will He not much more clothe you, O you of little faith?**" tell us that God cares for the plants (Matthew 6:28-30).

The words, "**Look at the birds of the air: for they do not sow, or reap, or gather into barns; yet your heavenly Father feeds them. Are you not much more valuable than they?**" tell us that God cares for the animals (Matthew 6:26).

The words, "**God... has made of one blood all nations of men to live on all the face of the earth, and has determined their appointed times, and the boundaries they live in; So that they should seek the Lord, in the hope that they might grope for Him, and find Him, although He is not far from any one of us,**" tell us that He cares for all men (Acts 17:24,26,27).

The words, "**Blessed is the nation whose God is the LORD; and the people whom He has chosen for His own inheritance. The LORD looks from heaven; He beholds all the sons of men. From His dwelling place He looks upon all the inhabitants of the earth. He sees the hearts of them all; He is aware of all they do,**" tell us that God cares about His people, and watches over them (Psalm 33:12-15). And, the words, "**The curse of the LORD is on the house of the wicked: but He blesses the home of the just,**" tell us that God's people are those who are justified by faith, for that is the only way to be just in the sight of God (Proverbs 3:33).

The words, "**O LORD, I know that a man does not control his own way: and no one who walks directs his own steps,**" // "**A man's steps are ordered by the LORD; so how can a man understand his own way?**" tell us that God is in control of our life whether we realize it or not (Jeremiah 10:23, Proverbs 20:24). The words, "**In all your ways acknowledge Him, and He will direct your paths.**" // "**All things work together for good for those who love God, for those who are the called according to His purpose,**" tell us that God's hand of providence is at work guiding and watching over His people (Proverbs 3:6, Romans 8:28). And, the words, "**To which of the angels has He ever said, Sit on my right hand, until I make your enemies your footstool? Are they not all spirits who serve Him, and are sent forth to help those who will be heirs of salvation?**" tell us that God cares for us and sends His angels to help us (Hebrews 1:13-14).

The words, "**That is the foundation upon which I will build my church; and the gates of hell will not prevail against it,**" tell us that nothing Satan devises to thwart the work of the gospel will prevail (Matthew 16:18). And, the words, "**The very hairs of your** head are all numbered," // "Not a hair of your head will perish," and, "**Are not five sparrows sold for two pennies, yet not one of them is forgotten by God?**" tell us that God is interested, and pays attention to, the smallest details of our existence (Matthew 10:30, Luke 21:18, Luke 12:6).

3. Divine Providence And Secondary Causes

Just as God uses His angels, He uses secondary causes, or intermediaries to carry out His will. The words, "**Unless the LORD builds the house, those who build it labor in vain: unless the LORD guards the city, the watchman stays awake in vain,**" tell us that God uses watchmen and builders as part of His providential care, and all of their efforts would be in vain without that care (Psalm 127:1). In short, **all who have honest and godly employment are serving the Lord,** and God is working through them to care for us. The plumber serves God by installing and fixing our pipes, The farmer and baker serve God by providing us with food etc.

The words, "**The LORD raised up judges, who delivered them out of the hand of those who plundered them,**" tell us that God used judges to deliver His people (Judges 2:16). The words, "**Be careful what you do: for you judge not for man, but for the LORD, who is with you in the judgment,**" warn judges not to pervert justice, because they are working for God (2Chronicles 19:6). And, the words, "**He who listens to you listens to me; and he who rejects you rejects me; and he who rejects me rejects Him who sent me,**" tell us that those who heard the Apostles were hearing Christ because He spoke through them (Luke 10:16).

The words, "**Submit yourselves to every ordinance of man for the Lord's sake: whether it be to the king, as supreme; Or to governors, as those sent by Him for the punishment of evildoers, and for the praise of those who do right,**" tell us that God uses earthly rulers to punish criminals and suppress crime (1Peter 2:13-14). And, the words, "**Can the throne of iniquity have fellowship with you, when he uses the law to mask evil? They band together against the life of the righteous, and condemn the innocent to death. But the LORD is my defense; and my God is the rock of my refuge. And He will turn their own iniquity back on them, and will wipe them out by means of their own wickedness,**" assure us that even when human government turns evil, **masking evil by making it legal and condemning the innocent to death,** God is in control (Psalm 94:20-23). And, **when Christians work within the system, as did Joseph, Daniel and Esther the hand of God will be with them** to protect His people and carry out His will.

4. Divine Concurrence In Good And Evil Actions

The words, **"The wrath of God is revealed from heaven against all ungodliness and unrighteousness of men,"** tell us that God opposes and condemns all of the evil done by men (Romans 1:18). It is man, not God, who brought evil into the world, and all of the bad that happens is in the world because of sin (Rom. 5:12).

Because of sin, believers make foolish decisions that sometimes get them into a predicament. One such predicament is described in the words, **"Abraham said of Sarah his wife, She is my sister: and Abimelech king of Gerar sent, and took Sarah. But God came to Abimelech in a dream by night, and said to him, Behold, you are a dead man, because of the woman that you have taken; for she is a man's wife. But Abimelech had not come near her: and he said, Lord... in the integrity of my heart and innocence of my hands have I done this. And God said to him in a dream, Yes, I know that you did this in the integrity of your heart; and I also kept you from sinning against me: for that reason I did not allow you to touch her"** (Genesis 20:2-6). In this case, God stepped in to protect Sarah and prevent an evil act from occurring. And, we pray for such protection when we pray, **"lead us not into temptation, but deliver us from evil"** (Matthew 6:13).

However, even though God does not cause men to do evil, He sometimes controls it, using it to bring His will to pass by causing all things to **"Work together for good for those who love God"** (Romans 8:28). One example of that is seen in the way God controlled and guided the brothers of Joseph. The words, **"Judah said to his brothers, What do we gain if we kill our brother, and conceal his blood? Come, let us sell him to the Ishmaelites, and let our hand not harm him; for he is our brother and our flesh. And his brothers agreed,"** tell us that the brothers of Joseph had planned to kill him (Genesis 37:26). However, the words, **"You planned evil against me; but God meant it for good, to bring about that many people should be kept alive, as they are to this day,"** tell us that God prevented them from killing Joseph, yet used their anger to send Joseph to Egypt (Genesis 50:20). And, God's words to Jacob, **"Do not be afraid to go down into Egypt; for there I will make of you a great nation,"** tell us that God used the sojourn of the children of Israel in Egypt to weld them into a nation (Genesis 46:2-3). A nation through which He would provide a Savior.

If man had never sinned, everything that God created and pronounced "very good" would work together in harmony (Genesis 1:31). The words, **"God saw that the wickedness of man was great in the earth, and that every imagination of the thoughts of his heart was only evil continually,"** reflect the fact that the sin of Adam destroyed that harmony (Genesis 6:5). From God's point of view,

He gave Adam and Eve exactly what they wanted; the freedom to act contrary to His will. But, from our point of view, that freedom has brought untold suffering into the world.

The words, "**His [God's] work is perfect: for all His ways are just: a God of truth without iniquity, just and right is He**," // "**The LORD is just: my rock, in whom there is no unrighteousness**," tell us that even though God sometimes makes the evil that men do work to accomplish His will, He is not the cause of that evil (Deuteronomy 32:4, Psalm 92:15). And, in many cases God causes an evil act to bring about the opposite of what the evildoer intended. We see one example of that in the account of Joseph and his brothers. Those brothers sold Joseph into slavery in order to prevent him from ruling over them, but what they did led to his rise to power, and put him in a position to rule over them.

"There are two consequences in history; an immediate one, which is instantly recognized, and one in the distance, which is not at first perceived. These consequences often contradict each other; the former are the results of our own limited wisdom, the latter, those of that wisdom which endures. The providential event appears after the human event. God rises up behind men. Deny, if you will, the supreme counsel; disown its action; dispute about words; designate, by the term, force of circumstances, or reason, what the vulgar call Providence; but look to the end of an accomplished fact, and you will see that it has always produced the contrary of what was expected from it, if it was not established at first upon morality and justice." (From Chateaubriand's Posthumous Memoirs, quoted in "That Which Is Seen, And That Which Is Not Seen", By Frederic Bastiat".)

The words, "**You are not a God who has pleasure in wickedness: nor will evil dwell with you. The foolish will not stand in your sight: you hate all who do evil. You will destroy those who tell lies: the LORD will detest the bloody and deceitful man**," tell us that even though God does not always punish evildoers immediately, that punishment is coming (Psalm 5:4-6). The words, "**The Lord is not slack concerning His promise, as some men count slackness; but is patient with us, not wanting anyone to perish, but all to come to repentance**," tell us that God is not tolerant of sin, but is giving us time to repent. (2Peter 3:9). Therefore, the words, "**The living God... Who in the past allowed all nations to go their own way**," are not telling us that God permitted those nations to sin, or condoned their sin, but that He refrained from destroying them so that millions could later be brought to repentance (Acts 14:15-16). At the same time, the words, "**God also gave them up to uncleanness through the lusts of their own hearts, to dishonor** their own bodies between themselves: For they changed the truth of God into a lie, and worshipped and served the creation more than the Creator, who is blessed forever. Amen. For this cause God gave them up to vile affections: for even their women exchanged the natural use for that which is contrary to nature: And likewise also the men, leaving the natural use of the woman, burned in their lust one toward another; men with men doing what is shameful, and receiving in themselves that recompense of their error that was fitting. And even as they did not like to retain God in their knowledge, God gave them over to a reprobate mind, to do those things that are not right,"** tell us that even though God does not immediately destroy a nation that rejects Him, that rejection does have consequences (Romans 1:24-28). As long as a nation worships God He works to bring its people to repentance, but once they reject Him their own innate depravity is unrestrained. As it is written, **"They did not want any of my advice: they rejected all my correction. Therefore they will eat of the fruit of their own way, and be fed with their own schemes"** (Proverbs 1:30-31).

5. Divine Providence And Free Will

One question that theologians struggle with has to do with the fact that God is fully in control, yet He does not approve of sin, or cause men to sin. In dealing with that question **it is important to never contradict or go beyond what the Bible plainly says**. Our mind is like the mind of an ant in comparison to God. Therefore, instead of professing ourselves to be wise, we need to faithfully teach what the Bible says, while acknowledging our own ignorance and limitations. As it is written, **"What we now see is like a dim reflection on a glass... Now I know in part; but then I will know even as I am known"** (1Corinthians 13:12). [See Jer. 17:9, Rom. 1:22.]

The words, **"O LORD, I know that a man does not control his own way: and no one who walks directs his own steps,"** tell us that God is fully in control (Jeremiah 10:23). At the same time, the words, **"Do not let anyone say when he is tempted, I am tempted by God: for God cannot be tempted with evil, nor does He tempt anyone: But every man is tempted, when he is drawn away by his own lust, and enticed,"** tell us that God does not cause us to sin (James 1:13-14). When Adam and Eve sinned, they chose to ignore God's direction. And, the words, **"They did not want any of my advice: they rejected all my correction. Therefore they will eat of the fruit of their own way, and be fed with their own schemes,"** apply to what they did (Proverbs 1:30-31).

The words, **"A man has many plans in his mind; nevertheless the LORD'S plan will stand," tell us that nothing can stop what God has determined to bring to pass (Proverbs 19:21). The words, **"Whoever commits sin is the servant of sin,"** tell us that sin has placed the human race in bondage (John 8:34). The words, **"Don't you know, that when you yield yourselves to someone to obey him as servants, you are the servants of the one you obey"** tell us that by obeying Satan, Adam and Eve became slaves of Satan (Romans 6:16). And, the words, **"But thanks be to God, you who were the slaves of sin, have obeyed from the heart the form of doctrine that was delivered to you. And having been freed from sin, you became the servants of righteousness,"** tell us that God's plan has, from the beginning, been to free us from that bondage through faith in Christ (Romans 6:16-18).

The words, **"I am deeply distressed; but should I pray, Father, save me from this hour? No, for this hour is the reason I came,"** tell us that it was God's plan from the beginning for Christ to die (John 12:27). And, the words, **"This is a faithful saying, and worthy of all acceptation, that Christ Jesus came into the world to save sinners; of whom I am chief,"** tell us that Christ came into the world to die for our sins (1Timothy 1:15). However, the words, **"You are of your father the devil, and you will do what your father desires. He was a murderer from the beginning, and did not abide in the truth, because there is no truth in him,"** tell us the Pharisees murdered Christ because they were under the control of Satan, not because God caused them to (John 8:44). Furthermore, Satan was not trying to do the will of God, but trying to thwart it. Satan thought that by killing Christ he could defeat Him. But, God caused the evil that Satan planned to bring about the opposite result; the result that God wanted.

The fact that God is in control should be a great comfort to those who trust in Christ. Having been freed from Satan's Control, we still need to struggle against the flesh. As it is written, **"I buffet my body, and bring it under my control: lest there be any way that I, after having preached to others, might be rejected"** (1Corinthians 9:27). And, the words, **"The flesh lusts against the Spirit, and the Spirit against the flesh: and they are opposed to each other: so that you cannot do the things that you would,"** then tell us that when we trust in Christ the Spirit of God is at work within us, helping us to resist the flesh (Galatians 5:17). Moreover, when we pray **"Lead us not into temptation, but deliver us from evil,"** we are praying **"Order my steps in your word: and do not allow any sin to have dominion over me"** (Matthew 6:13, Psalm 119:133). Therefore, God's assurance that, **"The steps of a good man are ordered by the LORD: and He delights in his way,"** should be a great comfort to us (Psalm 37:23). **"A man's heart devises his way: but the LORD directs his steps"** (Proverbs 16:9).

Some Questions Regarding Divine Providence

The words, "**Knowing the judgment of God, that those who commit such things are worthy of death**," tell us that **God hates sin** (Romans 1:32). And, the words, "**God cannot be tempted with evil, nor does He tempt anyone**," tell us that God does not lead anyone to sin (James 1:13). Yet the words, "**Herod and Pontius Pilate truly joined together, with the Gentiles, and the people of Israel, in opposition to your holy child Jesus, whom you anointed, To do everything your hand and counsel long ago decided should be done**," tell us that Pilate and the Pharisees were doing what God wanted done when they crucified Christ (Acts 4:27-28). How do we explain that?

In answering such questions we must always be willing to admit our own ignorance, and never profess ourselves to be wise. Knowing that "**the heart is deceitful above all things, and desperately wicked**," it would be foolish for us to pass off made up explanations as Bible doctrine (Jeremiah 17:9). Furthermore, any explanation that we tentatively advance must agree with everything the Bible says. As it is written, "**If they do not speak according to this word, it is because there is no light in them.**" (Isaiah 8:20).

That being said, one possible answer to the question of how God controlled things to the extent that Pilate and the Pharisees crucified Christ without God causing them to, may lie in the fact that God choose the time and place where Christ would be put on trial. For example, if that trial had taken place a century earlier, while Rome was still a republic, the cry "**If you let this man go, you are not Caesar's friend**," would not have intimidated Pilate (John 19:12). And, far from God causing Pilate to sentence Christ to death, the text itself tells us that Pilate was warned by God, and convinced of Christ's innocence. The words, "**While he [Pilate] was sitting on the judgment seat, his wife sent to him, saying, Have nothing to do with that just man: for I suffered much today in a dream because of Him**," tell us that Pilate was warned (Matthew 27:19). And, the words, "**From that time forth Pilate sought to release Him**," and "**I am innocent of the blood of this just person: see to it yourselves**," tell us that Pilate was convinced of Christ's innocence (John 19:12, Matthew 27:24). So Pilate did what he did out of self-interest, not because God made him do it.

Another question has to do with the fact that God long ago determined the length of our life, yet the Bible sometimes speaks of Him adding or subtracting years on the basis of what we do. For example: the words, "**Seeing his [a man's] days are determined, the number of his months are with you, you have set limits that he cannot pass;**" tell us that the length of our life is determined by God (Job 14:5). Yet the words, "**Honor your father and your mother: that your days may be long upon the land which the**

LORD your God gives you," // "My son, do not forget my law; but keep my commandments in your heart: For they will give you a long good life, and peace," and "Listen, O my son, accept what I say; and the years of your life will be many," promise long life to those who do God's will (Exodus 20:12, Proverbs 3:1-2 and 4:10). Now, reconciling the passages that I have just quoted is not a big problem because God knew from the beginning who would do His will and who would not. However, how do we square this with the fact that the godly often die young?

Here again, the Bible does not give us a direct explanation, so we need to humbly admit our ignorance without professing ourselves to be wise. In dealing with such questions we need to keep in mind God's plan for world evangelism, and the fact that the death of a believer is not the end, but the beginning of life with Christ. For example: I know of two young Christian girls who died in a car accident. Some saw that as a tragedy, but the words, **"The righteous dies, and no one cares: kind men are swept away, and no one realizes that the righteous is taken away from the evil to come. He will enter into peace,"** tell us that God may have spared those girls much pain and hardship (Isaiah 57:1-2).

The words, **"Er, Judah's firstborn, was wicked in the sight of the LORD; and the LORD slew him... And the thing that he [Onan] did displeased the LORD: therefore He slew him also,"** tell us that God sometimes shortens the life of those who do evil (Genesis 38:7-10). However, in understanding this we need to remember that whenever God shortens a life, that changes the world's timeline, and that could make a big difference over the centuries. At the same time, the words, **"A good man leaves an inheritance to his children's children: but the wealth of the sinner is stored up for the righteous,"** tell us that when God allows an evil person to prosper He has a purpose that we may not be able to understand (Proverbs 13:22).

The words, **"We believed that we had been sentenced to death, but that kept us from trusting in ourselves, rather than in God who raises the dead: He rescued us from so deadly a peril, and He will deliver us: He in whom we trust will continue to deliver us; As you also help us by praying for us,"** tell us that the hardship Paul endured strengthened his faith, that he was helped by the prayers of the church, and that God delivered him from death (2Corinthians 1:9-11). And, the words, **"I am torn between the two, I desire to depart, and to be with Christ; which is far better: Yet it is more important for you that I remain in the body,"** suggest that God saved Paul from death for the good of the church — not just then, but to this very day (Philippians 1:23-24).

The words, **"Whoever sheds man's blood, by man shall his blood be shed: for God made man in His own image,"** and "He who strikes another, so that he dies, shall be surely put to death," tell us that God sometimes works through government to shorten the lives of the wicked (Genesis 9:6, Exodus 21:12). While the words, **"The LORD preserved David wherever he went,"** tell us that God lengthened David's life by protecting him from danger, or possibly assassins (2Samuel 18:14).

The words, **"In those days Hezekiah became sick and was dying. And the prophet Isaiah the son of Amoz came to him, and said to him, The LORD says, Set your house in order; for you will not recover, but will die. Then he turned his face to the wall, and prayed to the LORD, saying, I beseech you, O LORD, remember now how I have walked before you in truth and with a perfect heart, and have done what is right in your sight. And Hezekiah wept bitterly. And before Isaiah had left the inner courtyard, the word of the LORD came to him, saying, Go back, and tell Hezekiah the leader of my people, The LORD, the God of David your father says, I have heard your prayer, I have seen your tears: behold, I will heal you: on the third day you will go up to the house of the LORD. And I will add to your days fifteen years,"** tell us that God lengthened the life of Hezekiah in answer to prayer (2Kings 20:1-6). But, God knew from eternity that Hezekiah would pray that prayer. In fact, God may have sent Isaiah to Hezekiah in order to get him to pray that prayer, and if so it was recorded for our benefit. So we have to keep God's eternal purpose in mind.

While keeping our focus on God's eternal plan, and the work of the gospel, we should never forget the fact that the day is coming when God will call all men to account for their sins. And, on that day only those whose sins have been washed away by the shed blood of Jesus Christ will escape God's eternal wrath. As it is written **"There is therefore now no condemnation for those who are in Christ Jesus,"** for **"The blood of Jesus Christ His Son cleanses us of all sin"** (Romans 8:7, 1John 1:7).

In contrast, God's warning to the unrepentant is that, **"Neither their silver or their gold will be able to deliver them on the day of the LORD'S wrath; but the whole world will be consumed by the fire of His jealousy: for He will make a quick end of all those who live on the earth."** // **"The earth will tremble at His wrath, and the nations will not be able to endure His indignation"** (Zephaniah 1:18, Jeremiah 10:10). And, the words, **"So man lies down, and does not arise: until the heavens are no more,"** tell us that the final judgment will take place after God has destroyed this universe (Job 14:12).

All Glory to God Alone

THE DOCTRINE OF THE ANGELS
(De Angelis)

1. The Existence Of Angels

The Bible tells us that angels are, **"Spirits who serve"** God (Hebrews 1:14). And, the words, **"A spirit does not have flesh and bones,"** tell us that they do not have physical bodies (Luke 24:39). While the Bible speaks of angels appearing at various times, conveying messages, and doing the will of God; in learning about them, **Scripture must be our sole source of knowledge.** The words, **"Satan himself masquerades as an angel of light,"** warn us of the danger in seeking spiritual truth apart from God's Word (2Corinthians 11:14). And, the words, **"If we, or an angel from heaven, preach any gospel to you other than what we have preached to you, let him be accursed,"** tell us that any angel (or spirit) that contradicts the gospel is under God's curse, and is not to be believed (Galatians 1:8).

The words, **"All things in heaven and earth, both visible and invisible, were created by Him,"** and **"Apart from Him nothing was created that was created,"** tell us that the angels are created beings (Colossians 1:16, John 1:3). And, even though the Bible does not tell us which day the angels were created on, the words, **"In six days the LORD made heaven and earth, the sea, and everything that is in them,"** // **"Thus the heavens and the earth, and everything in them, were finished,"** tell us that the angels were created during the six days (Exodus 20:11, Genesis 2:1).

The words, **"You, are LORD alone; you have made heaven, the heaven of heavens, with all their host,"** speak of angels as the "host" of heaven (Nehemiah 9:6). The words, **"I saw the LORD sitting on His throne, and the entire host of heaven standing by Him on His right hand and on His left,"** tell us that the angels [host of heaven] have access to God (1Kings 22:19). And, the words, **"Jacob went on his way, and the angels of God met him. And when Jacob saw them, he said, This is God's host,"** tell us that Jacob recognized the angels as the host of heaven (Genesis 32:1-2).

The words, "I saw the Lord sitting upon a high and lofty throne, and His train filled the temple. <u>Above it stood the seraphim</u>: each one had six wings; two to cover his face, two to cover his feet, and two to fly with," give the name "seraphim" to a specific kind of angel (Isaiah 6:1-2). Here the words, "I saw the

Lord," coupled with the words, "**No man has seen God at any time,**" tell us that Isaiah did not physically see God, but "**saw the Lord**" in a dream or vision (compare Isaiah 6:1 with John 1:18). And, the fact that angels are spirits that do "**not have flesh and bones,**" tell us that Isaiah's description of them is a description of what he saw in his dream or vision, not what they physically look like (Luke 24:39).

The words, "So He drove out the man; and He placed <u>Cherubim</u> at the east of the garden of Eden, and a flaming sword which turned every way, to guard the way to the tree of life," give the name "Cherubim" to another kind of angel (Genesis 3:24). And, when God told Moses to make the Ark of the Covenant, He said, "**You shall make two golden cherubim, you shall make them of hammered work, on the two ends of the mercy seat. One angel on the one end, and the other angel on the other end: making the cherubim of one piece with the mercy seat on the two ends of it. And, the cherubim shall spread out their wings above, covering the mercy seat with their wings, and their faces shall be facing each other; and looking down toward the mercy seat**" (Exodus 25:18-20). Here again, the angels are described as having wings. However, the words, "**A spirit does not have flesh and bones,**" tell us that this is a figurative way of portraying the cherubim, not a description of physical appearance.

In contrast, when "<u>**Two angels**</u> **came to Sodom... the men of the city, even the men of Sodom, surrounded the house... And they called to Lot, and asked him, Where are the men who came in to you this night?**" (Genesis 19:1-5). Those words tell us that the angels who appeared to Lot looked like men. Verse 12 even refers to them as men, saying, "**The men said to Lot**". And, none of those verses mention any wings. This leaves us with questions, such as, How were these angels (who are spirit beings) able to appear as men, and even eat food? (See Genesis 18:1-3.) However, since the Bible does not answer such questions, we should never add to God's Word by making up answers (Proverbs 30:6). What we can say for certain is that because angels are, "**spirits**" that do "**not have flesh and bones,**" the bodies that the angels appeared to have when they visited lot, were not a normal part of their nature, but virtual bodies that they assumed for the visit (Hebrews 1:14, Luke 24:39).

The words, "**The Son of man shall come in the glory of His Father with His angels**" // "**The Son of man shall send forth His angels, and they shall gather out of His kingdom all things that offend,**" and "**The angels shall come forth, and sever the wicked from among the just,**" tell us that God's angels will play an active part in the final judgment (Matthew 16:27, 13:41, and 13:49).

2. The Name "Angel"

While the words, "**Are they [angels] not all spirits who serve Him**," speak of angels as a certain class of beings, the term "angel" (in both Hebrew and Greek) simply means messenger (Hebrews 1:14). And, because the word "angel means messenger it is not limited to angelic beings. In the passage, "**A priest's lips should dispense knowledge, and they should seek the law from his mouth: for he is the messenger of the LORD of hosts**," the same Hebrew word that is elsewhere translated "angel" is here translated "messenger" (Malachi 2:7). In the words, "**This is he, of whom it is written, Behold, I send my angel/messenger ahead of you, who will prepare your way before you**," John the Baptist is referred to as an angel/messenger (Matthew 11:10). In the words, "**The Lord, whom you seek, will suddenly come to His temple, even the messenger of the covenant, whom you desire: behold, He will come, says the LORD of hosts**," Christ is referred to as "the angel/messenger of the covenant" (Malachi 3:1). And, we know that Christ is not one of the created angels, because the words, "**I will raise to David a righteous Branch, who will reign as King and prosper, and will execute judgment and justice in the earth... and this is the name by which He will be called, <u>Jehovah</u> Our Righteousness**," tell us that Jesus [the branch that sprang out of David] is Jehovah [Jahweh] (Jeremiah 23:5-6).

Since angels are created beings, whenever an angel/messenger is referred to as God, or credited with divine works such as redemption, that angel must be Christ. The very fact that Christ is the "WORD" of God makes Him the ultimate messenger. As it is written, "**In the beginning was the Word, and the Word was with God, and the Word was God. The same was with God in the beginning. All things were created by Him; and apart from Him nothing was created that was created. In Him was life; and that life was the light of men... He was in the world, and the world was made by Him, yet the world did not know Him. He came unto His own, but His own did not receive Him. But to as many as received Him, He gave power to become the sons of God, even to those who believe on His name: Who are not born of blood, or of the will of the flesh, or of the will of man, but of God. And the Word was made flesh, and dwelt among us**" (John 1:1-14).

3. The Nature Of The Angels

Because angels are spirit beings, having a body is not part of their nature, although, in a few cases, they seem to have appeared as men. The words, "**Look at my hands and my feet, and see that it is really me: handle me, and see; for a spirit does not have flesh and bones, as you see me have,"** tell us that spirits do not have "flesh and bones" (Luke 24:39). We see that again in the words, **"We wrestle not against flesh and blood, but against principalities, against powers, against the rulers of the darkness of this world, against spiritual wickedness in high places"** (Ephesians 6:12). The first phrase in that sentence, the words, **"We wrestle not against flesh and blood,"** tell us that the forces we "wrestle" against are spiritual, not corporeal. And, because the Bible refers to Satan as **"Your adversary the devil,"** we know that the spiritual forces that oppose us are **"the angels who did not keep their first estate"** (1Peter 5:8, Jude 1:6).

Although the words, **"God is a Spirit: and those who worship Him must worship Him in spirit and in truth,"** tell us that God is a spirit, the difference between God and angels is incomprehensibly great (John 4:24). It is the difference between infinite and finite, the difference between knowing everything, and knowing only in part etc. And, we know that the angels are limited in knowledge because the words, **"Reporting the things, that have now been proclaimed to you by those who are preaching the gospel to you with the Holy Spirit sent from heaven; things which angels long to look into"** tell us that the angels want to learn about the grace God has given unto us (1Peter 1:12). The words, **"That the manifold wisdom of God might now be made known through the church to the principalities and powers in heavenly places,"** tell us that the heavenly angels learn through what is proclaimed in the church (Ephesians 3:10). And, because angels think, speak, will, and learn we regard them as "persons," not just forces.

Although men have a spirit, those spirits are incomplete in that they exist in union with a body. In contrast, angels are complete spirits in that they exist as spirits, without "flesh and bones" (Heb. 1:14, Luke 24:39).

The words, **"The devil took Him up onto a very high mountain, and showed Him all of the kingdoms of the world, and their splendor; And said to Him, I will give you all of this, if you will fall down and worship me. Then Jesus said to him, Go away, Satan: for it is written, You shall worship the Lord your God, and Him only shall you serve,"** tell us that even the fallen angels have a will and intelligence (Matthew 4:8-10). And, the words, **"Your adversary the devil, prowls around like a roaring lion, looking for someone to devour,"** tell us that the fallen angels want to destroy us (1Peter 5:8).

Although any knowledge that angels possess is far less than that of God, the words, **"My lord is wise, like the wisdom of an angel of God, knowing everything on earth,"** tell us that angels know far more that any man (2Samuel 14:20). The words, **"The angel said,**

I am Gabriel, who stands in the presence of God; and have been sent to speak to you, and to tell you this good news," tell us that angels are capable of becoming acquainted with each other and with men (Luke 1:19). And, the words, "**Be careful that you do not despise one of these little ones; for I am telling you, That in heaven their angels continually behold the face of my Father who is in heaven,**" tell us that the holy angels "continually" look upon the face of God (Matthew 18:10). However, the words, "**Satan himself masquerades as an angel of light. Therefore it is not surprising if his servants also disguise themselves as ministers of righteousness,**" warn us that Satan and his followers can outwardly appear to be righteous (2Corinthians 11:14). The words, "**The Spirit specifically says, that in the future some will depart from the faith, giving heed to seducing spirits, and doctrines of devils,**" warn us against being deceived by them (1Timothy 4:1). The words, "**The things that the Gentiles sacrifice are sacrificed to devils, and not to God,**" equate worshiping idols with worshiping devils (1Corinthians 10:20). And, the words, "**If we, or an angel from heaven, preach any gospel to you other than what we have preached to you, let him be accursed,**" warn us that those who preach any other gospel [or another testament of Jesus] are under God's curse, even if they outwardly look like righteous men (Galatians 1:8).

Because angels are spirits, they do not have body parts (such as arms, legs, lungs etc.), they are ordinarily invisible, and they are not subject to physical decay. The words, "**In the resurrection they neither marry, nor are given in marriage, but are as the angels of God in heaven,**" tell us that angels do not marry or produce young (Matthew 22:30). The word "**continually,**" in the phrase, "**Their angels <u>continually</u> behold the face of my Father who is in heaven,**" tells us that holy angels do not die [if they did it would not be <u>continual</u>] (Matthew 18:10). And, the word "**everlasting,**" in the sentence, "**The angels who did not keep their first estate... have been kept by Him in darkness bound with everlasting chains,**" tells us that evil angels will not cease to exist (Jude 1:6).

Because angels are spirits, they can be present without occupying physical space, just as God is present without taking up space. And, the words, "**My name is Legion: for we are many,**" tell us that because they do not take up space, a great number of them were able to indwell one man (Matthew 5:9).

The words, "**The angels who did not keep their first estate, but went outside their bounds,**" tell us that angels have a will, and were not created evil, but some choose to do evil (Jude 1:6). The words, "**The angel of the Lord appeared to them, and the glory of the Lord shone round about them: and they were terrified. And the angel said to them, Do not be afraid: for, I bring you good** tidings of great joy, that will be for all people... And suddenly there was with the angel a multitude of heavenly host praising God," tell us that angels can appear, move about, speak, and praise God (Luke 2:9-13). And, the words, **"The Lord Jesus shall be revealed from heaven with His mighty angels,"** and **"Praise the LORD, you His angels, who excel in strength,"** tell us that angels are mighty (2Thessalonians 1:7, Psalm 103:20).

The words, **"How you are fallen from heaven, O Lucifer, son of the morning! how you are cut down to the ground, O you who laid the nations low! For you said in your heart, I will ascend into heaven, I will exalt my throne above the stars of God: I will sit on the mountain of the congregation, on the sides of the north: I will ascend above the highest clouds; I will be like the most High. But you will be brought down to hell, to the sides of the pit,"** tell us that Satan or Lucifer fell from his first estate because of his desire to exalt himself (Isaiah 14:12-15). Those who do not think that this passage is talking about Satan need to realize that the sin described here is the prototype for every sin. Like this sin, every sin is an attempt by the sinner to make himself God by exalting his will over God's will. And, the words, **"You are of your father the devil, and you will do what your father desires. He was a murderer from the beginning, and did not abide in the truth, because there is no truth in him. When he speaks a lie, he speaks on his own: for he is a liar, and the father of it,"** and **"Why has Satan filled your heart to lie to the Holy Ghost?"** tell us that even though those who sin imagine that they are doing what they want, they are actually doing what Satan wants (John 8:44, Acts 5:3). As it is written, **"Whoever commits sin is the servant of sin"** (John 8:34)

The words, **"Blessed is the LORD God, the God of Israel, who alone does wondrous things,"** tell us that it is **God alone** who performs miracles (Psalm 72:18). Therefore, whenever the Bible speaks of prophets, apostles, or even angels performing miracles it is God who is doing the miracles through them.

The words, **"They could not drink the waters, for they were bitter... and the LORD showed him [Moses] a tree, which he threw into the waters, and the waters were made sweet,"** tell of God working a miracle through Moses (Exodus 15:23-25). The words, **"As one was felling a log, the axe head fell into the water... And he [Elisha] cut down a stick, and threw it in at that place; and the iron floated,"** tell of God working a miracle through Elisha (2Kings 6:5-6). The words, **"Then Peter said, I have no silver or gold; but what I do have I give you: In the name of Jesus Christ of Nazareth rise and walk... And he jumped up stood, and walked, and went into the temple with them, walking, and jumping, and praising God,"** tell of God working a miracle through Peter (Acts 3:6-8). The words, "**My God has sent His angel, and has shut the lions' mouths, so that they have not hurt me,**" tell of God sending an angel to work a miracle (Daniel 6:22). The words, "**The angel of the LORD reached out the end of the staff that was in his hand, and touched the flesh and the unleavened cakes; and fire rose up out of the rock, and consumed the flesh and the unleavened cakes. Then the angel of the LORD vanished from his sight,**" again tell of God using an angel to work a miracle (Judges 6:22). And, all who trust in Christ have God's assurance that, "**The angel of the LORD encamps around those who fear him, and delivers them**" (Psalm 34:7).

Even though Satan has some strength, just as we have strength, because it is "**the God of Israel, who alone does wondrous things,**" Satan cannot perform miracles (Psalm 72:18)." However, the words, "**Even him, whose coming is after the working of Satan with all power and signs and lying wonders,**" tell us that like the magicians who opposed Moses, Satan is able to deceive people with "lying wonders" (2Thessalonians 2:9).

The Folly of Reading Man's Word into Scripture

The words, "**Do not go beyond what is written,**" // "**We have not written anything to you, other than what you read**" // "**No truth of scripture comes from any private explanation,**" tell us that God wants us to believe and teach exactly what the words of Scripture say, not made up explanations (1Corinthians 4:6, 2Corinthians 1:13, 2Peter 1:20). Yet because the "**heart is deceitful above all things,**" men usually do the opposite (Jeremiah 17:9). And, one such fairy-tale doctrine is the bogus claim that angels have in the past mated with humans.

Those who make this claim have to assume that these angels had bodies [man's word]. However, God tells us that **angels do not have bodies** by saying "**Are they [angels] not all spirits who serve Him?**" // "**A spirit does not have flesh and bones,**" (Hebrews 1:14, Luke 24:39). Nevertheless, those who want to believe that angels have mated with humans usually try to counter those passages by pointing out that angels have sometimes appeared as men, and were even thought to be men, such as when they appeared to Lot (Genesis 19:1 and 5). What they fail to see is that **looking like men is a far cry from actually being human.** In order to support their fairy-tale doctrine they have to assume that these angels not only looked like men, but had functioning sex organs [man's word]. They also have to assume that those sex organs had sperm with human DNA [man's word]. They also have to assume that God created those bodies [man's word], because angels do not have the knowledge or ability to create human bodies. Then, having fabricated a doctrine by piling one assumption upon another, they have to explain away what the Bible plainly says. For example: The very fact that the sin of Adam brought death **"upon all men,"** tells us that all men are the descendants of Adam (Romans 5:12). The Bible plainly tells us that God **"has made of one blood all nations of men"** (Acts 17:26). And, the words, **"When the dead rise, they neither marry, nor are given in marriage; but are like the angels who are in heaven,"** tell us that angels do not marry (Mark 12:25).

The passage this controversy centers around says, **"It came to pass, when men began to multiply on the face of the earth, and daughters were born to them, That the sons of God saw that the daughters of men were fair; and they took them wives of all whom they chose... And God saw that the wickedness of man was great in the earth"** (Genesis 6:1-5). These verses should warn every son of God [saved person John 1:12] of the importance of not just choosing a wife on the basis of looks, but choosing a godly wife. And, the fact that those **"sons of God"** married [**"took them wives"**] when the Bible plainly tells us that angels **"neither marry, nor are given in marriage,"** tells us that those **"sons of God"** were men, not angels (Matthew 22:30).

Of the "great-ones" or "Nephilim" spoken of in Gen. 6:4, The Keil and Delitzsch Commentary, which is generally regarded as the best in regard to the Hebrew, says, "Luther gives the correct meaning, 'tyrants:' they were called *Nephilim* because they fell upon the people and oppressed them" (Page 137).

> "In whatever matter Holy Scripture has definitely spoken the Christian theologian must suppress his own views, opinions, and speculations and adhere unwaveringly to the divine truths revealed in Holy Scripture. In no case is he permitted to inject into the body of divine truth **his own figments and fabrications**." (Christian Dogmatics, by J.T. Muller, page 39.)

4. The Number And Ranks Of Angels

The Bible tells us that the number of angels is great. The words, **"You have come to mount Zion, and to the city of the living God, the heavenly Jerusalem, and to an innumerable company of angels,"** tell us that the angels cannot be numbered (Hebrews 12:22). The words, **"I kept looking until thrones were brought down, and the Ancient of days took His seat... A stream of fire came out from Him: and thousands upon thousands served Him, and ten thousand times ten thousand stood before Him: the judge was seated, and the books were opened,"** tell us that at the final judgment (when the books are opened) "thousands upon thousands" who serve God will be present (Daniel 7:9-10). The words,

"God's chariots are twice ten thousand, even thousands upon thousands: the Lord is among them, as He was in Sinai, in the holy place," seem to be speaking of angels as "God's chariots," and, again their number is described as "thousands upon thousands" (Psalm 68:17). And, the words, "**Suddenly there was with the angel a multitude of heavenly host,**" tell us that many of the angels were present in Bethlehem when Christ was born (Luke 2:13).

The Bible indicates that there are different kinds, or ranks of angels. The words, "**So He drove out the man; and He placed Cherubim at the east of the garden of Eden, and a flaming sword which turned every way, to guard the way to the tree of life,**" refer to some angels as "Cherubim," a name that is also applied to the metallic angels that were part of the ark of the covenant (Genesis 3:24, see Exodus 25:18-22). The words, "**I saw the Lord sitting upon a high and lofty throne, and His train filled the temple. Above it stood the seraphim: each one had six wings,**" refer to another group of angels as "seraphim" (Isaiah 6:2). The words, "**By Him were all things created, that are in heaven, and that are in earth, visible and invisible, whether they be thrones, or dominions, or principalities, or powers,**" seem to be describing some angels as "principalities, or powers" (Colossians 1:16). And, in the words, "**The Lord himself will descend from heaven with a shout, with the voice of the archangel, and with the trump of God: and the dead in Christ will rise first,**" the use of the term "archangel" indicates that some angels have greater authority than others (1Thessalonians 4:16).

The Bible also indicates that there are differences of rank among the fallen angels. The words, "**We wrestle not against flesh and blood, but against principalities, against powers**" tell us that the "principalities, or powers" mentioned in the previous paragraph are not something with flesh and blood. And, the fact that the words, "**We wrestle not against flesh and blood, but against principalities, against powers, against the rulers of the darkness of this world,**" describe the forces that oppose us, tells us that some of the angels described as "principalities, or powers" have come under Satan's control (Ephesians 6:12).

The words, "**Then He will say to those on His left, Depart from me, you cursed, into everlasting fire, prepared for the devil and his angels,**" tell us that Satan has angels under him (Matthew 25:41). The words, "**Every kingdom divided against itself is laid waste; and a house divided against itself will fall. If Satan is divided against himself, how can his kingdom stand?**" tell us that Satan does not allow any dissention in the ranks (Luke 11:17-18)

Finally, even though the Bible describes the number of angels as "innumerable," it does not tell us how many there are (Hebrews 12:22). And, even though the Bible mentions different kinds or ranks of angels, it does not reveal their order of authority. In fact, the words, "**thrones, or dominions, or principalities, or powers,**" list them in a different order than the words, "**principality, and power, and might, and dominion**" (Colossians 1:16, Ephesians 1:21). And, because the Bible does not specify how many angels exist, or what their ranks are, we should never profess ourselves to be wise, by going beyond what the Bible says. As it is written, "**Do not add to His words, lest He reprove you, and you are found to be a liar**" (Proverbs 30:6).

5. Good And Evil Angels

Although all angels were created good, there are now both good and evil angels. The words, "**By Him were all things created, that are in heaven, and that are in earth, visible and invisible,**" tell us that invisible creatures [angels] were created by God (Colossians 1:16). And, the words, "**God saw every thing that He had made, and, behold, it was very good**" tell us that all of the invisible creatures [angels] were good when they were created (Genesis 1:31). However, the words, "**The angels who did not keep their first estate, but went outside their bounds, have been kept by Him in darkness**" tell us that some of the angels sinned (Jude 1:6).

While the dream or vision that John describes in the book of Revelation is highly figurative, the words, "**The great dragon was cast out, that old serpent, called the Devil, and Satan,**" tell us that the red dragon in John's vision signified Satan (Revelation 12:9). And, if the dragon is Satan, then the fact that, "**his tail swept away a third of the stars of heaven**" can be understood as telling us that Satan led one third of the angels into sin (Revelation 12:3-4).

The words, "**Be careful that you do not despise one of these little ones; for I am telling you, That in heaven their angels continually behold the face of my Father who is in heaven,**" tell us that the angels who did not sin "continually behold the face" of God (Matthew 18:10). Now, the fact that they "**continually** behold the face" of God tells us that they are no longer in danger of falling. And, the words, "**When the Son of man comes in His glory, and all the holy angels with Him, then He will sit on the throne of His glory,**" tell us that **all** of those angels will be with Christ when He returns (Matthew 25:31).

The words, "**I charge you before God, and the Lord Jesus Christ, and the elect angels,**" speak of some of the angels as being chosen [elect] (1Timothy 5:21). Since Christ, "**did not take on the nature of angels**" or make atonement for them, the election of certain angels seems to lie in the fact that God choose to keep them from being deceived or overpowered by Satan (Hebrews 2:16). While the words, "**You believe that there is one God; you do well: even the**

demons believe, and tremble," tell us that the angels who sinned have no hope of salvation, but live in fear and dread (James 2:19).

While the Bible does not tell us when the angels sinned, we know that Satan sinned before he tempted Adam and Eve, because it is evil to want others to do evil. Moreover, because angels are spirits any place where they are incarcerated will be a spiritual place, not a physical place. That being understood, a comparison of 2Peter 2:4, **"God did not spare the angels that sinned, but cast them down to hell, and delivered them to be kept in chains of darkness, until judgment,"** with Matthew 8:29, **"They cried out, saying, What do we have to do with you, Jesus, Son of God? have you come here to torment us before the time?"** tell us that, even though the angels who sinned have been cast "down to hell," their active torment will be greater after the final judgment. Of that torment Revelation 20:10 says, **"The devil who deceived them was thrown into the lake of fire and sulfur, where the beast and the false prophet are, and they will be tormented day and night for ever and ever"**.

6. The Holy Service Of The Good Angels

The Bible not only tells us that the holy angels serve God, but that many of the tasks they carry out are done for the sake of the gospel, and benefit of God's people. And, the words, **"Are they [angels] not all spirits who serve Him, and are sent forth to help those who will be heirs of salvation?"** tell us exactly that (Hebrews 1:14). But what do they do? The words, **"Praise the LORD, you His angels, who excel in strength, who listen when He speaks, and do what He says,"** not only tell us that the angels excel in strength, but that they listen to God and do His will (Psalm 103:20-21). The words, **"I saw another angel flying in the midst of heaven, having the everlasting gospel to preach to those who dwell on the earth, and to every nation, and kindred, and language, and people,"** describe an angel that helped spread the gospel (Revelation 14:6). And, when the Reformation began, Martin Luther observed that the gospel spread so fast it seemed like the angels were spreading the good news.

Since nothing is impossible with God, He does not need anyone to serve Him, nor does He lack anything. Therefore, the angels who serve God do so to their own benefit, not God's benefit. The words, **"Because you have made the LORD your refuge, and the most High, your dwelling place; No evil will befall you, nor will any plague come near your dwelling, for He will give His angels charge over you, to keep you in all your ways. They will bear you up in their hands, lest you stub your foot against a stone,"** speak of God's protection of those who trust in Him (Psalm 91:9-12). In fact, this is a passage that Satan quoted when he was tempting Jesus (See Matthew 4:6, Luke 4:11). And, in the resurrection all of that protection will be fully ours without any limitation.

The words, "**Do not despise one of these little ones; for I am telling you, that in heaven their angels continually behold the face of my Father,**" speak of those who trust in Christ [even small children] having angels (Matthew 18:10). The words, "**As Peter knocked at the door of the passage, a girl named Rhoda came to answer... and told everyone that Peter was standing outside the door. But they said to her, You are out of your mind. Yet she insisted that it was so. So they said, It must be his angel,**" tell us that some in the early church believed that Peter had an angel (Acts 12:13-15). And, the words, "**Paul stood up in their midst, and said, Sirs, you should have taken my advice, not to sail from Crete, and so prevented this damage and loss. But now I urge you to be of good cheer: for there will not be a single loss of life among you, only of the ship. For this night an angel from God, whose I am, and whom I serve, stood by me,**" tell of God sending an angel to Paul, when he was in danger, to assure him that there would be no loss of life (Acts 27:21-23).

The words, "**The beggar died, and was carried by the angels to Abraham's side,**" tell us that an angel carried the soul of the beggar [Lazarus] to be with Abraham in heaven (Luke 16:22) [See Mark 12:26-27.] The words, "**The angel of the LORD went out, and struck down one hundred and eighty-five thousand in the camp of the Assyrians: and those who got up early in the morning saw all the dead bodies,**" tell us that angels can fight on behalf of God's people (Isaiah 37:36). And, the words, "**The prince of the kingdom of Persia withstood me for twenty-one days: but then Michael, one of the chief princes, came to help me; and I left him there to oppose the kings of Persia,**" seem speak of one angel withstanding another angel (Daniel 10:13). Now, because no earthly prince could withstand an angel, the one referred to as "the prince of the kingdom of Persia," must have been an angel. Moreover, the fact that he opposed God's angel suggests that he was an evil angel. And, the fact that he is called "the prince of the kingdom of Persia," leads me to think that he might have been one of the angels that are described as "principalities" and "powers," that are not "flesh and blood" (Ephesians 6:12).

Things the Angels Do

The words, "**The things, that have now been proclaimed to you by those who are preaching the gospel to you with the Holy Spirit sent from heaven; things which angels long to look into,**" tell us that angels are interested in the salvation message

(1Peter 1:12).

The words, "The angel said to them, Do not be afraid: for, I bring you good tidings of great joy, that will be for all people. For unto you is born this day in the city of David a Savior, who is Christ the Lord," tell us that when Christ was born angels proclaimed the good news (Luke 2:10-11).

The words, "I saw another angel flying in the midst of heaven, having the everlasting gospel to preach to those who dwell on the earth, and to every nation, and kindred, and language, and people," tell of an angel that assisted in spreading the gospel (Revelation 14:6).

The words, "There is joy in the presence of the angels of God over one sinner who repents," tell us that angels rejoice when a sinner repents (Luke 15:10).

The words, "The angel of the LORD encamps around those who fear Him, and delivers them," tell us that angels protect those who fear God (Psalm 34:7).

The words, "I charge you before God, and the Lord Jesus Christ, and the elect angels, to keep these instructions without favoritism, and without partiality," tell us that angels are aware of what is going on in our churches (1Timothy 5:21). [See 1Corinthians 11:10.]

The words, "When the Son of man comes in His glory, and all the holy angels with Him, then He will sit on the throne of His glory," tell us that the angels will be present at the final judgment (Matthew 25:31).

The words, "He will send His angels with the sound of a great trumpet, and they will gather together His elect from the four winds, from one end of heaven to the other," tell us that angels will gather God's people together for the final judgment (Matthew 24:31).

The words, "The Son of man will send forth His angels, and they will weed out of His kingdom those who sin, and all who lead others to sin; And will throw them into a furnace of fire: where there will be weeping and grinding of teeth. Then the righteous will shine forth as the sun in the kingdom of their Father," tell us that angels will gather up the wicked and cast them into the lake of fire (Matthew 13:41-43).

The Danger of False Worship

While we should be aware of what the Bible says about angels, the words, "Let no man swindle you out of your reward through a false humility and the worship of angels, intruding into things that he has not seen, vainly puffed up by his fleshly mind," warn us not to worship angels (Colossians 2:18). The words, "I fell down to worship before the feet of the angel that showed me these things. And he said to me, Do not do it... worship God," tell us to worship God, not angels (Revelation 22:8-9). And, the words, "**The things that the Gentiles sacrifice are sacrificed to devils, and not to God.**" and "**They shall no longer offer their sacrifices to devils, after whom they have gone a whoring**" equate angel worship with idolatry and adultery (1Corinthians 10:20, Leviticus 17:7). And, because prayer is a form of worship, these passages forbid prayer to angels. In fact, because angels do the will of God, they will not do anything for us unless God tells them to, so any prayer that is not directed to God is futile.

7. The Evil Work And Eternal Punishment Of Evil Angels

It is important to understand that the evil angels are not evil because God created them that way, but because they sinned. The words, "**For all things in heaven and earth, both visible and invisible, were created by Him,**" tell us that God created "invisible" things, and that would include angels (Colossians 1:16). And, the words, "**God saw every thing that He had made, and, behold, it was very good,**" tell us that the angels that God created were all originally good (Genesis 1:31). While the words, "**And the angels who did not keep their first estate, but went outside their bounds, have been kept by Him in darkness bound with everlasting chains until the judgment of the great day,**" tell us that the first estate of angels was good, but they transgressed [i.e. "went outside their bounds"] (Jude 1:6).

Although the Bible does not tell us when the angels sinned, or how they sinned, the words, "**You said in your heart, I will ascend into heaven, I will exalt my throne above the stars of God: I will sit on the mountain of the congregation, on the sides of the north: I will ascend above the highest clouds; I will be like the most High. But you will be brought down to hell, to the sides of the pit,**" suggest that their fall originated with Satan's exalted opinion of himself (Isaiah 14:13-15). The words, "**The archangel Michael, when he disputed with the devil... did not dare to bring a railing accusation against him, but said, May the Lord rebuke you,**" suggest that Satan originally had great authority among the angels (Jude 1:9). The words, "**Everlasting fire, prepared for the devil and his angels,**" tell us that other evil angels are under his dominion (Matthew 25:41). And, the words, "**You are of your father the devil, and you will do what your father desires. He was a murderer from the beginning, and did not abide in the truth, because there is no truth in him. When he speaks a lie, he speaks on his own: for he is a liar, and the father of it,**" suggest that Satan used lies and deception to lead other angels astray, just as he used lies to lead Eve astray (John 8:44).

As to when Satan sinned, all we can say is that he sinned sometime after the six days of creation, but before Eve conceived a child. As to how long that was, the words, "**I will greatly multiply your… conception,**" imply that sin increased the sex drive, so Adam and Eve may have taken time to get to know each other before becoming intimate (Genesis 3:16). Another possibility is that what seems like a short time to us, could seem longer to the angels.

The words, "**Put on the whole armor of God, that you may be able to stand against the wiles of the devil,**" tell us that Satan is intelligent (Ephesians 6:11). However, the words, "**By the time of the supper, the devil had already put it into the heart of Judas Iscariot, Simon's son, to betray Him [Jesus]… And after he [Judas] took the bread Satan entered into him. Then Jesus said to him, What you do, do quickly,**" tell us that Satan is not wise, for what he moved Judas to do was his own undoing (John 13:2 and 27).

The words, "**There was war in heaven: Michael and his angels fought against the dragon; and the dragon and his angels fought back, But did not prevail; nor was there any longer any place for them in heaven. And the great dragon was cast out, that old serpent, called the Devil, and Satan, who deceives the whole world: he was thrown down to the earth, and his angels were thrown down with him,**" tell us that Satan and his angels have been thrown out of heaven (Revelation 12:7-9). The words, "**I saw Satan fall like lightning from heaven,**" indicate that it happened after Christ's incarnation, but before His death on the cross (Luke 10:18). The words, "**When I was daily with you in the temple, you did not lift a hand against me: but this is your hour, when darkness reigns,**" indicate that Satan's power on earth was greatest at the time of Christ's crucifixion (Luke 22:53). And, the words, "**Now is the judgment of this world: now the prince of this world will be cast out. And if I am lifted up from the earth, will draw all men to me,**" tell us that Christ triumphed over Satan through His death on the cross (John 12:31-32).

The words, "**Why has Satan filled your heart to lie to the Holy Ghost, and keep back part of the price of the land?**" tell us that those who choose to do evil, do so because Satan is within them (Acts 5:3). The words, "**Don't you know, that when you yield yourselves to someone to obey him as servants, you are the servants of the one you obey; whether of sin to death, or of obedience to righteousness?**" and "**Truly, truly, I tell you, Whoever commits sin is the servant of sin,**" tell us that those who choose to sin place themselves under Satan's power (Romans 6:16, John 8:34). The words, "**Jesus then replied, Have not I chosen you twelve, yet one of you is a devil? He spoke of Judas Iscar-**

iot the son of Simon: for it was he who would betray Him, although he was one of the twelve,"** tell us that Judas was a devil [indicating that Satan had control over him] (John 6:70-71). The words, **"One of His disciples, Judas Iscariot, Simon's son, who was going to betray Him, said, Why wasn't this valuable fragrance sold for three hundred denarii, and given to the poor? He did not say that because he cared for the poor; but because <u>he was a thief</u>, and had the bag, and would take what was put into it,"** tell us that Satan was in control of Judas because Judas had a long habit of choosing to do evil (John 12:4-6).

These facts raise a number of questions. For example: **If Satan is behind lies and theft, can anyone deny that he is behind rape, child molestation, adultery and murder? And, if that is the case wouldn't he also be behind all forms of sexual perversion, and abortion?** I am not saying that people who commit such sins cannot be saved, but if they sin willfully they are unrepentant and true faith cannot exist without repentance. That is why Christ said that, **"Repentance and remission of sins should be preached in His name among all nations, starting at Jerusalem"** (Luke 24:47). And, that is why the Apostle Paul wrote, **"Don't you know that the unrighteous will not inherit the kingdom of God? Do not be deceived: neither fornicators, nor idolaters, nor adulterers, nor sex perverts, nor homosexuals, nor thieves, nor covetous, nor drunkards, nor foulmouthed revilers, nor extortioners, shall inherit the kingdom of God"** (Corinthians 6:9-10.

The words, **"You formerly walked according to the way of this world, according to the prince of the power of the air, the spirit that now works in the children of disobedience,"** tell us that Satan is active in those who are unrepentant (Ephesians 2:2). The words, **"The minds of those who do not believe have been blinded by the god of this world, that the light of the glorious gospel of Christ, who is the image of God, might not reach them,"** tell us that Satan not only tries to defile us through specific sins, but actively seeks to destroy us through unbelief (2Corinthians 4:4). The words, **"While men slept, his enemy came and sowed weeds among the wheat, and went his way,"** tell us that Satan places unsaved people inside the church (Matthew 13:25). And, I believe that one way he does this, is by causing those who do not understand the way of salvation to place false definitions on the words of Scripture and Christian terminology, so they hear what is said but fail to understand it correctly.

The words, **"He has rescued us from the power of darkness, and transferred us into the kingdom of His dear Son,"** tell us that because we were under the power of darkness we could not save ourselves, but needed to be rescued (Colossians 1:13). The words, **"To open their eyes [the eyes of the Gentiles], and to turn them from darkness to light, and from the power of Satan to God, that they may receive forgiveness of sins, and inheritance among those who are sanctified through faith in me," tell us that the lost are under the power of Satan, and are delivered through faith in Christ (Acts 26:18). However, the Bible also makes a distinction between the kind of spiritual control that Satan had over Judas, and the sort of physical demon possession described in the words, **"As soon as Jesus got out of the boat, a man with an unclean spirit came out of the tombs to meet Him, This man lived in the tombs; and no one could bind him, no, not even with chains: For he had often been bound with shackles and chains, but the chains had been broken by him, and the shackles torn to pieces: and no one could tame him. And he was always in the mountains, and in the tombs, crying, and cutting himself with stones, night and day. But when he saw Jesus from a distance, he ran and prostrated himself before Him, and cried with a loud voice, What have I to do with you, Jesus, Son of the most high God? I implore you by God, do not torment me"** (Mark 5:2-7). In spite of what the Bible here says, western scholars often scoff at this account in Scripture. A son of missionary parents told of how his family encountered this sort of demon possession more than once, yet he was mocked when he told people in the States of his experience.

The words, **"If they do not speak according to this word, it is because there is no light in them,"** tell us that those who deny that Satan exists [or anything else that the Bible says] are in darkness, and, therefore, under Satan's influence (Isaiah 8:20). And, the words, **"The invisible things of Him from the creation of the world are clearly seen... so that they are without excuse,"** // **"When the Gentiles, who do not have the law, do by nature the things contained in the law, they... show the work of the law written in their hearts,"** tell us that being under Satan's dominion does not exempt the lost of responsibility for their actions (Romans 1:20 and 2:15).

Satan's Furious Attack on the Christian Church

Having been thrown out of heaven, Satan is fighting to keep control of this world. And, the words, **"That old serpent, called the Devil, and Satan, who deceives the whole world: he was thrown down to the earth, and his angels were thrown down with him. And I heard a loud voice in heaven say, Now the salvation, the power, and the kingdom of our God, and the authority of His Christ has come: for the accuser of our brethren has been thrown down, who accuses them before our God day and night. And they overcame him by the blood of the Lamb, and by the word of their testimony; and they did not love their** lives even unto death," tell us that Satan is being overcome by the blood of Christ, and the testimony of God's Word (Revelation 12:9-11).

The words, "**I [Jesus] came into the world, to testify to the truth. Every one who is of the truth hears my voice**," tell us that Christ's kingdom is a kingdom of truth (John 18:37). The words, "**Sanctify them through your truth: your Word is truth**," tell us that the Bible is the truth that Christ uses to destroy Satan's lies (John 17:17). And, the words, "**That is the foundation upon which I will build my church; and the gates of hell will not prevail against it**," tell us that God's people will triumph over all opposition (Matthew 16:18).

The words, "**I am not ashamed of the gospel of Christ: for it is the power of God to salvation to every one who believes**," tell us that God empowers His Word (Romans 1:16). The words, "**So will the word that goes out of my mouth be: it will not return to me empty, but it will accomplish what I want, and it will achieve what I sent it to do**," tell us that God's Word will achieve the results that He sent it to "accomplish" (Isaiah 55:11). The words, "**In every way we show ourselves to be servants of God, in enduring much, in sufferings, in hardships, in distresses, In beatings, in imprisonments, in riots, in labors, in nights without sleep, in days without food; By pure motive, by knowledge, by patience, by kindness, by the Holy Spirit, by sincere love, By the word of truth, by the power of God, with the armor of righteousness on the right hand and on the left, Through honor and dishonor, through slander and commendation: treated as deceivers, and yet true**," tell us that Satan will turn people against us, will portray the truth of Scripture as a lie and will label us as deceivers (2Corinthians 6:4-8). However, **our faith does "not rest in the wisdom of men, but in the power of God**," (1Corinthians 2:5). And, we "**are kept by the power of God through faith unto salvation**" (1Peter 1:5).

The words, "**Those by the way side are those who hear; then the devil comes, and removes the word from their hearts, lest they should believe and be saved**," tell us that Satan hinders the gospel by hardening the hearts of those who hear (Luke 8:12). That is why cult members and evolutionists are often quick to dismiss what we say.

The words, "**Now the Spirit specifically says, that in the future some will depart from the faith, giving heed to seducing spirits, and doctrines of devils**," tell us that Satan hinders the work of the gospel by leading some away from the faith (1Timothy 4:1). He does this every time someone joins a cult, or drops out of church because of what they were taught in college.

The words, "**Who opposes and exalts himself over everything that is called God, or is worshipped; so that he sits as God in** the temple of God, and says that he is God," tell us that Satan hinders the gospel by raising up false leadership in the church (2Thessalonians 2:4). The Pope is one example of this, but it applies to every cult leader, and to all who exalt their word over God's Word.

How God Uses Evil Angels

The words, "**The LORD has now put a lying spirit in the mouth of all your prophets** [idol worshipping prophets]," tell us that God uses evil angels to punish those who reject Him (1Kings 22:23).

The words, "**God will send them a powerful delusion, so that they will believe lies: That all who did not believe the truth, but had pleasure in unrighteousness, might be damned**," tell us that God sends delusion on those who harden their hearts to the gospel (2Thessalonians 2:11-12).

The words, "**To keep me from swelling with pride, because of the great and wonderful things that were revealed to me, I was given a thorn in the flesh, a messenger of Satan to afflict me, so that I would not become conceited**," (2Corinthians 12:7). And, the words, "**My grace is sufficient for you**," suggest that the messenger of Satan kept reminding Paul of his sin, in an attempt to convince him that God's grace was not sufficient to cover what he had done (2Cor. 12:9).

God's Wrath on the Evil Angels and Evil Men

The words, "**Then He will say to those on His left, Depart from me, you cursed, into everlasting fire, prepared for the devil and his angels**," tell us that the evil angels will be condemned to everlasting fire (Matthew 25:41). The question of whether this fire will be physical or spiritual is of little importance, because the torment will be real.

The words, "**The smoke of their torment ascends for ever and ever: and there is no rest day or night**," tell us that the torment will never lessen or cease (Revelation 14:11). And, just as those under judgment in this world often harm and torment each other, those in hell may cause additional pain by tormenting each other.

The words, "**The fearful, and unbelieving, the abominable, murderers, whoremongers, sorcerers, idolaters, and all liars, will have their part in the lake that burns with fire and sulfur: which is the second death**," should be a warning to all who think that they can continue in a sinful lifestyle, without a repentant heart, and never be called to account (Revelation 21:8).

And, the words, "**The day of the Lord will come as a thief in the night; in which the heavens will pass away with a great noise, and the elements will melt with intense heat, and the earth and everything in it will be burned up**," tell us that on the day of judgment the material world as we know it, including all of the things that men sinned to obtain, will cease to exist (2Peter 3:10-12).

"The Christian doctrine is not produced by the theologian; all that the Christian theologian does is that he compiles the doctrinal statements contained in Scripture (in the text and context), groups them under their proper heads, and arranges these doctrines in the order of their relationship." // "The whole Christian doctrine is revealed in Scripture passages that need no exegesis, but are an open book alike to the learned and the unlearned and can be so readily translated that the translator cannot go wrong unless he has made up his mind to depart from the original." (Dr. Francis Pieper, "Christian Dogmatics", Vol. 1, pg 52 & 347)

SCRIPTURE ALONE

THE DOCTRINE OF MAN
(DE ANTHXOPOLOGIA)

What the Bible tells us about man falls into two divisions: a) man before the fall into sin, and b) man after the fall into sin.

A. Man Before The Fall

1. Man Created In The Image Of God

When God created Adam, the words, "**God saw every thing that He had made, and, behold, it was very good,**" tell us that at that time Adam's nature was not corrupted by sin (Genesis 1:31). The words, "very good" in that passage stand out in stark contrast to Genesis 6:5, "**God saw that the wickedness of man was great in the earth, and that every imagination of the thoughts of his heart was only evil continually**". A comparison of those verses tells us that God did not create man with a heart that "was only evil continually," so that change must have taken place when Adam fell into sin. Therefore, when the Bible tells us that, "**God created man in His own image... male and female He created them,**" it is describing Adam and Eve before the fall (Genesis 1:27).

In the creation record the Bible uses the terms "image" and "likeness" as synonyms, and the use of plural pronouns in the phrase, "**Let us make man in our image, after our likeness,**" tell us that Adam was created in the image of the Triune God, not just the image of Christ (Genesis 1:26). Moreover, since the words, "**Now unto the King eternal, immortal, invisible, the only wise God**," tell us that God is invisible; we know that the terms "image" and "likeness" are not talking about outward appearance (1Timothy 1:17).

The words, "**When I consider your heavens, the work of your fingers, the moon and the stars, which you set in place; what is man, that you are mindful of him? And the son of man, that you visit him? For you made him a little lower than the angels, and crowned him with glory and honor. You made him to have dominion over the works of your hands; you have put all things under his feet**," speak of God's original intent for man (Psalm 8:3-6). And, the fact that man was given real dominion over all of the beasts suggests that before the fall all of them would have served man willingly, as eagerly as some dogs still do.

2. The Image Of A Righteous God

The fact that Adam was a finite being tells us that the divine image did not consist of an infinite nature. And, the fact that Adam and Eve were deceived by Satan tells us that they were not all-wise or all-knowing. In addition, the fact that Satan (who was **not** created in the image of God) has an intellect and is able to speak tells us that the divine image did not consist of such things. What Adam had that constituted the divine image was a righteous nature. That is why the Bible says, "**Put on the new <u>nature</u>, which after *the image of* God is created in righteousness and true holiness**" (Ephesians 4:24). Furthermore, because Adam had a righteous nature, he could look into his own heart and **know** the heart of God. That is why the Bible says, "**Put on the new man, who is renewed in knowledge after the image of the One who created him,**" (Colossians 3:10). That knowledge is why those who come to faith in Christ no longer see God as a harsh taskmaster, but as a loving Father.

The words, "**God has made men upright; but they have sought out many inventions,**" tell us that man did not have a sinful nature when he was created (Ecclesiastes 7:29). And, the words, "**The woman said to the serpent, We may eat of the fruit of the trees of the garden, but of the fruit of the tree that is in the middle of the garden, God has said, You shall not eat of it**," tell us that before Satan set to work Adam and Eve were perfectly willing to do what God told them to do (Genesis 3:2-3).

The words, "**Out of the ground the LORD God formed every beast of the field, and every fowl of the air; and brought them unto Adam to see what he would call them, and whatever Adam called each living creature, that was its name,**" tell us that far from being a brute, Adam was created with a good intellect (Genesis 2:19). And, the words, "**God said, Let us make man in our image, after our likeness, and let them have dominion over the fish of the sea, over the birds of the air, over the cattle, over all the earth, and over every creeping thing that creeps upon the earth. So God created man in His own image... and God said to them... have dominion over the fish of the sea, and over the fowl of the air, and over every living thing that moves upon the earth,**" tell us that God created man to have dominion over the earth and all of the animals (Genesis 1:26-28).

Since God originally intended for man to live forever, and since man was created to have dominion over the entire earth the immediate results of the divine image were immortality and dominion. Whether Adam and Eve would have lived forever on earth had they never sinned, or whether God would (in time) have translated them to a higher plain of existence as He did Enoch, the Bible does not say (Genesis 5:24). However, God knew that they would sin, and the words, "**The Lamb slain from the foundation of the world**," tell us that He planned from the beginning to provide salvation for us (Revelation 13:8).

3. The Divine Image And The Nature Of Man

Once we understand that righteousness is central to the image of God, the words, "**God created man in His own image**," tell us that the original righteousness that man had before the fall was a part of his created nature, not some sort of gift that was added on (Genesis 1:27). That means that the fall into sin brought about a change in man's nature. A change from having a righteous heart to having a heart that is, "**Deceitful above all things, and desperately wicked**," (Jeremiah 17:9). And, that fact tells us that fallen man no longer has the image of God. At most, all that remains of the divine image is a trace or impression, like the impression on paper of words that have been erased.

Because of that impression, fallen man seems to sense instinctively that there must be a God, even though he does not know who God is, and often prefers to believe that God does not exist. And, the words, "**That which may be known of God is known to them; for God has shown it to them**," tell us that God makes men aware of His existence (Romans 1:19).

Likewise, fallen man seems to recognize a difference between right and wrong, even though that difference is often blurred in his mind, rationalized away, and ignored. And, the words, "**When the Gentiles, who do not have the law, do by nature the things contained in the law, they... show the work of the law written in their hearts, their conscience also bearing witness**," tell us that the conscience of the lost tells them that they have done things that deserve condemnation (Romans 2:14-15).

Those passages tell us that if the lost would take that knowledge of God seriously, and call upon their creator, confessing their sins and seeking His mercy they could be saved. However, do not expect that to happen, because the Bible tells us that "**The natural man does not accept the things of the Spirit of God: for they are foolishness to him: and he cannot understand them, because they are spiritually discerned**" (1Corinthians 2:14). For, "**The fleshly mind is hostile to God: for it is not subject to the law of God, nor indeed can be**" (Romans 8:7). However, as hopeless as that sounds, God's remedy is to be found in His Word. As it is written, "**Since... the world through its wisdom did not know God, it pleased God to save those who believe through the foolishness of preaching**" (1Corinthians 1:20-21).

There are two passages that are sometimes cited by those who do not realize that man lost the image of God through the fall. As you read them, notice that neither of them say that man now bears the image of God, both say only that man was created in the image of God. The first passage is, Genesis 9:6, "**Whoever sheds man's blood, by man shall his blood be shed: for God <u>made man in His own image</u>**". The second is, James 3:6 and 9, "**The tongue is a world of evil... With it we bless our God and Father; and with it we curse men, who <u>were created in God's image</u>**".

The words, "**Remember that at that time you were without Christ, being aliens from the commonwealth of Israel, and strangers from the covenants of promise, <u>having no hope</u>, and without God in the world**," tell us that the unregenerate, those who have no knowledge of God's promise of forgiveness in Christ, are without God and without hope (Ephesians 2:12). And, the words, "**The things that the Gentiles sacrifice are sacrificed to devils, and not to God**," in complete contrast to the false claim that all religions lead to God, tell us that in their blindness (without the image of God) the religions of this world honor Satan, not God (1Corinthians 10:20).

Although the seat of the divine image (righteousness and knowledge of God) was the soul, not the body, because body and soul are a unit the body shared in the divine image. And, the body also shared in the loss of the divine image through sin. That loss resulted in man's loss of immortality, and that brought with it physical death and all that death entails. The words, "**But of the tree of the knowledge of good and evil, you may not eat of it: for in the day that you eat of it you will surely die**," were God's warning to Adam and Eve that death would result if they disobeyed (Genesis 2:17). The words, "**Just as sin entered the world by one man, and death by sin; so death passed upon all men, because all have sinned**," tell us that Adam's sin not only resulted in his death, but in the death of all of his descendants. (Romans 5:12). And, the words, "**The wages of sin is death; but the gift of God is eternal life through Jesus Christ our Lord**," make it clear that death is not in the world because it is a natural property of matter but because of sin, and faith in Christ is the remedy (Romans 6:23).

In theology a distinction is made between: **absolute immortality**, which is experienced not only by the saints in heaven, but also by the damned who will be conscious forever in hell; and the **conditional immortality** that Adam and Eve enjoyed before the fall. The fact that the Bible speaks of hell as the "second death" and of heaven as "everlasting life," tells us that all of the pains and suffering that we associate with death (and more) will be experienced by those in hell, "Where their worm does not die, and the fire is never put out" (Mark 9:44).

The words, "**LORD, cause me to know my end, and how many days I have left; so that I will know how fleeting my life is. Behold, you have made my days as short as a handbreadth; and my life is as nothing in your sight: truly every man at his best is merely a breath. Selah. Surely every man walks about like a mere shadow: surely they are troubled over nothing: each one heaps up riches, and does not know who will get them,**" speak of the futility of life because of man's loss of the divine image, death being the result (Psalm 39:4-6).

The words, "**To the woman He said, I will greatly multiply your sorrow and your conception; in sorrow you will bring forth children; and your desire shall be to your husband, and he will rule over you,**" tell us that before sin entered into the world, Adam and Eve did not experience painful and destructive sufferings (Genesis 3:16). And, the words, "**I will greatly multiply... your conception,**" suggest that the entrance of death into the world necessitated an increase in the sex drive.

> The original condition of man was therefore one of supreme happiness; for a) his soul was wise and holy; b) his body was free from suffering and death; c) his condition of life was most blessed; and d) his condition of habitation was most pleasant, since God placed him into a garden of pleasure, called Paradise, to dwell there and enjoy His goodness forever (Genesis 2:8-15). (John Theodore Mueller, "Christian Dogmatics," pages 207-208)

4. The Divine Image And Woman

At this point I want to focus specifically on the fact that the words, "**So God created man in His own image, in the image of God He created him; male and female He created them,**" tell us that Adam and Eve were both created in the image of God (Genesis 1:27). At the same time, the words, "**God said, It is not good that the man should be alone; I will make him a helper suitable for him,**" and the words, "**Neither was man created for woman; but woman for man,**" tell us that from the beginning Eve's role was that of a helper (Genesis 2:18, 1Corinthians 11:9).

God's words to Eve, "**Your desire shall be to your husband, and he will rule over you,**" tell us that before the fall, even though Eve was subject to her husband, and he was her leader, he did not "**rule over**" her (Genesis 3:16). At least not in the way the words "**rule over**" are understood in a sinful world. That tells me that God intended for man and wife to be a team, who work together in love, as friends, not rivals each fighting for their own way. When God's blessing is on the home, marriage and home life can be the closest thing to heaven that you can experience in this life. However, without God's blessing on the home, marriage and home life can be the closest thing to hell that you experience in this life. For that reason all Christians should seek God's blessing as fervently as Jacob sought it when he wrestled with the angel (Genesis 32:24, 26).

The words, "**Submitting yourselves one to another in the fear of God. Wives, submit yourselves unto your own husbands, as unto the Lord... Husbands, love your wives, even as Christ also loved the church, and gave himself for it**," (Ephesians 5:21, 22, 25) tell us that "This divine order must not be subverted; for it is the will of God that the woman should not usurp authority over the man by ruling over him. But, on the other hand, the woman should not be tyrannized or made a slave." (John Theodore Mueller, "Christian Dogmatics," page 209)

While the words, "**There is neither Jew nor Greek, there is neither bond nor free, there is neither male nor female: for you are all one in Christ Jesus**," tell us that men and woman are equal before God, and therefore equal in regard to salvation: the words, "**A woman should learn in silence with all subjection. But I do not allow a woman to teach, or to have authority over a man, but to remain silent. For Adam was first formed, then Eve**," tell us that just as God has given men and women different roles in the home, He has given them different roles in the church, and those roles should be respected (Galatians 3:28, 1Timothy 2:11-13). [See Gen. 2:21-22, Eph. 5:21-33, Titus 2:3-5, Proverbs 1:24-33, Titus 2:3-4.]

A Final Note

Although Adam and Eve knew the love of God before they fell into sin, they did not know God's plan to provide redemption for all mankind, or of the "seed" that would crush the serpents "head", for that was not yet revealed (Genesis 3:15). So even though they were not lost before they sinned, it would be inaccurate to say that they were saved, because someone has to be lost before they can be saved, and they have to trust in Christ. As it is written, "**The Son of man has come to seek and to save that which was lost**" (Luke 19:10).

B. The State Of Corruption

The words, "**By one man sin entered into the world, and death by sin**," tell us that there was no sin in the world before Adam and Eve disobeyed God (Romans 5:12). And, because there was no sin, Adam and Eve were righteous and holy in the sight of God. Therefore, contrary to the lie Satan told (Gen. 3:4-5), Adam and Eve's fall into sin was not something good, but the greatest evil that man has ever committed. It is the greatest evil, because every evil that has come into the world since, including Christ's betrayal and murder, are the result of that sin. All of the millions who have died in war, the millions killed by the Communists and Nazis, and the millions being murdered today by abortion suffer the consequences of Adam's sin.

If Adam and Eve had not sinned, the heart of man would not be **"Deceitful above all things, and desperately wicked,"** (Jeremiah 17:9). And, the heart of man would not be producing, **"Evil thoughts, murder, adultery, immorality, theft, false witness, blasphemy"** (Matthew 15:19).

Because the words, **"Christ Jesus came into the world to save sinners,"** and the words, **"Put on the new nature, which after *the image of* God is created in righteousness and true holiness,"** tell us that Christ came into the word to save us from our sins and restore us to the image of God; the doctrine of sin is an essential part of theology (1Timothy 1:15, Ephesians 4:24). And, we will deal with it under three heads: a) Sin in General; b) Original Sin; and c) Actual Sins.

a. Of Sin In General

1. Falling Short Of The Glory Of God

The words, **"God saw every thing that He had made, and, behold, it was very good,"** tell us that before sin entered the world the will of man was in complete conformity with the will of God (Genesis 1:31). The words, **"Be perfect, even as your Father who is in heaven is perfect,"** tell us that God does not have a double standard, but requires the same perfection from man that man had when he was created (Matthew 5:48). And the words, **"All have sinned, and come short of the glory of God,"** tell us that anything short of that high standard is sin (Romans 3:23).

A comparison of the words, **"Whoever sins breaks the law, for sin is a violation of the law,"** with the words **"Be perfect, even as your Father who is in heaven is perfect,"** tell us that anything short of the perfection God requires is **SIN** (1John 3:4, Matthew 5:48). **"All unrighteousness is sin"** (1John 5:17). And, that includes the unrighteousness of a heart that is, **"Deceitful above all things, and desperately wicked"** (Jeremiah 17:9).

The words, **"Being filled with unrighteousness of every kind, fornication, wickedness, covetousness, maliciousness; full of envy, murder, strife, deceit, malice; whisperers,"** tell us that sin involves not only wicked deeds [fornication, murder], but also wicked words [strife, deceit], and wicked thoughts and desires [covetousness, envy] (Romans 1:29). The words, **"If we confess our sins, He is** faithful and just to forgive us our sins, and to cleanse us from all unrighteousness,"** tell us that we should never excuse our sins, or hope that God will not notice, but should be willing to confess our sin to God (1John 1:9). The words, **"The LORD is near to those who are of a broken heart; and saves those who are of a contrite spirit,"** assure all who are contrite [sorry for their sin] of God's mercy (Psalm 34:18). And, the words, **"The blood of Jesus Christ His Son cleanses us of all sin,"** is God's promise of forgiveness to all who repent (1John 1:7).

2. The Divine Law And Sin

Since **"sin is a violation of the law,"** we need to know what the law says (1John 3:4). And, the words, **"There is only one lawgiver and judge, the one who is able to save and to destroy,"** tell us when it comes to sin, God's Law is the only law that counts (James. 4:12).

The words, **"You shall not add to the word which I command you, nor shall you take anything from it, that you may keep the commandments of the LORD your God which I command you,"** warn God's people not to add to or take from what His law says (Deuteronomy 4:2). That coupled with the words, **"Nor are you to be called masters: for you have one Master, even Christ,"** tells us that no church, no matter how large, has any authority to create new laws that are binding on God's people, or do away with those God has given us. (Matthew 23:10).

The words, **"Not one letter or stroke will pass from the law, until everything has been fulfilled,"** tell us that the Law is still in place (Matthew 5:18). And, the words, <u>**"The law is not meant for a righteous man, but for those who are lawless and rebellious**</u>**, for the ungodly and sinful, for the irreverent and profane, for those who strike or kill their fathers or mothers, for murders, for those who sin sexually, for sodomites, for kidnapers and slave traders, for liars and perjurers, and for any other thing that is contrary to sound teaching,"** tell us that **the unrepentant are still under the law** (1Timothy 1:9-10).

At this point let me digress from explaining the law in order to explain what the Bible says about freedom from the law.

It is important to know that those who trust in Christ have been freed from the law. As it is written, **"We have been released from the law, having died to that which once bound us; that we should serve in newness of spirit, and not in the oldness of the letter"** (Romans 7:6). For that reason, one of Satan's greatest attacks on our faith is aimed at confusing people as to what freedom from the law entails. On one hand Satan leads people to wrongly assume that if they are free from the law they are free to sin. But, the words, **"The law is not meant for a righteous man, but for those who are lawless and rebellious,"** tell us that those who use Christian freedom as an excuse to sin, wind up placing themselves back under the law and its condemnation (1Timothy 1:9). On the other hand, Satan leads people to react to Christian freedom by assuming that faith is not enough. **Those under that delusion place themselves back under the law by seeking righteousness through the law**. Against that error Paul warned, **"Stand fast in the liberty for which Christ set us free, and never again allow yourselves to be ensnared by the yoke of slavery... those of you who seek righteousness by the law; you are fallen from grace"** (Galatians 5:1,4).

Many people have a hard time understanding the freedom we have in Christ because they assume that the law makes them righteous. And, because they think that the law makes them righteous, they wrongly assume that freedom from the law is freedom to sin. However, nothing could be further from the truth! As it is written, **"No one will ever become righteous in God's sight by the deeds of the law: because the knowledge of sin comes by the law"** (Romans 3:20). Moreover, the words, **"All of our righteousnesses are like filthy rags,"** tell us that, apart from faith in Christ, the law condemns everything we do (Isaiah 64:6). In other words, far from making us righteous, it is the law that makes us sinners! And, it is only as we realize that the law is what condemns us that we can understand that freedom from the law is not freedom to sin, but the freedom to be righteous. **Because the purpose of God's law is to expose our sin, only those who acknowledge their sins and look to Christ for forgiveness are keeping God's law**. And, if keeping God's law involves condemning ourselves as sinners then freedom from the law is freedom from condemnation. In other words, freedom in Christ is not the freedom to sin, but the freedom to be a good citizen, a faithful husband, and a godly father without constantly being condemned by God's law. As it is written, **"There is therefore now no condemnation for those who are in Christ Jesus, who walk not after the flesh, but after the Spirit. For the law of the Spirit of life in Christ Jesus has set me free from the law of sin and death"** (Romans 8:1-2).

The Ceremonial Law

By the time of Christ's sojourn on earth Greek culture had spread over much of the Middle East, and many Greeks had embraced the God of Israel. In the book of John we read, **"Now there were some Greeks among those who went up to worship at the feast"** (John 12:20). The book of Acts tells us that "In Iconium, Paul and Barnabas went to the Jewish synagogue together, and spoke so effectively, that a great number of **Jews and Greeks believed**" (Acts 14:1). However, even though these Greeks worshiped the God of Israel, accepted the moral law of the Old Testament, and were living by the Ten Commandments; many of them had not become full-fledged Jews, (which involved keeping all of the Old Testament laws). These converts were referred to as "proselytes of the gate". And, when many of them embraced the Gospel and turned to Christ, the Apostle Paul saw no reason to require them to be circumcised and keep all of the ceremonial laws (those forbidding certain foods, and requiring ceremonial washings etc.). [See Acts 17:12 and 18:4.]

In the third chapter of Galatians the Apostle Paul explains why he did not require converts to become Jews by saying, "**Before faith came, we were imprisoned by the law, kept under guard by the law for the faith that would be revealed. Therefore, the law was our schoolmaster to bring us to Christ, that we might be declared righteous by faith. But now that faith has come, we are no longer under a schoolmaster, for you are all the children of God through faith in Christ Jesus**" (Galatians 3:23-26). Now, before going further let me make it clear that it was not the moral law that was being done away with, but the ceremonial law. When Paul was told of sexual sin in the Corinthian congregation he said, "**Among you one hears of immorality, and of a kind of immorality that does not even occur among the Gentiles, that one has his father's wife. And, you are still puffed up. Shouldn't you rather have been filled with sorrow, and have put out of your fellowship the man who did this**" (1Corinthians 5:1-2)?

The ceremonial law created a cultural barrier between Jews and gentiles. During the Old Testament era that was important. However, after Christ's resurrection it hindered the spread of the gospel. That is why God inspired Paul to say, "**If you died with Christ to the elemental things of this world, why, as though you still belonged to it, do you submit to its rules, Do not touch; do not taste; do not handle**" // "**Do not let anyone judge you by what you eat, or drink, or in regard to a holyday, or the new moon, or the Sabbath day**" (Colossians 2:20-21 and 2:16). That is why Peter said, "**I now realize how true it is that God is no respecter of persons, but in every nation those who fear Him, and do what is right, are accepted by Him**" (Acts 10:34-35). And, that is why the Council of Jerusalem said to the gentile converts, "**It seemed good to the Holy Ghost, and to us, to lay upon you no greater burden than these essential things: That you abstain from meats offered to idols, and from blood, and from things strangled, and from sexual immorality. If you keep yourselves from these things you will do well**" (Acts 15:28-29). And, no church has the authority to reinstitute what God has abolished.

In addition to what was just said, the book of Hebrews explains to the Jewish believers why animal sacrifice should be abolished, saying,

"The law being only a shadow of good things to come, and not the actual embodiment of those things, can never make those who come perfect by offering the same sacrifices continually year after year... Thus He does away with the first covenant, that He may establish the second. And by that will we are sanctified through the offering of the body of Jesus Christ once for all" (Hebrews 10:1,9,10).

Walking In Newness of Life

So, what law should we live by? Jesus answered that when He said, "**You shall love the Lord your God with all your heart, and with all your soul, and with all your mind. This is the first and greatest commandment. And the second is like it, You shall love your neighbor as yourself. On these two commandments hang all the law and the prophets**" (Matthew 22:37-40). So, "**Give to all men what you owe them: taxes to whom taxes are due; custom to whom custom; fear to whom fear; honor to whom honor. Owe no man any thing, but to love one another: for he who loves his neighbor has fulfilled the law. For this, You will not commit adultery, You will not kill, You will not steal, You will not bear false witness, You will not covet; and if there is any other commandment, it is summed up in this saying, namely, You will love your neighbor as yourself. Love does no harm to his neighbor: therefore love is the fulfilling of the law**" (Romans 13:7-01). Those words tell us that **love should never be twisted into an excuse to break God's commandments** [See 1John 5:3.]

The words, "**That we may lead a quiet and peaceable life in all godliness and honesty,**" tell us that the freedom we have in Christ is not the freedom to sin, but the freedom, "**to do what is right, and to love mercy, and to walk humbly with your God**" (1Timothy 2:2, Micah 6:8).

The words, "**Woe to those who call evil good, and good evil; who put darkness for light, and light for darkness,**" warn us that a Christian should never excuse or justify wrongdoing (Isaiah 5:20). The words, "**We are buried with Him [Christ] by baptism into death: that like as Christ was raised up from the dead by the glory of the Father, even so we also should walk in newness of life,**" tell us that we should walk in newness of life; **conducting ourselves as if sin has been removed from our nature** (Romans 6:4). The words, "**A bishop must be blameless,**" tell us that a Christian should conduct himself in a way that is **above reproach** (1Timothy 3:2). The words, "**Put aside all filthiness and every hint of naughtiness,**" tell us that we should not do anything that looks shady (James 1:21). And, the words, "**We are motivated by the love of Christ; because we are convinced, that if one died for all,** then all died: And He died for all, so that those who live should no longer live for themselves, but for Him who died for them, and rose again,"** tell us that our motivation in doing this should be our love for Christ, not some vain attempt to make ourselves righteous (2Corinthians 5:14-15). [See Romans 9:30-32 and 10:3-4] **"The fruit of the Spirit is in all goodness and righteousness and truth,"** and we should conduct ourselves accordingly (Ephesians 5:9).

Government

The words, **"Let everyone be subject to the governing authorities. For there is no authority except by God, and those that exist are established by God,"** tell us, not only that we should obey the law of the land, but that rulers are given their authority by God (Romans 13:1). However, any laws enacted by men are binding only if God Himself has given men authority to make them. And, **God has never given any ruler the authority to promote homosexuality or any other form of wickedness. Nor has He given them the authority to require us to send our children to schools that attack their faith and teach them the false religion of secularism.** In understanding how to deal with a government that actively promotes evil, the words, **"You need to be subject, not only to avoid wrath, but also for conscience sake,"** tell us that we need to work for reform in a way that will not bring down the wrath of government upon ourselves, or other Christians, and can be done with a clean conscience (Romans 13:5). If rulers actively try to force us to act contrary to God's Word, the rule is that, **"We ought to obey God rather than men"** (Acts 5:29).

Parents

Paul tells us that the words, **"Honor your father and your mother: that your days may be long upon the land which the LORD your God gives you,"** // **"is the first commandment with promise"** (Exodus 20:12, Ephesians 6:2). However, the words, **"All the promises of God in Him [Christ] are yea, and in Him Amen,"** tell us that God's promises can only be received through faith in Christ (2Corinthians 1:20). That fact tells us that the purpose of this commandment is not to make children our slaves, but to warn them to take our instruction seriously, so that they have a tender conscience before God, do not rationalize sin, and trust in His promise of forgiveness. On the other hand, **any father that teaches his son to sin ceases to be the child's father, and becomes an agent of Satan, who is trying to alienate the child from his true Heavenly Father.**

Conscience

The words, **"I know, and am persuaded by the Lord Jesus,**

that there is nothing unclean of itself: but if anyone regards something as unclean, then for him it is unclean. But if your brother is grieved because of what you eat, you are not walking according to love. Do not destroy with your food, him for whom Christ died,"** stress the importance of doing nothing that you cannot do with a **clean conscience** (Romans 14:14-15). I realize that when it comes to conscience people often either harden their conscience to the point that many sins do not bother them, or torment themselves over things that God has not forbidden. For that reason, it is important for every believer to train his or her conscience so that it condemns what God condemns, without either excusing sin or forbidding what God has not forbidden, while **"Casting down imaginations, and every high thing that exalts itself against the knowledge of God, and bringing into captivity every thought to the obedience of Christ"** (2Corinthians 10:5).

3. The Causes Of Sin

While Satan is the primary cause of sin in the world, the words, **"Every man is tempted, when he is drawn away by his own lust, and enticed,"** tell us that the efficient cause of sin is man's own corrupt will and sinful heart (James 1:14).

The words, **"God saw every thing that He had made, and, behold, it was very good,"** tell us that God did not create sin, nor was it part of His original creation (Genesis 1:31), while the words, **"Sin entered the world by one man, and death by sin,"** tell us that sin entered the world through the sin of Adam (Romans 5:12). Furthermore, the fact that man was created without a sinful nature tells us that God did not create man with an inclination to sin. On the contrary, as originally created Adam and Eve had no desire to sin. It was because they would not even think of lying to someone that they did not question what the serpent said (Genesis 3:4-5).

The words, **"In all this Job did not sin, or accuse God foolishly,"** tell us that those who blame God for the sin in the world, or for their own troubles are foolish (Job 1:22). And, the words, **"Do not let anyone say when he is tempted, I am tempted by God: for God cannot be tempted with evil, nor does He tempt anyone,"** tell us that those who excuse sin by claiming that God is tempting them are deluding themselves (James 1:13). The words, **"So these three men stopped answering Job, because he was righteous in his own eyes,"** tell us that God did not allow trouble to come upon Job to tempt him, but to humble him, and cure his self righteousness, so that he would not loose his salvation (Job 32:1). As it is written, **"Now to Him who is able to keep you from falling, and to present you faultless before His glorious presence with great joy,**

To the only wise God, our Savior, be glory and majesty, dominion and power, both now and forever" (Jude 24-25).

The words, **"For you are not a God who has pleasure in wickedness: nor will evil dwell with you. The foolish will not stand in your sight, <u>you hate all who do evil</u>**," tell us that God never approves of wickedness, or of those who do evil (Psalm 5:4-5). Those who condemn God for allowing wickedness to continue, foolishly assume that if God eliminated all evildoers they would be the exception, and that is just another form of self-righteousness. Most of the suffering in the world is caused by men, and the suffering caused by storms etc. is in the world because of sin. So for God to eliminate sin, He would have to judge the world, and destroy it. And, that will come to pass. However, the words, **"Therefore having overlooked the times of ignorance; God now commands all men every where to repent,"** tell us that God has not eliminated sin because He is giving you a chance to repent (Acts 17:30).

4. The Consequences Of Sin

Because Adam disobeyed God, his sin brought with it guilt and condemnation. The words, **"But you may not eat of the tree of the knowledge of good and evil, for in the day that you eat of it you will surely die,"** tell us that the immediate consequence of Adam's sin was death (Genesis 2:17). However, **there are three aspects to death**. The <u>**first aspect**</u> is **spiritual death**, and that is the death spoken of in the words, **"He has given you life, who were dead in trespasses and sins"** (Ephesians 2:1). The <u>**second aspect**</u> is **physical death**, and that is the death spoken of in the words, **"In the sweat of your face you will eat bread, till you return unto the ground; for out of it you were taken: for you are dust, and to dust you will return"** (Genesis 3:19). And, the <u>**third aspect**</u> is **eternal death**, and that is the death spoken of in the words, **"Who will be punished with unending destruction away from the presence of the Lord, and from the glory of His might"** (2Thessalonians 1:9).

The words, **"To the woman He said, I will greatly multiply your sorrow and your conception; in sorrow you will bring forth children; and your desire shall be to your husband, and he will rule over you. And to Adam He said, Because you have hearkened to the voice of your wife, and have eaten of the tree, of which I commanded you, saying, You shall not eat of it: cursed is the ground for your sake; in sorrow you will eat of it all the days of your life. Thorns also and thistles will it bring forth to you; and you will eat the herb of the field,"** tell us that another consequence of Adam's sin was the loss of God's blessing, the curse on creation, suffering and toil (Genesis 3:16-18).

The words, "**Adam lived an hundred and thirty years, and fathered a son in his own likeness, after his image,**" tell us that as a result of sin, Adam's descendants do not bear the image of God, but the image of sinful Adam (Genesis 5:3). And, the words, "**Just as sin entered the world by one man, and death by sin; so death passed upon all men, because all have sinned,**" tell us that as a result of Adam's sin all of his descendants are sinners (Romans 5:12). In fact, if they were not sinners they would never die of natural causes. As it is written, "**I was formed in iniquity; and sinful when my mother conceived me**" (Psalm 51:5).

However, God's words, "**I will put hostility between you and the woman, and between your seed and her seed; it will bruise your head, and you will bruise His heel,**" gave Adam and Eve the same promise of savor (a "seed") that was later given to Abraham (Genesis 3:15). The Apostle Paul tells us that God's promise of a "seed" was the promise of a savior, saying, "**God did not say, And to your seeds, as referring to many; but, And to your seed, referring to one which is Christ**" (Galatians 3:16). "**For the wages of sin is death; but the gift of God is eternal life through Jesus Christ our Lord**" (Romans 6:23). As it is written, "**If death reigned through one man's sin; how much more shall those who receive the abundance of grace and the gift of righteousness reign in life through one man, Jesus Christ. Therefore as through the sin of one judgment came upon all men to condemnation; even so through the righteousness of one the free gift abounds to all men bringing justification and life, for as by one man's disobedience many were made sinners, so by the obedience of one many will be made righteous**" (Romans 5:17-19).

Because sinful men continually make up excuses for their sins, deceive themselves, create false gods, and even deny that God exists rather than repent, Christian theologians need to constantly emphasize the importance of repentance. As it is written, "**God now commands all men every where to repent,**" and "**Repentance and remission of sins should be preached... among all nations**" (Acts 17:30, Luke 24:47).

The words, "**Who show the work of the law written in their hearts, their conscience also bearing witness, and their thoughts the mean while accusing or else excusing one another,**" simply describe what we see in everyday life (Romans 2:15). People are quick to accuse others, while excusing themselves. And, the words, "**Who knowing the judgment of God, that those who commit such things are worthy of death, not only do the same, but have pleasure in those who do them,**" describe the stubborn refusal to admit wrongdoing (Romans 1:32). The words,

"**Knowing the judgment of God**," apply to those millions who refuse to give up their immoral lifestyle. And, the words, "**Have pleasure in those who do them**," apply to the pulpit traitors who condone such wickedness, including those who perform "homosexual marriages".

All who refuse to repent need to know that Jesus will say, "**Depart from me, you cursed, into everlasting fire, prepared for the devil and his angels**" (Matthew 25:41). Nevertheless, warnings of God's judgement need to be tempered with His promise of forgiveness, for without God's assurance of mercy, the terrified sinner may well just try to find a false peace by shutting God out of his mind. The Bible tells us that, "**the goodness of God**" is what leads "**to repentance**," but there must be repentance (Romans 2:4).

While every Christian believer needs to take God's warning of eternal punishment seriously, and should never toy with sin, the words, "**But when we are judged, we are chastened by the Lord, so that we will not be condemned with the world**," tell us that any chastening a believer receives is not an expression of God's wrath, but of His mercy (1Corinthians 11:32). As it is written, "**Blessed is the man whom you chasten, O LORD, and teach from your word**" (Psalm 94:12). "**For the Lord disciplines those He loves**" (Hebrews 12:6). And, the words, "**As many as I love, I rebuke and chasten: therefore be zealous, and repent**," tell us that the reason for God's chastening is to bring us to repentance (Revelations 3:19). Not the false repentance of works righteousness, but **the true repentance that leads one to stop rationalizing sin, stop thinking that God is pleased because of works, and know that it is the forgiveness that is ours in Christ, and that forgiveness alone that cleanses us of all sin**, making us righteousness in the sight of God. As it is written, "**We have redemption through His blood, the forgiveness of sins, according to the riches of His grace**," and "**The blood of Jesus Christ His Son cleanses us of all sin**" (Ephesians 1:7 and 1John 1:7)

Because of what is going on in our society, let me add this thought. If anyone has sinful desires for someone of the opposite sex, or the same sex, those sinful desires need to be suppressed and repented of. A quick prayer might be, "Lord forgive me for wrong thoughts and get them out of my mind". Since God did not create anyone homosexual or bisexual, the claim that some people are born that way is an attempt to excuse sinful thoughts and desires instead of repenting. To all who experience such temptation God says, "**Blessed is the man who fears the Lord at all times: <u>but he who hardens his heart will fall into calamity</u>**" (Proverbs 28:14).

b. Original (Inherent) Sin

1. The Nature Of Original Sin

The words, "**Through the sin of one judgment came upon all men to condemnation**," tell us that Adam's sin did not just result in us having an inclination to sin, but brought judgment and condemnation "upon all men" (Romans 5:18). The words, "**By one man's disobedience many were made sinners**," tell us that we are all sinners because of Adam's "disobedience" (Romans 5:19). The words, "**Behold, I was formed in iniquity; and sinful when my mother conceived me**," tell us that even those in the womb are sinful (Psalm 51:5). And, the words, "**The wages of sin is death**," tell us that if infants were not sinners they would never die of natural causes (Romans 6:23).

The change to man's nature as a result of Adam's sin is itself sin. The words, "**The wicked are estranged from the womb: they go astray as soon as they are born, speaking lies**," tell us wickedness is not the result of bad influence, but is deeply rooted in our nature (Psalm 58:3). The words, "**The heart is deceitful above all things, and desperately wicked: who can know it?**" reveal how Adam's sin has changed our nature (Jeremiah 17:9). The words, "**God saw that the wickedness of man was great in the earth, and that every imagination of the thoughts of his heart was only evil continually**," describe that nature, and tell us that; to a Holy God **evil imaginations and thoughts are sinful** (Genesis 6:5). And, the words, "**Out of the heart proceed evil thoughts, murder, adultery, immorality, theft, false witness, blasphemy**," reveal the fruit of a sinful nature (Matthew 15:19).

The words, "**That which is born of the flesh is flesh**," tell us that we are born with a "**fleshly**" mind (John 3:6). The words, "**The fleshly mind is hostile to God**, for it is not subject to the law of God, nor indeed can be," tell us that as the result of sin, our mind is by nature hostile to God (Romans 8:7). The words, "**I see another law at work in my members, warring against the law of my mind, and making me a prisoner to the law of sin that is in my members**," describes the effect of sin in our nature (Romans 7:23). And, the words, "**Without the shedding of blood there is no forgiveness**," tell us that it is only through the shed blood of Jesus Christ that the wickedness of our nature can be forgiven (Hebrews 9:22). As it is written, "**The blood of Jesus Christ His Son cleanses us of all sin**" (1John 1:7).

The words, "**The son will not suffer for the sins of the father, nor will the father suffer for the sins of the son: the righteousness of the righteous person will be upon him, and the wickedness of the wicked person will be upon him**," tell us that the sentence of death that "passed upon all men" as a result of Adam's sin, is not punishment for Adam's sin, but for the wicked nature passed on to us as a result of Adam's sin (Ezekiel 18:20). And, the words, "**Do not let anyone say when he is tempted, I am tempted by God, for God cannot be tempted with evil, nor does He tempt anyone, but every man is tempted, when he is drawn away by his own lust, and enticed. Then when lust has conceived, it brings forth sin, and when sin is finished, brings forth death,**" tell us that all of the wickedness of men flows from that wicked nature (James 1:13-15).

The words, "**Whoever commits sin is the servant of sin,**" tell us that by choosing to sin the unrepentant place themselves under Satan's control (John 8:34). The words, "**He [Judas] did not say that because he cared for the poor; but because he was a thief, and had the bag, and would take what was put into it,**" tell us that by making excuses for sin Judas allowed Satan to take control of him (John 12:6). The words, "**Jesus then replied, Have not I chosen you twelve, yet one of you is a devil?**" tell us that by giving Satan control of his life Judas became a devil (John 6:70). The words, "**You are of your father the devil, and the lusts of your father you will do,**" tell us that the Pharisees' willingness to excuse sin allowed Satan to take control of them (John 8:44). [See Matt. 26:3-4, Mark 7:7-13, Luke 11:46] And, it is only through faith in Christ that we can escape that bondage (see John 8:31-32).

The words of the angel to Mary, "**The Holy Spirit will come upon you, and the power of the Highest will overshadow you: therefore the Holy One who will be born of you will be called the Son of God,**" tell us that because of His virgin birth, Christ did not inherit a sinful nature, but was "**the Holy One**" from conception (Luke 1:35). At the same time, Mary's words, "**My spirit delights in God my Savior,**" tell us that she was a sinner in need of a savior (Luke 1:47).

2. The Corrupt Mind And Will Of Man

Since man was created without sin, and, therefore, in perfect harmony with God, the words, "**The natural man does not accept the things of the Spirit of God: for they are foolishness to him: and he cannot understand them, because they are spiritually discerned,**" are not talking about man as he was originally created, but man as he is now (1Corinthians 2:14). As a result of the fall, and the corruption it wrought, those without the light of God's Word, "**Walk, in the futility of their mind, Having their understanding darkened, being alienated from the life of God through the ignorance that is in them, because of the blindness of their** heart" (Ephesians 4:17-18). Because of that blindness, **men would rather rationalize their sin than repent**, would rather deny God than seek His mercy, and would rather trust in works than admit that the law condemns them.

The words, **"All who trust in the law are under a curse: for it is written, Cursed is every one who does not continue to do everything that is written in the book of the law,"** and the words, **"There is none righteous, no, not one,"** tell us that the law of God condemns all who trust in it (Galatians 3:10, Romans 3:10). Moreover, the words, **"It is clear that no man is declared righteous in the sight of God by the law,"** tell us that no one can ever escape God's judgment through keeping the law (Galatians 3:11). Still, the sin-blinded heart of man continually leads men to seek God's favor through the law. That blindness exists because **our "heart is deceitful above all things, and desperately wicked"** (Jeremiah 17:9). And, because of that blindness, before God brought us to faith in Christ, we **"were dead in trespasses and sins... walked according to the way of this world, according to the prince of the power of the air, the spirit that now works in the children of disobedience... and were by nature the children of wrath,"** (Ephesians 2:1-3). Nevertheless, God in His mercy sent Christ to die for our sins, and caused the Gospel to be preached in order to open our eyes and turn us, **"From darkness to light, and from the power of Satan to God,"** that we might **"Receive forgiveness of sins"** (Acts 26:18).

The words, **"We do speak a wisdom among the perfected: but not the wisdom of this world, or of the rulers of this world, who will pass away. On the contrary, we speak the wisdom of God in a mystery, even the hidden wisdom that God ordained before the world to our glory. Which none of the rulers of this world knew, for had they known it they would not have crucified the Lord of glory. But as it is written, Eye has not seen, nor ear heard, nor has it entered into the heart of man, the things that God has prepared for those who love Him,"** tell us that the truth of the Gospel cannot be discovered by sinful man, and is alien to the sin-corrupted wisdom of this world (1Corinthians 2:6-9). And, the words, **"Because God, who once commanded light to shine out of darkness, made His light shine in our hearts, to give us the light of the knowledge of the glory of God in the face of Jesus Christ,"** tell us that it is only by the grace of God that we have been delivered from that darkness (2Corinthians 4:6). **"For you were once darkness, but now are light in the Lord: walk as children of light"** (Ephesians 5:8). Therefore, **hold fast to the truth of God's word at all times, "Lest any man take you captive through hollow and deceptive philosophy, after the tradition of men, after the basic principles of this world, and not after Christ... **Do not let any man swindle you out of your reward through a false humility and the worship of angels, intruding into things that he has not seen, vainly puffed up by his fleshly mind**" (Colossians 2:8 and 18).

3. The Cause And Universality Of Original Sin

In understanding original sin, it is important to keep in mind the words, "**God saw every thing that He had made, and, behold, it was very good**," and the words, "**By one man sin entered into the world, and death by sin; and so death passed upon all men, for all have sinned**" (Genesis 1:31, Romans 5:12). Those words tell us that sin is not in our nature because God made us that way, or because of what we are made of, but because our nature has been corrupted. That corruption not only produces blindness and ignorance of the truth, but actively fights against the truth. We find that taught in the words, "**I see another law at work in my members, warring against the law of my mind, and making me a prisoner to the law of sin that is in my members**," and in the words, "**The flesh lusts against the Spirit, and the Spirit against the flesh: and they are opposed to each other**" (Romans 7:23, Galatians 5:17).

The Bible tells us that the cause of sin is not God, who, "**Cannot be tempted with evil, and does not tempt anyone**," but the devil, and our first parents who listened to the devil (James 1:13). The words, "**The serpent deceived Eve through his craftiness**," compared with the words, "**That old serpent, called the Devil, and Satan, who deceives the whole world**," tell us that it was Satan working through the serpent who deceived Eve (2Corinthians 11:3, Revelation 12:9). The words, "**Adam was not the one deceived, but the woman being deceived led in transgression**," tell us Eve's part in man's fall into sin (1Timothy 2:14). And, the words, "**Therefore, just as sin entered the world by one man, and death by sin; so death passed upon all men, because all have sinned**," tell us that it was through the sin of Adam that death entered the world, and all men die because all have sinned (Romans 5:12). And, when the Bible says <u>all</u>, it means **ALL**. The words, "**I was formed in iniquity; and sinful when my mother conceived me**," tell us that the word "ALL" includes infants (Psalm 51:5). And, the words, "**The wages of sin is death**," tell us that if infants were not sinners, they would never die of natural causes (Romans 6:23).

Since this section deals with the universality of original sin, I need to point out again that Christ is the one exception. The words, "**For we do not have a high priest who is unable to sympathize with our weaknesses; but one who was in all points tempted just as we are, yet without sin**," tell us that Christ had no sin (Hebrews

4:15). And, the words, "**The Holy One who will be born of you will be called the Son of God**," tell us that Christ did not inherit a sinful nature, but was without sin "**holy**" from the very beginning (Luke 1:35).

4. The Effects Of Original Sin

The words, "**But of the tree of the knowledge of good and evil, you may not eat of it: for in the day that you eat of it you will surely die**," tell us that death is the primary effect of the first sin (Genesis 2:17). The words, "**She who lives for pleasure is dead while she lives**," tell us that a person can be alive physically, but dead spiritually (1Timothy 5:6). And, the words, "**He has given you life, who were dead in trespasses and sins... when we were dead in sins**," tell us that before we came to faith in Christ we were all dead spiritually (Ephesians 2:1,5). Therefore, one immediate consequence of mankind's first sin was that Adam and Eve died spiritually.

The words, "**By one man sin entered into the world, and death by sin**," and the words, "**And all the days that Adam lived were nine hundred and thirty years: and he died**," tell us that the second effect of the first sin was to begin the aging process that results in physical death (Romans 5:12 and Genesis 5:5). While the words, "**Then He will say to those on His left, Depart from me, you cursed, into everlasting fire**, prepared for the devil and his angels," and the words, "**Who will be punished with unending destruction away from the presence of the Lord, and from the glory of His might**," tell us that, apart from faith in Christ the final effect of original sin will be eternal damnation (Matthew 25:41, 2Thessalonians 1:9).

The words, "**The woman saw that the tree was good for food**," and that fact that Adam and Eve did not die physically until centuries later, tell us that death did not come because the fruit was poison, but because Adam and Eve disobeyed God (Genesis 3:6). The Bible does not tell us why God did not make another commandment the test of Adam and Eve's obedience. Some theologians believe that since the moral law was "written in their hearts" God chose to forbid something that would not appear to them as evil (Romans 2:15). However, when it comes right down to it, only God knows, and where the Bible has not spoken we should never profess ourselves "to be wise" (Romans 1:22).

In addition to all of the sorrows that have come into the world as a consequence of man's sin, **every specific sin that came after the first sin, is part of the effect of that first sin**. The words, "**We are consumed by your anger, and terrified by your fury. You have set our sins before you, our secret sins in the light of your face.**

For all our days ebb away under your wrath: we end our years like a story that is finished," describe the sorrows that have come into the world as a result of man's first sin (Psalm 90:7-9). And, the words, **"From within, out of men's hearts, proceed evil thoughts, adultery, fornication, murder, Theft, greed, malice, deceit, lewdness, envy, slander, pride, foolishness. All these evil things come from within, and defile a man,"** tell us that specific sins are the outgrowth of original [inherent] sin (Mark 7:21-23).

The words, **"You are not a God who takes pleasure in wickedness: nor will evil dwell with you... you hate all who do evil"** tell us that God does not take sin lightly (Psalm 5:4-5). And, the words, **"The LORD tries the righteous: but He hates the wicked and anyone who loves violence,"** tell us that God will not overlook wrongdoing (Psalm 11:5). However, those statements are warnings of God's law, and, **"We know that whatever the law says, it says to those who are under the law... because the knowledge of sin comes by the law"** (Romans 3:19-20). And, God wants us to know our sin, so that we will see our need for His forgiveness, repent, and look to Christ for mercy; for, "**As through the sin of one judgment came upon all men to condemnation; even so through the righteousness of one the free gift abounds to all men bringing justification and life**" (Romans 5:18).

c. Actual (Specific) Sins

1. The Nature Of Actual Sin

Since we have a "**Nature that is corrupt according to deceitful lusts**" actual sin consists of every transgression of the divine Law in desire, thought, word, and deed, that a heart "**Deceitful above all things and desperately wicked,**" produces in us (Ephesians 4:22, Jeremiah 17:9)

The words, **"Out of the heart proceed evil thoughts, murder, adultery, immorality, theft, false witness, blasphemy,"** tell us that sinful thoughts, words and deeds are evil in the sight of God (Matthew 15:19). And, the words, **"I am telling you, that whoever looks on a woman to lust after her has already committed adultery with her in his heart,"** condemn evil thoughts in no uncertain terms (Matthew 5:28).

The words, **"Who knowing the judgment of God, that those who commit such things are worthy of death, not only do the same, but have pleasure in those who do them,"** condemn those who, even without engaging in certain sins, encourage and take pleasure in those who do commit them, [and that includes those who excuse homosexuality] (Romans 1:32). And, the words, "**Whoever knows what is right, and does not do it, sins,**" condemn all who fail to do what is right (James 4:17).

The words, "**Abraham journeyed from there toward the south country, and settled between Kadesh and Shur, and lived for a time in Gerar. And Abraham said of Sarah his wife, She is my sister: and Abimelech king of Gerar sent, and took Sarah, but God came to Abimelech in a dream by night, and said to him, Behold, you are a dead man, because of the woman that you have taken; for she is a man's wife... restore the man's wife; for he is a prophet, and he will pray for you, and you will live: but if you do not restore her, know that you will surely die, you, and all who are yours,**" tell us that God condemns sins that we are not even aware of (Genesis 20:1-3 and 7). However, the words, "**And that servant, who knew his lord's will, and did not get ready, and did not do what his master wanted, will be beaten with many lashes. But the one who does not know, and committed deeds worthy of flogging, will be beaten with few lashes. For to whom much is given, much will be required: and from one who has been entrusted with much, more will be asked,**" tell us that God punishes willful sin far more harshly than sins of ignorance (Luke 12:47-48). And, the words, "**Blessed is the man to whom the LORD does not impute iniquity, and in whose spirit there is no self-deception,**" tell us that God does not impute sin to those who do not rationalize sin, deceiving themselves by making excuses for sin, but humbly look to Christ for mercy (Psalm 32:2, Romans 4:6).

The words, "**The works of the flesh are obvious, which are; Adultery, fornication, sexual filthiness, sensuality,**" refer to actual sins as "works of the flesh" (Galatians 5:19). The words, "**Have no fellowship with the unfruitful works of darkness, but rather reprove them,**" refer to actual sins as "works of darkness" (Ephesians 5:11). The words, "**Do not lie to each other, seeing that you have put off the old man with his deeds,**" refer to actual sins as the deeds of "the old man" (Colossians 3:9). The words, "**For that just man while living among them day after day, felt his righteous soul tormented by the lawless deeds he saw and heard,**" refer to actual sins as "lawless deeds" (2Peter 2:8). And, the words, "**How much more will the blood of Christ, who through the eternal Spirit offered himself without blemish to God, cleanse your conscience from dead works to serve the living God?**" refer to actual sins as "dead works" (Hebrews 9:14).

2. The Causes Of Actual Sin

Every specific sin flows from a heart that is corrupt according to deceitful lusts, lusts that reflect the nature of Satan. And, those lusts are inflamed, encouraged and promoted by Satan, the world, and our own flesh.

The words, "**It is no longer something that I do, but sin that dwells in me,**" tell us that the cause of actual sin is our corrupt nature (Romans 7:17). The words, "**Put off everything having to do with your former way of life, the old nature which is corrupt according to the deceitful lusts,**" identify sinful lusts with the corruption in our nature (Ephesians 4:22). The words, "**You are of your father the devil, and the lusts of your father you will do,**" tell us that those lusts reflect the will of Satan (John 8:44). And, the words, "**I was formerly a blasphemer, and a persecutor, and violent: but I was shown mercy, because I did it ignorantly in unbelief,**" describe the spiritual ignorance that results from the sin within us (1Timothy 1:13).

The words, "**And while Peter was below in the courtyard, one of the maids of the high priest came... and said, You were also with Jesus of Nazareth. But he denied it,**" give us an example of fear leading to sin (Mark 14:66-68), as do the words, "**For before certain men came from James, he would eat with the Gentiles: but once they came, he withdrew and separated himself, fearing those who were of the circumcision.**" (Galatians 2:12). And, the words, "**Upon hearing this, everyone in the synagogue became furious, and got up, and pushed Him out of the city, and brought him to the brow of the hill on which their city was built, in order to throw Him down the cliff,**" give us an example of anger leading to sin (Luke 4:28-29).

However, the words, "**Nor is there salvation in any other,**" make it clear that neither our ignorance, nor our passions are an excuse for sin (Acts 4:12). The apostle Paul sinned in ignorance [see 1Tim. 1:13], yet the words, "**Christ Jesus came into the world to save sinners; of whom I am the worst,**" tell us that he was saved through faith in Christ (1Timothy 1:15). So ignorance is no excuse. The words, "**Can the Ethiopian change his skin, or a leopard his spots? If so you might be able to do what is good, you who in whom evil is ingrained,**" are not being critical of the skin of an Ethiopian or the spots of a leopard, but are telling us that it is just as impossible for us to be sinless as it is for us to change our skin (Jeremiah 13:23).

The words, "**You formerly walked according to the way of this world, according to the prince of the power of the air, the spirit that now works in the children of disobedience,**" tell us that Satan is at work in those who are not saved (Ephesians 2:2). The words, "**Then Satan stood up against Israel, and provoked**

David to number Israel," and the words, "**The Lord said, Simon, Simon, Satan has desired to have you, that he may sift you as wheat,**" tell us that Satan works to seduce believers (1Chronicals 21:1, Luke 22:31). And, the words, "**He turned, and said to Peter, Get behind me, Satan: you are tempting me to sin: for you are not thinking as God thinks, but as men think,**" tell us that Satan sometimes uses other people to tempt us (Matthew 16:23).

The words, "**Make note of those who cause divisions and *soul destroying* offences contrary to the doctrine that you have learned; and avoid them, for such people are not serving our Lord Jesus Christ, but their own belly,**" tell us that Satan tempts us through those who spread false doctrine and cause division (Romans 16:17-18). The words, "**Their teaching will spread like gangrene,**" warn us against those who teach falsely (2Timothy 2:17). And, the words, "**Do not be deceived, bad company undermines good behavior,**" warn us against keeping company with those who tempt us (1Corinthians 15:33).

The words, "**The things that the Gentiles sacrifice are sacrificed to devils, and not to God: and I do not want you to have fellowship with devils,**" tell us that Satan is behind all false religion, and those who worship false gods are worshipping devils (1Corinthians 10:20). The words, "**There were also false prophets among the people, just as there will be false teachers among you, who will privately introduce damnable heresies, even denying the Lord who bought them, bringing swift destruction upon themselves. And many will follow their destructive ways; and because of them the way of truth will be portrayed as evil. And in their covetousness they will use deceptive words to swindle you: their condemnation has not been idle all this time, and their damnation is not asleep,**" warn us of the danger posed by those who teach contrary to the Word of God (2Peter 2:1-3). And, the words, "**They changed the truth of God into a lie, and worshipped and served the creation more than the Creator... For that reason God gave them up to vile affections: for even their women exchanged the natural use for that which is contrary to nature: And likewise also the men, leaving the natural use of the woman, burned in their lust one toward another; men with men doing what is shameful, and receiving in themselves that recompense of their error that was fitting,**" tell us that God draws all who worship Him to repentance, but gives those who reject Him up to serve their own degenerate lusts (Romans 1:25-27).

The words, "**I form light, and create darkness: I make peace, and create disaster: I the LORD do all these things,**" tell us that all of the disasters this world experiences are a judgment on sin (Isaiah 45:7). However, God is at work in all He does. Therefore, even those disasters can bring His mercy. For example, if a tank is coming toward a home, and a woman inside it is praying "God save me, God save me," she is calling on God to deliver her from evil. Furthermore, the words, **"The Lord disciplines those He loves, and scourges every son that He receives,"** tell us that God's chastening of believers is that of a loving father (Hebrews 12:6). And, the words, **"We know that all things work together for good for those who love God, for those who are the called according to his purpose,"** assure us that all we suffer works together for our good (Romans 8:28). As it is written, **"We must through much tribulation enter into the kingdom of God"** (Acts 14:22).

3. The Doctrine Of Offense

Just as it is a sin to do evil, the words, **"He who bids him God speed is a partaker of his evil deeds,"** tell us that it is a sin to bless those who do evil, for those who do so are encouraging them to do evil. And, when the Bible warns against giving offence, it is a warning against doing or saying things that encourage others to do evil, lead them to sin, harden their hearts, or result in their damnation.

The words, **"Make note of those who cause divisions and offences contrary to the doctrine that you have learned; and avoid them,"** tell us to avoid associating with those who cause division and offence (Romans 16:17). Christ's words, **"It is inevitable that offences will occur: but woe to him, through whom they come! It would be better for him to be thrown into the sea, with a millstone tied around his neck, than for him to cause one of these little ones to fall away,"** are a stern warning against giving offence; and the words, **"Cause one of these little ones to fall away,"** apply to every teacher and professor who ridicules the Christian faith (Luke 17:1-2). [See Matthew 18:6 and Mark 9:42.] What Christ said about Judas, **"Woe to that man by whom the Son of man is betrayed! It would be better for that man if he had never been born,"** applies to all who turn people away from Christ (Mark 14:21).

While encouraging others to sin or hardening them in unbelief is a serious matter, the Bible speaks of another way of giving offence. That is giving offence by leading others to go against their conscience. We find that in the words, **"Receive him who is weak in faith, but not to doubtful disputations. For one is confident that he may eat all things: another, who is weak, eats only vegetables... There is nothing unclean of itself, but if anyone regards something as unclean, then for him it is unclean. But if your brother is grieved because of what you eat, you are not walking according to love. Do not destroy with your food, him for whom**

Christ died. Do not allow your good be spoken of as evil... He who doubts is under condemnation if he eats, for his eating is not of faith: for whatever is not of faith is sin" (Romans 14:1-2, 14-16 and 23).

However, there is a difference between avoiding something perfectly harmless because it may give offence, and being told that you must avoid it. For example, if someone from a Jewish background comes to faith in Christ, but is troubled in conscience by the thought of eating ham, we should not push him to go contrary to his conscience. At the same time, if someone in the congregation begins to insist that everyone must give up ham, then he is a false teacher, and must be dealt with as such. In that situation the words, "**Do not let anyone judge you by what you eat, or drink, or in regard to a holyday, or the new moon, or the Sabbath day,**" apply (Colossians 2:16).

In Scripture we also see a distinction between giving offence, and taking offence. If we do something wrong, and someone else follows our example we have given offence. But if we are doing something that is not wrong (such as eating ham) and someone who sees us takes offence, then they are in the wrong. The Pharisees took offence at the words of Jesus when He said, "**It is not what goes into the mouth that defiles a man; but that which comes out of the mouth, that defiles a man,**" we know they took offence because the Bible says, "**His disciples came to him, and asked, Do you know the Pharisees were offended, when they heard you say that?**" (Matthew 15:11-12).

There is another aspect of taking offence, and that is those who take offence at the Gospel. Regarding such offence, Jesus said, "**Blessed is he, who does not take offence at me**" (Matthew 11:6). The words, "**We preach Christ crucified, a stumbling block to the Jews,**" speak of Christ as a "stumbling block" (1Corinthians 1:23). The words, "**Israel, that followed after the law of righteousness, has not attained to the law of righteousness. Why? Because they did not seek it through faith, but through the works of the law, for they stumbled at that stumbling-stone. As it is written, Behold, I lay in Zion a stumbling-stone and rock of offence: and whoever believes on Him will not be put to shame,**" Use, "stumbling-stone" and "rock of offence" as synonyms, and reveal that the Jews were offended at Jesus because they sought righteousness through the Law (Romans 9:31-33). The words, "**He [the LORD of hosts] will be a stone of stumbling and a rock of offence, and a snare and a trap for the inhabitants of Jerusalem,**" reveal that Christ [the rock of offence] is God (Isaiah 8:14). And, the words, "**Behold, I lay a stone in Zion, a chosen and precious cornerstone: and he who believes on Him will never be put to shame,**" assure all who trust in Christ that they will never be condemned (1Peter 2:6).

4. The Doctrine Of Obduration

The word "obdurate" not only describes hardness, but one who is stubbornly wicked, intractable, and unbending in their refusal to repent. We see such a refusal to repent described by the words, "**Even though He had done so many miracles in their presence, they did not believe in Him**" (John 12:37).

The words, "**He [Judas] did not say that because he cared for the poor; but because he was a thief, and had the bag, and would take what was put into it**," tell us that Judas had a habit of hardening his heart, by excusing his own wrongdoing (John 12:6). The words, "**Satan entered into Judas called Iscariot, who was one of the twelve**," tell us that because Judas was unrepentant Satan was able to enter into him, hardening his heart even more (Luke 22:3). And, the words, "**He threw the pieces of silver down in the temple, and left, and after leaving hung himself**," tell us that because Satan was in control, even when Judas was sorry for what he did he hardened himself more [to excuse self murder] instead of seeking forgiveness (Matthew 27:5). That fact tells us that even though Judas was sorry, his sorrow was not from God. "**For godly sorrow results in repentance leading to salvation, not regret: but the sorrow of this world brings death**" (2Corinthians 7:10).

Whenever men hear the Word of God, (whether it is through preaching, conscience, or some other source) and close their mind to what it says, either by excusing their sin or shutting it out of their mind, they are hardening their heart. The words of Stephen, "**You stiffnecked and uncircumcised in heart and ears, you always resist the Holy Ghost: as your fathers did, so do you**," speak of men hardening their own hearts in resistance to the Holy Ghost (Acts 7:51). And, the Bible tells us that those who heard Stephen's words "**Were cut to the heart and furious, and they gnashed their teeth because of him**" (Acts 7:54). Now, when the Bible tells us that they were, "cut to the heart," it is telling us that they were convicted of their sin. However, instead of repenting they became, "furious, and they gnashed their teeth," hardening their hearts in adamant refusal to admit their sin, repent and seek forgiveness.

When God's Word places someone under conviction, God is working through that Word to bring them to repentance. However, those who harden their hearts time after time can bring upon themselves God's judgment, which results in God withdrawing His gift of repentance. The words, "**With gentleness instructing those who oppose their own interest; in the hope that God will give them repentance bringing them to a realization of the truth**," tell us that repentance is a gift of God (2Timothy 2:25). The words, "**They [the scribes and Pharisees] do not do what they say. For they bind heavy burdens that are hard to bear, and lay them on men's** shoulders; but they will not move them with one of their fingers," reveal that even though the Pharisees warned others to keep the law, they made up excuses to get around it. (Matthew 23:2-4). The words, "**He [Jesus] said to them, You completely invalidate the commandment of God, in order to keep your tradition. For Moses said, Honor your father and mother; and, Anyone who curses his father or mother, let him be put to death. But you say, If a man will say to his father or mother, It is Corban, that is a gift, by which you might profit by me; he shall be free,**" give us an example of the kind of excuses they used (Mark 7:9-11). And, the words, "**He has blinded their eyes, and hardened their hearts; that they should not see with their eyes, nor understand with their hearts, and repent and turn to me, that I should heal them,**" speak of God hardening their hearts as a judgment on them (John 12:40). But, even though the Bible speaks of this hardening as an act of God, it is the devil that carries it out. God simply gives them up to his control. As it is written, "**The minds of those who do not believe have been blinded by the god of this world, that the light of the glorious gospel of Christ, who is the image of God, might not reach them**" (2Corinthians 4:4).

The words, "**God also gave them up to uncleanness through the lusts of their own hearts, to dishonor their own bodies between themselves, for they changed the truth of God into a lie, and worshipped and served the creation more than the Creator, who is blessed forever. Amen. For this cause God gave them up to vile affections: for even their women exchanged the natural use for that which is contrary to nature,**" speak of God rejecting those who have rejected Him (Romans 1:24-26). As long as one worships God, even without understanding the Gospel, the Holy Spirit is at work stirring up their conscience as a call to repentance. And, their conscience keeps them from committing many sins. But, when they turn to a false god, God gives them up.

The words, "**I will harden Pharaoh's heart, and multiply my signs and my wonders in the land of Egypt. But Pharaoh will not listen to you, then I will lay my hand upon Egypt, and bring the multitudes of my people, the children of Israel, out of the land of Egypt by great judgments,**" are speaking of a Pharaoh who had already hardened his heart against God by his devotion to false gods (Exodus 7:3). Therefore, the words "**I will harden Pharaoh's heart**" are not telling us that God hardened Pharaoh against salvation. All they say is that God hardened him against letting God's people go. After the first plague, Pharaoh could have told the Israelites to go. But, God continually hardened Pharaoh so He could reveal His power. And, although it is doubtful, after seeing that power displayed Pharaoh could have rejected the false gods of Egypt. At least, some of the Egyptian people may have accepted the God of Israel. We do not know, but God loves mercy and He does not cause anyone to be damned. Even though those who are saved are saved by grace alone, those who are lost are lost by their own fault. [Compare John 6:44 with Matthew 23:37.]

5. The Scriptural Doctrine Of Temptation

While the Bible tells us that, "**God cannot be tempted with evil, nor does He tempt anyone,**" it also tells us that God sometimes tests His children; but when He does so it is always done in love, and for their benefit (James 1:13).

The words, "**You, O God, have tested us: you have tried us, as silver is tried... but you brought us out into a place of plenty,**" speak of the entire nation of Israel being tried during their sojourn in Egypt (Psalm 66:10, 12). Yet as awful as that sojourn was, it welded them together and laid the foundation for their salvation as well as ours.

The words, "**God tested Abraham, and said to him... Take now your son, your only son Isaac, whom you love, and go into the land of Moriah, and offer him there for a burnt offering... And Abraham said to his young men, Wait here with the donkey; and I and the lad will go yonder and worship, and return again to you,**" speak of God's test of Abraham (Genesis 22:1,2,5). However, those who think this test was nothing more than a test of obedience miss the entire point. When they read the words, "**I and the lad will... return again to you,**" they assume that Abraham was lying. But, nothing could be further from the truth. The words, "**By faith Abraham, when he was tried, offered up Isaac: and he that had received the promises offered up his only begotten son, Of whom it was said, That in Isaac shall thy seed be called, believing that God was able to raise him up, even from the dead,**" tell us that Abraham acted on "faith," believing that God would "raise him up, even from the dead" (Hebrews 11:17-19). In other words, Abraham believed that Isaac was the promised "seed" that would die and rise again. And, through that test, God not only clarified and strengthened Abraham's faith, but uses Abraham's faith today to point us to Christ.

The words, "**If a prophet, or a dreamer of dreams, arises among you and gives you a sign or a wonder, And the sign or the wonder of which he spoke comes to pass, and then he says, Let us go after other gods, which you have not known, and let us serve them, you must not listen to the words of that prophet, or that dreamer of dreams: for the LORD your God is testing you, to know whether you love the LORD your God with all your heart and with all your soul," warn us not to listen to anyone who venerates other gods (Deuteronomy 13:1). The words, **"There must also be heresies among you, to reveal those who are approved by God,"** tell us that such tests reveal "those who are approved by God" (1Corinthians 11:19). And, one such heresy is Darwinism.

When it comes to the temptation to do evil, the words **"God cannot be tempted with evil, nor does He tempt anyone,"** make it clear that such temptation never comes from God, **"But every man is tempted, when he is drawn away by his own lust, and enticed"**(James 1:13-14). However, because lust can be initiated and amplified by the devil and the sinful world around us, we speak of the **world, the flesh and the devil** as the source of temptation.

The words, **"The Spirit led Jesus up into the desert to be tempted by the devil,"** and the words, **"Be sober, be vigilant; because your adversary the devil, prowls around like a roaring lion, looking for someone to devour,"** speak of temptation by the devil (Matthew 4:1, 1Peter 5:8).

The words, **"Do not love the world, or anything in the world. If any man loves the world, the love of the Father is not in him. For all that is in the world, the lust of the flesh, the lust of the eyes, and the pride of life, is not of the Father, but is of the world. And the world passes away, as do its lusts: but he who does the will of God remains forever,"** and the words, **"Those who are determined to be rich fall into temptation and a snare, and into many foolish and harmful desires, that plunge men into ruin and destruction,"** speak of the world as a source of temptation (1John 2:15-17, 1Timothy 6:9).

The words, **"Every man is tempted, when he is drawn away by his own lust, and enticed,"** and the words, **"Do not deprive one another, except by mutual consent for a time, that you may give yourselves to fasting and prayer; and come together again, that Satan may not tempt you through your lack of restraint,"** speak of lust as a source of temptation (James 1:14, 1Corinthians 7:5).

In all temptation it is important to look to God for the strength to resist and overcome. As it is written, **"Let him who thinks that he is standing take heed lest he fall. You have not experienced any temptation other than that which is common to man: but God who is faithful, will not allow you to be tempted beyond what you can bear; but when you are tempted, he will also provide a way out, giving you the ability to bear it"** (1Corinthians 10:12-13).

The words, **"The Lord said, Simon, Simon, Satan has desired to have you... But I have prayed for you, that your faith may not fail,"** tell us that Christ prayed for Simon so that he would be delivered from evil (Luke 22:31-32). And, we pray for the same deliverance whenever we pray the words of the Lord's Prayer, **"Lead us not into temptation, but deliver us from evil"** (Matthew 6:13). Therefore, **"Watch and pray, lest you enter into temptation"** (Mark 14:38). Knowing that, **"We do not have a high priest who is unable to sympathize with our weaknesses; but one who was in all points tempted just as we are, yet without sin"** (Hebrews 4:15). For He **"Knows how to deliver the godly from temptation, while keeping the wicked under punishment for the day of judgment"** (2Peter 2:9).

6. The Classification Of Actual Sins

Our classification of sins should never be used to excuse wrongdoing, but to reveal God's righteousness and our need for forgiveness in Christ. As believers we also need to train our conscience, so that we do not take sin lightly, excuse it, or delude ourselves into thinking that we need no forgiveness, or that we can earn God's favor.

Job asked, **"How can man be righteous before God?"** (Job 9:2). And, the Bible's answer to that question is that, **"No flesh will ever be justified [declared righteous] in God's sight by the deeds of the law: because the knowledge of sin comes by the law"** (Romans 3:20). Nevertheless, because, **"The heart is deceitful above all things, and desperately wicked,"** it is easy for men to blind themselves to their own faults, thinking that they are righteous when God says that they are not (Jeremiah 17:9).

The words, **"Watch and pray, that you do not enter into temptation: the spirit indeed is willing, but the flesh is weak,"** should remind us of our need to think before we speak or act (Matthew 26:41). And, the words, **"Let him who thinks that he is standing take heed lest he fall,"** warn us of our need for God's help in dealing with temptation (1Corinthians 10:12).

The words, **"Since we have these promises, dearly beloved, let us cleanse ourselves from everything that defiles body and soul, following holiness to its goal in the fear of God,"** make it clear that we should never twist God's promise of forgiveness in Christ into an excuse to sin, but should "cleanse ourselves from everything that defiles" (2Corinthians 7:1). And, the words, **"Seeing that we are a part of such a great company of martyrs, let us lay aside every weight, and the sin that so easily entangles us, and let us run with patience the race that is set before us, looking to Jesus the author and finisher of our faith; who for the joy set before Him endured the cross, indifferent to its shame, and sat down at the right hand of the throne of God,"** make it clear that we are not alone in our struggle against temptation and persecution, but are one with all believers who have gone before us, and with Christ who suffered for us (Hebrews 12:1-2).

The False Claim That All Sins Are the Same

One of the great heresies of our age is the claim that no one sin is greater than any other. While it is true that every unforgiven sin (no matter how small it seems) will bring damnation; that fact is being twisted around to excuse willful and unrepentant behavior. More than once, I have encountered people who, when confronted with their sin, say, "sin is sin" arguing that since we are all sinners they are no worse than anyone else. Nevertheless they are wrong, and the following passages tell us that they are wrong.

The words, "**If anyone sees his brother commit a sin that is not unto death, he shall ask, and God will give him life for those who do not sin unto death. There is a sin unto death: I am not saying that he should pray for it,**" tell us that there is a difference between a sin that is "unto death" and sin that is not (1John 5:16).

The words, "**Jesus answered, You would not have any power over me at all, unless it was given to you from above: therefore he who delivered me to you has the greater sin,**" tell us that God regards some sins as greater than others (John 19:11).

The words, "**Keep your servant back from presumptuous sins; let them not have dominion over me: then I will be upright, and I will be innocent of the great transgression,**" warn against "presumptuous sins" (Psalm 19:13).

The words, "**If we sin willfully or deliberately after we have received the knowledge of the truth, no sacrifice for sins remains, But only a fearful expectation of judgment and raging fire, that will devour the enemies of God,**" give a stern warning to all who think that they can harden themselves in unrepentance and never have to answer for it (Hebrews 10:26-27).

And, the words, "**I wrote to you in my letter not to associate with those who are sexually immoral: Not meaning that you must cut off all contact with the immoral people of this world, or the covetous, or extortioners, or idolaters; for in that case you would have to leave the world. But I am now writing you not to associate with anyone who calls himself a brother but is sexually immoral, or covetous, or an idolater, or a reviler, or a drunkard, or a swindler; do not even eat with such a man,**" draw a clear line between those who have a repentant heart and the unrepentant (1Corinthians 5:9-11).

Voluntary and Involuntary Sins

The words, "**You shall appoint cities to be cities of refuge for you; that the slayer, who kills any person unintentionally, may** flee there," recognize the fact that some sins are unintentional (Numbers 35:11). Likewise, the words, "**Abraham said of Sarah his wife, She is my sister: and Abimelech king of Gerar sent, and took Sarah. But God came to Abimelech in a dream by night, and said to him, <u>Behold, you are a dead man</u>, because of the woman that you have taken; for she is a man's wife. But Abimelech had not come near her**," also speak of unintentional sin, however, the words "Behold, you are a dead man" tell us that the fact a sin is unintentional is not an excuse. God condemns all sins (Genesis 20:2-4).

The words of the Apostle Paul, "**I was formerly a blasphemer, and a persecutor, and violent: but I was shown mercy, because I did it ignorantly in unbelief**," tell us that his persecution of Christians was an unintentional sin (1Timothy 1:13). However, his words, "**Christ Jesus came into the world to save sinners; of whom I am the worst**," tell us that without forgiveness in Christ, unintentional sins still merit God's condemnation and wrath (1Timothy 1:15). In contrast the words, "**He [Judas] was a thief, and had the bag, and would take what was put into it**," tell us that Judas was doing what he knew to be wrong (John 12:6).

When the Bible describes Peter's denial of Christ, saying, "**And the Lord turned, and looked at Peter, and Peter remembered the words of the Lord, how He had told him, Before the cock crows, you will deny me three times. And Peter went out, and <u>wept bitterly</u>**," the words "wept bitterly" tell us that Peter's sin was a sin of weakness, not a sin of intent (Luke 22:61-62). What Peter did was still a sin. However, the words, "**Blessed is the man to whom the Lord will not impute sin**," tell us that unintentional sins are not imputed to those who trust in Christ (Romans 4:8). In contrast, the words, "**David did what was right in the eyes of the LORD, and did not turn aside from any thing that he commanded him all the days of his life, except only in the matter of Uriah the Hittite**," tell us that when David sinned willfully in the matter of Uriah, that sin was imputed to David (1Kings 15:5). And, the words, "**David said to Nathan, I have sinned against the LORD. And Nathan said to David, The LORD has also put away your sin; you will not die**," tell us that David's sin in the matter of Uriah was not forgiven until he repented (2Samuel 12:13). There are a number of passages in the Psalms that show us that David's repentance was sincere. However, because of that sin **David lost the blessing of God that had been on his life and home prior to that sin**.

At this point we need to make a distinction between voluntary sins and willful sins. Peter surely knew that he was lying when he denied that he knew Christ [see Luke 22:55-62]. So his sin was voluntary, and without forgiveness it would have sent him to hell. Yet it was far different from David's sin. Nevertheless, the difference does not lie in the magnitude of the sin, "**For whoever keeps the whole law, yet fails in one point, is guilty of all**" (James 2:10). The difference lies in the hardness of the heart. When Peter lied about knowing Christ, he acted impulsively and was sorry for it. David hardened his heart many times before and after committing adultery. He hardened his heart when the thought first came to him. He hardened his heart when he sent for Bathsheba. He hardened his heart when he found out she was married. He hardened his heart when he tried to get her in bed. At each of those points he could have stopped, but he did not. The words, "**If we sin willfully or deliberately after we have received the knowledge of the truth, no sacrifice for sins remains,**" and the words, "**Her guests are in the depths of hell,**" tell us that if David had died while he was in bed with Bathsheba he would have gone to hell (Hebrews 10:26, Proverbs 9:18). God kept David from losing his salvation, but He kept him by bringing him to repentance, not by letting him sin.

[NOTE: The words, "<u>**Walk in the Spirit, and you will not fulfill the lust of the flesh, for the flesh lusts against the Spirit, and the Spirit against the flesh: and they are opposed to each other: so that <u>you cannot do the things that you would</u>**</u>," tell us that before David sinned he had lost the Holy Spirit's help (Galatians 5:16-17). He may have lost it because he began to think too highly of himself. If a person begins to think that God is pleased with him because of his own righteousness, the Holy Spirit cannot help him to resist sin without helping him to deceive himself.]

Sins of Commission and of Omission

The words, "**Whoever knows what is right, and does not do it, sins,**" are the basis for our distinction between sins of commission and sins of omission (James 4:17). Sins of commission involve doing what God has forbidden. Since God has said, "You shall not kill. You shall not commit adultery. You shall not steal. You shall not bear false witness against thy neighbor. You shall not covet etc.," those who do such things commit sin (Exodus 20:13-17). On the other hand, sins of omission involve failing to do something we should. One example is found in the words, "**Whoever stops his ears at the cry of the poor, will also cry out, but will not be heard**" (Proverbs 21:13). Therefore, we need God's forgiveness, not only for what we have done wrong, but also when we fail to do right.

Sins Against God, Against Our Neighbor, And Against Self

The words, "**You shall love the Lord your God with all your heart, and with all your soul, and with all your mind. This is the first and greatest commandment,**" specifically condemn all sins against the first table of the Ten Commandments as sins against God (Matthew 22:37-38). Nevertheless, the words, "**There is none greater in this house than I; neither has he kept back any thing from me but you, because you are his wife: how then can I do this great wickedness, and sin against God?**" tell us that those who commit adultery are also sinning against God (Genesis 39:9). And, the words, "**The children rebelled against me: they did not follow my law, or keep my instruction**," make it clear that every violation of God's Law is a sin against God (Ezekiel 20:21).

Now, the second table of the Ten Commandments is summarized in the words, "**You shall love your neighbor as yourself,**" and those who violate it sin against their neighbor (Matthew 22:39). However, the words, "**Flee from sexual immorality. All other sins that a man commits are outside his body; but he who sins sexually sins against his own body,**" (1Corinthians 6:18). Tell us that those who sin sexually not only sin against God and their neighbor, but also against their own body. Nevertheless, the words, "**Against you, you only, have I sinned, and done this evil in your sight: so you are right when you pass sentence, and blameless when you judge,**" were spoken by David after he committed adultery, and they make it clear that a sin against our own body is not a private matter, but a sin against God who made it (Psalm 51:4).

Grievous and Less Grievous Sins

The words, "**All who trust in the law are under a curse: for it is written, Cursed is every one who does not continue to do everything that is written in the book of the law,**" tell us that every violation of God's law is rebellion against God (Galatians 3:10). And the words, "**Whoever keeps the whole law, yet fails in one point, is guilty of all**," tell us that every unforgiven sin, no matter how small it seems to us will bring damnation (James 2:10). At the same time, the words, "**Jesus answered, You would not have any power over me at all, unless it was given to you from above: therefore he who delivered me to you has the greater sin,**" tell us that God sees some sins as greater than others (John 19:11).

The words, "**Moreover your little ones, which you said would be a prey, and your children, who in that day had no knowledge between good and evil, they will go in there, and I will give it to them, and they will own it,**" and the words, "**That servant, who knew his lord's will, and did not get ready, and did not do what his master wanted, will be beaten with many lashes. But the one who does not know, and committed deeds worthy of flogging, will be beaten with few lashes,**" tell us that God sees willful sin as more grievous than sins of ignorance (Deuteronomy 1:39, Luke 12:47). Nevertheless, the words, "**If there had been a law given that could have given life, righteousness** truly would have been by the law," tell us that when it comes to salvation, ignorance of the Law is no excuse (Galatians 3:21). If it was God would have never sent Christ to the cross.

The words, "**Whatever the law says, it says to those who are under the law: that every mouth may be stopped, and all the world may become guilty before God**," tell us that no one is righteous in the sight of God, all are guilty (Romans 3:19). And, the words, "**He who believes on Him [Christ] is not condemned: but he who does not believe is condemned already, because he has not believed on the name of the only begotten Son of God**," tell us that only those who trust in Christ will escape God's condemnation (John 3:18-19). Therefore, unbelief is the most grievous sin of all.

Sins unto Death and Sins That are Not Imputed

No one who sins willfully is truly sorry for his sin. And, **it is impossible for someone who wants to be a sinner to want to be delivered from sin** for those two wants are contradictory. The words, "**With gentleness instructing those who oppose their own interest; in the hope that God will give them repentance bringing them to a realization of the truth**," tell us that repentance is a gift of God (2Timothy 2:25). However, because repentance without faith is incomplete and cannot save anyone; **true repentance, the kind of repentance that comes from God, includes both contrition and faith**. Compare the words, "**God will not despise a heart that is broken and contrite [sorry for sin]**," with the words, "**Without faith it is impossible to please God**" (Psalm 51:17, Hebrews 11:6). Those words tell us that faith and contrition [sorrow for sin] go hand in hand. Therefore, when the Bible says, "**If anyone sees his brother commit a sin that is not unto death, he shall ask, and God will give him life for those who do not sin unto death. There is a sin unto death: I am not saying that he should pray for it**," we know that a "sin unto death" must be a willful sin, a sin that the perpetrator is not sorry for (1John 5:16).

Some think that the "sin unto death" spoken of by John is the sin of "**blasphemy against the Holy Ghost**," and that truly would be a sin unto death (see Matthew 12:31). I will deal with that sin later. However, the fact that Paul called for an unrepentant man to be delivered, "**Unto Satan for the destruction of the flesh**," tells me that man was guilty of a sin unto death (1Corinthians 5:5). For that reason, the words, "**The law is good, if one uses it lawfully; Understanding this, that the law is not meant for a righteous man, but for those who are lawless and rebellious, for the ungodly and sinful, for the irreverent and profane, for those who strike or kill their fathers or mothers, for murders, For those who sin sexually, for sodomites, for kidnapers and slave traders, for liars and perjurers, and for any other thing that is contrary to**

sound teaching," tell me that by committing the sins just listed the perpetrators of such sins place themselves back under the condemnation of the Law (1Timothy 1:8-10). And, sins that place one back under the condemnation of the Law are sins unto death, for the Law brings only death (Rom. 8:2). So if the perpetrator of such sins is unrepentant, the congregation has a responsibility to, **"Deliver such a one unto Satan for the destruction of the flesh that the spirit may be saved in the day of the Lord Jesus"** (1Cor. 5:5).

The idea that once a man comes to faith he can willfully engage in sin and still be saved is straight out of hell. Just as God brings us to faith solely by His grace, He keeps us in faith solely by His grace (1Peter 1:5). However, the words, **"The flesh lusts against the Spirit, and the Spirit against the flesh: and these are contrary the one to the other: so that you cannot do the things that you would,"** tell us that God keeps us from falling by keeping us repentant, not by letting us sin (Galatians 5:17).

In contrast, no sin is ever imputed to those who have a repentant heart; those who like David in his youth walk **"In integrity of heart, and in uprightness,"** trusting in the forgiveness that is ours in Christ (1Kings 9:4). In fact, it is only to those who so trust in Christ that the words, **"Blessed is the man to whom the Lord will not impute sin"** apply (Romans 4:8). That does not mean that we have no sin. On the contrary, the Bible tells us that, **"All have sinned, and come short of the glory of God"** (Romans 3:23). However, **"The righteousness of God apart from the law," does not consist of more laws, but of forgiveness** (Romans 3:21). That forgiveness is the reason that, **"Christ is the end of the law for righteousness to every one who believes"** (Romans 10:4). It is that forgiveness that makes us righteous in the sight of God, and because of that forgiveness no sin is ever imputed to those who trust in Christ. That is why the Apostle John could write, **"We know that whoever is born of God does not sin; but he who is born of God keeps himself, and the wicked one does not touch him"** (1John 5:18).

The False Distinction Between Mortal and Venial Sins

During the middle ages, someone who did not understand the Gospel, tried to rationalize an entire class of sins by claiming that they were too small to bring damnation. I have already explained why that idea is wrong, and why every unforgiven sin will damn. But in the past some have tried to sanctify that error by placing Biblical definitions on the terms "mortal" and "venial". However, whenever that terminology is used some people twist it to excuse certain sins. If you have ever heard someone use the phrase, "little white lie" they were excusing a sin. For that reason, the terms "mortal" and "venial" should be purged from our theological vocabulary. Of those terms C. F. W. Walther said:

The Word of God is not rightly divided when the preacher speaks of certain sins as if there were not of a damnable, but of a venial nature... The Lord says: *Verily I say unto you, Till heaven and earth pass, one jot or one tittle shall in no wise pass from the Law till all be fulfilled. Whosoever, therefore, shall break, one of these least commandments and shall teach men so, he shall be called the least in the kingdom of heaven; but whosoever shall do and teach them, the same shall be called great in the kingdom of heaven.*(Matthew 5:18-19) This is one of the most dreadful sayings found in Scripture. The Lord does not say: "He shall *be* the least," but: "He shall *be called* the least." "The least" means the most reprobate, or one whom God does not acknowledge as His own. That will be the *sentence* passed on him in the kingdom of God and Christ. Therefore you should with trembling approach the task of preaching both the Gospel and the Law. Do not speak of one jot of the Law, of one of the so-called least commandments, as of something about which a Christian need not be greatly concerned. ("Law and Gospel," pages 325 and 326.)

Sins That Cry Out For Judgment

The Bible tells us that some sins **cry** out to God for justice. Look for the words "**cry**," "**cried**" or "**cries**" in the following passages.

Genesis 4:10, "What have you done? the voice of your brother's blood **cries** to me from the ground."

Genesis 18:20, "The LORD said, Because the **cry** of Sodom and Gomorrah is great, and because their sin is very grievous."

Exodus 3:7, "The LORD said, I have surely seen the affliction of my people who are in Egypt, and have heard their **cry** because of their taskmasters; for I know their sorrows;"

Exodus 3:9, "Now behold, the **cry** of the children of Israel has come to me, and I have seen how the Egyptians are oppressing them."

Exodus 22:22-24, "You shall not afflict any widow, or fatherless child. If you afflict them in any way, and they **cry** to me, I will surely hear their **cry**, and my wrath will grow hot."

James 5:4, "Behold, the wages of the workers who reaped your fields, that you kept back by fraud, **cry** out: and the cries of those who did the harvesting have entered into the ears of the Lord of hosts."

Revelation 6:10, "And they **cried** with a loud voice, saying, How long, O Lord, holy and true, will you not judge and avenge our blood on those who dwell on the earth?"

Luke 18:7-8, "Will not God avenge his chosen, who **cry** to Him day and night, though he bears long with them? I tell you that he will avenge them speedily."

In general, sins that cry out for justice seem to be crimes against the innocent, the poor and the helpless.

Pardonable Sins and Blasphemy Against the Holy Ghost

The words, "**Men will be forgiven every sin and blasphemy: but blasphemy against the Holy Ghost will not be forgiven. Anyone who speaks a word against the Son of man, will be forgiven: but anyone who speaks against the Holy Ghost, will not be forgiven, not in this world, or in the world to come,**" tell us that every sin is pardonable, except for "blasphemy against the Holy Ghost" (Matthew 12:31-32).

However, the fact that most sins are pardonable should never be twisted into an excuse to sin. The words, "**A broken and a contrite heart, O God, you wilt not despise,**" tell us that forgiveness is only promised to those who are sorry for their sin (Psalm 51:17). In contrast, the man who <u>sins willfully</u> has treated "**The blood of the covenant, by which he was sanctified, as an unholy thing, and insulted the Spirit of grace**" (Hebrews 10:29).

Now we come to the question of what constitutes "**blasphemy against the Holy Ghost**". In order to answer that question let us first consider the words of Nicodemus who, when he came to Jesus by night said, "**Rabbi, we <u>know</u> that you are a teacher who has come from God: for no one could do these miracles that you do, unless God is with him**" (John 3:1-2). Those words of Nicodemus tell us that the Pharisees **knew** that Jesus performed miracles by the power of God. Therefore, when the Bible tells us that, "**The scribes that came down from Jerusalem said, He is possessed by Beelzebub, and casts out devils by the prince of the devils,**" we know that those scribes had so hardened themselves against Christ that they would rather claim that His miracles were done by the power of Satan than admit their own sin (Mark 3:22). That being the case, the fact that "**Jesus called them to Himself, and said to them in parables, How can Satan cast out Satan? If a kingdom is divided against itself, that kingdom cannot stand,**" tells us that Jesus was still reaching out to them, still trying to bring them to repentance (Mark 3:23-24). And, if they had already blasphemed the Holy Ghost that would have been a waste of time since they could not get forgiveness anyway. Therefore, His warning, "**I tell you truly, All sins will be forgiven to the sons of men, and all blasphemies they utter: But whoever will blaspheme against the Holy Ghost will never be forgiven,**" was aimed at keeping them from blaspheming the Holy Ghost (Mark 3:28-29). However, His warning tells us that **those who blaspheme the Holy Ghost are those who are so hardened against the truth of the Gospel that they portray everything the Holy Spirit does to bring them to faith as the work of Satan**. In short, "**blasphemy against the Holy Ghost**" involves a total **hardening of oneself in unbelief.** And, if that is the case, a person who is truly guilty of that sin will have no desire for Christ, or the forgiveness that is available through His death on the cross.

In the past there have been many Christians who have been tormented by a fear that they might blaspheme the Holy Ghost. If you are one of them, instead of worrying you need to entrust the safekeeping of your soul to God's grace, believing that you are "**kept by the power of God through faith unto salvation**" (1Peter 1:5). God's grace is fully able to keep us from that sin. As it is written, "**I know whom I have believed, and am persuaded that He is able to keep that which I have committed to him against that day**" (2Timothy 1:12).

Hidden Sins and Open Sins

The distinction between hidden and open sins is useful to pastors in dealing with matters of church discipline. For example, if one member of a family is guilty of a certain sin, to avoid bringing shame to the entire family a pastor might follow the steps of Matt. 18:15-18 while keeping the matter private (at least until the last step — see verse 17). If the sin is already known, then it can be dealt with publicly.

In Matthew 18 we read, "**If your brother sins against you, go and tell him his fault between you and him alone: if he will hear you, you have gained your brother. But if he will not listen, then take one or two others with you, so that every word may be established by the testimony of two or three witnesses. And if he refuses to listen to them, tell it to the church: but if he refuses to hear the church, let him be to you as a heathen man and a publican. I tell you truly, Whatever you bind on earth will be bound in heaven: and whatever you loose on earth will be loosed in heaven**" (verses 15-18).

The words, "Rebuke those who sin before all, that others also may fear," tell us that open sin by a member of the church needs to be dealt with swiftly and openly (1Timothy 5:20). And, the words, "**Among you one hears of immorality, and of a kind of immorality that does not even occur among the Gentiles, that one has his father's wife. And you are still puffed up. Shouldn't you rather have been filled with sorrow, and have put out of your fellowship the man who did this?**" command churches to put those who are **immoral yet unrepentant** out of their fellowship (1Corinthians 5:1-2).

Personal Sins and Sins in Whose Guilt We Share

Personal sins are sins that we are guilty of. However, the Bible also speaks of those who share in the guilt of sins committed by others. We partake in the sins of others whenever we command someone to sin, advise them to sin, help them to sin, or help them to cover up a sin.

The words, "Anyone who is partner with a thief hates his own soul: he is put under oath, but discloses nothing," call those who know of a crime, but refuse to testify, a "partner" in that crime

(Proverbs 29:24). In an American court of law, someone who helps cover up a crime is guilty of being an "accessory after the fact".

The words, "**If anyone sins, by hearing a public call to give sworn testimony, and is a witness, whether he has seen or learned of it; if he does not speak, then he shall bear his iniquity,**" again condemn those who have knowledge of a sin but refuse to testify (Leviticus 5:1).

The instructions that David gave to Joab, "**Set Uriah in the forefront of the hottest battle, and withdraw from him, so that he will be struck down and die,**" made David guilty of murder even though he did not commit the act (2Samuel 11:15).

The words, "**Come out of her, my people, so that you do not share in her sins,**" and the words, "**Do not be hasty in laying hands on any man, and do not share in the sins of others: keep yourself pure**" warn us against sharing in the sins of others (Revelation 18:4, 1Timothy 5:22).

The words, "**If there come any unto you, and bring not this doctrine, receive him not into your house, neither bid him God speed, for he who bids him God speed is partaker of his evil deeds,**" warn us against encouraging those who spread cultic doctrines and pervert the Gospel (2John 10-11).

The words, "**Who knowing the judgment of God, that those who commit such things are worthy of death, not only do the same, but have pleasure in those who do them,**" warn against friendship with evildoers (Romans 1:32). The words, "**Do not be deceived: bad company undermines good behavior,**" warn us against evil influence (1Corinthians 15:33). The words, "**Have no fellowship with the unfruitful works of darkness, but rather reprove them,**" warn us against fellowship with evil (Ephesians 5:11). And, the words, "**Blessed is the man who does not walk in the counsel of the ungodly, or stand in the way of sinners, or sit in the seat of the scornful.**" with the words "I have not sat with those who deceive, nor will I fellowship with hypocrites. **I hate the company of evil doers, and will not sit with the wicked,**" tell us what our attitude toward sin should be (Psalm 1:1 & 26:4-5).

The Freedom Of The Will

In the past there has been a great deal of controversy regarding freedom of the will, much of which stems from a failure to distinguish between freedom of the will from man's viewpoint, and freedom of the will from God's perspective. Man was created with a free will, and it appears to us like we still have it. In fact, when it comes to everyday choices, such as what we will wear or eat etc., we do have a free will – up to a point. I say "up to a point" because we cannot choose to wear or eat what we do not have. So even in everyday matters our freedom of choice is limited. However, the words, "**No one can say that Jesus is the Lord, but by the Holy Ghost**," and the words, "**No man can come to me, unless the Father who has sent me draws him**," tell us that from God's point of view we are no longer free to chose in spiritual matters, and no man can come to faith in Christ apart from the work of the Holy Spirit (1Corinthians 12:3, John 6:44). Having said this, the words, "**I will never turn away anyone who comes to me**," tell us that Christ is never going to turn away someone who truly wants to be saved (John 6:37). It is just that no one will want to be saved unless the Father "draws him".

Likewise, no one should ever be afraid that God does not want to save him. On the contrary, the words, "**The Lord is not slack concerning His promise, as some men count slackness; but is patient with us, not wanting anyone to perish, but all to come to repentance**," tell us that God does not want any one to be lost (2Peter 3:9). It is just that God works through His word to bring people to salvation. As it is written, "**Faith comes by hearing, and hearing by the word of God**" (Romans 10:17). And, all you have to do is look around you to see that the lost, for the most part, care nothing for God's Word

Much of the controversy regarding the doctrine of freedom of the will is generated by those who, on the basis of some passages, draw conclusions that contradict other passages. Then, when they realize that their conclusions contradict other passages, instead of rejecting their conclusions they reject what the Bible says by explaining it away. That is rebellion against God. And, the words, "**If they do not speak according to this word, it is because there is no light in them**," warn us against listening to those who contradict what the Bible says (Isaiah 8:20). **The doctrine that God wants us to learn is the doctrine He has plainly stated in the words of Scripture, "line upon line, line upon line; here a little, and there a little"** (Isaiah 28:10).

The words, "**There will be a bridle in the jaws of the people, causing them to err**," and the words, "**I will put my hook in your nose, and my bridle between your lips, and I will turn you back the way you came**," tell us that from God's point of view men are controlled by spiritual influences just as a horse is controlled by a bridle (Isaiah 30:28, Isaiah 37:29).

The words, "**You are of your father the devil, and you will do what your father desires. He was a murderer from the beginning, and did not abide in the truth, because there is no truth in him. When he speaks a lie, he speaks on his own: for he is a liar, and the father of it**," tell us that those who are not children of God are children of the devil, and will do his will (John 8:44). That does not mean that everyone who is lost will commit crimes like murder. However, if they do not commit such crimes it is only by the grace of God. In some cases God is reaching out to them through their conscience. In other cases He is protecting believers. In still other cases they are seeking righteousness through works. But, they are all guilty of the sins that stem from a fallen nature. They all lie, lust, and have imagined murdering someone they are angry at etc. And, the words, **"That they may come to their senses and escape from the devil's snare, having been taken captive by him to do his will,"** tell us that Satan is able to take control of them (2Timothy 2:26).

The words, **"The natural man does not accept the things of the Spirit of God: for they are foolishness to him: and he cannot understand them, because they are spiritually discerned,"** tell us that because of original sin it is contrary to nature for those who are lost to accept the things of God (1Corinthians 2:14). And, the words, **"The fleshly mind is hostile to God: for it is not subject to the law of God, nor indeed can be,"** tell us that when it comes to the Law of God, we do not have a free will (Romans 8:7).

The words, **"I know that you are Abraham's seed; but you want to kill me, because My Word has no place in you,"** tell us that God's Word is what works in us to change our hearts (John 8:37). The words, **"I am the vine, you are the branches: He who remains in me, and I in him, produces much fruit: for you can do nothing without me,"** and, the words, **"We are not adequate in ourselves to think that we can accomplish anything in our own strength; but our ability is from God,"** tell us that we are not able to accomplish anything spiritual in our own strength (John 15:5, 2Corinthians 3:5). As it is written, **"It is God who works in you both to will and to do His good pleasure"** (Philippians 2:13).

The words, **"You formerly walked according to the way of this world, according to the prince of the power of the air, the spirit that now works in the children of disobedience,"** again speak of those who are lost being under the influence of Satan (Ephesians 2:2). The words, **"They are all gone out of the way, they are together become unprofitable; there is no one who does good, no, not one,"** tell us that no one can make himself righteous in the sight of God (Romans 3:12). The words, **"The light shone in the darkness; and the darkness did not comprehend it,"** tell us that without the help of the Holy Spirit the lost do not understand (John 1:5). And, the words, **"He has rescued us from the power of darkness, and transferred us into the kingdom of His dear Son,"** tell us that we are saved by what God does, not by what we do (Colossians 1:13).

The Apostle Paul was not saved because he chose Christ, or because he resisted less than others, but because God chose him. At the time of Paul's conversion Christ said, **"I have appeared to you for this reason, to make you a minister and a witness not only to the** things that you have seen, but also to the things that I will let you see. I will deliver you from your people, and from the Gentiles, unto whom I now send you, to open their eyes, and to turn them from darkness to light, and from the power of Satan to God, that they may receive forgiveness of sins, and inheritance among those who are sanctified through faith in me" (Acts 26:16-18).

Speaking to Timothy, Paul said, "**The Lord's servant must not quarrel, but must be gentle toward all, able to teach, and patient when wronged. With gentleness instructing those who oppose their own interest, in the hope that God will give them repentance bringing them to a realization of the truth. That they may come to their senses and escape from the devil's snare, having been taken captive by him to do his will**" (2Timothy 2:24-26). Those words remind us that those who are lost, having been taken captive by Satan, oppose their own interest [i.e. salvation], and repentance is a gift of God.

A number of passages are commonly cited to support the idea that man has some part in his salvation. However, as you will see, that idea is not in the text, it is being assumed.

The words, "**Come to me, all you who labor and are carrying a heavy burden, and I will give you rest**," invite all who are lost to come (Matthew 11:28). The words, "**The kingdom of God is at hand: repent, and believe the gospel**," call on people to repent and believe (Mark 1:15). And, the words, "**Believe on the Lord Jesus Christ, and you will be saved**" were the words of Paul and Silas to the Philippian jailer (Acts 16:31). However, the words, "**The natural man does not accept the things of the Spirit of God: for they are foolishness to him: and he cannot understand them, because they are spiritually discerned**," and the words, "**No one can say that Jesus is the Lord, but by the Holy Ghost**," tell us that just because the Bible calls upon men to believe does not mean that they have the ability to believe (1Corinthians 2:14 and 12:3). Without the power of the Holy Spirit working through His Word they could never believe. Their sinful flesh would destroy faith before it got started by filling them with doubt

The words, "**He (Christ) is the propitiation for our sins: and not for ours only, but also for the sins of the whole world**," tell us that salvation is available to everyone (1John 2:2). However, the words, "**The minds of those who do not believe have been blinded by the god of this world, that the light of the glorious gospel of Christ, who is the image of God, might not reach them**," and the words, "**The world through its wisdom did not know God**," tell us that without God's Word the lost have no idea that they are lost, or that salvation is available (2Corinthians 4:4, 1Corinthians 1:21).

The words, "**It pleased God to save those who believe through the foolishness of preaching.**" // "**Faith comes by hearing, and hearing by the word of God,**" and "**No one can say that Jesus is the Lord, but by the Holy Ghost,**" then tell us that God works through His Word to bring multitudes to faith, in spite of their resistance (1Corinththians 1:21). And, the words, "**You are a chosen generation, a royal priesthood, a holy nation, a people valued by God; that you should show forth the praises of Him who has called you out of darkness into His marvelous light,**" tell us that we have not chosen Christ, He has chosen us (1Peter 2:9).

The Grace Of God Toward Fallen Mankind

1. The Necessity Of Divine Grace

The words, "**Sin entered the world by one man, and death by sin; so death passed upon all men, because all have sinned,**" tell us that everyone who is going to die is a sinner (Romans 5:12). The words, "**The wages of sin is death,**" tell us that the very reason that we are going to die is because we are sinners (Romans 6:23). And, the words, "**No flesh will ever be justified in God's sight by the deeds of the law: because the knowledge of sin comes by the law,**" tell us that no one will ever escape death by doing what the law says, because the Law is what condemns us (Romans 3:20). That is why Divine grace is necessary.

How then can we be saved? The Bible answers that question with the words, "**Now the righteousness of God apart from the law is revealed... Even the righteousness of God which comes through faith in Jesus Christ to all and upon all who believe**" (Romans 3:21-22). "**For God so loved the world, that He gave His only begotten Son, that whosoever believes on Him should not perish, but have everlasting life**" (John 3:16). Therefore, "**God has done what the law could not do, in that it was weak through the flesh. Sending His own Son in the likeness of sinful flesh, as an offering for sin... That the righteousness of the law might be fulfilled in us**" (Romans 8:3-4). So "**We have redemption through His [Christ's] blood, the forgiveness of sins, according to the riches of His grace**" (Ephesians 1:7). "**And the blood of Jesus Christ His Son cleanses us of all sin**" (1John 1:7). "**For as by one man's disobedience many were made sinners, so by the obedience of one many will be made righteous**" (Romans 5:19). "**All the prophets testify of Him, that through His name whoever believes in Him will receive forgiveness of sins**" (Acts 10:43). "**Nor is there salvation in any other: for there is no other name under heaven given among men, by which we must be** saved" (Acts 4:12).

[Note: believing that Christ died for our sins is more than just believing that He died. It is believing that He died for your sins, and that because of His death you have forgiveness and eternal life.]

2. The Nature Of Divine Grace

Because the Bible says, "**You are saved by grace through faith; and that not of yourselves: it is the gift of God, not of works, lest any man should boast**," we need to let the Bible tell us what grace is and what faith is (Ephesians 2:8-9). And, the Bible tells us what grace is through the words, "**He saved us, not by works of righteousness that we have done, but in keeping with His mercy**" (Titus 3:5). Notice that in Ephesians Paul says that we are saved by **grace**, in Titus he says that we are saved by **mercy**. That tells us that even though the word "grace" is a little broader in meaning than the word, "mercy," when it comes to salvation **grace and mercy can be viewed as synonyms**. Notice also that both passages emphasize the fact that grace or mercy is given **without works**. And, saying that God's **grace is unmerited** is another way of saying that grace is given to us without works.

The words, "**Whoever finds me [wisdom] finds life, and will obtain <u>favor</u> from the LORD**," define grace as "favor" **unmerited favor** (Proverbs 8:35). [Christ is the "the wisdom of God." 1Cor. 1:24]

The words, "**I have <u>trusted</u> in thy mercy; my heart shall rejoice in thy salvation**," tell us that David was saved by trust [faith] in God's mercy [grace] (Psalm 13:5 KJV). And, because the Bible uses **mercy and grace** as synonyms, that passage could be translated, "**I have placed my faith in your grace, my heart shall rejoice in your salvation**" (Ps. 13:5).

The words, "**God so <u>loved</u> the world, that He gave His only begotten Son, that whosoever believes in Him should not perish, but have everlasting life**," speak of us being saved through God's love, **thus defining divine grace as love**. (John 3:16).

The words, "**The <u>kindness</u> and <u>love</u> of God our Savior toward man appeared... according to His <u>mercy</u> He saved us**," define God's grace as kindness, love and mercy (Titus 3:4-5).

The words, "**To give His people the knowledge of salvation by the <u>remission</u> of their sins, through the <u>tender mercy</u> of our God;**" define the grace that saves us as **forgiveness of sins** (Luke 1:77-78). And, the words translated "tender mercy" could be translated as "bowels of compassion;" thus further **defining God's grace as compassion**.

The words, "**He [Jahweh] said, Surely they are my people,** children who will not deal falsely: so He was their Savior... in His love and in His <u>pity</u> He redeemed them," speak of God's deliverance of Israel from Egypt (Isaiah 63:8-9). However, since that deliverance is a prophetic type of our deliverance, it further **defines God's grace as pity.**

The words, "**In whom we have redemption through His blood, the <u>forgiveness</u> of sins, according to the riches of His grace**," again d**efine God's grace as the forgiveness of sins** (Ephesians 1:7).

The words, "**Scripture, having foreseen that God would justify the heathen through faith, proclaimed the gospel to Abraham in advance, saying, In you shall all nations be blessed**," tell us that Abraham knew and believed the gospel (Galatians 3:8). And, what is the gospel? The Apostle Paul answers that question by saying, "**I declare unto you the gospel which I preached unto you... that Christ died for our sins according to the scriptures. And that He was buried, and that He rose again the third day according to the scriptures**" (1Corinthians 15:1-4). Therefore, what Galatians 3:8 is telling us is that **Abraham understood and believed that his seed [descendant] would die for our sins, and rise again (Heb. 11:19)**. That being understood, when the Bible tells us that, "**Abraham believed God, and it was accounted to him for righteousness**," it is telling us that **Abraham was justified by believing the same gospel that we believe. That defines saving faith as believing that Christ died for our sins, and rose again the third day.** As it is written, "**Christ redeemed us from the curse of the law, receiving the curse in our stead, for it is written, Cursed is every one who hangs on a tree, that the blessing given to Abraham might come to the Gentiles through Jesus Christ, that we might receive the promise of the Spirit through faith... My point is this, the covenant concerning faith in Christ, that was confirmed by God at the time of Abraham, cannot be nullified by the law, which came four hundred and thirty years later, so as to make the promise of no effect, for if the inheritance comes by the law, it is not given by promise: but God gave it to Abraham by promise**" (Galatians 3:13,14,17,18).

The words, "**We have access by faith into this grace wherein we stand**," tell us that faith in **God's promise of forgiveness in Christ** [the gospel] is the hand that receives God's grace (Romans 5:2). And, the words, "**You are saved by grace through faith; and that not of yourselves: it is the gift of God, not of works**," tell us that even our faith is not something that we do, but is a gift of God (Ephesians 2:8-9). As it is written, "**Faith comes by hearing, and hearing by the word of God**" (Romans 10:17).

Those who oppose and compromise the gospel sometimes cite the words, "**Neither circumcision, or uncircumcision counts for anything; but faith which produces works through love,**" in a vain attempt to make faith include works (Galatians 5:6). However, those words are not saying that faith consists of works, but that **faith produces works** through love — in contrast to the Law which produces works through fear.

Those who oppose the gospel also often cite the words, "**By works a man is justified and not by faith only,**" and place those words in opposition to the words, "**A man is justified by faith without the deeds of the law**" (James 2:24, Romans 3:28). However, that is totally wrong. Because both statements are the Word of God, both statements are true. And, we cannot be faithful to the Word of God without accepting both of them without explaining either one of them away.

A careful examination of what James is saying makes it clear that Paul and James were talking about two different things. When Paul spoke of works **he was referring to "works of righteousness" (Titus 3:5).** In contrast, James was talking about not treating the wealthy that came to worship better than the poor (James 2:1-5). Furthermore, when James said, "**Was not Rahab the Harlot justified by works, when she had received the messengers, and had sent them out another way,**" he was <u>not</u> referring to works of righteousness that Rahab had performed, for she was a pagan harlot. However, her words, "**I know that the LORD has given you the land, and that the fear of you has fallen on us,**" reveal the faith she acted on, and it was not faith in Christ (Joshua 2:9). Therefore, James was not saying that faith in Christ is not enough, but that what we believe will affect the decisions we make, and if we have faith in Christ it should make a difference in the way we treat people.

3. Attributes Of Justifying Grace

The words, "**We have redemption through His blood, the forgiveness of sins, according to the riches of His grace,**" and the words, "**Nor is there salvation in any other, for there is no other name under heaven given among men, by which we must be saved,**" tell us that the grace by which we are saved is not ours because of a primal decision, but because Christ took our sins upon Himself and died on the cross to obtain it for us (Ephesians 1:7, Acts 4:12). Therefore, **the first attribute** of justifying grace, is that it is available to us through <u>Christ alone</u>.

The words, "**John saw Jesus coming to him, and said, Behold the Lamb of God, who takes away the sin of the world,**" and the words, "**He is the propitiation for our sins, and not for ours only, but also for the sins of the whole world,**" tell us that Christ did not just die for a few, but for all men (John 1:29, 1John 2:2). Therefore, **the second attribute** of justifying grace is that it is **available to all**. As it is written, "**For God so loved the world, that He gave His only begotten Son, that whosoever believes in Him should not perish, but have everlasting life**" (John 3:16).

The words, "**O Jerusalem, Jerusalem, you who kill the prophets, and stone those who are sent to you, how often I longed to gather your children together, as a hen gathers her chicks under her wings, and you would not**," and the words, "**You stiffnecked and uncircumcised in heart and ears, you always resist the Holy Ghost: as your fathers did, so do you**," tell us that God does not ignore the lost, but earnestly works through His Word to bring them to repentance (Matthew 23:37, Acts 7:51). Therefore, **the third attribute** of justifying grace is that **God actively works to bring men to repentance and faith** — so those who are lost are lost through their own fault, not because God wanted them to be lost. As it is written, "As I live, says the Lord GOD, **I have no pleasure in the death of the wicked; but want the wicked man to turn from his way and live**" (Ezekiel 33:11).

Salvation is Available Through Christ Alone

The words, "**When the time had fully come, God sent forth His Son, born of a woman, born under the law, To <u>redeem</u> those who were under the law, that we might receive the adoption of sons**," tell us that Christ came to redeem us (Galatians 4:4-5).

The words, "**Christ redeemed us from the curse of the law, receiving the curse in our stead: for it is written, Cursed is every one who hangs on a tree**," tell us that Christ redeemed us by taking upon Himself the curse that we deserved (Galatians 3:13).

The words, "**Being justified freely by His grace through the redemption that is in Christ Jesus**," tell us that the forgiveness Christ obtained for us is given to us **freely** (Romans 3:24).

The words, "**God has done what the law could not do, in that it was weak through the flesh. Sending His own Son in the likeness of sinful flesh, as an offering for sin, He condemned sin in the flesh; that the righteousness of the law might be fulfilled in us, who do not walk after the flesh, but after the Spirit**," tell us that Christ died as an offering for sin (Romans 8:3-4).

And, the words, "**God was in Christ, reconciling the world to himself, not counting their sins against them; and has committed to us the word of reconciliation**," tell us that we are reconciled to God by the forgiveness Christ won for us through His death on the cross (2Corinthians 5:19).

The words, "**It was fitting that we should have such a high priest, who is holy, blameless, pure, separated from sinners, and risen higher than the heavens; Who does not need to daily** offer up sacrifice, as do other high priests, first for his own sins, and then for the people's: for He did this once, when He offered up himself," tell us that Christ is our high priest, and that His death was the sacrifice for our sins (Hebrews 7:26-27).

The words, "**In Christ Jesus you who once were far away are made near by the blood of Christ. For He is our peace, who has made both Jew and Gentile one, and has broken down the wall of hostility that separated us. Having abolished in His flesh the law of commandments contained in ordinances; in order to make of the two one new body in Him, so making peace. And that He might reconcile both to God in one body by the cross, having thereby put the hostility to death,**" tell us that we are reconciled to God through Christ's death on the cross (Ephesians 2:13-16).

The words, "**Although you were previously alienated from Him [God the Father], and antagonistic in mind through your wicked works, He has now reconciled you, through the death of Christ's physical body, to present you holy, without fault and beyond reproach in His sight,**" tell us that God the father has reconciled us to Himself through Christ's death on the cross (Colossians 1:21-22).

And, the words "**In whom we have redemption through His blood, the forgiveness of sins, according to the riches of His grace,**" tell us that we have forgiveness through Christ's death on the cross ["His blood"] (Ephesians 1:7). As it is written, "**The blood of Jesus Christ His Son cleanses us of all sin**" (1John 1:7).

Salvation is Available to All

The words, "**For God so loved the world, that He gave His only begotten Son, that whosoever believes in Him should not perish, but have everlasting life,**" the words, "**This is good and acceptable in the sight of God our Savior; Who wants all men to be saved, and to come to the knowledge of the truth,**" the words, "**God has also granted to the Gentiles repentance unto life,**" and the words, "**The grace of God that brings salvation has appeared to all men,**" tell us that Christ died for the sins of **all men** (John 3:16, 1Timothy 2:4, Acts 11:18, Titus 2:11).

The words, "**The Lord is not slack concerning His promise, as some men count slackness; but is patient with us, not wanting anyone to perish, but all to come to repentance,**" the words, "**Say to them, As I live, says the Lord GOD, I have no pleasure in the death of the wicked,**" and the words, "**I have no pleasure in the death of him who dies, says the Lord GOD: therefore turn from sin, and live,**" and the words, "**God... has made of one blood all nations of men... So that they should seek the Lord, in the hope that they might grope for Him, and find Him, although

He is not far from any one of us," tell us that God does not want anyone to be damned (2Peter 3:9, Ezekiel 33:11, Ezekiel 18:32, Acts 17:26-27).

The words, "O Jerusalem, Jerusalem, you who kill the prophets, and stone those who are sent to you, how often I longed to gather your children together, as a hen gathers her chicks under her wings, and you would not," the words, "You stiffnecked and uncircumcised in heart and ears, you always resist the Holy Ghost: as your fathers did, so do you," and the words, "But there were also false prophets among the people, just as there will be false teachers among you, who will privately introduce damnable heresies, even denying the Lord who bought them, bringing swift destruction upon themselves," tell us that God does not want those who ultimately reject the gospel to be lost (Matthew 23:37, Acts 7:51, 2Peter 2:1).

God Earnestly Reaches Out to the Lost

The words, "To Israel He says, All day long I have stretched forth my hands to a disobedient and obstinate people," tell us that God earnestly reaches out to the lost (Romans 10:21)

The words, "Go into all the world, and preach the gospel to everyone," and the words, "Teach all nations... Teaching them to observe everything I have commanded you," tell us that God wants the gospel proclaimed to all men (Mark 16:15, Matthew 28:19-20).

The words, "Repent, and be baptized every one of you in the name of Jesus Christ for the forgiveness of sins, and you will receive the gift of the Holy Ghost," the words, "I will pour out my Spirit on all flesh; and your sons and your daughters will prophesy, your old men will dream dreams, your young men will see visions," and the words, "I will give them one mind, and I will put a new spirit in them; and I will take the stony heart out of their flesh, and will give them a heart of flesh, that they may walk in my statutes, and keep my ordinances, and do them: and they will be My people, and I will be their God," promise God's Spirit to all who believe (Acts 2:38, Joel 2:28, Ezekiel 11:19-20).

The words, "Being confident of this, that He who has begun a good work in you will continue it until the day of Jesus Christ," the words, "Kept by the power of God through faith unto salvation," the words "Him that is able to keep you from falling," and the words, "Looking to Jesus the author and finisher of our faith," tell us that God not only begins, but also finishes the work of His Spirit in those who believe (Philippians 1:6, 1Peter 1:5, Jude 24, Hebrews 12:2).

4. Accurately Describing The Divine Will Of Grace

Although we are saved by God's love, when we are describing that love, or the fact that God "Wants all men to be saved," **we should never give people the impression that God's love and salvation are available apart from faith in Christ.** As it is written, **"There is no other name under heaven given among men, by which we must be saved"** (Acts 4:12). [See John 3:16, 1Tim. 2:4.] Likewise, **we should never describe God's desire to save sinners in a way that leads men to believe that by praying a prayer the unrepentant and unbelieving can continue in sin without any danger of eternal punishment.** As it is written, **"Don't you know that the unrighteous will not inherit the kingdom of God? Do not be deceived: neither fornicators, nor idolaters, nor adulterers, nor sex perverts, nor homosexuals, nor thieves, nor covetous, nor drunkards, nor foulmouthed revilers, nor extortioners, shall inherit the kingdom of God."** // **"He who believes on the Son has everlasting life: and he who does not believe the Son will not see life; but God's wrath remains on him"** (1Corinthians 6:9-10, John 3:36).

Although God offers salvation to all who trust in Christ, and reaches out to the lost through His Word, **we should never give people the impression that faith is something they do to save themselves.** The words, **"You are saved by grace through faith; and that not of yourselves: it is the gift of God,"** tell us that even our faith is a gift of God (Ephesians 2:8). And, the words, **"Faith comes by hearing, and hearing by the Word of God,"** tell us that God gives us that gift through His Word (Romans 10:17).

Christ Himself said, **"No man can come to me, unless the Father who has sent me draws him"** (John 6:44). **However, we should never give people the impression that God might not want to save them.** Christ's words, **"I will never turn away anyone who comes to me,"** assure us that Christ's arms are open to all (John 6:37). On the other hand, even if it looks to you like you have chosen Christ, the words, **"No one can say that Jesus is the Lord, but by the Holy Ghost"** make it clear that apart from God's grace you would never have made the right choice (1Corinthians 12:3).

The words, **"I have no pleasure in the death of the wicked, but want the wicked man to turn from his way and live,"** tell us that it is not God's will for anyone to be lost (Ezekiel 33:11). However, the words, **"He who believes and is baptized will be saved; but he who does not believe will be damned,"** tell us that it is also His will for unbelievers to be damned (Mark 16:16). **Neither of these truths should be construed in a way that contradicts the other.** If these two facts seem contradictory to our puny finite minds, we need to accept what the Bible says without trying to manufacture explanations. When the Bible says, "Do not add to His words," that includes making up explanations and teaching them as doctrine (Proverbs 30:6). The words, "**Professing themselves to be wise, they became fools,**" apply to all who think that they can discover spiritual truths that God has not revealed (Romans 1:22). And, the words, "**How unsearchable are His judgments, and His ways past finding out,**" reveal the impossibility of discovering God's "hidden will" (Romans 11:33).

SCRIPTURE ALONE
GRACE ALONE
FAITH ALONE

THE DOCTRINE OF CHRIST
(CHRISTOLOGY)

The Doctrine Of The Person Of Christ

1. Introduction

The doctrine that God wants taught in His churches does not consist of opinions distilled from Scripture, but of the actual words of Scripture given to us, "Line upon line, line upon line; here a little, and there a little" (Isaiah 28:10). Therefore, we teach that Christ is both true God and true man because the Bible tells in one place that He is true God, and in another place that He is true man. For example, the words **"We know that the Son of God has come, and has given us understanding, so that we might know the one who is true, and we are in the one who is true, in His Son Jesus Christ. He is the true God, and eternal life,"** tell us that Christ is God (1John 5:20). At the same time, the words, **"There is one God, and one mediator between God and men, the man Christ Jesus,"** tell us that He is true man (1Timothy 2:5). Because God has given us both of those truths, He wants us to teach both without compromising them in a vain attempt to make them more palatable to our sin-corrupted little finite minds. For that reason we reject as false every attempt to deny Christ's deity, or His humanity, or to separate His divine nature from His human nature as if He were two beings.

The Bible tells us that, **"Christ died for our sins according to the scriptures, and He was buried, and He rose again the third day according to the scriptures"** (1Corinthians 15:1-4). And, because He died for our sins we have been, **"Reconciled to God by the death of His Son... by whom we have now received the atonement"** (Romans 5:10-11). That good news is the foundation of our faith. Faith is believing that we are, **"Justified freely by His grace through the redemption that is in Christ Jesus"** (Romans 3:24). And it is, **"By faith we have access into this grace wherein we stand"** (Romans 5:2). For that reason, the doctrine of the **atonement** cannot be separated from the doctrine that, **"A man is justified by faith without the deeds of the law"** (Romans 3:28). Together those two doctrines are the central truth of Scripture. [See 1Corinthians 3:11, 1Timothy 2:5-6.]

2. The True Deity Of Christ

The words, "**In the beginning was the Word [Christ], and the Word was with God, <u>and the Word was God</u>**," tell us that Christ is God (John 1:1). The book of John goes on to tell us that, "**All things were created by Him; and apart from Him nothing was created that was created**" (verse 3), and that, "**The Word [the Creator] was made flesh, and dwelt among us**" (verse 14). The Bible goes on to testify to Christ's deity by ascribing to Him:

a) **The Name God.** — The words, "**Unto us a child is born, unto us a son is given: and the government will be on His shoulders: and <u>His name will be called Wonderful, Counselor, The Mighty God, The Everlasting Father</u>**," tell us that Christ is, "**God**" (Isaiah 9:6). So do the words, "**We are in the one who is true, in His Son Jesus Christ. <u>He is the true God</u>, and eternal life**" (1John 5:20). The words, "**Peter answered and said, You are the Messiah, <u>the Son of the living God</u>**," tell us that Christ is the "Son" of God. And, the words, "**The Word was made flesh, and dwelt among us, (and we beheld His glory, the glory as of the only begotten of the Father,) full of grace and truth**," tell us that Christ is not an adopted son of God, but is the "**only begotten**" Son (John 1:14). In the book of Hebrews we read, "**To which of the angels did God ever say, You are my Son, today I have begotten you?... But to the Son He says, Your throne, <u>O God</u>, is for ever and ever**" (Hebrews 1:5,8). And, speaking through the prophet Jeremiah, God said, "**Behold, the days come, says the LORD, when I will raise to David a righteous Branch... and this is the name by which He will be called, JEHOVAH OUR RIGHTEOUSNESS**" (Jeremiah 23:5-6).

b) **Divine attributes.** — The words, "**Jesus said to them, Truly, truly, I tell you, Before Abraham was, I am**," and the words, "**O Father, glorify me at your side with the glory that I had with you before the world was**," ascribe to Christ the divine attribute of eternity (John 8:58 and 17:5). Peter's words, "**Lord, you know all things**," ascribe to Christ the attribute of omniscience (John 21:17). And, the words, "**My sheep hear my voice, and I know them, and they follow me: And I give to them eternal life; and they will never perish, neither will any man pluck them out of my hand. My Father, who gave them to me, is greater than anyone; and no one is able to pluck them out of my Father's hand. I and my Father are one**," ascribe omnipotence to Him (John 10:28-30).

c) **Divine works.** — The words, "**For all things in heaven and earth, both visible and invisible, were created by him**," tell us that Christ is the creator of all things (Colossians 1:16). The words, **"Just as the Father raises the dead, and gives them life; even so the Son gives life to whomever He will"** and the words, **"The hour is coming, in which all who are in the graves will hear His [Christ's] voice, and will come out;"** tell us that Christ raises the dead (John 5:21 and 28). And, the words, **"This the first of miracles was performed by Jesus,"** tells us that Jesus has the power to perform miracles (John 2:11).

d) **Divine adoration and worship.** — The words, **"Thomas answered and said unto him, My Lord and my God,"** tell us that Thomas honored Christ as God (John 20:28). The words, **"The Father does not judge anyone, but has committed all judgment to the Son, that all may honor the Son, even as they honor the Father. He who does not honor the Son does not honor the Father who sent him,"** tell us that we should honor Christ in the same way we honor God (John 5:22-23). The words, **"God has also highly exalted Him, and given Him a name that is above every name, that at the name of Jesus every knee should bow,"** tell us that God wants us to bow before Christ (Philippians 2:9-10). And, the words, **"Let this mind be in you, which was also in Christ Jesus, who, being by nature God, did not see equality with God as something to be used for self-glorification, but made himself of no reputation, and took upon him the nature of a servant, and was born as a man,"** tell us that Christ is by nature God (Philippians 2:5-7).

3. The True Humanity Of Christ

One of Satan's first attacks on Christianity was a denial of Christ's humanity. Those who held that heresy acknowledged that Christ was God, but claimed that He was a phantom person who did not have a body of flesh and blood. However, if Christ did not have blood, then His blood could never cleanse "us from all sin" (1John 1:7). That heresy arose at the time of the Apostles, and the Bible condemns it. The words, **"Do not believe every spirit... because many false prophets have gone out into the world... Every spirit who does not confess that Jesus Christ has come in the flesh is not of God: and this is the spirit of the antichrist,"** tell us to regard those who deny Christ's humanity as antichrists (1John 4:1,3). The words, **"Those who know God accept what we say; those who are not of God will not accept what we say,"** tell us that those who deny Christ's humanity are "not of God" (1John 4:6). That heresy is again condemned in the words, **"Many deceivers have gone out into the world, men who will not admit that Jesus Christ has** come in the flesh. Such is a deceiver and an antichrist. Beware of them, so that you do not lose the things that we worked for, but receive your reward in full. Whoever transgresses, and does not continue in the doctrine of Christ, does not have God... Do not receive him into your house, or bid him God speed, for he who bids him God speed is a partaker of his evil deeds**" (2John 7-11).

That denial of Christ's humanity was dangerous, and a serious attack on the Gospel, because a phantom Christ could never feel pain, and, therefore, could never truly suffer or die for our sins. The Muslim denial that Christ died on the cross merits the same condemnation, for it also undermines the Gospel.

Throughout history Satan has inspired a multitude of other attacks on what the Bible says about Christ's humanity. Some have denied that Christ had a human soul, others that He had a human will, others have claimed that He was not truly human, but brought His body from heaven. None of those views come from the Bible, but are **fantasies dreamed up by a heart that is, "Deceitful above all things, and desperately wicked"** (Jeremiah 17:9). That holds true for all of the other stories invented to get around what the Bible says. Of such fantasies Dr. John Theodore Mueller had this to say:

> In whatever matter Holy Scripture has definitely spoken the Christian theologian must suppress his own views, opinions, and speculations and adhere unwaveringly to the divine truths revealed in Holy Scripture. In no case is he permitted to inject into the body of divine truth his own *figments and fabrications*, and at no time must he allow his reason the prerogative of doubt, criticism, or denial, but every thought must everywhere be brought into captivity to the obedience of Christ, 2Corinthians 10:5. [*Christian Dogmatics.* (Page 39)]

In testifying to Christ's humanity the Bible ascribes to Him: a) manhood, b) human flesh, c) human descent, d) human (though miraculous) conception in the womb, e) human constituent parts, f) human emotions, g) human physical wants, h) human suffering and death.

- a) **Manhood**: The words, **"There is one God, and one mediator between God and men, the man Christ Jesus,"** say that Christ is a man (1Timothy 2:5); as do the words, **"But now you seek to kill me, a man who has told you the truth"** (John 8:40).
- b) **Human flesh**: The words, **"Since the children have flesh and blood, He in the same way took on flesh and blood; so that through His death He might destroy him who holds the**

power of death, that is, the devil," tell us that He had human flesh (Hebrews 2:14); as do the words, "**Look at my hands and my feet, and see that it is really me: handle me, and see; for a spirit does not have flesh and bones, as you see me have**" (Luke 24:39).

c) **Human descent**: The words, "**For they are Israelites... and of them as concerning the flesh Christ came**," tell us that Christ was an Israelite "as concerning the flesh" (Romans 9:4-5). The words, "**The lineage of Jesus Christ, the descendant of David, the descendant of Abraham**," say the same thing (Matthew 1:1). When the Bible says, "**The promises were made to Abraham and his seed. God did not say, And to your seeds, as referring to many; but, And to your seed, referring to one which is Christ**," it is telling us that Christ was a descendant (seed) of Abraham (Galatians 3:16, see Genesis 22:18). The Bible goes on to tell us that Jesus was the descendant (seed) of Eve, Isaac, Mary and David as well as Abraham (see John 7:42, Genesis 3:15, Hebrews 2:16, 2Timothy 2:8, Romans 9:7, Romans 1:3, and Luke 1:31).

d) **Human (though miraculous) conception**: The words, "**You will conceive in your womb, and bring forth a son, and will name him JESUS**," tell us that Mary conceived Christ in her Womb (Luke 1:31). And, Elisabeth's words to Mary, "**Blessed is the fruit of your womb**," tell us that Jesus was the fruit of Mary's womb (Luke 1:42). [See Isaiah 7:14, Matthew 1:23.]

e) **Human constituent parts**: The words, "**But He was speaking of the temple of His body**," tell us that Christ has a body (John 2:21). The words, "**He said to them, My soul is overwhelmed with sorrow**," tell us that He has a soul (Matthew 26:38). The words, "**Look at my hands and my feet, and see that it is really me: handle me, and see; for a spirit does not have flesh and bones, as you see me have**," tell us that He has hands, feet, flesh and bones (Luke 24:39). The words, "**When Jesus had cried with a loud voice, He said, Father, into thy hands I commend my spirit**," tell us that He has a spirit (Luke 23:46). And, the words, "**Father, if you are willing, remove this cup from me: nevertheless not my will, but yours, be done**," tell us that He has a will (Luke 22:42).

f) **Human emotions**: The words, "**After looking around at them in anger, being grieved because of the hardness of their hearts**," tell us that Jesus felt anger and grief (Mark 3:5). And, the words, "**Jesus... said to them, My soul is extremely sorrowful**," tell us that He experienced sorrow (Mark 14:34).

g) **Human physical wants**: The words, "**After fasting for forty days and forty nights, He was hungry**," tell us that Jesus experienced hunger (Matthew 4:2). The words, "**Jesus, knowing** that all was now complete, said, I thirst,"** tell us that Jesus experienced thirst (John 19:28). And, the words, **"As they were sailing He fell asleep,"** tell us that He grew tired (Luke 8:23).

   h) **Human suffering and death**: Because of His great suffering Jesus called out, **"My God, my God, why have you forsaken me?"** (Matthew 27:46). And, the words, **"Jesus said, It is finished: and He bowed His head, and gave up the ghost,"** tell us that Jesus died (John 19:30). The words, **"Christ physically suffered for us,"** and **"Christ died for our sins,"** also tell us that He suffered and died (1Peter 4:1, 1Corinthians 15:3).

Over the centuries Satan has inspired a multitude of heresies aimed at undermining what the Bible says about Christ's humanity. However, all of those heresies contradict something in the Bible. For example, the claim that Christ brought His body with Him from heaven not only contradicts all of the passages that tell us that Christ is the descendant (seed) of Eve, Abraham, David and Mary, or "The Son of man" (Matthew 9:6), it also contradicts all of the passages that tell us Christ was conceived by Mary (or a virgin). Isaiah wrote, **"A virgin will conceive"** (Isaiah 7:14, Matthew 1:23). The angel said to Mary, **"You will conceive in your womb, and bring forth a son, and will name him JESUS,"** and there is a big difference between conceiving a child and having one implanted in the womb (Luke 1:31). In fact, when Mary asked the angel, **"How can this be, since I have never been intimate with a man?"** he said, **"The Holy Spirit will come upon you, and the power of the Highest will overshadow you, therefore the holy one who will be born of you will be called the Son of God"** (Luke 1:34-35). Those words suggest that when Mary conceived, God created the genetic material that would have been supplied by the male sperm (including the Y chromosome), but even that is conjecture, not something that the Bible says. Moreover, that sort of conjecture leads more conjecture, like the question of whether God created that genetic material from Mary's egg, or from nothing. And, that leads us further and further from God's Word. For that reason conjecture should never be taught as doctrine, and should never be used to deny Christ's humanity. God wants us to teach what His word says, not what we imagine.

   "Those who know God accept what we [the inspired writers of Scripture] say, those who are not of God will not accept what we say. That is how we can distinguish the spirit of truth from the spirit of error" (1John 4:6).

   Furthermore, because the words, **"Forasmuch then as the children are partakers of flesh and blood, He also himself likewise took part of the same; that through death He might destroy** him that had the power of death, that is, the devil," tell us that Christ took our humanity (flesh and blood) upon Himself in order defeat Satan, those who deny that He was truly human call into question the atonement. As it is written, "**But when the fullness of the time had come, God sent forth His Son, <u>made of a woman</u>, <u>made under the law</u>, To redeem them that were under the law**" (Gal4:4-5). "**Surely He has taken on himself our pains, and carried our sorrows: yet we regarded him as condemned, struck down by God, and afflicted, but He was wounded for our transgressions, He was bruised for our iniquities: the punishment that brought us peace was upon Him; and by His stripes we are healed**" (Isaiah 53:4-5).

Those who argue that miracles such as a virgin birth are impossible because they would violate the "laws of nature" are extremely foolish. They are foolish because intelligent beings override the laws of nature all of the time. The laws of nature will never assemble wood, steel and plaster into a house. On the contrary, the laws of nature will cause a house to decay and fall apart. As intelligent beings, we cause the wood, steel and plaster to do what they never would do on their own. And, if we can override the laws of nature so can God! [See Luke 1:34-35.]

The words, "**Behold, I was formed in iniquity; and sinful when my mother conceived me**," the words, "**Just as sin entered the world by one man, and death by sin; so death passed upon all men, because all have sinned:**" and the words, "**We all... were by nature the children of wrath**," tell us that all men born in the natural way are sinners (Psalm 51:5, Romans 5:12, Ephesians 2:3). However, because of His virgin birth, Christ is without sin. As it is written, "**He committed no sin, nor was deceit ever found in His mouth**" (1Peter 2:22). Likewise, the words, "**The precious blood of Christ, as of a lamb without blemish and without spot,**" the words, "**God made Him who knew no sin, to be sin for us,**" the words, "**He had not committed any crime, nor was any deceit in His mouth,**" and the words, "**The holy one who will be born of you will be called the Son of God,**" all tell us that Christ is without sin (1Peter 1:19, 2Corinthians 5:21, Isaiah 53:9, Luke 1:35). And, He can be without sin, while still being truly human because sin is not a part of human nature, but a corruption of it. [**Compare** Genesis 1:31, "**God saw every thing that He had made, and, behold, it was very good,**" with Jeremiah 17:9, "**The heart is deceitful above all things, and desperately wicked: who can know it?**".] Even though Christ as true man was subject to the law, the words, "**The Son of man is Lord even of the Sabbath day,**" reveal that He was by nature above the Law.

The words, "**I am the LORD, I do not change,**" tell us that God never changes (Malachi 3:6). Therefore, when Christ became man, God did not change. Instead, the words, "**Since the children have** flesh and blood, He in the same way took on flesh and blood," and the words, "**Took upon him the nature of a servant, and was born as a man,**" tell us that without changing His nature, God took on flesh and blood (Hebrews 2:14). That is why the Athanasian Creed says that Christ, "While being both God and Man is not two individuals or two Christs, but one individual, one Christ. One, not by conversion of Deity into flesh, but by taking manhood into God; One altogether; not by mixing divinity with humanity, but by uniting the two in one person".

Because Christ is both true God and true man united in one person, He is both the branch that came out of David, and God. As it is written, "**I will raise to David a righteous Branch… and this is the name by which He will be called, The LORD [Jahweh] Our Righteousness**" (Jeremiah 23:5-6). "**All the fullness of God dwells in Christ bodily**" (Colossians 2:9). [See John 14:9.]

4. The Personal Union

The words, "**Great is the mystery of godliness: God was revealed in the flesh,**" tell us that the truth of Christ's incarnation is a mystery (1Timothy 3:16). And, because it is a mystery, man's puny finite sin corrupted mind will never be able to fully understand it (Jeremiah 17:9). For that reason, what God has revealed in Scripture must either be fully accepted or fully rejected. Made up explanations and compromise positions are not acceptable, for it is written, "**No truth of scripture comes from any private explanation**" (2Peter 1:20). There are only two choices, the way of Christian faith, or the way of pagan unbelief.

The words, "**Can anyone hide himself in a secret place where I will not see him? asks the LORD. Don't I fill heaven and earth? asks the LORD,**" and the words, "**In Him we live, and move, and have our being,**" tell us that God is present everywhere, including in all of creation (Jeremiah 23:24, Acts 17:28). However, when it comes to believers the Bible also tells us that God is present with them in a special way. As it is written, "**If a man loves me, he will keep my words: and my Father will love him, and we will come to him, and make our home with him**" // "**Don't you know that you are the temple of God, and that the Spirit of God dwells in you?**" // "**He who is joined to the Lord is one spirit with him**" (John 14:23, 1Corinthians 3:16 and 6:17). In contrast, the union of Christ's human nature with His divine nature goes far beyond God's presence. In Christ God and man are permanently united. The words, "**I will raise to David a righteous Branch… and this is the name by which He will be called, The LORD (Jahweh) Our Righteousness,**" tell us that a descendant (branch) of David will be

God (Jeremiah 23:5-6). The words, "**The Word (God) was made flesh, and dwelt among us**," also tell us that Christ is God (John 1:14). That is why Christ could say, "**He who has seen Me has seen the Father**" (John 14:9). And, that union is what Paul called a great mystery when he said, "**Great is the mystery of godliness: God was revealed in the flesh, justified in the Spirit, seen of angels, preached to the Gentiles, believed on in the world, received up into glory**" (1Timothy 3:16). [See Rom. 1:3-4 and 9:5.]

The words, "**I am the LORD, I do not change**," tell us that God did not change into Christ (Malachi 3:6). Furthermore, because there is only one God, Christ is that One God, not a third creature who is only half God and half man. If that were the case He would not truly be God or truly be man. Therefore, that idea contradicts all of the passages that tell us Christ is God, and all of the passages that tell us that Christ is man. In addition, the words, "**The Word (God) was made flesh**," tell us that God did not just join Himself to Christ, like two boards being glued together, but took upon Himself the nature of man (John 1:14). And, He took on that nature without changing (Malachi 3:6). The ideas just mentioned are some of the compromise positions invented by the deceitfulness of the human heart (Jeremiah 17:9). In contrast, God wants us to teach what His Word says, not man-made attempts to reconcile His Word with man's ignorance.

In opposition to all compromise positions, we teach what the words of Scripture actually say, while rejecting any view that goes beyond or contradicts the plain meaning of the words. In addressing such errors the Council of Chalcedon (451) declared: "We confess one and the same Jesus Christ, the Son and Lord only-begotten, in two natures without mixture, without change, without division, without separation."

5. The Communion Of Natures

The communion of the natures of Christ flows from the fact that there is only one Christ, not two. **Because there is only one Christ what happens to His human nature happens to His divine nature.** The words, "**Crucified the Lord of glory**," tell us that when Christ suffered, God suffered, when Christ was crucified, "**the Lord of glory**" was crucified (1Corinthians 2:8). And, that is true because Christ does not have two personalities or two consciousnesses but one. That is why He could say, "**He who has seen me has seen the Father**" (John 14:9). That is also why the Bible says, "**God was revealed in the flesh**" (1Timothy 3:16).

The words, "**That you might... know the mystery of God, and of the Father, and of Christ, in whom are hidden all the treasures of wisdom and knowledge**," speak of Christ, not just one of His natures, having all the knowledge of God (Colossians 2:2-3). When

Jesus was speaking to His disciples He said, "**All power is given to me**" Matthew 28:18). As God that power was always His, but because there is only one Christ that power belonged to Him as a unified person, not just one of His natures. When He said, "**I will be with you always, even to the end of the world,**" it was His body that was speaking (Matthew 28:20). And, His body could say "**I will be with you**" because His unified person is present with us, not just one of His natures. The same holds true for the words, "**Where two or three are gathered together in my name, there am I in the midst of them**" (Matthew 18:20). And, because there is only one Christ, after speaking to two disciples on the road to Emmaus He was able to vanish "out of their sight" (Luke 24:31).

6. The Communication Of Attributes

Since the personal union of Christ's two natures cannot be complete without a communication or sharing of attributes, that sharing is also revealed in Scripture. Although the truths that we will cover in this section have been mentioned in the section on "Personal Union" here they will be explained more fully.

Edward W. A. Koehler illustrated the communion of attributes between Christ's divine and human natures thus: "A person consists of body and soul; each of these has its own attributes and properties. But as both, body and soul, belong to the same person, the attributes of either body or soul are ascribed to the entire person... Christ has two distinct natures, a human and a divine, each of which has its own essential attributes, functions, and activities, But as both natures belong to the same Person, the attributes and properties of either may be ascribed to the Person." ("A Summary of Christian Doctrine," page 90.)

What Dr. Koehler is saying is that even though Christ is true man (Consisting of both body and soul) the union of His two natures (human and divine) joins the two natures into one person in a way that can be illustrated by the way our body and soul unite to form one person. In clarifying this we speak of the communication of attributes as three kinds or Genera.

The First Genus (Genus Idiomaticum)

The first genus has to do with properties peculiar to the divine or human nature being ascribed to the entire person. For example: Although Christ's human nature was nailed to the cross, the words, "**They... crucified the Lord of glory,**" ascribe the crucifixion to His entire person, both human and divine (1Corinthians 2:8). The same holds true for the words, "**You... killed the Prince of life**" (Acts 3:15). While the words, "**Jesus Christ is the same yesterday, and to day, and forever,**" ascribe eternity to the person of Jesus (Hebrews 13:8). And, communication of that attribute is why Christ (whose human nature was about 30 years old at the time) could say, **"Before Abraham was, I am"** (John 8:58).

The Second Genus (Genus Maiestaticum)

The second genus has to do with properties of the divine nature being communicated to the human nature. We see that in Christ's words, **"All power is given to me in heaven and in earth"** (Matthew 28:18). The words, **"The Father... has also given him (Christ) authority to execute judgment, because He is the Son of man,"** tell us that Christ's human nature ("the son of man") is given divine authority (John 5:26-27). The words, **"As the Father raises the dead, and gives them life; even so the Son gives life to whomever He will,"** were spoken by Jesus on earth and tell us that Jesus has the power to give life. (John 5:21). The words, **"The Son of man will come in the glory of His Father,"** attribute divine glory to Christ's human nature [the son of man] (Matthew 16:27). The words, **"All the fullness of God was pleased to dwell in Him, and through Him to reconcile all things to himself,"** ascribe all the fullness of God to Christ (Colossians 1:19). The words, **"He [God] has appointed a day, when He will judge the world in righteousness by <u>the man</u> He has appointed,"** not only tell us that "the man" will judge, but that He has all of the knowledge needed to judge (Acts 17:31). The Bible also tells us that, **"All the fullness of God dwells in Christ bodily"** (Colossians 1:9). And, **"God was revealed in the flesh"** (1Timothy 3:16). [See also, Col. 2:3,9, Matt. 18:20 and 28:20, John 3:13, Eph. 1:23 and 4:10, Matt. 11:27, Luke 1:33, John 6:62, Phil. 2:6, Heb. 2:7, Matt. 26:64, Mark 14:62, Rom. 8:34, Eph. 1:20 and 4:10, Heb. 8:1.]

The Third Genus (Genus Apotelesmaticum)

The third genus has to do with the entire person being involved in all official acts peculiar to either the divine or human nature. By official acts we mean all acts pertaining to His official work of dying for the sins of the world, destroying the works of the devil, protecting His church, ruling, judging and so forth. For example: the words, **"Jesus Christ... gave himself for our sins, that He might deliver us from this present evil world,"** and the words, **"Christ also has loved us, and gave himself for us an offering and a sacrifice to God,"** speak of Christ's body being sacrificed (Galatians 1:3-4, Ephesians 5:2). However, the words **"Since the children have flesh and blood, He in the same way took on flesh and blood; so that through His death He might destroy him who holds the power of death, that is, the devil,"** tell us that Christ's divine nature was involved, (Hebrews 2:14). As do the words, **"When the time had fully come, God sent forth His Son, born of a woman, born under** the law, to redeem those who were under the law, that we might receive the adoption of sons" (Galatians 4:4-5). In fact, the words, "**The reason the Son of God appeared, was to destroy the works of the devil,**" tell us that Christ's human nature could never have won the victory alone (1John 3:8).

The Doctrine Of The States Of Christ

1. Christ's State Of Humiliation

The doctrine of Christ's humiliation has to do with the fact that even though His two natures (divine and human) were inseparably united from the moment of His conception, He chose to live, suffer, and die as a man. That doctrine is summarized in the words, "**Let this mind be in you, which was also in Christ Jesus: Who, being by nature God, did not see equality with God as something to be used for self-glorification: But made Himself of no reputation, and took upon Him the nature of a servant, and was born as a man: And being found in human form, He humbled himself, and became obedient unto death, even the death of the cross**" (Philippians 2:5-8).

The angel's words to Mary, "**The holy one who will be born of you,**" tell us that Christ was God (the holy one) from the beginning (Luke 1:35). The Bible also describes the unity of Christ's divine and human natures in the words, "**The Word was made flesh, and dwelt among us,**" and "**All the fullness of God dwells in Christ bodily**" (John 1:14 and Colossians 2:9). What we want to concentrate on in this section is the fact that from His conception until His resurrection Christ refrained from the full and constant use of His divine attributes, and was, "**Obedient unto death, even the death of the cross**" (Phil. 2:8). The fact that in order to redeem us Christ was, "**Born under the law**" (Galatians 4:4). **Took upon, "Himself our pains, and carried our sorrows... He was wounded for our transgressions, He was bruised for our iniquities**" (Isaiah 53:4-5). **And, received, "The curse in our stead: for it is written, Cursed is every one who hangs on a tree: That the blessing given to Abraham might come to the Gentiles through Jesus Christ; that we might receive the promise of the Spirit through faith**" (Galatians 3:13-14). **That self-renunciation on the part of Christ is what we refer to as His state of humiliation.**

During His humiliation, Christ did not fully avail Himself of everything He, as God, had at His disposal. And, the reason He humbled Himself was for our sakes. The words, "**Do you think that I cannot call on my Father, and He would at once give me more than** twelve legions of angels?" tell us that He could have avoided capture, but did not (Matthew 26:53). The words, **"Jesus said... shall I not drink the cup that my Father has given me?"** tell us that He was willing to be captured and crucified for our sakes (John 18:11). The words, **"When the time had fully come, God sent forth His Son, born of a woman, born under the law, To redeem those who were under the law,"** tell us that He came into the world "to redeem" us (Galatians 4:4-5). The words, **"I lay down my life for the sheep... I am laying down my life, that I might take it again. No one takes it from me, but I lay it down voluntarily. I have the power to lay it down, and I have the power to take it back. That is the commandment that have I received from my Father,"** tell us that He willingly laid down His life for our sakes (John 10:15-18). The words, **"This is a trustworthy statement, worthy of complete acceptance, that Christ Jesus came into the world to save sinners,"** tell us the same thing (1Timothy 1:15). Therefore, even though Christ could have escaped crucifixion, He chose not to, but was **"obedient unto death, even the death of the cross"** (Philippians 2:8). Without that obedience, He could not have died for our sins, and we would be lost. [See Isaiah 53:1-6, 2Corinthians 5:19-21.]

However, even though Christ did not fully avail Himself of divine power during His state of humiliation, the power was still there, and He employed it when it was in our interest for Him to do so. For example, all of the miracles that He did were done by divine power. The words, **"These are written, that you might believe that Jesus is the Messiah, the Son of God; and that believing you might have life through His name,"** tell us that they were recorded for our salvation (John 20:31). And, because He endured the agony of the cross we can be, **"Justified freely by His grace... through faith in His blood"** (Romans 3:24-25).

2. Erroneous Views Regarding Christ's Humiliation

Christ's humiliation did not consist of the fact that He took upon Himself the nature of man, for He still has both natures. His humiliation is summarized in the words, **"Being found in human form, He humbled Himself, and became obedient unto death, even the death of the cross"** (Philippians 2:8). Those words tell us that He had "human form" before He "humbled Himself".

Likewise, Christ's humiliation did not involve a loss of His divine nature, or its attributes. Nor did it involve a reduction or diminishing of the divine nature. The words, **"I and my Father are one,"** and **"He who has seen me has seen the Father,"** tell us that while He was on earth He was still fully divine (John 10:30 and 14:9). The words, "**I am the LORD, I do not change,**" tell us that God can never be reduced or diminished (Malachi 3:6). The words, "**Whatever the Father does, the Son also does,**" tell us that while Christ was on earth He was able to do anything the Father did (John 5:19). And, the words, "**All the fullness of God dwells in Christ bodily,**" also make it clear that Christ was fully divine (Colossians 2:9). [See Psalm 102:27, 1Timothy 6:16.]

Whatever Christ does after His incarnation He does not do as God alone, but as the God-man, the incarnate Messiah. The words, "**How much more will the blood of Christ, who through the eternal Spirit offered Himself without blemish to God, cleanse your conscience from dead works to serve the living God?**" tell us that Christ "offered Himself" through "the eternal Spirit" (Hebrews 9:14). The words, "**God left nothing outside His control. However we do not yet see everything under His control. But we see Jesus, who was made a little lower than the angels, now crowned with glory and honor; because He suffered death so that by the grace of God He might taste death for every man,**" tell us that Christ (who was fully in control) willingly suffered death for us (Hebrews 2:8-9). And, the words, "**From now on the Son of man will be seated at the right hand of the power of God,**" and "**Who has entered into heaven, and is at God's right hand,**" Tell us that Christ's exaltation to the right hand of God came at the end of His humiliation (Luke 22:69, 1Peter 3:22).

3. The Several Stages Of The Humiliation

The humiliation of Christ extended throughout His earthly life from His conception to, and including, His burial. As I mentioned previously, Christ's humiliation did not consist of the fact that He took upon Himself the nature of man. However, because all men are subject to the devil through sin, He had to be born without sin in order to redeem us. That stage of His humiliation involved His willingness to be carried in a womb, born, and be subject to His parents. It is described in the words, "**You know the grace of our Lord Jesus Christ, that, though He was rich, yet for your sakes He became poor, that you through His poverty might be rich**" (2Corinthians 8:9).

The second stage of His humiliation was His willingness to be subject to the law. That involved His circumcision, education and life. The words, "**When eight days were accomplished for the circumcising of the child, His name was called JESUS,**" tell us that He was circumcised (Luke 2:21). His education is included in the words, "**And Jesus increased in wisdom and stature, and in favor with God and man**" (Luke 2:52). And, His life which undoubtedly included all of the hardships, dangers, temptations and reproaches common to this life, is described in the words, "**Foxes have holes, and birds of the air have nests; but the Son of man has no place to lay His head**" (Luke 9:58). [See Matt. 2:13, Luke 2:7, Matt. 8:17 and 20, Matt. 9:14, Matt. 17:27.]

The third stage of His humiliation includes all of the suffering leading up to and including His death on the cross. That stage of humiliation is described in the words, "**Surely He has taken on himself our pains, and carried our sorrows: yet we regarded him as condemned, struck down by God, and afflicted. But He was wounded for our transgressions, He was bruised for our iniquities: the punishment that brought us peace was upon him; and by His stripes we are healed. Like sheep we have all have gone astray; each of us has turned to his own way; and the LORD has laid on Him the iniquity of us all. He was oppressed, and He was mistreated, yet He did not open His mouth: He was led like a lamb to the slaughter, and as a sheep before her shearers is silent, so He did not open His mouth. He was taken from prison and from judgment: and who at that time understood? for He was cut off from the land of the living: and struck down for His people's sins. And He made His grave with the wicked, and with the rich in His death; because He had not committed any crime, nor was any deceit in His mouth**" (Isaiah 53:4-9).

The words, "**About the ninth hour Jesus cried with a loud voice, saying, Eli, Eli, lama sabachthani? that is, My God, my God, why have you forsaken me?**" describe the horror of His death (Matthew 27:46). The words, "**God made Him who knew no sin, to be sin for us; so that we might be made the righteousness of God in Him,**" tell us the reason for His death (2Corinthians 5:21). The words, "**He humbled himself, and became obedient unto death, even the death of the cross,**" tell us of His willingness to die for us (Philippians 2:8). And, the words, "**Jesus, having cried again with a loud voice, yielded up His spirit,**" describe His death (Matthew 27:50).

4. The State Of Exaltation

"Christ's state of exaltation began with His return to life in the grave, and exhibited itself to the lower world by His descent into hell, to the world by His glorious resurrection, and to the highest heavens by His ascension and session at the right hand of God the Father." (John Theodore Mueller, "Christian Dogmatics," page 295.) The words, "He humbled himself, and became obedient unto death, even the death of the cross. Therefore God has also highly exalted him, and given him a name that is above every name: That at the name of Jesus every knee should bow, in heaven, and on earth, and under the earth," summarize the doctrine of Christ's exaltation (Philippians 2:8-10). As do the words, "**He [God] raised Him [Christ] from the dead, and set Him at His own right hand in the heavenly places, Far above all principality, and power, and might, and dominion, and every name that is named, not only in this world, but also in that which is to come, and has put all things under His feet**" (Ephesians 1:20-22). [See Eph. 4:10.]

By telling us that Christ, "**Was raised again for our justification**," and that, "**If Christ did not rise, our preaching is a waste of time, and your faith is worthless**," the Bible tells us that Christ's exaltation also took place for our salvation (Romans 4:25). Thus our faith rests upon both Christ's crucifixion and His resurrection. As it is written, "**Brethren, I want to remind you of the gospel that I preached to you, that you believed, and upon which your faith rests... how that Christ died for our sins according to the scriptures, and that He was buried, and that He rose again the third day according to the scriptures**" (1Corinthians 15:1-4).

5. The Several Stages Of Christ's Exaltation

Following His resurrection Christ, a) descended into hell, b) left the tomb, c) spent forty days on earth, d) ascended unto heaven, e) sat down at the right hand of God, and f) will return to judge the living and the dead.

Regarding His descent into hell, Christ's words, "**It is finished**," tell us that He did not suffer in hell (John 19:30). Likewise, His words, "**Today you will be with me in paradise**," tell us that He was in heaven, not hell, while His body was in the grave (Luke 23:43). Because the Bible specifically defines "paradise" as "heaven" (2Corinthians 12:2-4), the idea that paradise was in hell is an unscriptural myth. That myth rests on a number of false assumptions. One of those assumptions is the myth (passed on as tradition in Catholic circles) that Old Testament saints could not receive forgiveness until Christ died. That myth flies in the face of all the Old Testament passages that speak of forgiveness. As it is written, "**There is forgiveness with you, that you may be feared**" and again "**You have forgiven the iniquity of your people**" (Psalm 130:4 and 85:2). In fact, **without forgiveness Abraham's faith could never have been "counted... to him for righteousness**," for it is forgiveness and forgiveness alone that makes us righteous in the sight of God (Genesis 15:6). And, the words, "**Being put to death in the flesh, but quickened by the Spirit, by which also He went and preached unto the spirits in prison, which sometime were disobedient, when** once the longsuffering of God waited in the days of Noah," tell us that it was after Christ was "quickened" [made alive] that He proclaimed His victory to those who are in hell awaiting the final judgment (1Peter 3:18-20). Moreover, the term translated "preached" in this passage, "Does not mean more than to proclaim... as the context shows, the term manifestly denotes Law-preaching" (John Theodore Mueller, "Christian Dogmatics," page 296.)

Regarding Christ's departure from the tomb, the words, "**The angel of the Lord descended from heaven, and going to the tomb rolled back the stone from the door, and sat on it... And the angel spoke and said to the women, Do not be afraid: for I know that you seek Jesus, who was crucified. He is not here: for He has risen, just as He said. Come, see the place where the Lord lay,**" tell us that Jesus left the tomb before the angel rolled back the stone (Matthew 28:2-6).

While the words, "**Christ was raised up from the dead by the glory of the Father,**" and "**He raised Him from the dead, and set Him at His own right hand,**" tell us that the father raised Christ from the dead (Romans 6:4, Ephesians 1:20); the words, "**I am laying down my life, that I might take it again. No one takes it from me, but I lay it down voluntarily. I have the power to lay it down, and I have the power to take it back,**" tell us that Christ was the cause of His own resurrection (John 10:17-18). The words, "**Destroy this temple, and in three days I will raise it up,**" also tell us that Christ rose under His own power (John 2:19). Both statements are true because what is done by one person of the Trinity is never done to the exclusion of the other two. And, for that reason, Christ's resurrection is in itself a powerful proof of His deity.

The words, "**Look at my hands and my feet, and see that it is really me: handle me, and see; for a spirit does not have flesh and bones, as you see me have,**" and the words, "**Bring your finger here, and examine my hands; and stretch out your hand, and thrust it into my side: and do not be faithless, but believing,**" tell us that Christ came out of the tomb with the same body that went into the tomb, the same body that was born of the Virgin Mary (Luke 24:39, John 20:27). However, the words, "**It is sown a natural body; it is raised a spiritual body. As there is a natural body, there is also a spiritual body,**" tell us that He rose with a glorified body (1Corinthians 15:44). And, the words, "**Who will transform our vile bodies, and make them like His glorified body, by the power by which He is able to bring everything under His control,**" tell us that we also will receive a glorified body like His (Philippians 3:21). [See, Acts 2:24, Heb. 2:14-15, Rom. 4:25, 1Peter 1:3-4, John 11:25-26 and 14:19, 2Cor. 4:14, 1Thess. 4:14, Rom. 6:4-5, 2Cor. 5:15.]

Regarding the forty days following Christ's resurrection, the words, "**He also showed that He was alive after His suffering by many** infallible proofs, being seen by them [His disciples] for forty days, and talking with them of things pertaining to the kingdom of God," tell us that He spent forty days on earth before His ascension (Acts 1:2-3). During those forty days Christ did not spend the majority of His time with His disciples as He had done before. However, He did appear to them a number of times, and the words, **"Look at my hands and my feet, and see that it is really me,"** emphasized to His disciples the fact that His resurrection was a physical resurrection (Luke 24:39). The words, **"So after they had eaten, Jesus said to Simon Peter,"** also tell us that Jesus ate with His disciples after the resurrection (John 21:15). That is significant because Jews believed that a being without flesh and blood (a phantom) could not eat food. And, the words, **"Every spirit who does not confess that Jesus Christ has come in the flesh is not of God: and this is the spirit of the antichrist,"** tell us why that fact was important (1John 4:3).

The words, **"He rose again the third day according to the scriptures, and that He was seen by Peter, then by the twelve, after that, He was seen by over five hundred brethren at once; most of whom are still alive, though some have fallen asleep. After that, He was seen by James; then by all the apostles,"** list some of Christ's appearances during the forty days (1Corinthians 15:4-7).

Regarding Christ's ascension unto heaven, the words, **"After He had said these things, while they watched, He was taken up; and a cloud received Him out of their sight,"** describe what happened (Acts 1;9). Although I could combine Christ's ascension with His sitting down at the right hand of the father, I have treated them as two steps in His exaltation because His ascension was seen by witnesses while His sitting down at the right hand of the father was not. The fact that Christ is with the Father tells us that the heaven He ascended into is not some place in space (which is part of God's creation) but the dwelling place of God who transcends both space and time. The ancient Jews referred to that place as "the third heaven" [the first being the place where the birds are, and the second being the place where the stars are] (2Corinthians 12:2). And, the words, **"In my Father's house are many mansions... if I go and prepare a place for you, I will come again, and receive you unto myself; that where I am, there you may be also,"** tell us that we will be in the same place (John 14:2-3).

Regarding Christ's position at the right hand of God, the words, **"Who being the brightness of His glory, and the true image of His nature, and sustaining all things by the word of His power, when He had by Himself made purification for our sins, sat down on the right hand of the Majesty on high,"** tell us that when the work of redemption was finished Christ sat down at the right hand of God (Hebrews 1:3). The words, "**Your right hand, O LORD, is glorious in power**," tell us that the right hand of God is a position of power (Exodus 15:6). And, the words, "**You will see the Son of man sitting on the right hand of power, and coming in the clouds of heaven**," tell us that when Christ returns He will be wielding the power of God (Matthew 26:64).

The words "**We have such an high priest, and He sat down on the right hand of the throne of the Majesty in the heavens, He is the minister of the true Holy Place, in the real tabernacle, that was set up by the Lord, and not by man**," tell us that sitting on the right hand of God is not a location that limits Him, but from there He officiates as our high priest (Hebrews 8:1-2). The words, "**If I take the wings of the morning, and stay at the most distant parts of the sea, even there your hand will lead me, and your right hand will hold me**," tell us that God's right hand is not a place, but a position of power that can be present wherever we are (Psalm 139:9-10).

The words, "**Who, being by nature God, did not see equality with God as something to be used for self-glorification**," tell us that as God Christ was equal to the Father and, therefore, over all things (Philippians 2:6). For that reason, when the Bible says that Christ will be subject to the Father, it is telling us that Christ's human nature will be subject to the divine. One such passage is 1Corinthians 15:25-28 where we read, "**For He must reign, until God has put all enemies under His feet. The last enemy that will be destroyed is death. For God has put everything under His feet. But when He says that everything has been put under Him, it is evident that this does not include the one who put all things under Him. And when all things are subject to Him, then <u>the Son Himself will also be subject to Him</u> who put all things under Him, that God may be all in all**". Another passage is Ephesians 1:20-23 where we read, "**He (God) raised Him (Christ) from the dead, and set Him at His own right hand in the heavenly places, far above all principality, and power, and might, and dominion, and every name that is named, not only in this world, but also in that which is to come. And has put all things under His feet, and appointed him to be the head over all things to the church, Which is His body, the fullness of him that fills all in all**". [See 1Peter 3:22, Acts 3:21, Eph. 4:10, Psalm 110:1, Heb. 2:7-8.]

Regarding Christ's second advent, the words, "**I charge you therefore before God, and the Lord Jesus Christ, who will judge the living and the dead at His appearing and His kingdom**," tell us that Christ will judge both the living and the dead when He returns (2Timothy 4:1-2). That topic will be dealt with in the chapter on Eschatology (the last things).

The Doctrine Of Christ's Office

The words, **"This is a trustworthy statement, worthy of complete acceptance, that Christ Jesus came into the world to save sinners; of whom I am the worst,"** tell us the reason Christ came into the world (1Timothy 1:15). You will notice that He did not come to make us righteous through works, He came to save us from our sins. As it is written, **"The Son of man has come to seek and to save that which was lost"** (Luke 19:10). [See Matt. 18:11.] And, the work of our salvation involves, 1) teaching us the way of salvation, 2) making satisfaction for our sins, and 3) reigning as head over those whom He has saved.

In teaching us the way of salvation He functioned as a **prophet**, and that prophetic role was foretold in the words. **"The LORD your God will raise up for you a Prophet like me from the midst of you, from your brethren; you must listen to him"** (Deuteronomy 18:15). In making atonement for our sins He functioned as a **priest**, and that priestly role was foretold in the words, **"The LORD has sworn, and will not change, You are a priest forever after the order of Melchizedek"** (Psalm 110:4). [See Hebrews 5:6.] As head over His church He functions as a **king**, and that role was foretold in the words, **"I installed my king upon my holy hill of Zion... Blessed are all those who put their trust in him"** (Psalm 2:6,12). That is why we say that Christ has a threefold office, the office of Prophet, Priest and King. [See, John 17:4 and 3:16, Matt. 18:11, Luke 1:30-31, Matt. 1:21,25, Luke 2:21, Luke 4:18, John 1:18, Heb. 1:1, Matt. 17:2, 2Cor. 5:18-19, Matt. 20:28, Rom. 5:10, 1John 2:2, Luke 1:33, Eph. 1: 20-23, John 18:33-37, Deut. 18:15-19, Ps. 110:2 and 6-12, Heb. 6:20 and 7:17.]

A. The Prophetic Office Of Christ

1. Executing This Office In The State Of Humiliation

Because Christ is **"The mighty God, The everlasting Father"** (Isaiah 9:6), when He taught He did not receive His message by inspiration, as did the prophets of old (2Timothy 3:16), but instead spoke as God Himself. As it is written, **"God, who in the past spoke to the fathers at many times and in various ways through the prophets, has spoken to us in these last days in the person of His Son**, whom He has appointed heir of all things, and through whom He made the universe" (Hebrews 1:1-2). For that reason, **"The people were astonished at His doctrine,** For He taught them as one who had authority, and not as the scribes" (Matthew 7:28-29). And, the authority He spoke with did not consist of acting like He had authority, but of the fact that, **"His word was with power"** (Luke 4:32). It was the power of the Spirit of God witnessing to the hearts of the hearers that astonished them.

The message Christ proclaimed was one of repentance and faith. As it is written, **"Jesus began to preach, and to say, Repent: for the kingdom of heaven is at hand."** // **"The Son of man did not come to be served, but to serve, and to give His life a ransom for many."** // **"As Moses lifted up the serpent in the wilderness, even so must the Son of man be lifted up, that whosoever believes on him should not perish, but have everlasting life."** // **"Every one who looks to the Son, and believes on him, may have everlasting life: and I will raise him up on the last day"** (Matthew 4:17 and 20:28, John 3:14-15 and 6:40). While Christ proclaimed the Law as part of His call to repentance, His focus was on the Gospel-truth of salvation through His death as our substitute. We see that in the words, **"He took the twelve aside, and said to them, Behold, we are going up to Jerusalem, and everything that is written by the prophets concerning the Son of man will come to pass, for He will be handed over to the Gentiles, and will be mocked, and treated spitefully, and spit on. And they will scourge him, and put him to death: and the third day He will rise again"** (Luke 18:31-33). [See, Matt. 16:21, Mark 8:31, Matt. 11:28-30, John 6:29,32,33,35.]

The words, **"I tell you truly, Until heaven and earth pass away, not one letter or stroke will pass from the law,"** tell us that Christ did not do away with the Law, or replace it with something else (Matthew 5:18). Instead, the words, **"Woe to you also, you lawyers! for you load men down with burdens they can hardly bear, and you yourselves do not touch those burdens with one of your fingers,"** tell us that the Pharisees, for all their legalism, rationalized God's Law and made excuses to get around it (Luke 11:46). Much of what Jesus said about the Law was aimed at correcting their false interpretations, while calling the People to repentance. We see an example of that in the words, **"You disregard the commandment of God, and hold to the tradition of men, such as the washing of pots and cups: and many other such things. And He said to them, You completely invalidate the commandment of God, in order to keep your tradition. For Moses said, Honor your father and mother; and, Anyone who curses his father or mother, let him be put to death, but you say, If a man will say to his father or mother, It is Corban, that is a gift, by which you might profit by me; he shall be free. And you no longer allow him to do any-**

thing for his father or his mother, making the word of God of no effect through your tradition, that you have handed down: and you do many things like that" (Mark 7:8-13).

The words, "**Jesus replied, You shall love the Lord your God with all your heart, and with all your soul, and with all your mind. This is the first and greatest commandment. And the second is like it, You shall love your neighbor as yourself. On these two commandments hang all the law and the prophets,**" and the words, "**The entire law is summed up in one command; You shall love your neighbor as yourself,**" tell us that the Law has not passed away (Matthew 22:37-40, Galatians 5:14). Moreover, the words, "**The law is not meant for a righteous man, but for those who are lawless and rebellious,**" tell us that those who are unrepentant are still under the Law, and will be condemned by the Law (1Timothy 1:9). So I repeat, "**Until heaven and earth pass away, not one letter or stroke will pass from the law**" (Matthew 5:18).

Another problem that Jesus had to deal with, was the idea that riches were evidence of God's favor. That idea often gave the wealthy a false assurance of salvation, while undermining the faith of the poor. We see that in the words, "**How hard is it for those who trust in riches to enter the kingdom of God**" and in the words, "**He (Jesus) looked at His disciples, and said, Blessed are you who are poor: for yours is the kingdom of God**" (Mark 10:24, Luke 6:20). Therefore, in reading passages like that we need to understand that the Bible is not saying that there is some virtue in being poor, but that we should not trust in riches. Whenever people derive their assurance of salvation from something other than God's promise of forgiveness in Christ, they have a false Gospel (1Corinthians 15:1-4).

2. The Prophetic Office In The State Of Exaltation

Since Christ has ascended unto heaven He is no longer here to proclaim the Gospel in person. However, He is still at work proclaiming the Gospel through His church, and the men He raises up to carry out the work of the church. The words, "**Jesus said, Peace be with you: as my Father has sent me, even so I am sending you,**" tell us that Christ sent His disciples to do that work (John 20:21). The words, "**The disciples went out, and preached everywhere, and the Lord worked with them, and confirmed the word through the signs that went with it,**" tell us that "**the Lord worked with**" those who preached the Gospel (Mark 16:20). And, the words, "**I will always be with you, even to the end of the world. Amen,**" tell us that Christ continues to be with us, and to work with those who preach the Gospel (Matthew 28:20).

The Apostle Paul said, "**Christ is speaking through me**" and

"Has saved us, and called us to a holy calling" (2Corinthians 13:3, 2Timothy 1:9). The words, "**His gift made some, apostles; and some, prophets; and some, evangelists; and some, pastors and teachers,**" tell us that His gift makes some "pastors and teachers" (Ephesians 4:11). When the Apostle Paul says, "**Let the word of Christ dwell in you richly,**" his words tell us that the Gospel message is the "word of Christ" (Colossians 3:16). The words, "**Jesus said to the Jews who believed on him, If you continue in my word, you are truly my disciples,**" tell us that He does not want us looking outside of His Word for doctrine, or teaching any ideas that do not come from His Word (John 8:31). The words, "**If any man speaks, let him speak according to God's Word; if any man serves, let him do it with the ability that God gives,**" again tell us that what we are to teach is what the Bible says, and God gives us ability (1Peter 4:11). And, the words, "**If anyone teaches otherwise, and will not agree with sound teaching, even the words of our Lord Jesus Christ, and the doctrine that is in accord with godliness, he is proud, knowing nothing,**" tell us that our Lord does not want anyone teaching any doctrine that is not in His Word or contradicts what His Word says (1Timothy 6:3-4).

The words, "**They worship me (Christ) in vain, teaching for doctrines the commandments of men,**" tell us that teaching the opinions of men hinders the work of salvation, and can destroy souls (Matthew 15:9). Therefore, all who do so are, "**false prophets, which come to you in sheep's clothing, but inwardly they are ravening wolves**" (Matthew 7:15). "**For such people are not serving our Lord Jesus Christ, but their own belly**; and by smooth words and flattering speech deceive the hearts of the simple" (Romans 6:18). Dr. A. Strong rightly says: "**All modern prophecy that is true is but the republication of Christ's message, the proclamation and expounding of truth already revealed in Scripture.**" (Syst. Theol, p. 389.)

Christ, as God the Son, is not only the true teacher of His church in this age, but was also the teacher before His incarnation. We see that in all of the passages where we read, "<u>**The Word of the LORD came**</u> **to Abram in a vision, saying**" or, "<u>**The Word of the LORD came**</u> **to Nathan, saying**" or, "<u>**The Word of the LORD came**</u> **to Solomon**" (Genesis 15:1, 2Samuel 7:4, 1Kings 6:11). We are also told of this in the words, "**Concerning this salvation the prophets who prophesied of the grace that would come to you, have inquired and searched diligently, seeking to know what person, or period of time the <u>Spirit of Christ</u> who was in them was indicating, when it testified in advance about the sufferings of Christ, and the glory that would follow**" (1Peter 1:10-11). [Notice the words, "**Spirit of Christ**" in that verse.]

B. The Priestly Office Of Christ

The same grace that Christ proclaimed as our divine Prophet He obtained for us as our divine priest. As it is written, **"We are sanctified through the offering of the body of Jesus Christ once for all... For by one offering He has perfected for ever those who are sanctified"** (Hebrews 10:10-14). For, He is, **"The Lamb of God, who takes away the sin of the world"** (John 1:29). He, **"Gave Himself a ransom for all"** (1Timothy 2:6). **"The LORD has laid on Him the iniquity of us all"** (Isaiah 53:6). And, **"He is the propitiation for our sins: and not for ours only, but also for the sins of the whole world"** (1John 2:2).

The words, **"Christ then arrived as a high priest of the good things about to come, through the greater and more perfect tabernacle, not made with human hands, that is to say, not a part of this creation, and it was not by the blood of goats and calves, but by His own blood that He entered once for all into the holy place, obtaining eternal redemption for us,"** tell us that what Christ obtained for us was obtained "by His own blood" (Hebrews 9:11-12). For, **"Christ redeemed us from the curse of the law, receiving the curse in our stead: for it is written, Cursed is every one who hangs on a tree"** (Galatians 3:13). He **"Gave himself for us, that He might redeem us from all iniquity, and purify for Himself a special people, eager to do good works"** (Titus 2:14). And, because of His sacrifice, **"We have redemption through His blood, the forgiveness of sins, according to the riches of His grace"** (Ephesians 1:7). **"For you were bought with a price. Therefore honor God with your body, and with your spirit, which are God's"** (1Corinthians 6:20). **"Knowing that you were not redeemed from the fruitless lifestyle handed down to you by tradition from your fathers, with corruptible things, such as silver and gold; But with the precious blood of Christ, as of a lamb without blemish and without spot"** (1Peter 1:18-19).

The Bible uses many different words to describe what Christ accomplished as our High Priest, and they all play an important role in understanding what He accomplished. For example:

a) If two parties are alienated and hostile to each other, a **mediator** is someone who goes to each party in order to work out a reconciliation. The words, **"There is one God, and one mediator between God and men, the man Christ Jesus,"** describe Christ as our Mediator (1Timothy 2:5). The words, **"The covenant of which He is mediator is superior to the old one, being founded on better promises,"** and the words, **"He is the mediator of a new testament, so that since a death has taken place that redeems them from sins committed** under the first testament, those who are called might receive the promise of the eternal inheritance," describe Him as "The **mediator** of the new covenant" (Hebrews 8:6, 9:15 and 12:24).

b) If you sell something, buying it back is called **redeeming** it. We see that word used in Leviticus 25:29, "**If a man sells a residence in a walled city, then he may redeem it within a whole year after it is sold**". The words, "**All have sinned, and come short of the glory of God, being justified freely by His grace through the redemption that is in Christ Jesus**," tell us that we are "justified" through the **redemption** Christ made for us – His own death being the price (Romans 3:23-24). The words, "**We have redemption through His blood, even the forgiveness of sins,**" and the words, "**In whom we have redemption through His blood, the forgiveness of sins, according to the riches of His grace,**" tell us that we were **redeemed** by the "blood" of Christ, that we are redeemed by the forgiveness of sins, and that it is ours through "grace" (Colossians 1:14 and Ephesians 1:7). "**You are in Christ Jesus, who has become for us wisdom from God, righteousness, sanctification, and redemption**" (1Corinthians 1:30). [See 1Timothy 2:6, Hebrews 9:12,15.]

c) If two parties are alienated from each other a propitiation would be something that would eradicate anger bringing peace and reconciliation. The words, "**God has shown His love for us... This is the love, not that we loved God, but that He loved us, and sent His Son to be the propitiation for our sins,**" tell us that what Christ did removed the anger that separated us from God (1John 4:9-10). For, "**Christ Jesus**" is the one, "**Whom God has set forth to be a propitiation through faith in His blood, to declare His righteousness for the remission of sins that are past, through the forbearance of God**" (Romans 3:24-25). And, Christ, "**Is the propitiation for our sins: and not for ours only, but also for the sins of the whole world**" (1John 2:2).

d) Christ's death has propitiated God's anger making **reconciliation** possible. And, "**If, we were reconciled to God by the death of His Son, when we were enemies, much more, having been reconciled, we will be saved by His life**" (Romans 5:10). "**For God was in Christ, reconciling the world to Himself, not counting their sins against them, and has committed to us the word of reconciliation**" (2Corinthians 5:19). As a result, "**You who once were far away are made near by the blood of Christ. For He is our peace, who has made both Jew and Gentile one... that He might reconcile both to God in one body by the cross**" (Ephesians 2:13-16).

"For all the fullness of God was pleased to dwell in Him [Christ], and through Him to reconcile all things to Himself" (Colossians 1:19-20).

e) Christ's death is also described as a ransom. In both Matthew 20:28 and Mark 10:45 we read, "**The Son of man did not come to be served, but to serve, and to give His life a ransom for many**".

f) The Bible tells us that Christ was made sin for us. As it is written, "**God made Him who knew no sin, to be sin for us; so that we might be made the righteousness of God in Him**" (2Corinthians 5:21). And by, "**Sending His own Son in the likeness of sinful flesh, as an offering for sin, He condemned sin in the flesh**" (Romans 8:3).

g) The Bible tells us that Christ became "a curse for us". As it is written, "**Christ redeemed us from the curse of the law, being made a curse for us [i.e. receiving the curse in our stead], for it is written, Cursed is every one who hangs on a tree**" (Galatians 3:13).

h) The Bible tells us that Christ took our sins and their punishment upon Himself. As it is written, "**Surely He has taken on Himself our pains, and carried our sorrows: yet we regarded Him as condemned, struck down by God, and afflicted. But He was wounded for our transgressions, He was bruised for our iniquities: the punishment that brought us peace was upon Him; and by His stripes we are healed. Like sheep we have all have gone astray; each of us has turned to his own way; and the LORD has laid on Him the iniquity of us all**" (Isaiah 53:4-6). For He, "**Bore our sins in His body on the tree, that we, being dead to sin, should live to righteousness**" (1Peter 2:24). And, that is why John the Baptist said that Christ was, "**The Lamb of God, who takes away the sin of the world**" (John 1:29).

i) The Bible tells us that Christ shed His blood for our sins. As it is written, "**It was not by the blood of goats and calves, but by His own blood that He entered once for all into the holy place, obtaining eternal redemption for us**" (Hebrews 9:12). For, "**The blood of Jesus Christ His Son cleanses us of all sin**" (1John 1:7). And, that is why Christ said, "**This is My blood, that of the new testament, which is shed for many for the forgiveness of sins**" (Matthew 26:28).

j) The Bible tells us that Christ's death **blotted out** the indictment against us. As it is written, "**He has made you, who were dead in your sins and the uncircumcision of your flesh, alive together with him, having forgiven all of your sins, blotting out the handwriting of ordinances that was against us, which was contrary to us, and took it out of** the way, nailing it to His cross" (Colossians 2:13-14).

k) The Bible tells us that Christ freed us from the **curse of the Law**. As it is written, "**Christ redeemed us from the curse of the law, receiving the curse in our stead: for it is written, Cursed is every one who hangs on a tree**" (Galatians 3:13). And, "**God sent forth His Son, born of a woman, born under the law, to redeem those who were under the law, that we might receive the adoption of sons**" (Galatians 4:4-5).

l) The Bible tells us that Christ freed us from the **wrath** of God. As it is written, "**You turned to God from idols to serve the living and true God, and to wait for His Son from heaven, whom He raised from the dead, even Jesus, who has rescued us from the wrath to come**" (1Thessalonians 1:9-10). "**For God has not appointed us to wrath, but to obtain salvation by our Lord Jesus Christ, who died for us, so that, whether we are watching or sleeping, we will live together with him**" (1Thessalonians 5:9-10).

m) The Bible tells us that Christ freed us from eternal **condemnation**. As it is written, "**Truly, truly, I tell you, He who hears My word, and believes on Him who sent me, has everlasting life, and will not come into condemnation; but has passed from death to life**" (John 5:24). "**There is therefore now no condemnation for those who are in Christ Jesus, who walk not after the flesh, but after the Spirit**" (Romans 8:1).

n) The Bible tells us that in Christ we are **righteous** and **beloved**. "**For God made Him who knew no sin, to be sin for us; so that we might be made the righteousness of God in Him**" (2Corinthians 5:21). And so, "**Beloved of God, called to be saints: Grace to you and peace from God our Father, and the Lord Jesus Christ**" (Romans 1:7).

In the Old Testament the priests offered lambs and goats for the sins of the people. However, in the third chapter of Galatians the Apostle Paul carefully explains to us that in every age salvation has always been through faith in Christ. As it is written, "**The Scripture, having foreseen that God would justify the heathen through faith, proclaimed the gospel to Abraham in advance, saying, In you shall all nations be blessed. So then those who have faith in Christ are blessed with Abraham, who also believed**" (Galatians 3:8-9). Why then was the Law given? Paul goes on to tell us that, "**The law was our schoolmaster to bring us to Christ, that we might be declared righteous by faith. But now that faith has come, we are no longer under a schoolmaster**" (Galatians 3:24-25). And, how did the law bring people to faith in Christ? Well it was divided into two parts. The purpose of the commandments and condemnation of sin was to reveal to us our sin and need of God's forgiveness. Which is why Paul said, "**The knowledge of sin comes by the law**" (Romans 3:20). The purpose of the sacrifices was to teach the people the importance of admitting their sin and seeking God's forgiveness. **It is important to understand that the sacrifices were not a different way of salvation, "For it is impossible for the blood of bulls and of goats to take away sins**" (Hebrews 10:4). By requiring animal sacrifice, God taught the people that forgiveness is not cheap. And, **because God instituted those sacrifices as a type of Christ's ultimate sacrifice, He counted faith in the promise of forgiveness that He had connected with that sacrifice as faith in Christ. For, "The covenant concerning faith in Christ, that was confirmed by God at the time of Abraham, cannot be nullified by the law, which came four hundred and thirty years later, so as to make the promise of no effect. For if the inheritance comes by the law, it is not given by promise: but God gave it to Abraham by promise**" (Galatians 3:17-18). David trusted in that promise, saying, "**I have placed my faith in your grace [mercy]; my heart will rejoice in your salvation**" (Psalm 13:5). And, that promise of grace (mercy) is why God said, "**I desired mercy, and not sacrifice**" (Hosea 6:6). **The actual sacrifices were just a means of giving people <u>God's promise</u> of mercy and forgiveness. Salvation has always been, and will always be, through faith in God's promise of forgiveness in Christ!**

The Bible describes Christ's saving work as obedience. That obedience can be seen as: **a) the active obedience** by which He placed Himself under the Law and fulfilled it in our stead, and; **b) the passive obedience** by which He allowed Himself to be crucified and placed under the curse of God for our sakes. Concerning His active obedience we read, "**God sent forth His Son, born of a woman, born under the law, to redeem those who were under the law**" (Galatians 4:4-5). "**For as by one man's disobedience many were made sinners, so by the obedience of one many will be made righteous**" (Romans 5:19). [See Matt. 3:15.] Concerning His passive obedience we read, "**And being found in human form, He humbled Himself, and became obedient unto death, even the death of the cross**" (Philippians 2:8). And, His blood, His death on the cross, is the purchase price of our salvation. As it is written, "**Feed the church of God, that He has purchased with His own blood**" (Acts 20;28).

By His obedience Christ Has delivered us from; a) **sin,** b) **death,** and c) **the dominion of sin** [power of the devil]. Concerning the first, we read, "**Who gave Himself for us, that He might redeem us from all iniquity**" (Titus 2:14). Concerning the second, we read, "**Forasmuch then as the children are partakers of flesh and blood, He also himself likewise took part of the same; that through death He might destroy him that had the power of death, that is, the devil" (Hebrews 2: 14). And, concerning the third, we read, "**For sin will not have dominion over you: because you are not under the law, but under grace**" (Romans 6:14).

1. The Vicarious Atonement

What Christ accomplished on the cross, the sacrifice He made for our redemption, is known in theology as His vicarious [i.e. substitutionary] atonement. Now, the word "atonement" is used throughout the Old Testament, and the blood sacrifices that were required of those under the law were designed help us to think of Christ as, "**The Lamb of God, who takes away the sin of the world**" (John 1:29). Isaiah speaks of God laying "**the iniquity of us all**" on Christ (Isaiah 53:6). And Paul uses the word "atonement" in reference to Christ's death (Romans 5:11). As it is written, "**For when we were yet without strength, in due time Christ died for the ungodly. For one will scarcely die for a righteous man: although perhaps some might even dare to die for a good man. But God demonstrates His love for us, in that, while we were yet sinners, Christ died for us. Much more then, being now justified by His blood, we shall be saved from wrath through Him. For if, when we were enemies, we were reconciled to God by the death of His Son, much more, being reconciled, we shall be saved by His life. And not only so, but we also rejoice in God through our Lord Jesus Christ, by whom we have now received the atonement**" (Romans 5:6-11). For, "**The Son of man did not come to be served, but to serve, and to give His life a ransom for many**" (Matthew 20:28). And, "**We have redemption through His blood, the forgiveness of sins, according to the riches of His grace**" (Ephesians 1:7).

2. The Finished Work Of Christ, And Faith

When the Bible says, "**This is a trustworthy statement, worthy of complete acceptance, that Christ Jesus came into the world to save sinners,**" it is telling us that Christ's reason for coming into the world was to save us from our sins (1Timothy 1:15). And, the words, "**The Son of man did not come to be served, but to serve, and to give His life a ransom for many,**" tell us that He came in order to save us through His death (Mark 10:45). Therefore, when, "**Jesus said, It is finished, and He bowed His head, and gave up the ghost,**" we know that He had accomplished what He set out to do (John 19:30). The words, **"The blood of Jesus Christ His Son cleanses us of all sin,"** tell us that the work of atonement is complete (1John 1:7). There is nothing more to be done! As it is written, **"The LORD has laid on Him [Christ] the iniquity of us all"** (Isaiah 53:6).

However, in understanding Christ's death, we should never assume that God just transferred our guilt to Christ and let Him take the blame for what we did. If our guilt could be removed simply by transferring it to someone else there would have been no reason for Christ to die. If that was all it took to remove our sins then no one on earth would be guilty because God placed the sins of everyone on Christ. And, if that was all it took to remove our sin, then it would not have mattered if Christ was sinless or not just as long as our guilt was transferred to Him. However, what God had in mind is far more glorious and far more profound. The Bible does say, **"The LORD has laid on Him the iniquity of us all"** (Isaiah 53:6). **But, the atonement for that sin was not complete until Christ died**. Therefore, from the moment that God laid our sins "on Him," while He was hanging on the cross, our sins were in two places, on us and on Him. Those sins condemned us, and they condemned Him as well. On the cross, He suffered the condemnation, punishment and death that we deserved. Then, when He died, something that was totally unexpected (from the world's point of view) happened. **Because Christ had no sin of His own, God forgave the sins that had been placed on Him, and pronounced Him innocent. For that reason, those sins no longer condemn Christ. They have been forgiven!** And, because they were our sins, and have been forgiven, **that forgiveness becomes ours when we place our faith in Christ**. As it is written, "Scripture has concluded all under sin, that the promise might be given to those who believe, through faith in Jesus Christ" (Galatians 3:22).

That means that Christ has already obtained forgiveness for every sin that has ever been committed. The forgiveness is already there for us! We do not have to earn it, or make ourselves worthy of it. We simply need to repent and believe that Christ has obtained forgiveness for us. Furthermore, repentance and faith is itself a gift of God, not something we do. The words, **"With gentleness instructing those who oppose their own interest; in the hope that God will give them repentance bringing them to a realization of the truth,"** tell us that repentance is a gift of God (2Timothy 2:25). The words, **"For you are saved by grace through faith; and that not of yourselves: it is the gift of God,"** tell us that faith is a "gift of God" (Ephesians 2:8). The words, **"Faith comes by hearing, and hearing by the word of God,"** tell us that God gives us His gift of faith through His "Word" (Romans 10:17). The words, **"For the wages of sin is death; but the gift of God is eternal life through Jesus**

Christ our Lord," tell us that salvation ("eternal life") is a "gift of God" (Romans 6:23). And, the words, "**We also have access by faith into this grace in which we stand,**" tell us that faith in Christ is the hand that receives God's gift of grace (Romans 5:2). In contrast, the words, "**Without faith it is impossible to please God,**" tell us that "without faith it is **impossible**" to be reconciled to God (Hebrews 11:6).

Repentance

The words, "**God will not despise a heart that is humbled and sorry for sin,**" tell us that those who are truly repentant will be sorry they have sinned (Psalm 51:17). And, the words, "**The Lord GOD says; Repent, and turn away from your idols; and turn your backs on all your abominations,**" tell us that those who repent will turn away from sin, (Ezekiel 14:6). Those passages of Scripture tell us that even though repentance is a gift of God, not a work, those who receive it will not want to continue in sin. Therefore, <u>**true repentance will produce a change in behavior**</u> as a fruit or by product. As it is written, "**Bring forth fruit that is consistent with repentance**" (Matthew 3:8). However, because it is faith in Christ's finished work that saves, repentance and faith go hand in hand, and without faith repentance is incomplete. As it is written, "**Repent and turn to God** [believing His promise of forgiveness in Christ (Gal. 3:18)], **and live lives consistent with repentance**" (Acts 26:20).

3. Errors Pertaining To Christ's Vicarious Atonement

Because the truth of Christ's atonement – His triumph over sin, death and the devil – is at the very heart of the Gospel, Satan has tried time and again to deny it, distort it, and undermine it. In the twelfth century, the Church of Rome began to claim that the priest was sacrificing Christ again every time He said a Mass; a claim that trivializes Christ's sacrifice while diverting faith from what Christ did to what the priest does. Another heresy of Rome is the idea that people can atone, in part, for their own sins or the sins of others through the things that they suffer. That heresy is at the root of their doctrine of purgatory. Both of those doctrines fly in the face of Christ's words, "**It is finished,**" contradict the words, "**For by one offering He has perfected for ever those who are sanctified,**" and are condemned by the words, "**If anyone preaches any gospel to you other than the one you received, let him be accursed**" (John 19:30, Galatians 1:9).

The words, "**He is the propitiation for our sins: and not for ours only, but also for the sins of the whole world,**" tell us that Christ atoned for the sins of all men, not just those who are saved

(1John 2:2). In contrast, the words, **"Without faith it is impossible to please God,"** tell us that even though Christ obtained forgiveness for the sins of the entire world, and it is offered to us as a free gift, that forgiveness does not become ours until God brings us to faith (Hebrews 11:6). Faith is the hand that receives God's grace, as it is written, we **"Have access by faith into this grace in which we stand"** (Romans 5:2).

The claim that God, at the time of Christ's death, declared all men righteous and was reconciled to the entire world does not come from Scripture. The words, **"He who does not believe the Son will not see life; but God's wrath remains on him,"** tell us that unbelievers are not reconciled to God, but are active recipients of His wrath (John 3:36). And, the words, **"Without faith it is impossible to please God,"** tell us that without faith it is impossible to please [be reconciled to] God (Hebrews 11:6). As I mentioned previously, during the time Christ hung on the cross, our sins were in two places, on us and on Him. Those sins condemned us, and they condemned Him as well. On the cross, He suffered the punishment that we deserved, and died in our place. But, when He died, because He had no sins of His own, God forgave the sins that had been placed on Him. As a result, those sins no longer condemn Him. He has been forgiven! And, because He has been forgiven we can be forgiven too. Because the sins that God laid on Him were our sins, the forgiveness that He received is already there for us, and becomes ours when we place our faith in Him. As it is written, **"Scripture has concluded all under sin, that the promise might be given to those who believe, through faith in Jesus Christ"** (Galatians 3:22).

Satan often tries to undermine faith in what Christ has done by redefining either faith or grace to include works. The words, **"You are saved by grace through faith; and that not of yourselves: it is the gift of God: <u>Not of works</u>, lest any man should boast,"** tell us that faith is "not of works" (Ephesians 2:8-9). The words, "When a man **does not work, but trusts in him who justifies the ungodly, his faith is counted for righteousness,"** tell us that faith excludes works (Romans 4:5). In the third chapter of Galatians, the Apostle Paul carefully explains to us that faith excludes works, saying, **"Scripture, having foreseen that God would justify the heathen through faith, proclaimed the gospel to Abraham in advance... For all who trust in the law are under a curse... But it is clear that no man is justified in the sight of God by the law, for, The just shall live by faith. However the law has nothing to do with faith... Christ redeemed us from the curse of the law, receiving the curse in our stead: for it is written, Cursed is every one who hangs on a tree: That the blessing given to Abraham might come to the Gentiles through Jesus Christ; that we might receive the promise of the Spirit through faith"**

(Galatians 3:6-14) And, the words, "**There is also at this present time a remnant according to the election of grace. And if by grace, then it is no longer by works: if it were grace would no longer be grace. For if it is by works, then it is no longer by grace: otherwise work is no longer work**," tell us that grace excludes works (Romans 11:5-6). All of those passages tell us that **true faith, faith in Christ, is believing that forgiveness and eternal life are ours because of what Christ did, not because of what we do**. As it is written, "**God so loved the world, that He gave His only begotten Son, that whosoever believes on Him should not perish, but have everlasting life**" (John 3:16).

Even though the Apostle Paul carefully explains why the law cannot make us righteous, those who want to be motivated by the law are continually trying to find some way around his words. Therefore, as soon as they learn that James said, "**By works a man is justified and not by faith only**," they assume that the words of James negate what Paul said (Romans 3:28, James 2:24). In their blindness they then feel free to ignore Paul's warnings against trusting in works. However, a careful examination of what James said makes it clear that **Paul and James were talking about two different things**. When Paul spoke of faith he was referring to faith in Christ. In contrast, the words, "**You believe that there is one God; you do well: the devils also believe and tremble**," are not speaking of faith in Christ. Christ did not die for the sins of devils. Likewise, when Paul spoke of works he was referring to works of righteousness, or obedience to the law. In contrast, the words, "**Was not Rahab the Harlot justified by works, when she had received the messengers, and had sent them out another way**," make it perfectly clear that the works James had in mind were not works of obedience, or righteousness, but what we would call the fruits of faith (James 2:19, 20, 25). He was saying that Rahab's actions were consistent with what she believed. Therefore, James was not saying that we need works of righteousness in addition to faith. Instead he was saying that if a man truly has faith in Christ it will make a difference in his life.

Those who claim to believe that salvation is through faith in Christ, but teach that God's favor depends on what we do, not what Christ did on the cross, are **double-minded**, and undermine the Gospel by making righteousness depend on works. I have dealt with people who profess to trust in Christ, but live in constant fear that God will punish them if they do not "obey" what He tells them through a "still-small-voice" in their heart. That doctrine is condemned by the words, "**If you continue in my word, you are truly my disciples**" (John 8:31). Those words tell us that those who are truly Christ's disciples will not look outside of His Word for direction. And the words, "**Christ is of no benefit to those of you who seek righteousness by the law; you are fallen from grace**," condemn everyone who trusts in what they do (rather than what Christ did on the cross) to make them righteous (Galatians 5:4). While it is true that those who are truly repentant will shun sin and seek righteousness, the improvement in behavior is not what saves them or makes them righteous. On the contrary, the words, "**Walk in the Spirit, and you will not fulfill the lust of the flesh. For the flesh lusts against the Spirit, and the Spirit against the flesh: and they are opposed to each other: so that you cannot do the things that you would**," tell us that the improvement in behavior does not come until after they are saved (Galatians 5:16-17). [See Gal. 3:2, 2Cor. 5:17.]

While Satan continually tries to undermine the Gospel by adding works to faith, he also tries to undermine it by twisting it into an excuse to sin. The words, "**Shall we continue in sin, that grace may abound? Absolutely not. How can we, who are dead to sin, continue living in it?**" tell us that the Apostle Paul had to deal with that heresy (Romans 6:1-2). And, it is becoming more and more prevalent today, with those who are openly immoral and even homosexual claiming that God accepts them without repentance. That lie is condemned by the words, "**How much more severely, do you think a man deserves to be punished, who has trampled the Son of God under foot, treated the blood of the covenant, by which he was sanctified, as an unholy thing, and insulted the Spirit of grace? For we know Him who said, Vengeance belongs to Me, I will repay, says the Lord. And again, The Lord will judge His people. It is a fearful thing to fall into the hands of the living God**" (Hebrews 10:29-31). "**Don't you know that the unrighteous will not inherit the kingdom of God? Do not be deceived: neither fornicators, nor idolaters, nor adulterers, nor sex perverts, nor homosexuals, Nor thieves, nor covetous, nor drunkards, nor foulmouthed revilers, nor extortioners, shall inherit the kingdom of God**" (1Corinthians 6:9-10). The words, "**The law is not meant for a righteous man, but for those who are lawless and rebellious, for the ungodly and sinful, for the irreverent and profane, for those who strike or kill their fathers or mothers, for murders, For those who sin sexually, for sodomites, for kidnapers and slave traders, for liars and perjurers, and for any other thing that is contrary to sound teaching**," tell us that all who sin willfully are under the condemnation of God's Law (1Timothy 1:9-10).

Another very common way Satan undermines the Gospel is with the antichristian doctrine of theistic-evolution and millions of years. The words, "**Just as sin entered the world by one man, and death by sin; so death passed upon all men, because all have sinned... Therefore as through the sin of one judgment came upon all men to condemnation; even so through the righteousness of one the free gift abounds to all men bringing** justification and life. For as by one man's disobedience many were made sinners, so by the obedience of one many will be made righteous," tell us that the fall of Adam and Christ's death on the cross go hand in hand (Romans 3:12 and 18-19). If sin and death were part of God's original creation, if God used evolution to create life, if the fall of Adam did not bring sin and death into the world, there would have been no reason for Christ to die on the cross. And, if the rocks of the earth formed slowly over millions of years as unbelievers assert, then the presence of fossil thorns in the rocks before Adam sinned would cast doubt upon all that the Bible says about Adam's sin and Christ's remedy for that sin. **Therefore, those who reject what the Bible says about creation and the age of the earth are undermining the Gospel and should be rejected as deceivers.** As it is written, "**O fools, and slow of heart to believe everything the prophets have said**" // "**To the law and to the testimony: if they do not speak according to this word, it is because there is no light in them**"(Luke 24:25, Isaiah 8:20). God gave us a clear doctrine of the age of the earth in Scripture because He loves us and does not want us to be deceived. Therefore, those who reject what His Word says are without excuse. And, those who actively promote theistic-evolution are false prophets.

Because we are, "**Justified by faith without the deeds of the law**," when the Bible tells us that Christ, "**Was raised again for our justification**," it is not saying that all men were justified at the time of Christ's resurrection. On the contrary, it is telling us that Christ was raised so that we might believe (Romans 3:28 and 4:25). In other words, if Christ had not risen we would have no reason to believe that He was successful.

4. The Priestly Intercession Of Christ

As our high priest, Christ has not only made atonement for our sins, but also makes intercession for us before the throne of God. As it is written, "**He takes upon Himself the sins of many, and makes intercession for the those who transgress**" (Isaiah 53:12).

The words, "**I do not pray for the world, but for those whom you have given to me,**" the words "**I have prayed for you, that your faith may not fail,**" and the words, "**I will ask the Father, and He will give you another Comforter,**" tell us that Christ was making intercession for believers before His resurrection (John 17:9, Luke 22:13, John 14:16). While the words, "**Who is there to condemn us? Christ who died, yea rather, who was raised from the dead, is at the right hand of God, and also intercedes for us,**" tell us that Christ continues to make intercession for us (Romans 8:34).

Christ's words, "**It is finished,**" tell us that His work of intercession is not part of our atonement, the atonement is complete (John 19:30). The words, **"Jesus... endured the cross, indifferent to its shame, and sat down at the right hand of the throne of God,"** tell us that since His ascension Christ has been at the right hand of God (Hebrews 12:2). The words, **"He is able to completely save those who come to God through Him, because He ever lives to make intercession for them,"** tell us that He intercedes for us (Hebrews 7:25). And, the words, **"We have an advocate with the Father, Jesus Christ the righteous,"** speak of Christ not only as our intercessor, but also as our advocate [i.e. lawyer] before the throne of God (1John 2:1).

The words, **"For Christ did not enter a man made sanctuary, that is only a type of the true one, but into heaven itself, now to appear in the presence of God for us: Nor did He enter heaven in order to offer Himself often, as does the high priest who enters into the sanctuary every year with blood that is not his own; Otherwise He would have had to suffer many times since the world was made: but now He has appeared once at the close of history to put away sin by the sacrifice of Himself,"** tell us that Christ's one sacrifice completed our atonement, that He did not enter heaven to continue that atonement, but He entered the heavenly temple [sanctuary] to apply His blood to the heavenly mercy seat for our forgiveness (Hebrews 9:24-26). As it is written, **"There is one God, and one mediator between God and men, the man Christ Jesus"** (1Timothy 2:5). [See Lev. 16:14-15.]

C. The Kingly Office Of Christ

The Bible not only testifies to Christ's kingly office (His Lordship) by telling us that He is King, but by telling us that God has given Him dominion over all of creation. For example: when the Bible says, **"Jesus came to them, and said, All power is given to me in heaven and in earth,"** we need to realize that as God that power was always His (Matthew 28:18). Therefore, those words are telling us that because He is both God and man, His human nature shares that power. The words, **"Our Lord Jesus Christ... is the blessed and only Sovereign, the King of kings, and Lord of lords,"** tell us that He is the King of Kings (1Timothy 6:14-15). Ephesians 1:20-23 tells us that God set Christ, **"At His own right hand in the heavenly places, Far above all principality, and power, and might, and dominion, and every name that is named, not only in this world, but also in that which is to come, and has put all things under His feet"**. The words, **"All things have been given to me by my Father,"** also tell us that "all things" are under Christ's authority (Matthew 11:27). The words, **"The LORD has said to me,**

You are my Son; this day have I begotten you. Ask me, and I will give you the heathen for your inheritance, and the uttermost parts of the earth for your possession,"** again testify to Christ's dominion (Psalm 2:7-8). As do the words, **"You made Him to have dominion over the works of your hands; you have put all things under His feet"** (Psalm 8:6). **"For God has put everything under His feet. But when He says that everything has been put under Him, it is evident that this does not include the one who put all things under Him"** (1Corinthians 15:27). [See Dan. 7:13-14, Psalm 110:2, Phil. 2:9-11.]

Although the words, **"God has put everything under His feet,"** tell us that Christ has one universal kingdom, theologians often speak of **His threefold kingdom**, the kingdom **of power**, the kingdom **of grace**, and the kingdom **of glory** (1Cor. 15:27). That is not because there are actually three different kingdoms, but because in governing He makes a distinction between the saved, the lost and those with Him in heaven. The words, **"The Lamb will conquer them: because He is Lord of lords, and King of kings: and those who are with Him are called, and chosen, and faithful,"** make a distinction between the lost [whom He will "conquer"], and the saved [who are with Him] (Revelation 17:14).

Strictly speaking, because God has put everything under Christ's feet, **all things are a part of Christ's kingdom of power**. However, we speak of the lost (including the fallen angels) as being under Christ's kingdom of power because they are not included in His kingdom of grace. As it is written, **"Don't you know that the unrighteous will not inherit the kingdom of God?"** (1Corinthians 6:9). In contrast, the words, **"He has rescued us from the power of darkness, and transferred us into the kingdom of His dear Son,"** speak of the kingdom of grace, which excludes unbelievers (Colossians 1:13). And, the words, **"The Lord will rescue me [Paul] from every evil plot, and will save me for His heavenly kingdom,"** speak of the kingdom of glory, of which Paul was not yet a part (2Timothy 4:18).

The words, **"Jesus said to him, Truly, truly, I tell you, Unless a man is born again, he cannot see the kingdom of God." // "For whoever is born of God overcomes the world, and this is the victory that overcomes the world, even our faith,"** tell us that we can only enter the kingdom of God through faith (John 3:3, 1John 5:4). And, since the kingdom of grace excludes unbelievers, the kingdom spoken of in these passages is the kingdom of grace. Moreover, the words, **"The kingdom of God is within you,"** apply to all who trust in Christ (Luke 17:21). **For, "Scripture has concluded all under sin, that the promise might be given to those who believe, through faith in Jesus Christ"** (Galatians 3:22).

Furthermore, because we enter Christ's kingdom of grace through faith in Him, every passage of Scripture that assures us of eternal life through faith in Christ is telling us that Christ's kingdom of glory is an extension of His kingdom of grace (or vise versa). Passages like, "**As Moses lifted up the serpent in the wilderness, even so must the Son of man be lifted up, that whosoever believes in Him should not perish, but have eternal life**" and, "**I was shown mercy... as an example for those who are going to trust in Him for everlasting life**" (John 3:14-15 and 1Timothy 1:16). Or the words, "**We believe that we will be saved through the grace of our Lord Jesus Christ**" (Acts 15:11). Or, "**Believe on the Lord Jesus Christ, and you will be saved**" (Acts 16:31). While the words, "**Father, I also want those, whom you have given me, to be with me where I am; and to see my glory, the glory that you have given me: because you loved me before the creation of the world,**" tell us that all who trust in Christ will experience the glory of heaven (John 17:24).

The words, "**If a man loves me, he will keep my words: and my Father will love him, and we will come to him, and make our home with him,**" tell us that Christ is at work in all who trust in Him (John 14:23). In contrast, the words, "**You formerly walked according to the way of this world, according to the prince of the power of the air, the spirit that now works in the children of disobedience,**" tell us that Satan is at work in all who do not trust in Christ (Ephesians 2:2). And, the words, "**We are now God's children, but what we are going to be like has not yet been revealed: however we know that, when He appears, we will be like Him; for we will see Him as He is,**" tell us that what God has planned for those who trust in Him is more than we can even imagine (1John 3:2). "**As it is written, Eye has not seen, nor ear heard, nor has it entered into the heart of man, the things that God has prepared for those who love Him**" (1Corinthians 2:9).

Because all power "**In heaven and in earth**" has been given to Christ, we know that He is in control (Matthew 28"18). Therefore, even though it often looks to us like Satan is in control, we need to keep our eyes on Jesus, knowing that, "**All things work together for good for those who love God, for those who are the called according to His purpose**" (Romans 8:28). That is why it is written, "**Let everyone be subject to the governing authorities. For there is no authority except by God: and those that exist are established by God**" (Romans 13:1). Now, of course, if political rulers begin to persecute Christians the words, "**We ought to obey God rather than men,**" apply (Acts 5:29). However, the words, "**The weapons we fight with are not the weapons of the world,**" tell us that we should not take up arms against the government (2Corinthians 10:4). If two governments are fighting, that is a different matter, and sometimes Christians are called upon to bear arms. But, we should not attempt to spread the Gospel by violence. On the other hand, because Christ is in control, we can expect political rulers to protect the church, make the streets safe, and punish crime so that we are free to spread the Gospel while living, "**A quiet and peaceable life in all godliness and honesty**" (1Timothy 2:2). As it is written, "**Rulers are not a terror to those who do right, but to those who do evil**" and are "**Sent by Him for the punishment of evildoers, and for the praise of those who do right**" (Romans 13:3, 1Peter 2:14). Moreover, the words, "**That is the foundation upon which I will build my church; and the gates of hell will not prevail against it**," tell us that Christ's church will prevail (Matthew 16:18). And the words, "**There is no other name under heaven given among men, by which we must be saved**," tell us that there is no salvation apart from faith in Christ's finished work, and His grace will never be withdrawn from the earth (Acts 4:12).

Errors Regarding The Kingly Office Of Christ

In our age, as in past ages, Satan is hard at work trying to lead people away from God's word. In regard to Christ's Kingly Office, what follows is a sampling of the many errors.

Those who deny that Christ is God not only deny that "**God was revealed in the flesh**," but also deny that His kingdom is God's kingdom (1Timothy 3:16). However, it is written, "**To the Son He says, Your throne, O God, is for ever and ever: and righteousness will be the scepter of your kingdom**" (Hebrews 1:8, Psalm 45:6).

Those who separate Christ's human nature from His divine nature have claimed that He is king only according to His divine nature. However, the words, "**I will raise to David a righteous Branch... and this is the name by which He will be called, The LORD (Jahweh) Our Righteousness**," tell us that the descendant (branch) of David is God "revealed in the flesh" (Jeremiah 23:5-6). [See 1Tim. 3:16.] And, the words, "**He [Jesus] will be great, and will be called the Son of the Highest: and the Lord God will give to him the throne of His father David, and He will reign over the house of Jacob forever; and His kingdom will never end**," tell us that it is the descendant of David (not just His divine nature) who is king (Luke 1:32-33).

Those who, "**Disregard the commandment [word] of God, and hold to the tradition of men**," reject Christ's authority by disregarding what He says (Mark 7:8). Those who teach, "**For doctrines the commandments [opinions] of men**," reject Christ's authority by adding to His Word when He has told us not to (Mark 7:7). [See Deut 4:2 and 12:32, Pr. 30:6, Rev.22:18-19 Matt. 15:9.]

Those who rebel against God by denying what the Bible says about the creation of the world, by explaining it away and twisting the Words of Scripture to fit their own man-made ideas about evolution, and by teaching the lie of theistic evolution and millions of years not only reject Christ as their king, but lie in His name. To all of them He says, "**O fools, and slow of heart to believe everything the prophets have said**" (Luke 24:25).

CHRIST ALONE

THE DOCTRINES OF SALVATION
(Soteriology)

The Doctrine Of Soteriology

Soteriology is the area of theology focusing on what Christ's death means for us, and specifically how the benefits of His sacrificial death on the cross are applied to us. Although this application of benefits is expressed differently in different languages, in English it is usually known as, "The Way of Salvation", or "The Order of Salvation".

When unbelievers read the words, **"The LORD has laid on Him [Christ] the iniquity of us all"** (Isaiah 53:6), they often assume that we believe that God just transferred our guilt to Christ and let Him take the blame for what we did. However, that would not be just, and that is not what the Bible says.

The words, **"The LORD has laid on Him [Christ] the iniquity of us all,"** tell us that God "laid" our sins on Christ (Isaiah 56:6). And, because He bore the punishment for our sins they have already been punished. However, the mere act of laying them on Christ is not what removes our guilt. On the contrary, while Christ hung on the cross our sins were in two places; they condemned us, and they condemned Christ as well. The words, **"He was wounded for our transgressions, He was bruised for our iniquities,"** tell us that He was under condemnation the entire time that He was on the cross (Isaiah 53:5). The words, **"Christ also suffered once for sins, the righteous for the unrighteous, that He might bring us to God,"** tell us that Christ, who was "righteous," suffered for us "the unrighteous" (1Peter 3:18). However, when Christ died, because He had no sin of His own, God forgave the sins that had been placed on Him. For that reason, those sins no longer condemn Christ. They have been forgiven! And, because they were our sins, and have been forgiven, that forgiveness extends to us when we place our faith in Christ. As it is written, **"Scripture has concluded all under sin, that the promise might be given to those who believe, through faith in Jesus Christ"** (Galatians 3:22).

"Being found in fashion as a man, He [Christ] humbled himself, and became obedient unto death, even the death of the cross. Wherefore God also has highly exalted Him, and given Him a name which is above every name" (Philippians 2:8-9). **"For God made Him who knew no sin, to be sin for us; so that we might be made the righteousness of God in Him"** (2Corinthians 5:21). **"Blotting out the handwriting of ordinances that was** against us, which was contrary to us... nailing it to His cross" (2Corinthians 2:14). "**Therefore as through the sin of one judgment came upon all men to condemnation; even so through the righteousness of one the free gift abounds to all men bringing justification and life**" (Romans 5:18). "**He who believes in Him is not condemned: but he who does not believe is condemned already, because he has not believed in the name of the only begotten Son of God**" (John 3:18).

The Means of Grace

Although Reformation theology usually describes the means of grace as "Word and Sacraments," that phrase is easily misunderstood because it appears to separate the "Word" from the "Sacrament," as if Sacraments were something entirely different from the Word. For that reason, I will be stressing the fact that the Word of God is the means of grace, the means by which God brings us to faith. As it is written, "**Faith comes by hearing, and hearing by the word of God**" (Romans 10:17).

> "There is but one means by which the knowledge of grace and salvation, and grace and salvation itself, are imparted to us; it is the Gospel, the glad tidings of the grace of God in Christ Jesus." ("A Summary of Christian Doctrine," by Edward W. A. Koehler, pages 189-190.) "Sacraments are nothing else than the Word of God attached to a symbol." ("Law And Gospel," by C. F. W. Walther, page 347.)

Through the Gospel, God not only offers us forgiveness in Christ, but brings us to faith by making us aware of what Christ has done for us, assuring us of forgiveness through His death in our stead, and enabling us to believe in spite of all the world, the flesh, and the devil do to create doubt and undermine our faith. The words, "**The natural man does not accept the things of the Spirit of God: for they are foolishness to him: and he cannot understand them, because they are spiritually discerned**," tell us that without God's help none of us would ever believe the gospel (1Corinthians 2:14). The words, "**What is the exceeding greatness of His power toward us who believe, according to the working of His mighty power**," tell us that we have faith in Christ, only because the power of God has enabled us to believe, and continues to enable us to believe (Ephesians 1:19).

The words, "**We also have access by faith into this grace in which we stand**," tell us that God's grace comes to us through faith in Christ (Romans 5:2). The words, "**In whom we have redemption through His blood, the forgiveness of sins, according to the riches of His grace**," tell us that the grace that we receive consists of the forgiveness Christ won for us through His death on the cross (Ephesians 1:7). The words, "**Believe on the Lord Jesus Christ, and you will be saved**," tell us that the grace that comes to us through faith in Christ is what saves us (Acts 16:31). The words, "**A man is justified by faith without the deeds of the law**," tell us that it is the forgiveness [grace] that we receive through faith in Christ, not what we do, that makes us righteous [just] in the sight of God (Romans 3:28). And, the words, "**Being justified by faith, we have peace with God through our Lord Jesus Christ**," tell us that we are reconciled to God through the forgiveness Christ won for us, (Romans 5:1).

Because "**The natural man does not accept the things of the Spirit of God**," men have in the past, "**Changed the truth of God into a lie, and worshipped and served the creation more than the Creator**," (1Corinthians 2:14, Romans 1:25). And, they do the same thing today. There is one cult that worships a god that they describe as an exalted man. However, it is more common in this country to find worship of the goddess "mother nature" disguised as science. Here are a few quotes that I found on the internet. "When it comes to efficient design, scientists are still learning from nature's smart evolutionary strategies." // "Nature gives us everything free – let's put it at the heart of everyday economic life." // "Nature has already solved many of the problems we are grappling with." Notice that those quotes ascribe intelligence and planning to nature, making it clear that men have not changed. Without peace with God they still try to escape guilt by inventing false gods, thereby changing "the truth of God into a lie" (Romans 1:25).

What it Means to be Justified

To justify someone is to absolve them of guilt, vindicate them of any wrongdoing, and pronounce them innocent or righteous in the sight of the law. For that reason, we describe our justification before God as "forensic justification" [i.e. legal or courtroom justification]. In other words, because Christ "**Suffered once for sins, the righteous for the unrighteous**," the forgiveness that He won for us through His death on the cross vindicates us of all guilt before the judgment seat of God (1Peter 3:18). Because He took our place under the law, we will be, "**blameless on the day of our Lord Jesus Christ**," (1Corinthians 1:8). As it is written, "**The blood of Jesus Christ His Son cleanses us of all sin**" (1John 1:7).

When the Bible says, "**God commends His love toward us, in that, while we were yet sinners, Christ died for us. Much more then, being now justified by His blood, we shall be saved from wrath through Him. For if we were reconciled to God by the death of His Son, when we were enemies, much more, having been reconciled, we will be saved by His life. And not only that,** but we also rejoice in God through our Lord Jesus Christ, by whom we have now received the atonement," those words tell us that the same forgiveness that removes our guilt before God, saves us from His wrath (Romans 5:8-11). The words, **"God, who has called you into fellowship with His Son Jesus Christ our Lord, is true to His promise"** // **"He will keep you strong to the end, that you may be blameless on the day of our Lord Jesus Christ,"** assure us that the same grace that saves us will keep us strong in the face of persecution (1Corinthians 1:9 & 8). And, because we are kept by the power of God, **"I am convinced, that neither death, nor life, nor angels, nor principalities, nor powers, nor things present, nor things to come, Nor height, nor depth, nor any other creature, will be able to separate us from the love of God, that is in Christ Jesus our Lord"** (Romans 8:38-39).

The Effects of Justification

Being cleansed of all sin by the forgiveness that is ours through faith in Christ, sin no longer separates us from God, and the Holy Spirit takes up residence in our heart. The words, **"Abraham believed God, and it was accounted to him for righteousness,"** tell us that Abraham was justified by faith, and the forgiveness that he received (through faith) is what made him righteous in the sight of God (Galatians 3:6, see Rom. 4:3). The words, **"The Scripture, having foreseen that God would justify the heathen through faith, proclaimed the gospel to Abraham in advance,"** tell us that Abraham believed the same gospel we believe (Galatians 3:8). The words, **"By faith Abraham, when he was tried, offered up Isaac... Believing that God was able to raise him up, even from the dead,"** tell us that Abraham was willing to sacrifice his son because he believed that his seed [descendant] would die as a sacrifice for sin and rise again (Hebrews 11:17-19). And, the words, **"Did you receive the Holy Spirit by the works of the law, or by the hearing of faith?"** and **"That Christ may dwell in your hearts by faith,"** tell us that all who have been cleansed of sin through faith in Christ receive the Holy Spirit (Galatians 3:2, Ephesians 3:17). As it is written, **"Don't you know that you are the temple of God, and that the Spirit of God dwells in you?"** (1Corinthians 3:16). (See also 1Cor. 6:19, John 14:23.)

The words, **"The flesh lusts against the Spirit, and the Spirit against the flesh: and they are opposed to each other: so that you cannot do the things that you would,"** tell us that another fruit or effect of our justification is ability to resist and overcome fleshly passion (Galatians 5:17). The words, **"The fleshly mind is hostile to God: for it is not subject to the law of God, nor indeed can be,"** tell us that apart from the help of God's Spirit, our thinking would be hostile to God (Romans 8:7). The words, **"When we were in the flesh,** the sinful passions, that were aroused by the law, were active in our members to bring forth fruit to death. But now we have been released from the law, having died to that which once bound us; that we should serve in newness of spirit," tell us that instead of trying to make ourselves righteous through the law, we should believe that we are already righteous through faith in Christ, and walking in that faith do what is what is right, and good, and godly as a way of letting the love of Christ shine forth in our lives [i.e. walk in newness of life] (Romans 7:5-6). The words, "**I have been crucified with Christ: nevertheless I live; yet not I, but Christ lives in me,**" tell us that when we walk by faith, Christ lives in us (Galatians 2:20). The words, "**Do not be conformed to this world: but be transformed by the renewing of your mind, that you may prove what is the good, and acceptable, and perfect, will of God,**" tell us that those who walk by faith will go through a process of transformation as their thinking is renewed through the influence of the Holy Spirit (Romans 12:2). The words, "**Put off everything having to do with your former way of life, the old nature which is corrupt according to the deceitful lusts, and be renewed in the spirit of your mind,**" also speak of that renewal (Ephesians 4:22-24). And, the words, "**Love does no harm to his neighbor. For this, You will not commit adultery, You will not kill, You will not steal, You will not bear false witness, You will not covet; and if there is any other commandment, it is summed up in this saying, namely, You will love your neighbor as yourself,**" tell us that those who are led by the Spirit will never twist the gospel into an excuse to sin (Rom 13:10 & 9).

Justification Joins Us to God's People

The words, "**By one Spirit we were all baptized into one body, whether we are Jews or Gentiles, whether we are slaves or free; and we have all been made to drink into one Spirit... God has arranged every one of the parts of the body, just as it He wanted them to be... That there should be no division in the body; but that the members should have equal concern for each another... You are the body of Christ, and each one of you is a part of it,**" tell us that all who trust in Christ have, through faith, been joined to Him and to everyone else who is joined to Him (1Corinthians 12:13-27). The words, "**We are members of His body, of His flesh, and of His bones,**" tell us that this union with Christ is physical as well as spiritual (Ephesians 5:30). The words, "**If we say that we have fellowship with Him [Christ], and walk in darkness, we are lying, and are not living the truth, but if we walk in the light, as He is in the light, we have fellowship with one another, and the blood of Jesus Christ His Son cleanses us of all sin,**" tell us that because we have been joined to Christ, we have fellowship with one another (1John 1:6-7). And, the words, "**Remember those who are imprisoned for the faith, as if you were in prison with them; and those who are mistreated, as being yourselves also in the body,**" tell us that we should care for those who are persecuted for the faith, for we are all members of the same body (Hebrews 13:3).

Election

The words, "**As I live, says the Lord GOD, I have no pleasure in the death of the wicked; but want the wicked man to turn from his way and live: turn, turn from your evil ways; why do you want to die, O house of Israel?**" tell us that God does not want anyone to be lost (Ezekiel 33:11). The words, "**O Jerusalem, Jerusalem, you who kill the prophets, and stone those who are sent to you; how often would I have gathered your children together, as a hen gathers her brood under her wings, but you would not have it!**" tell us that men are lost because they resist His efforts to bring them to repentance (Luke 13:34). The words, "**It pleased God to save those who believe through the foolishness of preaching,**" // "**Who has saved us, and called us to a holy calling, not because of anything we have done, but according to His own purpose and grace, which was given to us in Christ Jesus before the world began,**" tell us that God works through the preaching of the gospel to bring us to faith, not because of anything good in us, but solely according to His grace (1Corinthians 1:21, 2Timothy 1:9). And, the words, "**Compel them to come in, so that my house may be full,**" tell us that He brings us to faith, in spite of our resistance, so that Christ's death will not be in vain (Luke 14:23).

The Doctrine Of Saving Faith

1. The Necessity Of Faith

Although Christ secured forgiveness for us through His death on the cross, the words, "**Without faith it is impossible to please God,**" // "**He who believes on the Son has everlasting life: and he who does not believe the Son will not see life; but God's wrath remains on him,**" tell us that faith in Christ is not an option (Hebrews 11:6, John 3:36).

That raises a question as to what faith is. And, the Bible answers that question in many passages. For example: the words, "**The kingdom of God is at hand: repent, and believe the gospel,**" describe faith as believing "the gospel," and also tell us that repentance precedes faith (Mark 1:15). The words, "**I want to remind you of the gospel that I preached to you, that you believed, and upon which your faith rests... how that Christ died for our sins according to the scriptures; And that He was buried, and that He rose again the third day according to the scriptures**," tell us that faith in the gospel is believing that Christ **died for our sins and rose again** (1Corinthians 15:1-4). The words, "**In whom we have redemption through His blood, the forgiveness of sins, according to the riches of His grace**," tell us that believing that Christ died for our sins is believing that we have "redemption through His blood," (Ephesians 1:7). And, the words, "**We also have access by faith into this grace in which we stand**," tell us that trough "faith" in what Christ did we "have access" to the forgiveness He won for us by His death on the cross (Romans 5:2). Faith is the hand that receives what Christ did for us.

The words, "**No flesh will ever be justified in God's sight by the deeds of the law: because the knowledge of sin comes by the law. But now the righteousness of God apart from the law is revealed, being witnessed by the law and the prophets. Even the righteousness of God which comes through faith in Jesus Christ to all and upon all who believe: for there is no difference, for all have sinned, and come short of the glory of God being justified freely by His grace through the redemption that is in Christ Jesus**," tell us: 1) that the **"deeds of the law"** will never make anyone righteous [justify them] "**in God's sight;**" 2) God has revealed a new way to become righteous "**apart from the law;**" 3) that righteousness comes to us "**through faith in Jesus Christ;**" and 4) that we become righteous before God [are justified] "**through the redemption that is in Christ Jesus**" (Romans 3:20-24). In addition, the words, "**We have redemption through His blood, the forgiveness of sins**," tell us that the redemption that makes us righteous consists of "**the forgiveness of sins**" (Ephesians 1:7). In other words, it is forgiveness that makes us righteousness [or just] in the sight of God. As it is written, "**The blood of Jesus Christ His Son cleanses us of all sin**" (1John 1:7).

The words, "**God so loved the world, that He gave His only begotten Son, that whosoever believes on Him should not perish, but have everlasting life,**" // "**He who believes and is baptized will be saved; but he who does not believe will be damned,**" tell us that there is no salvation apart from faith in Christ (John 3:16, Mark 16:16). The words, "**Christ is of no benefit to those of you who seek righteousness by the law; you are fallen from grace**," should be a warning to all who profess to believe that they are saved by faith, yet trust in their own efforts to make them righteous (Galatians 5:4). Such thinking is "**double minded**" (James 1:7). Whatever gives you assurance of salvation is what you are putting your faith in. So if your assurance of salvation comes from what you do, then that is what you are trusting in. And, "**All who trust in the law are under a curse,**" because they are denying their own sin instead of seeking forgiveness (Galatians 3:10). "**There is no other name [than Jesus Christ] under heaven given among men, by which we must be saved,**" (Acts 4:12).

2. The Nature Of Saving Faith

Saving faith, the faith described in the words, "**Whosoever believes in Him should not perish, but have everlasting life,**" is not a matter of just believing something in general, but a matter of relying on someone, namely Christ (John 3:16). Those who trust in Christ are relying on what He did on the cross, His triumph over sin and death, to get them into heaven.

Because our faith in Christ involves believing that He, "**died for our sins,**" it is **impossible** for us to have faith in Him if we do not believe that we are sinners (1Corinthians 15:3-4). In other words: How can we believe that He died for our sins, if we do not believe that we have any sins? For that reason, **true repentance**, a humble willingness on our part to admit our sin and need of forgiveness, must precede faith. As it is written, "**Repent, and believe the gospel,**" // "**God will not despise a heart that is humbled and sorry for sin**" (Mark 1:15, Psalm 51:17).

Although Christ is the object of our faith, without the Bible we would not even know that He lived, and we certainly would not know that His death atoned for our sins. Moreover, our faith is not just in the knowledge of His death, but in **God's promise of forgiveness** to all who trust in Him. As it is written, "**If the inheritance comes by the law, it is not given by promise: but God gave it to Abraham by promise**" (Galatians 3:18). And, "**Christ redeemed us from the curse of the law, receiving the curse in our stead... that the blessing given to Abraham might come to the Gentiles through Jesus Christ, that we might receive the promise of the Spirit through faith**" (Galatians 3:13-14).

The words of John 3;16, "**Whoever believes on Him should not perish, but have everlasting life,**" <u>are God's promise</u> to all who trust in Christ. And, our faith is in that promise. The same can be said for the words, "**I am the door: if anyone enters through Me, he will be saved,**" // "**The sufferings of this present time are not worthy to be compared with the glory that will be revealed in us,**" // "**There is therefore now no condemnation for those who are in Christ Jesus,**" // "**Being now justified by His blood, we shall be saved from wrath through Him,**" // "**Whoever shall call upon the name of the Lord will be saved," and "The blood of Jesus Christ His Son cleanses us of all sin" (John 10:9, Romans 5:9, Romans 8:1&18, Romans 10:13, 1John 1:7).

While **faith in Christ** consists of knowledge, assent and trust, the inner confusion and struggles of life tend to blur those distinctions in the minds of many. However, let it be said that true faith in Christ involves knowing and believing that He died for your sins, coupled with the inner assurance that **because of what He did you will "not perish, but have everlasting life"** (John 3:16). That being said, I want to make it clear that someone does not need to understand the way of salvation to be saved. The essential thing is that they trust in Christ. I am not saying that understanding the way of salvation is not important, but it is possible for someone to come to faith before they realize that faith saves them. Take for example John the Baptist. The words of his mother Elisabeth, **"Why am I so favored, that the mother of my Lord should come to me? For, as soon as the sound of your greeting reached my ears, the babe leaped in my womb for joy,"** tell us that "the babe" [John] had a rudimentary faith while yet in the womb (Luke 1:43-44). The words, **"My sheep hear my voice, and I know them, and they follow me,"** tell us that the Jews who followed Christ were His sheep, even though many of them did not yet understand that He would die for their sins (John 10:27). In a similar vein, many Christians who do not understand the way of salvation endure persecution by Moslems, and they endure the persecution, because they believe Christ's promise, **"I am the resurrection, and the life: he who believes in me will yet live, even though he is dead. And whoever lives and believes in me will never die"** (John 11:25-26).

In saying this, I by no means want to downplay the importance of understanding the way of salvation. Many who came to faith before understanding the way of salvation have testified to the joy and the assurance of salvation that they experienced when they finally did understand it.

Satan's attack on the gospel is two pronged. On one hand he tries to convince people that faith in Christ is not enough. Paul's words, **"Christ is of no benefit to those of you who seek righteousness by the law"** is directed at that attack (Galatians 5:4). On the other hand, Satan leads people to twist the gospel into an excuse to sin. The book of Hebrews describes that error as, **trampling "the Son of God under foot,"** and **treating "the blood of the covenant, by which he was sanctified, as an unholy thing"** (Hebrews 10:29).

The words, **"Christ is the end of the law for righteousness to every one who believes... For with the heart man believes unto righteousness; and with the mouth confession is made unto salvation,"** tell us that the forgiveness that is ours through faith in Christ **"cleanses us of all sin"** making us righteous in the sight of

God (Romans 10:4,10, see 1John 1:7). And, if it makes us righteous it also makes us holy and obedient. As it is written, "**By one offering He has perfected for ever those who are sanctified**" (Hebrews 10:14). At the same time, because repentance and faith go hand in hand, a heart that is truly repentant, "**A heart that is humbled and sorry for sin,**" will never twist the gospel into an excuse to sin (Psalm 51:17).

3. Knowledge, Assent, and Confidence

I have mentioned that faith in Christ consists of knowledge, assent, and trust (or confidence), so let us take a deeper look at what the Bible says about those aspects of our faith.

Knowledge

The words, "**I have written these things to you who believe in the name of the Son of God; that you may know that you have eternal life,**" tell us that Scripture is a source of the knowledge that leads to eternal life (1John 5:13). The words, "**Faith comes by hearing, and hearing by the word of God,**" speak of that knowledge as the source of our faith (Romans 10:17). The words, "**To give His people the knowledge of salvation by the remission of their sins,**" tell us that salvation comes through "**knowledge**" (Luke 1:77). And, the words, "**This is life eternal, that they might know you the only true God, and Jesus Christ, whom you have sent,**" speak of faith in Christ although only knowledge is specifically mentioned (John 17:3). We know that faith in Christ is intended because the words, "**He who does not believe will be damned,**" tell us that we are not saved by knowledge alone, but by knowing and believing (Mark 16:16).

Ascent

The words, "**Whoever believes that Jesus is the promised Savior is born of God,**" tell us that we are born again through believing the Bible when it tells us that Christ "**is the promised savior**" (1John 5:1). The words, "**They have not paid attention to my words, says the LORD, which I sent to them by my servants the prophets, sending them time and again; but you would not listen, says the LORD,**" speak of people being lost because they refused to believe the knowledge given to them by God's Word (Jeremiah 29:19). And, the words, "**He who believes on Him is not condemned: but he who does not believe is condemned already, because he has not believed on the name of the only begotten Son of God,**" tell us that all who do not believe [asset to or accept] the gospel are under condemnation, not only for their sins, but also for their unbelief (John 3:18).

Confidence

The words, **"We are made partakers of Christ, if we hold firmly to the end the <u>confidence</u> that we had at first,"** // **"Christ as a son over His own house; whose house are we, if we continue to the end unshaken in our <u>confidence</u> and the hope of which we boast"** and **"Do not throw away your <u>confidence</u>, which has such a great promise of reward,"** all speak of faith in Christ as confidence" (Hebrews 3:14, 3:6, and 10:35). In those words Paul is urging Jewish believers not to turn away from the faith because of persecution. And, in the words, **"We both labor and suffer reproach, because we <u>trust</u> in the living God, who is the Savior of all men, especially of those who believe,"** Paul speaks of his faith as trust (1Timothy 4:10).

4. Why Saving Faith Justifies

The words, **"A man is justified by faith without the deeds of the law,"** plainly tell us that faith cleanses us of sin [justifies us] **"without the deeds of the law"** (Romans 3:28). As it is written, **"If we confess our sins, He is faithful and just to forgive us our sins, and to cleanse us from all unrighteousness"** (1John 1:9). It is true that **"faith... produces works through love,"** but those works come after we are "justified by faith," not before (Galatians 5:6). The words, **"Without faith it is impossible to please God,"** tell us that it is impossible for works to make us righteous (Hebrews 11:6). As it is written, **"No flesh will ever be justified in God's sight by the deeds of the law: because the knowledge of sin comes by the law."** (Romans 3:20). In fact, without the forgiveness that is ours in Christ, **"All of our righteousnesses are like filthy rags,"** in the sight of God (Isaiah 64:6).

The reason that faith justifies has nothing to do with any value or virtue in faith itself. In fact the words, **"You are saved by grace through faith; and that not of yourselves: it is the gift of God,"** tell us that our faith is itself a gift of God (Ephesians 2:8-9). **"No one can say that Jesus is the Lord, but by the Holy Ghost"** (1Corinthians 12:3). The words, **"We have access by faith into this grace wherein we stand,"** tell us that faith justifies us because it gives us access to God's grace (Romans 5:2). In other words, faith is like a hand that receives God's free gift of forgiveness.

It is only after **"the blood of Jesus Christ His Son cleanses us of all sin,"** that the Holy Spirit enters our heart through faith (1John 1:7). As it is written, **"After you believed, you were sealed with the Holy Spirit of promise,"** (Ephesians 1:13). And, the words, **"The flesh lusts against the Spirit, and the Spirit against the flesh: and they are opposed to each other: so that you cannot do the** things that you would," tell us that any improvement in our behavior comes after the Holy Spirit is at work in our heart (Galatians 5:17). In saying this, I do not want to imply that those who are saved never have to struggle against the flesh. The words, **"God who is faithful, will not allow you to be tempted beyond what you can bear; but when you are tempted, He will also provide a way out, giving you the ability to bear it,"** tell us that the Holy Spirit does not take away our sinful desires, but enables us to resist them (1Corinthians 10:13).

5. Faith Viewed As A Passive Act Or Instrument

The words, **"You are saved by grace through faith... Not of works, lest any man should boast,"** tell us that our faith is not a work, or something we do to please God (Ephesians 2:8-9). And, the words, **"We have peace with God through our Lord Jesus Christ, by whom we also have access by faith into this grace in which we stand,"** tell us that faith simply receives, or gives us access into, the grace Christ won for us by His death on the cross (Romans 5:1-2). That is why we view faith as a passive act or instrument. If God's grace was not already there for us, our faith would have nothing to receive.

Not only is faith not something we do, or something we deserve credit for, it is only by the power of the Holy Ghost that we are able to believe. The words, **"May the God of this hope fill you with all joy and peace as you trust in Him, so that you abound in this hope, through the power of the Holy Ghost,"** tell us that it is the power of God that enables us to trust [have faith] in the gospel (Romans 15:13). The words, **"I am not ashamed of the gospel of Christ: for it is the power of God to salvation to every one who believes;"** tell us that the power of God that enables us to believe comes to us through the gospel (Romans 1:16). The words, **"So will the word that goes out of my mouth be: it will not return to me empty, but it will accomplish what I want, and it will achieve what I sent it to do,"** also speak of God accomplishing His will [including bringing us to faith] through His Word (Isaiah 55:11). The words, **"My message and my preaching were not with enticing words of man's wisdom, but in demonstration of the Spirit and power, that your faith should not rest in the wisdom of men, but in the power of God,"** tell us that Paul's preaching was effective because of the power of God (1Corinthians 2:4). The words, **"Our gospel did not come to you only in word, but also in power, and in the Holy Ghost, and with much assurance,"** tell us that the power to produce faith came through the gospel (1Thessalonians 1:5). And, the words, **"Who are kept by the power of God through**

faith unto salvation which is waiting to be revealed at the end of time," tell us that we are not only brought to faith by the power of God, but are also kept in faith by that power (1Peter 1:5).

In other words, we are not only saved by what Christ accomplished for us on the cross, the very faith by which we have access to that salvation is a gift of God. As it is written, "**The wages of sin is death; but the gift of God is eternal life through Jesus Christ our Lord**" (Romans 6:23). In conversion we do not do anything to save ourselves, on the contrary, it is God who is at work bringing us to faith. The words, "**What is the exceeding greatness of His power toward us who believe, according to the working of His mighty power,**" plainly tell us that we are brought to faith by God (Ephesians 1:19). And, because our faith is like a hand that passively receives God's gift, the Bible sometimes speaks of faith as "**receiving**" Christ, or God's grace. The words, "**To as many as received Him,**" and "**By whom we have now received the atonement,**" are two examples (John 1:12, Romans 5:11). However, the passages quoted in this section make it clear that receiving Christ is not a work that we perform, or our part in salvation. Receiving God's gift of salvation is no more a work than receiving a Christmas present. We simply receive what Christ purchased for us by His blood. Therefore, saying that we receive it is a just another way of describing faith's passive reception of God's free gift.

6. Concerning True Faith And Living Faith

Because our faith in Christ is so different from the caricature of faith that we encounter in the world, many who are young or new to the faith have to deal with doubts about their faith, or fear that it might not be a true or living faith. Such fears are often amplified by the words of James, "**Faith, if it does not produce works, is dead, being alone,**" or Christ's warning, "**Many will say to me in that day, Lord, Lord, have we not prophesied in your name? and in your name cast out devils? and in your name done many wonderful works? And then I will declare to them, I never knew you: depart from me, you who do evil**" (James 2:17, Matthew 7:22-23). Therefore, we need to know how to deal with such doubts and fears.

Even though the words, "**A man is justified by faith without the deeds of the law,**" plainly tell us that faith makes us just [i.e. righteous] "**without the deeds of the law**" (Romans 3:28), a believer will sooner or later encounter the words, "**Faith without works is dead**" (James 2:20). And, the way of the world is to affirm one passage while explaining away the other. However, because both passages are the Word of God that approach is totally wrong. Both passages need to be accepted as true. And, both are true because they are talking about two different things. The words, "**A man is justified by faith without the deeds of the law,**" are speaking of works "of the law". In contrast, the statement, "**Faith without works is dead,**" is not talking about the works of the law, but about conduct that is consistent with faith. James makes that clear when he says, "**Wasn't Rahab the harlot also justified by works, when she received the spies, and sent them out another way?**" (James 2:25). Notice that Rahab's works had nothing to do with the law, but with acting in a way that was consistent with her faith. The second chapter of James begins by pointing out how wrong and inconsistent it is for believers to treat poor brethren as inferior, instead of showing to them the same love that Christ has shown for us, and James points to Rahab to illustrate his appeal to put our faith into action.

That being said, I need to make it clear that it is impossible for faith in Christ to ever be dead. Those who have faith have forgiveness, those who have forgiveness have the Holy Spirit, and the words, "**The flesh lusts against the Spirit, and the Spirit against the flesh: and they are opposed to each other: so that you cannot do the things that you would,**" tell us that those who trust in Christ have the Holy Spirit's help in resisting the flesh (Galatians 5:17). Therefore, John's statement, "**Anyone who claims to know Him, but does not keep his commandments, is a liar,**" is not talking about the struggles and shortcomings that beset a believer as he struggles against sin, but those who are unrepentant (1John 2:4). That would include those who claim to trust in Christ, but have no desire to give up their immoral lifestyle.

Just as those who have no desire to give up their immoral lifestyle are unrepentant, those who blind themselves to their own sins, convincing themselves that the rules they keep make them righteous or worthy of God's favor are equally unrepentant. The first group is condemned by the words, "**Anyone who claims to know Him, but does not keep his commandments, is a liar**" (1John 2:4). The second group is condemned by the words, "**Christ is of no benefit to those of you who seek righteousness by the law; you are fallen from grace**" (Galatians 5:4). True faith cannot exist without repentance, and true repentance is described in the words, "**God will not despise a heart that is humbled and sorry for sin**" (Psalm 51:17).

7. Faith And The Assurance Of Salvation

Consider the words, "**I have written these things to you who believe in the name of the Son of God; that you may know that you have eternal life, and that you may believe in the name of the Son of God**" (1John 5:13). Those words tell us that we can "**know**" (**not just feel certain, but know**) that we have eternal life. They also tell us that Scripture is the source of that **knowledge**, and that our faith rests upon that **knowledge**.

The words, "**Like sheep we have all have gone astray; each of us has turned to his own way; and the LORD has laid on Him [Christ] the iniquity of us all**," tell us that while Christ was hanging on the cross our sins were in two places, on Him and on us (Isaiah 53:6). Then, after He died, because He had no sins of His own, God forgave the sins that had been "**laid on Him**". And, because those sins were our sins, and because He received forgiveness for them, that forgiveness extends to us when we trust in Him. As it is written, "**All the prophets testify of Him, that through His name whoever believes in Him will receive forgiveness of sins**" (Acts 10:43).

Therefore, our salvation does not rest on anything that we do, but on what Christ has done for us. It does not even matter how strong our faith is. Even if it is "**faith like a mustard seed**," it is enough, because it is not our faith that saves us, but what Christ did (Luke 17:6). Our assurance of salvation should always rest on what Christ did, not how strong we imagine that our faith is.

The words, "**Scripture, having foreseen that God would justify the heathen through faith, proclaimed the gospel to Abraham in advance, saying, In you shall all nations be blessed**," tell us that Abraham was saved through believing the same gospel that we believe, namely God's promise of forgiveness in Christ (Galatians 3:8). And, the words, "**So then those who have faith in Christ are blessed with Abraham, who also believed... That the blessing given to Abraham might come to the Gentiles through Jesus Christ; that we might receive the <u>promise</u> of the Spirit through faith**," tell us that our faith is faith in God's promise (Galatians 3:9,14).

Now I have asked certain people about the doctrine of salvation only to have them say, "I just believe in Christ". And, that is fine if they truly are trusting in Christ. However, they would not even know that Christ existed if it were not for Scripture. And even if they did know; apart from Scripture they would not know that He died for their sins or that those who trust in Him receive forgiveness. That is why Jesus said, "**Search the scriptures; for in them you think that you have eternal life: and they are they that testify of me**" (John 5:39). And, that is why John wrote, "**These are written, that you might believe that Jesus is the Messiah, the Son of God; and that believing you might have life through His name**" (John 20:31). So I repeat, our faith is faith in God's promise of forgiveness in Christ. And, the words, "**God so loved the world, that He gave His only begotten Son, that whosoever believes on Him should not perish, but have everlasting life**," is one expression of that promise (John 3:16).

One of the problems that we encounter has to do with people who base their assurance of salvation on a "salvation experience" rather than on the Word of God. Now I do not deny that there are valid salvation experiences. Martin Luther had such an experience. The problem is false experiences. Suppose that you were to base your faith on the fact that an angel appeared to you and told you that you were saved. What would happen to that faith if, on your death bed, Satan appeared to you and told you that he was that angel disguised as an angel of light. Where would your faith be then? **That is why our faith must rest on the sure Word of God.** And, Luther's experience stemmed from the Joy that filled his heart when he understood what the Bible means when it says that we are justified by faith (see Rom. 3:28).

Hold fast to the Word of God. The opinions of men may contradict the words of Scripture, but the facts never do.

8. Can The Believer Be Sure He Has Saving Faith?

The words, "**I have written these things to you who believe in the name of the Son of God; that you may know that you have eternal life,**" tell us that we can "know" whether we have saving faith or not (1John 5:13). However, because of the inner confusion, doubts, and fears that are "**bound in the heart**" of man, many believers lack the "**full assurance of faith,**" (see Proverbs 22:15, Hebrews 10:22). And, we need to know how to deal with that lack of assurance.

The words, "**The natural man does not accept the things of the Spirit of God: for they are foolishness to him,**" coupled with the words, "**No man can come to me, unless the Father who has sent me draws him,**" tell us that God is dealing with those who seek assurance of salvation (1Corinthians 2:14, John 6:44). And, if they believe that there is forgiveness in Christ, and simply want assurance that they have it, then the seed of faith has already been planted in their hearts. A person with such doubts might be pointed to the words, "**If we confess our sins, He is faithful and just to forgive us our sins, and to cleanse us from all unrighteousness,**" and then asked to confess his sins to God, asking for forgiveness (1John 1:9).

However, it is not always that simple. There are always some who lack assurance of salvation because they are seeking righteousness by the law. Having gone through that struggle as a teenager, I know that it is possible for a person to profess to believe that salvation is by grace, while looking to works to make them righteous, because they are using the law as a motivation to resist the flesh. My deliverance from that double-mindedness came from realizing that God's standard of righteousness was so much higher than mine that it would condemn all my efforts at making myself righteous "**as filthy rags**" (Isaiah

64:6). And, realizing that I had to confess my sins and throw myself on God's mercy. It is only as I realized that the law would condemn me no matter how hard I tried, that I understood that freedom from the law is not freedom to sin, but freedom to be righteous. As it is written, "**By Him all who believe are justified from all things, from which you could not be justified by the law of Moses**" (Acts 13:39). And, "**Christ is the end of the law for righteousness to every one who believes**" (Romans 10:4).

God wants us to be sure of our faith. The words, "**Being justified by faith, we have peace with God through our Lord Jesus Christ**," tell us that our faith should bring us peace with God (Romans 5:1). But, we are not going to have that peace if we are not even sure that we have faith. The words, "**Let us draw near to God with a sincere heart in full assurance of faith**," tell us that faith should give us "full assurance" of salvation (Hebrews 10:22). And, the words, "**Being confident of this, that He who has begun a good work in you will continue it until the day of Jesus Christ**," tell us that God expects us to be "confident" that God will keep us safe unto salvation (Philippians 1:6). However, we cannot be confident if we are not even sure that we have faith.

God has not only given you His Word so that, "**You may know that you have eternal life**" (1John 5:13). The words, "**The Spirit Himself bears witness with our spirit, that we are the children of God**," tell us that the Spirit of God works through that Word to give us the inner assurance that what it says is true, and applies to us (Romans 8:16). The words, "**He who believes in the Son of God has this testimony in his heart**," again testify to the internal witness of the Holy Spirit (1John 5:10). However, the Bible also speaks of an external witness.

The words, "**He who is of God hears God's words: therefore you do not hear them, because you are not of God**," tell us that those who truly have faith are not going to reject what the Bible says (John 8:47). While the words, "**The fruit of the Spirit is love, joy, peace, patience, kindness, goodness, faith, meekness, self-control: against such there is no law. And they that are Christ's have crucified the flesh with its passions and lusts**," tell us that those who trust in Christ will see an improvement in their behavior (Galatians 5:22-24). However, the words, "**Who will transform our vile bodies, and make them like His glorified body, by the power by which He is able to bring everything under His control**," tell us that none of us is going to be totally free of sin in this life (Philippians 3:21). At the same time, even though the external witness exists; whenever people base their assurance of salvation on what they do, they are in danger of trusting in works rather than in Christ. And, they need to be reminded of the words, "**Satan himself masquerades as an angel of light. Therefore it is not surprising** if his servants also disguise themselves as ministers of righteousness" (2Corinthians 11:14-15). Those words tell us that even the unsaved are able to appear outwardly as righteous. And, those who look to external behavior for their assurance of salvation can easily deceive themselves. As it is written, **"You... outwardly appear righteous to men, but inwardly you are full of hypocrisy and wickedness"** (Matthew 23:28).

9. The Faith Of Infants

Many families over the centuries have had children that died in infancy or at a very young age. And, understandably, they wanted assurance that those children were in heaven. However, in giving comfort to such families it is important that we do not contradict Scripture, or go beyond what it says.

Matthew tells us that, **"Jesus called a little child to him, and set him in the midst of them, and said... Whoever offends one of these little ones who believe in me, it would be better for him if a millstone were hung around his neck, and he were drowned in the depth of the sea"** (Matthew 18:1-6). In those words, Jesus speaks of little children having faith in Him. And, that should be of great comfort to Christian families who have lost small children. However, Jesus was speaking of the children of believers. In contrast the words, **"The wicked are estranged from the womb: they go astray as soon as they be born, speaking lies,"** tell us that we cannot spin that comfort into a blanket rule that applies to all infants (Psalm 58:3).

The Augsburg Confession says, "Children, too, should be baptized, for in Baptism they are committed to God and become acceptable to him" (Tappert, page 33). And, we should commit our children to God. However, we should never assume that the mere act of baptism conveys grace apart from faith in Christ. Of that error, C.F.W. Walther says, "If the Word that is preached will not benefit a person unless he believes it, neither will being baptized and taking Communion benefit any one without faith". (Law and Gospel, page 351).

The words, **"Without faith it is impossible to please God,"** tell us that no infant will ever get to heaven without faith in Christ (Hebrews 11:6). The words, **"Nor is there salvation in any other: for there is no other name under heaven given among men, by which we must be saved,"** tell us the same thing (Acts 4:12). The words, **"If there had been a law given that could have given life, righteousness truly would have been by the law,"** tell us that no one, infants included, can be saved by their own innocence (Galatians 3:21). And, the words, **"He has given you life, who were <u>dead</u> in trespasses and sins... And were by nature the children of** wrath, even as others," tell us that all men are by "nature" spiritually "dead", and, therefore, in need of salvation (Ephesians 2:1-3). All of those passages tell us that infants are in need of salvation. How then can the Psalmist say, "**Out of the mouth of babes and sucklings you have ordained praise**"? (Psalm 8:2).

The Bible answers that question with the words, "**The LORD'S hand is not shortened, that it cannot save**" (Isaiah 59:1). The words, "**What is the exceeding greatness of his power toward us who believe, according to the working of his mighty power**," tell us that God's hand is not shortened because our faith is a gift of God (Ephesians 1:19). And, the words, "**When Elisabeth heard Mary's greeting, the babe leaped in her womb; and Elisabeth was filled with the Holy Spirit, and in a loud voice she exclaimed... why am I so favored, that the mother of my Lord should come to me? For, as soon as the sound of your greeting reached my ears, the babe leaped in my womb for joy**," tell us that John the Baptist leaped for "Joy" in the presence of Mary, and Christ who was in her womb (Luke 1:41-44). That leap on the part of John the Baptist tells us that he had faith, even while yet in the womb. And, if God can give an infant faith while yet in the womb, He can give our children faith.

So when it comes right down to it, we have to commit the spiritual well being of our children (born and unborn) to God's mercy, and entrust them to His justice. I prayed for my daughters while they were still in the womb. And, one of them would say, "Jesus died for my sins," before she was two years old. My point is that we should never neglect them spiritually, as if they are too young for it to matter.

Conversion, Or The Bestowal Of Faith

1. The Scriptural Basis Of The Doctrine

Jesus' words, "**I tell you truly, Unless you are converted, and become like little children, you will not enter into the kingdom of heaven**," tell us that conversion is not an option (Matthew 18:3). However, that raises two questions. What is conversion? And, why do we need it?

The words, "**Repent, and be converted, that your sins may be blotted out**," tell us that conversion brings forgiveness (Acts 3:19). The words, "**Just as sin entered the world by one man, and death by sin; so death passed upon all men, because all have sinned**," tell us that all men need forgiveness because all have sinned (Romans 5:12). **The proof that we have all sinned lies in the fact that we are all going to die. And, the very fact that you can do** nothing to prevent your death proves that you can do nothing to save yourself. "The wages of sin is death" (Romans 6:23). In short, we need to be converted because we are sinners who need forgiveness, and that forgiveness brings with it the promise of eternal life.

The words, "**Men are appointed to die once, and after that the judgment,**" tell us that death does not end our existence, but after death we will face God's judgment (Hebrews 9:27). The words, "**Men will account for every idle word that they speak, on the day of judgment,**" tell us that on that day we must account for everything that we have done (Matthew 12:36). **And, because we are all sinners, unless God forgives us we will all be condemned.** For God "**Is an holy God; He is a jealous God; He will not overlook your transgressions or your sins**" (Joshua 24:19).

However, the words, "**For God so loved the world, that He gave His only begotten Son, that whosoever believes on Him should not perish, but have everlasting life**," tell us that God has provided a way for us be forgiven, namely, through the death of His son (John 3:16). And, a comparison of the words, "**Whoever believes in Him will receive forgiveness of sins,**" with the words, "**Be converted, that your sins may be blotted out**," tell us that being "converted" and "believing in Christ" go hand in hand. **Conversion is the change from unbelief to faith**, and faith brings forgiveness (Acts 10:43 and Acts 3:19).

The words, "**What does a man profit, if he gains the whole world, and loses his own soul? or what will a man give in exchange for his soul?**" remind us that nothing we can gain in this world even comes close to the value of our soul (Matthew 16:20). The words, "**All who trust in the law are under a curse: for it is written, Cursed is every one who does not continue to do everything that is written in the book of the law,**" tell us that the law cannot save us, for it places us under a curse (Galatians 3:10). And, the words, "**None of them can by any means redeem his brother, or give God a ransom for him: (For the price to be paid for their soul is too costly, and what they give will never suffice,)**" tell us that no mere man could ever atone for his own soul, or the soul of anyone else (Psalm 49:7-8).

The words, "**When the time had fully come, God sent forth His Son, born of a woman, born under the law, To redeem those who were under the law, that we might receive the adoption of sons,**" tell us that even though we were in a hopeless mess, and could not save ourselves, God sent Christ into the world to save us (Galatians 4:4-5). The words, "**He was wounded for our transgressions, He was bruised for our iniquities: the punishment that brought us peace was upon Him; and by His stripes we are healed. Like sheep we have all have gone astray; each of us has** turned to his own way; and the LORD has laid on Him the iniquity of us all,"** tell us that Christ saved us by taking our sins upon Himself, and suffering the punishment that we deserved (Isaiah 53:5-6). **"For God has done what the law could not do, in that it was weak through the flesh.** *By* **sending His own Son in the likeness of sinful flesh, as an offering for sin, He condemned sin in the flesh: That the righteousness of the law might be fulfilled in us"** (Romans 8:3-4). **"And He has made you, who were dead in your sins and the uncircumcision of your flesh, alive together with Him, having forgiven all of your sins; Blotting out the handwriting of ordinances that was against us, which was contrary to us, and took it out of the way, nailing it to His cross,"** (Colossians 2:13-14). Faith is believing that Christ died for your sins, conversion is the beginning of faith, and the words, **"All the prophets testify of Him, that through His name whoever believes in Him will receive forgiveness of sins,"** tell us that faith brings forgiveness (Acts 10:43). So, to put it briefly, **conversion is the instantaneous change from being someone who is not forgiven to being someone who is forgiven.**

2. Conversion According To Scripture

The words, **"Jesus went into Galilee, preaching the gospel of the kingdom of God, and saying, The time has come, and the kingdom of God is at hand: repent, and believe the gospel,"** tell us that conversion involves both repentance and faith (Mark 1:14-15). And, the words, **"God will not despise a heart that is humbled and sorry for sin,"** describe a repentant heart as a heart that is "sorry for sin" (Psalm 51:17). However, the words, **"Godly sorrow results in repentance leading to salvation, not regret: but the sorrow of this world brings death,"** tell us that sorrow alone is not enough (2Corinthians 7:10). It is not sorrow that brings forgiveness, but faith in Christ. And, the words, **"Nor is there salvation in any other"** tell us that there is no other source of forgiveness (Acts 4:12).

When we compare the words, **"The sorrow of this world brings death,"** with the words, **"Judas, who had betrayed Him, having seen that He was condemned, repented, and brought the thirty pieces of silver back to the chief priests and elders, Saying, I have sinned for I have betrayed innocent blood... and after leaving hung himself,"** we see that Judas had "the sorrow of this world," he "repented," he was sorry for his sin (2Corinthians 7:10, Matthew 27:3-5). However, **his repentance was incomplete because it was not coupled with faith in Christ.** It was the sorrow that "brings death".

The "sorrow of this world" does not always result in suicide. Many times it leads those who are guilty to rationalize their sins. Instead of turning to God for forgiveness they make up excuses for their sins, as a way of easing their conscience. However, because they do not look to God for forgiveness they go into eternity unforgiven. My point is this, although being sorry for sin is part of repentance, **without faith that repentance is incomplete.** As it is written, "**Without faith it is impossible to please God**" (Hebrews 11:6).

It is a mistake to think of repentance as a one-time thing. While conversion is a one-time thing, just as the faith that begins at conversion will continue throughout our lifetime, the mental attitude that constitutes repentance, the attitude described in the words, "**God will not despise a heart that is humbled and sorry for sin,**" should continue throughout our lifetime (Psalm 51:17).

Those who are truly sorry for their sin will not want to repeat those sins. At the same time, because sin is in our very nature, there are many ways in which we all fall short. Sinful thoughts intrude into our minds even though we do not want them there. It is easy to fall into strife and contention. It is also easy for our sinful flesh to want to make excuses for those sins instead of looking to Christ for forgiveness. However, the words, "**Men will account for every idle word that they speak, on the day of judgment,**" tell us that instead of making excuses for such sins, we need to be sorry for them and humbly confess them to God, trusting in His promise of forgiveness in Christ (Matthew 12:36). As it is written, "**If we confess our sins, He is faithful and just to forgive us our sins, and to cleanse us from all unrighteousness**" (1John 1:9). At the same time, that forgiveness does not come because we confess our sins to God, but because we are trusting in Christ, for it is "**The blood of Jesus Christ His Son**" that "**cleanses us of all sin**" (1John 1:7).

The words, "**Whoever believes in Him will receive forgiveness of sins,**" tell us that forgiveness comes to us through faith in Christ (Acts 10:43). The words, "**We have redemption through His blood, the forgiveness of sins, according to the riches of His grace,**" tell us that the forgiveness that Christ won for us is ours through "grace" (Ephesians 1:7). And, the words, "**We also have access by faith into this grace in which we stand,**" tell us that faith is the hand that receives that grace (Romans 5:2). Therefore, because forgiveness comes to us through faith in Christ, **true conversion takes place the instant we come to faith in Christ.** It is faith that changes us from someone who is not forgiven to someone who is forgiven.

The words, "**Some of them... upon arriving in Antioch, spoke to the Grecians, preaching the Lord Jesus. And the hand of the Lord was with them, and a great number believed, and turned to the Lord,**" describe conversion as believing the gospel that was preached (Acts 11:20-21). The words, "**Philip opened his mouth,** and beginning at the same scripture, told him the good news about Jesus. And as they went on their way, they came to some water: and the eunuch said, Look, here is water; what prevents me from being baptized? And Philip said, If you truly believe, you may. And he said, I believe,"** describe conversion as believing the "good news about Jesus" (Acts 8:35-37). And the words, **"They said, Believe on the Lord Jesus Christ, and you will be saved, you and your household. And they spoke the word of the Lord to him, and to all who were in his house... and he and all his house were baptized,"** describe conversion as believing the "word of the Lord" regarding Jesus Christ (Acts 16:31-33).

The words, **"We have also come to believe in Jesus Christ, that we might be justified through faith in Christ, and not by the works of the law: for the works of the law will not make anyone righteous,"** tell us that our works [i.e. things done to make ourselves righteous] do not make us righteous, and, therefore, contribute nothing to our conversion (Galatians 2:16). At the same time, because **true repentance looks to God with "a heart that is humbled and sorry for sin,"** those who repent do not want to sin (Psalm 51:17). Moreover, the words, **"After you heard the word of truth, and were also sealed with the holy Spirit of promise, after you believed,"** tell us that once we come to faith in Christ we receive the Holy Spirit (Ephesians 1:13). And, the words, **"The flesh lusts against the Spirit, and the Spirit against the flesh: and they are opposed to each other: so that you cannot do the things that you would,"** tell us that the Holy Spirit works in us after we are saved to help us resist temptation (Galatians 5:17). Therefore, even though works cannot make us righteous, and contribute nothing to our conversion, they will follow faith, not as a part of faith, but as a fruit or by-product of faith. As it is written, **"If any man is in Christ, he is a new creation, the old things have passed away; behold, all things have become new"** (2Corinthians 5:17).

3. The Beginning And End Of Conversion

Because conversion is the inner change from unbelief to faith, the beginning point of conversion is unbelief, while its end is faith, faith in our Lord Jesus Christ.

Although **"The God who made the world and everything in it... has made of one blood all nations of men to live on all the face of the earth, and has determined their appointed times, and the boundaries they live in; So that they should seek the Lord, in the hope that they might grope for Him, and find Him"** (Acts 17:24-27). The words, **"There is a way that seems right to a man, but its end is the way of death,"** tell us that man's reason (the blind struggle of our sin-corrupted finite little minds to find the truth) regards the way of unbelief [death] as perfectly reasonable (Proverbs 14:12). That is true because, "**The natural [unbelieving] man does not accept the things of the Spirit of God: for they are foolishness to him**" (1Corinthians 2:14). "**For the minds of those who do not believe have been blinded by the god of this world, that the light of the glorious gospel of Christ, who is the image of God, might not reach them**" (2Corinthians 4:4). And, because of that unbelief the Apostle Paul described those "**without Christ**" as "**having no hope, and without God in the world**" (Ephesians 2:12). That is where conversion begins.

While the immediate end of conversion is faith in Christ, and the forgiveness that is ours through faith, Biblical descriptions of conversion sometimes include the fruits of faith [the change in our life and behavior that is the result of repentance and faith in Christ]. The words, "**There were some of them, men of Cyprus and Cyrene, who, upon arriving in Antioch, spoke to the Grecians, preaching the Lord Jesus. And the hand of the Lord was with them: and a great number believed, and turned to the Lord,**" describe the end of conversion as faith in Christ (Acts 11:20-21). The words, "**To open their eyes, and to turn them from darkness to light, and from the power of Satan to God, that they may receive forgiveness of sins, and inheritance among those who are sanctified through faith in me,**" describe conversion in terms of turning from darkness to light, being delivered from the power of Satan, forgiveness, and sanctification all of which come through faith in Christ (Acts 26:18). The words, "**You turned to God from idols to serve the living and true God,**" describe conversion as turning from idols to God, which is a fruit of repentance and faith (1Thessalonians 1:9). And, the words, "**You should turn from these fantasies to the living God, who made heaven, and earth, and the sea, and everything in them,**" describe the end of conversion as turning from fantasy [idol worship, or evolution] to God, which, again, is a fruit of repentance and faith (Acts 14:15). These descriptions of conversion all point to faith in Christ, and to the change that takes place as a result of that faith.

4. The Efficient Cause Of Conversion

Even though Jesus Himself said, "**No man can come to me, unless the Father who has sent me draws him,**" instead of giving God total credit for their salvation (the credit that is due Him) men, in their blindness, continually try to take some credit for their own salvation (John 6:44). [See Jeremiah 17:9.] One reason for this is lack of faith. Men who are not sure they are saved want something they can do to be sure. However, that does not really work, because we are saved by what Christ did, not by what we do. As a teenager, I would listen to radio preachers, and time after time would ask Jesus into my heart etc., yet nothing I did gave me assurance of salvation. That assurance only came when I actually placed my faith in Christ. Before that I thought that I believed in Him, but did not really understand. Assurance only came when I realized that all of my efforts were "**like filthy rags**" in the sight of God, and that I could only be saved by looking to Christ for mercy (Isaiah 64:6). And, the words, "**No one can say that Jesus is the Lord, but by the Holy Ghost,**" tell me that it was God who brought me to that point, and God who gave me faith in His promise of forgiveness in Christ (1Corinthians 12:3).

The words, "**What is the exceeding greatness of His power toward us who believe, according to the working of His mighty power,**" tell us that our faith is produced in us by God's power (Ephesians 1:19). The words, "**No man can come to me, unless the Father who has sent me draws him,**" tell us that no one can come to God without that power (John 6:44). The words, "**Giving thanks to the Father... For He has rescued us from the power of darkness, and transferred us into the kingdom of His dear Son,**" tell us that God has rescued us (Colossians 1:12-13). The words, "**You were without Christ... having no hope, and without God in the world,**" tell us that if God had not rescued us we would have had no hope of salvation (Ephesians 2:12). And, the words, "**You are saved by grace through faith; and that <u>not of yourselves</u>: it is the gift of God,**" tell us that our salvation does not come from us, but is a gift of God (Ephesians 2:8).

The words, "**It has been granted to you that for the sake of Christ, you should not only believe in Him, but also suffer for His sake,**" tell us that faith is something that God has granted to us (Philippians 1:29). The words, "**God, who once commanded light to shine out of darkness, made His light shine in our hearts, to give us the light of the knowledge of the glory of God in the face of Jesus Christ,**" compare God's act of filling our hearts with the light of faith, with His act of creating physical light (2Corinthians 4:6). The words, "**Whoever believes that Jesus is the promised Savior is born of God: and everyone who loves the Father also loves the child born of Him,**" tell us that we become God's children [are born again] through God's gift of faith in Christ (1John 5:1). [See Galatians 4:4-7.] The words, "**To as many as received Him, He gave power to become the sons of God, even to those who believe in His name,**" tell us that God gives those who believe the power to become the sons of God [be born again] (John 1:12). And, the words, "**Who are not born of blood, or of the will of the flesh, or of the will of man, but of God,**" tell us that our will plays no part in our becoming God's children [i.e. being born again] (John 1:13). At the same time, the words, "**I will never turn away anyone who comes to me**," tell us that God is not going to turn away anyone who wants to be saved (John 6:37).

Far from helping in our salvation, the Bible tells us that, "**The minds of those who do not believe have been blinded by the god of this world, that the light of the glorious gospel of Christ, who is the image of God, might not reach them**" (2Corinthians 4:4). Because of that blindness, "**The natural man does not accept the things of the Spirit of God: for they are foolishness to him: and he cannot understand them**," (1Corinthians 2:14). "**The heart is deceitful above all things, and desperately wicked**" (Jeremiah 17:9). And, "**The carnal [i.e. fleshly] mind is hostile to God: for it is not subject to the law of God, nor indeed can be**" (Romans 8:7).

5. The Means Of Conversion

The gospel is the means by which God brings us to faith, and the means by which He keeps us in faith. The words, "**The kingdom of God is at hand: repent, and believe the gospel**," point to the fact that we enter God's kingdom through believing the gospel (Mark 1:15). The words, "**Faith comes by hearing, and hearing by the word of God**," tell us that God brings us to faith through His Word (Romans 10:17). And, the words, "**Kept by the power of God through faith unto salvation**," tell us that God keeps us in faith "**through faith**," and thus through the gospel which produces that faith (1Peter 1:5).

Those who deny that the Gospel is the means by which God brings us to faith often point to Adam, Noah and Abraham. However, the words, "**Scripture, having foreseen that God would justify the heathen through faith, proclaimed the gospel to Abraham in advance**," tell us that Abraham was saved through believing the gospel (Galatians 3:8). The words, "**By faith Abraham, when he was tested, offered up Isaac... Believing that God was able to raise him up, even from the dead**," tell us that Abraham believed that his "seed" would die as a sacrifice for sin and rise again (Hebrews 11:17-19). The words, "**I will put hostility between you and the woman, and between your seed and her seed; it will bruise your head, and you will bruise His heel**," tell us God gave His promise of a Savior to Adam and Eve (Genesis 3:15). The words, "**That the blood of all the prophets, that was shed from the foundation of the world... From the blood of Abel to the blood of Zechariah**," tell us that Able was a prophet, and, therefore, one who understood the way of salvation (Luke 11:50-51). For, "**All the prophets testify of Him, [Christ] that through his name whoever believes in Him will receive forgiveness of sins**" (Acts 10:43). And, the words, "**Noah found grace in the eyes of the LORD**," tell us that Noah was saved through faith in Christ, for "**there is no other name under heaven given among men, by which we must be saved**" (Genesis 6:8, Acts 4:12).

However, the words, "**You are a chosen generation, a royal priesthood, a holy nation, a people valued by God; that you should show forth the praises of Him who has called you out of darkness into His marvelous light,**" tell us that those who are lost are in darkness (1Peter 2:9). The words, "**Being alienated from the life of God through the ignorance that is in them, because of the blindness of their heart,**" tell us that those who are lost are alienated from God and spiritually blind (Ephesians 4:18). The words, "**They are all estranged from me through their idols,**" tell us that those who worship idols are cut off from God. (Ezekiel 14:5). That means that even if they earnestly prayed to their idol for salvation they would never receive it, because an idol can never answer their prayer. And, the words, "**Of His own will He gave us life through the word of truth, that we should be a kind of first-fruits of His creation,**" tell us that God brings us to faith [i.e. gives us life] through "the word of truth" (James 1:18). All this points to the fact that the gospel is the means which God uses to convert the lost, and bring them to salvation. As it is written, "**The gospel of Christ... is the power of God to salvation to every one who believes**" (Romans 1:16). "**For the preaching of the cross is foolishness to those who perish; but it is the power of God to us who are saved... For since... the world through its wisdom did not know God, it pleased God to save those who believe through the foolishness of preaching**" (1Corinthians 1:18-21).

The words, "**repent, and believe the gospel,**" reveal that conversion requires both repentance and faith (Mark 1:15). The words, "**God will not despise a heart that is humbled and sorry for sin,**" describe repentance as being humbled and sorry for sin (Psalm 51:17). The words, "**No flesh will ever be declared righteous in God's sight by the deeds of the law: because the knowledge of sin comes by the law,**" tell us that the law is the means God uses to make us aware of our sin, and bring us to the point where we are "humbled and sorry for sin" (Romans 3:20). And, the words "**Christ did not send me to baptize, but to preach the gospel,**" compared with the words, "**Faith comes by hearing, and hearing by the word of God,**" tell us that hearing the gospel is the means that God uses to bring us to faith (1Corinthians 1:17, Romans 10:17).

The words, "**Whatever the law says, it says to those who are under the law: that every mouth may be stopped, and all the world may become guilty before God,**" tell us that God's law is designed to convict every last person on earth (Romans 3:19). Therefore, if they are not "**humbled and sorry for sin,**" it is only because they have hardened their heart (Psalm 51:17). And, the words, "**That repentance and remission of sins should be preached in His name among all nations," tell us that the purpose of preaching is to call all nations to repentance and faith in Christ (Luke 24:47).

The words, "**How many of my father's hired servants have food enough to spare, and I am dying with hunger! I will get up and return to my father, and will say to him, Father, I have sinned against heaven, and before you,**" and "**It is good for me that I have been afflicted; that I might learn your statutes,**" tell us that God sometimes uses affliction, together with His law, to bring us to repentance (Luke 15:17-18, Psalm 119:71). While the words, "**When you received the word of God that you heard from us, you did not receive it as the word of men, but as it is in truth, the word of God, which effectively works in you that believe,**" tell us that the word works in us to produce faith (1Thessalonians 2:13).

Rightly understood, baptism works together with preaching the Word, not as a work, but as a ceremonial proclamation of the gospel. To "**Repent, and be baptized... in the name of Jesus Christ for the forgiveness of sins,**" is to **repent and be baptized believing that there is forgiveness in Christ** (Acts 2:38). And, baptism is God's way of telling every convert who comes, believing that there is forgiveness in Christ, and that their sin has been washed away – not by the water, but by the blood of Jesus Christ and faith in that blood. As it is written, "**Scripture has concluded all under sin, that the promise might be given to those who believe, through faith in Jesus Christ,**" (Galatians 3:22). God designed that ceremony to give His promise of forgiveness in Christ to every convert, because preachers often fail to.

Likewise, rightly understood, the Lord's Supper works together with preaching as a ceremonial proclamation of the gospel. Christ's words, "**Take, eat: this is my body, which is broken for you,**" are saying "My body was broken [sacrificed] for you on the cross (1Corinthians 11:24). And, His words, "**This is my blood... which is shed for many for the forgiveness of sins,**" are saying "My blood was shed for you on the cross so that you can have forgiveness (Matthew 26;28). And, everyone who believes those words, everyone who believes that Christ's body was "**given**" for them (**on the cross**), and that His blood was "**shed**" for them (**on the cross**) so that they could have forgiveness, truly receives Christ's body and blood, not as something physical but as the atonement for their sin.

God designed that ceremony to give every believer who is, "**humbled and sorry for sin,**" His promise of forgiveness in Christ because churches often fail to.

6. The Internal Motions In Conversion

The Bible uses the word "repentance" in three ways. When the Bible says that, **"Judas... repented, and brought the thirty pieces of silver back to the chief priests and elders,"** it is telling us that Judas was sorry for what he had done (Matthew 27:3). However, his repentance was incomplete because it never led him to seek God's mercy or look to Christ for forgiveness. The words, **"Repent of this wickedness, and pray to God, that the thought of your heart may be forgiven you,"** again speak of repentance as sorrow for sin (Acts 8:22). However, the words, **"There will be more joy in heaven over one sinner who repents, than over ninety and nine just persons, who do not need to repent,"** use the word "repent" as a synonym of conversion – of complete repentance consisting of sorrow for sin coupled with faith in Christ (Luke 15:7). Without that faith in Christ there would be nothing for heaven to rejoice over. The words, **"Unless you repent, you will all perish,"** again speak of conversion as repentance (Luke 13:5). In contrast, the words, **"They should repent and turn to God, and live lives consistent with repentance,"** speak of a change in behavior that is **"consistent with repentance"** (Acts 26:20). That change of behavior is a fruit of repentance, not repentance itself. However, sometimes repentance is described by its fruits.

Because the focus of this section is conversion, we want to look at the internal change that leads to faith in Christ. And, the words, **"This is the man to whom I will look, even to him who is humble and of a contrite spirit, and trembles at my word,"** give us a description of that internal change (Isaiah 66:2). To be **"contrite"** is to be sorry for sin. Picture a young child who, upon being rebuked for wrongdoing, breaks into tears and cries "I'm sorry," meaning it from the heart. The words, **"Whoever will humble himself like this little child, the same is greatest in the kingdom of heaven,"** tell us that God wants us to come to Him as little children, who are truly sorry and want to do what is right (Matthew 18:4). At the same time God does not want us to take sin lightly as did King Saul, who said "I **have sinned: for I have transgressed the commandment of the LORD, and your words... Therefore, I pray, pardon my sin"** (1Samuel 15:24-25). Notice that Saul asked Samuel for pardon, not God, and did not indicate any fear of God or desire for God's forgiveness.

The words, **"If you love the LORD, hate evil,"** and **"The fear of the LORD is to hate evil,"** tell us that all who fear and love God will hate evil (Psalm 97:10, Proverbs 8:13). And, all who truly hate evil will not want it in their life. Moreover, the words, **"He who covers [excuses] his sins will not prosper: but whoever confesses and forsakes them will have mercy,"** tell us that those who truly fear and love God will not excuse their sins, but will confess and forsake them (Proverbs 28:13). In fact, we could say that those who excuse their sins, and try to justify wrongdoing, really love those sins, and that is the opposite of true repentance.

When Ezekiel said, "**If the wicked person turns from all the sins that he has committed, and keeps my law, and does that which is lawful and right, he will surely live, he will not die,**" he was describing repentance by its fruits (Ezekiel 18:21). What those who pull this verse out of context fail to realize is that God's law demands "**a heart that is humbled and sorry for sin,**" not just a heart that just puts on an outward show of righteousness. (Psalm 51:17). Christ condemned such outward show when He said, "**You also outwardly appear righteous to men, but inwardly you are full of hypocrisy and wickedness,**" (Matthew 23:28). However, that error can be avoided if we interpret those words of Ezekiel in the light of Christ's parable of the Pharisee and the publican. In fact, the words, "**He [Christ] spoke this parable to those who trusted in themselves that they were righteous, and looked down on others,**" tell us that this parable was directed against those who, like the Pharisees, would twist Ezekiel's words to support works-righteousness (Luke 18:9).

When "**The Pharisee stood up and prayed thus to himself, God, I thank you, that I am not like other men are, extortioners, evil doers, adulterers, or even like this publican. I fast twice in the week, I give tithes of everything I possess,**" he undoubtedly thought that he had turned from any sins he had committed, and was keeping God's law (Luke 18:11-12). However, Jesus did not share that opinion, and the reason He did not share it may be summarized in the following words by Dr. Walter A. Maier.

> The Pharisee lied when he posed as an example of goodness and obedience. He had harbored unclean, lust-filled, greedy, hate-charged thoughts. His soul, as every man's, was a source of vicious, destructive evil. Deny it though he did this Bible verdict condemned him: "From within, out of the heart of men, proceed evil thoughts, adulteries, fornications, murders, thefts, covetousness, wickedness, deceit, lasciviousness, an evil eye, blasphemy, pride, foolishness." (From the 1947 sermon, "The Prayer God Answers".)

In contrast, when "**the publican, standing afar off, would not even look up to heaven, but beat upon his breast, saying, God be merciful to me a sinner.**" He was doing what God's law required (Luke 18:13). And, the words, "**This man went down to his house justified,**" tell us that his repentance was coupled with faith (Luke 18:14). For, "**A man is not justified by the works of the law, but through faith in Jesus Christ... for the works of the law will not make anyone righteous"** (Galatians 2:16).

In short, the law prepares our heart for conversion by revealing our sin and need for forgiveness. The internal change that God works in us through the law takes place when we stop excusing our sin and come to God with a humble heart that is sorry for sin and wants to be delivered from it. Conversion then takes place when we believe God's promise of forgiveness in Christ. For, **"Scripture has concluded all under sin, that the promise [of forgiveness] might be given to those who believe, through faith in Jesus Christ"** (Galatians 3:22). As it is written, **"Repent, and be converted, that your sins may be blotted out,"** (Acts 3:19). Knowing that **"God will not despise a heart that is humbled and sorry for sin"** (Psalm 51:17). For **"If we confess our sins, He is faithful and just to forgive us our sins, and to cleanse us from all unrighteousness,"** and **"The blood of Jesus Christ His Son cleanses us of all sin"** (1John 1:7,9).

7. Conversion Is Instantaneous

The change that takes place in conversion, takes place the instant our sins are forgiven. Until we receive that forgiveness, we are **"dead in trespasses and sins"** (Ephesians 2:1). Those who fail to understand this often confuse incomplete repentance, or the works that follow repentance, with conversion, giving people the idea that conversion is some sort of process in which they determine the outcome. However that is clearly contrary to what the Bible teaches. The words, **"God, who is rich in mercy, because of His great love for us, Even when we were dead in sins, has made us alive together with Christ,"** tell us that it is God who **"has made us alive,"** not us (Ephesians 2:4-5). And, the Bible describes that change – from being **"dead in trespasses and sins,"** to being **"alive together with Christ"** – as a resurrection, saying that God, **"Has raised us up together with Him, and made us sit with Him in heavenly places in Christ Jesus"** (Ephesians 2:6). This resurrection – from being **"dead in trespasses and sins,"** to being **"alive together with Christ"** – is the **"first resurrection,"** and **"the second death [hell] has no power over,"** those who, **"have risen with Christ"** (Revelation 20:5-6, Colossians 3:1).

Conversion is also spoken of as a new birth. Here again, the change is from being **"dead in trespasses and sins,"** to being **"alive together with Christ"**. The words, **"Who are not born of blood, or of the will of the flesh, or of the will of man, but of God,"** tell us that man's will plays no part in the new birth (John 1:13). And, the words, **"Whoever believes that Jesus is the promised Savior is born of God,"** tell us that this new birth takes place the moment we come to faith in Christ (1John 5:1). "**He who believes on Him [Christ] is not condemned: but he who does not believe is condemned already, because he has not believed on the name of the only begotten Son of God**," (John 3:18).

8. The Grace Of Conversion Is Resistible

Although the Bible tells us that God, "**Wants all men to be saved, and to come to the knowledge of the truth**," He does not force them to be saved (1Timothy 2:4). On the contrary, the words, "**O Jerusalem, Jerusalem, you who kill the prophets, and stone those who are sent to you, how often I longed to gather your children together, as a hen gathers her chicks under her wings, and <u>you would not</u>**!" tell us that even though God reaches out to the lost, they resist His efforts to bring them to repentance (Matthew 23:37). The words, "**You stiffnecked and uncircumcised in heart and ears, you always resist the Holy Ghost: as your fathers did, so do you**," tell us the same thing (Acts 7:51). At the same time, the words, "**What is the exceeding greatness of His power toward us who believe, according to the working of His mighty power**," tell us that those who do believe, do so because they have been brought to faith by the **power of God**, not because of something in them (Ephesians 1:19). In fact, the words, "**Who are not born of blood, or of the will of the flesh, or of the will of man, but of God**," tell us that our own "will" plays no part in our salvation (John 1:13). "**No one can say that Jesus is the Lord, but by the Holy Ghost**" (1Corinthians 12:3). And, the fact that our own will plays no part in our salvation tells us that those who are saved, are not saved because they did not resist the Holy Ghost, but because **God chose to bring them to faith in spite of their resistance**. We do not know why He chose some and not others, but the words "**I know that nothing good dwells in me**," tell us that He does not choose us because of anything good in us, but solely because of His grace (Romans 7:18). As it is written, "**You are saved by grace through faith; and that not of yourselves: it is the gift of God: Not of works, lest any man should boast**" (Ephesians 2:8-9).

The words, "**John came to you in the way of righteousness, and you did not believe him: but the publicans and harlots believed him: and when you saw it, you did not repent, and believe him**," were spoken to the Pharisees, and the Pharisees resisted God's call to repentance by excusing and rationalizing their own sins (Matthew 25:32). They did not repent because they had convinced themselves "**that they were righteous**" (Luke 18:9). That is why Jesus told them that they had, "**Made the commandment of God of no effect**" (Matthew 15:6). However, what we want to make clear is that God is not going to turn anyone away. His words, **"Come to me, all you who labor and are carrying a heavy load, and I will give you rest,"** extend to all men (Matthew 11:28). Those who resist are **opposing "their own interest"**. However, we should still instruct them **"with gentleness... in the hope that God will give them repentance"** (2Timothy 2:25). Knowing that, **"It is God who works"** in both you and them **"to will and to do His good pleasure"** (Philippians 2:13).

9. Conversion According To Law And Grace

I have already mentioned the fact that the Law prepares our heart for conversion by showing us our sin and need of forgiveness. And, in reading the words, **"The law was our schoolmaster to bring us to Christ, that we might be declared righteous by faith,"** it is easy to assume that the Law does nothing more than show us our sins (Galatians 3:24). However, the Law not only condemned sin, it also required God's people to acknowledge their sin and seek forgiveness. We see that aspect of the Law in all of the sacrifices required by the Old Testament. At the same time, the words, **"If the inheritance comes by the law, it is not given by promise: but God gave it to Abraham by promise,"** tell us that forgiveness and salvation did not come to Abraham or anyone else because of the sacrifices, but because they believed God's promise of forgiveness in Christ (Galatians 3:18). As it is written, **"Scripture, having foreseen that God would justify the heathen through faith, proclaimed the gospel to Abraham in advance,"** (Galatians 3:8). And, **"Those who have faith in Christ are blessed with Abraham, who also believed,"** (Galatians 3:9).

God not only used the Law to show His people their sins, but also to teach them the necessity of repentance, and give them His promise of mercy. By requiring animal sacrifice, God taught His people that forgiveness is not cheap. However, because He instituted those sacrifices as a type of Christ's ultimate sacrifice, He counted faith in the promise of forgiveness connected with those sacrifices as faith in Christ. David trusted in that promise, saying, **"I have placed my faith in your grace [mercy]; my heart will rejoice in your salvation"** (Psalm 13:5). And, that promise of grace (mercy) is why God said, **"I desired mercy, and not sacrifice"** (Hosea 6:6). The actual sacrifices were just a means of teaching God's people to acknowledge their sin and look to God for mercy.

However, **"Now that faith has come, we are no longer under a schoolmaster. For you are all the children of God through faith in Christ Jesus"** (Galatians 3:25-26). Therefore, there is no longer any need for animal sacrifices. However, we still need to repent and look to Christ for forgiveness and salvation. The words, "**God now commands all men every where to repent**" // "**Repent, and be converted, that your sins may be blotted out,**" command us to repent (Acts 3:19). (Acts 17:30). And, all such commands are law. Nevertheless, because Christ said "**No man can come to me, unless the Father who has sent me draws him,**" we know that it is a law that we cannot keep, at least in our own strength (John 6:44). But, it does not depend on us! The words, "**What is the exceeding greatness of His power toward us who believe, according to the working of His mighty power,**" tell us that we are brought to faith and kept in faith by the power of God (Ephesians 1:19). So the Law commands us to repent, but both repentance and faith are gifts of God. For that reason, if we repent and look to Christ in faith, our action and God's action in us are one and the same.

Here we see a fine line of distinction between the grace that Christ won for us on the cross, and the grace that brings us to faith. Yet Christ is the reason for both. He not only died for our sins, He caused the Bible to be written, and sent the Holy Spirit to bring us to faith so that His death would not be in vain.

The words, "**Turn me, and I will be turned; for you are the LORD my God,**" call upon God to empower repentance (Jeremiah 31:18). The words, "**I will give them a heart to know me, and know that I am the LORD: and they will be my people, and I will be their God: for they will return to me with their whole heart,**" speak of repentance as a gift of God (Jeremiah 24:7). And, the words, "**It is God who works in you both to will and to do His good pleasure,**" tell us that God is at work in us (Philippians 2:13).

[Note: The words, "**The blood of all the prophets... From the blood of Abel to the blood of Zechariah,**" tell us that Able was a prophet (Luke 11:50-51). The words, "**Abel, also brought of the firstlings of his flock and of its fat. And the LORD had regard for Abel and his offering,**" tell us that Able instituted animal sacrifice. And, the words, "**All the prophets testify of Him [Christ], that through His name whoever believes in Him will receive forgiveness of sins,**" tell us that as God's prophet, Able instituted animal sacrifice as a way of testifying of Christ (Acts 10:43).]

10. Continued Conversion

When we speak of continued conversion we are not saying that people need to be converted over and over again, but that the change that comes over us when we come to faith in Christ will continue throughout our life. As it is written "**If any man is in Christ, he is a new creation: the old things have passed away; behold, all** things have become new" (2Corinthians 5:17).

Because repentance lays the groundwork for faith, a repentant heart, "**a heart that is humbled and sorry for sin**," will continue throughout our life (Psalm 51:17). Moreover, because the Holy Spirit comes into our heart "**through faith**" in Christ, once we come to faith the Holy Spirit will be at work in us (Galatians 3:14). That does not mean that there will not be a struggle. Our flesh will lust "**against the Spirit, and the Spirit against the flesh** (Galatians 5:17). But, because we are sorry for our sins **we will not want to do evil and will fight against it**. Those who are truly repentant do not want to be sinners. That is not to say that we never fall short. We all have unclean, lust-filled, greedy, and hate-charged thoughts. When we are angry it is easy to utter hateful and hurtful words, words that we are later sorry for. However, when that happens, instead of ignoring or excusing our sins like we did before we came to faith, we should confess them to God, looking to Christ for forgiveness. And, and since that is what happened when we came to faith in Christ, that is what I am calling "continued conversion". Here again, I am not saying that we need to be converted again every time we sin, but that being sorry for sin and looking to Christ for forgiveness is an attitude that should continue throughout our life.

The words, "**Put on the new nature, which after *the image of* God is created in righteousness and true holiness**," call upon us to conduct ourselves in a way that is in accord with the image of God (Ephesians 4:24). The words. "**Let us lay aside every weight, and the sin that so easily entangles us, and let us run with patience the race that is set before us**," urge us to avoid sin (Hebrews 12:1). The words, "**Just as Christ was raised from the dead through the glory of the Father, even so we should also walk in newness of life**," urge us to conduct ourselves as we would if we had no sinful desires (Romans 6:4). And, the words, "**Knowing this, that our old man was crucified with Him, that the body of sin might be destroyed, so that we would no longer serve sin**," tell us that we should no longer serve sin (Romans 6:6).

The words, "**The flesh lusts against the Spirit, and the Spirit against the flesh: and they are opposed to each other**," tell us that as we seek to do right there will be an inner struggle against the flesh (Galatians 5:17). And, the words, "**When I want to do good, evil is present with me**," // "**I buffet my body, and bring it under my control: lest there be any way that I, after having preached to others, might be rejected**," tell us that even the Apostle Paul had a struggle with sin (Romans 7:21, 1Corinthians 9:27).

The words, "**Have mercy upon me, O God, according to your loving-kindness: blot out my transgressions according to the multitude of your tender mercies. Wash me thoroughly from my iniquity, and cleanse me from my sin. For I acknowledge** my transgressions: and my sin is ever before me," reveal that David was truly sorry for his sin, and looked to God for forgiveness (Psalm 51:1-3). And, while we should never sin willfully as David did, like David we should all be sorry when we sin, instead of trying to excuse our sin.

Let me make it clear that I am not saying that our salvation depends upon confessing every sin. It is not through confession but through faith in Christ that we receive forgiveness. And, "**The blood of Jesus Christ His Son cleanses us of all sin**," not just some sins (1John 1:7). As Horatio Spafford put it, "**My sin not in part but the whole, is nailed to His cross and I bear it no more**" (From the Hymn, "It is Well With My Soul).

Just as the words "**faith comes by hearing**" tell us that Holy Spirit plants faith in our hearts through His Word: as we continue to humbly look at our sin, taking comfort daily in God's promise of forgiveness in Christ, the words, "**I planted, Apollos watered; but God gave the increase**," tell us that Holy Spirit continues to work through His Word to nurture and strengthen [water] our faith (Romans 10:17, 1Corinthians 3:6).

11. Sustained Conversion

It is a great comfort to know that we do not have to keep ourselves from falling away from the faith. On the contrary, the Bible plainly tells us that we "**are kept by the power of God through faith unto salvation**" (1Peter 1:5). Nevertheless, the only reason God needs to keep us from falling from faith is that without His help we would all fall away. As it is written, "**No one can keep his own soul alive**" (Psalm 22:29).

However, Satan is attacking that aspect of the gospel **on two fronts. On one hand** we have to deal with those who trust in works, rather than grace, to keep them from losing salvation. That error is refuted by the words, "**kept by the power of God**" and by the words "**To Him who is able to keep you from falling, and to present you faultless before His glorious presence with great joy, To the only wise God, our Savior**," which tell us that it is God who keeps us "**from falling**," not us (1Peter 1:5, Jude 1:24-25).

On the other hand, we have to deal with those who claim that once a person is saved they can live in sin and still be saved. And, that doctrine comes straight out of hell. Now many who teach that doctrine would never actually live in sin themselves. However, they have come from a background where they were in constant fear of losing salvation, and in trying to counter one false doctrine have created another. The vile fruit of that heresy is seen in congregations that tolerate fornication and abortion, accept unrepentant homosexuals, and even elevate those guilty of sexual sin to positions of leadership. That heresy is condemned by the words, "**They commit adultery, and walk in lies: they strengthen the hands of evildoers, so that no one repents of his wickedness: all of them are like Sodom in my sight**" (Jeremiah 23:14).

Because explaining away passages of Scripture is rebellious and irresponsible, we need to take a serious look at all of the passages that warn us of danger. At the same time, we should never interpret those passages contradict the passages that plainly tell us that we are "**kept by the power of God through faith unto salvation,**" not by our own efforts (1Peter 1:5). So let us look at some of those passages.

The first tells us that, "**Those on the rock are those, who, when they hear, receive the word with joy; but having no root, <u>believe for a while, and in time of temptation fall away</u>**" (Luke 8:13). This passage seems to be speaking of those who like the gospel message when they first hear it, but do not think that they have much to be forgiven of, and, therefore, do not value forgiveness. As it is written, "**He who** [*thinks that he*] **is forgiven little, loves little**" (Luke 7:47).

The second passage says, "**It is impossible for those who have once been enlightened, and have tasted the heavenly gift, and became partakers of the Holy Spirit, And have tasted the good word of God, and the powers of the world to come, And have then fallen away, to be brought back again to repentance**" (Hebrews 6:4-6). This passage was written as a warning to those from a Jewish background who were thinking about returning to Judaism, in order to escape persecution.

The third passage says, "**Christ is of no benefit to those of you who seek righteousness by the law; you are fallen from grace**" (Galatians 5:4). Those words are God's warning to anyone seeking to make himself righteous through obedience to the law.

The fourth passage says, "**I buffet my body, and bring it under my control: lest there be any way that I, after having preached to others, might be rejected**" (1Corinthians 9:27). Those words of Paul are God's warning to those who think that they can live in sin and still be saved.

And, the words, "**<u>The law is not meant for a righteous man, but for those who are lawless and rebellious</u>, for the ungodly and sinful, for the irreverent and profane, for those who strike or kill their fathers or mothers, for murders, For those who sin sexually, for sodomites, for kidnapers and slave traders, for liars and perjurers, and for any other thing that is contrary to sound teaching,**" tell us that those who sin willfully place themselves back under the condemnation of the Law (1Timothy 1:9-10).

Every one of the passages just quoted is the Word of God, and as such should be taken seriously. Far from letting us sin, the Bible tells us that "**The flesh lusts against the Spirit, and the Spirit against the flesh: and they are opposed to each other: so that you cannot do the things that you would," (Galatians 5:17). At the same time, none of those passages should ever be interpreted to contradict the fact that **we, "are kept by the power of God through faith unto salvation"** (1Peter 1:5). Or the words, **"Neither death, nor life, nor angels, nor principalities, nor powers, nor things present, nor things to come, nor height, nor depth, nor any other creature, shall be able to separate us from the love of God, which is in Christ Jesus our Lord"** (Romans 8:39-39). Because, **"The heart is deceitful above all things,"** God wants us to teach His Word faithfully instead of trying to make it agree with our ideas (Jeremiah 17:9). And, if some things seem contradictory to our puny finite minds, then we should admit our ignorance instead of trying to change what the Bible says.

How God Sustained Job

The book of Job tells us that God did not withdraw His blessing from Job because Job had sinned, but because Job was becoming self-righteous. And, everything that God allowed Job to suffer worked **"together for good,"** to keep Job from losing his salvation (Romans 8:28).

Because, **"No flesh will ever be declared righteous in God's sight by the deeds of the law,"** the words, **"There was a man in the land of Uz, whose name was Job; and that man was blameless and upright,"** are not telling us that Job was righteous because he kept the law, but because he trusted in Christ (Romans 3:20, Job 1:1). In fact, Job's own words, **"I know that my redeemer lives, and that He will stand at a future time upon the earth,"** tell us that he was trusting in Christ (Job 19:25). The words, **"So these three men stopped answering Job, because he was righteous in his own eyes... For Job has said, I am righteous: and God has treated me unjustly,"** then tell us that Job had become self-righteous, and, therefore, was in danger of losing his salvation (Job 32:1 and 34:5). And, the words, **"Then Job answered the LORD, and said... Who am I but one who obscures your purpose without understanding? I have spoken about things that I did not understand; things too wonderful for me... Therefore I am ashamed of myself, and repent in dust and ashes,"** tell us that what Job suffered led him to see his sin, humbled him, and kept him from losing his salvation (Job 42:1-6). As it is written, **"When we are judged, we are chastened by the Lord, so that we will not be condemned with the world"** (1Corinthians 11:32). [Note: The words, "After this Job lived for one hundred and forty years, and saw his sons, and his grandsons, even to the fourth generation," tell us that Job lived sometime after the flood, during the period when people lived far longer than they do now.]

12. Divine Monergism In Conversion

The words, "**No man can come to me, unless the Father who has sent me draws him,**" and "**No one can say that Jesus is the Lord, but by the Holy Ghost,**" tell us that we are brought to faith in Christ by the grace of God alone (John 6:44, 1Corinthians 12:3). And, the fact that our conversion and salvation is work of God alone (without any help on our part) is known in theology as divine monergism.

Some who oppose that doctrine do so because they assume that God would never command us to do something we are unable to do. However, that is a silly argument because the words, "**Keep my commandments, and live,**" command us to keep God's commandments, while the words, "**Whatever the law says, it says to those who are under the law: that every mouth may be stopped, and all the world may become guilty before God,**" tell us that no one can keep them (Proverbs 7:2, Romans 3:15). Is that unfair, as some contend? Absolutely not! The Bible plainly tells us that "**The law was our schoolmaster to bring us to Christ, that we might be declared righteous by faith**" (Galatians 3:24). And, how was the Law our schoolmaster? The words, "**The knowledge of sin comes by the law,**" tell us that God works through the Law to show us our sin, and, therefore, our need for the forgiveness that Christ won for us on the cross (Romans 3:20). For, "**Scripture has concluded all under sin, that the promise might be given to those who believe, through faith in Jesus Christ,**" (Galatians 3:22).

The words, "**The kingdom of God is at hand: repent, and believe the gospel,**" // "**Believe on the Lord Jesus Christ, and you will be saved**," command us to repent and believe (Mark 1:15, Acts 16:31). And, the words, "**Come to me, all you who labor and are carrying a heavy load, and I will give you rest,**" command us to come to Christ (Matthew 11:28). However, the words, "**No man can come to me, unless the Father who has sent me draws him,**" plainly tell us that coming to Christ is not something we are able to do (John 6:44).

The words, "**It is God who works in you both to will and to do His good pleasure,**" tell us that it is God who is at work in us bringing us to faith (Philippians 2:13). The words, "**Seeing that it has been granted to you that for the sake of Christ, you should not only believe in Him, but also suffer for His sake,**" tell us that our faith is a gift – something that has been granted to us (Philippians 1:29). And, the words, "**What is the exceeding greatness of His power toward us who believe, according to the working of His mighty power,**" tell us that it is the power of God that brings us to faith (Ephesians 1:19).

This brings us to the question: If we are brought to faith by the power of God, why doesn't He bring everyone to faith? And, the Biblical answer to that question is that in bringing us to faith He does not deal with us directly in a way that we cannot resist, but deals with us through His Word. The words, "**As I live, says the Lord GOD, I have no pleasure in the death of a wicked**," tell us that God does not want people to be lost (Ezekiel 33:11). At the same time, the words, "**O Jerusalem, Jerusalem, you who kill the prophets, and stone those who are sent to you, how often I longed to gather your children together, as a hen gathers her chicks under her wings, and you would not**," tell us that He does not try to bring them to faith by force but deals with them through His Word (Matthew 23:37)

The words, "**So will the word that goes out of my mouth be: it will not return to me empty, but it will accomplish what I want, and it will achieve what I sent it to do**," tell us that the Word of God has power (Isaiah 55:11). The words, "**You stiff necked and uncircumcised in heart and ears, you always resist the Holy Ghost: as your fathers did, so do you**," tell us that men resist that power (Acts 7:15). The words, "**The natural man does not accept the things of the Spirit of God: for they are foolishness to him: and he cannot understand them, because they are spiritually discerned**," tell us that resistance to the truth of God is rooted in our sinful nature (1Corinthians 2:14). And, the words, "**The fleshly mind is hostile to God: for it is not subject to the law of God, nor indeed can be**," tell us that our sinful nature is actively hostile to the truth (Romans 8:7).

The words, "**It pleased God to save those who believe through the foolishness of preaching**." // "**For the preaching of the cross is foolishness to those who perish; but it is the power of God to us who are saved**," tell us that God works through preaching to save the lost (1Corinthians 1:21, 18). The words, "**Faith comes by hearing, and hearing by the word of God**," tell us that God works through His Word to bring us to faith (Romans 10:17). And, the words, "**I have planted, Apollos watered; but God gave the increase**," tell us that God not only brings us to faith by His Word, but also nurtures [waters] our faith through the regular preaching of His Word (1Corinthians 3:6). At the same time, the words, "**Let the little children come to me, and do not hinder them: for of such is the kingdom of God**," tell us that God works through parents and families to overcome sinful resistance to the gospel (Luke 18:16).

The words, "**Whoever commits sin is the servant of sin**," and "**When you yield yourselves to someone to obey him as servants, you are the servants of the one you obey; whether of sin to death, or of obedience to righteousness?**" suggest that sin increases our natural resistance to spiritual truth (John 8:34 and Romans 6:16). At the same time, the words, "**I tell you truly, That the**

publicans and harlots will enter the kingdom of God before you," suggest that social condemnation that agrees with the Word of God, can reinforce the Word of God in bringing people to repentance (Matthew 21:31). However, even though there are many things in our lives that can increase or decrease our resistance to the Word of God, the words, "**But God, who is rich in mercy, because of His great love for us, Even when we were dead in sins, has made us alive together with Christ, (you are saved by grace,)**" and the words, "**To as many as received Him, He gave power to become the sons of God, even to those who believe in His name: Who are not born of blood, or of the will of the flesh, or of the will of man, but of God.**" Make it clear that our conversion is the work of God alone (Ephesians 2:4-5, John 1:12-13).

The Pernicious Character of Synergism

Even though the Bible plainly tells us that we are, "**Not born of blood, or of the will of the flesh, or of the will of man, but of God,**" there are some who seem driven to teach that man has some part in his salvation (John 1:13). In theology that error is known as synergism.

Some who hold that error would make works play a role, others would reduce man's part to "making a decision for Christ," "asking Jesus into their heart," "praying for God to tell them that they are saved," or "ceasing to resist". Now, some who seek God in this way do wind up coming to faith in Christ, and they are often the most passionate defenders of synergism. Having come to faith in Christ, they do not see what the problem is. So let me explain it.

Having come to faith in Christ, they are blind to the fact that many who "make a decision for Christ," or "ask Jesus into their heart," etc. fail to actually place their faith in Christ. Many ask Jesus into their heart expecting Him to help them live a more righteous life – thus earning God's favor by works. Young people who are told to ask Jesus into their heart, often do so without understanding what faith is. And when those same unsaved young people are told that they cannot lose salvation no matter what they do, that can become a way of rationalizing immorality.

A man once told me that after praying and praying for God to tell him that he was saved he saw sunlight making a circle on the floor and when he moved into that circle and began to pray he just knew that he was saved. He said nothing about Christ dying for his sins, forgiveness, or faith. His entire assurance of salvation rested on that experience. And that is the heart of the problem! Whenever synergists teach that man has some role in his own salvation, there will always be some whose faith will be in what they did, rather that in what Christ did on the cross.

What you are counting on to get you into heaven is what you are placing your faith in. If you believe that God will let you into heaven because; on a certain date you "gave your life to Christ," "asked Him to come into your heart," or "prayed to receive Him" then you are placing your faith in what you did, rather than what Christ did for you. Faith in Christ consists in believing that God will let you into heaven because Christ took our sins upon Himself and suffered in our stead, **"The just for the unjust, that He might bring us to God"** (1Peter 3:18).

13. Synonyms Of Conversion

Our conversion involves far more than just a change of opinion. It is a transformation that changes our standing with God, our spiritual nature, and the place where we will spend eternity. For that reason, in order to fully appreciate conversion we need to understand the synonyms of conversion used in Scripture.

While the Bible sometimes speaks of repentance as nothing more than sorrow for sins, one example being when it tells us that Judas "**repented**," at other times it uses repentance as a synonym for conversion, such as when it tells us that, "**There will be more joy in heaven over one sinner who repents, than over ninety and nine just persons, who do not need to repent**" (Matthew 27:3, Luke 15:7). [See Mark 14:21.]

Whenever the Bible speaks of repentance bringing salvation, such as when it says, "**Unless you repent, you will all perish**," repentance is being used as a synonym for conversion (Luke 13:5). However, whenever it separates repentance from faith or forgiveness, it is speaking only of sorrow for sins. For example: The words, "**The kingdom of God is at hand: repent, and believe the gospel**," separate repentance from faith (Mark 1:15). The words, "**Testifying... of repentance toward God, and faith in our Lord Jesus Christ**," separate repentance from faith (Acts 20:21). And, the words, "**That repentance and remission of sins should be preached in His name among all nations, starting at Jerusalem**," separate repentance form forgiveness (Luke 24:47).

The words, "**Unless a man is born of water and of the Spirit, he cannot enter the kingdom of God**," use the phrase "born of water and of the Spirit" as a synonym for conversion (John 3:5,6). The words, "**Whoever believes that Jesus is the promised Savior is born of God**," use the phrase "born of God" as a synonym for conversion (1John 5:1). And, the words, "**To as many as received Him, He gave power to become the sons of God, even to those who believe in His name: Who are not born of blood, or of the will of the flesh, or of the will of man, but of God**," use the phrases "become the sons of God" and "born... of God," as synonyms of conversion (John 1:12,13).

The words, "**You formerly... were by nature the children of wrath, even as others. But God, who is rich in mercy, because of His great love for us, Even when we were dead in sins, has made us alive together with Christ,**" speak of conversion as a transformation from being "**dead in sins**" to being "**alive together with Christ**" (Ephesians 2:2-5). The words, "**He has made you, who were dead in your sins and the uncircumcision of your flesh, alive together with Him, having <u>forgiven</u> all of your sins,**" again speak of conversion as a transformation from being ""dead in your sins" to being "alive together with" Christ (Colossians 2:13). Telling us also, that the transformation is the result of forgiveness.

The words, "**To open their eyes, and to turn them from darkness to light, and from the power of Satan to God, that they may receive forgiveness of sins, and inheritance among those who are sanctified through faith in me [Christ],**" speak of conversion as being brought "from darkness to light" and "from the power of Satan to God" (Acts 26:18). The words, "**I [Jesus] have come into the world as a light, so that no one who believes in me will remain in darkness,**" speak of conversion [i.e. believing in Christ] as a change from darkness to light (John 12:46). And, the words, "**You were once darkness, but now are light in the Lord: walk as children of light,**" again speak of conversion as a change from darkness to light (Ephesians 5:8).

The words, "**Many are called, but few are chosen,**" separate being "called" from actual conversion (Matthew 22:14). In that context, to be called is to hear the gospel. In contrast, the words, "**Who has saved us, and called us to a holy calling, not because of anything we have done, but according to His own purpose and grace, which was given to us in Christ Jesus before the world began,**" equate being called with being converted (2Timothy 1:9). The words, "**You are also the called of Jesus Christ,**" also equate being called with being converted (Romans 1:6). As do the words, "**Those He predestinated, He also called: and those He called, He also justified: and those He justified, He also glorified**" (Romans 8:30).

Justification By Faith

1. Justification According To Scripture

To be justified in the sight of God is to be absolved of all guilt, vindicated of any wrongdoing, and declared innocent and blameless before the court of divine justice. Now, in regard to justification, the Bible plainly tells us that even though we all deserve God's condemnation and wrath, "**The blood of Jesus Christ His Son cleanses us of all sin**" (1John 1:7). And, the phrase "Justification by Faith" points to the fact that we receive that cleansing through faith in Christ. Therefore, to be justified by faith is to be justified by what Christ did [His shed blood], rather than by what we do.

The Doctrine of Universal Condemnation
Romans 3:9-20 "**All men, both Jews and Gentiles, are all under sin; As it is written: There is none righteous, no, not one; There is none who understands; there is none who seeks after God. They have all gone out of the way; they are together become unprofitable; there is none who does good, no, not one. Their throat** *is* **an open sepulcher; with their tongues they have used deceit. The poison of serpents** *is* **under their lips, whose mouth** *is* **full of cursing and bitterness. Their feet** *are* **swift to shed blood; Destruction and misery** *are* **in their ways, and the way of peace have they not known. There is no fear of God before their eyes. Now we know that whatever the law says, it says to those who are under the law, that every mouth may be stopped, and <u>all the world may become guilty before God</u>. Therefore by the deeds of the law no flesh shall be justified in His sight, for the knowledge of sin comes by the law,**" and "<u>**All of our righteousnesses are like filthy rags**</u>" (Isaiah 64:6).

The Doctrine of Justification by Faith
Romans 3:21-28 "**But now <u>the righteousness of God without the law</u> is revealed, being witnessed by the law and the prophets, Even the righteousness of God,** *that is* **by faith in Jesus Christ, unto all and upon all those who believe. For there is no difference, For all have sinned, and come short of the glory of God, Being justified freely by His grace through the redemption that is in Christ Jesus. Whom God has set forth** *to be* **a propitiation <u>through faith in His blood</u>, to declare His righteousness for the remission of sins that are past, through the forbearance of God;**

To declare, *I say*, at this time His righteousness: that He might be just, and the justifier of him who believes in Jesus. Where *is* boasting then? It is excluded. By what law? of works? No: but by the law of faith. Therefore we conclude that a man is <u>justified by faith without the deeds of the law</u>." [Note: faith without "the deeds of the law" is **faith alone**.]

In understanding what the Bible is saying about our justification it is important to understand that **we are justified by the forgiveness Christ secured for us by His death on the cross, not our faith**. There is no particular virtue in faith. Our faith can be described as a hand that passively accepts God's free gift of forgiveness. Or as Christ Himself put it, **"This is my blood... which is shed for many for the forgiveness of sins"** (Matthew 26:28). **"For Christ also suffered once for sins, the righteous for the unrighteous, that He might bring us to God,"** (1Peter 3:18). And, **"God was in Christ, reconciling the world to Himself"** (2Corinthians 5:19).

That being understood, the Bible describes our justification both in terms of the sin and condemnation that is removed when we come to faith in Christ, and the righteousness that is imputed to us as a result of our sin being removed.

The words, **"The blood of Jesus Christ His Son cleanses us of all sin,"** testify to the forgiveness that Christ won for us through His death on the cross (1John 1:7). The words, **"All the prophets testify of Him, that through His name whoever believes in Him will receive forgiveness of sins,"** again testify to that forgiveness (Acts 10:43). While the words, **"David also describes the blessedness of the man, to whom God imputes righteousness without works, Saying, Blessed are they whose iniquities are forgiven, and whose sins are covered. Blessed is the man to whom the Lord will not impute sin,"** speak of our justification both in terms of forgiveness, and the righteousness that is imputed to us because our sins are forgiven (Romans 4:6-8).

The following passages all testify to the fact that, we are absolved of all guilt, and declared righteous before the court of divine justice because of the forgiveness that is ours in Christ – forgiveness that we receive through faith in His blood (Romans 5:2).

"For I am not ashamed of the gospel of Christ... For in it the righteousness of God is revealed from faith to faith: as it is written, The just will live by faith" (Romans 1:16-17).

"But now the righteousness of God apart from the law is revealed, being witnessed by the law and the prophets; Even the righteousness of God which comes through faith in Jesus Christ to all and upon all who believe" (Romans 3:21-22).

**"What does the scripture say? Abraham believed God, and it was counted to him for righteousness" (Romans 4:3).

"These are those who... have washed their robes, and made them white in the blood of the Lamb" (Revelation 7:14).

"When a man does not work, but trusts in Him who justifies the ungodly, his faith is counted for righteousness" (Romans 4:5).

2. Justification By Faith Alone

In the third chapter of his Epistle to the Romans, the Apostle Paul describes Justification by Faith, as, **"The righteousness of God which comes through faith in Jesus Christ"** (Romans 3:22). And, to prevent all misunderstanding, he goes on in the next chapter to describe it as **imputed righteousness**. A righteousness that is ours, not because of anything we have done, but because when we trust in Christ, no sin is imputed to us. In that chapter he tells us that:

Righteousness Was imputed to Abraham

Romans 4:3-5 "For what does Scripture say? Abraham believed God, and it was counted (imputed) to him for righteousness. Now to him who works is the reward not reckoned of grace, but of debt. But to him who does not work, but believes on Him who justifies the ungodly, his faith is counted for righteousness."

Righteousness Was Imputed To David

Romans 4:6-8 "Even as David also describes the blessedness of the man, to whom God imputes righteousness without works, *Saying*, Blessed *are* those whose iniquities are forgiven, and whose sins are covered. Blessed *is* the man to whom the Lord will not impute sin."

Righteousness is Imputed Apart From The Law

Romans 4:9-12 "Does this blessedness *only come* upon the circumcised, or also upon the uncircumcised? for we say that faith was reckoned to Abraham for righteousness. How was it reckoned? when he was circumcised, or uncircumcised? Not circumcised, but uncircumcised. And he received the sign of circumcision, a seal of the righteousness of the faith that *he had* while *still* uncircumcised: that he might be the father of all those who believe, though they are not circumcised; that righteousness might be imputed to them also: And the father of circumcision to those who are not of the circumcision only, but who also walk in the steps of that faith of our father Abraham, that *he had* while *still* uncircumcised."

Righteousness is Imputed by Faith

Romans 4:13-16 "The promise, that he should be the heir of the world, *was* not to Abraham, or to his seed, through the law, but through the righteousness of faith. For if those who are of the law *are* heirs, faith is made void, and the promise made of no effect: Because the law works wrath: for where no law is, *there is* no transgression. Therefore *it is* by faith, that *it might be* by grace; that the promise might be sure to all the seed; not only to those who are of the law, but also to those who are of the faith of Abraham; who is the father of us all,"

Righteousness is Imputed To All Who Trust In Christ

Romans 4:23-25 "Now it was not written for his sake alone, that it was imputed to him; But for us also, to whom it will be imputed, if we believe on Him who raised up Jesus our Lord from the dead; Who was delivered for our offences, and was raised again for our justification."

Righteousness is Imputed Without Works

The words, "God... did not save us by works of righteousness which we have done, but according to His mercy... Which He shed on us abundantly through Jesus Christ our Savior," specifically say that we are saved by mercy, not works (Titus 3:4-6). The words, "I [Paul] have suffered the loss of all these things, and regard them as dung, that I may win Christ, And be found in Him, not having any righteousness of my own, which is of the law, but that which is through faith in Christ, the righteousness that comes from God by faith," tell us that righteousness comes from God by faith, not by "the law" (Philippians 3:8-9). The words, "The Gentiles, who did not pursue righteousness, attained to righteousness, even the righteousness that is by faith. But Israel, which followed after the law of righteousness, has not attained to the law of righteousness. Why? Because they did not seek it through faith, but through the works of the law. For they stumbled at that stumbling-stone... For I bear witness that they have a zeal for God, but not according to knowledge. For being ignorant of God's righteousness, and seeking to establish their own righteousness, they have not submitted to the righteousness of God. For Christ is the end of the law for righteousness to every one who believes," tell us that the Gentiles who looked to God for mercy had their sins forgiven, while the Jews who sought to make themselves righteous were condemned (Romans 9:30 – 10:4). And, the words, "**We have redemption through His blood, the forgiveness of sins, according to the riches of His grace,**" tell us that we have forgiveness through the blood of Christ, the same blood that "**cleanses us of all sin**"

(Ephesians 1:7, 1John 1:7).

Although the Bible plainly tells us that works do not make us righteous, and play no part in our salvation, **Satan attacks that doctrine on two fronts**. On one hand he attacks it through those who say, **"Let us do evil that good may come. Whose damnation is just"** (Romans 3:8). On the other hand he attacks it through those who, seek **"to establish their own righteousness"** (Romans 10:3). Furthermore, because Satan blinds whomever he can to **"The light of the glorious gospel,"** those who believe that the law makes them righteous cannot understand how we can be righteous apart from the law (2Corinthians 4:4). And, they will not be able to understand it until they can say with Paul, **"I know that nothing good dwells in me (that is, in my flesh,)"** and truly see that all of their own **"righteousnesses are like filthy rags"** in the sight of God (Romans 7:18, Isaiah 64:6). For it is only as we see that the law condemns everything we do to make ourselves righteous, that we can understand that **freedom from the law is not freedom to sin, but freedom to be righteous**. It is freedom to walk in a clean conscience without constantly being condemned. It is the freedom to **"lead a quiet and peaceable life in all godliness and honesty"** (1Timothy 2:2). And, **"The goal of our instruction is love flowing from a pure heart, a good conscience, and a sincere faith"** (1Timothy 1:5).

3. Why Justification By Faith Is Central

The doctrine of justification by faith is central to everything that the Bible says, because it is central to the work of Christ, and everything that the Bible says was written to testify of Christ. As it is written, **"All the prophets testify of Him, that through His name whoever believes in Him will receive forgiveness of sins,"** (Acts 10:43).

The Bible Was Written to Testify of Christ

The words, **"I have written these things to you who believe in the name of the Son of God; that you may know that you have eternal life, and that you may believe in the name of the Son of God,"** tell us that Scripture was given so that we might know about Christ and believe in Him (1John 5:13). The words, **"For whatever things were written in the past were written for our learning, that we through patience and comfort of the scriptures might have hope,"** say the same thing (Romans 15:4). The words, **"These are written, that you might believe that Jesus is the Messiah, the Son of God; and that believing you might have life through His name,"** tell us that Scripture was written so that we might believe, and through faith receive eternal life (John 20:31). The words,

"He [John] who saw it [Christ's death] bears witness to it, and his witness is true: and he knows that what he says is true, so that you might believe," again tell us that Scripture was written so that we might know and believe (John 19:35). And, Christ Himself said of Scripture, "They are they that testify of me," // "When I was still with you I said, that everything must be fulfilled, that was written in the law of Moses, in the prophets, and in the psalms, concerning me" (John 5:39, Luke 24:44).

Christ Came Into the World to Save Sinners

The words, "This is a trustworthy statement, worthy of complete acceptance, that Christ Jesus came into the world to save sinners," tell us that Christ came into the world to save sinners (Titus 1:15). "For God so loved the world, that He gave His only begotten Son, that whosoever believes on Him should not perish, but have everlasting life. For God did not send His Son into the world to condemn the world; but that the world through Him might be saved" (John 3:16-17). In short, "God has shown His love for us, by sending His only-begotten Son into the world, that we might live through Him" (1John 4:9).

The words, "Just as sin entered the world by one man [Adam], and death by sin; so death passed upon all men, because all have sinned," tell us that sin entered the world through Adam (Romans 5:12). And, because of Adam's sin "judgment came upon all men to condemnation" (Romans 5:18). Therefore, according to God's plan, just as "many were made sinners by one man's disobedience, so by the obedience of one [Christ] many will be made righteous" (Romans 5:19).

Christ Died in Our Place to Secure Forgiveness for Us

In order to save us, Christ "Suffered once for sins, the righteous for the unrighteous, that He might bring us to God, being put to death in the flesh, but made alive in the Spirit" and "by *that* one offering He has perfected forever those who are sanctified" (1Peter 3:18, Hebrews 10:14).

Rom 5: 6-11 "For when we were yet without strength, in due time Christ died for the ungodly. For one will hardly die for a righteous man: although it is possible that some would even dare to die for a good man. But God commends His love toward us, in that, while we were yet sinners, Christ died for us. Much more then, being now justified by His blood, we shall be saved from wrath through Him. For if, we were reconciled to God by the death of His Son, when we were enemies, much more, having been reconciled, we will be saved by His life. And not only that, but we also rejoice in God through our Lord Jesus Christ, by whom we have now received the atonement." Or as Isaiah put it.

Isaiah 53:4-11 "Surely <u>He has taken on Himself our pains</u>, and carried our sorrows: yet we regarded Him as condemned, struck down by God, and afflicted. But He was wounded for our transgressions, He was bruised for our iniquities: the punishment that brought us peace was upon Him; and by His stripes we are healed. Like sheep we have all have gone astray; each of us has turned to his own way; and the LORD has laid on Him the iniquity of us all. He was oppressed, and He was mistreated, yet He did not open His mouth: He was led like a lamb to the slaughter, and as a sheep before her shearers is silent, so He did not open His mouth. He was taken from prison and from judgment: and who at that time understood? for He was cut off from the land of the living: and struck down for His people's sins. And He made His grave with the wicked, and with the rich in His death; because He had not committed any crime, nor was any deceit in His mouth. Yet it was the will of the LORD to bruise Him; He has caused Him to suffer: and <u>when you make Him an offering for sin</u>, He will see His seed, He will prolong His days, and the will of the LORD will succeed by His hand. He will see it out of His anguish, and will be satisfied: by His knowledge my righteous servant will justify many; for <u>He will bear their iniquities</u>."

Forgiveness is What Justifies Us

The words, "**Justified freely by His grace through the redemption that is in Christ Jesus,**" tell us that we are "justified" [i.e. absolved of guilt and declared righteous] by God's "grace" [God's mercy] (Romans 3:24). While the words, "**We have redemption through His blood, the forgiveness of sins, according to the riches of His grace,**" tell us that the "grace" by which we are justified consists of "the forgiveness of sins" (Ephesians 1:7). In short, **we are not justified by works, but by forgiveness; the same forgiveness that Christ won for us on the cross**. Moreover, because Christ came into the world so that we could be forgiven [i.e. justified], **and**, because we are "justified by faith," **the doctrine of "justification by faith" is central to everything the Bible says** (Romans 3:28).

Interpreting Scripture in the Light of Justification

Furthermore, because we should never interpret any passage of Scripture to contradict what the Bible plainly says, we should never interpret any passage to contradict the doctrine of justification by faith. For example: A comparison of the words, "**He who has my commandments, and keeps them, loves me**," with the words "**No flesh will ever be justified in God's sight by the deeds of the law**," tells us that those who truly keep God's commandments are not those who seek righteousness through the law, but those who have their sins washed away by the blood of Christ (John 14:21, Romans 3:20). That being the case, while we should never sin willfully, and should try to do what is right, we need to realize that **it is not our works, but the forgiveness that Christ won for us, that cleanses us of all sin and makes us righteous and obedient in the sight of God**. [Compare Isaiah 64:6, Romans 16:26, 1John 1:7-9, Hebrews 10:14, Romans 9:30 – 10:4.]

4. Terminology That Guards Against Error

Even though the Bible plainly tells us that, "**All of our righteousnesses are like filthy rags**," that **no one, "Will ever be justified in God's sight by the deeds of the law**," and that we are, "**Justified by faith without the deeds of the law**," Satan continually works to blind people to that glorious good news, and get them to trust in themselves, and what they do, rather than in Christ (Isaiah 64:6, Romans 3:20 and 28). For that reason, **we need to hold fast to sound words, and sound terminology, when telling others of** "**the faith and love that are in Christ Jesus**" (2Timothy 1:13). Those who have been blinded to the truth continually try to twist the gospel message in a vain attempt to make salvation depend in part on what they do.

Satan often uses a person's own sinful desires to blind them to the gospel. He can do this by leading young people who want to be righteous, and are struggling against sin, to seek motivation in the lie that resisting sexual temptation makes them righteous. They can be argumentative, disrespectful to parents, and nasty yet still think that they are righteous because they resist sexual temptation. These are the kind of people who desperately want salvation to depend on works, and pervert the gospel in their own minds in order to convince themselves that God is pleased with them because of their works. What they fail to see is that if they were truly righteous they would not have any sinful desires to begin with.

It is right and good for believers to resist sexual temptation. "**For this is the will of God, even your sanctification, that you abstain from sexual immorality**," (1Thessalonians 4:3). The Apostle Paul said, "**I buffet my body, and bring it under my control: lest there be any way that I, after having preached to others, might be rejected**" (1Corinthians 9:27). At the same time, those who think that resisting sexual desire is what makes them righteous in the sight of God are under a delusion. And, as long as they think that works make them righteous they will not be able to see justification by faith as anything other than an excuse to sin, when nothing could be further from the truth. That is one way that Satan blinds people to the gospel (2Corinthians 4:4).

Because of this constant assault on the gospel: in teaching the gospel we need to make it clear; **1)** that God's grace is His mercy and forgiveness, not some ability to resist temptation, **2)** that we are saved by the blood of Christ and faith in what He did, not what we do, and **3)** that salvation is a "**gift of God, Not of works**" (Ephesians 2:8-9).

The words, "**If by grace, then is it no longer by works: if it were grace would no longer be grace. For if it is by works, then it is no longer by grace: otherwise work is no longer work,**" place grace in opposition to works (Romans 11:6). That means that when the Bible says, "**You are saved by grace through faith; and that not of yourselves,**" it is stressing the fact that we are not saved by works (Ephesians 2:8-9). And, when the Bible says, "**He did not save us by works of righteousness that we have done, but because of His mercy,**" it not only stresses the fact that we are not saved by works, but defines grace as mercy (Titus 3:5). At the same time, the words, "**In whom we have redemption through His blood, the forgiveness of sins, according to the riches of His grace,**" tell us that we are saved by the blood of Jesus Christ, and that His grace consists of forgiveness, not works (Ephesians 1:7).

The words, "**Being now justified by His blood, we shall be saved from wrath through Him,**" tell us that we are "justified" [i.e. absolved of guilt and pronounced innocent] by the blood of Jesus Christ, not by what we do (Romans 5:9). "**The blood of Jesus Christ His Son cleanses us of all sin,**" (1John 1:7). However, "**Christ is of no benefit to those... who seek righteousness by the law**" (Galatians 5:4).

The words, "**Being justified freely by His grace through the redemption that is in Christ Jesus**" // "**So that being justified by His grace, we became heirs having the hope of eternal life,**" tell us that we are justified freely by God's grace, and being justified by that grace, have the assurance of eternal life (Romans 3:24, Titus 3:7).

The words, "**Having come to know that a man is not justified by the works of the law, but through faith in Jesus Christ, we have also come to believe in Jesus Christ, that we might be justified by faith in Christ, and not by the works of the law: for the works of the law will not make anyone righteous,**" tell us that we are not justified by works, but through faith in Christ (Galatians 2:16). And, the words, "**Being justified by faith, we have peace with God through our Lord Jesus Christ: By whom we also <u>have access by faith</u> into this grace in which we stand,**" tell us that faith receives the forgiveness that is already there for us (Romans 5:1-2). In response to that cult which pronounces a curse on those who believe that we are saved through out trust (faith) in God's mercy (grace), David said, **"I have trusted in your mercy; my heart will rejoice in your salvation"** (Psalm 13:5).

That being said, I want to make it clear that those who are saved will experience an Improvement in their behavior. It will not come all at once, and it will never be complete in this life. However, **it cannot even begin until we are saved**, for the Holy Spirit does not come into our hearts until we have been justified by faith. As it is written, **"Did you receive the Holy Spirit by the works of the law, or by the hearing of faith?... Did God give you His Spirit, and work miracles among you, because you observed the law, or because you heard and believed the gospel?"** You were **"Sealed with the Holy Spirit of promise, after you believed"** (Galatians 3:2,5, Ephesians 1:13).

After you have received the Spirit, **"Walk in the Spirit, and you will not fulfill the lust of the flesh. For the flesh lusts against the Spirit, and the Spirit against the flesh: and they are opposed to each other: so that you cannot do the things that you would. But if you are led by the Spirit, you are not under the law"** (Galatians 5:16-18). **"Understanding this, that the law is not meant for a righteous man, but for those who are lawless and rebellious"** (1Timothy 1:9).

5. Justification And Works

The words, **"Whoever keeps the whole law, yet fails in one point, is guilty of all,"** tell us that in the eyes of God there are no shades of gray (James 2:10). A person is **either totally condemned, or totally innocent**, there is no middle ground. Therefore, if a person has not been justified by faith [forgiven] God sees no good in him. Even his **"righteousnesses are like filthy rags;"** (Isaiah 64:6). In contrast, once a person has been justified by faith [forgiven] God sees no fault in him. His **"iniquities are forgiven,"** his **"sins are covered,"** and **"the Lord will not impute sin"** to him (Romans 4:7-8).

That means that there are **two ways of looking at those who trust in Christ**. In the light of God's law, we are all sinners. **Judged by the law, none of us "will ever be declared righteous in God's sight... because the knowledge of sin comes by the law"** (Romans 4:20). We stress that fact because we are saved by "the forgiveness of sins," and Satan does all he can to keep people from seeking forgiveness (Ephesians 1:7).

At the same time, **because no sin is imputed to those who trust in Christ**, apart from willful sin **God sees all who are justified by** faith as righteous. That is why we read that, "**David did what was right in the eyes of the LORD, and did not turn aside from any thing that He commanded him all the days of his life, except only in the matter of Uriah the Hittite**" (1Kings 15:5). And, that is why John said, "**Whoever is born of God does not sin; but he who is born of God keeps himself, and the wicked one does not touch him**" (1John 5:18).

That being understood, the words, "**Joseph her husband, being a just man,**" are telling us that Joseph was **justified by faith** [in the promised Messiah] (Matthew 1:19). We know that because the Bible plainly tells us that **no one will ever, "be justified in God's sight by the deeds of the law"** (Romans 3:20). And, the same holds true for all of the passages in which someone is said to be just. [See Proverbs 9:9, 13:22, 24:16 and 29:27.] At the same time, **when judged by the law, "There is not a just man on earth, who does good, without sinning"** (Ecclesiastes 7:20).

Since the only way to be righteous in the sight of God is to be justified by faith, the words, "**Don't you know that the unrighteous will not inherit the kingdom of God?**" are telling us that those who are not justified by faith "will not inherit the kingdom of God" (1Corinthians 6:9). Likewise, the words, "**They were both righteous before God, walking in all the commandments and ordinances of the Lord blameless,**" tell us that Zacharias and Elisabeth were justified by faith (Luke 1:5-6).

The same holds true in every place where the Bible speaks of a particular work bringing God's favor. Without forgiveness that work would be "**like filthy rags**" in the sight of God (Isaiah 64:6). For example: When God said to Abraham, "**In your seed shall all the nations of the earth be blessed; because you have obeyed my voice,**" we know that without forgiveness Abraham's "obedience" would have been "**like filthy rags**" in the sight of God. Likewise, when the Bible says, "**If you forgive men their trespasses, your heavenly Father will also forgive you,**" we know that without faith any forgiveness would be "**like filthy rags**" in the sight of God (Matthew 6:14). The words, "**Without faith it is impossible to please God,**" tell us that **no work will ever be acceptable** to God unless it is done in faith, that is, by one who trusts in Christ.

At the same time, those who truly have "**a heart that is humbled and sorry for sin,**" will not sin willfully, and if they did they would be grieved over it as David was (Psalm 51:17). For that reason, those who are truly justified by faith (and not double-minded) conduct themselves in a way that reflects the righteousness that they already have through faith in Christ.

6. The Effects Of Justification

To be justified by faith is to be **cleansed "of all sin,"** by the blood of Jesus Christ (1John 1:7). However, Christians all too often fail to realize the full significance of that cleansing. Therefore, **I would like you to try to visualize your sins being washed away by the blood of Christ. Close your eyes if necessary and picture all of your sins being washed away.** Picture a cleansing flood coming in, swirling all around you and washing away every filthy stain. Picture that flood flowing right through you, **washing away every foul thought and every evil desire so that you begin to shine with a righteous glow. Picture yourself standing before God radiant with holiness.** Radiant not because of your works, but because every sin has been washed away. **That is true holiness!** That is how God sees us when we trust in Christ! That is the perfect righteousness of Christ Himself (Romans 10:4). And, nothing that we do, **no set of rules that we keep, could ever improve one bit on that perfection.** Therefore, when we stand before God it is as if Christ Himself were standing there in our place, for **His righteousness has become our righteousness** (Galatians 3:6). He took our sin upon Himself and has given us His righteousness in exchange for it. As it is written, **"By one offering He has perfected for ever those who are sanctified"** (Hebrews 10:14).

Because all of our sins have been washed away, **"All things work together for" our "good"** (Romans 8:28). And, everything God has promised in His Word is ours. Or as Paul put it, **"All the promises of God in Him are yea, and in Him Amen,"** (2Corinthians 1:20). For that reason, we do not need a different faith for each prayer or each promise of God, they are all ours through faith in Christ.

The Bible tells us that without justification we **"were dead in trespasses and sins,"** and **"walked according to the way of this world, according to the prince of the power of the air, the spirit that now works in the children of disobedience. Among whom we all likewise formerly lived in the lusts of our flesh, fulfilling the desires of the flesh and of the mind; and were by nature the children of wrath,"** (Ephesians 2:1-3). However, because forgiveness removes God's condemnation, when we are justified we rise from being spiritually **"dead in trespasses and sins,"** to new life in Christ (Ephesians 2:1,6). That new life is, in effect, a new birth, for through it **we are born, "Not of blood, nor of the will of the flesh, nor of the will of man, but of God"** (John 1:13). And, being born of God we are **"the children of God," "and if children, then heirs; heirs of God, and joint-heirs with Christ"** (Romans 8:16-17). [See Gal. 3:26.]

"Being justified by faith, we have peace with God through our Lord Jesus Christ" (Romans 5:1). **"Who has blessed us with**

all spiritual blessings in heavenly places" (Ephesians 1:3). And, one of those blessings is the Spirit of God. The words, "**Did you receive the Holy Spirit by the works of the law, or by the hearing of faith?**" tell us that when we come to faith in Christ the Holy Spirit comes into our heart (Galatians 3:2). However, the words, "**God has sent the Spirit of His Son into your hearts, crying, Abba, Father,**" tell us that Christ Himself dwells in our heart (Galatians 4:6). And, the words, "**If a man loves me, he will keep my words: and my Father will love him, and we will come to him, and make our home with him,**" tell us that when we trust in Christ both the Father and the Son reside in us (John 14:23).

Furthermore, the words, "**He who is joined to the Lord is one spirit with Him,**" tell us that having received God's Spirit we are joined to God (1Corinthians 6:17). The words, "**We are members of His body, of His flesh, and of His bones,**" tell us that being joined to Christ we are His offspring, His flesh and bone (Ephesians 5:30). And, the words, "**Don't you know that you are the temple of God, and that the Spirit of God dwells in you?**" tell us that our bodies are God's temple (1Corinthians 3:16).

The words, "**The Spirit Himself bears witness with our spirit, that we are the children of God,**" tell us that the Spirit of God strengthens our faith (Romans 8:16). And, part of that faith is the assurance that Christ is "**The resurrection, and the life**" (John 11:25). And, that "**Neither death, nor life, nor angels, nor principalities, nor powers, nor things present, nor things to come, Nor height, nor depth, nor any other creature, shall be able to separate us from the love of God, which is in Christ Jesus our Lord**" (Romans 8:38-39).

The words, "**We have been released from the law, having died to that which once bound us; that we should serve in newness of spirit, and not in the oldness of the letter,**" tell us that having been justified by faith, cleansed of all sin by the blood of Jesus Christ, the law no longer condemns us. (Romans 7:6). On the contrary, we are free from the law, not so that we can sin, but so that we can serve God in love rather than fear. **For faith "Produces works through love."** (Galatians 5:6). And, because, "**The Spirit of life in Christ Jesus has set**" us "**free from the law of sin and death**" (Romans 8:2). We "**have been called to liberty; but do not use your freedom as an excuse to serve the flesh, instead serve one another in love**" (Galatians 5:13). [See Eph. 2:10]

The words, "**If we walk in the light, as He is in the light, we have fellowship with one another,**" tell us that we are not only united with God through our faith in Christ, we are united with all true believers (1John 1:7). For God has not called us to live in seclusion, but we are "**called to be saints, together with all those everywhere who call upon the name of our Lord Jesus Christ**"

(1Corinthians 1:2) And, "**We, being many, are one body in Christ, and every one members one of another**" (Romans 12:5).

The words, "**Do not call anyone on earth father: for you have one Father, who is in heaven**" (Matthew 23:9). And, **do not seek** "**to be called Master: for one is your Master, even Christ; and you are all brethren**" (Matthew 23:8). Tell us that all who trust in Christ, all who are justified by faith, are brethren. And there is no clergy class that is over everyone else.

The words, "**He [Christ] breathed on them, and said to them, Receive the Holy Ghost. If you forgive the sins of anyone, they are forgiven; and if you retain the sins of anyone, they are retained**," apply to all who have received the Holy Spirit (John 20:22-23). And, the words, "**He [Jesus] said to him, Friend, your sins are forgiven. And the scribes and the Pharisees began to think, Who is this man who speaks blasphemies? Who can forgive sins, but God alone?**" tell us that we are to forgive sins by assuring those who repent that they have forgiveness in Christ (Luke 5:20-21).

"**Eye has not seen, nor ear heard, nor has it entered into the heart of man, the things that God has prepared for those who love Him**" (1Corinthians 2:9).

SCRIPTURE ALONE
GRACE ALONE
FAITH ALONE

THE DOCTRINE OF SANCTIFICATION AND GOOD WORKS
(De Sanctificatione et Bonis Operibus.)

1. The Nature Of Sanctification

Sanctification has to do with what sets believers apart from the world as holy; both in the eyes of God and from man's perspective. Therefore, in its broadest sense sanctification includes being **cleansed "of all sin"** by **"the blood of Jesus Christ"** (1John 1:7); **receiving "the Holy Spirit"** (Acts 2:38); **being "raised incorruptible" from the dead** (1Corinthians 15:42); and **a life of perfect righteousness in "a new heavens and a new earth"** (2Peter 3:13). However, much that we will deal with in this section has to do with sanctification in its narrower sense, which is **the improvement in behavior that takes place in the life of a believer.**

The words, **"We are sanctified through the offering of the body of Jesus Christ once for all... For by one offering He has perfected for ever those who are sanctified,"** tell us that we are sanctified [set apart in the eyes of God as holy] by the blood of Christ, and the forgiveness He won for us by His death on the cross (Hebrews 10:14). And, because, **"All of our righteousnesses are like filthy rags,"** that is the only sanctification that makes us holy in the eyes of God (Isaiah 64:6). However, do not misunderstand me. I am not saying that the improvement in behavior that comes as a result of sincere repentance and the work of the Holy Ghost is not important. Some people who turn to Christ come from a background **so perverse** that they cannot continue in it without bringing condemnation down on themselves. As it is written, **"The unrighteous will not inherit the kingdom of God. Do not be deceived: neither fornicators, nor idolaters, nor adulterers, nor sex perverts, nor homosexuals, nor thieves, nor covetous, nor drunkards, nor foulmouthed revilers, nor extortioners, shall inherit the kingdom of God. And that is what some of you <u>were</u>: but you are washed, but you are <u>sanctified</u>, but you are justified in the name of the Lord Jesus, and by the Spirit of our God"** (1Corinthians 6:9-11). That being said, we must never lose sight of the fact that it is the blood of Christ and faith in His finished work not improvement in our behavior that makes us righteous, holy and obedient in the sight of God. **"Christ is the end of the law for righteousness to every one** who believes" (Romans 10:4).

The words, "**This is the will of God, even your sanctification, that you abstain from sexual immorality: That every one of you should know how to <u>control his body</u> and take a wife in a way that is holy and honorable; Not in the passion of lust, like the heathen who do not know God**," tell us that a key aspect of our sanctification is sexual self-control (1Thessalonians 4:3-5). Nevertheless, evil is so rampant in our society that many Christians and even churches no longer are shocked by sexual sin, and even tolerate it. That is totally unacceptable! **Christian couples are to begin marriage in a way that is "holy and honorable,"** and that excludes living together before marriage.

Fornication is so serious that the Apostle Paul commanded the Corinthian congregation to excommunicate those who were unrepentant, saying, "**It is reported commonly that there is fornication among you... And you are puffed up. Shouldn't you rather have been filled with sorrow? and have put out of your fellowship the man who did this?... Deliver such a man over to Satan for the destruction of the flesh, in order that the spirit may be saved in the day of the Lord Jesus**" (1Corinthians 5:1-5). And, to every pastor and congregation that is tolerant of such wickedness, the following words of Ezekiel apply. "**I have appointed you as a watchman for the house of Israel; you will hear the word from my mouth, and warn them for me. When I say to the wicked, O wicked man, you will surely die; if you do not speak to warn the wicked from his way, that wicked man will die in his sin; but I will require his blood at your hand**" (Ezekiel 33:7-8).

> "Faithfulness in Christian marriage entails that: great mortification. For a Christian man there is no escape. Marriage may help to sanctify and direct to its proper object his sexual desires; its grace may help him in the struggle; but the struggle remains.... No man, however truly he loved his betrothed and bride as a young man, has lived faithful to her as a wife in mind and body without deliberate conscious exercise of the will, without self-denial." (J.R.R. Tolkien, from a letter to his son.)

Having said this, I want to make it clear that there is far more to sanctification than just dealing with sexual sin. The words, "**The goal of our instruction is love flowing from a pure heart, a good conscience, and a sincere faith**," tell us that the goal of all instruction is a right heart before God, as well as sincere faith (1Timothy 1:5). And, having a right heart and clean conscience before God excludes all attempts to excuse or rationalize sin.

While a clean conscience is of key importance to our sanctification, you should never confuse conscience with guilt. Our conscience is our inner knowledge that something is, or could be, wrong. Guilt is the inner condemnation that we may or may not feel if we do something we believe to be wrong. The way of the world is to deal with guilt by making up some excuse or reason to justify wrongdoing in an attempt to alleviate guilt. A shoplifter may ease feelings of guilt by saying, "The store will never miss it". A slanderer may use the excuse, "What he doesn't know won't hurt him," and so forth. A woman who caused much strife in her home excused it by saying "Everybody argues". A man who had certain sins pointed out to him, excused them by saying, "That isn't sin, that's human nature". Rationalizing sin is the way of the world. However, God says, **"He who excuses his sins will not prosper: but whoever confesses and forsakes them will be treated mercifully"** (Proverbs 28:13). A Christian should never excuse sin, for by excusing it you are denying your need for forgiveness. For that reason, a Christian should always be willing to confess his sin to God, and should even be willing to ask forgiveness for thoughts or behavior that he is not sure are sinful. If even **"our righteousnesses are like filthy rags,"** there is nothing we do that does not need some forgiveness (Isaiah 64:6). And, we should be more interested in admitting our sin, than excusing it. In fact, when it comes to confessing sin, Christ set an example for us by going to John for baptism. Christ, who had "no sin" was not afraid to be seen being baptized "for the remission of sins" (Mark 1:4, see 2Corinthians 5:21). Moreover, if Christ had refused to be baptized, He would not have been setting a good example for us. Likewise, we should not be denying sin or putting on airs, even in our own mind.

The words, **"Do not be conformed to this world: but be transformed by the renewing of your mind, that you may prove what is the good, and acceptable, and perfect, will of God,"** tell us that improvement in our behavior starts in our mind (Romans 12:2). We need to bring our thinking into agreement with the word of God. And, a big part of that involves **learning to recognize our sins, and stop excusing them**. However, another part involves **training the conscience**, so that we recognize sin as sin, and are sorry when we fall short.

Passages That Address Sanctification

"I now send you, to open their eyes, and to turn them from darkness to light, and from the power of Satan to God, that they may receive forgiveness of sins, and inheritance among those who are sanctified through faith in me" (Acts 26:17-18).

"Let us cleanse ourselves from everything that defiles body and soul, following holiness to its goal in the fear of God." (2Corinthians 7:1).

"As He who has called you is holy, so you should be holy in everything you do" (1Peter 1:15).

"Let us walk honestly, as in the day; not in rioting and drunkenness, not in sensuality and debauchery, not in strife and envying. But put on the Lord Jesus Christ, and make no provision for the flesh, to fulfill its lusts" (Romans 13:13-14).

"For the grace of God that brings salvation has appeared to all men, Teaching us that, denying ungodliness and worldly lusts, we should live soberly, righteously, and godly, in this present world" (Titus 2:11-12).

"The fruit of the Spirit is love, joy, peace, longsuffering, gentleness, goodness, faith, Meekness, temperance: against such there is no law. And they that are Christ's have crucified the flesh with the affections and lusts. If we live in the Spirit, let us also walk in the Spirit" (Galatians 5:22-25).

"I am being frank with you because of the weakness of the flesh: for as you have yielded your members as slaves to uncleanness and to iniquity leading to more iniquity; even so now yield your members as servants to righteousness to sanctification. For when you were the slaves of sin, you were free from righteousness. Yet what benefit did you get out of those things that you are now ashamed of? For those things result in death. But now having been <u>freed from sin</u>, and become servants of God, you have your <u>fruit unto holiness</u>, and the result is everlasting life" (Romans 6:19-22). [Notice that the "**fruit unto holiness**" comes after we are "**freed from sin**" (i.e. saved).]

2. The Efficient Cause Of Sanctification

The words, "**Walk in the Spirit, and you will not fulfill the lust of the flesh. For the flesh lusts against the Spirit, and the Spirit against the flesh: and they are opposed to each other: so that you cannot do the things that you would,**" tell us that the improvement in our behavior that follows justification comes as a result of the Holy Spirit working in us (Galatians 5:16-17). As it is written, "**It is God who works in you both to will and to do His good pleasure**" (Philippians 2:13).

The words, "**Having been freed from sin, and become servants of God, you have your fruit unto holiness,**" tell us that sanctification is a fruit or by-product of our salvation (Romans 6:22). The words, "**May the God of peace sanctify you entirely... He who calls you is faithful, and will bring it to pass,**" tell us that it is God who sanctifies us (1Thessalonians 5:23-24). However, in contrast to our justification – which is totally the work of God; even our faith being a "gift of God" Eph. 2:8-9 – in our sanctification we cooperate with God; not in the sense that we produce the improvement in our behavior, but in the sense that we yield to the Holy Spirit. As it is written, "**It is God who works in you both to will and to do His good pleasure**" (Philippians 2:13).

The words, "**Yield your members as servants to righteousness to sanctification**," // "**Being confident of this, that He who has begun a good work in you will continue it until the day of Jesus Christ**," tell us that in sanctification we are to yield to righteousness, but it is God who is working in us to produce that righteousness (Romans 6:19, Philippians 1:6). That means that no matter how hard we struggle with the flesh, if God is not at work in us we will not have the will or strength to resist the flesh.

The words, "**Sin will not have dominion over you: because you are not under the law, but under grace**," tell us that because we are saved sin no longer has the power to overwhelm us (Romans 6:14). As it is written, "**God who is faithful, will not allow you to be tempted beyond what you can bear; but when you are tempted, He will also provide a way of escape, that you may be able to endure it**" (1Corinthians 10:13).

Having "**these promises, dearly beloved, let us cleanse ourselves from everything that defiles body and soul, following holiness to its goal in the fear of God**," and, "**let us lay aside every weight, and the sin that so easily entangles us, and let us run with patience the race that is set before us**" (2Corinthians 7:1, Hebrews 12:1).

3. The Inner Motions Of Sanctification

The Bible describes the change which takes place in a man when he comes to faith in Christ as a transformation. And, the words, "**He has given you life, who were dead in trespasses and sins**," describe that transformation as a change from spiritual death to new life in Christ (Ephesians 2:1). At the same time, the Bible does not give us any details about that change. However we are told that, "**If any man is in Christ, he is a new creation: the old things have passed away; behold, all things have become new**," (2Corinthians 5:17). And, those words describe a transformation that goes far beyond receiving life. What is being described is a new nature. And, the words, "**Put on the new nature, which after *the image of* God is created in righteousness and true holiness**," // "**Put on the new man, who is renewed in knowledge after the image of the One who created him**," tell us that the new nature restores us to the image of God (Ephesians 4:24, Colossians 3:10). [An image lost through the fall, Jer. 17:9, John 8:44, Matt. 15:19.]

The words, "**I inwardly delight in the law of God: But I see another law at work in my members, warring against the law of my mind**," tell us that our new nature assents to the will of God, but still struggles against the old nature (Romans 7:22-23). **However, the struggle that we endure should never cause us to "lose heart; on the contrary, even though our outward man dies, our inner man is being renewed day by day"** (2Corinthians 4:16). And, that renewal should lead you to **"put off everything having to do with your former way of life, the old nature which is corrupt according to the deceitful lusts; and be renewed in the spirit of your mind"** (Ephesians 4:22-23). **"Regard yourselves as dead to sin, but alive to God through Jesus Christ our Lord"** (Romans 6:11).

The words, **"The flesh lusts against the Spirit, and the Spirit against the flesh: and they are opposed to each other: so that you cannot do the things that you would,"** tell us that the struggle with our old nature can be very intense (Galatians 5:17). And, because of the deceitfulness of sin, men who are struggling with the flesh can easily puff themselves up in their own minds, telling themselves that the effort they make to resist sin is what makes them righteous. However, what they fail to see is that if they were really righteous they would not have to make an effort to resist sin, it would come naturally. **What they are resisting is the wickedness of their own heart; a heart that the Bible describes as, "Deceitful above all things, and desperately wicked"** (Jeremiah 17:9).

Christians who are undergoing an intense struggle with the flesh should never assume that they are struggling because they have fallen from grace. It is the lost who have no struggle; the lost just give into the flesh, or water down the law and excuse transgressing it (Luke 11:46). And, they are condemned by the words, **"If you live according to the flesh, you will die: but if <u>by the Spirit</u> you <u>put to death</u> the deeds of the body, you will live"** (Romans 8:13). And, because only those who trust in Christ have the Holy Spirit, only those who trust in Christ can "put to death the deeds of the body" "<u>by the Spirit</u>".

Because the Apostle Paul had to struggle with the flesh, and was describing his struggle when he said, **"I inwardly delight in the law of God: But I see another law at work in my members, warring against the law of my mind,"** no one should ever think that they are lost because they have to struggle (Romans 7:22-23). On the other hand, if you assume that your struggle with the flesh makes you righteous it can greatly intensify that struggle, because the Holy Spirit will not help you to deceive yourself. The Holy Spirit wants you to say with Paul **"I know that nothing good dwells in me,"** while admitting your sin and trusting in Christ [rather than your own efforts] for righteousness (Romans 7:18). As it is written, **"Christ is the end of the law for righteousness to every one who believes"** (Romans 10:4).

Even though we receive a new nature when we come to faith in

Christ, the old nature is still present. And, the words, **"The dead shall be raised incorruptible,"** tell us that our old corruptible nature will continue in us until the resurrection (1Corinthians 15:52). Moreover, because that old nature is present in us, we endure the same sinful desires and passions as the lost; and in that regard are no better than them. The words, **"The heart is deceitful above all things, and desperately wicked"** tell us that we should not be surprised if our old nature tempts us to do horrible things (Jeremiah 17:9). **What sets us apart from the world is the fact that we struggle against sinful thoughts and desires. And, the following passages describe that struggle. "If you live according to the flesh, you will die: but if by the Spirit you put to death the deeds of the body, you will live"** (Romans 8:13). **"They that are Christ's have crucified the flesh with its passions and lusts"** (Galatians 5:24). **"Put to death whatever belongs to your earthly nature; sexual immorality, impurity, lust, evil desires, and covetousness, which is idolatry"** (Colossians 3:5). **"I buffet my body, and bring it under my control: lest there be any way that I, after having preached to others, might be rejected"** (1Corinthians 9:27). **"If your hand or your foot offends you, cut it off, and throw it away: it is better for you to enter into life crippled or maimed, than to have two hands or two feet and be thrown into everlasting fire. And if your eye offends you, pluck it out, and throw it away: it is better for you to enter into life with one eye, than to have two eyes and be thrown into hell fire"** (Matthew 18:8-9). **"Let us lay aside every weight, and the sin that so easily entangles us, and let us run with patience the race that is set before us"** (Hebrews 12:1).

In our struggle with the flesh we need to remember the promise **"God who is faithful, will not allow you to be tempted beyond what you can bear; but when you are tempted, He will also provide a way of escape, giving you the ability to bear it"** (1Corinthians 10:13). And, when we are tempted we should meet each temptation with the Word of God and prayer. Moreover, in praying for strength against the flesh, **do not forget to ask God to forgive your wrong thoughts and get them out of you mind.**

The words, **"Lead us not into temptation, but deliver us from evil,"** // **"Watch and pray, that you do not enter into temptation,"** tell us that it is God's will for us to pray to escape temptation (Matthew 6:13 and 26:41). At the same time, the words, **"Take the helmet of salvation, and the sword of the Spirit, which is the word of God,"** tell us that the Word of God is a weapon that we can use in fighting temptation (Ephesians 6:17).

4. The Means By Which We Are Sanctified

Just as the Holy Spirit works through His Word to bring us to faith, He works through that same Word to produce the improvement in our behavior which we call sanctification.

The words, "**Faith comes by hearing, and hearing by the word of God**," tell us that God works through His Word to bring us to faith (Romans 10:17). The words, "**That we might receive the promise of the Spirit through faith**," tell us that when we are brought to faith by the Word of God we receive the Holy Spirit (Galatians 3:14). And, the words, "**The flesh lusts against the Spirit, and the Spirit against the flesh: and they are opposed to each other: so that you cannot do the things that you would**," tell us that the Holy Spirit that we receive through faith in Christ works in us to improve our behavior (Galatians 5:17).

Now, just as the Holy Spirit brought us to faith by bringing us to repentance – producing in us "**a heart that is humbled and sorry for sin**," once we come to faith that same sorrow for sin causes us to desire a sin-free life (Psalm 51:17). Without faith a person who is sorry for sin might rationalize sin in order to escape its condemnation. However, once we have the assurance of forgiveness in Christ, sin is no longer a terror to us. That should make us willing to examine ourselves, stop making excuses for sin, and shun sinful behavior. Now, although our lives will never be perfect in this world, the words, "**Neither fornicators, nor idolaters, nor adulterers, nor sex perverts, nor homosexuals, nor thieves, nor covetous, nor drunkards, nor foulmouthed revilers, nor extortioners, shall inherit the kingdom of God. And that is what some of you were: but you are washed, but you are sanctified**," tell us that we can and should be free of gross sinful behavior (1Corinthians 6:9-11). And, the words, "**Now, brethren, I commit you to God, and to the word of His grace, which is able to build you up, and to give you an inheritance among all those who are sanctified**," tell us that it is "the word of His grace" that builds us up producing sanctification in us (Acts 20:32).

As the Holy Spirit works in us, both Law and Gospel play a part in our sanctification. While the words, "**No flesh will ever be justified in God's sight by the deeds of the law: because the knowledge of sin comes by the law**," tell us that the law makes us aware of our sin, they also tell us that the law cannot make us righteous (Romans 3:20). At the same time, the words, "**We have been released from the law, having died to that which once bound us; that we should serve in newness of spirit, and not in the oldness of the letter**," tell us that being released from the law through faith in Christ enables us to serve with a new attitude as the Spirit works in us (Romans 7:6). **Walking in the Spirit we should desire to do** what is right and praiseworthy and good, and our fruit will be "**love, joy, peace, patience, kindness, goodness, faith, meekness, self-control**" (Galatians 5:22-23). At the same time, the words, "**Love one another: for he who loves his neighbor has fulfilled the law. For this, You will not commit adultery, You will not kill, You will not steal, You will not bear false witness, You will not covet; and if there is any other commandment, it is summed up in this saying, namely, You will love your neighbor as yourself. Love does no harm to his neighbor: therefore love is the fulfilling of the law**," tell us that the law is our guide to expressing love in a godly way (Romans 13:8-10).

The words, "**The knowledge of sin comes by the law,**" tell us that the law makes us aware of our sins (Romans 3:20). The words, "**I buffet my body, and bring it under my control,**" tell us that the law lets us know what behavior we should fight against (1Corinthians 9:27). And, the words, "**How can a young man keep his life pure? By taking heed to it according to your word,**" tell us that the law is a guide to our conduct (Psalm 119:9).

At the same time, the words, "**The days come, says the LORD, when I will make a new covenant with the house of Israel... I will put my law in their inward parts, and write it in their hearts; and will be their God, and they will be my people**," tell us that it is the gospel that inscribes the law upon our heart (Jeremiah 31:31-33).

5. The Necessity Of Sanctification And Good Works

As Christians we need to continually be on guard because **our "adversary the devil, prowls around like a roaring lion, looking for someone" he can destroy** (1Peter 5:8). And, his attack on the doctrine of sanctification is twofold. On one hand he promotes the idea that one can live in sin and still be saved, while on the other hand promoting the idea that salvation depends on works. This has led to a confused debate over the question of whether good works are necessary for salvation. So let us look at what the Bible says.

First of all, the Bible plainly tells us that a person can be saved without works. We not only have the example of the thief on the cross, to whom Christ said, "**Today you will be with me in paradise**" (Luke 23:43). We are plainly told that "**A man is justified by faith without the deeds of the law**" (Romans 3:28). **We are also told that we "Are saved by grace through faith... Not of works,**" and that, "**if it [salvation] is by grace, then is it no longer by works**" (Ephesians 2:8-9, Romans 11:6). Therefore, the real question is not whether a person can be saved without works, but: **Can a person who is living in sin – with no desire to change his sinful life-**

style –be truly repentant? And, the Biblical answer to that question is a resounding **NO**.

The words, "**Among you one hears of sexual immorality... And you are still puffed up. Shouldn't you rather have been filled with sorrow? and have put out of your fellowship the man who did this?**" tell us of a man who claimed to be saved, yet was unrepentant and living in sin (1Corinthians 5:1-2). The fact that the Holy Spirit instructed the congregation to deliver him "to Satan" tells us that he was not saved (1Cor. 5:5). And, the words, "**Don't you know that the unrighteous will not inherit the kingdom of God? Do not be deceived: neither fornicators, nor idolaters, nor adulterers, nor sex perverts, nor homosexuals, Nor thieves, nor covetous, nor drunkards, nor foulmouthed revilers, nor extortioners, shall inherit the kingdom of God. And that is what some of you were: but you are washed, but you are sanctified, but you are justified in the name of the Lord Jesus, and by the Spirit of our God,**" tell us that those who are "sanctified" do not continue to commit those sins (1Corinthians 6:9-11). In addition, the words, "**The law is not meant for a righteous man, but for those who are lawless and rebellious, for the ungodly and sinful, for the irreverent and profane, for those who strike or kill their fathers or mothers, for murders, For those who sin sexually, for sodomites, for kidnapers and slave traders, for liars and perjurers, and for any other thing that is contrary to sound teaching,**" tell us that those who engage in such sins place themselves back under the law, **and thus under condemnation and outside of God's grace** (1Timothy 1:9-10).

When the Bible says, "**If we sin willfully or deliberately after we have received the knowledge of the truth, no sacrifice for sins remains, But only a fearful expectation of judgment and raging fire, that will devour the enemies of God. Anyone who despised Moses' law died without mercy on the testimony of two or three witnesses: How much more severely, do you think a man deserves to be punished, who has trampled the Son of God under foot, treated the blood of the covenant, by which he was sanctified, as an unholy thing, and insulted the Spirit of grace? For we know Him who said, Vengeance belongs to me, I will repay, says the Lord. And again, The Lord will judge His people. It is a fearful thing to fall into the hands of the living God,**" those words are a warning to anyone who would trample Christ "under foot" by twisting the forgiveness He offers into an excuse to sin (Hebrews 10:26-31). That warning from the book of Hebrews comes straight from the Old Testament, where we read, "**If any soul sins through ignorance, then he shall bring a she goat of the first year as a sin offering... But the soul that does anything presumptuously, whether he is born in the land, or a** stranger, the same reproaches the LORD; and that soul shall be cut off from among his people" (Numbers 15:27-31)

The words, "**He [Christ] is the one whom God has exalted to His own right hand to be a Prince and a Savior, to give to Israel repentance, and forgiveness of sins**," tell us that "repentance and forgiveness" go hand in hand (Acts 5:31). Now while it is possible for someone who is sorry for a particular sin to rationalize that sin rather than seeking forgiveness, because our faith is a "gift of God" it is impossible for someone who is unrepentant to truly have faith in Christ (Ephesians 2:8). It is impossible because **the idea that a person can live in sin and still be saved is a false gospel**, and God does not give anyone faith in a false gospel.

Because one who is truly repentant will have, "**A heart that is humbled and sorry for sin**," he will not want to sin (Psalm 51:17). And, his desire to lead a sin-free life will produce works. However, **those works come after he repents, and thus after he is saved**. For that reason those works are a fruit or by-product of repentance and salvation, not what saves us. They are necessary only in the sense that true repentance will always produce an improvement, but that improvement is not what makes us righteous, and it is not what saves us.

Furthermore, because works cannot save us, they cannot keep us saved. On the contrary, the words, "**Kept by the power of God through faith unto salvation**," tell us that we are kept by the power of God (1Peter 1:5). For even though the improvement in our behavior after we are saved is pleasing to God, the words, "**All of our righteousnesses are like filthy rags**," tell us that it is only because the "**The blood of Jesus Christ His Son cleanses us of all sin**," that the improvement in our behavior is acceptable to God, without that forgiveness it is worthless (Isaiah 64:6, 1John 1:7).

The following passages tell us that just as God has saved us by His grace, He will keep us by His grace. "**He who hears my word, and believes on Him who sent me, has everlasting life, and will not come into condemnation; but has passed from death to life**" (John 5:24). "**The Lord is faithful, and will strengthen you, and keep you from evil**" (2Thessalonians 3:3). "**He who has begun a good work in you will continue it until the day of Jesus Christ**" (Philippians 1:6). "**I know whom I have believed, and am persuaded that He is able to keep that which I have committed to Him against that day**" (2Timothy 2:12). "**Now to Him who is able to keep you from falling, and to present you faultless before His glorious presence with great joy, To the only wise God, our Savior, be glory and majesty, dominion and power, both now and forever. Amen**" (Jude 1:24-25).

6. The Imperfection Of Sanctification In This Life

The Bible tells us that the very purpose of the law is to show us our sins, and tells us that because the law was given to expose our sins no one **"Will ever be declared righteous in God's sight by doing what the law requires,"** (Romans 3:20). That should be perfectly clear. However the Bible goes further to tell us that, **"If there had been a law given that could have given life, righteousness truly would have been by the law"**. But because no law can make us righteous, the law was given as **"Our schoolmaster to bring us to Christ, that we might be declared righteous by faith"** (Galatians 3:21,24). Nevertheless, because **"The heart is deceitful above all things,"** some try to get around what the Bible says by calling their efforts to **"establish their own righteousness"** "sanctification," "obedience" or "holiness" (Jeremiah 17:9, Romans 10:3). In saying this I want to make it clear that Biblical "sanctification" is very real, and will result in an improvement in our behavior. However, the words, **"No man living is righteous in your sight,"** tell us that it will never improve our behavior enough to make us righteous or obedient in the sight of God (Psalm 143:2). For that reason, we need to beware of the false claim that men can make themselves "holy" or "obedient" by their own effort. It should be obvious that if we cannot make ourselves "righteous," we cannot make ourselves "holy". Calling "righteousness," "holiness" or "obedience" does not change a thing. The words, **"When you have done everything that you were commanded to do, say, We are unworthy servants: for we have only done what it was our duty to do,"** tell us what our attitude should be (Luke 17:10).

The words, **"The blood of Jesus Christ His Son cleanses us of all sin,"** tell us that we cannot possibly improve on the cleansing from sin that is already ours through faith in Christ (1John 1:7). There is **"No condemnation for those who are in Christ Jesus,"** // **"For by one offering He has perfected for ever those who are sanctified"** (Romans 8:1, Hebrews 10:14). At the same time the words, **"Do not enter into judgment with your servant: for no man living is righteous in your sight,"** tell us that it is not our works, but the forgiveness that is ours in Christ, that makes us acceptable to God (Psalm 143:2).

The words, "I inwardly delight in the law of God: But I see another law at work in my members, warring against the law of my mind," are just another way of saying **"The flesh lusts against the Spirit, and the Spirit against the flesh: and they are opposed to each other,"** for both passages describe the struggle we have with the flesh (Romans 7:22-23, Galatians 5:17). The words, "**The works of the flesh are obvious, which are; Adultery, fornication, sexual filthiness, sensuality, Idolatry, witchcraft, hatred, discord, rivalry, rage, strife, divisions, heresies, Envy, murder, drunkenness, orgies, and such like: of which I forewarn you, as I have in the past, that those who do such things will not inherit the kingdom of God," describe the kind of behavior that a believer should strive to eliminate in thought word and deed (Galatians 5:19-21). In contrast, the words, "**The fruit of the Spirit is love, joy, peace, patience, kindness, goodness, faith, Meekness, self-control: against such there is no law. And they that are Christ's have crucified the flesh with its passions and lusts. Since we live by the Spirit, let us also walk in the Spirit,**" describe the kind of behavior that a believer should cultivate (Galatians 5:22-25).

Because our sanctification is never perfect in this life, it is easy for us to fall short. Strife, contention, and bickering seem especially hard to eliminate. Nevertheless, Paul's words, "**You are still carnal: for as long as there is jealously, strife, and division among you, are you not walking after the flesh, and acting like unsaved men?**" sternly rebuke such sins (1Corinthians 3:3). And, the words, "**The fleshly mind is hostile to God,**" warn us that such behavior needs to be taken seriously (Romans 8:7).

"**Therefore, my beloved brethren, be steadfast, unmovable, always abounding in the work of the Lord**" (1Corinthians 15:58). "**That you might walk worthy of the Lord pleasing in every way, being fruitful in every good work, and increasing in the knowledge of God; Being strengthened with all power, according to His glorious might, so that you might endure all with joyfulness and patience**" (Colossians 1:10-11). And, "**Speaking the truth in love, may in every way grow up in respect to Him, who is the head, even Christ**" (Ephesians 4:15). Now, "**May the Lord cause you to increase and abound in love for one another, and for all men, just as we also do for you**" (1Thessalonians 3:12). "**And this is my prayer, that your love may abound yet more and more in knowledge and in all discernment**" (Philippians 1:9). Knowing that, "**God is able to make every blessing abound to you; that you, always having everything you need, may abound to every good work**" (2Corinthians 9:8).

At the same time, do not let Satan deceive you into thinking that the things you do are what make you righteous or obedient, but keep your eyes on Christ, being ready to confess your sin as did David, saying: "**Have mercy upon me, O God, according to your lovingkindness: blot out my transgressions according to the multitude of your tender mercies**" (Psalm 51:1). "**Do not enter into judgment with your servant: for no man living is righteous in your sight**" (Psalm 143:2). "**O LORD, do not rebuke me in your wrath: or chasten me in your hot displeasure**" (Psalm 38:1). "**I acknowledged my sin to you, and I did not hide my iniquity. I said, I will confess my transgressions to the LORD; and you forgave the iniquity of my sin" (Psalm 32:5). For, "**If we confess our sins, He is faithful and just to forgive us our sins, and to cleanse us from all unrighteousness**" (1John 1:9).

The Doctrine Of Good Works

1. The Nature Of Good Works

<u>Because</u> "**No living person is righteous**" in the sight of God, <u>because</u> no one "**Will ever be justified in God's sight by the deeds of the law**," and <u>because</u> "**All of our righteousnesses are like filthy rags**" in the sight of God; **the only people who can do works that are truly good in the sight of God are those who trust in Christ, those whose sins have been washed away through faith in His blood** (Psalm 143:2, Romans 3:20, Isaiah 64:6, 1John 1:7). And, <u>unlike the law</u>, which motivates by fear, **faith "produces works through love"** (Galatians 5:6).

Those who seek righteousness through the law know that they fall short, although they usually try to block it out of their mind. Sometimes they delude themselves into thinking that God will somehow overlook their shortcomings because of their intent or effort. However, Joshua warned them saying, "**God... will not overlook your transgressions or your sins**" (Joshua 24:19). And, the words, "**Whoever keeps the whole law, yet fails in one point, is guilty of all**," add another warning (James 2:10). They need to seek God's mercy instead of deluding themselves. For God assures us that, "**If we confess our sins, He is faithful and just to forgive us our sins, and to cleanse us from all unrighteousness**" (1John 1:9). And, David said, "**I have trusted in your mercy; my heart will rejoice in your salvation**" (Psalm 13:5).

One important part of our sanctification involves training our conscience in order to bring it into agreement with the Word of God. This is important because our "**heart is deceitful above all things, and desperately wicked**," (Jeremiah 17:9). And, because the heart is deceitful, people are more likely to rationalize their sin than seek God's forgiveness. The words, "**Do not be conformed to this world: but be transformed by the renewing of your mind**," tell us that we need to stop making excuses for sin (Romans 12:2). On the other hand, the words, "**The entire law is summed up in one command, You shall love your neighbor as yourself**," warn us against twisting God's law into an excuse to be mean (Galatians 5:14). For example: I once was talking with a young man when an obese woman walked by. At that moment he said, "Boy is she fat" in a voice loud enough for her to hear. When I asked him why he would say such a thing, he replied, "We are supposed to be honest". That kind of "honesty" is totally unchristian. God does not want us to deceive each other, but He does not want us to be rude and unkind either.

The words, "**By one offering He [Christ] has perfected for ever those who are sanctified**," tell us that every thought, word, and deed of believers who **walk in love, having "a pure heart, a good conscience, and a sincere faith**," is a good work in the sight of God (Hebrews 10:14, 1Timothy 1:5). As it is written, "**There is therefore now no condemnation for those who are in Christ Jesus, who walk not after the flesh, but after the Spirit**" (Romans 8:1). And, again, "**Blessed is the man to whom the Lord will not impute sin**" (Romans 4:8).

The following passages testify to the importance of a clean conscience before God. "**To the pure everything is pure: but to those who are defiled and unbelieving nothing is pure; both their mind and conscience is defiled**" (Titus 1:15 see 3:9). But, "**We... have renounced the hidden things of dishonesty, not resorting to craftiness, nor handling the word of God deceitfully; but by clearly speaking the truth we commend ourselves to every man's conscience in the sight of God**" (2Corinthians 4:1-2). And, "**Our rejoicing is this, our conscience testifies that we have conducted ourselves, in the world and especially toward you, in sincerity and singleness of heart, not in accord with fleshly wisdom, but in accord with the grace of God**" (2Corinthians 1:12). "**Holding the mystery of the faith in a clean conscience**," // "**which some by disregarding have made shipwreck of their faith**" (1Timothy 3:9 and 1:19).

Furthermore, as Christians, **Scripture is to be our sole source, standard, and judge of what is right and what is wrong in the sight of God**. The words, "**Do not turn aside from any of the words which I command you this day, to the right hand, or to the left**," warn us not to add to or take from what the Bible says (Deuteronomy 28:14). I stress this because there are many outside influences working to twist, distort and pervert our ideas of right and wrong. At the time of Christ, the Pharisees boasted of being "the strictest sect" of the Jewish religion (Acts 26:5). Yet the words, "**You load men down with burdens they can hardly bear, and you yourselves do not touch those burdens with one of your fingers**," reveal the fact that whenever keeping the law was inconvenient, the Pharisees rationalized sin (Luke 11:46). Jesus gave one example of that, when He said, "**You hypocrites... You completely invalidate the commandment of God, in order to keep your tradition. For Moses said, Honor your father and mother; and anyone who curses his father or mother, let him be put to death: But you say, If a man will say to his father or mother, It is Corban, that is a gift, by which you might profit by me; he shall be free. And you no longer allow him to do anything for his father or his mother; Making the word of God of no effect through your tradition,"** (Mark 7:6-13). And, just like it was then, there are many today who want to **"load men down with burdens they can hardly bear,"** by making righteousness depend on works (Luke 11:46). At the same time, there are others who justify, rationalize and encourage wickedness, including all manner of sexual sin and perversion. **Such rationalization is totally anti-Christian, and training the conscience includes totally eradicating that kind of thinking from your heart.**

Christ accused the Pharisees of **"Making the word of God of no effect,"** by their rationalizations (Mark 7:13). And, they made it of "no effect" by teaching men to excuse sin, rather than repent. Because **the law was given as a "schoolmaster to bring us to Christ,"** excusing sin rendered it ineffective (Galatians 3:24). That is why contradicting God's Word, or trying to get around what it says, is such a serious matter.

By rationalizing sin the Pharisees, **"Rebelled against the words of God, and despised the counsel of the most High,"** and in the eyes of God, **"Rebellion is as the sin of witchcraft, and defiance is as iniquity and idolatry"** (Psalm 107:11, 1Samuel 15:23). By exalting their own word over the Word of God, the Pharisees were usurping God's authority, in effect deifying themselves. **And, all who add to God's Word by teaching made-up doctrines [such as theistic evolution etc.] as the Word of God, or explaining away what the Bible plainly says, are guilty of the sin of self-deification.** Of this sin Luther said:

> "Scripture calls it a most horrible sorcery, idolatry, and idol-service not to listen to the Word of God, but to purpose to do something without or against God's Word; and this is indeed a most dreadful verdict, especially when you see how common this is and how much it is done in the world." (Martin Luther, St. L., I, 866.)

At the same time, as long as we are not being told to do something wrong, we need to go along with what our leaders say. This is important, because having a clean conscience is important. That is why we are told to **be subject to rulers, "Not only for wrath, but also for conscience sake"** (Romans 13:5). Furthermore, in the past, evil rulers have used rebellion on the part of some Christians as an excuse to persecute all Christians, and that is the devil's work. However, we always need to beware of those who would make God's favor depend on what we do, or rationalize and excuse sin. And, the words, "**We ought to obey God rather than men,**" tell us that whenever man's word contradicts God's Word, we are to obey God (Acts 5:29).

With the words, "**Observe and practice whatever they tell you; but do not do what they do: for they do not do what they say,**" Jesus told His disciples to go ahead and comply with the rules required by the Pharisees (Matthew 23:3). That was good advice for Jewish believers, not only for conscience sake, but because non-compliance would only become an excuse for persecution. At the same time, they were not to pervert the rules the way the Pharisees did, by imagining that rule keeping would bring God's favor, or by excusing sin.

The words, "**Listen to those who lead the congregation, and follow their guidance: for they watch for your souls, as men who must give account, so that they may do this with joy, and not with grief: for that is not to your advantage,**" tell us to comply with the leaders of the congregation (Hebrews 13:17). That is important for those who are spiritually immature, because they are not going to learn if they ignore what they are being taught. At the same time, those who are spiritually mature need to set a good example, and not hinder the work of the congregation with unnecessary controversy. However, the words, "**Beware of false prophets,**" and "**We ought to obey God rather than men,**" warn us that when congregational leaders teach or do what is contrary to the Word of God we must take action. And, in most cases that will involve following the steps of Matthew eighteen, "**If your brother sins against you, go and tell him his fault between you and him alone: if he will hear you, you have gained your brother. But if he will not listen, then take one or two others with you, so that every word may be established by the testimony of two or three witnesses. And if he refuses to listen to them, tell it to the church: but if he refuses to hear the church, let him be to you as a heathen man and a publican**" (Matthew 18:15-17). Or the words, "**I speak as to wise men; judge for yourselves what I say,**" and "**Reject a man who is a heretic after the first and second warning**" (1Corinthians 10:15, Titus 3:10).

2. The Works Of The Heathen

The Bible tells us that "**When the Gentiles, who do not have the law, do by nature the things contained in the law, they... show the work of the law written in their hearts**" (Romans 2:14-15). And, because the law of God is in their hearts, they can conduct themselves in a way that is praiseworthy, at least from man's point of view. **However, it would be a mistake for us to assume that any praiseworthy behavior on their part could ever make** them acceptable to God. I am not saying that the good things they do are not good. That is not the issue. What I am saying is that the whole idea that good works somehow merit a blessing is a delusion. The words, **"When you have done everything that you were commanded to do, say, We are unworthy servants: for we have only done what it was our duty to do,"** tell us that our best is only what is expected of us, not something exceptional (Luke 17:10).

Furthermore, because **"No man living is righteous"** in the sight of God, no heathen person is going to be free of sin (Psalm 143:2). And, the very idea of balancing good works against sins is as silly as a bank robber saying to the judge, "Don't the banks that I did not rob make up for the ones that I did rob?" Because we are all sinners the Bible tells us that, **"Without faith [and thus without the forgiveness that is ours through faith in Christ] it is impossible to please God"** (Hebrews 11:6).

Another thing to consider is that the heathen, **"are all estranged from"** God **"through their idols"** (Ezekiel 14:5). Because the heathen are breaking the first commandment, the words, **"Whoever keeps the whole law, yet fails in one point, is guilty of all,"** apply (James 2:10). And, the very fact that the words, **"All of our righteousnesses are like filthy rags,"** tell us that the righteous deeds of believers are not acceptable apart from forgiveness, should make it clear **apart from forgiveness in Christ it is impossible for anyone to gain God's favor**.

That being said, if God chooses to bless an unbeliever because that unbeliever has shown kindness to one of His children, it is not because that kindness merits a blessing, but because God is trying to bring that person to repentance (Rom. 2:4).

3. The Christian's Growth In Good Works

Because it is **the "blood of Jesus Christ"** God's Son, and the forgiveness that He won for us on the cross, that **"cleanses us of all sin,"** it is the blood of Jesus Christ and His blood alone that makes us righteous in the sight of God (1John 1:7). As it is written, **"By one offering He has perfected for ever those who are sanctified"** (Hebrews 10:14). And, that forgiveness frees us from the law's condemnation. However, the freedom we have in Christ is not the freedom the world craves (the freedom to gratify the flesh), but the freedom to be a respectful child, a responsible parent, a faithful spouse, a reliable employee, an honest employer, and so forth without being condemned because we cannot be "perfect" as the law requires (Matthew 5:48). In short it is **the freedom to "lead a quiet and peaceable life in all godliness and honesty"** (1Timothy 2:2). It is only when that is understood that our motivation for doing what is right becomes our love for Christ, rather than a vain attempt to make ourselves righteous. That is important because **faith "produces works through love," and "whatever is not of faith is sin."** (Galatians 5:6, Romans 14:23).

That being understood, the Bible, time after time, urges believers to perform good works. God wants us to, **"Walk in newness of life"** (Romans 6:4). And, to **"Do good to all men, especially to those who are of the household of faith"** (Galatians 6:10). It is true that we have, **"Been called to liberty; but do not use your freedom as an excuse to serve the flesh, instead serve one another in love"** (Galatians 5:13). At the same time, **"Do not nullify the grace of God, [by thinking that good works make you righteous] for if the law could make us righteous, then Christ died for nothing"** (Galatians 2:21).

The law, with all of its warnings, produces works through fear, while faith **"produces works through love"** (Galatians 5:6). And, the love that God has shown us in Christ should move us to be thoughtful, kind and helpful to others. Nevertheless, when it comes to fighting against our sinful flesh, fear and love need to work together. Although Christ's love for us should move us to want to do what is right and good and holy at all times, the fear of God should make us tremble at the thought of willfully violating God's commandment, as David did with Bathsheba, for, **"It is a fearful thing to fall into the hands of the living God."** (Hebrews 10:31).

Years ago it was common to hear someone say, "My conscience would never let me do that," but I have not heard anyone say that in years. In fact, our entire culture has become so comfortable with sexual wickedness of the worst kind, that few people are shocked by behavior that would have brought almost universal condemnation just a few decades ago.

Because our culture has become so comfortable with sin, it is more important than ever for believers to train their conscience so that it condemns what God condemns. Because this generation is, **"A wicked and adulterous generation,"** many church members have lowered their standards, and gloss over sins that would have shocked their grandparents (Matthew 16:4). And, before we can train our conscience we must be willing to look at our sins, and search out the sins that we usually do not even notice. To give just one example: Years ago, I heard a church member using vulgar language outside of church. When I said something, he said, "That's not cussing". He knew it was wrong. That is why he did not talk that way in church. However, he chose to rationalize rather than conduct himself in a way that is above reproach. As Christians our desire should not be to do the bare minimum that is required, but to **conduct ourselves in a way that will cause, "The name of our Lord Jesus Christ" to "be glorified"** (2Thessalonians 1:12). And, Jesus is not glorified by anything that is shady, questionable, or naughty on the part of His followers. That is why the Bible says, "**Let no corrupt communication proceed out of your mouth, but that which is good for building others up as needed, that it may give grace to those who hear**" (Ephesians 4:29). "**Rid yourselves of... anger, wrath, malice, blasphemy, and filthy language**" (Colossians 3:8). And, "**Put aside all filthiness and every hint of naughtiness**" (James 1:21).

Because congregational leaders are to set an example for the flock, every believer should want to live up to the standard God has given for leaders. The standard that says, "**An overseer must be blameless, the husband of one wife, vigilant, sober-minded, of good behavior, given to hospitality... Not given to wine, not a striker, but one who is patient and gentle not a brawler, not covetous or greedy for gain; One who does a good job of running his own house, having his children under control, yet dealing with them in a dignified way... He must also be well thought of by those who are outside the church**" (1Timothy 3:2-7).

The words, "**Do not be conformed to this world: but be transformed by the renewing of your mind**," // "**Casting down imaginations, and every high thing that exalts itself against the knowledge of God, and bringing into captivity every thought**," tell us that God wants us to correct our thinking, and bring it into agreement with the Word of God (Romans 12:2, 2Corinthians 10:5). As it is written, "**To the law and to the testimony: if they do not speak according to this word, it is because there is no light in them**" (Isaiah 8:20). And, one aspect of bringing your thinking into accord with the Word of God is, "**Not to think of yourself more highly than you ought; but think of yourself soberly** (Romans 12:3). For leaders that includes not seeking to be "**lords over the congregation, but... examples to the flock**" (1Peter 5:3).

The words, "**Those who are being led by the Spirit of God, are the sons of God**," // "**But if you are led by the Spirit, you are not under the law**," tell us that those who have received the Spirit of God through faith in Christ, **walk by faith, which "Produces works through love**" (Romans 8:14, Galatians 5:6, 18). And, because they "walk by faith," and are "not under the law," **they do not live under the constant fear of God's wrath.** However, I have encountered Christians who have gotten this truth so twisted around in their minds that they live in constant fear that God will punish them if they do not obey "still small voices" in their head. And, **that is satanic, because it is nothing more than works righteousness**, in another guise. If our "obedience" could bring God's favor, "**Then Christ died for nothing**" (Galatians 2:21). The Holy Spirit does not work outside of us, telling us what to do, but works inside of us, producing the faith and love that causes us to want to do what is right and holy and good. For that reason, "**The fruit of the Spirit is love,** joy, peace, patience, kindness, goodness, faith, Meekness, self-control," and not fear (Galatians 5:22-23). And, those who are truly led by the Spirit will want to, "**Be kind to one another, tenderhearted, forgiving one another, even as God for Christ's sake has forgiven**" them (Ephesians 4:32).

At the same time, **the love that comes from God is not the false love that condones and allows wickedness**. God condemned Eli because he did not take action when his sons were doing evil. By doing nothing to restrain or punish his sons, Eli sent them to hell. Had he really loved them, he would have made certain that they not only knew that their behavior was evil but regretted ever behaving that way. As it is written, "**I will perform against Eli all the things that I have said concerning his house... because his sons made themselves vile, and he did not stop them**" (1Samuel 3:12-13).

Because some in our society would like to see all religions worship together, they want Christians to tolerate falsehood and condone those who contradict God's Word. However, because "**there is no other name under heaven given among men, by which we must be saved**," that would be hate not love (Acts 4:12). God's will is revealed in the words, "**You shall not forget the covenant that I have made with you; nor shall you worship other gods**" (2Kings 17:38).

The following passages urge us to do good works. As you read them you should never just interpret them to justify yourself, so that you wind up thinking that you are a good person. Instead you need to look at the many ways that you fall short. Then, instead of trying to make yourself righteous, **humbly whisper "God be merciful to me a sinner," while reminding yourself of how much you need and appreciate the forgiveness that is yours in Christ**; taking comfort in the fact the He is "**The Lamb of God, who takes away the sin of the world**" (Luke 18:13, John 1:29). **Because the human "Heart is deceitful above all things," the aim in reminding yourself of your sin is to combat the inborn inclination to assume that you are righteous, while cultivating a humble and grateful attitude that wants to do good when the opportunity arises**.

"**Conduct yourselves in a manner worthy of the gospel of Christ: so**" // "**that the name of our Lord Jesus Christ may be glorified in you**," (Philippians 1:27, 2Thessalonians 1:12). For "**The grace of God that brings salvation has appeared to all men, teaching us that, denying ungodliness and worldly lusts, we should live soberly, righteously, and godly, in this present world; Looking for that blessed hope, and the glorious appearing of our great God and Savior Jesus Christ; Who gave Himself for us, that He might redeem us from all iniquity, and purify for Himself a special people, eager to do good works**"

(Titus 2:11-14).

Therefore, "**Conduct yourself in a manner worthy of the life to which you have been called, With all lowliness and meekness, with patience, bearing with one another in love; Being diligent to keep the unity of the Spirit in the bond of peace**" (Ephesians 4:1-3). And "**Have no fellowship with the unfruitful works of darkness, but rather reprove them. For it is a shame to even speak of those things which are done by them in secret. But all things that are reproved are exposed by the light: for whatever exposes evil is light... See then that you walk circumspectly, not as fools, but as wise, redeeming the time, because the days are evil. For that reason do not be foolish, but understand what the will of the Lord is. And do not be drunk with wine, wherein is excess; but be filled with the Spirit, speaking to yourselves in psalms and hymns and spiritual songs, singing and making melody in your heart to the Lord; Always giving thanks for all things unto God the Father in the name of our Lord Jesus Christ; Submitting yourselves one to another in the fear of God. Wives, submit yourselves unto your own husbands, as unto the Lord... Husbands, love your wives, even as Christ also loved the church, and gave Himself for it**" (Ephesians 5:11-25).

"Put off everything having to do with your former way of life, the old nature which is corrupt according to the deceitful lusts; And be renewed in the spirit of your mind. And... put on the new nature, which after *the image of* God is created in righteousness and true holiness. Therefore putting away lying, let every man speak the truth with his neighbor: for we are members one of another. When angry, do not sin: do not let the sun go down on your anger, nor give place to the devil. Let him who stole steal no more: but rather let him labor, working with his own hands that which is good, that he may have something to give to those in need. Let no corrupt communication proceed out of your mouth, but that which is good for building others up as needed, that it may give grace to those who hear. And do not grieve the Holy Spirit of God, by whom you were sealed for the day of redemption. Let all bitterness, and wrath, and anger, and yelling, and evil speaking, be put away from you, with all malice, and be kind to one another tenderhearted, forgiving one another, even as God for Christ's sake has forgiven you" (Ephesians 4:22-32).

"I want you to continually stress these things, so that those who have trusted in God might be careful to maintain good works. Such things are good and beneficial for everyone" (Titus 3:8). For Christ "**Gave Himself for us, that He might redeem us from all iniquity, and purify for Himself a special people, eager** to do good works" (Titus 2:14). "**Therefore, as you abound in everything, in faith, and utterance, and knowledge, and in all diligence, and in your love to us, see that you abound in this gracious giving also**" (2Corinthians 8:7). For "**God is able to make every blessing abound to you; that you, always having everything you need, may abound to every good work**" (2Corinthians 9:8).

"**Do not be deceived; God is not mocked: for whatever a man sows that shall he also reap. For he who sows to his flesh will reap corruption from the flesh; but he who sows to the Spirit will from the Spirit reap everlasting life**" (Galatians 6:7-8).

4. The Reward Of Good Works

The Bible plainly tells us that, "**No one will ever become righteous in God's sight by the works of the law, because the law was given to reveal our sins**" (Romans 3:20, a paraphrase). And, the idea that the law can make us partway righteous, or even a little righteous is blown away by the words, "**Whoever keeps the whole law, yet fails in one point, is guilty of all**" (James 2:10). So, if those who are trying hard to keep that law are "**guilty of all**," it should be obvious that there is nothing we can do, no work that we can perform, that will make us worthy of God's blessing or reward. Therefore, **whenever the Bible speaks of works being rewarded, those rewards only apply to those, "To whom God imputes righteousness without works, saying, Blessed are they whose iniquities are <u>forgiven</u>, and whose sins are covered**," // "**The righteousness that is by faith**" (Romans 4:6-7, Romans 9:30). That being understood let us look at some of the passages that speak of good works and reward.

The words, "**The hour is coming, in which all who are in the graves will hear His voice, And will come out; those who have done good, to the resurrection of life; and those who have done evil, to the resurrection of damnation**," are misunderstood by everyone who assumes that the law is what makes "Those who have done good" good (John 5:28-29). The words, "**If the law could make us righteous, then Christ died for nothing**," tell us that assumption is wrong (Galatians 2:21). In fact, Christ was trying to correct that wrong idea when He said, "**Two men went up to the temple to pray; one a Pharisee, and the other a publican. The Pharisee stood up and prayed thus to himself, God, I thank you, that I am not like other men are, extortioners, evil doers, adulterers, or even like this publican... And the publican, standing afar off, would not even look up to heaven, but beat upon his breast, saying, God be merciful to me a sinner. I tell you that this man went down to his house justified rather than the other" (Luke 18:10-14). Now, as we compare John 5:29 with Luke 18:10-14, the words, "**This man went down to his house justified rather than the other,**" tell us that Christ regarded the publican as one of "**those who have done good,**" but not the Pharisee. That tells us that those who will be counted as having "**done good,**" on the day of judgment, are not those who seek to make themselves righteous through works, but those who humbly acknowledge their sin while looking to Christ for mercy. As it is written, "**God will not despise a heart that is humbled and sorry for sin**" and "**There is therefore now no condemnation for those who are in Christ Jesus**" (Psalm 51:17, Romans 8:1).

Believers who are troubled by the words of John 5:29 [see the preceding paragraph] often wonder why Christ would make a statement that sounds like works righteousness. What they fail to understand is that the words of John 5:29 are law not gospel. And, because they are law, God expects those who read those words to admit their sin and look to God for mercy; as did David who said, "**I have trusted in your mercy, my heart will rejoice in your salvation**" (Psalm 13:5). For all who trust in God's mercy, "**Are not under the law, but under grace**" (Romans 6:14). However, because "**The heart is deceitful above all things,**" most people who read John 5:29 try not to think about it, explain it away, excuse their sins, and hope that they are good enough (Jeremiah 17:9). That sort of self-deception is what Jesus had in mind when He said to Nathaniel, "**Behold an Israelite indeed, in whom is no deceit [self-deception]**" (John 1:47).

The words, "**I have been crucified with Christ: nevertheless I live; yet not I, but Christ lives in me: and the life which I now live in the flesh I live by faith in the Son of God, who loved me, and gave himself for me,**" speak of good works flowing out of the Apostle Paul freely cheerfully and willingly without any coercion (Galatians 2:20). And, that is the way it should be in the life of a believer.

The words, "**If you do not forgive men their trespasses, neither will your Father forgive your trespasses,**" are a warning of the law, not a promise of the gospel (Matthew 6:15). And, that warning should be taken seriously by any church member who holds grudges and refuses to forgive. Not because forgiving is a work that brings grace, but because a refusal to forgive is evidence of an unrepentant heart, and an indication that he is not saved.

The words, "**He who has shown no mercy, will be judged without mercy,**" are again a warning of the law, not a promise of God's mercy (James 2:13). And, that warning should be taken seriously by any church member who shows no mercy (such as one who forecloses on widows' houses, Matt. 23:14). However, the words, "**Without faith it is impossible to please God,**" tell us that being merciful will never get an unbeliever into heaven (Hebrews 11:6). In fact, any good works that we perform before we come to faith in Christ are themselves a gift of God (not something that deserves a reward). Moreover, because our sense of right and wrong, including our conscience, is a gift of God, if there is any good in us it is only there because God put it there, so He deserves the credit for it, not us. On the other hand any bad in us is there because of sin.

The words, "**May the Lord show mercy to the house of Onesiphorus; for he often showed me kindness... May the Lord grant to him that he find mercy with the Lord in that day**," are Paul's prayer for a man who had shown him kindness (2Timothy 1:16-18). The fact that Paul's prayer is for mercy "in that day" suggests that Onesiphorus had not yet joined the church, otherwise there would have been no need for Paul's prayer. At any rate, his act of showing kindness was not a work that automatically brought mercy.

There are many passages in Scripture that speak of reward. However, the words, "**When you have done everything that you were commanded to do, say, We are unworthy servants: for we have only done what it was our duty to do**," tell us that any reward that we receive is a gift of God's grace, not something He owes us (Luke 17:10).

The words, "**And everyone who has left houses, or brothers, or sisters, or father, or mother, or wife, or children, or lands, for my name's sake, will receive a hundredfold, and will inherit everlasting life**," were not written to tell us how to earn eternal life, but to assure those who face adversity for Christ's sake, that God will take care of them, and that what they have to look forward to in heaven is worth far more than anything they give up here (Matthew 19:29).

The words, "**Blessed are you, when men revile you, and persecute you, and say all sort of evil things against you falsely, for my sake. Rejoice, and be very glad: because your reward in heaven is great**," promise a reward (Matthew 5:11-12). However, that reward is not something we earn. On the contrary, the words, "**Kept by the power of God through faith**," tell us that it is only by the grace and power of God that anyone is able to endure persecution (1Peter 1:5). The reward being spoken of is that described in the words, "**The sufferings of this present time are not worthy to be compared with the glory that will be revealed in us**," for "**Eye has not seen, nor ear heard, nor has it entered into the heart of man, the things that God has prepared for those who love Him**" (Romans 8:18, 1Corinthians 2:9).

The words, "**Be careful not to do your good works before men, to be seen by them: otherwise you will have no reward from your Father in heaven**," tell us that God will reward certain things that we do (Matthew 6:1). However, the purpose of this passage is not to tell us how to get those rewards, but to warn us against doing good works to impress others. God wants us to show kindness to others, but that kindness should be an out-flowing of the kindness God has shown us in Christ, not an outward show. And, any reward that God chooses to give us is a gift of His grace, not something we deserve.

The words, "**The wicked man earns a deceitful wage: but the man who sows righteousness receives a sure reward**," promise a reward to the righteous (Proverbs 11:18). While the words, "**The inheritance you will receive from the Lord is a reward: for you serve the Lord Christ**," tell us that heaven itself is our reward, not a reward that we earn but a reward that belongs to all who trust in Christ (Colossians 3:24). Anything beyond that (such as who will sit on Christ's right hand or left) is determined by God, not by what we do. And, the words, "**Let no man swindle you out of your reward through a false humility and the worship of angels, intruding into things that he has not seen, vainly puffed up by his fleshly mind**," are a warning against being led astray (Colossians 2:18).

The words, "**Bring all your tithes into the storehouse, so that there will be food in my house, and prove me in this way, says the LORD of hosts, see if I will not open to you the windows of heaven, and pour out a blessing to you, that there will not be room enough to receive**," speak of God pouring out a blessing (Malachi 3:10). However, that blessing was not something the people deserved, but a blessing that had been withheld because of their stinginess. Sometimes God does pour out a blessing in response to unselfish giving. However, that blessing is not something that comes mechanically because of what we do, or every time we give. It is an expression of God's grace, and "**if by grace, then it is not by works**" (Romans 11:6).

The Beatitudes

The blessings listed in Christ's Sermon on the Mount were never intended to be viewed as works that bring reward. The final one, "**Blessed are those who are persecuted for righteousness' sake**," should make that obvious, since we cannot persecute ourselves (Matthew 5:10). The rest of them all relate to the fruits of repentance and faith.

Consider the words, "**Blessed are the poor in spirit: for theirs is the kingdom of heaven**" (Matt. 5:3). One of the problems that Christ had to deal with was people who derived a false assurance of salvation from their material wealth. They assumed that their wealth was evidence of God's favor. That is what Christ was talking about when He said, "**How hard is it for those who trust in riches to enter the kingdom of God**" (Mark 10:24). In contrast, someone who is poor in spirit is someone who has "**A heart that is humbled and sorry for sin**" (Psalm 51:17). And, because the words, "**In the hope that God will give them repentance**," tell us that repentance is a gift of God's grace, being poor in spirit is a gift of God's grace (2Timothy 2:25).

Consider the words, "**Blessed are those who mourn**" (Matt. 5:4). There are untold millions of unsaved people who mourn, but their mourning brings no blessing. **The only kind of mourning that brings God's blessing has to do with being sorry for your sins**. That is the "**godly sorrow**" that "**results in repentance leading to salvation**" (2Corinthians 7:10).

Consider the words, "**Blessed are the meek: for they will inherit the earth**" (Matt. 5:5). In the parable of the Pharisee and the publican, the Pharisee was proud, and the publican was meek (Luke 18:9-14). And, that is the only kind of meekness that has anything to do with inheriting the earth.

Consider the words, "**Blessed are those who hunger and thirst after righteousness**" (Matt. 5:6). The only people who truly hunger and thirst after righteousness are those who have "**A heart that is humbled and sorry for sin**" (Psalm 51:17)..

Consider the words, "**Blessed are the merciful: for they will obtain mercy**" (Matt. 5:7). The words, "**Scripture has concluded all under sin, that the promise might be given to those who believe, through faith in Jesus Christ**," tell us that the only people who receive God's promise of mercy are those who trust in Christ (Galatians 3:22). Therefore, if someone is merciful, that virtue is itself a gift of God, and a fruit of faith in Christ. At the same time, Christ's words are a warning to any church member who shows no mercy (such as one who forecloses on widows' houses, Matt. 23:14).

The only people who are "**pure in heart**," are those who do not deceive themselves by rationalizing sin, and, therefore, those whose sins have been washed away by the blood of Christ (Matt. 5:8). As it is written, "**By one offering He has perfected for ever those who are sanctified**" (Hebrews 10:14). And, being "**a peacemaker**" is a fruit of faith, that flows from the peace that we have in Christ.

Combating Works Righteousness

As we have seen, the Bible does speak of rewards, but the words, "**All of our righteousnesses are like filthy rags**," and "**Without faith it is impossible to please God**," tell us that we do not deserve anything from God other than His condemnation (Isaiah 64:6, Hebrews 11:6). It is only the forgiveness we have in Christ that changes our status with God. For that reason, any reward that God chooses to give us is a gift of His grace, not something we can earn. That also applies to the "crowns" mentioned in the New Testament. For example: the words, "**Continue in faith unto death, and I will give you a crown of life**," are not telling us how to earn a golden crown (Revelation 2:10). On the contrary, **eternal "life" itself is the crown being spoken of**. And, every believer will receive that crown at death. Likewise, the words, "**When the chief Shepherd appears, you will receive a crown of glory that will never fade away,**" are not telling us how to earn a golden crown (1Peter 5:4). Instead "**glory**" itself is the crown. And, the words, "**the sufferings of this present time are not worthy to be compared with the glory that will be revealed in us,**" tell us that every believer will receive that glory (Romans 8:18). The same holds true for the words, "**A crown of righteousness is reserved for me**" (2Timothy 4:8). Righteousness itself is the crown! And, the words, "**The dead will be raised incorruptible, and we shall be changed. For our corruptible nature must be made incorruptible, and our mortal nature must become immortal,**" tell us that every believer will receive that righteousness at the resurrection (1Corinthians 15:52-53).

5. The Great Value Of Good Works

On one hand, we have to deal with people who want to make God's favor depend on what we do; on the other hand, we have to deal with those who insist that good works are worthless. However, both of those views contradict the Bible. **Just because our works are not good enough or perfect enough to earn God's favor, does not change the fact that they are of great value to other people**. Ask yourself what life would be like if we lived in a world where there were no good works: a world where others were constantly trying to cheat us, steal from us, lie to us, beat us up, and even kill us, a world where everyone lived in fear. The very fact that we do not live in such a world is a gift of God's grace. And, do not assume that I am only talking about good works done by Christians. The words, "**When the Gentiles, who do not have the law, do by nature the things contained in the law, they... show the work of the law written in their hearts,**" tell us that even the unbelievers who do what is right and good, only do so by the grace of God, because He put His law in their heart (Romans 2:14-15). Therefore, even though good works will not save us, they are of great value to all who benefit from those works. In fact it is those works that make it possible for us to "**Lead a quiet and peaceable life in all godliness and honesty**" (1Timothy 2:2).

God uses everyone who does an honest day's work to bless others. God works through the businessman who provides us with good products or reliable services. He works through the car repairman who does a good job without trying to cheat us. When it comes to unbelievers He works through His law, moving them to do what is right while at the same time using that law to show them their sins and need for repentance. And, that is true for believers as well. However, the words, "**It is God who works in you both to will and to do**

His good pleasure," for "**The fruit of the Spirit is love, joy, peace, patience, kindness, goodness, faith, meekness, self-control: against such there is no law,**" tell us that the Holy Spirit works within believers to produce even more good works [i.e. fruit] (Philippians 2:13, Galatians 5:22-23).

The words, "**You are the light of the world. A city that is on a hill cannot be hidden. Nor do they light a lamp, and put it under a basket, instead they put it on a stand; and it gives light to everyone in the house. Let your light so shine before men, that they may see your good works, and glorify your Father who is in heaven,**" tell us that the works God produces in us should be a light to the world (Matthew 5:14-16).

The words, "**We are His workmanship, created in Christ Jesus for good works, that God determined in advance that we should do,**" tell us that God has determined in advance what He would accomplish through us. (Ephesians 2:10). That means that we do not have to figure out what His plan for our life is. If we tried we would probably get it wrong. As long as we walk in a clean conscience, leading "**A quiet and peaceable life in all godliness and honesty,**" God will work out His plan in our life (1Timothy 2:2).

The words, "**The truth of the gospel... has come to you, bringing forth fruit in you, as in all the world, since the day you heard it, and knew the truth of God's grace,**" tell us that God's work in us began as soon as we came to faith in Christ (Colossians 1:5-6).

The words, "**The grace of God that brings salvation has appeared to all men, Teaching us that, denying ungodliness and worldly lusts, we should live soberly, righteously, and godly, in this present world; Looking for that blessed hope, and the glorious appearing of our great God and Savior Jesus Christ; Who gave Himself for us, that He might redeem us from all iniquity, and purify for Himself a special people, eager to do good works,**" mention God's desire for us to do good works (Titus 2:11-14).

The words, "**Instruct those who are rich in this world, not to think highly of themselves, or trust in uncertain riches, but to trust in the living God, who richly gives us all things to enjoy. And that they do good, and are rich in good deeds, glad to give and to share, and show friendliness,**" urge those who have been blessed to show the love of Christ in their lives (1Timothy 6:17-19).

The words, "**I heard a voice from heaven saying, Write, Blessed are the dead who die in the Lord from now on: Yes, says the Spirit, that they may rest from their labor; for their deeds follow them,**" tell us that our deeds will follow us (Revelation 14:13). That may include many things that we were unaware of. Things we said or did that seemed to be ignored at the time, but that

God used. My point is that everything God does through us has value. **So we should never say that Good works are worthless.** Nothing done by God (either through us or through His law inscribed on the heart) is worthless!

6. Perversion Of The Doctrine Of Good Works

Having looked at what the Bible says about good works, the purpose of this section is to look at four ways that Satan attacks and perverts the truth of Scripture regarding works. Those four perversions consist of: **1-** making righteousness and salvation depend on works; **2-** teaching that we can sin willfully and live in sin and still be saved; **3-** teaching that our standing with God depends upon our obedience to men (leaders) and their commandments; **4-** and teaching that leaders are to be obeyed even if they tell you to do something wrong.

First of all, the Bible plainly tells us that we are cleansed of sin and made righteous in the sight of God and saved through the blood that Christ shed on the cross, and the forgiveness that is ours through faith in Him. The words, "**The blood of Jesus Christ His Son cleanses us of all sin,**" tell us that our sin is removed by what Christ did, by His blood (1John 1:7). The words, "**Being now justified by His blood, we shall be saved from wrath through Him,**" tell us that the same blood that "**cleanses us of all sin**" makes us just [i.e. righteous] and **saves us "from wrath"** (Romans 5:9). The words, "**We have redemption through His blood, the forgiveness of sins, according to the riches of <u>His grace</u>**," tell us that the forgiveness we have "**through His blood**" is ours through "**His grace**" (Ephesians 1:7). And, the words, "**If by grace, then is it no longer by works: if it were grace would no longer be grace. For if it is by works, then it is no longer by grace: otherwise work is no longer work,**" plainly tell us that grace is not a work (Romans 11:6). Anyone who rejects these truths is teaching a false gospel, and is, therefore, an antichrist [See Galatians 1:6-9, Romans 3:20-28 and 5:1, Luke 1:77, Acts 10:43.]

Secondly, the Bible plainly tells us that we cannot continue a sinful lifestyle, sinning willfully, and still be saved. [Historically that heresy is known as antinomianism.] The words "**Some slanderously claim that we say, Let us do evil, that good may come. Whose damnation is just,**" tell us that those who continue in sin without repentance will be damned (Romans 3:8). The words, "**Whoever believes that Jesus is the promised Savior is born of God,**" tell us that all who believe in Christ are "**born of God**" (1John 5:1). And, the words, "**Whoever has been born of God does not continue in sin,**" tell us that those who are born of God **do not continue** a sinful lifestyle (1John 3:9). While the words, "**Walk in the Spirit, and you will not fulfill the lust of the flesh. For the flesh lusts against the Spirit, and the Spirit against the flesh: and they are opposed to each other: so that you cannot do the things that you would,**" tell us that the Spirit is at work within us to help us overcome temptation (Galatians 5:16-17). At the same time the words, "**I buffet my body, and bring it under my control: lest there be any way that I, after having preached to others, might be rejected,**" warn us of the importance of fighting against the flesh (1Corinthians 9:27). While the words, "**Anyone who despised Moses' law died without mercy on the testimony of two or three witnesses: How much more severely, do you think a man deserves to be punished, who has trampled the Son of God under foot, treated the blood of the covenant, by which he was sanctified, as an unholy thing, and insulted the Spirit of grace? For we know Him who said, Vengeance belongs to me, I will repay, says the Lord. And again, The Lord will judge His people. It is a fearful thing to fall into the hands of the living God,**" warn all who think that they can continue a sinful lifestyle without repentance of God's wrath (Hebrews 10:28-31).

Thirdly, the Bible strongly **warns us against, "Teaching for doctrines the commandments of men"** (Matthew 15:9). While on one hand we are instructed to "**Listen to those who lead the congregation, and follow their guidance: for they watch for your souls,**" the fact that overseers are **not to be "lords over God's heritage,"** but "**examples to the flock,**" tells us that the authority of leaders is to teach people what the Bible says, not to exalt themselves (Hebrews 13:17, 1Peter 5:3). Therefore, any Church or church leader who demands to be "obeyed" is in rebellion against God. And, the words, "**Paying no attention to… the commandments of men, who have turned from the truth,**" tell us that **those who teach the "commandments of men" are leading their followers away from God's Word and thus away from the truth, so we are not to pay any attention to them** (Titus 1:14).

Fourthly, some false prophets and cult leaders are so deeply under the influence of Satan that they tell their followers that they are to obey the leadership, even if they are told to do something evil. In contrast, the Bible plainly tells us that, "**We ought to obey God rather than men**" (Acts 5:29). The words, "**Beware of false prophets, who come to you in sheep's clothing,**" warn us against listening to false teachers (Matthew 7:15). The words, "**I speak as to wise men; judge for yourselves what I say,**" tell us that we are to judge what we are being taught (1Corinthians 10:15). The words, "**If they do not speak according to this word, it is because there is no light in them,**" tell us that if they contradict the Bible [by telling us to obey them rather than God] they are in spiritual darkness (Isaiah 8:20). And, the words, "Those who know God accept what we [the inspired writers of Scripture] say; those who are not of God will not accept what we say. **That is how we can distinguish the spirit of truth from the spirit of error**," tell us that those who refuse to hear the word of God [by telling people to do something sinful] do not have the Holy Spirit, and thus are unsaved, and should be regarded as antichrists (1John 4:6).

The Index Oeneralis [of the Jesuit order] declares expressly: "The superiors may obligate [members] to sin by virtue of the obedience (which is due them), provided this will confer great benefits." (Cp. Index Oeneralis, Vol. II, sub Obedient tiae et Obedire; also, Christl. Dogmatik, III, p. 80ff.)

Sanctification And The Christian Life

1. The Christian Life And The Cross

As Christians every blessing of God is ours, for, "**You are all the children of God through faith in Christ Jesus**," // "**And if children, then heirs; heirs of God, and joint-heirs with Christ**," (Galatians 3:26, Romans 8:17). Furthermore, much of what God has in store for us, "**Has not yet been revealed**" (1John 3:2). So we have much to look forward to. Nevertheless, **Christ has warned us to expect persecution**, saying, "**I send you forth like sheep in the midst of wolves.**" // "**If the world hates you, you know that it hated me before it hated you**" (Matthew 10:16, John 15:18). The words, "**The apostles left the presence of the Sanhedrin, rejoicing that they were counted worthy to suffer shame for His name**," tell us that it is an honor to suffer for Christ's sake (Acts 5:41). And, He has called any hardship or persecution that we endure for His sake our "cross," saying, "**If any man will come after me, let him deny himself, and take up his cross, and follow me.**" // "**Anyone who does not bear his cross, and follow me, cannot be my disciple**" (Matthew 16:24, Luke 14:27).

However, it is important to understand that the Bible only uses the word "cross" in reference to the suffering of believers. While the words, "**The sorrows of those who choose another god will be multiplied**" and "**Many are the sorrows of the wicked**," tell us that the wicked suffer many things, the Bible never calls the suffering of the wicked a "cross" (Psalm 16:4 and 32:10).

The following words describe some of the things that believers may be called on to endure for Christ's sake. "**I send you forth like sheep in the midst of wolves: therefore be as wise as serpents, and** harmless as doves. But beware of men: for they will hand you over to their courts, and they will scourge you in their synagogues; And you will be brought before governors and kings for my sake, as a testimony to them and to the Gentiles... And brother will deliver up brother to death, and a father his child: and children will rise up against their parents, and cause them to be put to death. And you will be hated by all men for my name's sake: but he who endures to the end will be saved" (Matthew 10:16-22).

Throughout history, many believers have suffered in that way, and many are suffering today. But, the persecution seems to be most fierce when the Holy Spirit is bringing a nation to faith, and Satan is fighting against it tooth and claw – such as when the Holy Spirit brought the Roman empire to faith. Nevertheless, there is always a certain level of persecution, even if it is sometimes more subtle. However, we should never confuse the cross that we may be called on to bear with the punishment or chastening for sin.

The words, **"The Lord disciplines those He loves"** and **"When we are judged, we are chastened by the Lord, so that we will not be condemned with the world,"** tell us that God sometimes does chasten His people (Hebrews 12:6, 1Corinthians 11:32). Job was chastened in order to keep him from becoming self righteous. In contrast, when we suffer for Christ's sake we are being attacked by Satan, Christ Himself endured Satan's wrath. However, just as God used Satan's attack on Christ to defeat Satan (winning salvation for all); **God will use Satan's attacks on us to spread the gospel.** That is why the blood of the martyrs has always resulted in more converts. God wants the world to know that Christianity will triumph, **"Not by might, nor by power, but by"** His **"Spirit"** (Zechariah 4:6). And, in all of this we have God's own promise that, **"All things work together for good for those who love God,"** and that includes both chastening, and any cross that we might bear (Romans 8:28).

There are many passages of Scripture which tell us that God blesses those who are persecuted for Christ's sake. The words, **"If you are reproached for the name of Christ, you are blessed; for the Spirit of glory and of God rests upon you: on their part He is blasphemed, but on your part He is glorified,"** tell us that if we suffer reproach for His sake we are blessed (1Peter 4:14). The words, "Blessed are you, when men revile you, and persecute you, and say all sort of evil things against you falsely, for my sake. Rejoice, and be very glad: because your reward in heaven is great: for that is how they persecuted the prophets who were before you," again associate persecution with blessing (Matthew 5:11-12). The words, **"The sufferings of this present time are not worthy to be compared with the glory that will be revealed in us,"** tell us that what God has in store for us is worth more than all the riches in the world (Romans 8:18). The words, **"Our light affliction, which lasts but a moment, is preparing for us an eternal glory that is far beyond all comparison,"** again speak of the great glory that God has in store for us (2Corinthians 4:17). The words, **"If your enemy is hungry, feed him; if he is thirsty, give him drink: for in so doing you will heap coals of fire on his head,"** tell us how we should deal with persecution (Romans 12:20). And, the words, **"Seeing it is a righteous thing with God to recompense tribulation to them that trouble you,"** tell us that when we return good for evil God will "recompense tribulation" to those who persecute you – as the Spirit works to bring them to repentance (2Thessalonians 1:6). [Pastor Richard Wurmbrant, who was tortured for Christ by Marxists, told of persecutors who came to faith, and then were themselves tortured.]

The words, **"Blessed be the God and Father of our Lord Jesus Christ, the Father of mercies, and the God of all comfort; Who comforts us in every trial, so that we are able to comfort others who are suffering, with the same comfort that God gives to us,"** tell us that God will comfort us in every trial, in a way that will help us to comfort others (2Corinthians 1:3-4). The words, **"I delight in weaknesses, in insults, in hardships, in persecutions, and difficulties for Christ's sake: for when I am weak, then am I strong,"** tell us that even when we are at our weakest, God is at work strengthening us (2Corinthians 12:10). The words, **"God who is faithful, will not allow you to be tempted beyond what you can bear; but when you are tempted, He will also provide a way out, giving you the ability to bear it,"** tell us that God will not let us receive greater temptation than we can bear (1Corinthians 10:13). The words, **"My sheep hear my voice, and I know them... And I give to them eternal life; and they will never perish, neither will any man pluck them out of my hand,"** tell us that no one will ever be able to take away our faith (John 10:27-28). And, the words, we **"Are kept by the power of God through faith unto salvation,"** tell us that we are kept by the power of God Himself "unto salvation" (1Peter 1:5). [If you face persecution; instead of wondering if you will have the strength to bear it, look to God's grace for strength, confident that **God "is able to keep you from falling"** (Jude 1:24).]

Having said this it should be obvious that we should never try to impose crosses upon ourselves, as a way of gaining God's favor, for that is just another form of works righteousness. This warning is only necessary because in the past there have been monks, hermits and others who have spent years sitting on a pole, refraining from talking to anyone, inflicting torture on themselves, wearing a hair shirt and so forth, in a vain attempt to atone for their own sins. They are all condemned by the words, **"Being ignorant of God's righteousness, and seeking to establish their own righteousness, they have** not submitted to the righteousness of God. For Christ is the end of the law for righteousness to every one who believes" (Romans 10:3-4).

The following words give us a good summary of how God wants those of us who trust in Christ to live. "**All of you should be like-minded, sympathetic, loving each other as brothers, being compassionate, and courteous: Not rendering evil for evil, or insult for insult: but instead bless; knowing that you were called for this purpose, that you should inherit a blessing. For let him who wants to enjoy life, and see good days, keep his tongue from evil, and his lips from uttering deception: Let him shun evil, and do good; let him seek peace, and pursue it. For the eyes of the Lord are upon the righteous, and His ears are open to their prayers: but the face of the Lord is against those who do evil. Who will harm you, if you are eager to do good? But if you do suffer for righteousness' sake, you are blessed: do not fear their intimidation, and do not be troubled; But in your hearts acknowledge Christ as Lord: and be ready at all times to answer everyone who asks you to explain the hope that is in you, answering gently and respectfully: Keeping a clean conscience; so that those who continue to speak against you may be ashamed, as they slander your good behavior in Christ. It is better, if it is the will of God, for you to suffer for doing right, than for doing wrong**" (1Peter 3:8-17). Keeping those words in mind, and remembering that Satan not only attacks us through the world, but also through our own flesh, let us run the race set before us keeping our eyes always on "**The cross of our Lord Jesus Christ**" (Galatians 6:14).

2. The Christian Life And Prayer

For a Christian, prayer is not a work! We are not doing God a favor by praying to Him. On the contrary, He is doing us a favor by allowing us to approach Him in prayer. And, any answer that we receive is not a reward for praying, but a gift of His grace.

Because those who are lost do not have any assurance of God's grace, they tend to be afraid of God. In contrast, we who know the love of Christ have His own assurance that our prayers will be heard. The words, "**They [Adam and Eve] heard the voice of the LORD God walking in the garden in the cool of the day: and Adam and his wife hid themselves**," reveal the natural inclination of those who have done wrong to hide from God (Genesis 3:8). In contrast, the words, "**Whatever you ask the Father in my name, He will give to you. Up to now you have not asked anything in my name: ask, and you will receive, that your joy may be full... For the**

Father Himself loves you," assure all who trust in Christ that because their sins have been washed away, God will hear their prayers (John 16:23-27). Furthermore, praying in Christ's name is not just a matter of tacking the words, "in Christ's name" on the end of a prayer, but approaching God in the confidence that your prayer will be heard because your sins have been washed away by the blood of Christ. As it is written, "**Christ is the end of the law for righteousness to every one who believes,**" for "**The blood of Jesus Christ His Son cleanses us of all sin**" (Romans 10:4, 1John 1:7).

The words, "**Since the children have flesh and blood, He [Christ] in the same way took on flesh and blood; so that through His death He might destroy him who holds the power of death, that is, the devil; And free those, who throughout their lives were enslaved by fear of death**," tell us that those without the assurance of forgiveness in Christ live in fear of death (Hebrews 2:14-15). While the words, "**You have not received the spirit of bondage again to fear; but you have received the Spirit of adoption, whereby we cry, Abba, Father**," tell us that while those who are under the law [bondage] are motivated by fear, we can approach God without fear, as a child approaches a loving Father (Romans 8:15). For that reason, Christian prayer presupposes a relationship between God and man that only those who have been born again have. And, the words, "**Whoever believes that Jesus is the promised Savior is born of God**," tell us that we are "born of God" [born again] through faith in Christ (1John 5:1).

Therefore, Christian prayer involves more than just dependence on God. Why even the heathen can be dependent on their gods. However, as Christians we have no need to fear God [unless we do evil] or appease His wrath [Christ has already taken care of that]. We come to God as to a friend, a loving Father, who cares for us. And, if you do not know what to say, just talk to Him about it. Thank Him for forgiveness, thank Him for His blessings, ask for His help in dealing with life's difficulties, ask for wisdom and greater faith, pray for those in authority, think of Him as a constant companion, and no matter what happens keep in mind the words, "**All things work together for good for those who love God**" (Romans 8:28).

The words, "**Whatever you ask in prayer, believing, you will receive**," give us a promise on condition of faith (Matthew 21:22). However, the faith being spoken of is not just a matter of believing it will happen, but **believing that "the blood of Jesus Christ" has cleansed you "of all sin"** (1John 1:7). For, the forgiveness that you have in Christ includes forgiveness for any imperfection in your prayer. Now, the words, "**If we ask anything according to His will, He hears us**," tell us that our prayer has to be in accord with the will of God (1John 5:14). But that does not mean that we need to figure out what the will of God is. On the contrary, the words, "**The Spirit** also helps our weakness: for we do not know what we should pray for as we should: but the Spirit Himself makes intercession for us," assure us that the Holy Spirit will move us to pray for those things that are in accord with the will of God (Romans 8:26). And, the words, "**Continue steadfast in prayer, being watchful therein with thanksgiving,**" urge us to pray for help before problems arise (Colossians 4:2).

The words, "**Seek the welfare of the city to which I have caused you to be taken... and pray to the LORD for it: for when it fares well it will be well with you,**" tell us that it is God's will for us to pray for our land (Jeremiah 29:7). The words, "**I urge that requests, prayers, intercession, and giving of thanks, be made on behalf of all men; For kings, and for all who are in authority; so that we may lead a quiet and peaceable life in all godliness and honesty. For this is good and acceptable in the sight of God our Savior,**" tell us that it is God's will for us to make those requests necessary for us to "lead a quiet and peaceable life in all godliness and honesty" (1Timothy 2:1-3). And, the words, "**Pray without ceasing.**" // "**Praying always with all prayer and supplication in the Spirit,**" are not telling us to pray twenty four hours a day, but are telling us not to give up on prayer, or stop praying and seeking God's help (1Thessalonians 5:17, Ephesians 6:18).

The words, "**Pray to the Lord of the harvest, asking Him to send forth workers into His harvest,**" tell us that the Lord expects our prayers to play a part in world evangelism (Matthew 9:38). Therefore, we know that such prayers are in accord with the will of God. The words, "**When you said, Seek my face; my heart said to you, I will seek your face, LORD,**" tell us that the Holy Spirit, which is in every believer, makes us responsive to the will of God, and that would include being responsive in prayer (Psalm 27:8). The words, Pray "**for me, that utterance might be given unto me, that I may open my mouth fearlessly, to make known the mystery of the gospel,**" tell us that it is God's will for us to pray for those who spread the gospel (Ephesians 6:19). The words, "**Pray for us, that the word of the Lord may continue to spread, and be received and honored, even as it is with you,**" tell us that it is God's will for us to pray that the gospel be received and embraced by those who hear (2Thessalonians 3:1). And, the words, "**I urge you, brethren, for the sake of our Lord Jesus Christ, and by the love of the Spirit, that you strive with me in your prayers to God on my behalf; That I may be delivered from those in Judea who do not believe,**" tell us that it is the will of God for us to pray for God's protection for those who spread the gospel (Romans 15:30-31).

The words, "**Whatever you ask in my name, I will do, so that the Father may be glorified in the Son,**" tell us that God is glorified by answered prayer (John 14:13). And, the words, "**Ask, and it** will be given to you; seek, and you will find; knock, and it will be opened to you: For every one who asks receives; and he who seeks finds; and to him who knocks it will be opened," encourage us to pray for every need (Matthew 7:7-8). However, Christ's prayer, "**O my Father, if it is possible, let this cup be taken from me: nevertheless not as I will, but as you will,**" tells us that we should want our prayer to be answered in the way God thinks best (Matthew 26:39).

It should be obvious that God will not hear prayers addressed to false gods, as the words, "**They are all estranged from me through their idols,**" indicate (Ezekiel 14:5). However, the words, "**If I make excuses for sin in my heart, the Lord will not hear me,**" tell us that God will also not hear the prayers of those who are unrepentant (Psalm 66:18). Of course that can change if a person repents, as the words, "**If we confess our sins, He is faithful and just to forgive us our sins, and to cleanse us from all unrighteousness,**" tell us (1John 1:9).

The Bible also says, "**When you pray, do not use empty repetitions, as the heathen do: for they think that they will be heard because of their many words**" (Matthew 6:7). This verse is not talking about regular use of the Lord's Prayer. What this verse is talking about, is repeating a prayer over and over again. Because those who worship idols have no assurance that their prayer will be answered – to use modern terminology – they keep repeating their prayer in the hope that they will hit on a time when the line isn't busy.

Although the Bible speaks of people praying in different positions the Bible does not require us to be in a specific position. The words, "**He arose from before the altar of the LORD, from kneeling on his knees with his hands spread up to heaven,**" speak of kneeling in prayer with hands uplifted (1Kings 8:54). The words, "**Abram fell on his face: and God talked with him,**" speak of praying face down (Genesis 17:3). And, the words, "**A little folding of the hands to sleep**" mention folding the hands before going to sleep (Proverbs 24:33). Likewise, the Bible does not tell us how to pray. The words, "**The effectual fervent prayer of a righteous man can accomplish much,**" speak of fervent prayer, yet it would be wrong to assume that you can manipulate God by faking fervency (James 5:16). The seventeenth chapter of John records a prayer in which Christ talked with God. In the garden of Gethsemane, Jesus pleaded with God (Matthew 26:36, Luke 22:44). Yet when His disciples asked Him to teach them to pray, He gave them the Lord's Prayer (Matthew 6:9-13). And, its use of plural words [i.e. **OUR** Father] indicates that it is to be a group prayer. Reciting group prayers was a part of Jewish worship that Jesus never criticized. All of that tells us that many kinds of prayer are acceptable to God, and each of them has its place. I might also add that our prayers do not need to be loud or even audible to those around us. We should pray throughout the day, even if our prayers are quietly whispered as we speak to God in our heart.

Finally, Christians have no business praying to saints. The words, "Surely you are our father, <u>even though Abraham does not know us</u>, and Israel does not recognize us: you, O LORD, are our father, our redeemer; your name is from everlasting," tell us that saints – namely Abraham and Israel – are not even aware of us (Isaiah 63:16). The words, **"I fell down to worship before the feet of the angel that showed me these things. And he said to me, Do not do it: for I am your fellow servant, and of your brethren the prophets… worship God,"** warn us not to pray to anyone other than God (Revelation 22:8-9). And, the words, **"Whatever you ask the Father in my name, He will give to you,"** assure us that God hears our prayers (John 16:23). The idea of praying to saints [or asking them to pray] was invented by Satan to keep people from seeking God's help and forgiveness. The proponents of that heresy not only keep people from praying to God, they destroy faith by telling them that the saints are more willing to hear their prayers than God is. That heresy is refuted by the words, **"God so loved the world, that He gave His only begotten Son, that whosoever believes on Him should not perish, but have everlasting life,"** which tell us that God loves us far more than any of the saints ever could (John 3:16). Besides, those who claim that a saint can be present to hear their prayer and know what they are saying are ascribing divine attributes to that saint, which is idolatrous. **Christian prayer is made to God alone, and is heard because, "The blood of Jesus Christ His Son" has cleansed "us of all sin"** (1John 1:7).

Our Father in heaven,
May your name be exalted.
May your kingdom come.
And your will be done on earth, as it is in heaven.
Give us this day our daily bread.
And forgive us our wrongs, as we forgive those who wrong us.
Lead us not into temptation, but deliver us from evil:
For the kingdom, the power, and the glory is yours forever,
Amen.

3. The Christian Life And The Hope Of Eternal Life

As Christians, **"We should live soberly, righteously, and godly, in this present world; Looking for that blessed hope, and the glorious appearing of our great God and Savior Jesus Christ, who gave Himself for us"** (Titus 2:12-14). However, because Christ, **"Will judge the living and the dead at His appearing,"** the only

Christians who can look forward to His appearing with eager expectation, **are those who know that they will not be condemned because, "The blood of Jesus Christ... cleanses us of all sin"** (2Timothy 4:1, 1John 1:7). As it is written, **"There is therefore now no condemnation for those who are in Christ Jesus,"** // **"For Christ is the end of the law for righteousness to every one who believes"** (Romans 8:1 and 10:4).   All who have that blessed hope, **"Wait eagerly for the coming of our Lord Jesus Christ"** (1Corinthians 1:7). **"Knowing that, while we are at home in the body, we are absent from the Lord,"** and that **"To be with Christ... is far better"** (2Corinthians 5:6, Philippians 1:23). For, **"It is written, Eye has not seen, nor ear heard, nor has it entered into the heart of man, the things that God has prepared for those who love Him"** (1Corinthians 2:9).

Because our sins have been washed away by **"the blood of Jesus Christ,"** // **"our citizenship is in heaven"** (1John 1:7, Philippians 3:20). And, **"Because of the hope that is laid up for"** us **"in heaven,"** we look forward to being there with Christ (Colossians 1:5). The words, **"I urge you as strangers and pilgrims in the world, to abstain from fleshly lusts, that war against your soul,"** remind us that heaven is our home (1Peter 2:11). The words, **"We do not have any permanent city here, but we seek one to come,"** tell us that **"the Jerusalem which is above,"** is our eternal city (Hebrews 13:14, Galatians 4:26). The words, **"The world as we know it will pass away,"** remind us that the life we are experiencing now is only temporary (1Corinthians 7:31). The words, **"Let your kindness be known to all men. The Lord may come at anytime,"** remind us that we do not know when Christ will come, just as we do not know when our death will be (Philippians 4:5). Therefore we should be ready. As it is written, **"No one knows the day and hour, no, not even the angels of heaven"** (Matthew 24:36). And, the words, **"The sufferings of this present time are not worthy to be compared with the glory that will be revealed in us,"** remind us again of why we should look forward to being with Christ (Romans 8:18).

Having that hope, and knowing that **"The coming of the Lord draws near,"** should motivate us to **conduct ourselves, "In a manner worthy of the gospel of Christ,"** in a way that is **"Above reproach,"** so that those who do not believe, **"May see the good that you do, and glorify God in the day of visitation"** (James 5:8, Philippians 1:27, 1Peter 2:12).

ALL GLORY TO GOD ALONE

THE DOCTRINE OF THE MEANS OF GRACE
(De Medlis Gratiae)

1. Identifying The Means Of Grace

Speaking of Christ, the Apostle Paul said, "**We have redemption through His blood, the forgiveness of sins, according to the riches of His grace**" (Ephesians 1:7). Those words tell us that we have been redeemed through Christ's "blood" [the blood He shed on the cross], a redemption consisting of forgiveness given to us freely "according to the riches of His grace" – "**not of works, lest any man should boast**" (Ephesians 2:9). As it is written, "**The wages of sin is death; but the gift of God is eternal life through Jesus Christ our Lord**" (Romans 6:23). The doctrine of the means of grace looks at how the forgiveness won for us by Christ's death on the cross is applied to our life and becomes ours.

In the past, one of Satan's tricks has been to make "works" [something we do] into a means of grace. However, the words, "**If by grace, then is it no longer by works: if it were grace would no longer be grace. For if it is by works, then it is no longer by grace: otherwise work is no longer work**," plainly tell us that grace excludes works (Romans 11:6). We "**are saved by grace through faith**" (Ephesians 2:8). Furthermore the Bible tells us that, "**The gospel... is the power of God to salvation to every one who believes**" (Romans 1:16). Therefore, **the gospel is the means of grace!** Of that truth Dr. Edward Koehler said, "There is but one means by which the knowledge of grace and salvation, and grace and salvation itself, are imparted to us; it is the Gospel, the glad tidings of the grace of God in Christ Jesus." ("A Summary of Christian Doctrine," pages 189-190.)

In his epistle to the Galatians, the Apostle Paul identifies the means of grace as God's promise of forgiveness in Christ. He begins by telling us that the Word, "**Proclaimed the gospel to Abraham in advance**" (Galatians 3:8). Those words tell us that Abraham knew the gospel, **the glorious news that, "Christ died for our sins... And that He was buried, and that He rose again the third day according to the scriptures**" (1Corinthians 15:3-4). In fact, the words, "**By faith Abraham, when he was tried, offered up Isaac... Accounting that God was able to raise him up, even from the dead**," tell us that Abraham was willing to sacrifice his son because of his belief that his descendant would die as a sacrifice for sin and that God would raise him from the dead (Hebrews 11:17-19). That fact tells us that God did not ask Abraham to sacrifice his son as some morbid test of subservience, but as a witness to us of Abraham's faith in God's promise of forgiveness in Christ – as well as a way of telling Abraham that Isaac was not the one who would die for the sins of the world. Then, many years later, Zacharias described the good news of forgiveness in Christ as, **"the knowledge of salvation by the remission of their sins, Through the tender mercy of our God"** (Luke 1:77-78). God's promise of forgiveness in Christ is the means of grace. And, the words, **"Those who have faith in Christ are blessed with Abraham, who also believed,"** tell us that faith is the hand that receives the forgiveness God offers (Galatians 3:9). As it is written, **"We have access by faith into this grace"** (Romans 5:2).

2. The Means Of Grace In General

The Bible tells us that we are saved, **"By grace through faith,"** faith in God's promise of forgiveness in Christ. (Ephesians 2:8). However there are many ways in which God gives us that promise.

The words, **"God... has committed to us the word of reconciliation... as if God were appealing to you by us,"** speak of oral communication as a way that God uses to give us His promise of forgiveness in Christ (2Corinthians 5:19-20). The words, **"It pleased God to save those who believe through the foolishness of preaching,"** speak of preaching as a specific kind of oral communication (1Corinthians 1:21). The words, **"These are written, that you might believe that Jesus is the Messiah, the Son of God; and that believing you might have life through His name,"** speak of the written word as a way in which God communicates His promise (John 20:31). And, the words, **"The gospel of Christ... is the power of God to salvation to every one who believes,"** tell us that the power of God works through the gospel, in whatever form it is communicated (Romans 1:16).

However, the words, **"All the promises of God in Him are yea, and in Him Amen, to the glory of God,"** tell us that faith in Christ brings us everything that God has promised us (2Corinthians 1:20). And, if every promise of forgiveness or salvation that God gives is received by faith in Christ, that means that every promise of forgiveness and salvation that God gave to His people during the Old Testament era, was a promise of forgiveness in Christ. In fact that is exactly what the Apostle Paul was trying to explain when he said, **"The covenant *concerning faith* in Christ, that was confirmed by God at the time of Abraham, cannot be nullified by the law, which came four hundred and thirty years later, so as to make the promise of no effect. For if the inheritance comes by the law, it is not given by promise: but God gave it to Abraham by promise"** (Galatians 3:17-18). Paul goes on to explain that, **"The law was our** schoolmaster to bring us to Christ, that we might be declared righteous by faith" (Galatians 3:24). **Notice the reference to faith in Christ!** The law consisted of two parts. 1-The purpose of the commandments and warnings was **"the knowledge of sin,"** (Romans 3:20). 2-The purpose of the sacrifices and offerings was to give God's people His promise of forgiveness. However, because there is no forgiveness apart from faith in Christ, and because God instituted those sacrifices as a way of pointing people to Christ, the words, **"All the promises of God in Christ are yea, and in Him Amen"** tell us that God counted faith in the promise of forgiveness He had connected with those sacrifices as faith in Christ (2Cor. 1:20).

The same holds true for the serpent **"Moses lifted up...in the wilderness"** (John 3:14). Because God told Moses to make the serpent as a type of Christ, His promise of deliverance to all who would look upon it was a promise of deliverance in Christ, and He counted faith in that promise as faith in Christ (Compare Numbers 21:6-9 with John 3:14).

For us today, that means that any promise of forgiveness that God has connected with baptism or the Lord's Supper is a promise of forgiveness in Christ. And, **that means that any forgiveness that is promised to us in Scripture comes to us through faith in Christ**, not because the ceremony has any power. The power is in the gospel [God's promise of forgiveness in Christ] connected with the ceremony, not in the ceremony itself. Martin Luther and his coworker Philip Melanchthon explained it this way.

"**The first thing in baptism to be considered is the divine promise**, which says: " He that believes and is baptized shall be saved... **The second part of baptism is the sign**, or sacrament, which is that immersion into water from this also it derives its name. For the Greek baptizo means "I immerse," and baptisma means "immersion." For, as has been said, signs are added to the divine promises to represent that which the words signify" This promise must be set far above all the glitter of works, vows, religious orders, and whatever man has added to it." (Martin Luther, from *"The Babylonian Captivity of the Church"*.)

"I have said that the gospel is the promise of grace. Moreover next to promises is the place of signs. For in the Scripture signs are added to the promises for a mark. These signs remind us of the promises and are sure testimonies of the divine will toward us. They also bear witness that of a certainty we will receive what God has promised unto us... Signs do not justify, as Paul says in I Corinthians 7:19: "Circumcision is nothing," and so baptism and participation in the Lord's table are nothing but witnesses of the divine will toward you. And your conscience, if at all in doubt, is rendered certain by them of the grace and benevolence of God toward it. As Hezekiah could not doubt the fact that he would recover when he had both heard the promise and had seen it confirmed by a sign; as Gideon could not doubt the fact that he would be a victor, when he was confirmed by so many signs; just so, ought you not doubt the fact that you have attained mercy, when you have heard the gospel preached and received its baptism, and the body and blood of the Lord. But if you will, Hezekiah could have been restored to his health even without a sign had he been willing only to believe the bare promise. Likewise Gideon would have been victorious without a sign, if he had believed. So you can be justified without a sign provided you believe." (Philip Melanchthon, "*The Loci Communes,*" 1521 edition.)

God intends for baptism and the Lord's Supper to work together with the preaching of the Word, not as works, but as ceremonial proclamations of the gospel. On the day of Pentecost, every Jewish man who stepped forward to be baptized was saying by his action that he believed that Jesus was the promised Messiah, and that there was forgiveness in Him. Baptism then, was God's way of telling each of those men that He had washed away his sin. So rightly understood, being baptized was an act of faith on the part of each man who came forward, not an act of obedience. Those who were baptized were never commanded to be baptized. Peter's words, "Repent, and be baptized," were the answer to a question, not a command. And an answer to a question is never imperative (Acts 2:38). In the same way, every man who comes to the Lord's Supper, believing what Christ said, namely that Christ's body was "given" for him [on the cross], and that Christ's blood was "shed" for him [on the cross] comes as an act of faith. And, through faith he truly does receive Christ's body and blood, not as something physical, but as the atonement for his sin.

3. Errors Regarding The Means Of Grace

The words, "**Be sober, be vigilant; because your adversary the devil, prowls around like a roaring lion, looking for someone to devour,**" are a warning that Satan will do everything he can to thwart, and subvert the means of grace (1Peter 5:8). And, over the centuries he has come up with dozens of ways to make the means God has put in place ineffective.

Those who carry out one of his attacks deny that God needs any means. And, it may be true that God does not need means. However, the Bible plainly tells us that God uses means. The words, "**Faith comes by hearing, and hearing by the word of God,**" tell us that the Word of God is the means of grace (Romans 10:17). And, that verse is preceded by the words, "**How shall they believe in Him of whom they have not heard? And how shall they hear without a preacher?**" (Romans 10:14). Now, it is true that God spoke to Abraham directly. And, it is written, "**Abraham believed God, and it was counted to him for righteousness**" (Romans 4:3). But, the words, "**Scripture, having foreseen that God would justify the heathen through faith, proclaimed the gospel to Abraham in advance,**" tell us even with Abraham God used means, namely "the gospel" (Galatians 3:8).

That brings us to those who deny that the written or spoken Word is needed. Instead of pointing people to God's promise of forgiveness in Christ, those who hold this error urge them to wrestle with God in prayer for assurance of salvation. However, feeling "saved" is not the same as trusting in Christ. What if you had an experience that made you feel absolutely sure that you were saved, and then Satan appeared to you on your death bed, and told you that he had given you that experience to deceive you. What would happen to your confidence then? The only people who have a valid "salvation experience" are those who trust in Christ. And, their confidence is not in what they felt at some point in time, but in the sure Word of God, and His promise, "**He who believes on Him [Christ] is not condemned**" (John 3:18).

There is at least one cult that tries to change grace itself from God's mercy in Christ, into an ability to keep the law. Those who hold this error pay lip service to what the Bible says about Christ's sacrificial death, and victory over death, but deny it by their emphasis on works. Like most cults, they make their own leaders the authority, and explain away any Bible passages that do not agree with their ideas. However, the words, "**If by grace, then is it no longer by works,**" make it clear that saving grace does not consist of works, and, in fact, excludes works (Romans 11:6). And, the words, "**To give His people the knowledge of salvation by the remission of their sins,**" tell us that God's saving grace consists of forgiveness, not works (Luke 1:77).

There is another sect that undermines the means of grace, and robs people of assurance of salvation by denying that God's promise of forgiveness in Christ is meant for everyone. The limitation that they place on Christ's atonement is a perversion of the gospel, and as such is condemned by the words, "**Some who want to pervert the gospel of Christ are troubling you,**" (Galatians 1:7). The words, "**The Lord is... patient with us, not wanting anyone to perish, but all to come to repentance,**" tell us that God does not want anyone to go to hell (2Peter 3:9). The words, "**They should seek the Lord, in the hope that they might grope for Him, and find Him,**" tell us that God wants all men to seek Him (Acts 17:27). And, the words, "**Go into all the world, and preach the gospel to every creature,**" tell us that God wants everyone to know that there is forgiveness in Christ (Mark 16:15).

When the Bible tells us that Christ's church is, **"Built upon the foundation of the apostles and prophets,"** it is telling us that it is built on the Word of the apostles and prophets (Ephesians 2:20). And, Christ's own words, **"Nor do I pray for them alone, but also for those who will believe on me through their word,"** tell us that people are brought to faith through the word of the apostles (John 17:20). The words, **"So will the word that goes out of my mouth be: it will not return to me empty, but it will accomplish what I want, and it will achieve what I sent it to do,"** tell us that God works through His Word (Isaiah 55:11). And, the words, **"What is the exceeding greatness of His power toward us who believe, according to the working of His mighty power,"** tell us that those who believe the gospel do so because of the power of God working through the gospel (Ephesians 1:19). As it is written, **"The gospel of Christ...is the power of God unto salvation to every one who believes,"** (Romans 1:16).

4. The Importance Of The Means Of Grace

Those who lack understanding sometimes scoff at the means of grace. Since they do not see the phrase "means of grace" in Scripture, they either ignore the phrase entirely, or call certain works the "means of grace," even though the Bible plainly tells us that, **"If it is by works, then it is no longer by grace"** (Romans 11:6). In contrast, the following passages plainly tell us that the gospel is the means of grace.

The words, **"Being born again, not of corruptible seed, but of incorruptible, by the word of God, that lives and abides forever,"** for **"The seed is the word of God"** tell us that the "word of God" is the means by which we are "born again" (1Peter 1:23, Luke 8:11). And, the words, **"My message and my preaching were not with enticing words of man's wisdom, but in demonstration of the Spirit and power: That your faith should not rest in the wisdom of men, but in the power of God,"** tell us that the power of God works through His Word to produce faith in formerly unbelieving hearts (1Corinthians 2:4-5). That is why the Bible says, **"Faith comes by hearing, and hearing by the word of God"** (Romans 10:17).

Now does that mean that deaf people cannot be saved? Of course not! The words, **"These are written, that you might believe"** tell us that the Word of God is the means of grace, irregardless of whether it is written or spoken (John 20:31). And, that brings us to the ceremonies of baptism and the Lord's Supper, which God has connected to the gospel.

I previously quoted Philip Melanchthon as saying, "These signs [baptism and the Lord's Supper] remind us of the [gospel] promises and are sure testimonies of the divine will toward us. They also bear witness that of a certainty we will receive what God has promised unto us". ("*The Loci Communes,*" 1521 edition.) Now the reason he calls baptism and the Lord's Supper "signs" is because; just as "**The sign of circumcision**" was "**a seal of the righteousness of the faith**" under the Old Covenant, baptism, and the Lord's Supper are seals "**of the righteousness of the faith**" under the New Covenant (Romans 4:11).

Therefore, to understand the role that God intends for baptism and the Lord's Supper to play in bringing people to Christ, you need to realize that many people have no idea of what faith actually is. Our culture conditions people to think of faith as "believing something without evidence" when that is not at all what the Bible means by "faith". To have faith in Christ is to rely on Him, to believe that we have forgiveness through His death on the cross.

That being understood, visualize yourself in the place of Peter on the day of Pentecost. After your sermon a man comes to you who has no idea of what faith is. However, having heard you preach, he feels condemned and wants assurance of forgiveness. You say to him, "**Repent, and be baptized... in the name of Jesus Christ for the forgiveness of sins,**" so he is baptized (Acts 2:38). He still has no idea of what faith is, but after being baptized he believes that when he accepted Jesus as the Messiah his sins were washed away, and that is faith. It was not the ceremony that washed his sins away, but his faith in Christ. And, baptism gave him that faith by convincing him that when he accepted Jesus as the Messiah his sins were washed away. Understood this way you can see how important baptism is, and the role God intended it to play.

Now, don't react to what I have just said by saying "I do not need baptism to believe". Perhaps that is the case. Philip Melanchthon went on to say, "Hezekiah could have been restored to his health even without a sign had he been willing only to believe the bare promise. Likewise Gideon would have been victorious without a sign, if he had believed. So you can be justified without a sign provided you believe." ("*The Loci Communes,*" 1521 edition.) However, don't hinder the work of salvation by assuming that because you understand what faith in Christ is, that signs have no purpose. God instituted them for a reason, and He expects us to use them.

The words, "**Go into all the world, and preach the gospel to every creature. He who believes and is baptized will be saved; but he who does not believe will be damned,**" tell us that salvation comes to those who believe the gospel [the means of grace], and baptism follows faith as evidence that one has accepted the gospel (Mark 16:15-16). In contrast, a refusal to be baptized can be evidence of unbelief. As it is written, "**The Pharisees and lawyers rejected the counsel of God against themselves, by refusing to be baptized by him**" (Luke 7:30).

The words, "**The preaching of the cross is foolishness to those who perish; but it is the power of God to us who are saved**," tells us that preaching [the Word of God] has power as the means of grace (1Corinthians 1:18). The words, "**Then Paul and Barnabas grew bold, and said, We had to speak the word of God to you first: but seeing that you reject it, and do not consider yourselves worthy of everlasting life, we turn to the Gentiles**," tell us that those who reject the Word of God [means of grace] reject salvation (Acts 13:46). And, the words, "**If anyone does not receive you, or hear your words, leave that house or town, and shake the dust off of your feet. I tell you truly, It will be more tolerable for the land of Sodom and Gomorrah on the day of judgment, than for that city**," warn of the danger of rejecting the means of grace [the gospel] (Matthew 10:14-15).

5. The Means Of Grace And Forgiving Sin

Jesus made certain statements about forgiving and retaining sin that were twisted during the Middle Ages into a way of making forgiveness depend on works. For that reason, we need to look closely at what the Bible does say, while allowing Scripture to interpret itself.

One of those statements reads, "**At evening on that same day, which was the first day of the week, after the doors to the place where the disciples had gathered were locked, for fear of the Jews, Jesus came and stood among them, and said to them, Peace be with you. And after saying that, He showed them His hands and his side. Then the disciples were overjoyed, when they saw the Lord. Again Jesus said, Peace be with you: as my Father has sent me, even so I am sending you. And after He had said this, <u>He breathed on them, and said to them, Receive the Holy Ghost. If you forgive the sins of anyone, they are forgiven; and if you retain the sins of anyone, they are retained</u>. But Thomas, called Didymus, who was one of the twelve, was not with them when Jesus came**" (John 20:19-24)

Notice that all of the Apostles were not present [Thomas was missing]. Furthermore, a comparison of this passage with Luke 24:13-36 reveals that two other disciples (who were not apostles) were present when Christ made these statements. That tells us that Christ's words, "**If you forgive the sins of anyone, they are forgiven; and if you retain the sins of anyone, they are retained**" were not meant for the Apostles alone. Likewise, there is nothing in the text to indicate that forgiving and retaining sins is limited to the "clergy" or is passed on by ordination. On the contrary, if we look at the context, Christ's words, "**Receive the Holy Ghost**," suggest that the power of forgiving and retaining sins is extends to all who have received the Holy Ghost.

If we look at Christ's example we read, "**They brought to Him a paralyzed man, lying on a bed: and having seen their faith, Jesus said to the paralyzed man; Son, be of good cheer; your sins are forgiven.** At this, some of the scribes said within themselves, This man blasphemes. And Jesus knowing their thoughts said, Why do you think evil in your hearts? For which is easier, to say, Your sins are forgiven; or to say, Arise, and walk? But that you may know that the Son of man has power on earth to forgive sins, (He then said to the paralyzed man,) Get up, pick up your bed, and go to your house" (Matthew 9:2-6).

The fact that Christ told the paralyzed man that his "**sins**" were "**forgiven**," tells us that the paralyzed man desperately needed assurance of forgiveness. And, that is understandable because the words, "**Who sinned, this man, or his parents, that he was born blind?**" tell us that in their society affliction was often seen as punishment for sin (John 9:2)

In our society the words that Christ spoke to the paralyzed man would be viewed as assuring him of forgiveness, rather than forgiving his sin. And, that tells us that **whenever we assure people of forgiveness we are forgiving sin in the sense Christ intended when He said, "If you forgive the sins of anyone, they are forgiven**" (John 20:23). That being understood, we need to realize that Christ never said, "**Be of good cheer; your sins are forgiven**," when speaking to those who were self-righteous, unrepentant or unbelieving. Those words were spoken to believers who were burdened by guilt and desperately needed assurance of forgiveness. And, when we say to people like that, "God has forgiven your sins," we know it is true because the sacrifice for sin has already been made. As it is written, "**By one offering He has perfected for ever those who are sanctified**" (Hebrews 10:14). [See Luke 7:48-49.]

There is a clear parallel between the forgiving and retaining of sins that Christ spoke of in John 20:19-24, and the binding and loosing that He spoke of in Matthew eighteen. In that chapter He said, "**If your brother sins against you, go and tell him his fault between you and him alone: if he will hear you, you have gained your brother. But if he will not listen, then take one or two others with you, so that every word may be established by the testimony of two or three witnesses. And if he refuses to listen to them, tell it to the church: but if he refuses to hear the church, let him be to you as an heathen man and a publican. I tell you truly, Whatever you bind on earth will be bound in heaven: and whatever you loose on earth will be loosed in heaven**" (Matthew 18:15-18).

In those words of Christ we see the power to retain sin used in the context of congregational discipline. And, its purpose is not to impose the will of some on others, but to bring the unrepentant person to repentance by removing any false assurance of forgiveness [See 1Cor. 5.] In theology, exercising this authority is referred to as the "office of the keys". Of those keys Lenski says, "How the keys are to be used is shown with great clearness in Matt. 18:18. Always the power in them is Christ's won for us to use only in accord with his will. Only repentant sinners are to be freed of their sins, only the impenitent are to be sent away unforgiven. The keys are stronger than we; they will never work according to any man's perverted will." (R.C.H. Lenski's commentary on Matthew, page 630.)

The Keys Of The Kingdom

There is a clear parallel between Christ's words to Peter, "**I will give to you the keys of the kingdom of heaven: and whoever you will bind on earth will be bound in heaven: and whoever you will loose on earth will be loosed in heaven,**" and His words in Matthew eighteen (Matthew 16:19). However, notice that the words "**I will** give to you," tell us that Peter did not receive the keys at that time, but later when they were given to all the apostles (see John 20:22-23). That tells us that the keys do not belong to Peter alone. And, there is certainly no mention of his successors. However, Christ's use of the same terminology in Matthew eighteen does make it clear that the power of the keys resides with the congregation. Furthermore, the words, "**Woe to you, lawyers! for you have taken away the key of <u>knowledge</u>: you did not go in yourselves, and you hindered those who were entering,**" tell us that the keys consist of knowledge [law and gospel] (Luke 11:52). And, the words, "**I am He who lives, and was dead; and, behold, I am alive forevermore, Amen; and have the keys of hell and of death,**" tell us that the keys belong to Christ, and we exercise them only as His agents (Revelations 1:18). Of that Lenski says, "It is still Jesus who dismisses and who holds sins, yet by his act which empowers the disciples he makes them his agents – he acts through them. They are thus by their very commission bound to dismiss and hold sins only in accord with the will of Jesus. They can dismiss, yea. Must dismiss, the sins of all those who repent and believe; they cannot and dare not do otherwise. To attempt to do so is to forfeit their commission and their power. They can, yea, must hold the sins of all the impenitent and unbelieving; they cannot dismiss them unless they would lose their authorization." (R. C. H. Lenski's commentary on John, page 1377.)

6. The Means Of Grace In The Old Testament

Because there is no salvation apart from faith in Christ, the only way of salvation both in the Old Testament and the New was and is through faith in Christ. The words, "**Nor is there salvation in any** other: for there is no other name under heaven given among men, by which we must be saved," testify to that fact (Acts 4:12). The words, "**I will put hostility between you [the serpent] and the woman, and between your seed and her seed; He will bruise your head, and you will bruise His heel,**" give us God's first promise of a deliverer (Genesis 3:15). And, the words, "**All the prophets testify of Him, that through His name whoever believes in Him will receive forgiveness of sins,**" tell us that all of God's prophets looked to Christ for forgiveness (Acts 10:43).

The words of Job, "**I know that my redeemer lives, and that He will stand at a future time upon the earth,**" testify to the fact that Job was saved through faith in Christ (Job 19:25). The words of David, "**Let the words of my mouth, and the meditation of my heart, be acceptable in your sight, O LORD, my strength, and my redeemer,**" testify to the fact that David looked to Christ for redemption (Psalm 19:14). And, because God is not bound by time, the words, "**The Lamb slain from the foundation of the world,**" tell us that the blood of Christ, and the forgiveness that He won for us, has been available from the very beginning (Revelation 13:8).

Now as to the means of grace, the words, "**If Abraham was justified by works, he would have a reason to boast; but now he has none before God. For what does the scripture say? Abraham believed God, and it was counted to him for righteousness,**" testify to the fact that grace came to Abraham through faith in God's promise of forgiveness in Christ (Romans 4:2-3). The words, "**The covenant *concerning faith in Christ*, that was confirmed by God at the time of Abraham, cannot be nullified by the law, which came four hundred and thirty years later, so as to make the promise of no effect,**" tell us that the law of Moses did not change the fact that salvation came through believing God's promise (Galatians 3:17). And, the words, "**Scripture, having foreseen that God would justify the heathen through faith, proclaimed the gospel to Abraham in advance, saying, In you shall all nations be blessed,**" tell us that the promise Abraham believed is the same promise we believe, the gospel promise of forgiveness in Christ (Galatians 3:8).

The words, "**He [Abraham] received the sign of <u>circumcision, a seal of the righteousness of the faith</u> that he already had while uncircumcised: that he might be the father of all who believe, yet are not circumcised; that righteousness might be imputed to them... For the promise, that he should be the heir of the world, was not to Abraham, or to his seed, through the law, but through the righteousness of faith,**" tell us that circumcision was a "sign" and "seal" of the righteousness that comes through faith in Christ (Romans 4:11-13). That raises the question: Why then did the Apostle Paul object so strongly to circumcising the gentiles?

And, the answer is found in the words, "**I again remind every man who is circumcised, that he is a debtor obligated to do everything the law requires**" (Galatians 5:3). Those words tell us that circumcision was being promoted as part of a system of works righteousness that was rooted in a total misunderstanding of the Old Testament. And, it was that doctrine of works righteousness [the doctrine of the Pharisees] that Paul recognized as a danger, saying, "**Christ is of no benefit to those of you who seek righteousness by the law; you are fallen from grace**" (Galatians 5:4).

The words, "**Christ our Passover is sacrificed for us: Therefore let us keep the feast, not with old leaven, neither with the leaven of malice and wickedness; but with the unleavened bread of sincerity and truth**," tell us that Christ is the true Passover lamb, who was sacrificed for our deliverance (1Corinthians 5:7-8). Therefore, the Passover sacrifice itself, was a sign and testimony instituted by God to point forward to (and explain) Christ's sacrifice.

To institute the Passover sacrifice, "**Moses called for all the elders of Israel, and said to them, Go out and select a lamb according to your families, and kill the passover. And you will take a bunch of hyssop, and dip it in the blood that is in the basin, and strike the lintel and the two side posts with the blood that is in the basin; and none of you shall go out of the door of his house until morning. For the LORD will pass through to slay the Egyptians; and when He sees the blood on the lintel, and on the two side posts, the LORD will pass over the door, and will not allow the destroyer to come in to your houses to slay you. And you shall observe this rite as an ordinance for you and for your sons forever**" (Exodus 12:21-24).

Notice that just as the children of Israel were delivered from God's wrath by the blood of the Passover lamb, we are delivered from God's wrath by the blood of Christ. And, just as they ate the lamb that was sacrificed, we partake of Christ's body and blood in the Lord's Supper. Moreover, all who partake of the Lord's Supper believing the words that Christ spoke – namely that His body was "given" for them [on the cross], and that His blood was "shed" for them [on the cross] – through faith truly receive Christ's body and blood, not as something physical, but as the atonement for their sin.

7. The Means Of Grace And Prayer

Since the Bible plainly tells us that we, "**Have access by faith into this grace in which we stand**," faith is the primary means of grace (Romans 5:2). However, because faith and grace go hand in hand, our doctrine of the means of grace deals more specifically with the means by which God brings us to faith. And, in that regard the words, "**The gospel of Christ... is the power of God to salvation to every one who believes,**" tell us that the gospel is the means by which we are brought to faith (Romans 1:16). As it is written, "**Faith comes by hearing, and hearing by the word of God**" (Romans 10:17). Nevertheless, there are some who regard prayer as a means of grace, and I need to explain why it is not.

In His parable of the Pharisee and the publican Christ said, "**Two men went up to the temple to pray; one a Pharisee, and the other a publican. The Pharisee stood up and prayed thus to himself, God, I thank you, that I am not like other men are, extortioners, evil doers, adulterers, or even like this publican. I fast twice in the week, I give tithes of everything I possess. And the publican, standing afar off, would not even look up to heaven, but beat upon his breast, saying, God be merciful to me a sinner. I tell you that this man went down to his house justified rather than the other: for every one who exalts himself will be humbled; and he who humbles himself will be exalted**" (Luke 18:10-14).

That parable plainly tells us that the publican "went down to his house justified". However, the fact that we are, "**Justified by faith,**" and "**Without faith it is impossible to please God,**" tells us that the publican received God's grace "by faith" not by praying a prayer [which would be a work] (Romans 3:28, Hebrews 11:6, Rom. 5:2). If he had not had faith, he would not have been justified. Now it is true that when believers pray for mercy (as the publican did), God answers that prayer. As it is written, "**If we confess our sins, He is faithful and just to forgive us our sins, and to cleanse us from all unrighteousness**" (1John 1:9). But we are not forgiven because we ask for it, but because we believe God's promise of forgiveness in Christ. Faith is the hand that receives God's grace (Romans 5:2).

One verse that is often cited by those who regard prayer as a means of grace does say that, "**Whoever will call upon the name of the Lord will be saved**" (Romans 10:13). However, the context is talking about believers. Starting in verse eleven we read, "**Whoever believes in Him will not be ashamed. For there is no difference between the Jew and the Greek: for the same Lord is Lord of all, and is rich to all who call upon Him. For whoever will call upon the name of the Lord will be saved**" (Romans 10:11-13). So in context, Verse thirteen is not telling how to be saved, but that salvation is extended equally to both Jew and gentile. As it is written, "**It will come to pass, that whoever calls upon the name of the LORD will be saved: for on mount Zion and in Jerusalem there will be deliverance, as the LORD has promised**" (Joel 2:32).

Without faith in Christ our prayer will not be heard, for "**Without faith it is impossible to please God**" (Hebrews 11:6). However, if we do have faith, our prayer is a fruit of faith, not the means by which

God gives us faith. That being understood, the words, "**Lord, I believe; help my unbelief**," tell us that there is nothing wrong with asking God to strengthen your faith (Mark 9:24). We can, and should, ask God to give us faith, or strengthen our faith. However, the words, "**Faith comes by hearing, and hearing by the word of God**," tell us that God uses His Word to bring us to faith, and strengthen our faith (Romans 10:17).

The Law And The Gospel

1. The Difference Between Law And Gospel

One of the ways that Satan attacks, and attempts to subvert, the gospel is by confusing the law with the gospel. The words, "**A man is not made righteous by the works of the law, but through faith in Jesus Christ**," tell us that it is through the gospel [the good news of forgiveness in Christ] that we are made righteous in the sight of God (Galatians 2:16). As it is written, "**Christ is the end of the law for righteousness to every one who believes**" (Romans 10:4). For that reason, the words, "**Being ignorant of God's righteousness, and seeking to establish their own righteousness, they have not submitted to the righteousness of God**," tell us that whenever someone assumes that the law will make him righteous he is confusing law and gospel (Romans 10:3).

What then is the purpose of the law? The Bible answers that question by saying, "**The law was our schoolmaster to bring us to Christ, that we might be declared righteous by faith**" (Galatians 3:24). And, the words, "**The knowledge of sin comes by the law**," tell us that the law brings us to Christ by showing us our sin and need for the forgiveness that He won for us on the cross (Romans 3:20). However, the law is not a means of grace because it does not produce faith. It may prepare our hearts for faith, by bringing us to repentance, but without the gospel that would just leave us in despair, without any hope of salvation. It is the gospel that gives us hope, by telling us that Christ died for our sins, and by assuring us that, "**Whoever believes in Him should not perish, but have everlasting life**" (John 3:16). And, faith is believing the gospel.

The words, "**The law has nothing to do with faith**," tell us that our faith does not consist of believing the law, and has nothing to do with the law (Galatians 3:12). In fact the words, "**All who trust in the law are under a curse: for it is written, Cursed is every one who does not continue to do everything that is written in the book of the law**," tell us that the law brings condemnation, not righteousness (Galatians 3:10). And the words "**Whatever the law says,** it says to those who are under the law: that every mouth may be stopped, and all the world may become guilty before God," tell us that everyone on earth is condemned by the law (Romans 3:19). "As it is written, There is none righteous, no, not one" (Romans 3:10).

However, the words, "**But now the righteousness of God <u>apart from the law</u> is revealed, being witnessed by the law and the prophets; Even the righteousness of God which comes through faith in Jesus Christ to all and upon all who believe: for there is no difference,**" tell us that there is a different way of becoming righteous, namely, through faith in Jesus Christ (Romans 3:21-22). For, "**The blood of Jesus Christ His Son cleanses us of all sin**" (1John 1:7).

To put it briefly, the law consists of everything in the Bible that reveals our sin, condemns it, or contrasts it with God's holiness. The gospel, on the other hand, consists of everything in the Bible that testifies of Christ, assuring us of forgiveness in Him. Furthermore, everything God has written in the Bible is either law or gospel. Even the simple statement, "Jesus wept," is gospel because it reveals Christ's compassion (John 11:35). While the words, "Cain rose up against Abel his brother, and killed him," are law because they reveal and condemn sin (Genesis 4:8).

Because both law and gospel are inspired by God, and apply to all men, they need to be preached side by side. Since the purpose of the law is to reveal our sin and point us to Christ, that is the way in which the law should be used. And, since the purpose of the gospel is to assure all who look to Christ for mercy that they have forgiveness in Christ, that is the way in which the gospel should be used. **The law and gospel need to work together. They are not being used properly whenever the unrepentant are given a false assurance of salvation, or those who repent are robbed of their assurance of salvation by being told that their faith in Christ is not enough.**

2. The Law And The Gospel Considered As Opposites

The law is God's message to the unrepentant, the gospel is God's message to those who repent. The law reveals God's condemnation of sin, while warning the sinner of His wrath. The Gospel reveals God's grace while assuring those who repent of forgiveness in Christ.

The words, "**As through the sin of one judgment came upon all men to condemnation; even so through the righteousness of one the free gift abounds to all men bringing justification and life**" tell us that sin brings the condemnation of the law, while the gospel frees us from condemnation (Romans 5:18). The words, "**If the ministry of condemnation is glorious, the ministry of righteousness is far more glorious,**" call the law a "ministry of condemnation," and the gospel a "ministry of righteousness" (2Corinthians 3:9). And, the words, "**As sin has reigned unto death, even so grace might reign through righteousness to eternal life by Jesus Christ our Lord,**" tell us that the law [sin] brings death, while the gospel [grace] brings righteousness and life to all who trust in Christ (Romans 5:21).

The words, "**All who trust in the law are under a curse: for it is written, Cursed is every one who does not continue to do everything that is written in the book of the law... However... Christ redeemed us from the curse of the law, receiving the curse in our stead,**" tell us that the law condemns all who trust in it, while the gospel assures us of God's mercy in Christ; assuring us that "**we have redemption through His blood, the forgiveness of sins, according to the riches of His grace**" (Galatians 3:10-14, Ephesians 1:7).

The words, "**No flesh will ever be justified in God's sight by the deeds of the law: because the knowledge of sin comes by the law. But now the righteousness of God apart from the law is revealed, being witnessed by the law and the prophets. Even the righteousness of God which comes through faith in Jesus Christ to all and upon all who believe,**" tell us that the law cannot make anyone righteous, but there is another way of becoming righteous, namely through the forgiveness that comes through faith in Christ (Romans 3:20-22). As it is written, "**Christ is the end of the law for righteousness to every one who believes**" (Romans 10:4). And, how does faith in Christ make us righteous? When we look to Christ for mercy "**The blood of Jesus Christ His Son cleanses us of all sin**" (1John 1:7). "**We have access by faith into**" that cleansing (Romans 5:2). And, because of that cleansing, there is "**no condemnation for those who are in Christ Jesus**" (Romans 8:1). [See Luke 1:77-78.]

The law makes us sinners; the gospel frees us from sin. The law condemns us; the gospel frees us from condemnation. The law brings death, the gospel brings life.

3. The Close Connection Between Law And Gospel

Although the law and gospel are, in many ways, opposites they need to work together like the two blades of a scissors. Without the gospel, the law will bring only despair. And, without the law, the gospel will give the unrepentant a false assurance of salvation.

The words, "**Do not think that I have come to destroy the law,** or the prophets: I have not come to destroy, but to fulfill. For I tell you truly, Until heaven and earth pass away, not one letter or stroke will pass from the law, until everything has been fulfilled," tell us that God has not changed His law, or made it easier to keep (Matthew 5:17). The words, **"The law is not meant for a righteous man, but for those who are lawless and rebellious, for the ungodly and sinful, for the irreverent and profane, for those who strike or kill their fathers or mothers, for murders, For those who sin sexually, for sodomites, for kidnapers and slave traders, for liars and perjurers, and for any other thing that is contrary to sound teaching,"** tell us that the unrepentant are still under the law, and are still condemned by the law (1Timothy 1:9-10). While the words, **"There is therefore now no condemnation for those who are in Christ Jesus, who walk not after the flesh, but after the Spirit. For the law of the Spirit of life in Christ Jesus has set me free from the law of sin and death,"** tell us that the freedom from the law that we have in Christ is freedom from condemnation, not license to sin (Romans 8:1-2).

In his Epistle to the Romans the Apostle Paul shows us how law and gospel should work together by first condemning sin, and then pointing those who are guilty to Christ. In chapter three we read, "Whatever the law says, it says to those who are under the law: that every mouth may be stopped, and the entire world may become guilty before God. Therefore no flesh will ever be declared righteous in God's sight by the deeds of the law: because the knowledge of sin comes by the law. <u>But now the righteousness of God apart from the law is revealed</u>, being witnessed by the law and the prophets; Even the righteousness of God which comes <u>through faith in Jesus Christ</u> to all and upon all who believe: for there is no difference: For all have sinned, and come short of the glory of God; Being cleansed of sin freely by His grace through the forgiveness that is in Christ Jesus... Therefore we conclude that a man is justified by faith without the deeds of the law" // "For Christ is the end of the law for righteousness to every one who believes" (Romans 3:19-28 and 10:4).

Having been freed from the law through the forgiveness that Christ won for us, the words, **"Just as Christ was raised from the dead through the glory of the Father, even so we should also walk in newness of life,"** tell us that we should not allow our flesh to control our behavior, but should try to behave as we will after we are **"raised incorruptible,"** and all sinful desire has been removed from our nature (Romans 6:4, 1Corinthians 15:52)

The words, **"God...has also made us able ministers of the new testament; not of the letter [the law], but of the spirit [i.e. faith 1Cor. 12:3]: for the letter [law] kills, but the spirit gives life,"** tell us that the law brings death, but the gospel brings life (2Corinthians 3:5-6). However, having been freed from the law the Bible says, "Walk in the Spirit [that is by faith, believing that it is the forgiveness that is ours in Christ, and not the law that makes us righteous in the sight of God], and you will not fulfill the lust of the flesh. For the flesh lusts against the Spirit, and the Spirit against the flesh: and they are opposed to each other: so that you cannot do the things that you would. But if you are led by the Spirit, you are not under the law. Moreover the works of the flesh are obvious, which are; Adultery, fornication, sexual filthiness, sensuality, Idolatry, witchcraft, hatred, discord, rivalry, rage, strife, divisions, heresies, envy, murder, drunkenness, orgies, and such like: of which I forewarn you, as I have in the past, that <u>those who do such things will not inherit the kingdom of God</u>. But the fruit of the Spirit is love, joy, peace, patience, kindness, goodness, faith, meekness, self-control: against such there is no law. And they that are Christ's have crucified the flesh with its passions and lusts. Since we live by the Spirit, let us also walk in the Spirit. Let us not be desirous of vain glory, provoking one another, envying one another" (Galatians 5:16-29).

4. The Art Of Distinguishing Between Law And Gospel

Once the difference between law and gospel has been explained, it would be a mistake to assume that distinguishing between the two will always be easy. Because the gospel is the means that God uses to bring us to faith, Satan is continually at work confusing law and gospel, deceiving as many as possible, and trying as hard as he can to undermine faith in Christ. Moreover, his attack is always twofold.

At Corinth, Satan did not try to get the congregation to deny the gospel. Instead, he perverted the gospel by using it to rationalize sin. The words, "**Among you one hears of immorality... And you are still puffed up**," tell us that the church members were tolerating immorality in their midst (1Corinthians 5:1-2). And, the Apostle Paul condemned them for it, saying, Do not "**associate with anyone who calls himself a brother but is sexually immoral**" (1Corinthians 5:11). However, there are many congregations in our own nation who are tolerating evil in their midst. I have heard young people argue in favor of accepting homosexuals, by yelling we are all sinners. What those young people failed to understand is that no one who is truly repentant is a sinner by choice! While those young people claimed to trust in Christ, by using the gospel as an excuse to sin they, "**Trampled the Son of God under foot, treated the blood of the covenant... as an unholy thing, and insulted the Spirit of grace**"

(Hebrews 10:29). Moreover, they erred because they confused the gospel with the law, assuming that the gospel simply lowered the standard of behavior. In fact, that is a mistake that many make. Therefore, it is important to stress the fact that, **"Until heaven and earth pass away, not one letter or stroke will pass from the law"** (Matthew 5:18). The words, **"The law is not meant for a righteous man, but for those who are lawless and rebellious, for the ungodly and sinful,"** tell us that those who sin by choice place themselves back under the law, and are condemned by the law (1Timothy 1:9).

In Galatia, Satan, again, did not try to get the congregation to deny the gospel. Instead he perverted the gospel by denying that the forgiveness we have in Christ is enough to make us righteous in the sight of God. He led the congregation to believe that it was fine to think that faith would save, but that only obedience [keeping the law] would make them righteous. In response Paul said, **"Are you so foolish, that after beginning in the Spirit, you now seek perfection [righteousness] through your own effort?"** (Galatians 3:3). And, there are many people in American churches who make the same mistake. They assume that they must either try to make themselves righteous, or just give up and sin by choice. What they fail to understand is that the law does not make us righteous. On the contrary, the law is what makes us sinners!

I was not able to understand that until I realized the importance of seeing myself as God sees me. Then, since, **"All of our righteousnesses are like filthy rags"** in the sight of God, I asked God to help me to see all of my sins. It was only when I came to the point where I saw that everything that I did was so imperfect that it would be condemned by a Holy God, that I could see that freedom from the law was not freedom to sin, but freedom to be righteous. That is why the Apostle Paul said, **"The letter [law] kills, but the Spirit gives life,"** and called the law a, **"ministry of death,"** and a, **"ministry of condemnation"** (2Corinthians 3:6-9). As long as I saw myself as fifty or even twenty percent righteous, I could not see freedom from the law as anything other than freedom to sin. However, after God enabled me to see that the law condemned everything I did; I could see that freedom from the law is not freedom to sin but the freedom to be righteous. **Christ has freed us from the law so that we can be righteous**, not so that we can sin. He has freed us so that we can be law-abiding citizens, faithful husbands or wives, and godly parents without being condemned by the law. In short, **Christ has freed us from the law so that we can each, "Lead a quiet and peaceable life in all godliness and honesty"** (1Timothy 2:2).

Satan also confuses law and gospel, by denying that we can be sure that we are saved, or claiming that we are not saved until we get to heaven. However, both of those claims contradict God's Word. The words, **"I have written these things to you who believe in the** name of the Son of God; that you may <u>know</u> that you have eternal life, and that you may believe in the name of the Son of God," tell us that we can "know" that we have eternal life [are saved] (1John 5:13). Moreover, the words, "**Who has saved us, and called us to a holy calling, not because of anything we have done, but according to His own purpose and grace**" and "**He saved us, not by works of righteousness that we have done, but because of His mercy,**" tell us that we are saved now [past tense] (2Timothy 1:9, Titus 3:5).

While many other ways of confusing law and gospel could be listed, there is no end to the ways Satan may come up with. The important thing is for pastors, who are entrusted with the care of souls, to be watchful. And, one book that may be helpful is *"Law And Gospel,"* by C.F.W. Walther.

The Doctrine Of Preservation

One important area in which law and gospel are often confused has to do with divine preservation. That is, with the fact that just as God has saved us by His grace, He keeps us by His grace. As it is written, "**You... are kept by the power of God through faith unto salvation,**" (1Peter 1:4-5).

When a man who does not understand the gospel reads the words, "**The soul that sins will die,**" or "**The wages of sin is death,**" he may assume that he can only be saved by not sinning (Ezekiel 18:20, Romans 6:23). And, if he believes that, he may live in fear of slipping up. However, once we understand the gospel, that fear is gone! Why? Because the words, "**The blood of Jesus Christ His Son cleanses us of all sin,**" tell us that our salvation does not depend on us (1John 1:7).

The same holds true when it comes to divine preservation. God's promise to keep us from falling is part of the gospel. However, when one who fails to understand that reads the words, "**Those on the rock are those, who... believe for a while, and in time of temptation fall away,**" or "**I buffet my body, and bring it under my control: lest... I, after having preached to others, might be rejected,**" he may assume that he has to keep himself from falling from grace (Luke 8:13, 1Corinthians 9:27). And, if he believes that, he may live in fear of slipping up. However, once we understand that God has not only saved us by His grace, but also keeps us by His grace, that fear is gone. Why? Because the words, "**You... are kept by the power of God through faith unto salvation,**" tell us that "staying saved" does not depend on us (1Peter 1:4-5).

I am not saying that a believer cannot lose salvation. If I did I would be contradicting the Bible. What I am saying is that it is God who keeps you from losing salvation. The danger of loosing salvation is very real, and God wants you to know that. However, the words, **"All the promises of God in Him [Christ] are yea, and in Him Amen,"** tell us that if you have faith in Christ, you also have His promise to **"keep you from falling,"** (Jude 1:24).

Just as the words, **"The wages of sin is death,"** are law, while the words, **"The blood of Jesus Christ His Son cleanses us of all sin,"** are gospel; the words, **"I buffet my body, and bring it under my control: lest... I, after having preached to others, might be rejected,"** are law, while the words, **"You... are kept by the power of God through faith unto salvation,"** are gospel (Romans 6:23, 1John 1:7, 1Corinthians 9:27, 1Peter 1:4-5). And, because, **"The law is not meant for a righteous man, but for those who are lawless and rebellious,"** the warnings of the law do not apply to those who trust in Christ (1Timothy 1:9). On the contrary, the words, **"Blessed is the man to whom the Lord will not impute sin,"** tell us that no sin is imputed to those who trust in Christ (Romans 4:8). That means that the passages that warn us of the danger of losing salvation are there as a curb, to keep any church members who do not fully understand the gospel from doing something that could harden their heart and result in their destruction.

The following passages warn us of the danger of falling.

"Let him who thinks that he is standing take heed lest he fall" (1Corinthians 10:12).

"Christ is of no benefit to those of you who seek righteousness by the law; you are fallen from grace" (Galatians 5:4).

"It is impossible for those who have once been enlightened, and have tasted the heavenly gift, and became partakers of the Holy Spirit, And have tasted the good word of God, and the powers of the world to come, And have then fallen away, to be brought back again to repentance" (Hebrews 6:4-6)

"Many will say to me in that day, Lord, Lord, have we not prophesied in your name? and in your name cast out devils? and in your name done many wonderful works? And then I will declare to them, I never knew you: depart from me, you who do evil" (Matthew 7:22).

"If after they have escaped the pollutions of the world through the knowledge of the Lord and Savior Jesus Christ, they are again entangled therein, and overcome, the latter end is worse with them than the beginning" (2Peter 2:20).

The following passages assure us that God will keep us by His grace.

"I am convinced, that neither death, nor life, nor angels, nor principalities, nor powers, nor things present, nor things to come, nor height, nor depth, nor any other creature, shall be able to separate us from the love of God, that is in Christ Jesus our Lord" (Romans 8:38).

"Being confident of this, that He who has begun a good work in you will continue it until the day of Jesus Christ" (Philippians 1:6).

"You... are kept by the power of God through faith unto salvation" (1Peter 1:4-5).

"I give to them eternal life; and they will never perish, neither will any man pluck them out of my hand. My Father, who gave them to me, is greater than anyone; and no one is able to pluck them out of my Father's hand. I and my Father are one" (John 10:28-30).

"The Lord is faithful, and will strengthen you, and keep you from evil" (2Thessalonians 3:3)

"May... the God of peace sanctify you entirely; and your whole spirit and soul and body be preserved blameless unto the coming of our Lord Jesus Christ. He who calls you is faithful, and will bring it to pass" (1Thess. 5:23-24).

The Doctrine Of Holy Baptism

1. The Divine Institution Of Baptism

Because Jesus has instructed us to, "**Teach all nations, baptizing them in the name of the Father, and of the Son, and of the Holy Ghost,**" baptism is not just some rite the church has come up with, but is a divine institution with the authority of God behind it (Matthew 28:19).

When Christ said, "**Go into all the world, and preach the gospel to every creature. He who believes and is baptized will be saved; but he who does not believe will be damned,**" the words "He who believes and is baptized" tell us that baptism is to be an expression of faith, not a work (Mark 16:15-16).

On the day of Pentecost, when "Peter said, "**Repent, and be baptized every one of you in the name of Jesus Christ for the forgiveness of sins, and you will receive the gift of the Holy Ghost,**" everyone who came forward to be baptized "**In the name of Jesus Christ,**" knew that by being baptized in His name they were accepting Him as the Messiah [and thus as the source of forgiveness] (Acts 2:38). For that reason, coming forward was **an act of faith** on their part. And after being baptized they went away believing that when they accepted Christ as the Messiah their sins were washed away – and that is the very essence of faith. In contrast, the words, **"The Pharisees and lawyers rejected the counsel of God against themselves, by refusing to be baptized,"** tell us that everyone who refused to be baptized did so as an expression of their unbelief (Luke 7:30).

How Satan Tries to Muddy the Water

Even though the Bible plainly tells us that people were baptized in water, there have been many who have placed themselves in opposition to the Word of God by trying to change what God set in place. So here are a few of the passages that speak of water in connection with baptism.

"I indeed baptize you with water for repentance: but the one who comes after me, whose shoes I am not worthy to carry, is mightier than I: He will baptize you with the Holy Spirit, and with fire" (Matthew 3:11).

"Having been baptized, Jesus immediately went up out of the water" (Matthew 3:16).

"I have baptized you with water: but He will baptize you with the Holy Ghost" (Mark 1:8). [See Luke 3:16, John 1:26, Acts 1:5, Acts 11:16.]

"The one who sent me to baptize with water told me, The man upon whom you see the Spirit descending, and remaining, is He who baptizes with the Holy Ghost" (John 1:31,33).

"John was also baptizing in Aenon near to Salim, because there was plenty of water there: and people were coming, and being baptized" (John 3:23).

"They came to some water: and the eunuch said, Look, here is water; what prevents me from being baptized?... And he commanded the chariot to stop: and they both went down into the water, both Philip and the eunuch; and he baptized him" (Acts 8:36, 38).

"Can any man forbid water, for these people, who have received the Holy Ghost just as we did, to be baptized?" (Acts 10:47)

Not only is the human mind corrupted by sin, the mind of the most brilliant man who ever lived is like the mind of a worm when compared to the mind of God. For that reason, I find it difficult to understand how some people can be so naive as to think that the petty reasons they come up with for changing baptism, or for dispensing with the entire ceremony will not be condemned by God. How can they fail to see that they are in rebellion against God. By trying to exalt their own will over God's will they are trying to exalt themselves over God, and that is self-deification – which is a form of idolatry.

2. Baptism In The Light Of The Gospel

Christian baptism began with John the Baptist. And, because John was sent by God to "**prepare the way for**" Christ, baptism has always been a divinely instituted way of pointing those who repent to Christ, as, "**The Lamb of God, who takes away the sin of the world**" (John 1:29, see Luke 1:76-78). In addition, the words, "**That we might receive the promise of the Spirit through faith,**" tell us that any forgiveness promised in connection with baptism comes to us "through faith" in Christ, not through the outward act of applying water (Galatians 3:14). Do not misunderstand me. I am not saying that baptism is not important. God instituted it for a reason, and He works through it in ways that we do not always understand. What I am saying is that because the ceremony of baptism was instituted to point people to Christ as the source of forgiveness, God intended for Christ to be the object of our faith. And, it is through faith in Him that we have access to forgiveness. As it is written, "**There is no other name under heaven given among men, by which we must be saved**" (Acts 4:12).

The words, "**John did baptize in the wilderness, and preach the baptism of repentance for the remission of sins,**" tell us that John the Baptist used baptism in calling the people to repentance (Mark 1:4). The words, "**John saw Jesus coming to him, and said, Behold the Lamb of God, who takes away the sin of the world,**" tell us that John pointed all who were baptized to Christ as the source of forgiveness (John 1:29). And, the words, "**I [John] have baptized you with water: but He [Christ] will baptize you with the Holy Ghost,**" tell us that John pointed those whom he baptized to Christ as the source of spiritual cleansing (Mark 1:8).

Because it is "**the blood of Jesus Christ**" that "**cleanses us of all sin,**" the baptism of the Holy Spirit is the spiritual cleansing [washing] that takes place when our sins are washed away (1John 1:7). And, the words, "**We have access by faith into this grace wherein we stand,**" tell us that we receive that cleansing when the Holy Spirit brings us to faith in Christ (Romans 5:2).

The words, "**After this Jesus and His disciples went out into the countryside of Judea; and there He spent some time with them, and baptized,**" tell us that Jesus continued the work of John the Baptist (John 3:22). However, the words, "**Although it was not**

Jesus who baptized, but His disciples," tell us that Christ did not personally baptize those who came, but let His disciples do it (John 4:2). And, a comparison of the words, **"Preaching the baptism of repentance for the remission of sins,"** with the words, **"Repent, and be baptized... in the name of Jesus Christ for the forgiveness of sins,"** tells us that just like John the Baptist, Jesus and His disciples were calling people to **repent and be baptized** for the forgiveness of sins (Luke 3:3, Acts 2:38). In fact, Christ's disciples were baptized by John (John 1:35-42).

Because baptism is a **"baptism of repentance,"** the words, **"Go therefore, and teach all nations, baptizing them in the name of the Father, and of the Son, and of the Holy Ghost,"** are telling us to baptize those who repent (Matthew 28:19). That is why Christ told His disciples that, **"Repentance and remission of sins should be preached in His name among all nations, beginning at Jerusalem"** (Luke 24:47). And, all who are baptized receive the promise, "He who believes and is baptized will be saved" (Mark 16:16).

Because baptism is a **"baptism of repentance,"** when Jesus said, "Unless a man is born of water and the Spirit, he cannot enter into the kingdom of God" His words "born of water," were a reference to the baptism of repentance, with the emphasis on **repentance** (John 3:5). However, Christ not only referred to "water," but also to, "the Spirit," for it is the Spirit who brings us to faith (1Cor. 12:3). **So what Jesus was saying is that "Unless a man is born of repentance [water] and faith [the Spirit], he cannot enter into the kingdom of God**.

While the Greek word "baptizo" does not appear in Titus 3:5, **"He saved us because of His mercy, through the washing of regeneration [i.e. rebirth], and renewing of the Holy Ghost,"** because being "born again" is a "rebirth," there is a clear parallel between this passage and John 3:5. Therefore, if the word, "washing," is a reference to baptism it is also a reference to repentance. At the same time, the phrase "renewing of the Holy Ghost" is a reference to faith, for the Holy Spirit renews our life by bringing us to faith in Christ. Understood that way, this passage is telling us that we are saved through repentance and faith. [See John 1:12-13.]

Because baptism is a baptism of repentance, and because repentance is incomplete without faith in Christ, to **"Repent, and be baptized... in the name of Jesus Christ for the remission of sins,"** is to repent and be baptized believing that there is forgiveness in Christ (Acts 2:38).

Because baptism is a baptism of repentance, and because repentance is incomplete without faith in Christ, the words, **"Be baptized, and wash away your sins, calling on the name of the Lord,"** tell us that the Apostles saw baptism as a way of "calling on the name of the Lord" for forgiveness (Acts 22:16). At the same time, the words,

"Jesus... loved us, and washed us from our sins in His own blood," tell us that it is the blood of Christ, not the water, that cleanses us of sin (Revelations 1:5). **The water is God's way of assuring all who come to Christ that He has washed away their sins.**

Because the Bible describes baptism as a baptism of repentance, when Peter said, "**Baptism... also now saves us (not by removing the filth of the flesh, but the promise of a good conscience toward God,) through the resurrection of Jesus Christ**," his definition of baptism was broad enough to **include** repentance and faith in Christ (1Peter 3:21). Therefore, when he said, "baptism... also now saves us," he was talking about baptism in its context of repentance and faith, not water alone. That is why Dr. Walter A. Maier said:

> "Do not be misled by those who say that Baptism is not important. They contradict Christ. They put their own opinion above Scripture. Take Jesus at His word, and you will find that through Baptism — and I mean of course, not merely the performance of the ritual itself, but by your personal faith in Jesus and in His promise — the Holy Ghost unmistakably comes to you." (From the sermon, *"The Power of Pentecost,"* 1943.)

3. What Makes A Baptism Valid

For a valid baptism to take place there must be an application of water. However, because baptism consists of far more than water, that water must also be applied in accord with the Word of God; which says, "**Go, and teach all nations, baptizing them in the name of the Father, and of the Son, and of the Holy Ghost**" (Matthew 28:19).

Now if the President were to authorize me to do something in his name, he would be authorizing me to do it as his representative, with his authority backing me. Therefore, to baptize "in the name of the Father, and of the Son, and of the Holy Ghost," not only involves using those words, but using them as God's representative, with His authority behind them. For that reason, when we baptize, God is baptizing through us. We are only His representatives. Furthermore, because we are to baptize in the name of the Father, Son, and Holy Ghost, a valid baptism can only be performed by someone who believes in the triune God.

In theology, any group that is not worshipping the God of the Bible is designated a cult. That includes groups that deny the deity of Christ, worship a god that they describe as an exalted man, or in any way falsify what God has revealed about Himself. And, because they are not worshipping the God of the Bible, we do not regard any baptism performed by them as valid.

The Promise of Baptism

When baptism is carried out as God intended, it is more than just water, it is a ceremonial proclamation of the gospel. And, just as the gospel conveys God's promise of forgiveness in Christ, baptism carries with it God's promise of forgiveness in Christ. However, in order to avoid being misunderstood, let me make it clear that **baptism is not a requirement** for receiving forgiveness. If you repent, God does not withhold His forgiveness until you are baptized. And, forgiveness does not come to you through the performance of the ritual, but through your personal faith in Jesus and in His promise. As it is written, **"We... receive the promise of the Spirit through faith"** (Galatians 3:14). Therefore, baptism holds the same place in our salvation as a sermon that promises forgiveness in Christ. Baptism differs only in that it is a sermon proclaimed by a ceremony. In both cases we receive the forgiveness being offered, through faith in Christ.

"If the Word that is preached will not benefit a person unless he believes it, neither will being baptized and taking Communion benefit anyone without faith... Let me offer you a few passages that treat, in particular, of the Sacraments. Mark 16, 16 the Lord says: *"He that* BELIEVETH AND IS BAPTIZED *shall be saved."* He does not say: "He that is baptized and believeth," but the reverse. Faith is the primary necessity; Baptism is something to which faith holds. Moreover, the Lord continues: *But he that believeth not shall be damned."* This shows that even if a person could not have Baptism administered to himself, he would be saved, as long as he believed.

Acts 8,36. 37 we read: *And as they went on their way, they came unto a certain water; and the eunuch said, See, here is water; what doth hinder me to be baptized? And Philip said,* IF THOU BELIEVEST WITH ALL THINE HEART, THOU MAYEST. *And he answered and said, I believe that Jesus Christ is the Son of God."* The only thing that Philip required was faith, as if he had said to the eunuch: "If you do not believe, being baptized will not benefit you at all." At our baptism it is not we that are performing a work, but God.

Gal. 3, 26. 27 Paul writes: For ye are all the children of God by faith in Christ Jesus. For as many of you as have been baptized into Christ have put on Christ. This text shows that Christ is put on in Baptism only if a person believes. The current interpretation is that any one that is baptized has put on Christ; however, that is not what the apostle says, but: "As many of you," namely, of you who are "the children of God by faith." Such people, indeed, put on Christ in Baptism. An unbeliever who receives Baptism does not put on Christ, but keeps on the spotted garment of his sinful flesh." (C.F.W. Walther, *"Law and Gospel,"* pages 351-353)

The Importance of Sticking to God's Word

There are any number of sects that try to assert their own authority by changing baptism in some way. One such sect seizes on the passages that speak of baptizing "in the name of Jesus," and argues that when the Apostles actually baptized they did it in the name of Jesus, not in the name of the Father, Son and Holy Ghost. However, they are wrong because in the examples they cite no one is actually being baptized. When Peter said, **"Repent, and be baptized every one of you in the name of Jesus Christ for the forgiveness of sins,"** he was not performing a baptism, but holding up the promise of forgiveness in Christ (Acts 2:38). All who come to baptism are to come believing that there is forgiveness in Christ. However, that does not change the fact that when Peter actually baptized someone he would have done it just like Jesus told him to, **"In the name of the Father, and of the Son, and of the Holy Ghost"** (Matthew 28:19). [See Acts 8:16, and 10:48.] Those who depart from the accepted Scriptural practice cause needless division and contention while undermining faith, and for that reason they should be condemned.

4. Baptism A True Means Of Grace

The gospel, the good news of forgiveness in Christ, is the means by which God brings us to faith, and, therefore, the means by which God gives us His grace. As it is written, **"The gospel... is the power of God to salvation to every one who believes"** (Romans 1:16). **And, "We have access by faith into this grace"** (Romans 5:1).

That being the case, baptism is a means of grace because it is a ceremonial proclamation of the gospel. There is no mysterious power in the ceremony itself. Apart from the gospel it would be nothing but water. Rightly understood, and rightly used, the promise of baptism is the promise of forgiveness in Christ. When Peter said, **"Repent, and be baptized every one of you in the name of Jesus Christ for the forgiveness of sins,"** he was saying, **repent and be baptized believing that there is forgiveness in Christ** (Acts 2:38). The words, **"If you truly believe, you may [be baptized],"** tell us that faith is of primary importance (Acts 8:37). And, when baptism is performed as God intended, the ceremony is God's way of telling the new believer that He has washed away his sin.

The Bible tells us that on the day of Pentecost, the people who heard Peter preach, **"Were cut to the heart** [i.e. convicted of sin]," (Acts 2:37). Desiring forgiveness they cried out, **"what shall we do?"** and Peter said, **"Repent, and be baptized... in the name of Jesus Christ for the forgiveness of sins"** (Acts 2:38). For that reason, everyone who came forward to be baptized came believing that there was forgiveness in Christ, and went away, believing that when they came to Christ for forgiveness their sins were washed away. Like the gospel, the purpose of baptism was to assure them that when they looked to Christ for forgiveness their sins were washed away. As it is written, "**Every one who looks to the Son, and believes on Him, may have everlasting life: and I will raise him up on the last day**" (John 6:40).

Satan's Attack on Baptism

Because baptism is a means of grace, Satan does all that he can to pervert it and make it ineffective. And, one of the ways he perverts baptism is by turning it from gospel into law, from God's promise of forgiveness in Christ to an "act of obedience". However, those who hold that view fail to see that the Bible never commands anyone to be baptized. Christ commanded His church to baptize converts, but He never commanded anyone to be baptized. Coming to baptism should be an act of faith on the part of those who come, not a work. When Peter said, "Repent, and be baptized," he was answering a question, not giving a command, and the answer to a question is never imperative.

Another way that Satan attacks baptism is by shifting the focus of faith from Christ to the ceremony, as if the ceremony had power to forgive simply by performing the act. Instead of turning baptism into law, this view turns it into a false gospel; a gospel that offers forgiveness through the rituals of a church rather than through faith in Christ. Worse yet, the church of the antichrist, which promotes that view, has pronounced a curse on everyone who says that the divine grace offered in baptism is only received through faith in Christ.

Bible Passages That Connect the Gospel with Baptism

Romans 6:3 "**Don't you know, that all who were baptized into Jesus Christ were baptized into His death?**"

Acts 2:38 "**Repent, and be baptized every one of you in the name of Jesus Christ for the forgiveness of sins, and you will receive the gift of the Holy Ghost.**"

Mark 16:16 "**He who believes and is baptized will be saved; but he who does not believe will be damned.**"

Acts 22:16 "**What are you waiting for? get up, and be baptized, and wash away your sins, calling on the name of the Lord.**"

Ephesians 5:26 "**That He might sanctify and cleanse it with the washing of water by the word.**"

Titus 3:5 "**He saved us, not by works of righteousness that we have done, but because of His mercy, through the washing of rebirth, and renewing of the Holy Ghost.**"

1Peter 3:21 "**That water prefigured baptism which also now

saves us (not by removing the filth of the flesh, but as the promise of a good conscience toward God,) through the resurrection of Jesus Christ."

John 3:5 "**Unless a man is born of water and of the Spirit, he cannot enter the kingdom of God.**"

1Peter 1:23 "**Being born again, not of corruptible seed, but of incorruptible, by the word of God, that lives and abides for ever.**"

1John 5:1 "**Whoever believes that Jesus is the promised Savior is born of God: and everyone who loves the Father also loves the child born of Him.**"

Galatians 3:26-27 "**For you are all the children of God through faith in Christ Jesus. For as many of you as were baptized into Christ have put on Christ.**"

5. The Use Of Baptism

Although baptism and the Lord's Supper are both ceremonial proclamations of the gospel, they are not the same. God designed each one for a different role. That is why we partake of the Lord's Supper often, but are only baptized once.

Just as Abraham, "**Received the sign of circumcision, a seal of the righteousness of the faith that he already had while uncircumcised**" (Romans 4:11). All who are baptized believing that there is forgiveness in Christ, receive baptism as a sign and seal of the righteousness that they already have through faith in Christ. Therefore, just as Abraham could only be circumcised once, a believer should only be baptized once. And the Christian church has always followed that practice.

In the past some have mistakenly assumed that they needed to be rebaptized every time they sinned. However, because that error assumes that forgiveness comes through the water, rather than through faith in Christ, the Christian church has always condemned it. Furthermore, when we come to baptism believing that there is forgiveness in Christ, our coming to baptism is a public testimony to our faith in Christ [not faith in baptism]. And, because it is a public testimony, the promise, "**Whoever confesses me before men, I will also confess before my Father who is in heaven,**" belongs to all who come (Matthew 10:32). Then, after being baptized, we continue to confess Christ before men, not only by our words, but by attending church and receiving the Lord's Supper.

The words, "**You are all the children of God through faith in Christ Jesus. For as many of you as were baptized into Christ have put on Christ,**" use baptism as a synonym for conversion (Galatians 3:26-27). And, we **put on Christ** by being clothed in His righteousness, the righteousness that God imputes to us "without works". As it is written, **blessed is "The man, to whom God imputes righteousness without works,"** (Romans 4:6). That same symbolism [of being clothed in Christ's righteousness] is found in the words, **"She [Christ's church] should be arrayed in fine linen, clean and white: for the fine linen is the righteousness of saints"** (Revelation 19:8). Moreover, the righteousness that we receive when we "put on Christ" is the **"wedding garment"** spoken of in Matthew 22:12-13. The wedding garment that makes us acceptable to God. Therefore, once we come to faith in Christ there is no need to be rebaptized, because the righteousness that we receive at conversion is always ours through faith. For that reason, if we do something that we need to repent of, then we should repent, looking to Christ for forgiveness, believing that **"Christ is the end of the law for righteousness to every one who believes"** (Romans 10:4). And, believing His promise, that **"If we confess our sins, He is faithful and just to forgive us our sins, and to cleanse us from all unrighteousness"** (1John 1:9).

6. Whom The Church Should Baptize

When an adult comes to us for baptism, we do not baptize them simply because they want baptism. Wanting baptism is not enough. The words, **"He who believes and is baptized will be saved,"** tell us that all who come must come believing that there is forgiveness in Christ (Mark 16:16). And, the words, **"Without faith it is impossible to please God,"** tell us that without faith baptism is incomplete (Hebrews 11:6). That is why Martin Luther said, "It is not baptism that justifies or benefits anyone, but it is faith in the word of promise, to which baptism is added. This faith justifies, and fulfils that which baptism signifies" (from *The Babylonian Captivity of the Church*).

Furthermore, the Bible calls baptism a **"baptism of repentance,"** because those who believe that there is forgiveness in Christ must want forgiveness. Any man who wants to be baptized, but is not sorry for his sins, and does not want to give up his sinful lifestyle, does not want God to forgive his sin. Instead he wants God to accept his sin. However, that is something that God will never do! And, any church that does accept his sin is condemned by the words, **"He who justifies the wicked, and he that condemns the innocent, are both an abomination to the LORD.** (Proverbs 17:15).

The words, "<u>Repent</u>, **and be baptized... in the name of Jesus Christ for the remission of sins,"** // **"Be baptized, and wash away your sins, calling on the name of the Lord,"** tell us that Christian baptism is a, **"Baptism of repentance for the remission of sins"** (Acts 2:38, Acts 22:16, Mark 1:4). While the words, **"He who**

believes and is baptized will be saved," // "Many of the Corinthians who heard **believed**, and were baptized," // "When they **believed** Philip... they were baptized, both men and women," and "the eunuch said, Look, here is water; what prevents me from being baptized? And Philip said, If you truly **believe**, you may," tell us that Christian baptism is a baptism of believers (Mark 16:16, Acts 18:8, Acts 8:12 and 36-37). Repentance and faith go hand in hand. That is why Dr. Francis Pieper said:

> "Scripture expressly points out that only such adults are to be baptized as have previously come to faith in Christ. Of those baptized on the First Pentecost we read: "Then they that gladly received his word were baptized" (Acts 2:41); and when the eunuch, having been instructed by Philip, desired Baptism, his wish was granted after he had confessed his faith in Christ (Acts 8:36-38)." ["*CHRISTIAN DOGMATICS*", Volume 3, page 277.]

Infant Baptism

"Luther freely admitted that infant baptism is neither explicitly commanded or explicitly mentioned in Scripture. There are no 'specific passages' referring to infant baptism. The direct witness of Scripture is by itself not strong enough to provide an adequate basis for beginning infant baptism were it not already practiced." ("*THE THEOLOGY OF MARTIN LUTHER*", by Paul Althaus, page 361). Why then did Martin Luther vigorously defend infant baptism? That is a question that I will try to answer.

In order to understand the thinking behind Luther's defense of infant baptism, we need to begin by comparing the words, "**Be baptized... and you will receive the gift of the Holy Ghost**," with the words, God "**has sealed us**, and **sent the Spirit into our hearts as a pledge**" (Acts 2:38, 2Corinthians 1:21-22). Taken together, those passages tell us that baptism (and the "gift of the Holy Ghost" that accompanies it) is a "**seal**" of the righteousness that we have through faith in Christ. Comparing those passages with the words, **Abraham**, "**received the sign of circumcision, a seal of the righteousness of the faith**," tells us that there is a clear parallel between baptism and circumcision (Romans 4:11). For that reason, Martin Luther saw baptism as the New Testament replacement for circumcision. Both were given as a "**seal**" of the righteousness that is ours through faith in Christ.

That being understood, the words, "**You shall circumcise the flesh of your foreskin; and it will be a token of the covenant between me and you. And he that is eight days old shall be circumcised among you, every man child in your generations**," tell us that even though circumcision was a "**seal of the righteousness of the faith**," that Abraham had as an adult, God wanted the infant male offspring of Abraham to receive it (Genesis 17:11-12). In fact, Exodus 4:24-26 tells us that God was angry at Moses because he had not circumcised his son. All of that, coupled with the fact that infant baptism can be traced back to the earliest days of the Christian church, Convinced Martin Luther that God wanted the infant offspring of believers baptized.

Another fact that we need to consider is that Luther lived in a nation in which Christianity was the established religion. If the male offspring of Abraham had been allowed to wait until adulthood to decide if they wanted to be circumcised, in every generation there would have been some men who refused to be circumcised. And, if they refused, in most cases their sons would refuse. And, because more would join their ranks in every generation, there would come a time when much of the nation was uncircumcised. In saying that, I realize that the nation of Israel still had many problems, but because of circumcision the male infants grew up believing that they had a responsibility to seek God's mercy and pass on the faith. In a similar vein, Luther realized that his country would quickly cease to be Christian, if Christian parents were not required to have their children baptized. Again, I realize that, like Israel, Europe and America have always had many problems. However, the millions of immigrants that spread across this land over a century ago, filling it with churches, were Christians because the nations that they came from were Christian.

What I have just said, explains why Martin Luther saw the words, "Teach **all nations, baptizing them** in the name of the Father, and of the Son, and of the Holy Ghost," as requiring infant baptism (Matthew 28:19). Living in a country that was officially Christian, he believed that God wanted everyone in the nation baptized, just as God wanted everyone in Israel circumcised.

God's Gift of Faith

The words, "**You are saved by grace through faith; and that not of yourselves: it is the gift of God,**" tell us that faith is a "gift of God" (Ephesians 2:8). And, the words, "**The LORD your God will circumcise your heart, and the heart of your descendants,**" tell us that God is fully able to give His gift of faith to infants (Deuteronomy 30:6). In fact, the words, "**He** [John the Baptist] **will be filled with the Holy Ghost, even from his mother's womb,**" tell us that John the Baptist had faith in Christ before he was born (Luke 1:15). And, because he had faith, **he "leaped in" the "womb for joy," upon hearing the voice of the mother of his Savior** (Luke 1:44).

The words, "**Behold, I was formed in iniquity; and sinful when my mother conceived me,**" tell us that infants are sinners from conception (Psalm 51:5). And, the words, "**Sin entered the world by one man, and death by sin; so death passed upon all men, because all have sinned,**" tell us that if infants were not sinners they would never die of natural causes (Romans 5:12). At the same time, the words, "**The wicked are estranged from the womb,**" tell us that the children of unbelievers are "estranged [from God] from the womb" (Psalm 58:3). As do the words, "**We… were by nature the children of wrath,**" (Ephesians 2:3).

However, the fact that Jesus encouraged believing parents to bring their babies to Him, saying, "**Let the little children come to me, and do not hinder them: for of such is <u>the kingdom of God</u>**," tells us that those children had faith (Luke 18:15-17). We know they had faith because the words, "**Without faith it is impossible to please God,**" tell us that without faith they would not be included in "the kingdom of God" (Hebrews 11:6). And, the words, "**He and all his house were baptized right away,**" tell us that entire households were baptized (Acts 16:33). [See, 1Cor. 1:16, Acts 11:14, Acts 16:15, Acts 18:8.]

When the children of believers die before baptism, we must commend them to God's mercy, knowing that He is fully able to give them faith, just as He gave it to John the Baptist. However, I encourage parents to begin praying for their children while they are yet in the womb. Ask God to give them faith, and commit them to His care, knowing that "**He is able to keep that which**" you "**have committed to Him**" (2Timothy 1:12).

If someone who is baptized does not have faith, and later comes to faith, he does not need to be rebaptized, because faith completes his baptism and makes it valid.

Christians should never do anything underhanded like baptizing children without the knowledge or consent of their parents.

The cultic idea that someone can be baptized in the place of someone else is as unscriptural as the idea that one person can believe for someone else. The words, "What shall they do which are baptized for the dead, KJV" are not talking about being baptized in place of someone else, but being baptized [i.e. becoming a Christian] in order to be reunited with a believing loved one who has passed on (1Corinthians 15:29). That verse could be paraphrased as saying "**What will those who are baptized in the hope of being reunited with the dead do, if the dead do not actually rise? why are they baptized on account of them?**" (1Cor. 15:29).

7. The Administrants Of Baptism

Just as the words, "**Go, and teach all nations, baptizing them in the name of the Father, and of the Son, and of the Holy Ghost,**" authorize every believer to spread the good news of forgiveness in Christ; they also authorize every believer to baptize those who come to faith (Matthew 28:19). In saying this, I am by no means giving my approval to those who separate themselves from other Christians. Every Christian who is led by the Holy Spirit will want baptism to be carried out by the congregation that he or she is a member of, simply because that is the way that is honorable and above reproach. At the same time, there are occasions (such as Philip's baptism of the Ethiopian eunuch) when that is not possible (Acts 8:26-39). And, in such cases every Christian has not only the privilege, but the duty to baptize. As it is written, "**You are a chosen generation, a royal priesthood, a holy nation, a people valued by God; that you should show forth the praises of Him who has called you out of darkness into His marvelous light,**" (1Peter 2:9).

The words, "**All things are yours**" and "**All the promises of God in Him are yea, and in Him Amen,**" tell us that all of the spiritual blessings that Christ has secured for us by His death on the cross, belong to every believer (1Corinthians 3:21, 2Corinthians 1:20). And, we should all want the affairs of the Christian church to be carried out "**decently and in order**" (1Corinthians 14:40).

8. The Necessity Of Baptism

While the words, "**He who believes and is baptized will be saved; but he who does not believe will be damned,**" tell us that faith in Christ is absolutely necessary for salvation, they also tell us that baptism is not absolutely necessary (Mark 16:16). In saying this I want to make it clear that baptism is not an indifferent matter that we can dispense with on a whim. The visible church is God's earthly kingdom, and those who refuse to join themselves to it through baptism place themselves in opposition to His will. The words, "**All the people, even the publicans, who heard John <u>agreed with God</u>, by being baptized with the baptism of John. But the Pharisees and lawyers <u>rejected the counsel of God</u> against themselves, by refusing to be baptized by him,**" tell us that just as coming to baptism is an act of faith, a refusal to be baptized is evidence of unbelief, and that is a serious matter (Luke 7:29-30).

9. Regarding Baptismal Customs

Let me make it clear from the start that when I speak of baptismal customs, I am not talking about anything God has commanded in regard to baptism. While Christ has commanded us to, "**Teach all nations, baptizing them in the name of the Father, and of the Son, and of the Holy Ghost,**" many customs have arisen over the centuries (Matthew 28:19). Not only are there differences in the way the water is applied, or the wording that is used, there are also a number of other practices, such as stating the name of the person being baptized, that are not commanded by Scripture, yet should be kept because they serve a good purpose and rejecting them would cause needless controversy.

One of the customs has to do with the way the water is applied. Regarding that, Martin Luther made the following statements.

> The first thing in baptism to be considered is the divine promise, which says: 'He that believes and is baptized shall be saved'... The second part of baptism is the sign, or sacrament, which is that immersion into water from this also it derives its name. For the Greek baptizo means "I immerse," and baptisma means "immersion." (From *"The Babylonian Captivity of the Church"* by Martin Luther, 1520.)
>
> The act or rite [of baptism] consists in being placed into the water, which flows over us, and being drawn from it again. These two things, the placing in the water and emerging from it signify the power and efficacy of baptism; which is simply the mortifying of the old Adam in us and the resurrection of the new man, both of which operations continue in us as long as we live on the earth. (*"Large Catechism"*, Dr. Lenker's translation, pages 168-169.)

Notice that Luther speaks of immersion. He even translated an ancient baptismal liturgy that called for immersion. At the same time, he never insisted on immersion, and stressed the fact that faith in Christ is of primary importance, not the way the water is applied. In order to understand his reasons, we need to understand that there is a difference between immersion and submersion. Immersionists who understand this sometimes use the term, "total-immersion". Furthermore, the Greek Church, which still baptizes by "immersion," does so by sitting or standing a person in water while pouring water over his or her head. For that reason (and others) Luther saw nothing wrong with baptism by pouring.

In many American churches, a person is baptized by laying them backward, which is based on an interpretation of the words, "**We are buried with Him [Christ] through baptism... If we have been planted together in the likeness of His death, we will also continue together in the likeness of His resurrection**" (Romans 6:4-5). However, a more traditional approach would be to have the person being baptized kneel in water, and have the pastor push his head down (under the water) while saying, "I baptize you etc". The point that I want to stress is that the efficacy of baptism is not determined by the way the water is applied, but by faith in Christ. Because baptism is a ceremonial proclamation of the gospel, we only receive what is promised (the washing away of sin) through faith in Christ.

There are many other customs that could be mentioned; such as referring to the sin of Adam, making the sign of the cross, reading Mark 10:13-16, and praying. And, there is nothing wrong with those customs. However, they are not necessary.

The practice of having sponsors, or God parents, dates back to a time when the Christian church was being persecuted. Parents who could become martyrs were eager to have their children baptized, and the Godparents were fellow Christians who promised to see that the children received a Christian upbringing should the parents be killed. However, sadly, many parents today do not take the idea of Godparents seriously, and sometimes even invite unbelieving friends and relatives to be sponsors. In such cases the pastor cannot seriously ask them to see that the children receive a Christian upbringing, and can only list them as witnesses, not Godparents. And, enemies of the faith [atheists, cultists] should not even be admitted as witnesses.

10. The Baptism Of John The Baptist

As I have already explained, Christian baptism began with John the Baptist, and baptism has always been a divinely instituted way of pointing those who repent to Christ.

The words, "**After this Jesus and His disciples went out into the countryside of Judea; and there He spent some time with them, and baptized. And John was also baptizing in Aenon near to Salim, because there was plenty of water there: and people were coming, and being baptized**," tell us that Jesus and John were baptizing in the same area (John 3:22-23). Even though, "**It was not Jesus who baptized, but His disciples**," they were working together (John 4:2). Furthermore, even though the Apostles, and even Apollos, were baptized by John the Baptist, they were never rebaptized (John 1:35-42, Acts 18:24-25). Therefore, when the Apostle Paul baptized certain men who had been baptized, "**unto John's baptism**," it is fairly obvious that they had not actually been baptized by John the Baptist. John not only did not baptize anyone "unto John's baptism," he pointed all who came to him to Christ, saying "**He will baptize you with the Holy Ghost**," and they had not even heard of the Holy Ghost (Mark 1:8). That is why Dr. John Theodore Mueller said, "We may not be wrong in assuming that the "certain disciples" at Ephesus had not been baptized by John himself, but by some of his followers, who discarded their master's command to join Jesus as "the Lamb of God." ("*CHRISTIAN DOGMATICS*," page 505.) Such groups did exist.

The Doctrine Of The Lord's Supper

1. The Divine Institution Of The Lord's Supper

Our Lord Jesus Christ, the same night in which He was betrayed, took bread and when He had given thanks, He broke it and gave it to His disciples saying, "**Take eat this is My body which is given for you.** This do in remembrance of Me." (Matt. 26:26, Mark 14:22, Luke 22:19, 1Cor. 11:23-24.)

After the same manner, He took the cup when He had supped, and when He had given thanks, He gave it to them saying, "**All of you drink of it; this cup is the New Testament in My blood, which is shed for you for the remission of sins.** This do**, as often as you drink it, in remembrance of Me.**" (Matt. 26:27-28, Mark 14:23-24, Luke 22:20, 1Cor. 11:25-26.)

With those words, Christ instituted "The Lord's Supper" as a perpetual observance of the Christian Church, something we can expect to see observed wherever Christians gather for worship. And, because it was instituted by Christ Himself, it should not be regarded as some rite that the church has come up with, but as a divine institution with the authority of God behind it.

As we look carefully at what Christ said when He instituted His Supper, the words, "**this do**" are significant, because they tell us to do exactly what He did every time we celebrate the Lord's Supper. Just as He said, "**Take eat this is My body which is given for you,**" we should say, "Christ said, '**Take eat this is My body which is given for you**'. And, just as He said, "**This cup is the New Testament in My blood, which is shed for you for the remission of sins** etc." we should say exactly that. The first two paragraphs of this section frame those quotes in a way that provides context. However, the actual words spoken by Christ are of primary importance because **Christ's words are the GOSPEL**. If you do not see that, think about what Christ said. When He said, "**This is My body which is given for you,**" you need to realize that **Christ's body was given for you on the cross**. Likewise, when He said, "**This cup is the New Testament in My blood, which is shed for you for the remission of sins,**" you need to realize that **Christ's blood was shed for you on the cross**. Therefore, when He said, "**This do, as often as you drink it, in remembrance of Me,**" **He was telling us to do it as a ceremonial way of reminding all of us that He died for our sins**, while assuring us of "**the remission of sins**" through His sacrifice. In short, the Lord's Supper was instituted as a ceremonial proclamation of the gospel.

Some Christians have a tender conscience, and need assurance that their sins are forgiven. And, whenever the Lord's Supper is administered as Christ intended, they should go to the Lord's Supper believing that there is forgiveness in Christ, and come away **believing that they have forgiveness through the blood of Christ** – and that is the very essence of faith. In that way, God uses the Lord's Supper to give faith to those who do not understand what faith is. And, **everyone who believes that Christ's body was given for them (on the cross), and that His blood was shed for them (on the cross) so that they could have forgiveness, truly receives Christ's body and blood, not as something physical but as the atonement for their sin.**

Ways Satan Attacks the Lord's Supper

Christ instituted His Supper during Passover so that it would point to Him as the true Passover sacrifice. Therefore, the bread and wine that He used would have been the same unleavened bread and Passover wine that all Jews used at that time. So one way that Satan attacks the Lord's Supper is by eliminating the bread and wine, or replacing it with something else.

One perversion of the Lord's Supper eliminates the wine entirely. Another replaces the wine with water. In one cult almost no one partakes because they are told that it is not for everyone. Some sects have eliminated it entirely. I have even heard of milk and cookies being used. And, in every case where this happens, it happens because some men are exalting their will over God's will, and replacing His Word with their word. When Christ instituted His Supper He was dead serious. And, **even if we do not fully understand how Christ uses His Supper to further His kingdom, no one has the right to disregard what He said, or to treat what He instituted in a flippant and irresponsible way.**

2. A Ceremonial Proclamation Of The Gospel

Christ instituted His Supper as a way of telling each one of us that His body was "**given for**" us and that His blood was "**shed for**" us, "**for the remission of sins**". And, that promise is the very heart of the gospel. In other words, there is no difference between saying that Christ's body and blood were "given" and "shed for you," and saying that **Christ died for your sins**. That is why Christ said, "**This cup is the New Testament [i.e. gospel] in My blood**" (Luke 22:20). Those words of Christ are very important because they tell us that the gospel ["**New Testament**"] is **the good news of forgiveness in Christ**, not a new set of rules.

"The whole virtue of the Lord's Supper consists in those words of Christ, in which He testifies that **forgiveness is granted to all who believe that His body is given and His blood shed for them.**" (Martin Luther, *"The Babylonian Captivity of the Church,"* 1520.)

"The promise of the New Testament is the promise of the forgiveness of sins, as the text says, "this is my body, which is given for you"; "this is the cup of the new testament with my blood, which is poured out for many for the forgiveness of sins." (Luke 22:19, Matt. 26:28) **Therefore the Word offers forgiveness of sins, while the ceremony is a sort of picture or "seal," as Paul calls it** (Rom. 4:11), showing forth the promise." ("*The Book of Concord*," Tappert edition, page 262.)

"In the Lord's Supper, the word of Christ is the testament; the bread and wine are the sacrament [i.e. sign]. And as there is greater power in the word than in the sign, so is there greater power in the testament than in the sacrament. **A man can have and use the word or testament without the sign** or sacrament. 'Believe,' says Augustine, 'and you have eaten;' but in what do we believe except in the word of Him who promises? Thus I can have the Lord's Supper daily, nay hourly; since, as often as I will, I can set before myself the words of Christ, and nourish and strengthen my faith in them; and **this is in very truth the spiritual eating and drinking**." (Martin Luther, "*The Babylonian Captivity of the Church*," 1520.)

The words just quoted raise one important question. If Martin Luther regarded the bread and wine that we receive in the Lord's Supper as "signs" of Christ's body and blood, why was he so adamant in his opposition to Ulrich Zwingli? The two of them met in the German City of Marburg, but they could not agree regarding the Lord's Supper. And, many today wrongly assume that they could not agree because they each had a different interpretation. However, the words of Luther that I have just quoted prove that was not the case. Zwingli and Luther both agreed that the bread and wine were "signs" of Christ's body and blood. **The problem arose when Zwingli said** that the bread (in the Lord's Supper), "is not really Christ's body, it just represents Christ's body," **Luther did not object** to the claim that the bread represented Christ's body, but to the, words, "It is not really Christ's body". That was the real point of contention! **Zwingli was contradicting Christ**. In other words, Christ said, "This is My body" and Zwingli replied, "It is not really His body". That is what Luther objected to, and that is why Luther simply quoted Christ's words ("This is My body") and made it clear that he was not going to budge from what they said.

Luther was not afraid that someone might assume that they were receiving actual flesh and blood with the bread and wine, that would not affect their salvation. However, he knew that doubting Christ's words, "**My body is given for you**" and "**My blood is shed for you**" would.

Zwingli was totally clueless as to why Luther was upset by what he taught. He could not see beyond the Romish claim that actual flesh and blood are present. And, because he failed to see that the Lord's Supper is a ceremonial proclamation of the gospel, he could not understand that **by contradicting Christ's words, he was making the "Word of God of no effect"** (Mark 7:13). In saying this I realize that the gospel is not limited to the Lord's Supper. However, Christ instituted His Supper for reasons that we might not fully understand, and **when He said, "this do" He was telling us to repeat and affirm what He said, not contradict it.**

Luther stood firmly on the Word of God, and **everyone who believes that Christ's body was given for them (on the cross), and that His blood was shed for them (on the cross) so they can have forgiveness, truly receives Christ's body and blood, not as something physical but as the atonement for their sin.**

3. The Words Of Institution

Scripture records the words that Christ used to institute His Supper in four places. In each of those accounts the inspired writer briefly recounts what was said, and every student of Scripture knows that there are minor differences in the accounts.

In the past, skeptics have used those differences to attack the Bible, and deny its inspiration. However, police investigator J. Warner Wallace found the minor differences in the various accounts to be evidence of their truthfulness, and one of the things that led him to become a Christian. As a police investigator, he found that whenever witnesses agree perfectly, it is because they have agreed on what to say. But, when there is no collusion there are always minor, but easily reconcilable, differences. [His testimony is on youtube.]

The Words Take Eat This Is My Body
Matthew 26:26 **As they were eating, Jesus took bread, and blessed** *it*, **and broke** *it*, **and gave** *it* **to the disciples, saying, Take, eat; this is my body.**
Mark 14:22 **As they ate, Jesus took bread, and blessed, and broke** *it*, **and gave to them, saying, Take, eat: this is my body.**
Luke 22:19 **He took bread, and gave thanks, and broke** *it*, **and gave it to them, saying, This is my body which is given for you: this do in remembrance of me.**
1Corinthians 11:23-24 **The Lord Jesus the** *same* **night in which He was betrayed took bread: And after giving thanks, He broke** *it*, **and said, Take, eat: this is my body, which is broken for you: this do in remembrance of me.**

While all four of these accounts tell us that Christ said, "**This is**

My body," the words, "**Whosoever shall eat this bread,**" tell us that the bread remained bread, and the fact that Christ's physical body was doing the talking tells us that He was not passing out His physical flesh (1Corinthians 11:27). At the same time, we should never contradict what He said! Through the words of His Supper He truly gives us His body, not as something physical, but as the atonement for our sin. And, all who receive it are, "**Members of His body, of His flesh, and of His bones**" (Ephesians 5:30).

The Words This Is My Blood

Matthew 26:27-28 **He took the cup, and gave thanks, and gave** *it* **to them, saying, Drink from it, all of you; for this is my blood of the new testament, that is shed for many for the remission of sins.**

Mark 14:23-24 **He took the cup, and when He had given thanks, He gave** *it* **to them: and they all drank of it. And He said to them, This is my blood of the new testament, that is shed for many.**

Luke 22:20 **Likewise also the cup after supper, saying, This cup** *is* **the new testament in my blood, which is shed for you.**

1Corinthians 11:25 **In the same way** *He* **also** *took* **the cup, after He had eaten, saying, This cup is the new testament in my blood: do this, as often as you drink** *it*, **in remembrance of me.**

While all four of these accounts tell us that Christ said, "**This is My blood,**" His presence tells us that He was not passing out physical blood. Yet we should never contradict what He said (Isaiah 8:20). **His words, "Which is shed for you," tell us that He was talking about the blood that was "shed" on the cross (not a symbol).** And, through the words of His Supper He truly does give us His blood, not as something physical, but as the atonement for our sin. The ceremony promises us Christ's body and blood as the atonement for our sin, while faith receives what is promised (Galatians 3:6,22).

The words, "**The cup of blessing which we bless, is it not the communion of the blood of Christ? The bread which we break, is it not the communion of the body of Christ? For we being many are one bread, and one body: for we are all partakers of that one bread,**" tell us that all who partake are bound together in one body through faith in Him (1Corinthians 10:16-17).

4. The Material Elements In The Lord's Supper

It should be obvious that Christ wants us to affirm the truth of what He said when He instituted His Supper. And, it should also be obvious that we cannot be honest in our affirmation of what He said, and at the same time contradict what He said whenever the Lord's Supper is offered. **Because we want everyone who partakes of the Lord's Supper to believe that Christ's body was given for them (on the cross), and because we want everyone who partakes to believe that Christ's blood was shed for them (on the cross), we want them to believe every word that Christ spoke as He gave out the bread and wine.** And, after they partake we want them to believe that they have received Christ's body and blood [i.e. His sacrifice] as the atonement for their sin. But, that is not what they are going to believe if they are being told that they did not really receive His body and blood. For that reason, we need to assure them that they have truly received Christ's body and blood as the atonement for their sin.

However, we do not want to depart from Scripture in the other direction by claiming that the bread and wine change into Christ's body and blood. As I have said, because Christ instituted His Supper during Passover, the bread and wine that He used would have been the same unleavened bread and Passover wine that all Jews used at that time. And, the words, **"Whoever eats the bread, and drinks the cup of the Lord,"** tell us that when we partake, what we eat and drink is bread and wine (1Corinthians 11:27). That means that whenever we partake of the Lord's Supper in the way that Christ intended, we eat and drink bread and wine while truly receiving Christ's body and blood, not as something physical but as the atonement for our sins.

Let's Not Confuse The Issue

The following discourse by Christ is sometimes confused with the Lord's Supper. "**Jesus said to them, Truly, truly, I say unto you, unless you eat the flesh of the Son of man, and drink His blood, you have no life in you. Whoever eats my flesh, and drinks my blood, has eternal life; and I will raise him up on the last day**" (John 6:53-54). These verses are not describing the Lord's Supper, because it had not yet been instituted when Christ made those statements. Furthermore, the grammar is different. In these verses, He calls His body "bread" (which is a metaphor), yet in the Lord's Supper He calls bread His "Body" (which is the opposite of a metaphor). In fact, calling bread His "body," is the equivalent of saying, "that door is me" instead of saying "I am the door". For that reason, we should never use John 6:51-59 as an explanation of the Lord's Supper.

However, these verses do describe our faith in Christ as a spiritual eating and drinking. Through faith we partake of His sacrifice. And, that does take place when we partake of the Lord's Supper.

5. The Lord's Supper As A Means Of Grace

Because **"the gospel of Christ... is the power of God unto salvation to every one who believes,"** it is the gospel message proclaimed by the Lord's Supper – the good news that Christ's body was given for us on the cross, and that His blood was shed for us on the cross so that we could have forgiveness – that makes the Lord's Supper a means of grace. And, the purpose of the Lord's Supper is to assure us that we have received Christ's body and blood [His death] as the atonement for our sin.

At the same time, **because Christ only died once, every offer of the Lord's Supper can be viewed as a continuation of what Christ did when He instituted it – as opposed to an imitation or copy of what He did.** Viewed that way, there has only been one celebration of the Lord's Supper in history; because the one that Christ started is still going on. In other words, just as Christ passed the elements (the bread and cup) to the Apostles, they passed them to others, who passed them to still others all the way down through history to us. And, just as Peter repeated Christ's words as he passed the elements on to others, pastors today repeat Christ's words as they pass the elements on to us. Viewed that way, the blessing that Christ placed on the elements [see Matt. 26:26] remains upon the elements, and every time we partake we are partaking of that first Lord's Supper. Moreover, every time we partake we are reminded that His body was given, and His blood was shed [on the cross], to secure forgiveness for us.

That being understood, **we only have a valid celebration of the Lord's Supper when those administering it are doing what Christ told them to do** when He said, **"This do"** (Luke 22:19). That means that just as Christ used bread and wine, we should use bread and wine. And, just as Christ said, **"Take, eat: this is my body, which is broken for you,"** and **"This cup *is* the new testament in my blood, which is shed for you,"** those administering Christ's Supper should repeat His words (1Corinthians 11:24, Luke 22:20).

When it comes to the elements being used, although the Bible refers to the contents of the cup as, **"The fruit of the vine,"** that phrase is a Jewish synonym for wine (Luke 22:18). And, Christ would have used Passover wine. However, because it is now possible to pasteurize grape juice (in order to prevent fermentation) many American churches are using grape juice in the Lord's Supper. That has resulted in some controversy. However, because grapes are the fruit of the vine, using grape juice is less objectionable than using wine made from something other than grapes, such as peaches.

In order to do the will of God, the words that Christ spoke when He instituted His Supper must be taken seriously, not explained away. And, those who come should come respectfully, with **"a heart that is** humbled and sorry for sin" (Psalm 51:17). That rules out all attempts to alter the Lord's Supper by eliminating the cup, changing the elements, or failing to repeat what Christ said etc. Because such changes call into question the validity of what is being done they undermine the very purpose Christ intended for His Supper to serve, and should be condemned by all.

6. Who May Be Admitted To The Lord's Supper

In administering the Lord's Supper, the words, "**Let a man examine himself... For he who eats and drinks unworthily, eats and drinks damnation to himself,**" need to be taken very seriously (1Corinthians 11:28-29). Those words tell us that we should never just pass out the bread and wine willy-nilly with no regard for who might partake. Nevertheless, that happens all the time in American churches. Unbaptized children partake because the bread and cup are just passed around without regard for the spiritual state of those who partake. I know of one child who said that he only took the cup because he did not like the bread. And, I know of one case where a Moslem who was visiting the church was allowed to partake. That is totally irresponsible!

Because "**The blood of Jesus Christ His Son cleanses us of all sin,**" **it is the blood of Jesus Christ and His blood alone that makes us worthy to partake of His Supper.** That fact excludes unbelievers, and all who have not publicly accepted Christ by being baptized. At the same time, all who do come should first examine themselves, with a willingness to look at their faults and repent of any wrongdoing. In short, those who come to the Lord's Supper should **come with "a heart that is humbled and sorry for sin"** (Psalm 51:17). It is the unrepentant and unbelieving who are unworthy, and the self-righteous [those who think that their works make them worthy] are just as unrepentant as those who defend and excuse their sin.

The words, "**If your brother sins against you, go and tell him his fault between you and him alone: if he will hear you, you have gained your brother. But if he will not listen, then take one or two others with you, so that every word may be established by the testimony of two or three witnesses. And if he refuses to listen to them, tell it to the church: but if he refuses to hear the church, let him be to you as a heathen man and a publican,**" tell us that any man who will not repent, even after these steps have been followed, should be regarded "**as a heathen man**" (Matthew 18:15-17). **And, "as a heathen man," he should not partake of the Lord's Supper.**

Here is God's warning. "**Whoever eats the bread, and drinks *the* cup of the Lord, unworthily, will be guilty of the body and blood of the Lord. But let a man examine himself, then let him eat of *the* bread, and drink of *the* cup. For he who eats and drinks unworthily, eats and drinks damnation to himself, not recognizing the Lord's body. That is why many among you *are* weak and sickly, and many sleep. For if we would judge ourselves, we would not be judged. But when we are judged, we are chastened by the Lord, so that we will not be condemned with the world" (1Corinthians 11:27-32).

In the verses just quoted, the words, **"Not recognizing the Lord's body,"** point to those who fail to recognize Christ's body [His Sacrifice] as the source of forgiveness (1Corinthians 11:29). At the same time, the words, **"If we would judge ourselves,"** can be explained by Christ's parable of the Pharisee and the publican (Luke 18:10-14). In that parable, the publican judged himself, saying, **"God be merciful to me a sinner"** (Luke 18:13). In contrast, the Pharisee thought that his works made him worthy.

Because the Lord's Supper is not open to unbelievers, it should never be offered to atheists, those who have not been baptized, the members of pagan religions, cults, and lodges, or those too young to examine themselves.

> "In general, it may be said that all baptized Christians who heartily repent of their sins, truly believe in Jesus Christ, regard the ordinance of Holy Communion as Christ instituted it, are open to Christian instruction on every point of doctrine and life, are able to examine themselves, lead a Christian life, and purpose to amend their lives by the aid of the Holy Spirit should be admitted to the Lord's Table." (*"Christian Dogmatics,"* by John Theodore Mueller, page 539.)

7. The Necessity Of The Lord's Supper

Since the Lord's Supper is a ceremonial proclamation of the gospel, we are saved by believing the gospel message that it proclaims, not by receiving the bread and the wine. And, because the same gospel promise is proclaimed through preaching, the Lord's Supper is not absolutely necessary for our salvation in the same sense that faith in Christ is necessary. At the same time, because Christ works through His Supper to plant and nurture faith, if someone neglects it and has no interest in receiving it, he is rejecting the gospel promise that it conveys, and that could be the sign of a deeper problem.

Now, because partaking of the Lord's Supper is not absolutely necessary for our salvation, when a congregation excommunicates someone, they are warning that person of a very real danger to their soul, not keeping them from being saved. The words, **"Whoever you will bind on earth will be bound in heaven,"** convey a very serious warning (Matthew 16:19). And, that warning should never be twisted into a tool for imposing the will of one man on another. In fact, when the Apostle Paul commanded the Corinthian congregation to, **"Expel that wicked man from your congregation,"** it was only done because he was unrepentant and **"in order that his soul might be saved"** (1Corinthians 5:1-12). And, because anyone who is placed under church discipline in that way is to be regarded **"as a heathen man and a publican,"** they are no longer welcome to partake of the Lord's Supper (Matthew 18:17-18).

Examine yourselves, to see if you are in the faith.
2Corinthians 13:5

SCRIPTURE ALONE

THE DOCTRINE OF THE CHURCH AND MINISTRY
(Ecclesiology)

The Doctrine Of The Christian Church

A. The Church Universal

1. God's Heavenly Kingdom

The kingdom of God is not the same thing as the visible church. Visible church organizations and congregations are a part of God's earthly kingdom. While only believers are citizens of God's heavenly kingdom.

Christ's words, **"Unless a man is born of water and of the Spirit, he cannot enter the kingdom of God,"** tell us that God's heavenly kingdom only includes those who are born again (John 3:5). The words, **"To as many as received Him, He gave power to become the sons of God, even to those who believe in His name,"** tell us that we are born again [become "the sons of God"] through faith in Christ (John 1:12). And because we cannot look into anyone's heart, to see if they are born again, **"The kingdom of God does not come in a way that is seen... for, the kingdom of God is within you"** (Luke 17:20-21). That is why Christ's heavenly kingdom is sometimes called "**the invisible church**".

"The Church, which is truly the kingdom of Christ, is properly the congregation of saints. For the wicked are ruled by the devil and are captives of the devil; they are not ruled by the Spirit of Christ." ("*Apology of the Augsburg Confession,*" articles 7-8, #16.)

Now some people see the words, **"The unrighteous will not inherit the kingdom of God,"** and assume that their own efforts at making themselves righteous will get them into God's heavenly kingdom (1Corinthians 6:9). However, the words, **"No man living is righteous in your sight,"** tell us that no one is good enough to get into God's kingdom on the basis of their own righteousness (Psalm 143:2). The only righteousness that will get anyone into the kingdom of heaven is, **"The righteousness of God which comes through** faith in Jesus Christ to all and upon all who believe" (Romans 3:22). That is why the Bible tells us that, "**Christ is the end of the law for righteousness to every one who believes**" (Romans 10:4).

Although the words, "**No flesh will ever be justified in God's sight by the deeds of the law**," tell us that our own efforts at making ourselves righteous will never make us sinless [righteous] in the sight of God, and, therefore, will never get us into God's heavenly kingdom (Romans 3:20): The words, "**I am the vine, you are the branches: He who remains in me, and I in him, produces much fruit: for you can do nothing without me**," tell us that as soon as we are saved Christ will begin working in us to produce fruit (John 15:5).

The words, "**For you are all the children of God through faith in Christ Jesus**," again tell us that we become the "children of God" [i.e. are born again] through faith in Christ (Galatians 3:26). The words, "**If any man is in Christ he is a new creation: the old things have passed away; behold, all things have become new**," tell us that being born again will result in a change in our conduct (2Corinthians 5:17). And the words, "**He has given you life, who were dead in trespasses and sins; in which you formerly walked according to the way of this world, according to the prince of the power of the air, the spirit that now works in the children of disobedience**," tell us that change in our conduct is the result of receiving the Holy Spirit (Ephesians 2:1-2). As it is written, "**Walk in the Spirit, and you will not fulfill the lust of the flesh. For the flesh lusts against the Spirit, and the Spirit against the flesh: and they are opposed to each other: so that you cannot do the things that you would**" (Galatians 5:16-17).

The words, "**Your body is the temple of the Holy Ghost who is in you, who you have received from God**," tell us that, because the Holy Spirit dwells in all who trust in Christ our bodies are now the temple [dwelling place] of God (1Corinthians 6:19). The words, "**You are a chosen generation, a royal priesthood, a holy nation, a people valued by God; that you should show forth the praises of Him who has called you out of darkness into His marvelous light**," tell us that we have been chosen by God (1Peter 2:9). And, the words, "**You also are being built, as living stones, into a spiritual temple, to be holy priests**," tell us that because our bodies are the temple [dwelling place] of God we are all priests of God, as His witnesses to a lost and dying world (1Peter 2:5).

Before concluding this section I want to make it clear that those who have truly come to faith in Christ, and received the Holy Spirit, will want to be baptized. In some cases they may have been baptized before coming to faith. In other cases they may have come to faith before baptism. However, even though they become citizens of God's heavenly kingdom as soon as they come to faith, the words, "**All the people, even the publicans, who heard John, agreed with God, by being baptized... But the Pharisees and lawyers rejected the counsel of God against themselves, by refusing to be baptized," tell us that if a person claims to have faith in Christ, yet refuses to be baptized, he may not actually have faith (Luke 7:29-30).

2. Erroneous Doctrines Concerning The Church

Since we become citizens of God's heavenly kingdom through faith in Christ, what the Bible tells us about Christ's church must be understood in the light of what it says about Christ's sacrificial death, the gospel as the means of grace, and our faith as the hand that receives God's grace.

Concerning Christ's sacrificial death the words, "**Christ was once offered to bear the sins of many,**" and "**We were reconciled to God by the death of His Son,**" tell us that "**We have redemption through His blood, the forgiveness of sins, according to the riches of His grace**" (Hebrews 9:28, Romans 5:10, Ephesians 1:7). Anyone who denies these truths about Christ is bound to err regarding His church.

Concerning faith and the means of grace, the words, "**No man can come to me, unless the Father who has sent me draws him,**" tells us that we can do nothing to save ourselves (John 6:44). The words, "**The gospel of Christ... is the power of God unto salvation to every one who believes,**" and the words, "**Faith comes by hearing, and hearing by the word of God,**" tell us that the gospel is the means that God uses to bring us to faith (Romans 1:16). And, the words, "**We... have access by faith into this grace,**" tell us that faith is the hand that receives the forgiveness [grace] Christ won for us by His death on the cross (Romans 5:2). Anyone who denies these truths is bound to err regarding the church.

Regarding those who err — A number of cults confuse their own organizations with God's heavenly kingdom. And, because they equate their own organization with God's heavenly kingdom they regard everyone outside of their organization as lost.

Those who err in regard to Christ's atonement tend to see the promotion of outward works or moral reform as the purpose of their organization; and see outward piety [infused grace] as proof of the work of the Holy Spirit, and thus, citizenship in God's heavenly kingdom.

Those who err in regard to faith tend to equate salvation with a decision or experience rather than faith in Christ. Those under that influence will sometimes seek assurance so desperately that they convince themselves that they are saved when they are not. If they do not deceive themselves, their experience is, at best, a fruit of faith, not faith itself.

The words, "**Christ is of no benefit to those of you who seek righteousness by the law; you are fallen from grace,**" are God's warning to all who seek "**to establish their own righteousness**" (Galatians 5:4 and Romans 10:3). And, the words, "**All who trust in the law are under a curse: for it is written, Cursed is every one who does not continue to do everything that is written in the book of the law,**" are God's warning to all who delude themselves into thinking that they can make themselves righteous without doing everything that the Law requires (Galatians 3:10).

The words, "**Abraham believed God, and it was counted to him for righteousness,**" tell us that righteousness comes through faith, not works (Romans 4:3). And, the words, "**All the prophets testify of Him, that through His name whoever believes in Him will receive forgiveness of sins,**" tell us that salvation has always been through faith in Christ and always will be through faith in Christ (Acts 10:43). As it is written, "**There is no other name under heaven given among men, by which we must be saved**" (Acts 4:12).

3. The Properties Of The Christian Church

From the Bible we learn that God's heavenly kingdom has the following characteristics or properties.

First of all, the Bible tells us that, "**The kingdom of God does not come in a way that is seen... for, the kingdom of God is within you**" (Luke 17:20-21). In other words, because we cannot see into the hearts of those who profess to believe, we cannot see who the members of God's heavenly kingdom are. So the first characteristic of God's heavenly kingdom is that **it is invisible**. That is why Christ's heavenly kingdom is sometimes called "**the invisible church**". In theology we stress that fact in order to make it clear that the one true church is not a visible organization.

However, even though God's heavenly kingdom is invisible to us, the words, "**You, and you alone, know the hearts of all the children of men,**" tell us that it is not invisible to God (1Kings 8:39). The words, "**I am the good shepherd, and know my sheep, and they know me,**" tell us that "**The Lord knows those who are His**" (John 10:14, 2Timothy 2:19). And, the words, "**When Christ, who is our life, appears, then you will also appear with Him in glory,**" tell us God's heavenly kingdom will remain invisible to us until the resurrection (Colossians 3:4).

Secondly, because Christ's heavenly kingdom includes everyone God has brought to faith in Christ, it is not divided. The words, "**There is one body, and one Spirit, just as you were called to one hope in your calling,**" tell us that all who share the "one hope" [i.e. trust in Christ] are one body, the body of Christ (Ephesians 4:4).

As it is written, "**We, being many, are one body in Christ,**" and again, "**For you are all one in Christ Jesus**" (Romans 12:5, Galatians 3:28). So the second characteristic of God's heavenly kingdom is that **it is one**.

Because "**The blood of Jesus Christ His Son cleanses us of all sin,**" everyone who is a citizen of God's heavenly kingdom is sinless in the sight of God (1John 1:7). The words, "**I have suffered the loss of all these things, and regard them as dung, that I may win Christ, And be found in Him, not having any righteousness of my own, which is of the law, but that which is through faith in Christ, the righteousness that comes from God by faith,**" tell us that the cleansing from sin that is ours in Christ makes us righteous in the sight of God (Philippians 3:8-9). And the words, "**By one offering He [Christ] has perfected for ever those who are sanctified,**" tell us that Christ's death on our behalf makes us holy in the sight of God (Hebrews 10:14). So the third characteristic of God's heavenly kingdom is that **it is holy**.

The words, "**All the prophets testify of Him [Christ], that through His name whoever believes in Him will receive forgiveness of sins,**" and the words, "**Nor is there salvation in any other: for there is no other name under heaven given among men, by which we must be saved,**" tell us that God's heavenly kingdom includes everyone who has been saved in every period of history (Acts 10:43 and 4:12). So Christ's heavenly kingdom is not only "one," it is "universal". Therefore, the fourth characteristic of God's heavenly kingdom is that **it is universal**. Moreover, because the word "catholic" means "universal," and no earthly organization can honestly claim to be "universal," only Christ's heavenly kingdom is truly catholic.

The words, "**Built upon the foundation of the apostles and prophets, Jesus Christ himself being the chief corner stone,**" tell us that Christ's church [see Matt. 16:18] is built on the foundation of the apostles and prophets [i.e. the ones God inspired to write Scripture] (Ephesians 2:20). The words, "**His gift made some, apostles; and some, prophets; and some, evangelists; and some, pastors and teachers,**" list the apostles first because the things that the prophets wrote are to be interpreted to agree with what the apostles taught (Ephesians 4:11). The words, "**They devoted themselves to the apostles' doctrine,**" tell us that the apostles' doctrine is the doctrine that Christ wants taught (Acts 2:42). And, the words, "**I pray for... those who will believe in me through their [the apostles] word,**" tell us that those who "believe in" Christ, believe through the word of the apostles (John 17:20). So the fifth characteristic of God's heavenly kingdom is that **it is apostolic**.

Originally there was no difference in rank between pastors, priests and bishops. Congregations chose some of the elder men in the congregation [presbyters] to be overseers [bishops] of the congregation, and these elder/overseers were called pastors [shepherds]. So the idea that bishops are above priests and pastors, or that "apostolic succession" is passed on through bishops, does not come from the Bible. **Only those congregations where the doctrine of the apostles is taught can honestly claim to be "apostolic"**. [Our English word "priest" originated as a slur of the Greek term "prēsbyter," and both words mean "elder".]

Finally, because Christ's heavenly kingdom includes everyone who ever has or ever will be "born again," **no saved person is outside of it**. Since I have already given the passages that tell us that God's heavenly kingdom is "one" and "universal" I will not repeat those passages here. However, the sixth characteristic of God's heavenly kingdom is that **there is no salvation outside of it**.

4. The Glory Of The Christian Church

Having been delivered from the power of Satan by the blood of Christ, the words, **"We ought to obey God rather than men,"** tell us that no one has the authority to stop us from preaching the gospel (Acts 5:29). While the words, **"Don't you realize that the saints will judge the world?"** tell us that in the eyes of God those who trust in Christ are masters of all and servants of none (1Corinthians 6:2). The words, **"Let this mind be in you, which was also in Christ Jesus, who... being found in human form... humbled himself, and became obedient unto death, even the death of the cross,"** tell us that we are not to defy earthly authorities, [unless they command us to disobey God] but are to, **"Submit... to every ordinance of man for the Lord's sake"** (Philippians 2:5-8, 1Peter 2:13). In short, for Christ's sake we are to appear to men as servants of all and masters of none.

The words, **"You are Christ's; and Christ is God's,"** // **"You were bought with a price; do not become the servants of men,"** tell us that we are not to blindly follow men (1Corinthians 3:23 and 7:23). On the contrary, the words, **"Beware of false prophets, who come to you in sheep's clothing, but inwardly are ravening wolves,"** // **"I speak as to wise men; judge for yourselves what I say,"** tell us that we are not to blindly accept any teaching that is contrary to the Word of God (Matthew 7:15 and 1Corinthians 10:15). Instead we are to **search "the scriptures daily, to see,"** if what we are being **taught agrees with what the Bible explicitly says"** (Acts 17:11).

The words, **"You are not to be called Rabbi: for one is your Master, even Christ; and you are all brethren. And do not call anyone on earth father: for you have one Father, who is in heaven. Nor are you to be called masters: for you have one Master, even Christ,"** tell us that all believers are equal before God

(Matthew 23:8-10). That means that no religious leader can command us to accept his authority over the word of God. And, the words, "**The son of perdition, who opposes and exalts himself over everything that is called God**," tell us that anyone who does exalt his word over the Word of God should be regarded as an antichrist (2Thessalonians 2:3-4).

Because the Bible tells us that **Christ's "gift made some... pastors and teachers**," we know that Christ does provide those who trust in Him with godly pastors and teachers (Ephesians 4:11). And, the words, "**If any man speaks, let him speak according to God's Word; if any man serves, let him do it with the ability that God gives**," tell us that those teachers that God provides will not use their position to exalt themselves, or teach contrary to Scripture, but will "speak according to God's Word," letting God's Word be the authority (1Peter 4:11).

However, the words, "**Do not listen to what the prophets who prophesy to you say: they give you empty hopes: they tell you about visions from their own imagination, and not from the mouth of the LORD**," warn us against assuming that every pastor or teacher is of God (Jeremiah 23:16). And, the words, "**If anyone teaches otherwise, and will not agree with sound teaching, even the words of our Lord Jesus Christ, and the doctrine that is in accord with godliness; He is proud, knowing nothing**," tell us that we are not to listen to anyone who contradicts what the Bible plainly says (1Timothy 6:3-4). In short, we are not to listen to pastors or teachers because they are called and ordained, but because they speak the Word of God. In fact, the words "**He who listens to you [the Apostles] listens to me; and he who rejects you rejects me; and he who rejects me rejects Him who sent me**," tell us that those who reject the word of the Apostles reject God (Luke 10:16).

Furthermore, the fact that those who trust in Christ are to judge what is being taught tells us that pastors are not mediators between God and His people, but servants of the flock. As it is written, "**Feed the flock of God that is under your care... Not as lords over those in your care, but as examples to the flock**" (1Peter 5:2-3). And, the words, "**I tell you truly, Whatever you [the congregation] bind on earth will be bound in heaven: and whatever you loose on earth will be loosed in heaven**," remind us that the power of the keys rests with the congregation (Matthew 18:18). God's people have a responsibility to see that the gospel is faithfully taught, and that the Word of God is not corrupted.

5. How The Church Is Founded And Preserved

While Christ's words, "**Unless a man is born of water and of the**

Spirit, he cannot enter the kingdom of God," tell us that God's heavenly kingdom only includes those who are born again; the words, "**Not born of blood, or of the will of the flesh, or of the will of man, but of God**," tell us that the new birth is solely the work of God (John 3:5 and 1:13). And, because we are born again by the work of God, and not "**the will of man**," the Christian church exists solely because God has brought it into existence and sustains it. However, the words, "**It pleased God to save those who believe through the foolishness of preaching**," and "**Faith comes by hearing, and hearing by the word of God**" tell us that God works through "preaching" to build and sustain His church (1Corinthians 1:21, Romans 10:17). As it is written, "**The gospel of Christ… is the power of God to salvation to every one who believes**" (Romans 1:16).

Because we receive the new birth through the work of believers [i.e. the citizens of God's heavenly kingdom], the Bible tells us that God's heavenly kingdom [**the Jerusalem which is above**] "**is the mother of us all**" (Galatians 4:26).

The words, "**What is the exceeding greatness of His power toward us who believe, according to the working of His mighty power**," tell us that we have been brought to faith [believe] through God's "mighty power," the same "**power of God unto salvation**" that is expressed through the gospel (Ephesians 1:19, Romans 1:16). The words, "**No one can say that Jesus is the Lord, but by the Holy Ghost**," but "**You are a <u>chosen</u> generation, a royal priesthood, a holy nation, a people valued by God**," tell us that if it seemed to us like we were choosing God, in reality He was choosing us (1Corinthians 12:3, 1Peter 2:9). And, the words, "**Kept by the power of God through faith unto salvation**," tell us that we are not only brought to faith by the power of God, but are kept in faith by His power (1Peter 1:5).

The Spiritual Warfare of God's Saints

The words, "**Even though we live in the flesh, we do not carry on our war according to the flesh: For the weapons we fight with are not the weapons of the world, but through God they have the power to break down strongholds**," tell us that we are involved in a war, not a war fought with guns and bombs, but a war of light against darkness in which our weapon is the Word of God (2Corinthians 10:3-4). **Why** does this war exist? The words, "**Whoever commits sin is the servant of sin**," and "**Sin entered the world by one man, and death by sin**," tell us that sin brought Adam [along with everything under Adam's authority] under Satan's dominion (John 8:34, Romans 5:12). And, the words, "**Because you have done this, you are cursed above all cattle, and above every beast of the field**," tell us that Adam's sin brought a curse upon all creation (Genesis 3:14).

The power of the gospel is removing that curse from the world one believer at a time, and Satan is fighting against it tooth and nail. However, **God wants us to win this war by doing "good to those who hate you" and praying "for those who spitefully use you, and persecute you"** (Matthew 5:44). That is important because <u>we are not fighting</u> "**against flesh and blood, but against principalities, against powers, against the rulers of the darkness of this world, against spiritual wickedness in high places**" (Ephesians 6:12): And, when Christianity triumphs, God wants the world to know that it has triumphed "**not by might, nor by power, but by**" His "**Spirit**" (Zechariah 4:6).

B. Concerning Local Churches

1. God's Earthly Kingdom

It is important to distinguish between God's heavenly kingdom, **the kingdom that "is within you,"** and His earthly kingdom (Luke 17:21). Although God's earthly kingdom began as the nation of Israel, because of wickedness, the children of Israel were carried captive into Babylon – where congregational worship began. And, the development of congregations [synagogues] made it possible for Jews to spread throughout the Mediterranean area without losing their identity. That is why, by the day of Pentecost, there were, "**Devout Jews from every nation under heaven, present in Jerusalem**" (Acts 2:5). Many of those Jews were the first Christians, and the congregations that they started were patterned after the synagogues they were familiar with. Furthermore, just as each synagogue, irregardless of the country it is located in, is part of the nation of Israel, every Christian congregation is part of God's earthly kingdom – and Christ is our king.

While it is possible for a person to come to faith in Christ without being the member of any church organization, God does not want it to stay that way. For that reason, God instituted baptism as a way of joining every new believer to His earthly kingdom. No one can baptize himself (at least it would not be valid if he did). So we must all be baptized by someone who is already a member of a Christian congregation, and baptism joins us to that congregation.

On the day of Pentecost, over three thousand Jews came to faith in Christ, and the words, "**The Lord added to the congregation daily those who were being saved,**" tell us that after Pentecost God continued to add believers to that congregation (Acts 2:47). The words, "**To God's congregation in Corinth, to those who have been set apart in Christ Jesus,**" tell us that those whom God adds to the congregation have been set apart from the world through faith in Christ

(1Corinthians 1:2). And, the words, "**Take heed to yourselves, and to all the flock, over which the Holy Ghost has made you overseers, to feed the church of God, that He has purchased with His own blood**," tell us that God gathers believers into congregations, and provides them with pastors, in order to feed them spiritually (Acts 20:28). [See John 21:15-17 and 1Corinthians 3:6.]

The words, "**They came to some water: and the eunuch said, Look, here is water; what prevents me from being baptized? And Philip said, If you truly believe, you may**," tell us that every church member should be a believer (Acts 8:36-37). Nevertheless, the words, "**The kingdom of heaven is like a man who sowed good seed in his field: But while men slept, his enemy came and sowed weeds among the wheat, and went his way**," tell us that Satan will sow falsehood and unbelief within the church (Matthew 13:24-25). However, the fact that the words, "**Do you want us to pull the weeds up?**" were answered with the words, "**No; lest while you are pulling up the weeds, you root the wheat up with them**," tell us that even though unsaved people should not be members of a Christian congregation, more souls will be lost it we try to root them out than if we just leave them be (Matthew 13:28-29).

At the same time, the words, "**Expel that wicked man from your congregation**," tell us that we dare not condone the wickedness of those who are openly immoral or allow them to corrupt others in the congregation (1Corinthians 5:13). The Bible clearly teaches the importance of church discipline. However, the authority in all discipline must be the Word of God. And, the purpose of church discipline is not to make everyone bow to the will of the leaders, or accept their interpretations, but to warn the unrepentant of God's judgment.

The words, "**Put out of your fellowship the man who did this**," // "**If he refuses to hear the church [repent], let him be to you as a heathen man and a publican**," tell us that we are "**Not to associate with anyone who calls himself a brother but is sexually immoral, or covetous, or an idolater, or a reviler, or a drunkard, or a swindler**," we should, "**Not even eat with such a man**" (1Corinthians 5:2, Matthew 18:17, 1Corinthians 5:11).

Notice that the Apostle Paul did not excommunicate the unrepentant man, but called on the congregation to do it. That tells us that spiritual discipline is the responsibility of the local congregation (1Cor. 5).

2. The Divine Institution Of Local Churches

Every believer has a responsibility to find a congregation in which the gospel is faithfully taught, or to start one.

Christ said, "**Feed my sheep**," and His sheep are not fed spiritually, "**By bread... but by every word that proceeds out of the mouth of God,**" including those words proclaimed through good Biblical preaching (John 21:16, Matthew 4:4). That is why the Bible tells us that, **God has chosen to save those who believe, "Through the foolishness of preaching**" (1Corinthians 1:21). It is by preaching that the seed of faith is planted, and "**The seed is the word of God**" (Luke 8:11). Of that seed, Paul's words, "**I planted, Apollos watered; but God gave the increase,**" tell us that just as God uses preaching to plant the seed of faith in our heart, He uses it to water and nourish our faith, enabling us to grow spiritually (1Corinthians 3:6). And, through it all **we are, "Kept by the power of God through faith unto salvation**" (1Peter 1:5). That is why the Apostles, led by the Holy Spirit, organized congregations, ordained elders, and gathered believers into those congregations, and that is why we need to be in church (Acts 14:23, Titus 1:5, Acts 2:47, Acts 15:41 and 16:5, 1Corinthians 1:10).

The words, "**They devoted themselves to the apostles' doctrine and fellowship, and to the breaking of bread, and to prayers,**" describe the actions of those filled with the Holy Spirit (Acts 2:42). And, the words, "**Let us be concerned about one another and so promote love and good works: <u>Not forsaking the assembling of ourselves together</u>, as the habit of some is; but encouraging one another,**" tell us that those who are led by the Spirit of God will want to be with other believers (Hebrews 10:24-25).

Within the congregation, "**Let the peace of God rule in your hearts, for you have been called to peace as one body in Christ; and be thankful. Let the word of Christ dwell in you richly in all wisdom; as you teach and counsel one another singing psalms, hymns and spiritual songs to the Lord, with grace in your hearts**" (Colossians 3:15-16).

3. Church And State

One of the biggest problems the church faces today is the secularization of government and society. And, the wedge being used to eliminate Christian influence from the public sector, effectively reducing Christians to second-class status, is the unbiblical claim that Church and State should be absolutely separate.

Those who disagree with what I have just said need to realize that when Martin Luther called for separation of church and state he wanted to prevent bishops from sentencing people to death, not exclude all Christian influence from government. The atheist doctrine of "separation of church and state," is totally opposed to what Luther wanted, and to what the Bible teaches. For that reason we need to take a serious look at what God's Word actually says.

First of all, the cliché, "separation of church and state," is the word of man, not the word of God. You will not find those words anywhere in Scripture. The Bible passage usually cited, "**Render therefore unto Caesar the things which are Caesar's, and unto God the things which are God's,**" does not command us to separate anything (Luke 20:25). In fact, in that passage Christ's words are an answer to a question, and an answer to a question is never imperative! A command for separation is being read into the text, contrary to the plain grammatical meaning of the words.

A truly Biblical understanding of church and state begins with a look at the government that God provided for the nation of Israel. That government was divided into two realms, one political, the other religious. The political realm was an instrument of God's wrath; in the sense that God worked through it to judge His people, enforce His Law and punish crime. In contrast, the priesthood was an instrument of God's mercy; in that God used it to show His people their sins, teach them the necessity of repentance, and give them His promise of mercy. Therefore, in ancient Israel church and state were separate; not separate in the modern sense – which would separate sacred from secular – but separate in the fact that they were separate institutions.

There was an official priesthood, which, by calling God's people to repentance while giving them His promise of forgiveness, carried out the same function that the church does today. But, it was not a tax-supported "state church". It is true that the people were to give a tithe. But, that was not a tax, because it was not taken by force and they were not punished by the government if it was not paid (Malachi 3:8). Furthermore, the fact that God provided for His church to be supported independently of the state, tells us that God does not want His churches to be supported by the state. Government should never be able to control the church by threatening to cut off its funds. At the same time, the fact that the priesthood was hereditary, tells us that rulers should not decide who can preach or hold church office.

While Christian believers who have been chosen to fill governmental offices must not conceal or deny their faith, we cannot expect a pagan nation to follow the same rules, or be governed the same way as a nation that is officially Christian. The people need to see the benefit of the laws they are being asked to keep. Here is where wisdom is called for.

The words, "**When you come to the land which the LORD your God gives you, and you possess it, and live in it, and then say, I will set a ruler over me... you may not set a foreigner over you, who is not one of your brethren,**" tell us that once a nation is Christian, God wants it ruled by Christians (Deuteronomy 17:14-15). But, that only applies to a nation that calls itself Christian. While any country can choose a Christian as its ruler; attempting to force a Christian ruler upon a nation of unbelievers would only produce resentment.

The words, "**When he [the ruler] sits on the throne of his government, he shall write down for himself in a book a copy of this law... And he shall keep it with him, and read from it all the days of his life: that he may learn to fear the LORD his God**," tell us that God wants rulers to be guided by His Word (Deuteronomy 17:18-20). But here again, that rule would only be faithfully carried out by rulers who want to do the will of God.

The words, "**It seemed good to the Holy Ghost, and to us, to lay upon you no greater burden than these essential things; That you abstain from meats offered to idols, and from blood, and from things strangled, and from sexual immorality: if you keep yourselves from these things, you will do well**," tell us that Christian rulers should never attempt to impose the laws of ancient Israel on any nation (Acts 15:28-29). At the same time, because rulers study and copy the laws of other nations, the English system of common law originated when **King Alfred** adopted a legal code that included the Ten Commandments along with other excerpts of Mosaic Law (871-899 A.D.). And, Blackstone's commentaries on the laws of England (which grew out of King Alfred's legal code) are basic to American jurisprudence. Referring to that Biblical influence upon our law, lawyer and columnist David Limbaugh once said, "Biblical laws were also foundational to our system of jurisprudence. In the Book of Exodus following the Ten Commandments are further laws, sometimes collectively referred to as the Book of the Covenant. As a lawyer I was fascinated to discover just how much of our law - torts, contracts, property and criminal law - is obviously traceable to this section of scripture." (From his column, used by permission.)

The words, "**When the Gentiles, who do not have the law, do by nature the things contained in the law, they... show the work of the law written in their hearts, their conscience also bearing witness**," tell us that God has written His law on our heart (Romans 2:14-15). And, because the Ten Commandments summarize that law, every ruler should be guided by the Ten Commandments. At the same time, the freedom that we have in Christ allows us to apply those commandments in a way that is reasonable, and conforms to the customs and culture of our nation, without compromising morality. A Christian ruler should never compromise morality, or legitimatize sin.

The words, "**The weapons we fight with are not the weapons of the world, but through God they have the power to break down strongholds**," tell us that God's church does not need the government behind it to triumph. (2Corinthians 10:4). In fact, the words, "**The gates of hell will not prevail against it**," tell us that it will triumph in spite of persecution (Matthew 16:18). For that reason, when a formerly pagan nation [such as ancient Rome] does become

Christian, we should regard it as a triumph of the gospel, and a gift of God.

When a government makes Christianity the official religion, God's people have a situation very similar to that which existed in ancient Israel under the kings. If that government uses its power to protect Christians, the Biblical admonition to pray, **"For kings, and for all who are in authority; so that we may lead a quiet and peaceable life in all godliness and honesty,"** tells us that protection is a blessing from God (1Timothy 2:2). When it comes to separating church and state, it is religious institutions and congregations that should be separate, not Christians. Those who trust in God (His heavenly kingdom) should be at work inside both church and state, like a hand in a glove, spreading Christian influence, and doing His will. And where that situation exists, if earthly rulers promote idolatry, then in the eyes of God it is no different than when the kings in ancient Israel promoted idolatry. Likewise, if earthly rulers suppress idolatry, then it is no different in the eyes of God than when the kings in ancient Israel suppressed idolatry. If earthly rulers do evil or promote evil, believers should condemn that evil. And, if church leaders are corrupt, or pawns of the state, believers should condemn that corruption like the prophets of old. Nevertheless, in all things they should act with prayer and wisdom.

The Bible does not call for a specific form of government because every government can be corrupted by evil and selfish men. The words, **"He [the ruler] shall write down for himself in a book a copy of this law... And he shall keep it with him, and read from it,"** tell us that the government that God gave Israel was a rudimentary republic [a government in which rulers must obey the law] (Deuteronomy 17:18-20). However, having a republican form of government is no guarantee of freedom. Having a republic in this land did not automatically bring freedom to the slaves, and our freedom is being slowly subverted. If we had true freedom, a Christian congressman could stand up in congress and say, "I am introducing this bill to stop abortion, because I believe that abortion is contrary to the Word of God," and everyone would say, "Put it to a vote, he has just as much right to his opinion as anyone else". Rulers need to have a tender conscience before God, and Christians need to work within the system to hold rulers accountable when they do evil. "Luther wanted neither autocracy nor mobocracy, but 'lawocracy' book law, a constitution. He admired the ancient republics and Switzerland. If the Emperor broke the law, he was to be fought as a common robber." (Lutheran Cyclopedia, page 598)

The words, **"We ought to obey God rather than men,"** tell us that whenever rulers tell us to do evil we are not to comply (Acts 5:29). However, the words, **"Submit yourselves to every ordinance of man for the Lord's sake: whether it be to the king, as supreme;**

or to governors, as those sent by him for the punishment of evildoers, and for the praise of those who do right. For it is the will of God, that by doing good you may put to silence the ignorance of foolish men: Live as free men, without using your liberty as an excuse for evil, live as servants of God. Show proper respect to everyone. Love the brotherhood. Fear God. Honor the king,"** tell us that as long as the government is not telling us to do evil we should comply (1Peter 2:13-17). **God wants you to "seek the welfare of the" nation in which He has placed you, "for when it fares well it will be well with you"** (Jeremiah 29:7).

4. Orthodox And Heterodox Churches

The words, orthodox and heterodox come from Hebrew. The word "orthodox" conveys the idea of right or correct thinking, while the word "heterodox" conveys the idea of wrong or errant thinking.

When it comes to churches, **what is orthodox or heterodox must be determined by the Word of God.** That means that when the Bible says, "**In six days the LORD made heaven and earth, the sea, and everything that is in them, and rested on the seventh day**," those who are orthodox will say, "That is what we should believe and teach" (Exodus 20:11). When the Bible says, "**A man is justified by faith without the deeds of the law**," those who are orthodox will say, "That is what we should believe and teach" (Romans 3:28). When God says, "**I have no pleasure in the death of a wicked; but want the wicked man to turn from his way and live**," those who are orthodox will say, "That is what we should believe and teach" (Ezekiel 33:11). When the Bible says, "We have an advocate with the Father, Jesus Christ the righteous. **He is the propitiation for our sins: and not for ours only, but also for the sins of the whole world**," those who are orthodox will say, "That is what we should believe and teach" (1John 2:1-2). When Christ says, "**No man can come to me, unless the Father who has sent me draws him**," those who are orthodox will say, "That is what we should believe and teach" (John 6:44). When the Bible says, "**No one can say that Jesus is the Lord, but by the Holy Ghost**," those who are orthodox will say, "That is what we should believe and teach" (1Corinthians 12:3). When Christ says, "**Every one who looks to the Son, and believes on Him, may have everlasting life: and I will raise him up on the last day**," those who are orthodox will say, "That is what we should believe and teach" (John 6:40). And, when Christ says, "**My kingdom is not of this world**," those who are orthodox will say, "That is what we should believe and teach" (John 18:36). In contrast, any church that explains away those passages, or anything else that the Bible says, is heterodox.

I once tried to explain this to a cult member, only to have him say, "You explain away the words, '**If anyone comes to me, and does not hate his father, and mother, and wife, and children, and brothers, and sisters, yes, and his own life also, he cannot be my disciple**'" (Luke 14:26). Of course, what he said was not true. I do not explain away those words. However, I do reject any interpretation of those words that contradicts what the Bible says about love and respect for parents. I reject those interpretations because they are the word of man, not the Word of God, and any opinion of man that contradicts the Word of God should be rejected (Isaiah 8:20). Once those wrong interpretations are rejected, it becomes obvious that Luke 14:26 is addressed to those who are accused of hating their family because they have come to faith in Christ – and that does happen.

The reason heterodox churches find it necessary to explain away many statements of Scripture lies in the fact that their doctrine does not consist of what the Bible explicitly says, but of interpretations, ideas deduced from those interpretations, and, in some cases, ideas from outside of Scripture. Of those who teach their own opinions as the Word of God, the Bible says, "**I am against the prophets, says the LORD, who steal my words every one from his neighbor. I am against the prophets, says the LORD, who use their tongues, and say, He says. I am against those who prophesy false dreams, says the LORD, and tell them, causing my people to err by their lies, and by their lightness**" (Jeremiah 23:30-32).

The words, "**If anyone teaches otherwise, and will not agree with sound teaching, even the words of our Lord Jesus Christ, and the doctrine that is in accord with godliness; He is proud, knowing nothing… from such withdraw yourself,**" tell us to avoid those who contradict Scripture (1Timothy 6:3-5).

The words, "**Beware of false prophets, who come to you in sheep's clothing, but inwardly are ravening wolves,**" and "**They worship me in vain, teaching for doctrines the commandments of men,**" warn us that teaching the word of man as the Word of God can destroy souls (Matthew 7:15 and 15:9).

The words, "<u>**Earnestly contend for the faith**</u> **that has now been entrusted to the saints. For there are certain men who have slipped in unnoticed,** <u>**ungodly men**</u>**, whose condemnation was recorded long ago, who** <u>**pervert the grace of our God into licentiousness**</u>**,**" condemn all churches that condone immorality and homosexuality (Jude 1:3-4).

The words, "**Keep that which has been entrusted to you, avoiding profane and godless chatter, and the opposition of what is falsely called science: For some who have followed it have erred from the faith,**" warn us of the danger of a false science that contradicts the Word of God (1Timothy 6:20-21). And, that is a very ominous danger today when false science is being touted as fact.

"Many deceivers have gone out into the world," and "There will be false teachers among you, who will privately introduce damnable heresies," so if anyone, even "An angel from heaven, preaches any gospel to you other than what" the Apostles taught, he should be condemned (2John 7, 2Peter 2:1, Galatians 1:8).

5. Heterodox Churches And True Discipleship

Our Lord Jesus Christ does not want any church to teach falsehood, contradict His Word, or twist His Word in a vain attempt to make it agree with the opinions of men. **What He wants taught is nothing "other than what you read" in Scripture** (2Corinthians 1:13). Therefore, heterodox churches only exist because of sin. All of the errors being taught as the Word of God, or in place of the Word of God, are rooted in satanic deception, and **a heart that "is deceitful above all things, and desperately wicked"** (Jeremiah 17:9).

The words, **"If you continue in my word, you are truly my disciples, and you will know the truth,"** tell us that those who are truly Christ's disciples will not depart from His Word (John 8:31-32). Because the Bible says, **"Do not add to His words,"** // **"No truth of scripture comes from any private explanation,"** they will not depart from His Word by adding man-made explanations to His Word [including man-made explanations of Bible prophesy] (Proverbs 30:6, 2Peter 1:20). And, because the Bible says, **"If they do not speak according to this word, it is because there is no light in them,"** they will not depart from His Word by contradicting or explaining away anything it says (Isaiah 8:20).

The words, **"The prophet, who shall presume to speak any word in my name, that I have not commanded him to speak... shall die,"** tell us that passing man-made explanations of Bible prophesy off as the Word of God is a very serious sin (Deuteronomy 18:20).

The words, **"I have also seen a horrible thing... they commit adultery, and walk in lies: they strengthen the hands of evildoers, so that no one repents of his wickedness,"** should be a warning to every church that condones immorality and homosexuality (Jeremiah 23:14).

The words, **"I have heard what the prophets say, who prophesy lies in my name... they are prophets of the deceit of their own heart,"** condemn all who add to God's Word by claiming that the Holy Spirit told me this or that (Jeremiah 23:25-26). While the Holy Spirit does help us to understand His Word, He uses one passage of Scripture to explain another, not private explanations (2Peter 1:20).

The words, **"Woe to the foolish prophets, who follow their own spirit, and have seen nothing,"** should be a warning to all who look into their own heart for doctrine, instead of to the written Word of God (Ezekiel 13:3).

The words, "**There must also be heresies among you, to reveal those who are approved by God**," tell us that God allows heresies to become controversial to expose those who are teaching falsely (1Corinthians 11:19). And, the words, "**God will send them a powerful delusion, so that they will believe lies: That <u>all who believed not the truth</u>, but had pleasure in unrighteousness, might be damned**," warn us that God will destroy those who reject the gospel [believe not the truth] and refuse to repent (2Thessalonians 2:11-12).

6. The Limits Of Spiritual Fellowship

The words, "**They devoted themselves to the apostles' doctrine and fellowship, and to the breaking of bread, and to prayers**," tell us that God wants us to have fellowship with other Christians (Acts 2:42). And, the words, "**If we walk in the light, as He is in the light, we have fellowship with one another, and the blood of Jesus Christ His Son cleanses us of all sin**," tell us that those whom we are to have fellowship with are those who are cleansed of all sin by the blood of Christ (1John 1:7). At the same time, the words, "**Do not be unequally yoked together with unbelievers: for what fellowship is there between righteousness and wickedness? and what do light and darkness have in common?**" warn us against having fellowship with those who are wicked and those who reject the gospel (2Corinthians 6:14).

The words, "**God... has called you into fellowship with His Son Jesus Christ our Lord**," tell us that all believers have been called into fellowship with Jesus Christ (1Corinthians 1:9). However, the words, "**If we say that we have fellowship with Him, and walk in darkness, we are <u>lying</u>, and are not living the truth**," tell us that anyone who claims to trust in Christ while continuing in a sinful lifestyle, is "lying" (1John 1:6).

The Bible tells us that **we are "not to associate with those who are sexually immoral"** (1Corinthians 5:9). **That does not mean "that you must altogether *cut off contact with* the immoral people of this world, or the covetous, or extortioners, or idolaters; for in that case you would have to leave the world"** (1Corinthians 5:10). But, the fact that we should "**not even eat with such a man**," tells us that we should not seek out their company, run with them, or let them influence us in any way (1Corinthians 5:11). We are to, "**have no fellowship with the unfruitful works of darkness, but rather reprove them**" (Ephesians 5:11).

Just as we are not to have fellowship with those who are sexually immoral, the Bible tells us that we are not to have fellowship with those who worship false gods. The words, **"What fellowship is there between righteousness and wickedness?"** tell us that we should not have any fellowship with them (2Corinthians 6:14). Furthermore, because **"The things that the Gentiles sacrifice are sacrificed to devils, and not to God,"** those who worship false gods are worshipping devils, and God does not **"want you to have fellowship with devils"** (1Corinthians 10:20). I am not saying that unbelievers can never join us in worshipping the True God, but we should never join with them in worshipping their god. Nor should we worship with Lodges or cults that claim to be worshipping the God of the Bible but are not. Idolatry is a very serious sin.

False Prophets

The words, **"Many false prophets have gone out into the world,"** // **"Who will... introduce damnable heresies, even denying the Lord who bought them, bringing swift destruction upon themselves,"** warn us of the danger posed to souls by those who teach religious falsehood (1John 4:1, 2Peter 2:1). Yet, our nation is full of religious falsehood: falsehood that is actively promoted by the media, by publishers, by schools and universities, and even by some churches. As Christians we should never condone such falsehood, either by allowing those who teach it to speak in our churches, or by failing to speak out against it.

We should never assume that only errors taught in churches constitute false prophesy. Although some false teachers spread their poison in Christian churches, the words, **"They are of the world: therefore what they say is of the world, and the world listens to them,"** tell us that they are more likely to find a following outside of churches (1John 4:5). Many colleges offer courses on the Bible and Christianity that are taught from an atheist perspective. Furthermore, everything that is being taught about "millions of years," the origin of life, and even space aliens is false religion. If it was not false religion it would not contradict the Bible! Remember! No matter how many opinions contradict what the Bible says, the facts never do.

The false prophets that Jeremiah and Ezekiel condemned were not priests or pastors. On the contrary, they were teachers who were misleading God's people. The words, **"They prophesied by Baal, and caused my people Israel to err,"** are not talking about false doctrine being taught in churches, but those who poison the culture with false religion (Jeremiah 23:13). The words, **"I have also seen a horrible thing in the prophets of Jerusalem: they commit adultery, and walk in lies: they strengthen the hands of evildoers, so that no one repents of his wickedness: all of them are like Sodom in my sight, and the people of the city like Gomorrah,"** describe the effects of the poison they spread, and it describes perfectly what we see today (Jeremiah 23:14). The only difference between then and now is the god false prophets claim to be getting their knowledge from. Then it was Baal, now it is Nature – for all who claim that nature created us and gave us life are deifying nature.

Christian churches should condemn and expose the soul destroying lies being spread by schools and universities. Christian children should not be unequally yoked with false teachers in the classroom, and Just as Christian pastors need to be grounded in the Word of God, those who teach in Christian schools need to be trained in exposing and refuting the soul destroying lies that the children are sure to encounter.

As to the differences between denominations: While we should regard those who trust in Christ as brothers, we would not be showing love for those we attend church with if we allowed men who create doctrines out of interpretations, or contradict Scripture, to teach in our churches.

7. Separatists, Or Schismatics

In an ideal world, the Word of God would be faithfully taught in every congregation, there would be no division, and Christian believers would be welcomed as brothers by every congregation in the world. However, that is not the case, and the words, **"There will be false teachers among you, who will privately introduce damnable heresies,"** make it clear that we should not expect it to be the case (2Peter 2:1).

The words, **"damnable heresies"** tell us that many of the errors that cause division will be so serious that we cannot remain in fellowship with congregations where they are taught without endangering souls. In contrast, many congregations separate themselves from other Christians over unscriptural or trivial matters, and we call those who do so, separatists or schismatics. In saying this I want to make it clear that any errors that contradict Scripture, or add to what it says, are never trivial. The matters that I am calling trivial are matters which the Bible leaves free. Matters such as the use of musical instruments in worship, the day on which we worship, clerical vestments, customs, and so forth.

The book, "The Small Sects in America," by Elmer T. Clark, lists hundreds of small sects that arose during the nineteenth and early twentieth centuries. Some may be listed only because they are small, but many separated themselves from others for unscriptural reasons. Reasons that all too often consist of nothing more than some silly "doctrine" cobbled together from interpretations. Furthermore, the importance that they attach to those doctrines seems to be rooted in the idea that having a distinctive "doctrine" makes them more righteous than those who do not have it – and that is just another form of works righteousness.

8. The Representative Church

While the Apostles started many congregations, no organizational structure above the congregational level is mentioned in Scripture.

The words, **"His gift made some, apostles; and some, prophets; and some, evangelists; and some, pastors and teachers,"** list the offices in order of authority (Ephesians 4:11). The Apostles are listed first because the Old Testament [what the prophets wrote] is to be interpreted in the light of what the apostles taught. And, by listing the Apostles and prophets first, this verse is telling us that their word – the Old and New Testaments – is the highest authority. Next in authority are the evangelists. Today we would call them missionaries. And, their authority is listed above that of pastors and teachers because they have the authority to straighten out any problems that arise in congregations that they start.

Those in positions of leadership in the synagogues, as well as in the congregations started by the Apostles, were referred to as "Pastors" or "teachers". The pastors were lay-elders chosen by the congregation to oversee things. The teachers (rabbis) were trained men hired by the congregation and elders as instructors. The teachers not only led worship on the Sabbath day, but also taught the boys to read and write during the week. [The word translated "teachers" in Eph. 4:11 is used in John 1:38 to translate the word "rabbi".]

When there are many congregations in a particular area, it is natural for them to cooperate, and help each other out. And, if some congregations are teaching contrary to Scripture it is natural for like-minded congregations to form associations. However, because those associations, (no matter what they are called) do not derive their authority from Scripture, they have no authority over the local congregation. Since the highest authority in every controversy must be the Word of God, not the word of man, what is called for is cooperation, not coercion. **All things should "be done decently and in order"** (1Corinthians 14:40). And, men who exalt their own authority over the Word of God [including earthly rulers] should be regarded as antichrists.

The Doctrine Of The Public Ministry

1. The Christian Pastor

Christ's words, **"You are not to be called Master: for one is your Master, even Christ; and you are all brethren. And do not call anyone on earth father: for you have one Father, who is**

in heaven," tell us that all believers are equal before God (Matthew 23:8-9).

> "Self-exaltation is a moral offence in the Christian Church. It has produced the great pope, a large number of little popes, and men and women 'bosses' in congregations. But all self-exalted men 'shall be humbled.' There is no question about it." (R.C.H. Lenski's commentary on Matthew, Page 902.)

For that reason, those whom the congregation calls to positions of responsibility **are not to act like "lords over those in" their care, but are to be "examples to the flock"** (1Peter 5:3). And, "**he who is greatest" should think of himself "as one who serves"** (Luke 22:26). That being said, the role of a pastor, elder or deacon is distinct from the priesthood of all believers, in that men called to those positions carry out certain aspects of the great commission on behalf of the congregation.

The words, "**I left you in Crete... to set right what was left undone, and to ordain elders in every city,**" tell us that Titus, working as an assistant to Paul, ordained elders in each of the congregations that they had started. And, the words, "**A bishop must be blameless,**" refer to those elders as bishops [overseers] (Titus 1:5,7). That fact tells us that the terms "elder" and "overseer" are synonyms, and that their job was to oversee the affairs of the congregation.

The words, "**After they had ordained elders... in every congregation, and had prayed with fasting, they commended them to the Lord, <u>in whom they had put their trust</u>,**" tell us that only those who trust in Christ are to be elders (Acts 14:23). The words, "**If a man does not know how to lead his own house, how can he take care of God's church?**" tell us that the role of elders is to care for God's people [the people are the church] (1Timothy 3:5). And, the words, "**Take heed to yourselves, and to all the flock, over which the Holy Ghost has made you overseers, to feed the church of God, that He has purchased with His own blood,**" tell us three things (Acts 20:28). 1- The Holy Ghost made those men overseers, 2- their job included spiritually feeding the flock, and 3- the flock consisted of those whom God purchased with His own blood.

Finally, the words, "**Not as lords over those in your care, but as examples to the flock,**" remind us again that those who have positions of responsibility are not to abuse their position by a carnal display of self-exaltation (1Peter 5:3).

2. Pastors And The Priesthood Of All Believers

Since the great commission can only be carried out by those who are saved through faith in Christ – and believe what He has said in His Word – the role of a minister within the congregation is not opposed to the priesthood of all believers, but is itself an expression of it. In other words, the priesthood of believers does not exist apart from congregational ministry, but includes it. At the same time, **the words, "A bishop must be etc." tell us that the role of a minister is not open to every believer**, but only to those who meet the qualifications and have been called by the congregation (1Timothy 3:2, Titus 1:7).

The words, "**You are a chosen generation, a royal priesthood, a holy nation, a people valued by God; that you should show forth the praises of Him who has called you out of darkness into His marvelous light,**" tell us that all believers [those called out of darkness] are priests before God (1Peter 2:9): While the words, "**A bishop must be blameless, as the steward of God; not self-willed, not quick tempered, not given to wine, not one who hits, not covetous or greedy for gain; But a lover of hospitality, a lover of good men, sober-minded, upright, moral, and self-controlled; Holding fast to the faithful word as he has been taught, so he will be able to comfort people with sound teaching and convict those who oppose it,**" tell us that all believers are not pastors, nor should they be (Titus 1:7-9)

The words, "**It is written in the prophets, They will all be taught by God,**" therefore "**You should show forth the praises of Him who has called you out of darkness into His marvelous light,**" and "**Let the word of Christ dwell in you richly in all wisdom; as you teach and counsel one another singing psalms, hymns and spiritual songs to the Lord, with grace in your hearts,**" tell us that every believer is to know and profess the divine truth (John 6:45, 1Peter 2:9, Colossians 3:16).

However, the words, "**A bishop must be blameless, as the steward of God... sober-minded, upright, moral, and self-controlled, holding fast to the faithful word as he has been taught, so he will be able to comfort people with sound teaching and convict those who oppose it,**" tell us that a pastor needs to have a thorough knowledge of God's Word (Titus 1:7-9).

The words, "**I will give to you the keys of the kingdom of heaven: and whoever you will bind on earth will be bound in heaven: and whoever you will loose on earth will be loosed in heaven,**" tell us that the power of the keys is the power to bind and loose (Matthew 16:19). And, the words, "**If he refuses to hear the church, let him be to you as a heathen man and a publican,**" // "**Expel that wicked man from your congregation,**" tell us that the power to bind and loose belongs to the entire congregation (Matthew 18:17). However, the words, "**Not many of you should be teachers, knowing that we will be judged more severely**" // "**His gift made <u>some</u>, apostles; and <u>some</u>, prophets; and <u>some</u>, evangelists; and <u>some, pastors and teachers</u>, for the perfecting of the saints, for the work of the ministry, for the edifying of the body of Christ**," tell us God only wants "**some**" [not all] to be pastors and teachers (James 3:1, Ephesians 4:11-12).

Finally, although the Bible plainly tells us that all believers are equal before God, it also tells us to show gratitude respect and love to those whom God has placed in positions of leadership.

The words, "**Different gifts are distributed, but the Spirit is the same. And different ministries are given, but the Lord is the same. And power is given, but it is the same God who works all in all. But the gift of the Spirit is given to every man for the profit of all**," tell us that God gives different people different gifts, and the purpose of those gifts is to benefit the church, not exalt those who have them (1Corinthians 12:4-7). The words "**There should be no division in the body; but... the members should have equal concern for each another**," tell us that we should care for everyone in the congregation (1Corinthians 12:25). And, the words, "**Do not go beyond what is written. Then you will not be taking pride in one man over against another**," tell us that if we stick to what the Bible says we will not be glorifying one man over another (1Corinthians 4:6). At the same time, the words, "**Remember your leaders, who have taught you the word of God**: and emulate their faith, considering the outcome of their life," and "**Let the elders who preside well be counted worthy of double honor, especially those who labor in the word and doctrine**," tell us that we should respect and honor those who faithfully serve us in Christ (Hebrews 13:7, 1Timothy 5:17).

3. The Public Ministry Is A Divine Appointment

While the words, "**One is your Master, even Christ; and you are all brethren**," tell us that those who carry out the public ministry are not superior to other Christians, it would be wrong to assume that their role is only of human origin (Matthew 23:8). The fact that the public ministry is a divine appointment is revealed by the fact that God's Apostles ordained those who would carry it out, and God's Word lists their qualifications, describes their duties, and urges us to honor them.

The words, "**I left you in Crete... to ordain elders**," and "**After they had ordained elders for them in every congregation, and had prayed with fasting, they commended them to the Lord,** in whom they had put their trust," tell us that the Apostles and their assistants [in this case Titus] set up congregations and invested qualified men with the responsibility of overseeing those congregations (Titus 1:5, Acts 14:23). Moreover, the words, "**He sent to Ephesus from Miletus, and summoned the elders of the congregation,**" tell us that like the synagogues that the Apostles grew up in, each congregation had a board of elders (Acts 20:17).

The words, "**A bishop must be blameless, the husband of one wife, vigilant, sober-minded, of good behavior, given to hospitality, able to teach; Not given to wine, not a striker, but one who is patient and gentle not a brawler, not covetous or greedy for gain; One who does a good job of running his own house, having his children under control, yet dealing with them in a dignified way; (For if a man does not know how to lead his own house, how can he take care of God's church?) Not a new convert, or he may be lifted up with pride and so fall into the same condemnation as the devil. Moreover he must also be well thought of by those who are outside the church; or he may fall into disgrace and the devil's snare,**" list qualifications for those who hold the public ministry, thereby setting apart the role of a minister (1Timothy 3:2-7).

The words, "An overseer [bishop] must be blameless... Holding fast to the faithful word as he has been taught, so he will be able to <u>comfort</u> people with sound <u>teaching</u> and convict those who oppose it," // "Take heed therefore to yourselves, and to all the flock, over the which the Holy Ghost has made you overseers, to <u>feed</u> the church of God, which He has purchased with His own blood," // "Not as dictators over those in your care, but as examples to the flock," describe the function and duties of a minister (Titus 1:7-11, Acts 20:28, 1Peter 5:3).

The words, "**His gift made some... pastors and teachers,**" // "**Notice those who labor among you... And because of their work hold them in the highest regard in love,**" // "**emulate their faith**" // "**and follow their guidance: for they watch for your souls, as men who must give account, so that they may do this with joy, and not with grief: for that is not to your advantage,**" make a distinction between those who hold the ministry and other believers, and urge us to "hold them in the highest regard" (Ephesians 4:11, 1Thessalonians 5:12-13, Hebrews 13:7 and17).

4. Is The Public Ministry Necessary?

Although the public ministry has been instituted by God, and plays an important role in the salvation of souls, it should never be regarded as being necessary for salvation, as if the salvation of souls depends upon the work of the church rather than faith in Christ alone.

The words, "**Abraham shall surely become a great and mighty nation... He will command his children and his household after him, and they shall keep the way of the LORD**," tell us that the faith of Abraham was passed on to his descendants, from father to son, long before the public ministry was instituted (Genesis 18:18-19). And, throughout history there have been times when persecution was so severe that the faith could only be preserved by passing it from parents to children within the family.

The words, "**I am the vine, you are the branches: He who remains in me, and I in him, produces much fruit: for you can do nothing without me**," tell us that because believers have been joined to Christ, He works in and through believers to produce fruit (John 15:5). And, the words, "**Let the word of Christ dwell in you richly in all wisdom; as you teach and counsel one another singing psalms, hymns and spiritual songs to the Lord, with grace in your hearts**," list some of the things that Christ does through us (Colossians 3:16).

Nevertheless, even though the public ministry is not absolutely necessary to salvation, it should never be despised because God has set it in place and works through it to plant and nurture the seeds of faith. As it is written, "**Since... the world through its wisdom did not know God, it pleased God to save those who believe through... preaching**" (1Corinthians 1:21). And, again, "**The gospel of Christ... is the power of God to salvation to every one who believes**," // "**I planted, Apollos watered; but God gave the increase**" (Romans 1:16, 1Corinthians 3:6).

Therefore, "**Remember your leaders, who have taught you the word of God: and emulate their faith, considering the outcome of their life**," // "**Listen to those who lead the congregation, and follow their guidance: for they watch for your souls, as men who must give account, so that they may do this with joy, and not with grief: for that is not to your advantage**" (Hebrews 13:7-17). And, **do not forsake "the assembling of" yourselves "together, as the habit of some is; but" encourage "one another: and all the more, as you see the day approaching**" (Hebrews 10:25).

5. The Call Into The Ministry, And Ordination

Although God spoke to Moses and the prophets with an audible voice, and explicitly called them to specific tasks, His calling of pastors is far less dramatic. Because God has warned Christian congregations to, "**Beware of false prophets**," no one should ever be allowed to just take over a congregation, without being called by the congregation (Matthew 7:15). At the same time, the fact that God does provide those who trust in Him with godly pastors, is revealed by the words, "**Take heed to yourselves, and to all the flock, over which the Holy Ghost has made you overseers**" (Acts 20:28).

The words, "**If a man <u>desires</u> the office of a bishop, he desires a good work. However, a bishop must be blameless, the husband of one wife, vigilant, sober-minded, of good behavior, given to hospitality, able to teach**," tell us that simply wanting to be a pastor is not a call into the ministry (1Timothy 3:1-2). If it was, then everyone who wanted to be a minister would meet the qualifications, and that is not the case. The words, "**No man can come to me, unless the Father who has sent me draws him**," suggest that some who are being drawn to God's Word may assume it is a call (John 6:44). The words, "**Some... want to be teachers of the law; but they do not know what they are talking about, or understand the things they so confidently assert**," tell us that some who want to pastor a church are more interested in promoting works than saving souls (1Timothy 1:6-7). And, the words, "**I have not sent these prophets, yet they ran**," tell us that those whom God has not called, and even false prophets, may want to be pastors (Jeremiah 23:21). Therefore, even though the words, "**Take heed to yourselves, and to all the flock, over which the Holy Ghost has made you overseers**," tell us that godly pastors are a gift of God, the words, "**There will be false teachers among you, who will privately introduce damnable heresies**," warn of the importance of screening those who are called (Acts 20:28, 2Peter 2:1).

The words, "**His gift made some... pastors and teachers**," tell us that it is God who makes "some pastors and teachers" (Ephesians 4:11). The words, "**The things that you have heard me say... pass on to faithful men, who will also be able to teach others**," tell us that those whom God has made pastors and teachers will faithfully pass on what the Apostles have taught (2Timothy 2:2). The words, "**Discharge carefully the duties of the ministry that you have received in the Lord**," tell us that those whom God has made pastors and teachers will be conscientious about carrying out their duties (Colossians 4:17). And, the words, "**Keep close watch on yourself, and on your doctrine; and hold to it: for by doing so <u>you will both save yourself, and those who hear you</u>**," tell us that those whom God has made pastors and teachers will faithfully proclaim the gospel, to the salvation of souls (1Timothy 4:16).

Although the New Testament does not specifically mention pastors being called, the right of a congregation to call pastors is inferred from God's command to "**Beware of false prophets**," and from other instances of men being chosen by the congregation (Matthew 7:15). The words, "**Select seven men of good reputation from among you... And they chose Stephen, a man full of faith and of the Holy Ghost, and Philip, and Prochorus, and Nicanor, and Timon, and

Parmenas, and Nicolas a proselyte of Antioch," speak of men being chosen by the congregation (Acts 6:2-6). As do the words, "**He was also chosen by the churches to travel with us**" (2Corinthians 8:19).

Of Ordination

Congregational worship began after the Jewish people were carried captive into Babylon. As they gathered into communities and set aside places [synagogues] where they could meet, certain elders [older men] of the community were chosen to oversee those meeting places, lead Sabbath worship and teach the youth. The congregation then ordained those elders as a way of publicly investing them with responsibility. Later, because the first Christian congregations were organized along the same lines as the synagogue, the elders whom they chose were also ordained, and the Bible mentions that fact. However, since God never commanded ordination, and no divine promise is connected with it, it is only a public ratification of the call, not some mysterious ceremony that empowers the one being ordained.

The words, "**After they had ordained elders for them in every congregation, and had prayed with fasting, they commended them to the Lord, in whom they had put their trust,**" tell us that Paul and Barnabas ordained elders in every congregation that they started (Acts 14:23). The words, "**The reason I left you in Crete, was to set right what was left undone, and to ordain elders in every city, as I instructed you,**" tell us that Paul instructed Titus to ordain elders (Titus 1:5). The words, "**They chose Stephen... and Philip, and Prochorus, and Nicanor, and Timon, and Parmenas, and Nicolas... Whom they brought before the apostles: and after they had prayed, they laid their hands on them,**" tell us that they were ordained after they had been chosen to positions of responsibility (Acts 6:5-6). And, the words, "**Select seven men of good reputation from among you, <u>full of the Holy Ghost</u> and wisdom,**" tell us that the men who were chosen were "<u>**full of the Holy Ghost**</u>" before they were ordained" (Acts 6:3).

In regard to the laying on of hands, the words, "**They laid their hands on them, and they received the Holy Ghost,**" are speaking of the laying on of hands following conversion (Acts 8:17). In light of that fact the words, "**Do not neglect the gift that is in you, which was given to you by prophecy, with laying on of the hands,**" should be seen as a reference to the laying on of hands at conversion, not ordination (1Timothy 4:14).

6. The Christian Ministry Is Not A Spiritual Estate

Because the lust for self-exaltation is deeply rooted in our sinful nature, you are going to encounter men who want to make Christ's kingdom into their kingdom. The Apostle Paul referred to that desire for self-exaltation as the "**mystery of iniquity,**" and it leads some to portray the "office of the ministry" as a spiritual estate that entitles all who hold it to special reverence – as if being ordained places them in a class by themselves, or gives them a higher rank than other Christians (2Thessalonians 2:7). However, that is clearly contrary to what the Bible plainly says.

The words, "**Notice those who labor among you... And because of their work hold them in the highest regard in love,**" tell us to show love to those who "labor among" us, "because of their work," not because of their rank or position (1Thessalonians 5:12-13). On the contrary, the words, "**Let us be regarded as servants of Christ, and stewards of the mysteries of God,**" tell us that the Apostle Paul himself only wanted to be regarded as a servant of Christ, not a master or lord over other believers (1Corinthians 4:1). And, the attitude expressed by the words, "**We do not preach ourselves, but Christ Jesus as Lord; and ourselves as your servants for Jesus' sake,**" will be the attitude of every godly pastor (2Corinthians 4:5).

Although men may anoint with oil, every believer has been anointed with the Holy Spirit of God. As it is written, "**Did you receive the Holy Spirit when you came to faith?**" (Acts 19:2) And, again, "**Did you receive the Holy Spirit by the works of the law, or by the hearing of faith?**" (Galatians 3:2) And, because you were anointed with the Holy Spirit when you came to faith in Christ, "**The anointing that you have received from Him remains in you,**" making all believers "**A royal priesthood, a holy nation, a people valued by God**" (1John 2:27, 1Peter 2:9).

Therefore, even though we should be willing to, "**Listen to those who lead the congregation, and follow their guidance,**" (Hebrews 13:17). We are not to follow them blindly, but are to "**Beware of false prophets,**" and reject those who contradict what the Bible says (Matthew 7:15, see Titus 3:10, Romans 16:17, Acts 17:11).

7. The Authority Of The Public Ministry

The authority of the public ministry is not the authority of this world, the authority of rank and position, but the authority of the Word that is proclaimed! God's Word is, and must be, the highest authority in every Christian congregation, and in the life of every believer.

The words, "**One is your Master, even Christ; and you are all brethren,**" not only tell us that all believers are equal, but that all ministers are equal (Matthew 23:8). Therefore, there are no ranks within the public ministry. I am not saying that a congregation cannot assign positions [such as pastor and assistant pastor], but that such positions are man-made, and carry no weight with God.

Because those who hold the public ministry have been called to teach the Word of God, it is fitting and right for those who are taught to "**Listen to those who lead the congregation, and follow their guidance,**" (Hebrews 13:17). And, the words, "**It would not make sense for us to neglect the word of God, to serve tables,**" tell us that it is perfectly reasonable for a congregation to have other men in positions that do not involve teaching the Word of God (Acts 6:2). At the same time, those who are taught should be encouraged to **search "the scriptures daily, to see whether" the things they are taught square with the Word of God** (Acts 17:11).

The words, "**He who listens to you listens to me; and he who rejects you rejects me; and he who rejects me rejects Him who sent me,**" should never be pulled out of context (Luke 10:16). Christ spoke those words when He empowered seventy to "**heal the sick... and tell them, The kingdom of God has come near to you**" (Luke 10:1, 9). Therefore, those who rejected what the seventy said were rejecting the gospel, not just disagreeing over some matter. However, while the words of Luke 10:16 should never be twisted to give divine authority to the word of man; they do condemn those who reject what the Bible plainly says. The words, "**They rebelled against the words of God, and despised the counsel of the most High,**" and "**Rebellion is as the sin of witchcraft, and defiance is as iniquity and idolatry,**" condemn both the layman who justifies his sin, and the pastor who explains away what the Bible plainly says (Psalm 107:11, 1Samuel 15:23).

While godly pastors are often loved and appreciated by those they serve, the words, "**The time will come when they will not endure sound doctrine,**" warn us that will not always be the case (2Timothy 4:3). The words, "**If the world hates you, you know that it hated me before it hated you,**" could be cited to describe the way self-righteous or unrepentant church members sometimes treat a godly pastor (John 15:18). While the words, "**Woe to you, when all men speak well of you! for that is how their fathers treated the false prophets,**" could be cited to describe how false teachers are often treated (Luke 6:26). At the same time, those who are teaching falsehood are quick to condemn any godly Christians who speak out. For that reason Christians need to be watchful and have their faith firmly grounded in the Word of God. As it is written, "**Be sober, be vigilant; because your adversary the devil, prowls around like a roaring lion, looking for someone to devour**" (1Peter 5:8).

Because the real world is often complex and difficult, I am aware of some congregations that have chosen a retired pastor to be on call in case of a controversy. His role is not intended to be one of authority, but that of a neutral mediator. And, his job is to help settle any controversy in a way that is in accord with God's Word. That sounds like a good idea to me.

8. Antichrists And The Antichrist

We live in a world that is full of religious falsehood, and bogged down in the mire of deception and lies. "**You have undoubtedly heard that an antichrist is coming, however, those who talk the most about it seem blind to the fact that there are already many antichrists at work in the world**" (a paraphrase of 1John 2:18). In fact, **everyone "who denies that Jesus is the Messiah… is an antichrist**" (1John 2:22). So let us identify them.

It is obvious that the Pharisees denied that Jesus was the Messiah. However, because the words, "**Unto us a child is born, unto us a son is given… and His name shall be called… The mighty God**," tell us that the Messiah is God; all who deny that Jesus is God are denying that He is the Messiah (Isaiah 9:6). That not only includes any cults that deny the deity of Christ, but also all of the "liberal" and atheist professors and teachers who deny His deity.

Because the words, "**All things in heaven and earth, both visible and invisible, were created by Him… all things were created by Him, and for Him: And He is before all things**," tell us that Christ is our creator, all who deny that Christ is our creator are denying that He is God and therefore that He is the Messiah (Colossians 1:16-17). That includes all who claim that life came into existence through evolution.

Because the words, "**He was wounded for our transgressions, He was bruised for our iniquities: the punishment that brought us peace was upon Him; and by His stripes we are healed. Like sheep we have all have gone astray; each of us has turned to his own way; and the LORD has laid on Him the iniquity of us all**," foretold that the Messiah would die for the sins of His people, all who deny that Christ died for our sins are denying that He is the Messiah (Isaiah 53:5-6). That not only includes any false religion that denies that Christ died on a cross, but also the "liberal" churchmen who mock the idea of blood atonement. [See Psalm 22:16-19.]

Because the words, "**Search the scriptures; for in them you think that you have eternal life: and they are they that testify of me**," tell us that the Bible was written to testify to Christ, all who undermine the truth of that testimony by denying messianic prophesy and the reliability of Scripture are antichrists (John 5:39). And, that includes many seminary professors.

In contrast to the multitude of antichrists in our society, the Bible speaks of **one man, "who opposes and exalts himself over every-**

thing that is called God, or is worshipped; so that he sits as God in the temple of God, and says that he is God" (2Thessalonians 2:4). Many who read those words today assume they speak of a future ruler. However, there was a time when people coming before the Pope were expected to kiss his feet. And, "According to Innocent III, 'the Pope holds the place of the true God'" (*The Papacy Evaluated*," by E.G. Bhem, page 98.) And, while those aspects of the Papacy are played down today, especially in America, they have never been repudiated.

The Papacy further identifies itself with the antichrist by pronouncing a curse on all who teach that we are saved by faith alone, by claiming that Mary plays a part in salvation, and by encouraging its people to pray to the dead. Furthermore, the angel that spoke to John in his vision, used the present tense when he identified "Babylon The Great," as "That great city, which reigns [present tense] over the kings of the earth" (Revelation 17:1, 5, 18). And, the city that reigned at that time was Rome.

SCRIPTURE ALONE
GRACE ALONE
FAITH ALONE

The Doctrine Of Eternal Election
(De Electione)

1. Chosen By God

While the Bible plainly tells us that **God has "Chosen us in" Christ "before the foundation of the world,"** that truth should never be construed in a way that contradicts what the Bible says elsewhere, namely that those who are saved are saved solely by the forgiveness that Christ won for them on the cross, while those who are lost are lost solely through their own fault (Ephesians 1:3-4).

The words, **"God... has saved us, and called us to a holy calling, not because of anything we have done, but according to His own purpose and grace, which was given to us in Christ Jesus before the world began,"** plainly tell us that we are not saved because of anything we have done, but solely through the "grace" [i.e. mercy] of God (2Timothy 1:8-9). Furthermore, the words, **"We have redemption through His [Christ's] blood, the forgiveness of sins, according to the riches of His grace;"** tell us that God's grace, the grace that saves us, consists of the forgiveness that Christ won for us through His death on the cross (Ephesians 1:7). And, the words, **"And if by grace, then is it no longer by works: if it were grace would no longer be grace,"** stress the fact that works play no part in our salvation (Romans 11:6). We are saved by the grace of God alone.

The words, **"They should seek the Lord, in the hope that they might grope for Him, and find Him,"** tell us that salvation is available to all who seek God's mercy (Acts 17:27). The words, **"As I live, says the Lord GOD, I have no pleasure in the death of the wicked; but want the wicked man to turn from his way and live,"** tell us that God wants the wicked to repent and look to Him for mercy (Ezekiel 33:11). And, the words, **"O Jerusalem, Jerusalem, you who kill the prophets, and stone those who are sent to you; how often would I have gathered your children together, as a hen gathers her brood under her wings, but you would not have it,"** tell us that those who resist God's efforts to bring them to salvation, do so against the will of God (Luke 13:34). They are lost solely through their own fault.

God has revealed the fact that He has chosen us in Christ **"before the foundation of the world,"** to comfort us and assure us of His mercy (Eph. 1:4). Nevertheless, just as Satan tries to pervert everything that is good, he twists those words of comfort to create fear in people, a fear that they might not be one of God's elect, or that God might not want them. He then uses that fear to rob them of their assurance of forgiveness. Those who labor under that fear need to know that **Christ has not only obtained forgiveness for their sins, "but also for the sins of the whole world"** (1John 2:2). And, that **He has said, "I will never turn away anyone who comes to me"** (John 6:37).

2. How Believers Are To Consider Their Election

Although the Bible plainly tells us that **God has "Chosen us in"** Christ **"before the foundation of the world,"** because the Bible says, **"If they do not speak according to this word, it is because there is no light in them,"** we must reject any interpretation of those words that contradicts what the Bible says elsewhere (Ephesians 1:3-4, Isaiah 8:20).

Since Scripture is our only source and standard of doctrine, rejecting interpretations that contradict Scripture should be automatic. Nevertheless, **because we have a heart that "is deceitful above all things," men are far more likely to explain away what God has said, than to admit that they are wrong** (Jeremiah 17:9). And, that certainly holds true when it comes to the doctrine of election. In fact, that is why a debate has raged over the doctrine of election for over four-hundred years.

John Calvin (1509-1564) drew certain conclusions from the words, **"God... has chosen us... before the foundation of the world,"** of which we will examine two (Ephesians 1:3-4). First he assumed that if God has chosen those who are saved, He must not want to save those whom He did not choose. Then he assumed that Christ only died to atone for the sins of those whom God had chosen. Both of those conclusions are the word of man, not the Word of God, and both of them should be rejected because they contradict what the Bible plainly says.

The words, **"God... wants all men to be saved, and to come to the knowledge of the truth,"** // **"As I live, says the Lord GOD, I have no pleasure in the death of the wicked; but want the wicked man to turn from his way and live,"** tell us that God **"wants all men to be saved"** (1Timothy 2:3-4, Ezekiel 33:11). Therefore we know that those who assume that He does not want everyone to be saved are wrong. At the same time, the words, **"Jesus Christ... is the propitiation for our sins: and not for ours only, but also for the sins of the whole world,"** tell us that Christ's death atoned for the sins of all men [**"the whole world,"**] and not just for some (1John 2:1-2). Therefore, we know that those who assume that Christ did not die to atone for the sins of all men are wrong.

The fact that those two conclusions contradict the Bible proves that they are wrong. However, we have to ask why they are wrong. And, in answering that question it is important to realize that conclusions always have more than one premise. In this case, the words, "**God... has chosen us... before the foundation of the world**," constitute the **first premise**, and that premise cannot be wrong because it is the Word of God (Eph. 1:3-4). Therefore, there must be another premise, (a false premise) that is leading to the false conclusions. That hidden premise must be identified and eliminated. Once that is done, a correct understanding can be determined by taking a view that does not lead to conclusions that contradict the Bible.

For example: If we assume that God first decided to save certain people and afterward decided to send Christ to die for the sins of those He had chosen, we would draw the same unbiblical conclusions that Calvin did. So **that assumption is the hidden premise**. In contrast, if we instead hold that God first decided to send Christ to die for the sins of all men, and then, because no one could or would believe without His help, chose to bring millions to faith through the preaching of the gospel, that view does not lead to those conclusions.

Therefore, **a Biblical view of election** starts with the fact that 1- God did not want man to sin in the first place. 2- However, because God knew that man would sin, He decided from eternity to send Christ to die for the sins of all mankind. 3- Then, since no one would ever know that Christ had died for their sins without divine revelation, He also decided to cause the Bible to be written and the gospel to be preached. 4- And finally, knowing that no man left to himself could or would believe, He determined to bring untold millions of people to faith (in spite of their resistance) through the preaching of the Word.

I am not saying that this is the way God thinks of election, but that **this view of election does not lead to conclusions that contradict Scripture.**

It agrees with the passages that tell us that Christ died for the sins of all. It agrees with the words, "**There is one God, and one mediator between God and men, the man Christ Jesus; who gave Himself a ransom for all**" (1Timothy 2:5-6). It agrees with the words, "**God was in Christ, reconciling the world to Himself**," He is "**The Savior of all men, especially of those who believe**" (2Corinthians 5:19, 1Timothy 4:10). And, it agrees with the words, "**Behold the Lamb of God, who takes away the sin of the world**" (John 1:29).

It agrees with the passages that tell us that God wants all men to be saved. It agrees with the words, "**I have no pleasure in the death of him who dies, says the Lord GOD: therefore turn from sin, and live**" (Ezekiel 18:32). It agrees with the words, "**I have no pleasure in the death of the wicked; but want the wicked man to turn from his way and live**" (Ezekiel 33:11). And, it agrees with the words, "**God our Savior... wants all men to be saved, and to come to the knowledge of the truth**" (1Timothy 2:3-4).

It agrees with the passages that tell us that faith is a gift of God, and that no man could or would believe without God's help. It agrees with the words, "**No one can say that Jesus is the Lord, but by the Holy Ghost**" (1Corinthians 12:3). It agrees with the words, "**You are saved by grace through faith; and that not of yourselves: it is the gift of God**" (Ephesians 2:8). And, it agrees with the words, "**What is the exceeding greatness of His power toward us who believe, according to the working of His mighty power**" (Ephesians 1:19).

It agrees with the passages that tell us that no one is saved unless God chooses to save him. It agrees with the words, "**No man can come to me, unless the Father who has sent me draws him**" (John 6:44). It agrees with the words, "**No one can come to me, unless the Father enables him**" (John 6:65). And, it agrees with the words, "**Those He predestinated, He also called: and those He called, He also justified: and those He justified, He also glorified,**" thus "**The elect obtained it, and the others were hardened**" (Romans 8:30 and 11:7).

It agrees with the passages that tell us that the lost are lost because of their own fault, not because God wanted them to be lost. It agrees with the words, "**O Jerusalem, Jerusalem, you who kill the prophets, and stone those who are sent to you, how often I longed to gather your children together, as a hen gathers her chicks under her wings, and you would not**" (Matthew 23:37). It agrees with the words, "**To Israel He says, All day long I have stretched forth my hands to a disobedient and obstinate people**" (Romans 10:21). And, it agrees with the words, "**They should seek the Lord, in the hope that they might grope for Him, and find Him**" (Acts 17:27).

Because it often seems to us that we are making a choice, even though we know from Scripture that apart from God's grace we would never make the right choice, it also agrees with the passages that indicate that we have a free will, or must make a choice. It agrees with the words, "**Choose this day whom you will serve... but as for me and my house, we will serve the LORD**" (Joshua 24:15). It agrees with the words, "**Today if you hear Him speak, do not harden your hearts**" (Hebrews 3:7-8). And, it agrees with the words, "**I have set before you life and death, blessing and cursing: therefore choose life**" (Deuteronomy 30:19).

It even agrees with the words, "**The race is not to the swift, or the battle to the strong... but time and chance happen to all,**" for a man born in seventeenth century England would have a far better chance of being saved than a man born in seventeenth century Algeria, or first century England. (Ecclesiastes 9:11).

3. The Objects Of Eternal Election

One source of the controversy surrounding the doctrine of election stems from the egotistic assumption that **God thinks the same way we do**, or that His mind reasons along the same lines of logic that He has given to us. However, nothing could be further from the truth! **We only need to reason because we do not KNOW!** The words, **"My thoughts are not your thoughts, nor are your ways my ways, says the LORD. For as the heavens are higher than the earth, so my ways are higher than your ways, and my thoughts than your thoughts,"** tell us that God's mind is so far above our mind that we cannot begin to understand why He has chosen some and not others (Isaiah 55:8-9). For that reason, humility requires us to stop professing ourselves to be wise, admit our ignorance, and simply accept what He has revealed about eternal election even if it seems confusing and contradictory to our puny finite little minds.

We need to accept what the Bible says when God tells us that: 1- He wants all men to be saved, and; 2- we are chosen solely by His grace, yet; 3- God has not chosen everyone. If that is what God has revealed, then that is what He wants us to believe and teach; even though it is a stumbling block to those unwilling to admit their own ignorance.

The Bible tells us that God chooses to save individuals, not just anyone who believes. The words, **"Many are called, but few are chosen,"** tell us that God calls many to salvation, and chooses to bring some to faith in spite of their resistance (Matthew 22:14). The words, **"God chose you from the beginning unto salvation,"** tell us that God has chosen those who will be saved from the beginning (2Thessalonians 2:13). The words, **"Those He predestinated, He also called: and those He called, He also justified: and those He justified, He also glorified,"** tell us that God calls certain people and brings them to faith because it was part of His plan from the beginning (Romans 8:30). And, the words, **"No man can come to me, unless the Father who has sent me draws him,"** tell us that no person can come to faith in Christ unless God first chooses to draw him (John 6:44).

The Bible tells us that those who are saved are not chosen because of anything they have done. On the contrary, we all deserve damnation. The words, **"All men, both Jews and Gentiles, are all under sin,"** tell us that we are all under sin, and no sinner is worthy of anything other than damnation (Romans 3:9). The words, **"Whoever keeps the whole law, yet fails in one point, is guilty of all,"** tell us that there are no degrees of condemnation, even one unforgiven sin will send a person to hell (James 2:10). The words, **"He did not save us because of works of righteousness that we have done, but** because of His mercy," tell us that we are not saved because of things we do (Titus 3:5). And, the words, **"Then it [salvation] is no longer by works: if it were grace would no longer be grace,"** tell us that works play no part in our salvation (Romans 11:6).

The Bible tells us that God actively brings those whom He has chosen to faith, and keeps them from falling. The words, **"God... has saved us, and called us to a holy calling, not because of anything we have done, but according to His own purpose and grace, which was given to us in Christ Jesus before the world began,"** tell us that God actively saves us, and chose to save us before the world began (2Timothy 1:8-9). The words, **"I am convinced, that neither death, nor life, nor angels, nor principalities, nor powers, nor things present, nor things to come, nor height, nor depth, nor any other creature, shall be able to separate us from the love of God, that is in Christ Jesus our Lord,"** tell us that because God has chosen us, no one will be able to take our faith from us (Romans 8:38-39). And, the words, **"You... are kept by the power of God through faith unto salvation,"** tell us that God actively enables us to endure to the end (1Peter 1:4-5).

Those who deny that Christ has atoned for the sins of all men, rob believers of their assurance of salvation, because when the words, **"He is the propitiation for our sins: and not for ours only, but also for the sins of the whole world."** are explained away, no one can be certain that his sins were atoned for (1John 2:2). Likewise, those who claim that God has only chosen those He knew would endure to the end also rob believers of their assurance of salvation, because if it depends on us then no one can be certain that he will endure to the end.

4. The Relation Of Faith To Eternal Election

A great controversy over the doctrine of eternal election began when Jacob Arminus (1560-1609) tried to correct the unbiblical conclusions Calvin had come up with without understanding why those conclusions were wrong. Lacking that understanding, he failed to get to the root of the problem. Instead, he sidestepped Calvin's conclusions by coming up with counter conclusions.

First of all, he assumed that God's elect were those that God knew would come to faith of their own free will; and then assumed that every sinful, lost human being has within himself the ability to choose to believe or reject the gospel. Those two conclusions not only contradict the passages that tell us that God chooses to save individuals, not just anyone who believes, but also contradicts the passages that tell us that faith is a gift of God. For example: The words, **"You are saved by grace through faith; <u>and that not of yourselves: it is the gift of God</u>,"** plainly tell us that faith does not come from some inner ability to believe, but is a gift of God (Ephesians 2:8). The words, "**What is the exceeding greatness of His power toward us who believe, according to the working of His mighty power**," reinforce that truth by telling us that it is the power of God that brings us to faith, not some ability in us (Ephesians 1:19). While men do have the ability to make many choices, because all of the lost are in Satan's kingdom Satan will not let them come to faith in Christ unless God intervenes. The words, "**Who are not born of blood, or of the will of the flesh, or of the will of man, but of God**," tell us that we are not saved by our "free will," but by the will "of God" (John 1:13). The words, "**So then salvation is not of him who wills, nor of him who runs, but of God who shows mercy**," again tell us that we are not saved by our will, but by God's will (Romans 9:16). And, the words, "**No man can come to me, unless the Father who has sent me draws him**," // "**No man can say that Jesus is the Lord, but by the Holy Ghost**," tell us that "no man" has in himself the ability to chose to believe (John 6:44, 1Corinthians 12:3).

Those who make salvation dependent upon a choice made by man shift salvation from what Christ did to what we do. As a result, Christ is not seen as saving us, but instead as making it possible for us to save ourselves by choosing to believe. For that reason, every Christian should reject that idea.

Calvinists err because they put God's choice of who should be saved (election) prior to His decision to provide atonement for the sins of mankind. Arminians err because they place God's choice of who should be saved (election) after faith (that is after He knew that a person would believe). The Biblical doctrine that I have presented avoids those errors by placing God's election between God's decision to provide atonement for all, and His bestowal of the gift of faith.

5. The Purpose Of The Doctrine Of Eternal Election

The purpose of the doctrine of eternal election is not to make us smug, but to assure us that our salvation is solely a gift of God's grace. As it is written, "**Salvation is not of him who wills, nor of him who runs, but of God who shows mercy**" (Romans 9:16). And, again, "**God... has saved us, and called us to a holy calling, not because of anything we have done, but according to His own purpose and grace, which was given to us in Christ Jesus before the world began**" (2Timothy 1:9). "**And if [salvation is] by grace, then is it no longer by works: if it were grace would no longer be grace. For if it is by works, then it is no longer by grace: otherwise work is no longer work**" (Romans 11:6).

In fact, God's choice of the nation of Israel gives us a type of our election, because just as our salvation is solely by His grace, His Word to Israel was, "It is not because of your righteousness, or because of the uprightness of your heart, that you are going in to possess their land: but the LORD your God is driving them out before you because of the wickedness of those nations, that He may keep the promise which He swore to your fathers, Abraham, Isaac, and Jacob. Understand therefore, that the LORD your God is not giving you this good land to possess because of your righteousness; for you are a stubborn people" (Deuteronomy 9:5-6).

Even though the doctrine of election was given to assure us of God's grace, Satan does all he can to rob us of that assurance. **By denying that Christ "died for all," he robs many of the assurance that Christ died for their sins** (2Corinthians 5:15). **Then by portraying salvation as dependent on man's ability to endure to the end, he robs others of the assurance that God will keep them "from falling"** (Jude 24). Furthermore, whenever people lack assurance of salvation, (either because they fear that Christ may not have died for their sins, or that they will not be able to endure to the end) they look to works to regain that assurance. And, looking to works for assurance is the opposite of faith.

The words, **"If one died for all, then all died. And Christ died for all, so that those who live should no longer live for themselves, but for Him who died for them, and rose again,"** tell us that Christ "died for all," not just some (2Corinthians 5:14-15). The words, **"Christ... is the propitiation for our sins: and not for ours only, but also for the sins of the whole world,"** tell us that Christ's death is the propitiation [atonement] for the "sins of the whole world" (1John 2:1-2). And, that is what the Bible says because that is what God wants us to believe and teach.

The words, **"The only wise God, our Savior,"** // **"is able to keep you from falling, and to present you faultless before His glorious presence,"** tell us that it is God who keeps us from falling, not our free will (Jude 24-25). The words, **"Blessed is the God and Father of our Lord Jesus Christ, who in His great mercy has caused us to be born anew... To an inheritance... reserved in heaven for you who are kept by the power of God through faith unto salvation,"** tell us that just as God has saved us by His grace, He will keep us from falling by His grace (1Peter 1:3-5). And, that is what the Bible says because that is what God wants us to believe and teach.

6. Holy Scripture Teaches No Election To Damnation

The Bible plainly tells us that God is solely responsible for our salvation, our will and works play no part in it whatsoever. At the same time, the Bible plainly tells us that those who are damned bear the sole responsibility for their damnation.

The argument that God chooses to damn some by not choosing to save them is as silly as claiming that the governor sentences people to prison by not choosing to pardon them. The truth is that those in prison are in prison because of what they did, and those in hell are in hell not only because of what they did, but because they rejected every attempt that God made to bring them to salvation.

The words, "**They are all estranged from me through their idols,**" tell us that those who worship idols cut themselves off from God (Ezekiel 14:5). The words, "**To Israel He says, All day long I have stretched forth my hands to a disobedient and obstinate people,**" tell us that even those who outwardly worship God often fight against Him by justifying sin and doing what they know to be wrong (Romans 10:21). The words, "**O Jerusalem, Jerusalem, you who kill the prophets, and stone those who are sent to you, how often I longed to gather your children together, as a hen gathers her chicks under her wings, and you would not!**" tell us that God actively seeks the salvation of those who resist Him (Matthew 23:37). And, the words, "**Israel, you have destroyed yourself; and none can help you but me,**" tell us that those who are lost are lost because they reject God's help (Hosea 13:9).

Speaking in a parable, Jesus said, "**The kingdom of heaven is like a certain king, who prepared a wedding banquet for his son, and sent forth his servants to call those who were invited to the wedding: but they would not come. Again, he sent forth other servants, saying, Tell those who have been invited... all things are ready: come to the wedding. But those who made light of it went their way... and the rest seized his servants, mistreated them, and killed them... He then said to his servants, The wedding is ready, but those who were invited were not worthy. Therefore / Go out into the roads and country lanes, and compel them to come in, so that my house may be full / For many are called, but few are chosen**" (Matthew 22:1-14, Luke 14:23). That parable illustrates the fact that God sincerely calls many to come to Him for forgiveness, but "compels" few to come in spite of their resistance.

Those who limit atonement make God responsible for both the salvation and damnation of souls. Those who make salvation depend on man's choice make man responsible for both the salvation and damnation of souls. In contrast, the Bible tells us that God is solely responsible for the salvation of souls, and men are solely responsible for their own damnation.

GRACE ALONE

The Doctrine Of The Last Things
(Eschatology)

1. Temporal Death

The words, "**Do not fear those who kill the body, but are not able to kill the soul: but rather fear him who is able to destroy both soul and body in hell,**" tell us that our existence does not end with physical death (Matthew 10:28). And, the words, "**It is better for you to enter into the kingdom of God with one eye, than to be cast into hell fire having two eyes: Where their worm does not die, and the fire is never put out,**" tell us that there will be no end to the suffering of those in hell (Mark 9:47-48).

Through the words, "**The hour is coming, in which all who are in the graves will hear His [Christ's] voice, And will come out; those who have done good, to the resurrection of life; and those who have done evil, to the resurrection of damnation,**" Christ tells us that even though the bodies of the dead return to dust, they will rise to face God's eternal judgment (John 5:28-29). The words of Daniel, "**Many of those who sleep in the dust of the earth will awake, some to everlasting life, and some to shame and everlasting contempt,**" teach the same thing (Daniel 12:2).

The words, "**You fool, your <u>soul</u> will be required from you tonight: then who will own the things you have prepared?**" tell us that physical death takes place when the soul is separated from the body (Luke 12:20). The same doctrine is also taught in the words, "**Jesus, having cried again with a loud voice, yielded up His spirit,**" (Matthew 27:50). And, in the words, "**When He had received the vinegar, Jesus said, It is finished: and He bowed His head, and gave up the ghost,**" (John 19:30).

The Death of a Believer

The words, "**Then Abraham gave up the ghost, and died at a good old age, an old man, and full of years; and was gathered to His people,**" portray the death of a believer as a reunion with those who have gone before (Genesis 25:8 see also verse 17). The words, "**Let your servant now depart in peace,**" tell us that there is no terror associated with the death of a believer (Luke 2:29). The words, "**The righteous dies, and no one cares: kind men are swept away, and no one realizes that the righteous is taken away from the evil to come. He will enter into peace,**" tell us that those who die in faith are delivered from the "the evil to come" (Isaiah 57:1-2). The words, "**The girl is not dead, but asleep,**" describe death as a sleep (Matthew 9:24). However, the words, "**To be absent from the body, and present with the Lord," tell us that it is the body not the soul that is being described as asleep (2Corinthians 5:8). [See also 1Thessalonians 4:13-14.] For a believer, death is the gateway into eternal life (John 11:26).

The Death of an Unbeliever

On the other hand, the words, "**Woe to that man by whom the Son of man is betrayed! it would have been better for that man if he had not been born,**" portray the death of the wicked and unbelieving in terms of horror and dread (Matthew 26:24). The same goes for the words, "**Where their worm does not die, and the fire is never put out**" (Mark 9:48). As it is written, "**It is a fearful thing to fall into the hands of the living God**" (Hebrews 10:31).

The Reason Death is in the World

The words, "**In the day that you eat of it you will surely die,**" and the words, "**Just as sin entered the world by one man, and death by sin; so death passed upon all men, because all have sinned,**" tell us that death is not in the world because God created it that way, but because of sin (Genesis 2:17; Romans 5:12). As it is written, "**The wages of sin is death,**" (Romans 6:23).

Because death came into the world as a result of sin, all instrumental causes of death such as murder, disease, storms, famines, floods and war are only in the world because of sin. And, the world rightly fears all of those things, and should be calling on God for deliverance. However, the words, "**What shall separate us from the love of Christ? tribulation, or distress, or persecution, or famine, or nakedness, or peril, or sword? As it is written, For your sake we are killed all the day long; we are accounted as sheep for the slaughter. Nay, in all these things we are more than conquerors through him that loved us,**" tell us that as believers we have nothing to fear (Romans 8:35-37). I am not saying that such things are not unpleasant, or that we should desire them. But, the words, "**All things work together for good for those who love God, for those who are the called according to His purpose,**" assure us that all that happens works together for our good in Christ Jesus.

As Christians we must constantly remember that death is only in the world as "**the wages of sin**" (Romans 6:23). Those who deny that death is a punishment for sin cannot rightly understand or properly appreciate Christ's atoning death on the cross. In fact, those who deny what the Bible says about sin being the sole cause of death quite consistently also deny Christ's vicarious atonement.

The Sentence of Death

The words, "**Death passed upon all men, because all have sinned,**" tell us that all of the descendants of Adam are under the sentence of death (Romans 5:12). Those words as well as the words, "**The wages of sin is death,**" also tell us that if infants were not sinners they would never die of natural causes, and that every attempt by man to find a cure for death will end in failure. However, the words, "**Jesus Christ, who has abolished death, and brought life and immortality to light through the gospel,**" and the words, "**If a man keeps my word, he will never see death,**" tell us that there is one way in which sinful man can be freed from death, and that is through faith in Christ (2Timothy 1:10; John 8:51). And, Christ's promise to all who believe is, "**I am the resurrection, and the life: he who believes in me will yet live, even though he is dead: And whoever lives and believes in me will never die**" (John 11:25-26).

The fact that we are freed from death through faith in Christ raises the question: Why then must believers also die? And, the Scriptural answer to that question is that we who believe are also sinners according to the flesh. So even for believers, "**The wages of sin is death,**" (Romans 6:23). However, the words, "**O death, where is your sting? O grave, where is your victory? The sting of death is sin; and the strength of sin is the law. But thanks be to God, who has given us the victory through our Lord Jesus Christ,**" tell us that for a believer death is not joined with a sense of divine wrath (1Corinthians 15:55-57). On the contrary, through faith we have assurance of God's mercy and forgiveness. And, the words, "**I do not want you to be ignorant concerning those who are asleep, that you may not grieve, as do those who have no hope. For as we believe that Jesus died and rose again, even so God will bring those who have fallen asleep in Jesus with him,**" describe the death of the believer as a blessed sleep (1Thessalonians 4:13-14). However, the words of Stephen, "**Lord Jesus, receive my spirit,**" remind us again that it is the body, not the soul, that is described as being asleep (Acts 7:59). For "**to be absent from the body**" is to be "**present with the Lord,**" (2Corinthians 5:8). And, to be with the Lord is to be "**in paradise**" (Luke 23:43; 2Corinthians 12:4; revelation 2:7).

The words, "**He who believes on Him is not condemned,**" tell us that there is no condemnation for those who trust in Christ (John 3:18). Even though we were, "**dead in trespasses and sins**" and "**by nature the children of wrath,**" God has "**raised us up together with Him [Christ]**" (Ephesians 2:1,3; Colossians 2:12-13). And, having "**risen with Christ,**" // "**the second death has no power over**" us (Colossians 3:1; Revelation 20:6 and 14). Therefore, temporal death holds no terror for us. As it is written, "**Blessed are the dead who die in the Lord from now on: Yes, says the Spirit, that they may rest from their labor" (Revelation 14:13)

2. The Soul Between Death And The Resurrection

Although the Bible focuses the attention of believers on Christ, while looking forward to the Day of Judgment and the promise of eternal life, it says comparatively little about the state of blessedness that believers enjoy immediately after death. The Bible speaks of believers waiting "**eagerly for the coming of our Lord Jesus Christ**" (1Corinthians 1:7). It also reminds us that Christ "**will transform our vile bodies, and make them like His glorified body**" (Philippians 3:21). And, for that reason, we should always look forward to Christ's second coming. At the same time, the Bible warns the unbeliever of the coming judgment and the need to repent. [See 1Corinthians 1:7; Philippians 3:20-21; Colossians 3:4; 1Thessalonians 4:13; 2Timothy 4:7-8; Titus 2:13; 2Thessalonians 1:9-10; Hebrews 10:27; 2Peter 2:3-6; Jude 6-7; Matthew 25:31-46.]

Nevertheless, the Bible does speak of the condition of soul after death. The words, "**He [Christ] also proclaimed His victory to the spirits in prison**," describe the souls of the wicked and unbelieving as being in "prison" (1Peter 3:19). The words, "**I am tormented in this flame**," tell us that they suffer torment (Luke 16:24). And, the words, "**Into hell, into the fire that shall never be put out**," tell us that there will be no end to their torment (Mark 9:43).

On the other hand, the Bible assures us that the souls of the godly are in God's hand. At death, Stephen cried out, "**Lord Jesus, receive my spirit**," (Acts 7:59). At death Jesus cried out, "**Father, into your hands I commend my spirit**," (Luke 23:46). Paul said, "**I desire to depart, and to be with Christ; which is far better**" (Philippians 1:23). And, Christ said to the thief on the cross, "**Today you will be with me in paradise**" (Luke 23:43). In the Book of Revelation we read, "**Blessed are the dead who die in the Lord**" (Rev. 14:13). The psalmist writes, "**At your right hand there are pleasures for evermore**" (Psalm 16:11). Jesus prayed, "**Father, I also want those, whom you have given me, to be with me where I am; and to see my glory**" (John 17:24). And, Paul writes, "**I reckon that the sufferings of this present time are not worthy to be compared with the glory that will be revealed in us**" (Romans 8:18). Therefore, because the souls of those who have died in faith are with God, the words, "**The dead do not praise the LORD**," are speaking of unbelievers, or bodies in the grave, not the souls of believers (Psalm 6:5 and 115:17). As it is written, "**I heard the voice of a great multitude in heaven, shouting, Hallelujah**" (Revelation 19:1).

The Bible tells us that "**The righteous**" are "**taken away from** the evil to come" (Isaiah 57:1). And, the words, "**You are our Father, even though Abraham does not know us**," make it clear that those who have passed on are not even aware of us, or of all of the wickedness and misery going on in this world (Isaiah 63:16). Those who deny this truth in order to justify prayer to the saints are not only engaging in an idolatrous practice, but such behavior borders on an attempt to contact the dead which Scripture clearly forbids. As it is written, "**There shall not be found among you any one who... talks with those who are dead, for all that do such things are abomination unto the LORD**" (Deuteronomy 18:10-12).

Some see the appearance of Moses and Elijah at the transfiguration of Christ, or the appearance of "Samuel" at Endor as an exception to this rule (Matthew 17:3; 1Samuel 28:11-16). However, that is not necessarily the case. There is much we do not understand, and it would be wrong to just let our imaginations run wild. There is nothing in the account of Christ's transfiguration to indicate that Moses and Elijah were aware of the apostles, much less of anything else going on in the world at that time. And, what the witch saw at Endor may have been a vision of Samuel, rather than Samuel himself. That is indicated by the fact that Saul could not see Samuel. Furthermore, the message Saul received was clearly one of condemnation. Therefore, because Scripture is the source and standard of our faith, we should never interpret unclear passages to contradict its clear condemnation of those who attempt to contact the dead (Isaiah 8:20); nor should we ever attempt to supplement what the Bible says with human speculation or other revelations (Proverbs 30:6; 2Peter 1:20).

Between death and resurrection, all souls exist in one of two states; the state of being forgiven, or the state of being unforgiven. The words, "**Today you will be with me in paradise**," tell us that those who die forgiven experience the joy and light of God's presence (Luke 23:43). While the words, "**Throw him into outer darkness; where there will be weeping and gnashing of teeth**," tell us that those who die without forgiveness will experience the horror and torment of hell (Matthew 22:13). Since these souls are no longer in the physical realm, the idea of them residing in physical places is unrealistic. Christ said that He was going to "prepare a place for" us, and we will be with Him "in paradise," but idle speculation about the nature of such a place will not give us any facts beyond what is plainly stated in Scripture. Furthermore, the words, "**Where their worm does not die, and the fire is never put out**," make it clear that there is no forgiveness after death (Mark 9:48). Therefore, when Christ, "preached to the spirits in prison," He was not offering them forgiveness, but proclaiming His victory as the Greek word *kerusso* indicates, and as the context shows (1Peter 3:19).

The claim that Old Testament saints could not get into heaven because Christ had not yet obtained forgiveness, flies in the face of all that the Old Testament says about forgiveness. As it is written, **"The Lord our God is merciful and forgives,"** (Daniel 9:9). **"The sin which he has done shall be forgiven him"** (Leviticus 19:22). **"You have forgiven the iniquity of your people,"** (Psalm 85:2). Just as God is not limited by time, the forgiveness that He has provided for us is not limited by time. In fact, because it is forgiveness and forgiveness alone that makes us righteous in the sight of God, without forgiveness Abraham's faith could never have been counted to Him for righteousness (Galatians 3:6).

Likewise, the claim that infants that die without baptism are kept in "limbo" unable to enter either heaven or hell is not taught anywhere in Scripture, but is just a figment of someone's imagination. The words, **"The wicked are estranged from the womb,"** apply to all who die without forgiveness. While the words, **"As the sound of your greeting reached my ears, the babe leapt in my womb for joy,"** tell us that God is able to impart faith [and thus joy in the presence of the Lord] to the smallest of infants (Luke 1:42-44). **"The LORD'S hand is not shortened, that it cannot save;"** (Isaiah 59:1). Therefore, instead of professing ourselves to be wise, we need to admit our ignorance while trusting infants to God and His justice.

The words, **"Christ is the end of the law for righteousness to every one who believes,"** tell us that it is the forgiveness that is ours in Christ, not the law, that makes us righteous in the sight of God (Romans 10:4). And, the words, **"The blood of Jesus Christ His Son cleanses us of all sin,"** tell us that all of our sin is completely removed by Christ's sacrifice and atoning death on our behalf (1John 1:7). For that reason the claim that Christ's death is not sufficient to pay for some sins, or that those who are guilty must atone for those sins by suffering in purgatory is not only unscriptural, it is anti-Christian. Worse yet, because it offers the guilty a false hope it is a false gospel. And, the words, **"If anyone preaches any gospel to you other than the one you received, let him be accursed,"** tell us that all who teach it are under God's curse.

3. The Second Advent Of Christ

The Bible clearly tells us that Christ will return. As it is written, **"This same Jesus that has been taken up from you into heaven, will come back in the same way that you saw him go into heaven"** (Acts 1:11). We are also told to, **"be ready"** for He will return **"at a time when you do not expect him,"** (Matthew 24:44). And, we need to be watchful, for we **"do not know either the day or the hour when"** He will return (Matthew 25:13). However, when He does return, **"every eye will see him"** including **"those who pierced him"** (Revelations 1:7). For He will, **"come in His glory, and all the** holy angels with him, then shall He sit upon the throne of His glory, and all nations will be gathered before Him" (Matthew 25:31), and He, "**will judge the living and the dead [after their resurrection] at His appearing**" (2Timothy 4:1). [See Matt. 24:27-30; 1Thess. 5:2; Matt. 25:31; 1Thess. 4:16; Matt. 13:41-42; 1Cor. 15:51; Dan. 12:2; John 5:28-29.]

The words, "**I know that he will rise again in the resurrection [singular] on the last day**," tell us that there will be one general resurrection "**on the last day**" (John 11:24). The words, "**He who rejects me, and does not receive my words, has one who judges him: the word that I have spoken, will judge him on the last day**," tell us that judgment will take place on that same day ["**the last day**"] (John 12:48). And, the words, "**These shall go away into everlasting punishment: but the righteous into life eternal**," tell us that on the Day of Judgment the wicked will "**go away into everlasting punishment**," while the righteous enter "**into life eternal**" (Matthew 25:46). [See Hebrews 9:28.] Let me also add that, when we are judged those who trust in Christ will not be condemned, not because they do not deserve condemnation, but because, "**The blood of Jesus Christ His Son cleanses us of all sin**" (1John 1:7). As it is written, "**There is therefore now no condemnation to those who are in Christ Jesus**," and "**Whoever believes in him will not be ashamed**" (Romans 8:1 and 10:11).

We must emphasize the truth of Christ's return in opposition to all who scoff, "**Saying, Where is the promise of His coming?**" (2Peter 3:4). And also as a reminder to Christians, lest they say in their heart, "**My lord delays His coming**," and begin to behave as if they will never have to answer to God (Luke 12:45). For, none of us know when Christ will return, as it is written, "**Of that day and hour no one knows, no, not the angels in heaven**" (Mark 13:32). "**Therefore you should be ready also: for the Son of man will come at a time when you do not expect him**" (Matthew 24:44). "**For you know perfectly well that the day of the Lord will come like a thief in the night. For when they are saying, Peace and safety; destruction will come upon them suddenly, as travail comes upon a woman with child; and they will not escape. But you are not in darkness, brethren, that that day should catch you unprepared as a thief**" (1Thessalonians 5:2-4). And, even if Christ does not come in our lifetime, at any time He could say to us "**Your soul will be required from you tonight**," (Luke 12:20). So be ready! [See Matt. 24:36; Matt. 24:44; Mark 13:33-36; Acts 1:6-7.]

At the same time, even though we should be ready we should never try to compute the time of Christ's return. As it is written, "**Do not add to His words, lest He reprove you, and you are found to be a liar**" (Proverbs 30:6). Because Christ said, "**Of that day and hour no one knows, no, not the angels in heaven**," we know that God has not revealed the date (Mark 13:32). Therefore, every attempt to find it in Scripture, or anywhere else, is doomed to failure. And, the words, "**No truth of scripture comes from any private explanation,**" apply to every attempt (2Peter 1:20).

However, the Bible has listed certain "signs of the times" that we should be aware of (Matthew 16:3). And, they should arouse in us greater watchfulness and preparedness. The Bible tells us that, "**There shall be signs in the sun, and in the moon, and in the stars; and upon the earth distress of nations, with perplexity; the sea and the waves roaring; Men's hearts failing them for fear, and for looking after those things which are coming on the earth: for the powers of heaven shall be shaken**" (Luke 21:25-27). We are also told that, "**They will hand you over to persecution, and kill you: and you will be hated by all nations for my name's sake. And then many will turn away from the faith, and will betray each other, and will hate each other. And many false prophets will rise up, and deceive many. And because iniquity will abound, the love of many will grow cold. But he who endures to the end, will be saved. And the gospel of the kingdom will be preached in all the world as a testimony to all nations; and then the end will come**" (Matthew 24:9-14). But, "**Let no one deceive you by any means: for that day will not come unless it is preceded by a great apostasy, and that man of sin is revealed, the son of perdition; Who opposes and exalts himself over everything that is called God, or is worshipped; so that he sits as God in the temple of God, and says that he is God**" (2Thessalonians 2:3-4).

As a sign of the time, persecution of Christ and His Gospel is most telling. For even though Christians have been persecuted through the centuries, and persecution is going on today, it suggests a time when men turn away in ingratitude, harden their hearts, and show only contempt for the love Christ has shown them. Of this time the Bible says, "**Because iniquity will abound, the love of many will grow cold**" (Matthew 24:12). We are also told, "**That day will not come unless it is preceded by a great falling away,**" (2Thessalonians 2:3). Despite this opposition, "**The gospel of the kingdom will be preached in all the world as a testimony to all nations**" before the end comes (Matthew 24:14). [See Matt. 24:9; John 16:2; Matt. 10:17; Rom. 8:36; Acts 14:5-6, 19:16-22.]

After Jesus told His disciples that the Temple was going to be destroyed, they asked Him, "**When will these things take place? and what will be the sign of your coming, and of the end of the world?**" (Matthew 24:2-3). That question asked two things, **1-** when the Temple would be destroyed, and **2-** what would be the sign of Christ's coming and the end. His answer to those two questions indicates that many of the signs foreshadowing the destruction of Jerusalem are the same as those foreshadowing His return and the end (Matthew 24:2-51). It also indicates that the Lord was viewing both events, one near in time the other further away in a way that revealed their similarities. And, in the words, "**They went up on the breadth of the earth, and compassed the camp of the saints about, and the beloved city: and fire came down from God out of heaven, and devoured them**," the reference to "the beloved city" gives us another parallel between the destruction of Jerusalem and the end. Therefore, because many of the signs were fulfilled when the Temple was destroyed, Christ could come at any time, and we should be ready.

The Thousand Years

The claim that Christ will reign on this world for one thousand years, comes from the words, "**I saw the souls of those who had been beheaded for their testimony of Jesus,... and they lived and reigned with Christ for a thousand years**" (Revelation 20:4). In response to that claim it needs to be pointed out that 1- **those words say nothing about Christ reigning on this world**, 2- **the context, which speaks of souls reigning with Christ suggests that this reign is taking place in heaven**, and 3- **these words are describing something John saw in a dream or vision, not earthly events**. Furthermore, because this passage says nothing about Christ reigning on this world, those who claim that He will reign on this world are adding their own opinions to what the Bible says. And, because the claim that He will reign on this world contradicts Christ's own words, "**My kingdom is not of this world**," those who teach it are rejecting what Christ said (John 18:36). And, by rejecting what He said, they are taking away from what the Bible says. Therefore, that doctrine only exists in disobedience to God's Word, which says, "**You shall not add to the word which I command you, nor shall you take anything from it**" (Deuteronomy 4:2; Revelation 22:18-19).

Because the claim that Christ will reign on this world does not come from Scripture, every passage that Millennialists interpret to support that claim is being interpreted to teach an unscriptural doctrine, and that is "private interpretation" at its worst (2Peter 1:20). Furthermore, those who teach that doctrine often teach a number of other unscriptural doctrines. One of those is the claim that Christ will raise up believers before the last day. That claim contradicts Christ's own words, "**This is the will of the Father who sent me, that I should not lose any of those He has given me, but should raise them up again <u>on the last day</u>**" (John 6:39, 40, 44, 54). Moreover, when they interpret the words, "**Then we which are alive and remain will be caught up together with them in the clouds, to meet the Lord in the air**," to contradict Christ's words, "**raise them up again on the last day**," they are teaching contrary to God's Word (1Thessalonians 4:17). It should be obvious that if Christ will raise up believers **on the last day**, then the rapture will take place **on the last day.** [Compare John 6:39-40 with 1Thessalonians 4:17 and Job 14:12.]

Worse yet, the claim by some that God's offer of grace will be withdrawn in the future and people will go back to the sacrificial system of the Old Testament is satanic, and is condemned by the words, "**If anyone preaches any gospel to you other than the one you received, let him be accursed**" (Galatians 1:9). Those who hold that doctrine need to read the third chapter of Galatians, for that chapter plainly tells us that salvation has always been through faith in Christ. As it is written, "**The covenant *concerning faith in Christ* that was confirmed by God at the time of Abraham cannot be nullified by the law, which came four hundred and thirty years later, so as to make the promise of no effect. For if the inheritance comes by the law, it is not given by promise: but God gave it to Abraham by promise.**" (Galatians 3:17-18).

Another mistake that they make is to assume that Christianity is not the religion of Ancient Israel. What they fail to see is that because God gave the inheritance to Abraham through faith in God's promise, "**Those who trust in Christ are the children of Abraham**" (Galatians 3:7). "**For he is not a Jew, who is one outwardly; neither is that circumcision, which is outward in the flesh: But he is a Jew, who is one inwardly; and circumcision is that of the heart, in the spirit, and not in the letter; whose praise is not of men, but of God**" (Romans 2:28-29). "**For not all who are descended from Israel belong to the spiritual Israel: And they are not all Abraham's children, just because they are descended from him: on the contrary, Through Isaac shall your descendants come. That is, It is not the children of the flesh who are the children of God: but the children of the promise are counted as the descendants**" (Romans 9:6-8). As it is written, "**There is neither Jew nor Greek, there is neither bond nor free, there is neither male nor female: for you are all one in Christ Jesus. And if you belong to Christ, then you are Abraham's seed, and heirs according to the promise**" (Galatians 3:28-29). Thus, "**All Israel will be saved: as it is written, There shall come out of Zion the Deliverer, He will turn ungodliness away from Jacob**" (Romans 11:26).

4. The Resurrection Of The Dead

The words, "**Christ died for our sins according to the scriptures; and He was buried, and He rose again the third day according to the scriptures**" (1Corinthians 15:3-4), tell us that our hope not only rests on the fact that Christ "**died for our sins,**" but also on the fact that He, "**Was raised again for our justification**" (Romans 4:25). He is, "**The resurrection, and the life**" (John 11:25), "**As in Adam all die, so in Christ all will be made alive**" (1Corinthians 15:20), and, "**Whoever lives and believes in**" Him "**will never die**" (John 11:26).

This glorious hope is not only taught in the New Testament, but also in the Old, where we read, "**Your dead will live, together with my dead body they will arise. Awake and sing, you who dwell in the dust: for your dew is like the dew of the fields, and the earth will deliver up the dead**" (Isaiah 26:19), and, "**Those who sleep in the dust of the earth will awake, some to everlasting life, and some to shame and everlasting contempt**" (Daniel 12:2). Having that hope we can say with Job, "**I know that my redeemer lives, and that He will stand at a future time upon the earth: And after the skin worms have destroyed this body, yet in my flesh I will see God**" (Job 19:25-27). Or with the Psalmist, "**I will behold your face in righteousness: I will be satisfied, when I awake, with your likeness**" (Psalm 17:15). As it is written, "**You will know that I am the LORD, when I open your graves, O my people, and bring you up out of your graves**" (Ezekiel 37:13). "**I will ransom them from the power of the grave; I will redeem them from death: O death, where are your plagues; O grave, where is your destruction**" (Hosea 13:14).

In dealing with skeptics who denied the resurrection, Jesus said, "**Have you not read what God said to you, saying, I am the God of Abraham, and the God of Isaac, and the God of Jacob? God is not the God of the dead, but of the living**" (Matthew 22:31-32). The same holds true for all of God's people, for Christ said, "**If a man keeps my word, he will never see death**" (John 8:51). In fact, resurrection is even implied by God's words to the serpent, "**I will put hostility between you and the woman, and between your seed and her seed; He will bruise your head, and you will bruise His heel**," for destruction of the serpent implies a reversal of what the serpent caused (Genesis 3:15).

While the words, "**Your soul will be required from you tonight**," tell us that the soul departs from the body at death (Luke 12:20). The fact that Christ will "**raise**" bodies "**up again on the last day**," tells us that the soul will be reunited with the body at the resurrection (John 6:39). And, the fact that, "**Those who sleep in the dust of the earth will awake**," tells us that even if the molecules of which we consist are scattered among the dust of the earth, they will reassemble at the resurrection (Daniel 12:2).

"**When the dead rise, the body that is sown in corruption; is raised in incorruption: It is sown in dishonor; it is raised in glory: it is sown in weakness; it is raised in power: It is sown a natural body; it is raised a spiritual body. As there is a natural** body, there is also a spiritual body. And so it is written, The first man, Adam, was made a living soul; the last Adam a life giving spirit. However the spiritual did not come first, but the natural; and after that the spiritual. The first man *is* of the earth, earthy: the second man *is* the Lord from heaven. As *was* the earthy *man*, so also *are* those who are of the earthy: and as *is* the heavenly *man*, so also *are* those who are of the heavenly. And as we have borne the image of the earthy one, we will also bear the image of the heavenly one" (1Corinthians 15:42-49). "Christ... will transform our vile bodies, and make them like His glorified body" (Philippians 3:20-21). And, we will be "as the angels of God in heaven" (Matthew 22:30).

Now not all of us will die, "But all of us will be changed, In a moment, in the twinkling of an eye, at the last trump: for the trumpet shall sound, and the dead will be raised incorruptible, and we shall be changed, for our corruptible *nature* must be made incorruptible, and our mortal *nature must* become immortal. So when the corruptible has put on incorruption, and the mortal has put on immortality, then the Scripture that says, Death is swallowed up in victory, will be fulfilled. O death, where *is* your sting? O grave, where *is* your victory?" (1Corinthians 15:51-55). "For as we believe that Jesus died and rose again, even so God will bring those who have fallen asleep in Jesus [i.e. the souls of those who have died in Christ, see 2Cor. 5:8] with him. For we are telling you only what the Lord has told us, that we who are alive and remain at the coming of the Lord will not precede those who are asleep. For the Lord himself will descend from heaven with a shout, with the voice of the archangel, and with the trump of God: and the dead in Christ will rise first [i.e. the souls that Christ brings with Him will be reunited with their resurrected bodies]: Then we which are alive and remain will be caught up together with them in the clouds, to meet the Lord in the air: and so shall we ever be with the Lord" (1Thessalonians 4:14-17).

The passages just quoted make it clear that all of the effects of sin will be removed from those who trust in Christ. **Our incorruptible resurrection bodies will have no physical defects or any traces of age or suffering for all of those things are the consequences of sin.** God will give us "**beauty for ashes**" (Isaiah 61:3). Our bodies will no longer be subject to earthly infirmities. They will no longer be disfigured, corrupt, imperfect, maimed, and unsightly, but will be perfect in every way. In contrast, because the ungodly remain in their sin, and are under a divine curse, their bodies will come forth from the grave "**Unto shame and everlasting contempt**" (Daniel 12:2). "**Where their worm does not die, and the fire is never put out**" (Mark 9:44). Having been raised from the dead they will be immortal, but will be subject to all of the pains of life, and destined for eternal disgrace and darkness as vessels unto dishonor (Romans 9:21, 2Timothy 2:20).

Because the Father, Son, and Holy Spirit are One God, what one does they all do. We see that in connection with Creation, where the words, **"Don't we all have one father? Hasn't one God created us?"** tell us that the Father is our Creator: while the words, **"Who created all things by Jesus Christ,"** tell us that Christ is our Creator (Ephesians 3:9). We see that again in what the Bible says about the resurrection, for it is written, **"Just as the Father raises the dead, and gives them life; even so the Son gives life to whomever He will... The hour is coming, and now is, when the dead will hear the voice of the Son of God: and those who hear will live"** (John 5:21, 25).

5. The Final Judgment

The lord Jesus Christ has told us that He will raise up believers, **"On the last day"** (John 6:40). And, that He **"Will judge the living and the dead at his appearing"** (2Timothy 4:1). For Christ **"is the one whom God has appointed to be the Judge of the living and dead"** (Acts 10:42). We are told that, **"When the Son of man comes in His glory, and all the holy angels with Him, then He will sit on the throne of His glory, and all nations will be gathered before Him"** (Matthew 25:31-32). **"For we must all appear before the judgment seat of Christ; that every one may receive the things done in his body, according to what he has done, whether it be good or bad"** (2Corinthians 2:10).

However, even though **"everyone"** will **"be judged according to their works,"** // **"judged according to what they have done"** (Revelation 20:12-13) there will be **"no condemnation for those who are in Christ Jesus"** (Romans 8:1). On the contrary, no sin will be imputed to those who trust in Christ. As it is written, **"Blessed is he whose transgression is forgiven"** // **"Blessed is the man to whom the Lord will not impute sin"** (Psalm 32:1; Romans 4:8). For God has, **"cast all our iniquities into the depths of the sea,"** (Micah 7:19) and only takes into account the good we have done (Matthew 25:34-40). As it is written, **"He who hears my word, and believes on Him who sent me, has everlasting life, and will not come into condemnation; but has passed from death to life"** (John 5:24). [See John 12:48; Revelation 12:11; Romans 2:16.]

Furthermore, the words, **"God did not spare the angels that sinned, but cast them down to hell, and delivered them to be kept in chains of darkness, until judgment,"** and the words, **"The angels who did not keep their first estate, but went outside** their bounds, have been kept by Him in darkness bound with everlasting chains until the judgment of the great day," tell us that on the Day of Judgment, God will not only judge men, but also all of the angels that sinned (2Peter 2;4; Jude 6).

When the Bible warns us that the day is coming when, **"All who are in the graves will hear His voice, and will come out; those who have done good, to the resurrection of life; and those who have done evil, to the resurrection of damnation,"** those words are Law, not Gospel (John 5:28-29). Because they are Law, their purpose is not to terrify believers, but to warn unbelievers of the coming judgment and call them to repentance. As it is written, **"The law is not meant for a righteous man, but for those who are lawless and rebellious"** (1Timothy 1:9). In contrast, the same section of Scripture comforts those who trust in Christ with the words, **"He who hears My word, and believes on Him who sent me, has everlasting life, and will not come into condemnation; but has passed from death to life"** (John 5:24). The first statement is Law, the second is Gospel. Furthermore, because believers have already **"passed from death to life,"** their future is already determined. At death, they will be with Christ in paradise, and that can never change (Luke 23:43). In contrast, those who die without faith in Christ will be in hell, and that can never change (Matthew 9:46).

The words, **"In a moment, in the twinkling of an eye, at the last trump... the dead shall be raised incorruptible, and we shall be changed,"** tell us that our judgment will not be a long drawn out process (1Corinthians 15:52). On the contrary, the fact that believers are changed, **"in the twinkling of an eye"** tells us that our judgment is already determined. Furthermore, the words, **"Don't you know that the saints will judge the world?... Don't you know that we will judge angels?"** tell us that once Christ has raised us up, and separated the saved for the lost, we will join Him in judging not only the lost, but also the angels (1Corinthians 6:2-3).

6. The End Of The World

In regard to the end of world, the doctrine that God has given us, the doctrine that He wants us to believe and teach, consists of what His Word explicitly says. And, it says, **"The day of the Lord will come as a thief in the night; in the which the heavens shall pass away with a great noise, and the elements shall melt with fervent heat, the earth also and the works that are therein shall be burned up"** (2Peter 3:10). That same doctrine is taught in a number of other passages. In Luke 21:33 we read, **"Heaven and earth shall pass away: but my words shall not pass away"**. In Psalm 102:25-26 we read, **"Long ago you laid the foundation of** the earth: and the heavens are the work of your hands. They will perish, but you will endure: yea, all of them will grow old like a garment; you will change them like clothes, and they will pass away". And, in Hebrews 1:10-12 we read, "**In the beginning, Lord, you laid the foundation of the earth; and the heavens are the works of your hands. They will perish; but you remain; they will all grow old like a garment, And you will fold them up like a robe, and they will be changed: but you remain the same, and your years will never end**".

The passages just quoted do not describe a mere alteration or cleansing of this world, but a total destruction of both heaven and earth. Our Lord Jesus Christ has plainly said, "**The stars will fall from heaven**" (Matthew 24:29 see Mark 13:25). Job said, "**Man lies down, and does not arise: until the heavens are no more**" (Job 14:12). In the book of Isaiah we read, "**And all the heavenly bodies will vanish, and the heavens will be rolled together like a scroll: all its stars will fall, like leaves falling from a vine, or figs falling from a fig tree**" (Isaiah 34:4), and again, "**Behold, I create a new heavens and a new earth: and the former will not be remembered, or come into mind**" (Isaiah 65:17). In the book of Revelation we read, "**The sky departed like a scroll when it is rolled up**" (Revelation 6:14); and again, "**I saw a new heaven and a new earth: for the first heaven and the first earth had passed away**" (Revelation 21:1). That is what the Bible says, and that is what God wants us to teach (see Jeremiah 23:28).

When Peter said, "**In keeping with His promise, we look for a new heavens and a new earth, in which righteousness dwells,**" he was not speaking prophetically, but was stating what he believed, and what he expected others to believe (2Peter 3:13).

7. Eternal Damnation

The words, "**These shall go away into everlasting punishment: but the righteous into life eternal,**" make it clear that at the last judgment there will be a complete and eternal separation of those who are saved from those who are lost (Matthew 25:46). And, the words, "**He who believes on the Son has everlasting life: and he who does not believe the Son will not see life; but God's wrath remains on him,**" tell us that it is faith in Christ, not works, that determines where we will spend eternity (John 3:36).

As to the lost, the words, "**The wrath of God is revealed from heaven against all ungodliness and unrighteousness of men… Because that which may be known of God is known to them; for God has shown it to them**," make it clear that the lost are without excuse, "**For the invisible things of Him from the creation** of the world are clearly seen, being understood by the things that are made, even His eternal power and Godhead" (Romans 1:18-20). So, "**When the Gentiles, who do not have the law, do by nature the things contained in the law, they... show the work of the law written in their hearts, their conscience also bearing witness, and their thoughts meanwhile accusing or else excusing one another**" (Romans 2:14-15). Yet, instead of being sorry for their sins, repenting of those sins and seeking God's forgiveness, they "**suppress the truth in unrighteousness**" (Romans 1:18). And, "**knowing the judgment of God, that those who commit such things are worthy of death, not only do the same, but have pleasure in those who do them**" (Romans 1:32).

Now even though those words tell us that the lost know of the existence of God, and that their conscience warns them of God's judgment, the natural knowledge of God alone is not enough to save, because it tells them nothing about Christ and the forgiveness available through His death and resurrection (1Corinthians 15:3-4). And, while God can reveal that to them, because "**The heart is deceitful above all things, and desperately wicked**," the natural knowledge of God is easily denied and perverted by man's sinful imagination (Jeremiah 17:9).

A Place of Torment

The Bible makes it clear that those who have rejected the Gospel will, "**Be punished with everlasting destruction from the presence of the Lord, and from the glory of His power**" (2Thessalonians 1:9). That punishment is elsewhere described as, "**everlasting fire**" (Matthew 18:8), a fire that will never be "**put out**" (Isaiah 66:24), where, "**they will be tormented day and night for ever and ever**" (Revelation 20:10).

While the terms "Sheol" (Hebrew) and "hades" (Greek) may denote the "grave," the "hereafter" or "the place of the dead," they are general terms, not the names of specific places. In contrast, our English word "hell" is the name we give to the place where the lost suffer eternal torment. And, that torment is very real. The words, "**Jesus, Son of God have you come here to torment us before the time?**" tell us that the demons who followed Satan will be tormented (Matthew 8:29). And, the words, "**I am tormented in this flame**," and "**I have five brothers; [send Lazarus] that he may testify to them, lest they also come into this place of torment**," tell us that the lost will also suffer torment (Luke 16:24 and 28).

At the time of Christ, the residents of Jerusalem dumped their refuse into the valley of Hinnom (Gehenna). The perpetually burning fires in that valley led some New Testament writers to use the name "Gehenna" as a synonym for hell. [See Matthew 5:22, 29, 30; 10:28; 18:9; 23:15, 33; Mark 9:43, 45, 47; Luke 12:5; and James 3:6.]

The words, **"Depart from me, you cursed,"** tell us that the damned are separated from God (Matthew 25:41). The words, **"Who shall be punished with everlasting destruction from the presence of the Lord,"** tell us that separation from God will be eternal (2Thessalonians 1:9). The words, **"Cast out into outer darkness: where there will be weeping and gnashing of teeth,"** tell us that the lost will be totally cut off from the light of God's presence – including all of the joy and beauty that is ours through faith in Christ (Matthew 8:12). And, the words, **"He also proclaimed His victory to the spirits in prison, who were disobedient, long ago,"** tell us that the lost are prisoners, and prisoners have no control over what they are allowed to do (1Peter 3:19-20).

In addition to this separation from God, the Bible also describes the suffering of the damned as, **"tribulation and anguish"** (Romans 2:9, **"being in torments"** (Luke 16:23), **"tormented in this flame"** (Luke 16:24), **"where their worm does not die, and the fire is never put out"** (Mark 9:43-46), **"weeping and gnashing of teeth"** (Matthew 8:12), **"wailing and grinding of teeth"** (Matthew 13:50), and so forth. Moreover, the words, **"the rich man also died, and was buried, and in hell he lifted up his eyes, being in torment,"** tell us that the lost begin to experience the torment of hell as soon as they die (Luke 16:22-23). In short, the Bible uses the strongest language to warn people of the horror of hell.

In addition, the words, **"I beg you, father, that you send him to my father's house,"** tell us that those in hell will remember their former life, and that memory will carry with it all of condemnation and guilt that goes with knowing the reason they are cursed by God and in hell (Luke 16:27). [See Galatians 3:13.] Whether the fire of hell is physical or spiritual does not matter. If the Bible uses the word **"fire"** to describe the torment of hell, it does so because that is the most accurate way to describe it. Therefore, those who deny the reality of hell, or try to convince themselves that it is not as horrible as the Bible says, are deluding themselves. Instead of trying to downplay what the Bible says about hell, they ought to seek God's mercy so that they do not wind up there.

Since much of the suffering that we endure in this world is caused by sin and the harm that men do to other men, some wonder if those in hell will continue to sin. That may be the case since they will not have the Holy Spirit. And, the fact that their punishment never ends tells us that they will not be improved by punishment. Therefore, if they do sin they will suffer torment because of it, and nothing they do will be acceptable to God (Isaiah 64:6). If they refrain from sin they will do so only under coercion in endless agony.

The words, **"That servant, who knew his lord's will... and did not do what his master wanted, will be beaten with many lashes, but the one who does not know, and committed deeds** worthy of flogging, will be beaten with few lashes," seem to indicate that there will be degrees of punishment in hell (Luke 12:47-48). Hell will still be horrible for everyone who is there, but certain passages make it clear that it will be far worse for those who knew God's word and rejected the gospel. That is why we read, "**And you, Capernaum... it will be more tolerable for the land of Sodom on the Day of Judgment than for you**" (Matthew 11:23-24), or "**Woe to you, Chorazin, woe to you, Bethsaida... I tell you, It will be more tolerable for Tyre and Sidon on the Day of Judgment, than for you**" (Matthew 11:21-22).

The words, "**Warn them, lest they also come into this place of torment**," tell us that hell is a place (Luke 16:28). Peter describes that place as a "prison" (1Peter 3:19). However, the fact that those passages are talking about disembodied spirits indicates that they are in a spiritual place, not a physical place. That place is just as real to them as our world is to us, and the torment is very real, but we should not expect to find it anywhere in the physical realm. In fact the words, "**We look for a new heavens and a new earth, in which righteousness dwells**," indicate that hell (which is full of unrighteousness) will not be a part of the new universe [i.e. the new heaven and new earth] (2Peter 3:13). The words, "**Outside of it are dogs, and sorcerers, and whoremongers, and murderers, and idolaters, and whoever loves and makes a lie**," tell us the same thing (Revelation 22:15). That being the case, hell may exist in a different plain of existence, a different dimension.

While the lost need to be warned of God's coming judgment, and of hell, they also need to know that God offers them forgiveness in Christ. Without God's promise of forgiveness, a terror of hell may only lead them to close their mind to God's Word and try to shut it out of their thinking.

8. Eternal Salvation

The words, "**These shall go away into everlasting punishment: but the righteous into life eternal**," tell us that after the last judgment, the righteous [those whose sins have been washed away by the blood of Christ, compare Romans 10:4 with 1John 1:7] will enter into eternal life (Matthew 25:46). Now the words, "**Today you will be with me in paradise**," tell us that those who trust in Christ begin that eternal life at death (Luke 23:43). However, after the resurrection and final judgment they begin eternal life with their resurrected and glorified bodies. Of that life we are told that there will be, "**A new heavens and a new earth in which righteousness dwells**" (2 Peter 3:13). And, of that existence we are told, "**Behold, the dwelling place of God is with men, and He will live with them, and they** will be His people, and God himself will be with them, and be their God, and God will wipe every tear from their eyes; and there will be no more death, or sorrow, or crying, neither will there be any more pain: for the former things have passed away" (Revelation 21:3-4).

The words, "**We... rejoice in hope of the glory of God,**" and the words, "**God, who is rich in mercy... has raised us up together with Him, and made us sit with Him in heavenly places in Christ Jesus,**" give us a glimpse of what God has in store for those who are saved (Romans 5:2, Ephesians 2:6). Paul says, "**I desire to depart, and to be with Christ; which is far better**" (Philippians 1:23). John says of those who are with Christ, "**They will never again hunger, nor will they thirst; nor will the sun beat down on them**" (Revelation 7:16), for, "**God shall wipe away all tears from their eyes; and there shall be no more death, neither sorrow, nor crying, neither shall there be any more pain: for the former things are passed away**" (Revelation 21:4). The Psalmist writes, "**In your presence is abundant joy; at your right hand there are pleasures for evermore**" (Psalm 16:11). And, Jesus prayed, "**I also want those, whom you have given me, to be with me where I am; and to see my glory, the glory that you have given me: because you loved me before the creation of the world**" (John 7:24). In short, "**The sufferings of this present time are not worthy to be compared with the glory that will be revealed in us**" (Romans 8:18). All of those statements tell us of the glory and blessedness that God has waiting for those who trust in Christ.

At the same time, the words, "**We speak the wisdom of God in a mystery, even the hidden wisdom that God ordained before the world to our glory,**" tell us that these truths cannot be known apart from Divine Revelation (1Corinthians 2:7). As it is written, "**Eye has not seen, nor ear heard, nor has it entered into the heart of man, the things that God has prepared for those who love him**" (1Corinthians 2:9). For that reason, the truth that God has revealed to us in Scripture should never be confounded with the twisted and distorted ideas about the soul and heaven held by pagan philosophers and unbelievers. On the contrary, the Bible warns us that, "**The heart is deceitful above all things and desperately wicked**" (Jeremiah 17:9), and that, "**There is a way that seems right to a man, but its end is the way of death**" (Proverbs 14:12 and 16:25).

Although the heathen have always speculated about the immortality of the soul and life after death, all of their speculation is at best only a caricature of the truth. The sensual "heaven" of the Moslems and Mormons has more in common with sexual fantasy than the glory God has prepared for those who love Him. The Bible plainly says, "**In the resurrection they neither marry nor are given in marriage but are as the angels of God in heaven" (Matthew 22:30). Furthermore, all who hope to gain eternal life apart from faith in Christ are deluding themselves. The words of the Apostle Paul, **"Strangers from the covenants of promise, having no hope, and without God in the world,"** tell us that there is no hope of Salvation among the heathen (Ephesians 2:12; see Acts 4:12). Also, the words, **"Where is the scholar? Where is the debater of this world? Hasn't God made the wisdom of this world foolish?"** tell us that there is more eternal wisdom in the heart of those who trust in Christ, than in all of the unbelieving philosophers (1Corinthians 1:20).

Historically, seeing God has been described as a **"beatific vision,"** that is, a seeing that is inseparable from supreme bliss. The words, **"You will show me the path of life: in your presence is abundant joy; at your right hand there are pleasures for evermore,"** equate all the joy and pleasure of heaven with God's presence (Psalm 16:11). The words of Job, **"After the skin worms have destroyed this body, yet in my flesh I will see God: Whom I will see for myself, my eyes will see him, not the eyes of someone else; though my reins are consumed within me,"** tell us that he believed in the resurrection and equated seeing God with salvation (Job 19:25-27). Christ said, **"Blessed are the pure in heart: for they will see God"** (Matthew 5:8). However, the words, **"Moses said, I beseech you, show me your glory... But He [God] said, You cannot see my face: for no man shall see me and live,"** make it clear that no sinner can ever see God and live (Exodus 33:18-20). And no sinner ever shall! The words of the Psalmist, **"I will behold your face in righteousness: I will be satisfied, when I awake, with your likeness,"** tell us that when the saved see God no sin will remain in them (Psalm 17:15). Furthermore, the words, **"What we are going to be like has not yet been revealed: however we know that, when He [Christ] appears, we will be like him; for we will see him as He is,"** tell us that we will be transformed by seeing Christ (1John 3:2). Therefore, seeing God involves far more than just seeing Him with our eyes.

In this life we only see God through His Word, a seeing that Scripture describes as, **"Like a dim reflection on a glass,"** but, as Paul puts it, **"Then we will see face to face: now I know in part; but then I will know even as I am known"** (1Corinthians 13:12). All who see God, having been cleansed of sin through **"the blood of the Lamb... will never again hunger, nor will they thirst; nor will the sun beat down on them, nor any heat, because the Lamb who is in the midst of the throne will feed them, and will lead them to fountains of living water: and God will wipe away every tear from their eyes"** (Revelation 7:14, 16, 17). And, because the **"devil who deceived them"** will be **"thrown into the lake of**

fire" there will never again be any spiritual foe to interfere with their bliss (Revelation 20:10).

The heavenly blessing that all Christian believers will enjoy consists not only of the fact that we will never again have to experience the suffering brought on by sin, but also of great joy and "**pleasures for evermore**" in the presence of God (Psalm 16:11).

Concerning the things that we will never again suffer, Isaiah says, "**The Lord GOD will wipe away tears from all faces; and He will remove the reproach of His people from all the earth**" (Isaiah 25:8). And, again, "**They will not hunger or thirst; nor will the heat or sun strike them: for He who has mercy on them will lead them, and guide them to the springs of water**" (Isaiah 49:10). In the book of Hosea we read, "**I will ransom them from the power of the grave; I will redeem them from death: O death, where are your plagues; O grave, where is your destruction**" (Hosea 13:14). [See also Rev. 21:4; 1Cor. 15:26 and 55-57; Rev. 2:7, 11; Rev. 7:16-17; Matt. 22, 30.]

Concerning the positive blessings of heaven, the words, "**We know in part, and we prophesy in part, but when that which is perfect is come, then that which is in part shall be done away**," tell us that our intellect will be enlightened (1Corinthians 13:9-10). The words, "**Who will transform our vile bodies, and make them like His glorified body**," tell us that sin will be removed from our nature (Philippians 3:21). The words, "**When the dead rise. The body that is sown in corruption; is raised in incorruption, it is sown in dishonor; it is raised in glory: it is sown in weakness; it is raised in power, it is sown a natural body; it is raised a spiritual body. As there is a natural body, there is also a spiritual body**," also speak of our resurrection body (1Corinthians 15:42-44). The words, "**In a moment, in the twinkling of an eye, at the last trump: for the trumpet shall sound, and the dead shall be raised incorruptible, and we shall be changed. For this corruptible must put on incorruption, and this mortal must put on immortality**," assure us that our spiritual bodies will be incorruptible and immortal (1Corinthians 15:52-53). And, the words, "**To give to them beauty for ashes, the oil of joy for grief, the garment of praise for the spirit of heaviness**," tell us of the beauty, joy and happiness that will belong to all who are saved through faith in Christ (Isaiah 63:3).

In addition to all of those blessings, we will dwell in the presence of God which is the greatest blessing of all. The words, "**Behold, the dwelling place of God is with men, and He will live with them, and they will be His people, and God himself will be with them, and be their God**," tell us that God will dwell among us (Revelation 21:3). Jesus said, "**If I go and prepare a place for you, I will come back, and take you with me; so that where I am, you may be** also," and "**If anyone serves me, my Father will honor him**" (John 14:3, John 12:26). The Apostle Paul said, "**We have courage, and would prefer to be absent from the body, and present with the Lord**" (2Corinthians 5:8). In the book of Hebrews we read, "**You have come to mount Zion, and to the city of the living God, the heavenly Jerusalem, and to an innumerable company of angels**" (Hebrews 12:22). And, the words, "**So shall we ever be with the Lord**," tell us that we will never cease to be in God's presence (1Thessalonians 4:17). [See Luke 23:43, John 17:24, Phil. 1:23, Matt. 8:11, Luke 13:29.]

Because all who are saved through faith in Christ will dwell in God's presence, they will all be equally happy and blessed in every way. However, the words, "**Those who are wise will shine like the brightness of the heavens; and those who turn many to righteousness as the stars forever and ever**," seem to indicate that there will be degrees of glory (Daniel 12:3). The parable of the talents (Matthew 25:14-23) may also indicate this, however, the words, "**Whoever believes on him should not perish, but have everlasting life**," (John 3:16) tell us that no one who trusts in Christ will ever be cast "**into outer darkness: where there will be weeping and gnashing of teeth**" (Matthew 25:30). Regarding this, there is much that we do not know, but we do know that there will be no envy among the saved for sin will no longer be part of our nature.

While the Bible portrays heaven as "a place," (John 14:2) we should not think of it as a physical place. Because God created the physical universe, He transcends the universe. At the same time, because He is present everywhere angels are in His presence even when they are doing His will on earth, and Christ was in heaven at the same time He was on earth. As it is written, "**No one has ascended up to heaven, but He who came down from heaven, even the Son of man who is in heaven**" (John 3:13). And, again, "**The angel said, I am Gabriel, who stands in the presence of God**" (Luke 1:19). [See Matt. 18:10.]

Because it is only those who are justified through faith in Jesus Christ who are saved, ministers need to be faithful to their calling lest any be lost through neglect. Moreover, Because Christians often endure hardship and persecution in this world, we all need to keep our eyes on Christ, and the promise of eternal life that is ours through His death burial and resurrection. Walking in that faith we have God's own assurance that He will keep us by His grace. As it is written, "**What shall separate us from the love of Christ? tribulation, or distress, or persecution, or famine, or nakedness, or peril, or sword?... Nay, in all these things we are more than conquerors through him that loved us. For I am convinced, that neither death, nor life, nor angels, nor principalities, nor powers, nor things present, nor things to come, nor height, nor depth, nor** any other creature, shall be able to separate us from the love of God, that is in Christ Jesus our Lord." (Romans 8:35-39) [See John 3:36, Mark 16:15-16, Luke 24:47, Acts 26:18, Ezek. 3:18-19, 2Tim. 2:23-26 and 4:1-2, 1Tim. 4:15-16, Matt. 18:15-17, 1Cor. 5.]

ALL GLORY TO GOD ALONE

If you have found understanding in the pages of this book, and been blessed by reading it, know that the wisdom it imparts was not revealed to me because I am especially wise, but to help you to grow in faith and understanding. I am just an ordinary believer that has spent many years in prayerful study of God's Word. [See Daniel 2:30.]
Gary Ray Branscome

www.ingramcontent.com/pod-product-compliance
Lightning Source LLC
Chambersburg PA
CBHW070456120526
44590CB00013B/659